ISBN 978-0-656-85592-6
PIBN 10470212

San Francisco Blue Book

AND

Pacific Coast Elite Directory

BEING THE

FASHIONABLE PRIVATE ADDRESS DIRECTORY AND
LADIES' VISITING AND SHOPPING GUIDE

Containing the Names, Addresses, Reception Days and Country
Residences of the Elite of San Francisco, Oakland,
Alameda, Los Angeles, Menlo Park, Portland, Red-
wood City, San Mateo, Sacramento, San Diego,
San Jose and Santa Clara, San Rafael,
Santa Rosa, Sausalito, Stockton.
and California Colony
in New York

SEASON 1890–91

SAN FRANCISCO
THE BANCROFT COMPANY
1890

Reynolds & Adams

I237 MARKET STREET
SAN FRANCISCO
Near Ninth Street

Wood Carpet, Parquetry

:

Inlaid Hardwood Floors AND Borders

MANUFACTURERS OF

Artistic Fretwork for Arches and Portieres

DESIGNS AND ESTIMATES FURNISHED ON APPLICATION

G. W. CLARK & CO.
Frescoing
A Specialty

IMPORTERS AND JOBBERS

Foreign AND American Wall Paper

INTRODUCTORY

A BLUE BOOK has always been deemed an essential adjunct to the literature of every prominent family in the leading Eastern Cities and European Capitals; and in supplying this undoubted want, we feel assured of doing a duty to society which will be appreciated.

In submitting this publication to our subscribers, we have endeavored to give a full and complete list of the society people of San Francisco, Oakland, etc., and of those whose position or wealth has made their names familiar; together with their City and Country residences. It also contains a list of the names and addresses of the California Colony in New York and vicinity, together with their Summer Residences.

The Reception Days of society ladies in San Francisco are, in most cases, given, but when not mentioned, we desire to call attention to the following: Monday is the Reception Day at all Hotels and Boarding Houses, with the exception of the Berkshire, which has both Monday and Thursday; and the Bella Vista, Thursday. Tuesday for Nob Hill, (California street) and Taylor street to the North. Wednesday for Rincon Hill, South Park and streets near the Mission. Thursday for Pine, Bush, Sutter, and parallel streets south (a few having Tuesday), and the greater part of Van Ness Avenue. Friday for Pacific Avenue, the upper part of Van Ness Avenue and streets west of Van Ness Avenue as far as the Presidio.

In the Oakland Division will be found those living in Oakland, Berkeley, Alameda, Fruitvale, and a few at San Leandro and San Lorenzo.

As there are many gentlemen prominently identified in Commercial and Social Circles in this city who reside in Oakland or adjacent towns, their names will be found classified in their respective divisions.

We particularly desire to call attention to the *Additional List*, which contains not only names received too late for classification, but also changes of residences made since the printing of the main portion.

Table of Contents

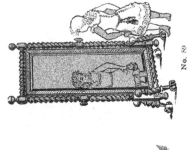

No. 80.
CHEVAL GLASS

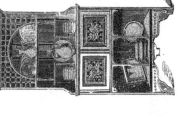

No. 29.
CHINA CLOSET

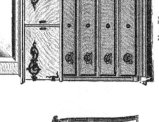

No. 77
CHIFFONIER

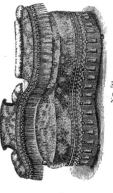

No. 50.
CONVERSATION CHAIR

If you want House your Furnished

Or if you want to buy a Single Piece of **Furniture**, or if you want to make a Wedding or Holiday **PRESENT** visit the immense Furniture Emporium of

 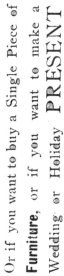

No. 41.
WEST PARIS CHAIR

  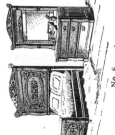

No. 36.
DINING-CHAIR

No. 6
CHAMBER SUITE

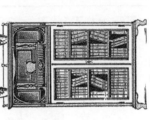

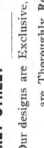
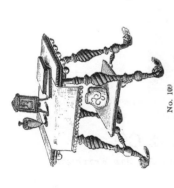
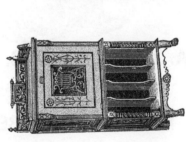

CLUBS

HOTELS

PERSONNEL OF THE PRESS

DIAGRAMS OF THE THEATRES

SHOPPING GUIDE

ADDITIONAL LIST

White Star Laundry Co.

 **EXTRA DRY**

Famous Vintage of 1884

J. F. PLUMEL

18 Stockton St, SAN FRANCISCO

SOLE AGENT PACIFIC COAST

ALSO *FINE COGNACS*

PIÈRRE CHABANMEAU & CO.

COGNAC

FINE BORDEAUX WINES

PIÈRRE
CHABANMEAU
& CO

BORDEAUX

Rare Foreign Wines ———— of Authentic Vintages

Alphabetical List of Advertisers

*

ADDITIONAL LIST

*

Additional List

CONTAINING THE NAMES RECEIVED TOO LATE FOR CLASSI-
FICATION ; ALSO CHANGES OF RESIDENCE OF PARTIES
IN MAIN PORTION OF THE BOOK SINCE
GOING TO PRESS

———

Abrams, Albert; 2426 Fillmore st.
Armes, Mr and Mrs Geo. W.; Dwight Way, Berkeley   *Wednesday*
———William D.

Barnes, Mr and Mrs W. P.; Lick House
———Miss Bessie
Bates,. Mr and Mrs B. W.; 803 Golden Gate ave.   *Thursday*
———Miss Luella
Beans, Mr and Mrs T. Ellard; 489 N. First st., San Jose, Cal.   *Friday*
———Miss Frances L.
———Miss Mary V.
———Miss Rowena
Bee, Frederick A.; 1923 Pine st,   *Thursday*   **Martinez** *Not as on page 6*
———Frank M.
———Mrs S. Louise
———Everett N.
Benjamin, Miss Ruth E.; 1222 Pine st., Van Ness Seminary   **San Rafael**
Boerieke, Dr and Mrs Wm.; 330 Sutter st. **Santa Barbara** *Not as on page 8*
Buckleton, Mr and Mrs E. E.; 1449 McAllister st.   *Thursday*
Butler, Mrs Rosa F.; 1222 Pine st.; Van Ness Seminary.
Brown, A. Page; 2024 Jackson st. *Not as on page 11.*
Brown, Clinton; care of W. F. Bowers & Co., Front and Stark sts., Portland
                              Not as on page 4, Portland
Burke, Mrs M. N.; Naglee Place, San Jose
———Miss E.
———Miss C.
———Miss M.
———Mr and Mrs J. Naglee
———Miss Marie Naglee

Carroll, Mr and Mrs Edgar B.; 1027 H st., Sacramento. *1st and 3d Thursdays*
                                                       Del Monte

Castner, Mrs C. A.; 813 Haight st.   *Thursday*   **Mountain View**

Cheney, J. V.; 900 O'Farrell st.   *Tuesday. Not as on page 15*

Church, Rev and Mrs E. B.; Hill and Valencia sts.   *Monday*

Coffee, Mr and Mrs; 704 Larkin st.   *Tuesday*   **Sunol**

————Mr Walter A.

————Mr Ernest H.

————Miss Florence E.

Coltere, Mrs E. A.; 105 Stockton st.

Conger, Miss Kate E.; 604 Haight st.   **Santa Rosa**

Corter, Madam Marie A.; 1222 Pine st., Van Ness Seminary

Crothers, Miss Jennie; S. F., Cal. *Thursday* **Niles, Ala. Co.** *Not as on p. 19*

————Mr R. A.

Crux, Mr and Mrs Geo. A.; 1447 McAllister st.   *Wednesday*

Currier, Mr and Mrs Chas. H.; 816 Grove st.   *Wednesday*

————Miss Carrie

————Miss Rose

Dornin, Mr and Mrs Geo. D.; 1026 Pine st.   *Tuesday*   **"Oakmead"**

————Miss Julia

————Miss Alice

————John C.; U. S. S.; Patterson Coast Survey, S. F.   **Alaska**

Drexler, Mrs L. P.; 1603 Van Ness ave.   *Tuesday*   *Not as on page 24*

————L. P.

————Harvey D.

————Miss Marion Bybee

————Miss Gertrude Bybee

————Master Louis Horne

Eitel, Mr and Mrs Edward E.; 1931 Ellis st.   *Wednesday*

Elbert, Mr and Mrs L. R.; 1512 Larkin st.   *Wednesday*

Felton, Mr and Mrs Walter W.; Palace Hotel *Thursday* **Mazatlan, Mex.**
                                                      Not as on page 28

Finley, Mrs M. J.; SE cor. Francisco & Leavenworth sts. *Friday* **Santa Cruz**

————Mr Peter J.   *Not as on page 29*

————Miss M.

————Miss Jennie

Finn, Judge and Mrs John F.; Palace Hotel   *Monday Not as on page 29*

Gamble, Mrs S. B.; 1222 Pine St., Van Ness Seminary

Glen, Mr and Mrs John Q.; Cor. Julia and Monroe   *Tuesday*   **Fruitvale**

Goodfellow, Dr and Mrs Geo. E.; 1353 Webster st.   *Tuesday*   **Oakland**

————Mrs M. J.

————Miss

————Miss Bessie

Hague, Mr & Mrs James D.; 175 W. 58th st., New York **Stockbridge, Mass.**

ii

Diaries. Publishers of the Pacific Coast Diaries containing specially prepared information for the Pacific coast. *The Bancroft Company, 721 Market st.*

Hall, Mr and Mrs Wm. P.; Petaluma   *Thursday.   Not as on page 37*
———Miss Hattie
———Will S.
Hamilton, Mr and Mrs W. B.; The Berkshire
Hatch, Mr and Mrs Stephen D.; Murray Hill Hotel, New York
———Miss Gertrude   *Friday*   **Swanton**
Hayes, Mrs E. P.; Hotel Pleasanton   *Monday*   **Del Monte**
Hewlett, Mr and Mrs H. H.; Palace Hotel   **Hotel Del Monte**
Hibbard, Mr and Mrs A. A.; 604 Haight st.   **Santa Rosa**
Holden, Mr and Mrs S. P.; 2622 Gough st.
———Miss
———Miss May

Ives, Stephen D.; 2407 Pacific ave.   *Tuesday.   Not as on page 47*

Jackson, Mr and Mrs P. H.; Eighth ave. and Eighteenth st., East Oakland
James, Mr and Mrs N. T.; 721 Ashbury st.   *1st and 3d Thursdays* *Not as on page 47*
———Miss
———Miss Madge
James, Mrs J.; 113 Page st.   · *Thursday*
Jewett, Mrs J. H.; 931 Bush st.   *Thursday*   **Oak Ridge**
Jobson, Mr & Mrs W. G.; 1029 Dolores st. *1st and 3d Tuesdays, not as on p. 48*

Keane, Mrs Thomas; 340 Page st. *Wednesday* **Santa Cruz**, *Not as on page 49*
———Miss Florence M.
———Mr Jas.
———Tom
———Emmet
———Harry
———Edmund
———Charles

Lathrop, John; Bohemian Club
Levy, Mrs John; 518½ Eddy st.   *Not as on page 53*

Macgregor, Mrs Marguerite; 1222 Pine st., Van Ness Seminary
Marston, Frank W.; Hotel Pleasanton
McGlynn, Mr & Mrs Peter J.; SE cor. Francisco & Leavenworth sts.   *{Not as on page 61}*
McKenty, Mrs Lita; 1222 Pine st., Van Ness Seminary
Miller, Mr and Mrs Wm. H.; 20 Pearl st.   *Tuesday*
Monteverde, Mrs F. E.; 1618 Sutter st.   *Thursday*
———Miss Lolita
Moulten, Mr and Mrs F. F.; "The California"   **Fair Oaks**

Oxnard, Robert; 2014 Webster st.   *Not as on page 69*
Otis, Mr and Mrs Frank; Santa Clara ave. near Paru, Alameda, Cal. *Thursday*   **Lake Tahoe**
Otis, Mr and Mrs Stephen; 2121 Larkin st.   *Thursday*
———Miss Ara

Park, Mrs M. B.; 489 N. First st., San José   *Friday*
Pickering, Mr and Mrs L.   *Thursday*   **Niles, Alameda Co.**
Pray, Mrs Annie B.; 1222 Pine st., Van Ness Seminary

Rawson, C. H.; Stockton and San Francisco
Ridgely, Mrs A. N.; Strathmore opp. New City Hall   **London, England**
Russell, Mr and Mrs John A.; 724 Gough st., Alameda
———Miss Ada
———John A., Jr.

Sahlein, Mr and Mrs M. J.; 407 Devisadero st.
Sawyer, F. E ; 819 Bush st
Schell, Mr and Mrs Geo. W.; 1017 Twenty-first st.   *Tuesday* **Redwood City**
———Miss Lena
Scruggs, Miss Sarah W.; 1036 Valencia st.   *Not as on page 81*
Steel, W. G.; 132½ First st. cor. Alder   *Not as on page 18, Portland*
Stevens, Mr and Mrs C.; The Renton, 712 Sutter st.
———W. E.
Stevenson, Robert Bruce; 1419 Clay st.
Summers, Lieut.-Col. O.; 189, 191 First st., Portland
Stinson, W. H.; 3136 Washington st.   *1st and 3d Thursdays*
———Fannie J.
———Ida M

Tevis, Mr and Mrs Hugh; Cal. House **Hotel Del Monte** *Not as on page 91*
Thurston, Mr and Mrs Geo. P.; Hotel Pleasanton   *Not as on page 92*
Toland, Dr and Mrs C. G.; 2332 Pacific ave. *Thursday* **Yo Semite or Alaska**
    Not as on page 93
Tubbs, R. M.; 519 McAllister st.

Van Norden, Mrs R. I.; 210 Broderick st.

Winslow, Chauncey R.; 2115 California st.
Williams, Miss Carrie ; Petaluma   *Thursday*
Wolff, Mr J.; 116 California st.

Wilshire, Mr and Mrs W. B.; 2616 Buchanan st. *Friday Not as on page 100*
———Eaton, Mrs A. A.; 2616 Buchanan st.   *Friday*
West, Mary B.; 2014 Van Ness ave.   *Friday*   *Not as on page 98*

CHOICE CONFECTIONERY

Telephone 1007

ALL ORDERS BY MAIL OR TELEPHONE
PROMPTLY ATTENDED TO

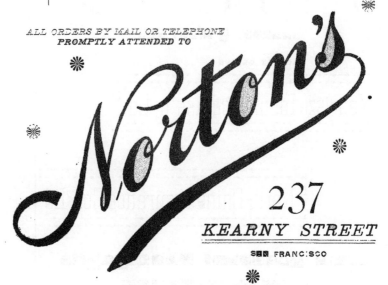

237 KEARNY STREET

SAN FRANCISCO

Chocolate and Bon Bons

*A Full Line of Imported Silk
Boxes and Baskets*

ICE CREAM, SODA, ETC.

HOT CHOCOLATE, HOT BOUILLON AND
HOT CLAM BROTH
During the Winter Season

MACONDRAY & CO.

IMPORTERS

Teas, Mattings, Silks

MARKET & FIRST STREETS

AGENCY OF THE

Yangtsze Insurance Ass'n, Ld.

North China Insurance Co., Ld.

LOUIS ROEDERER Champagne

THE HIGHEST GRADE CHAMPAGNE IN THE WORLD

White Label   **Brown Label**

"CARTE BLANCHE"   "GRAND VIN SEC'

A Magnificent Rich Wine   Perfection of a Dry Wine

"BRUT" Extra Dry

SEE THAT EVERY BOTTLE BEARS THE
PRIVATE LABEL OF

MACONDRAY & CO.   SOLE AGENTS FOR
THE PACIFIC COAST

THE

San Francisco Blue Book

and

Pacific Coast Elite Directory

1890

NOTE—The *Italics* designate the Reception Day, the **Bold Face Type**
the Country Residence

Abbott, Augustus; Cosmos Club   **Sacramento**
Abbott, Mr and Mrs S. Leonard, Jr.; 2411 Pierce st.   *Friday*
Abbott, Mr and Mrs Wm.; 311 Haight st.   *Tuesday*   **Pacific·Grove**
——Miss Carrie B.
——William **M.**
Acker, Nicholas A.; 1502 Jones st.
Ackerson, Miss L. F.; Hotel Pleasanton   *Monday*
Adams, J. M.; 2510 Washington st. or Pacific-Union Club
Adams, Mr John Quincy; 734 Sutter st.
Adams, Miss Aggie; 1211 Mission st.   *Tuesday*
——Hattie
——Will P.
Adams, L. L.; 401 California st.
Adams, Mr and Mrs S. L.; 822 Shotwell st.   **Menlo Park**
Adams, Mr and Mrs L. S.; 825 Bush st.   *Thursday*
——Miss Ella
——E. D.
Adams, Mr and Mrs W. J.   **Menlo ·Park**
Adolphson, Mr and Mrs; 836 O'Farrell st.
Ager, Capt John E.; 214 Sansome st.
Albertson, Dr and Mrs Joseph A.; Hotel Pleasanton   *Monday*
Albright, George W.; 36 New Montgomery st.
Alexander, Mr and Mrs Chas. O.; 2028 Scott st.   *Friday*   **San Rafael**
Alexander, Joseph; 1408 McAllister st.
Alexander, S. Cameron; Cosmos Club
Allen, Mrs E. T.; 2204 Jackson st.   *Friday*

BOVININE Gives Children Rosy Lips and Cheeks

Allen, Miss Elsie H.; 1912 Vallejo st.   *Friday*
Allen, Mr and Mrs Henry F.   **Ross Valley**
——John DeWitt
Allen, Judge J. M.; 305 Sansome st.   **San Mateo**
Allison, Mr and Mrs D. E.   **Del Monte**
Alverson, Mrs Blake; 1619 Geary st.   *Thursday*
Alvord, Mr and Mrs William; New California Hotel   *Monday*
Alvord, H. B.; Cosmos Club   **San Jose**
Ames, Mrs E. C.; Hotel Pleasanton   *Monday*
Ames, Mr and Mrs E. E.; 1019 Buchanan st.   *Wednesday* **Pacific Grove**
——Eddie M.
Ames, Mr and Mrs H. C.; Hotel Fairmount   *Thursday*   **Monterey**
Ames, Mr and Mrs Fisher; Palace Hotel   *Monday*   **Del Monte**
Amoreaux, Miss Mamie C. L.; 830 Haight st.   *Wednesday*   **San Rafael**
Anderson, Miss; 1222 Pine st.
Anderson, Capt and Mrs A.; 119 Capp st.
——Miss Minnie
——Harry
Anderson, Mr and Mrs Thomas; 2209 Devisadero st.
Anderson, Mr and Mrs W. G.; 2209 Devisadero st.
Andrews, Col and Mrs A.; Lick House   *Monday*
Angus, Mr and Mrs J. S.; 2211 Devisadero st.
Archibald, F. A.; 419 California st.
Arey, Mr and Mrs Walter; 2225 California st.   *Tuesday*   **Santa Clara**
——Miss Ruby W.
Arguello, Miss Tula; 912 Bush st.   *Tuesday*   **San Diego**
——Miss Lola
Armstrong, Mrs; Haight and Baker sts.
Armstrong, Mrs H. W.; 814 Fulton st.
Arnold, Mrs Austin; 413 Van Ness ave.   *Thursday*
Arnold, George H.; Rodondo Beach Hotel
Arthur, Charles S.; Purser O. & O. S. S. Co.; Occidental Hotel
Ashburner, Mrs William; 1014 Pine st.
Ashton, Mr and Mrs George F.; 1606 Larkin st.
Ashworth, Mr and Mrs Thomas; 806 McAllister st.   *Thursday*
Atherton, Mr and Mrs Faxon D.; 2020 Buchanan st.   **Menlo Park**
Ashe, Mr and Mrs William L.; Occidental Hotel   **Santa Cruz**
Ashe, Mrs Caroline L. 2315 Sacramento st.   *Thursday*   **Santa Cruz**
——Miss Linie
——Miss Millie
——Miss Bettie
——R. Porter
——Gaston N.
Atkinson, Thomas T.; 1444 McAllister st.

2

Austin, Dr and Mrs H.; SE cor McAllister and Gough sts.
Austin, Joseph; Palace Hotel
Auzal, Dr E. W.; Cosmos Club   **Mare Island**
Ayer, Dr Washington; 1622 Clay st.
———Miss Mabel
Ayers, Capt J. C.; U. S. A.   **East**
Ayers, Mrs E.; 1208 Sutter st.   *Tuesday*
———Miss Anna

Babcock, John P.; The Westminster, 614 Sutter st.
Bach, Charles; 1583 Folsom st.
Bachelder, Mr and Mrs Horace; 309 Sanchez st.   *Thursday*
Bachelder, Mr and Mrs T. F.   *Thursday*   **Sunol**
Bachman, Mr and Mrs S.; The Berkshire   *Monday*
Backus, Gen and Mrs Samuel W.; 2398 Howard st.
Babin, Mr Landry C.; 534 California st.
Bacon, Joseph S.; 806 Jones st.
———Miss Mae Helene
Badger, William G.; 1921 Sacramento st.   *Tuesday*
———Miss
Badlam, Mr and Mrs Alexander; 1024 Franklin st.   *Friday*
———Miss Maud
———Alexander T.
———Edgar
Baggs, Mr and Mrs Montgomery; The Westminster
Bagley, Mrs Angeline D.; 28 Liberty st.
———Miss Adele
———Miss Sarah N.
———David B.
———Albert N.
Bailey, Dr E. I.; Phelan Building
Bailey, Mr and Mrs James D.; 1915 Franklin st.
Bailey, Mrs Mary; 1001 Fillmore st.   *1st & 3d Mondays*
———Miss
———Miss Agnes
———Miss Dollie
Bailey, Mrs Maria; American Legation   **Tokio, Japan**
Baird, Mr and Mrs B. H.; 1458 Franklin st.   *First Thursday of Month*
———Miss Marie
Baker, Mr and Mrs Abijah; Hotel Pleasanton   *Monday*
Baker, Mr and Mrs L. L.; 1822 Washington st.   *Thursday* **Del Monte**
———Wakefield, Mr and Mrs   **Sausalito**
Baldwin, Mr and Mrs A. S.; 2201 Scott st.   *Friday*
Baldwin, Mrs; 26 McAllister st.

Baldwin, Charles A.; Pacific-Union Club   **Mountain View**
Baldwin, Mr and Mrs Alex. R.; 2006 Washington st.
Baldwin, Mr and Mrs E. J.; 1217 Cal. st.   *Tuesday*   **Mountain View**
Baldwin, Geo. W.; Baldwin Hotel
Baldwin, Mrs Janet; NE cor. Gough and Broadway
Baldwin, Mr and Mrs D.; SE cor. Pacific ave. and Buchanan st. **Oroville**
Baldwin, Mr and Mrs A. S.; 830 Haight st.   *Thursday*
Balfe, M. J.; 2446 Jackson st.
Balfour, Mr and Mrs Robert; 2120 Broadway   **Menlo Park**
Ball, Mr and Mrs Gardner; Occidental Hotel
Ball, Capt H. M.; 1908 Stockton st.
Ball, William K.; 1317 Larkin st.
Ballard, Irwin; The Berkshire
Bancroft, Mr and Mrs H. H.; 1298 Van Ness ave. *Thursday* **Walnut Creek**
Bancroft, Mr and Mrs W. B.; 3118 Washington st. *1st and 3d Fridays*
Bandman, Mr and Mrs Julius; 514 Lombard st.   *Wednesday*
——Miss Antonia F.
Bandman, Mr and Mrs Charles J.; 2215 Broadway *Friday* **Larkspur**
Barklay, Peter T.; 927 Haight st.
Barkan, Dr A.; 1808 Gough st.
Barnard, Mr and Mrs George B.; 1516 Leavenworth st.
Barnell, Mr and Mrs Robert; The Berkshire   *Monday*
Barnes, General and Mrs W. H. L.; 821 Sutter st.   **Santa Cruz**
——William S.
Barnes, Mr and Mrs W. P.; Lick House   *Monday*
——Miss Bessie
Barnes, C. L.; 306 Stockton st.
Barnett, Lieut G.; Mare Island
Barnhart, Mr Geo.; 613 Clay st.
Barr, Mr and Mrs John D.; 1214 Mason st.   *Thursday*
——Miss Lottie
——Miss Fannie
——Milton H.
Barr, Stewart A.; 1211 Mission st.
Barra, E. J.; 738 Sixteenth st.
Barreda, Mrs F. L.; 2121 Buchanan st.   *Tuesday*   **East**
——Miss Rose
Barrett, Miss M. G.; 302 Montgomery st.
Barrett, W. G.; cor. First and Natoma sts.   **Sausalito**
Barriolhet, Mr and Mrs Henry; 1209 Sutter st. *Monday* **Menlo Park**
Barron, Mr and Mrs Edward; 1404 Sutter st. *Monday* **Mayfield Park**
Barry, Thomas F.; 806 Lombard st.
Barry, Lieutenant and Mrs F. A.; Angel Island

Barry, Thos. F.; 260 Clara st.
Barstow, Mrs George; 927 Pine st.
Bartlett, George H.; 501 Geary st.
Bartlett, Mrs M. A.; Hotel Pleasanton
——Miss
Bartling, Major and Mrs H.; 826 Powell st.   *Monday*
——Miss Emma
Barton, Benj. F.; 612 Bush st.
Bass, Dr. Frederick; 1401 Folsom st.
Bass, Mr and Mrs Thomas J.; SE cor. Noe and 15th sts.   **Lake Tahoe**
Bassett, Mr and Mrs George H.; 712 Sutter st. (The Renton)
Bates, Mr and Mrs Frank D.; 2218 Webster st.   *Friday*
Bates, Mrs A. B.; 1619 Washington st.   *Friday*   **Santa Cruz**
——Miss Mary D.
Bates, Mr and Mrs Dudley C.; 1705 Octavia st.   *Friday*
——Miss Bernice P.
——George W.
——Miss
Bates, Morris U.; 1112 Powell st.
Bauer, Mrs John A.; 509 Post st.   *Monday*
Batchelder, Mr Nathaniel; 36 New Montgomery st.
Bauer, Miss Nellie; 1838 Geary st.   *Thursday*
——John E., Jr.
Baum, Mrs Charles; 1705 Powell st.
——Alexander
Bausman, Mr and Mrs William; 10 Bond st.
——Miss H.
——Miss Laura
——Henry S.
Beach, Mr and Mrs Chilion; 1301 Taylor st.   *Thursday*
Beach, Thomas B.; Bohemian Club
Beale, Truxton; 1007 California st.
Beauregard, A. T.; Cosmos Club   **San Diego**
Beaver, Samuel E.; 118 Grant ave.
Beaver, Mr and Mrs George W.; 1300 Taylor st.   *Tuesday*   **Del Monte**
——Miss Ethel
——Miss Kate
——Miss Anna
——Frederick H.
——Mr K. W.
Beazley, F. C.; 316 California st.   **Saratoga, Santa Clara County**
Beck, Mr and Mrs F. E.; 1716 Bush st.   *Tuesday*
Beck, Harry M.; 1919 Sutter st.
Beck, Mr and Mrs Milton W.   **San Jose**
——Miss Myrtle

Beers, Rev and Mrs Hiram W.; Occidental Hotel   *Monday*   St. Helena
Beck, Mr Thomas; U. S. Appraiser's Building
Becker, Prof George; U. S. Geological Building
Beford, Miss Fannie; Hotel Pleasanton   *Monday*
Belcher, Edward Augustus; Union League Club, or 234 Montgomery st.
Belcher, Judge W. C.; Palace Hotel
Belcher, Judge and Mrs   Marysville
——Miss
Belden, Mr and Mrs Charles A.; 2004 Gough st.
Belden, Mrs D.; Hotel Pleasanton
Belknap, Mr and Mrs David P.; 24 Metcalfe Place
Belknap, Admiral and Mrs Geo. C.   Mare Island
Bell, Lieut J. A.; U. S. N.   Mare Island
Bell, Mr and Mrs Thomas; 1661 Octavia st.
  emis, Mr and Mrs Charles C.; 419 Bryant st.
Bender, Miss Ella   Carson, Nevada
Bendixen, C. Edward; 808 Leavenworth st.
Benedict, W. E.; 102 Ellis st.
Benedict, Mrs E. L.; Hotel Rafael
Benjamin, Mr and Mrs A. F.; 2712 Pine st.   *Wednesday*
Bee, Frederick A.; 1923 Pine st.
——Frank M.
——Everett N.
Benjamin, Lieut E. E.; U. S. A.   Angel Island
Benjamin, Mr and Mrs Edward J.; 907 Pine st.
Bennett, Mr and Mrs Clement; 2419 California st.   *Monday*
Bennett, James G.; San José   Costa Rica, Central America
Bennett, Major and Mrs F. T., U. S. A.; Presidio or 1713 Baker st.
   Friday   Santa Cruz
Bennett, T. A.; Grand Hotel
Bennett, Dr William; 2213 Webster st.   *Thursday*   New Hope
Bennett, William; 105 Grove st.   New Hope
Benson, John; 803 Stockton st.
Bent, Mr and Mrs E. F.; The Berkshire   *Monday*
Benyaurd, Major W. H. H.; Pacific-Union Club
Bergin, T. J.; 2012 Jackson st.
Bermingham, John; 611 Chestnut st.
——Miss Charlotte
Berry, Mr and Mrs Fulton G.; 1812 Van Ness ave.
——Miss Maude
Berry, Mr and Mrs Washington; Angel Island
Berry, Thomas C.; 202 California st.   San Rafael
——T. B.
Bertheau, C.; 26 McAllister st.

Berton, Mr and Mrs Geo. A.; 913 Jones st.
Best, Mrs K. R.; 1023 Hyde st.   *Friday*
Bermingham, Capt; 611 Chestnut st.   *Friday*
——Miss J.
Beveridge, Mr and Mrs H.; 729 Ashbury st.   *Wednesday*
——Miss A.
Bigelow, Mr and Mrs J. H.; 816 Powell st.
Bigelow, Mr and Mrs S. C.; NW cor. McAllister and Steiner   *Monday*
Biggs, Mr and Mrs Harry C.; 1240 Sutter st.
Billings, Mr and Mrs George E.; 1612 Clay st.   *Tuesday*
Bingham, Mr and Mrs A. C.; Marysville
Bingham, Lindsley G.; 1119 Leavenworth st.
Bird, Dr and Mrs N. J.; 136 McAllister st.   *Wednesday*
Bishop, Mr and Mrs Ira; Hotel Pleasanton
Bishop, Mr and Mrs Thomas B.; 1503 Larkin st.
——Mr and Mrs W. A.
Bissell, Mrs H. B.; 1408 California st.   **Del Monte**
——H. M.
——Miss Julia
——Miss Theresa
Bixler, Mr and Mrs David; SW cor. Union and Pierce sts.   *Friday*
Blacker, Miss Lizzie; 1827 Pacific ave.
Blair, Capt and Mrs Samuel M.; 1315 Van Ness ave.   *Thursday* **Del Monte**
——Miss Jennie
——William S.
Blaisdell, C. J.; The Renton
Blake, Lieut E. M.; Presidio
Blake, Dr and Mrs Alfred E.; 2142 Post st.   *Monday*
Blake, Mrs Geo. M.; 1922 Franklin   *Thursday*
Blake, Mr Wm. E.; 1619 Geary st.
Blake Dr and Mrs Charles E.; 1614 Geary st.
Blake, Dr and Mrs Charles E., Sr.; 1414 Hyde st.
Blake, Charles T.; 4 Vernon Place
Blake, Maurice C.; 325 Seventeenth st.
Blakeman, Mr and Mrs T. Z.; 2420 Pacific ave.   *Friday*   **Santa Cruz**
Blakeney, Thomas J.; 137 Montgomery st.
Blanchard, Mr and Mrs Henry P.; 2006 Jackson st.
——Miss Kittie
——John O.
Blanchard, Mrs L. A.; 1008 Bush st.
Blanding, Mr and Mrs Gordon; 1900 Franklin st.   *Friday* **Del Monte**
——Miss Lena
Blaney, Mr and Mrs E. W.; 922 Van Ness ave.   *Tuesday*   **Lake Tahoe**
Blankman, Dr and Mrs William; Nucleus Building
Blethen, Mr and Mrs C.; The Renton   *Monday*   **Del Monte**
Blethen, Mr Clement; 1014 Pine st.
Block, Mr and Mrs E. M.; 1613 Larkin st.   *Tuesday*
——Miss

Block, Mr and Mrs James N.; 1533 Sacramento st.
Blood, Dr and Mrs John N.; 324 Noe st.
Bloodgood, Miss Annie; Hotel Pleasanton   *Monday*
Bloom, S.; 230 Seventh st.
Blount, Mrs A. K.; The Berkshire   *Monday*
Blow, Mr and Mrs A. W.; 899 Pine st.
Blum, Mrs. A.; 526 Ellis st.
Blum, Mr Simon; 818 Market st.
Blunt, Lieut and Mrs A. C.; Presidio
Boardman, Mr and Mrs Geo. C.; 1750 Franklin st.   *Tuesday*
——Samuel H.
——George C., Jr.
Bode, William; Hotel Pleasanton
Boalt, Judge and Mrs John H.; 332 Haight st.   *Tuesday*.   **Del Monte**
Boericke, Dr and Mrs William; 824 Sutter st.
Bogart, Mrs W. F.; 830 Haight st.   *Wednesday*   **San Rafael**
Boggs, Hon and Mrs John; Palace Hotel   **Princeton, Colusa Co.**
Boggs, Miss Alice   **East**
Bolado, Mr and Mrs Joaquin; 528 Sutter st.   *Monday*   **Salinas City**
——Miss Dulce
Bolton, Mr J. R.; 2201 Jones st.
——Miss Lizzie
——Robert C.
Bond, C. A.; The Bella Vista; 1001 Pine st.
Bonelli, Mr and Mrs E. S.; Hotel Fairmount   *Wednesday*
Bonestell, Chelsey K.; 907 Sutter st.
Bonestell, Mrs John T.; 1506 Sacramento st.
Bonestell, Mr and Mrs Louis H.; 512 Stockton st.
——Louis Cutler
Bonnell, Mr and Mrs Edwin; 1709 Gough st.
——Allison C.
Bonner, Mr and Mrs John; 1900 Vallejo st.
——Miss Geraldine
Bonney, Miss Callie; Oriel Hotel   *Monday*
Bonny, George; 106 Montgomery st.; Pacific-Union Club
Boomer, Mr and Mrs A. H.; 948 Haight st.   *Monday*
Booth, Mr and Mrs A. G.; 1522 Broadway   *Monday*
Booth, Mr Edgar H.; 209 Geary st.   **San Mateo**
Borden, Mr and Mrs Ivy; 1501 Van Ness ave.
Borden, Rhodes; 957 Broadway   **Oakland**
——Miss Helen
Borel, Mr and Mrs Antoine; 606 Stockton st.   *Thursday*   **San Mateo**
——Miss Chonita
——Miss Sophia

8

Borhyte, Miss Belle; 1418 Sutter st.
Boruck, Mr and Mrs Marcus D.; 2125 California st. Sacramento
-———Miss Belle
———Miss Florence
———Leland S.
Bosqui, Mr and Mrs Edward Ross Valley
———Miss Helen
———Miss Katie
———Miss Emma
-———Edward L.
———Frank
Bothin, Mr and Mrs H. E.; NE cor. Van Ness and Jackson *Friday*
Botsford, Mrs. E.; The Berkshire *Monday* San Jose
Bourn, Mr and Mrs William B.; 1300 Hyde st. St. Helena
Bourn, Mrs W. B.; NW. cor. Pacific ave. and Gough st. *Friday*
———Miss Ida
———Miss Maude
———Miss May
Bourne, John B.; 2516 California st.
Bouton, Mrs C. W.; 1421 Webster st. *Tuesday* Reno, Nev.
———Miss Lillian
———Miss Cloy
Bouvier, Mr and Mrs Alfred; 2524 Broadway *Friday*
Bovee, Mr and Mrs Wm. H.; Hotel Pleasanton
Bowen, Mr and Mrs E. J.; 2018 Franklin st. *Friday* Del Monte
———Miss Mary
———Miss Edith
Bowen, Mr and Mrs J.; 1306 Jones st.
Bowers, G. W.; 2610 Jackson st.
———Miss Clare Louise
Bowers, W. F.; 712 Pine st.
Bowie, Mr and Mrs A. J.; 1913 Clay st. *Friday*
———Miss Bessie
Bowie, Allan St. John; cor. Gough and Jackson sts.
-———Miss Jessie
Bowie, Dr and Mrs Hamilton C.; 2221 Sutter st. San Mateo
Bowie, Dr Robert I.; 2202 California st. or 313 Kearny st.
Bowman, George F.; 2640 Pacific ave.
Bowman, Mr and Mrs John ; 1832 Sutter st.
Bowman, Prof M. L.; Hotel Pleasanton
Bowman, Mrs May; 828 Union st.
Boyd, Mr and Mrs Alexander; 2020 Washington st.
———George Davis
Boyd, Mr and Mrs Colin M.; American Exchange
Boyd, James T.; Pacific-Union Club

BOVININE the Blood Maker

9

Boyd, Mr and Mrs James T., Jr.; 738 Treat ave.   *Wednesday*
Boysen, Edward C.; 911 Valencia st.   *Wednesday*
——Miss Minnie
Boysen, Dr and Mrs J. Thomas; Baldwin Hotel   *Monday*   **Oakland**
Bradley, Mr and Mrs George L.; Hotel Pleasanton   *Monday* **San Rafael**
Bragg, Mr and Mrs Robert; NE cor. Castro and Beaver sts.   *Wednesday*
——Miss Mary
——Miss Lizzie
——Miss Adah
——Miss Ethel
——John S.
——Robert, Jr.
Brand, Mr A.; 534 California st.
Brahane, Mr and Mrs G.; 1225 Fulton st.
Brandenstein, M. J.; 1611 Bush st.
Bradford, Mr A. C.; 611 Commercial st.
Bradshaw, Miss Sue Ella; 424 Haight st. } *Wednesday* **Syracuse, N. Y. Portland, Me.**
Branch, Mr and Mrs L. C.; 3009 Sacramento st.   *Wednesday*
Brant, Lieut L. P.; U. S. A.   **Presidio**
Brastow, Mrs S. D.; 1116 Hyde st.   *Thursday*
Braverman, Mr and Mrs Louis; 1016 Eddy st.
Breed, Mrs L. N.; Hotel Pleasanton
Breede, Henry L.; 1014 Stockton st.
Breeze, Charles K.; Cosmos Club   **Concord, Cal.**
Breeze, Mrs Thomas   **Abroad**
——Miss Mary
Breon, Mr and Mrs Paul; Lick House   *Monday*   **Coronado**
Breyfogle, Dr and Mrs Edwin S.; Palace Hotel and 209 Geary st.
Brewer, Dr and Mrs B. B.; 1221 Jones st.   *Wednesday*
——Miss Libbie
——Mr Wm. W.
Brewster, Mr Charles H.; 2517 Sutter st.
——Mrs Julia
Briel, M.; 226 Stockton st.
Briggs, Mr and Mrs A. R.; Hotel Pleasanton   *Monday*
Brigham, Dr and Mrs C. B.; 2202 Broadway   **Lake Tahoe**
Brison, William M.; 539 Geary st.
Bristol, Miss Maude K.; 919 O'Farrell st.
——Miss Helen
——Mr and Mrs Robert D.
Bristol, Mrs J. K.; 801 Leavenworth st.   *Monday*
——Mr and Mrs R. D.
——Miss Helen
——Miss Maude
Brittan, Mr and Mrs Wm. G.; 600 Bush st.   *Monday*
——Miss

Brittan, Mr and Mrs N. J.; Pacific-Union Club   **Redwood City**
Britton, Joseph; 829 Union st.
Britton, George W.; 1313 Taylor st.
Brooks, Samuel M.; 611 Clay st.
Brooks, Samuel H.; 634 Polk st.   **Santa Cruz**
———Miss Maggie
———Miss Lucy
Brooks, William A.; 621 Bush st.
Brooks, Mrs M. J.; 621 Bush st.
Brooks, Mr. George H.; 611 Commercial st.
Brown, Mr and Mrs A. Page; 318 Pine st.
Brown, Dr Charlotte Blake; 1212 Sutter st.
Brown, Henry A.; 1212 Sutter st.
———Philip K.
———Miss Adelaide
Brown, Miss M. R.; 322 Eighteenth st.
Brown, George C.; 1026 Washington st.
Brown, Mr and Mrs J. William; 603 Bush st.   **Highland Springs**
Brown, Mr and Mrs S. H.; 903 Treat ave.   *Thursday*
Brown, Mr and Mrs Thos.; 1019 Bush st.   *Thursday*
———Miss Lizzie
———Miss Grace
———Miss Fannie
Brown, Mr and Mrs J. W.; 902 Pine st.
Brown, James N.; 1019 Bush st.
Brown, Mrs L. W.; 712 Sutter st.
Brown, Lieut R. A.; Presidio
Brown, William E.; Palace Hotel
Brown, Mr and Mrs W. S.; 426 Ellis st.   *Thursday*
Brown, Mr and Mrs William G.; 732 Treat ave.   *Wednesday*
Brown, Mr and Mrs Winsor L.; 2016 California st.   *1st and 3d Fridays*
Browne, Mr J. Lewis; 616 Folsom st.
Brownstone, Mrs Jacob; 309 Powell st.   *last Wednesday*   **Menlo Park**
Bruce, Mr and Mrs Robert; 2122 Pacific ave.
Bruguiere, Mr and Mrs E. A.; 1800 Franklin st.   *Tuesday*   **Del Monte**
Brumagim, J. W.; 1604 Van Ness ave.   *Thursday*
———Miss Minnie
———Stuart M.
Brune, Mr and Mrs Henry; 324 Grove st.   *Tuesday*
Brunswick, Mr and Mrs E.; 2109 California st.
Brunt, Walter N.; 621 Twenty-first st.
Brush, Miss Lillie; Hotel Bella Vista
Bryan, Capt and Mrs William J.; 1822 Pine st.   *Wednesday*
———Mr and Mrs William V.
Bryant, Mrs A. J.; 2001 California st.   *Thursday*

Bryant, Mr and Mrs George H.; 2315 California st.   *Tuesday*
Bryant, Dr and Mrs W. August; 819 Post st.
Bryde, Mrs; The Berkshire   *Monday*
——The Misses
Buckbee, Spencer C.; 1906 Laguna st.   *Thursday*
——Miss Annie
——Samuel G.
Buckingham, A. E.; 1016 Franklin st.   *Tuesday*
——Miss Edith
Buckingham, Mrs Elise P.; Grand Hotel   *Monday*   { Suguintie'sRanch Vacaville
Buckingham, Thomas H.; Palace Hotel   Kelseyville
Buckingham, Mr and Mrs W. P.; { 1904 Market st.   *Monday* White Sulphur Springs
Buckley, Dr C. F.; 811 O'Farrell st.
Buckley, Mrs E. P.; 1103 Jackson st.
Buckley, Mr D. J.; cor. Market and Montgomery sts.
Bucknall, Dr and Mrs George J.; 1121 Laguna st.   *Thursday*   St. Helena
——Miss Marguerite H.
Bufford, Mr and Mrs Samuel F.; 1814 Sutter st.   *Wednesday*
Bull, Mrs Alpheus; Francisco and Leavenworth sts.
——Alpheus, Jr.
Bundschu, Charles; 125 Chestnut st.
Bunker, Mr and Mrs Robert F.; 1116 Golden Gate ave.
——Miss Ella
Bunker, Mr and Mrs William M.; The Bella Vista   *Thursday*
Burbank, Mr and Mrs M. B.; 1114 Clay st.
Burdick, George R.; 1523 Scott st.
——Miss Fannie
Burgess, Mr and Mrs George H.; 2505 Fillmore st.
Burgess, Dr and Mrs O. O.; 329 Geary st.   *Friday*
Burgin, Mrs Kate; 801 Golden Gate ave.   *Friday*   Litton Springs
——Miss Burgin
——Miss Kate
——Miss Agnes
——J. Fred, Jr.
Burke, Judge and Mrs Ethelbert; 824 Powell st.   *Friday*
Burling, Mr and Mrs William; 1618 Washington st.
Burling, Mr Benjamin L.; 1618 Washington st.   *Tuesday*
——Miss Mamie H.
——G. B.
——Fred
——Augustus B.
Burling, J. W.; The Bella Vista
Burnett, J. C.; U. S. N.; Cosmos Club, 1121 Geary st.   "McArthur"
Burnett, Mr and Mrs J. M.; 1713 Larkin st.   *Friday*
Burnett, Mrs W. C.; 1916 Broadway st.   *Friday*
——Miss
——Miss Gertrude

Burns, Capt and Mrs A. M.; 1506 Washington st.   *Tuesday*
———Miss Daisy
Burns, Clayton J.; Hotel Pleasanton   Los Angeles
Burns, Mr and Mrs Isidore; Grand Hotel   *Monday*
Burns, Paul O.; Cosmos Club   San Jose
Burns, W. F.; Hotel Pleasanton
Burr, Lieut George W.; Presidio
Burrell, Mr and Mrs ; 1322 Mission st.
———Miss Nellie E.
Burrows, Frank D.; 737 Market st.
Burton, Mr and Mrs C. H.; 1024 Washington st.   *Tuesday*
Bush, Capt Hyman P.; 1011 Golden Gate ave.
Bush, Mr Chas. S.; 210 Bush st.
Butler, Mr and Mrs H. B.; 2101 Pacific ave.   *Friday*   Fresno
Butterworth, Mr and Mrs Thos. C.; 818 Treat ave. *Thursday* Victoria, B.C
Buxton, O. W.; Palace Hotel
Byrne, J. W.; Occidental Hotel
Caduc, Mrs P.; 2123 Sacramento st.
———Miss Cora
Cachot, Miss Minnie; 207 Taylor st.
Cachot, Dr Maximilian A; 207 Taylor st.
Cahalin, Miss G. H.; 616 Jones st.
Cahill, E. J.; Grand Hotel
Cahill, Edward; 706 Stockton st.
———Miss Mamie
Cahn, Mr David; 205 Sansome st.
Callaghan, Mr and Mrs Chas. W.; 830 Eddy st.
Callaghan, Mrs D.; 830 Eddy st.
———The Misses
Cammeyer, Mr; 607 Market st.
Cammock, J. M.; Grand Hotel
Campbell, Mr Vernon; Eddy and Powell sts.
Campbell, Alexander, Jr; 1415 Mason st.
Campbell, Donald Y.; 130 Sansome st. and Oakland
Campbell, Mr and Mrs H. J.; 1310 Hyde st.
Campbell, Mr and Mrs John F.; 1519 Van Ness ave.
———Miss Isabel
Campbell, Mr and Mrs P. C.; 417 Lyon st.
Campbell, Mr and Mrs Walter C.; 1820 Turk st.   *Monday*
Campbell, W. S.; Cosmos Club   New York
Campbell, William H., Jr; 2301 Devisadero st.
Cantin, Eugene; 613 Clay st.
Capp, Prof. A. B.; 1148 Sutter st.
Carey, General and Mrs J. T.; Grand Hotel   *Monday*
Card, Dr Egerton F.; 2406 Sutter st.
Carlin, Lieut John W.; U. S. N., Bohemian Club   Mare Island

Carlton, Miss Ida; 1822 Sacramento st.
Carlson, Mrs Lars; 523 Pine st.   *Saturday*
——Miss Mary
——Mr Chas. J.
Carmany, Mr and Mrs John W., 514 Hyde st.   *Tuesday*
Carmody, Mr and Mrs Arthur F.; 1606 Washington st.   *Friday*
Carolan, Mr and Mrs James; 1714 Cal. st.   *Tuesday*   **Hotel del Monte**
——Miss Evelyn
— —Miss Genevieve
——Miss Emily
——Frank J.
——Herbert C.
Carpenter, Edwin W.; 1311 Taylor st.
Carpenter, Mrs M. A.; 926 Clay st.
Carr, Mr J. S.; U. S. Postoffice
Carr, Colonel and Mrs B. O.   **St. Helena**
Carrey, Mr and Mrs Edmond; 522 Ellis st.
——Miss
Carrigan, Mrs Andrew; 2124 California st.   **San Rafael**
——Miss
——Andrew
——William
Carroll, Miss; 2028 Scott st.   *Friday*
——Miss Leila
Carroll, John; Palace Hotel   *Monday*
— —Miss
——Miss F.
——G. L.
Carroll, Mrs R. T.; 1520 Van Ness ave.   *Friday*
Carroll Thomas P.; 518 Lombard st.
Casa, A. Della; Grand Hotel
Case, George A.; 2338 Washington st.
Casey, Mr. John; U. S. Building, City
Casey, Mr and Mrs Maurice; 1329 Sutter st.
Cassell, Mr and Mrs John F.; 2118 Pacific ave.   *Friday*
Casserly, Mrs Eugene; 2123 Buchanan st.   *Friday*   **Del Monte**
——Miss
Casserly, John B.; bus. 201 Sansome st.
Casserly, Augustin; bus. 507 Montgomery st.
Castelazo, Arthur; 826 Bush st.
— ——Miss
Castle, Mr and Mrs Michael; Washington & Laguna sts. *1st & 3d Fridays*
——Neville H.; Washington and Laguna sts.   **San Jose**

14

Castle, Mr and Mrs Frederick L.; Van Ness ave & Sutter st. **Healdsburg**
——Miss Eva
——Miss Blanche
——Miss Hilda
——Albert E.
——Arthur H.

Castle, Mr and Mrs Walter M.; 1720 Bush st. *Friday* **Healdsburg**
Castle, Hon and Mrs William R. **Honolulu**
Caswell, Mr and Mrs George; 1921 Sacramento st. *Tuesday*
Castner, Mrs C. A.; 813 Haight st.
Catherwood, Mr and Mrs R. B.; Palace Hotel *Monday*
Center, Mr and Mrs Wm.; 214 Shotwell st.
——John
Chadbourne, Mr and Mrs F. S.; 1106 Bush st. *Thursday*
Chamberlain, S. S.; 1008 Jones st.
Chamberlain, Mrs Eloise; 306 Stockton st.
——Miss Cherry
——Miss Belle
——Miss Charlotte

Chamberlain, Col and Mrs W. H.; 921 Valencia; Union League Club
Chambers, Mr and Mrs R. C.; 2220 Sacramento st.
Champion, Mr and Mrs Charles Noble; 1823 Broadway.
Champion, Miss Gertrude; cor. Clay and Laguna sts.
Chapman, Mr and Mrs Frank; 816 Powell st. *Thursday*
Chapman, Miss Mattie; 118 Liberty st. *Tuesday*
Chapman, Mr and Mrs W. S.; Palace Hotel *Monday*
Chapman, Mr and Mrs Wilfrid B.; 1123 California *Tuesday*
Chapman, Mr and Mrs R.; 1602 Taylor st. *Tuesday* **San Rafael**
Chappell, Mr J. J.; Cosmos Club
Chase, Miss; 1222 Pine st.
Chase, Mr and Mrs H. P.; Hotel Pleasanton
Chase, Mr and Mrs Horace Blanchard; { Hotel Pleasanton { "Stag's Leap," **Yountville**
Cheeseman, Mrs Morton; Palace Hotel *Monday*
——Miss Jennie
——George S.

Cheney, Mr and Mrs John Vance; 908 Sutter st. "Solitude" **Napa Co.**
Chesebrough, Mr and Mrs A.; 2428 Jackson st.
Chevassus, Mr and Mrs Edward; 2321 Scott st.
Chevers, Miss Helena; 2311 Jackson st. *Friday*
——Mrs O. W.
——Miss Emma
——Miss Ruth

15

Chinn, Mrs Thomas; 2928 Clay st.

Chismore, Dr George; 920 Market st.

Chown, Mr and Mrs James G.; 922 Geary st.

Chown, Mr and Mrs James V.; 1411 Post st.

Choynski, Herbert; 1209 Golden Gate ave.

Chretien, Mr and Mrs John M.; 804 Bush st.   *Tuesday*

Chrystal, James B.; 310 Stockton st.

Chrystal, Pierre J.; 214 O'Farrell st.

Church, Rev and Mrs Edward B.; 1036 Valencia st.

Church, Seymour R. 209 Geary st.

Church, Mrs T. R.; 1016 Franklin st.   *Tuesday*

Cicott, Mr Frank X.; Lick House

Clapp, Mr and Mrs Milton B.; 923 Hyde st.

Clark, Mr and Mrs C. H.; Palace Hotel   *Monday*

Clark, Joseph; Union Club

Clark, Mrs George W.; 720 Union st.

——George W.

——Harry L.

Clark, Mr & Mrs Robert C.; NE cor.16th & Castro *Thursday* **Santa Barbara**

Clark, Mr and Mrs W. C.; 1703 Broderick st.

Clark, Mr and Mrs John J.; 327 Fremont st.   *Wednesday* **Santa Clara**

Clark, Warren D.; NE cor. California st. and Van Ness ave.

Clark, Mrs Z. P.; 2612 California st.   *Tuesday*   **Blithedale**

——Miss

Clark, Dr J. G: Office, 238 Kearny st.

Clarke, Mrs Jeremiah; 2119 California st.

——Miss Lottie

——Edward K.

Clarke, T. D.; Grand Hotel

Clawson, Leonard E.; 129 Oak st.

Clayton, Mrs C.; Hotel Pleasanton   *Monday*

Clement, Mr and Mrs L. H.; The Bella Vista   *Thursday*   **Lake Co.**

——Miss Ethel

Clements, John; Lick House

Cline, Mr Walter B.; cor. Annie and Stevenson sts.

Clough, Charles L.; Cosmos Club

Cluff, Mr and Mrs William; 1916 Vallejo st.

Cloman, Lieut S. A.; Angel Island

Clover, Lieut and Mrs Richard; U. S. N.   U. S. Steamer "Dolphin"

Clunie, Mr and Mrs Thomas J.; 836 Turk st.

Coats, Mr Geo. K.; 105 Montgomery st.

Cochran, Dr and Mrs John; The Berkshire   *Monday*

Cochrane, Dr and Mrs E. O.; 850 Market st.   *Monday*   **Santa Clara**

Code, Mr and Mrs James A.; 624 Haight st.   *Wednesday*

Code, Mr and Mrs Philip D.; 930 Valencia st.   *Tuesday*   **Del Monte**
——Miss May
——Miss Gladys M.
——Philip Jr.
Codman, H. L.; Menlo Park
Coe, Miss Grace E.; 1408 Bush st.   *Wednesday*
Coffey, Hon J. V.
Coffin, Mrs D. B.; 1614 Post st.
Coffin, Lieut W. U.; Presidio
Cofran, Mr and Mrs John W. G.; 1126 Hyde st.
Coggins, Edward B.; The Westminster, 614 Sutter st.
Cohen, Edward A.; 1706 Fillmore st.
Cohen, Mr and Mrs R.; Hotel Pleasanton   *Monday*
Cohn, Mrs David; 1404 Sutter st.
Colburn, Mrs C. H.; Palace Hotel   *Monday*
Cole, Hon Cornelius; Hotel Pleasanton   **Los Angeles**
Cole, Foster P.; 1707 Gough st.
Cole, Mr and Mrs N. P.; 1801 Franklin st.   *Monday*
——Charles M.
Cole, Dr and Mrs R. Beverly; 218 Post st.   ·   **Cosmos Club**
——Schuyler   **Los Angeles**
Cole, Mr and Mrs Thomas; 2006 Bush st.
——Miss Gussie
——Miss Etta
——Rudolph Y.
Coleman, Mrs E. B.; 1900 Franklin st.   **San Jose**
Coleman, Mr and Mrs Evan J.; 1450 Sacramento st. *Tuesday* **Del Monte**
Coleman, Mrs J. H.; Lick House   *Monday*
Coleman, Mrs Maria   **Washington, D. C.**
——James V.; Nevada Block
Coleman, Nicholas D.; Cosmos Club   **Los Angeles**
Coleman, Mr and Mrs Wm. T.; Pacific ave. and Fillmore   **San Rafael**
——Robert L.
Colley, F. A.; 202 San Jose ave.   ·
Collins, Mr and Mrs T. W.; 1824 Eddy st.
Colton, Mrs D. D.; California and Taylor sts.   *Tuesday*   **Santa Cruz**
Condit-Smith, Mrs J. C.
——Miss Alice
Condict, J. Elliot; 620 Sutter st. · *Thursday*
Connell, Miss Nora; 2221 Sutter st.
Conner, Mrs Julia W.; 1455 Franklin st.   *Friday*
——Miss Julie
——Fred
Conrad, Mr and Mrs David; 441 Golden Gate ave.
Conrad, Mr and Mrs J. G.; 1316 Buchanan st.

Conrad, Samuel; 317 Bush st.
Conroy, Miss; 2024 California st.
Cook, Dr A. S.; 224 Post st.
——Miss C. L.
——Mrs C. A.
Cook, Mr and Mrs H. N.; 809 Hyde st.
Cooke, Mrs Wm. B.; 522 O'Farrell st.   *Wednesday*
——Walter B.
Cook, Mrs J. E.; Hotel Pleasanton
Cook, Mr and Mrs William Hoff; Sixteenth and Hoff avenue
——Dr Channing H.
Coon, F. H.; 1239 Pine st.
Coon, Mr and Mrs Harry I.; 3014 Sacramento st.
Cooper, George D.; 1456 Franklin st.
Cooper, Mr and Mrs J. B. H.; 1926 Octavia st.   *Wednesday* **Del Monte**
——Miss Alice
Cooper, Mrs S. M.; 1608 Van Ness ave.
Cooper, Mrs Sarah B.; 1902 Vallejo st.
Cooper, William; 330 O'Farrell st.
Cope, Miss Anna; 826 Powell st.
Cope, Warner W.; 614 Sutter st.
Corbitt, Wm.; New California Hotel   *Monday*   **San Mateo**
——Miss Minnie
——Miss Nellie
Cormack, Mr and Mrs C. F.; 2508 Folsom st.
Corning, Mrs Phœbe; 843 Mission st.
Cornwall, Mr and Mrs P.; SE cor. Buchanan & Page *Wednesday* Glenwood
——Miss
Corran, Mr and Mrs W. H. L.; 626 Haight st.
Cortez, Madame Marie A.; Van Ness Seminary
Cory, Mr and Mrs I. H.; 326 Oak st.   *Wednesday*
Cosgrave, J. O'H.; 1227 Pine st.
——Miss Millicent
Cotton, Mrs Aylett R.; 837 Post st.
Coulson, Dr Nat T.; Hotel Marquette   *Tuesday*   **Lassen Co.**
Coulter, Mrs Clarence H.; Hotel Pleasanton   *Monday*
Coulter, Mr and Mrs Robt.; 1921 Clay st.   *Thursday*
——W. W.
Coursen, Miss Ellen; 1060 Fulton st.
Cousins, Mr and Mrs J. J.; 624 Golden Gate ave.
Cowie, Wallace M. ; 1224 Twenty-first st.
Cowles, Mr and Mrs Samuel W.; 35 Twelfth st.
Cowles, Wm. Northrope; Bohemian Club   **Santa Barbara**
Cox, Capt J. B.; 2740 California st.
Cox-Edwards, Mr J. F.; Hotel Pleasanton

18

Coxe, Major and Mrs F. M.; Hotel Beresford *Monday* **Hotel Ben Lomond**

Crabbé, Mrs Elise; 2406 Washington st.

——Miss Jeanne

Cragin, Geo. A.; Hotel Pleasanton

Craig, Mrs Wm.; Clay near Fillmore

Craigin, Mrs A. E.; 912 Pine st.

Cramer, Walter H.; 1123 Devisadero st.

Crane, A. E.; Hotel Pleasanton

Creighton, Mr and Mrs T. F.; 623 Shotwell st.   *Thursday*

Crane, Mr and Mrs Lemuel P.; 210 Fillmore st.   *Wednesday* **Santa Cruz**

——Miss Daisy L.

——Miss Lilabel

——Douglas B.

Crawford, Mrs J.; 1502½ California st.

Cressey, E. P.; Occidental Hotel

Creswell, Mr and Mrs Harry T.; 1123 Leavenworth st.

Crim, Mrs Samuel; 2320 Howard st.

——George S.

Crim, Mr and Mrs Wm. H.; 2526 Howard st.

Christy, Mrs H. P.; Hotel Pleasanton   *Monday*

Crittenden, C. S.; 305 Jones st.

Crocker, Col Charles F.; 915 Leavenworth st.

Crocker, Mrs Clark W.; 1609 Sutter st.   *Thursday*

——Miss Fanny

Crocker, Mrs E. B.; Sacramento

Crocker, Mr and Mrs H. S.; New California Hotel   *Monday*

——Charles H.

Crocker, Mr & Mrs Henry J.; NW cor. Washington & Laguna sts.   *Monday*

Crocker, Mr and Mrs John H.; 1422 Clay st.

Crocker, Mr & Mrs Wm. H.; California & Jones sts. *Tuesday* **Del Monte**

Crocker, George; 1100 California st.

Crockett, Mr and Mrs J. B.; 2029 California st.   *Friday*

Crooks, Mrs Susan; Palace Hotel   *Monday*   **Moscow Cottage**

——Miss Olive

Cropper, Mrs Minnie; Palace Hotel

Cropper, Mrs Thornburg; Pacific ave.

Crosett, Mr and Mrs J. F.; 2525 Folsom st.   *Tuesday*   **Pacific Grove**

Crothers, R. A.; 1018 Bush st.

——Miss Jennie

Crowley, Mr and Mrs Patrick; 1629 Sacramento st.

——Miss Daisy

——Miss Josie

Cummings, Francis; 1722 Sutter st.

Cunningham, Mrs James; 2518 Broadway st.

——John

Cunningham, John; 209 Gough st.

Curran, Mr Hugh ; SE cor Sansome and Pacific sts.
Currey, Judge and Mrs Montgomery ; Palace Hotel   *Monday*   **Dixon**
Currier, Mr and Mrs J. P. ; Hotel Pleasanton   *Monday*   **Sausalito**
——Miss Marie L.
——Miss Florence G.
Currey, Judge and Mrs John ; Palace Hotel   *Monday*
Currey, Montgomery ; 1920 Franklin st.   **Dixon**
Currey, Robert J. ; 1906 Laguna st.
Curtaz, Mr and Mrs Harry J. ; 2517 Fillmore st.   *Monday*
Curtis, Edward ; Grand Hotel
Curtis, Mrs Grace Taylor ; 709 Bush st.   *Thursday*
Curtis, Mr and Mrs John M. ; 2321 Webster st.   *Thursday*
——Miss
Curtis, Dr and Mrs R. H. ; 634 Sutter st.
Curtis, Mr and Mrs Jonathan ; 1720 Baker st.
Curtis, Mr and Mrs J. B. ; 1419 Hyde st.   *Thursday*
——Miss Agnes D.
Curtis, Mr and Mrs W. G. ; 811 Polk st.   *Thursday*
Cusheon, Miss L. ; 830 Bush st.   *Wednesday*
Cushing, Dr and Mrs Clinton ; 636 Sutter st.   **Coronado Beach**
Cushing, Mr and Mrs Sidney B. ; 508 California st.   **San Rafael**
Cuspenera, Madame ; The Berkshire   *Monday*
Cutlar, Dr and Mrs Roger ; 421 Ellis st.
Cutler, Mr and Mrs Ben A. ; 503½ Broderick st.   *Thursday*
Cutter, Mrs B. B. ; 500 Van Ness ave.   *Friday*   **Los Medanos**
Cutter, Mr and Mrs C. G. ; The Bella Vista   *Thursday*
Cutter, Mr and Mrs Edward B. ; 2422 Clay st.
Cutter, Mrs J. H. ; 2532 Washington st.
Cutting, General and Mrs John T. ; Occidental Hotel   *Monday*

Daggett, Mr and Mrs ; Bush and Mason sts.
——Miss Grace
Dallam, Mr and Mrs R. B. ; 1731 Sutter st.   *Thursday*
——Miss Ella
——Miss Annie
——Fred
Danforth, Mr and Mrs Edwin P. ; 1200 Mason st.   **Napa Soda Springs**
——Miss Fanny
——Mr and Mrs Edward P.
Daniels, Mr and Mrs John ; 2013 Polk st.   *Saturday*
——Miss May W.
——Miss L.
——John, Jr.
Daniels, Sam Houston ; 1321 Leavenworth st.   { *1st, 2d, & 3d Tuesdays* **Yosemite or Alaska**
——Miss Josephine Fanny
Danneviller, Prof Marc J. ; Hotel Pleasanton
Darling, Mr and Mrs George L. ; 515 Fell st.   *Tuesday*
Darling, Major John A. ; Pacific-Union Club   **Fort Mason**

Davidson, Prof and Mrs George; 2221 Washington st., after Jan., '91
——George F.
——Thomas D.
Davidson, Rev H.; 417 Mason st.
Davidson, Miss Della
Davis, Mrs Addie M.; 1120 Gough st.   *Wednesday*   Blithedale
Davis, Mr and Mrs A. G.; 1605 Scott st.   *Wednesday*
Davis, Mr J. M.; 17 Fremont st.
Davis, Mr and Mrs J. W.; 1635 Sacramento st.   *Wednesday* {Olympia {Wash. Ty.
——Miss Amelia
——Benj. F.
Davis, C.; 591 Ellis st.
Davis, Mr and Mrs E. G.; Hotel Pleasanton   *Monday*
Davis, Mr and Mrs George A.; 1109 Bush st.   *Wednesday*
——Mr and Mrs A. M.
Davis, Dr and Mrs G. E.; 107 Ridley st.
Davis, Dr and Mrs Henry C.; 2203 Sacramento st.   *3d and 4th Fridays*
Davis, Mr and Mrs Horace; 1011 Bush st.   *Thursday*
Davis, Mrs Isaac E.; 1802 Pacific ave.
Davis, Mr and Mrs John B. F.; 920 Guerrero st.
Davis, Mr and Mrs P. L.; 2317 Sutter st.   *Wednesday*
Davis, Mr and Mrs Robert J.; 2515 Broadway st.   *Friday*
Davis, Rev and Mrs Wm. W.; 2108 Jackson st.   *Tuesday*   San Rafael
——Miss Mary Converse
Day, Ben W.; 610 Commercial st.
Dayan, Mr and Mrs J. W.; 644 Oak st.   *Thursday*
Deacon, William; 811 Twentieth st.
Deacon, Mr and Mrs Geo. T.; 1912 San Carlos ave.   *Wednesday* Stockton
——M. G.
——F. C.
Deady, Miss Nellie M.; 216 Waller st.   *Thursday*
Dean, Mrs E. J.; Van Ness ave and Clay   *Monday*
——Miss Flora
——Miss Ethel
Dean, Mr and Mrs Walter E.; Baldwin Hotel   *Monday*
——Walter L.
Deane, Mrs M.; 1919 California st.   *Thursday*   San Rafael
——Miss Mamie
——J. J.
——William
Deane, Mr and Mrs Coll.; 1124 McAllister st.
Deane, Dr Charles Tenison; 1003 Sutter st.   *Tuesday*
——Louis C.
Dearborn, Capt and Mrs H. C.; Palace Hotel   *Monday* **"City of Pekin"**
Dearborn, Irving A.   **"City of New York"**
Debney, Capt Girard; 917 McAllister st.
——Charles G.

Decker, Mrs. Peter; Pacific ave.
———Miss Alice
Deering, Mrs K. A.; 413 Mason st.
———Miss Minnie
Deering, Mrs C. J.; 711 Jones st.
Deering, F. P.; 929 Fillmore st.
———Miss Annie
———J. H., Jr.
De Forrest, Mr and Mrs W. F.; Grand Hotel   *Monday*
Degener, L. E. (Consul of Guatemala); Cosmos Club
De Greyer, Mrs J. A.; 707 Mason st.   *Tuesday*
De Guigne, Mr and Mrs C.; 517 Sutter st.   **San Mateo**
Deitzler, Mrs George; 3309 Clay st.   *Wednesday*
———Miss Mamie
———Miss Georgie
Deitzel, Mrs; 19 Webster st.
———Miss
De Krafft, J. C.; Hotel Pleasanton
De la Montanya, Mr and Mrs James; 1508 Taylor st.   *Tuesday*
———Miss Jennie
De la Montanya, Mr and Mrs Jas., Jr.; 1508 Taylor { *Tuesday* **MarkWest Springs**
Delane, Charles; 105 Montgomery st.
De La Requena, Madame; The Berkshire   *Monday*
De Laveaga, Mr and Mrs M. A.; 1228 Geary st.   *Friday*
Delehanty, Lieut and Mrs Daniel; 707 Chestnut st.
Delmas, Mr and Mrs D.M.; Taylor and Washington sts. { *Tuesday* **Mountain View**
———Miss Delphine
———Miss A
———Miss Josie
Deming, Halleck; 714 Ellis st.
Dempsey, Miss; Palace Hotel   *Monday*
Denicke, E. A.; 819 Turk st.
Deming, Joseph G.; 225 Page st.
Denigan, Mr and Mrs Thos.; 1715 Octavia st.
Denman, Mr and Mrs James; 2101 Webster st.   *Friday*
———Miss May
———William
Denman, Miss Kate   *Wednesday*   **Petaluma**
Dennis, Dr and Mrs Frank H.; Palace Hotel   *Monday*
Dennis, Madame Zeiss; Palace Hotel   *Monday*
De Noon, Mrs; The Berkshire   *Monday*
———Miss Emma
———Miss Dottie
Denver, Miss Jennie; 320 Turk st.

BOVININE has Cured many Cases of St. Vitus' Dance

22

DePue, Elmer H.; Bohemian Club
DeRussey, Colonel Isaac D.; Pacific-Union Club
De Ruyter, Mr and Mrs John E.; 2206 Devisadero st.   San Rafael
De Sabla, Mr and Mrs Eugene; 219 Geary st.
De Sabla, Mr and Mrs Eugene, Jr.
Descalso, Mr and Mrs Luke M.; 1920 Howard st.
Deuprey, Mr and Mrs Eugene N.; 2629 Bush st.
De Vecchi, Dr and Mrs Paolo; 1715 Jackson st.   *Friday*
Devine, John; SE cor. Kearny and Clay sts.
DeVoe, Mrs B. O.; 1116 Powell st.   *Wednesday*
Dewey, Lieut and Mrs Theodore G.; U. S. N.   Washington, D. C.
Dexter, Mr and Mrs Frank   Saratoga
De Young, Mr and Mrs M.H.; 1919 California st.   *Thursday* San Rafael
Dibbern, J. Henry; 217 Sansome st.
Dibble, Mr and Mrs Henry C.; 1916 Sacramento st.
Dibblie, Mrs H. C.; 1719 Clay st.   *Thursday*
——Miss
Dickerson, Mr and Mrs W. L.; Hotel Pleasanton
Dickson, Mr and Mrs Robert; Baker and Haight sts.   *Thursday*
Dillenback, Captain J. W.   New York
Dillon, Mrs Nano; 501 Van Ness ave.
——Miss Kate
——Miss Marie
——Thomas I.
Dillon, Miss Kate May; 1329 Sutter st.
Dimond, Harry P.; Cosmos Club
Dimond, Gen W. H.; 2204 Pacific ave.   *Friday*   Menlo Park
——Miss Eleanor
——Miss Mae
-——Mr and Mrs E. R.
——Mr H. W.
Doane, Mr and Mrs W. G.; 2013 Bush st.   *Friday*
Dobinson, J. H.; 305 Sansome st.
Dodge, Mr and Mrs N.; 1019 Twenty-first st.
Dodge, Dr H. Washington; 2742 California st. *Friday* Hotel del Coronado
Dodge, Dr H. Washington; 2742 California st.
Dodge, Zenas U.; 225 Post st.
——Miss M.
Doe, John S.; Grand Hotel
Doe, Mr and Mrs Loring B.; Cosmos Club, 1727 Pine st. { Fish Rock, Mendocino Co.
Dolbeer, John; 828 Lombard st.
Dole, Miss Sarah L.; 1036 Valencia st.
Donahue, Mrs Annie; cor. Bryant and Second sts.   *Wednesday*
Donahue, Mrs Isabelle Wallace; 799 Van Ness ave.   San Rafael

Donahue, Mr Peter J.; 346 First st.	Laurel Wood
Donaldson, Mr and Mrs R. A.; 1151 Octavia st.	*Wednesday*
Donnels, H. C.; 101 Scott st.	
Donohoe, Mr and Mrs Jos. A.; 526 Harrison st.	} *Wednesday* }Menlo Park
——Edward	
——Mr and Mrs Jos. A., Jr.; 2117 Pacific ave.	
Doolan, Thomas; 1424 Mission st.	Santa Cruz
——R. P.	
Dooly, Miss Mary E.; 1321 Sutter st. *Thursday*	
Dore, Mrs Elizabeth; 2900 California st.	
——Miss Ruby	
Dore, Maurice; 1215 Jones st.	
——Miss Charlotte	
——Miss Nellie	
——Mrs Charles	
Dorland, Mr and Mrs T. A. C.; 623 Seventeenth st.	
——Miss Leonora	
Dorn, Lieut and Mrs Edward J., U. S. N.; The Bella Vista	*Thursday*
Dorr, Dr and Mrs L. L.; 1030 Post st. *Wednesday*	
Dornitt, Miss Ellen; 818 Powell st. *Tuesday*	
Dougherty Mrs A. B.; 1115 Geary st.	San Rafael
Doughty, Rev John; 1508 Leavenworth st.	
Douglass, Mr and Mrs Mark W.; Palace Hotel *Monday*	Sausalito
Douglass, W. A.; 809 O'Farrell st.	
Douty, Mr and Mrs Frank S.; 509 Webster st.	Del Monte
Dowling, Thomas H.; 1300 Pine st.	
Downey, Gov. and Mrs John G.	Los Angeles
Doxey, Mr and Mrs Wm.; 916 Fulton st.	
Dozier, Mr and Mrs Thomas B.	Redding
Dressel, Dr and Mrs G.; 1819 Clay st.	
Dreypolcher, Wm. S.; 1511 Pierce st.	
Drexler, Mr and Mrs Louis P.; 1603 Van Ness ave.	
Drinkhouse, Mr and Mrs J. A.; 42 South Park	
——Miss Lulu	
——John A., Jr.	
——Frederick R.	
Drown, Mr and Mrs A. N.; NE cor. Jackson and Pierce sts.	
Dubedat, Eugene; 1014 Sutter st.	
——Edward; 217 Grant ave.	
Duff, Miss A. M.; Hotel Pleasanton *Monday*	
Dugan, Albert D.; 416 Oak st.	
Duggan, James B.; 105 Montgomery st.	
Duisenberg, C. A. C.; 1031 Harrison st.	

24

Duncan, Mr and Mrs Hilarion; 1823 Turk st.   Clayton
——Miss Marion
Duncan, Mr and Mrs U. J.; Strathmore House
Duncan, Mr and Mrs William L.; 1501 Jones st.
Dunn, H. L.; 105 Montgomery st.
Dunning, W. B.; U. S. N.; Cosmos Club
Dunbar, Chaplain and Mrs. G. W.; U. S. A., Presidio *Friday*
——Miss
——A. W.
Dunphy, Mr and Mrs W. H.; Palace Hotel *Monday*
Dunphy, Mr and Mrs William ; 2122 Washington st. Cupertino
——Miss Jennie
——James C.
Dunsmuir, Alexander ; Pacific-Union Club
Dunwoody, Lieut and Mrs F. M.; U. S. N. "Bear"
Durand, Mr and Mrs Joseph A. ; 17 South Park
——Miss Gabrielle
Durbrow, Mr and Mrs A. K.; 1615 Washington st. *Tuesday*
——Miss Katharine
Durbrow, Mr and Mrs Elbridge; 1706 Buchanan st. *Friday*
Durbrow, Mrs Joseph; 1124 Bush st. *Thursday*
——Miss Emma
——Harry
Durden, Henry S.; 1720 Union st.
Dutard, Mr and Mrs Hyppolite; 2510 Fillmore st.
Dutton, Mrs Henry; 1732 Pacific ave.
Dutton, Mr and Mrs Samuel E.; 2511 Sacramento st. *Friday*
——Miss Lottie
——Miss Louise
Dutton, Mr and Mrs Wm. J.; 2007 Devisadero st. *Tuesday*
Duval, Geo. L. Peru
Du Val, Mr and Mrs W. S.; 1012 Pine st. *Thursday* Oakville, Napa

Eagan, Capt and Mrs Chas. P.; Occidental Hotel *Monday* Monterey
——Miss Estelle M.
——Charles E.
Eagleson, J. G.; 317 Stockton st.
——R.; 328 Geary st.
Earl, Mrs Edwin; Hotel Pleasanton
Earl, Mrs D. W.; 2297 Sacramento st.
Earl, Mr and Mrs John O.; 2440 Jackson st.
Eastland, Mr and Mrs Joseph G.; Palace Hotel.
Easton, Mr and Mrs Ansel M. Millbrae
Easton, Mrs A. M.; Leavenworth and Pine sts. San Mateo
Easton, George D.; Hotel Pleasanton

Easton, Mr and Mrs George; 2608 California st.
Easton, Mrs O. W.; Hotel Pleasanton   *Monday*
——Miss E. B.
Easton, Mr and Mrs Wendell
Eaton, Mrs Hester A.; 2102 Mason st.   *Thursday*
Eaton, Mrs J. A.; 1804 Sutter st.
Eberle, Lieut and Mrs Edward Walter; 1912 Vallejo st. *Friday* **U. S. N.**
Ebbets, Mr and Mrs Arthur M.; 1401 Jones st.   *Tuesday*
——Miss Carry
——Miss Annie
Eccleston, Miss; care Lieut A. C. Blunt; Presidio
Eddy, Miss Mabel; 1420 California st.
Edgar, William M.; 12 Mason st.
Edgerton, Mrs Frances B.; 1001 Leavenworth st.   *Thursday*
Edmunds, Miss Emily; The Bella Vista   *Thursday*   **Del Monte**
Emonds, Lieut Frank H.; U. S. A.   **Angel Island**
Edston, George; 423 California st.
Edwards, Miss; Scott st. near Haight st.
Edwards, Mrs M. A.; 609 Post st.
—— –Miss Mercy
Edwards, Miss Lucy; Steiner and O'Farrell sts.
——Miss Georgie
Eells, Mrs James; 1920 Franklin st.   *Friday*   **Calistoga**
Eells, Mr and Mrs John S.; 2508 Folsom st.
——Miss Lulu M.
Eells, Mr and Mrs Charles P.
Eells, Miss; 2524 Washington st.
Eggers, George H.; 1130 Eddy st.
——The Misses
Ehrenberg, Dr A. T.; 918 Hyde st.
——Thomas E.
Ehrman, Mr and Mrs M; 519 Van Vess ave.
Einstein, Mrs M.; 1457 Franklin st.   *3d and 4th Thursdays*
Elam, Mrs R. H.; 1902 Broadway st.
Eldridge, Oliver; 615 Sutter st.
Eliot, Joseph B.; 325 Seventeenth st.
Elliot, Mr and Mrs Charles; 516 Sutter st.
Elliott, Mrs W. L.; 1827 Sacramento st.   *Friday*
——Miss
——Miss Frances V.
——Miss Mary B.
Ellis, Rev and Mrs John W.; The Renton, 712 Sutter st.
Ellis, Asa; Int. Revenue Collector
Ellis, Mr and Mrs A. C.; 2524 Washington st.

Ellis, Mrs W. T.; Occidental Hotel   Marysville
——Miss Hope
Ellis, Mrs Leila; 930 Sutter st.
——Miss
Ellsworth, Mrs; 712 Sutter st., The Renton
Eloesser, Mr and Mrs Arthur; 2702 Laguna st.   *2d and 4th Thursdays*
Elwell, Frank D.; 24 Fell st.
Emeric, Mr and Mrs H. F.; 1115 Geary st.
Emmerich, Mr E.; 36 New Montgomery st.
Emery, W. H.; 1632 Post st.
Emmal, Joseph B.; 612 Jones st.
——The Misses
Emmons, Elmer S.; 1023 Valencia st.
Endres, Jacob; 408 Haight st.
Engelbrecht, H.; 1523 Webster st.
Engelbrecht, Mr and Mrs H. A.; 106 Webster st.
Engelbrecht, R. T.; 834 Turk st.
English, Mr and Mrs John F.; 2417 Howard st.
Eppinger, Mr and Mrs J.; 1102 Van Ness ave.   *Monday*
Erickson, Miss E.; 117 Jones st.   *Thursday*
Estee, Mr and Mrs Morris M.; Palace Hotel *Monday* "Hedgeside," Napa
Erwin, Lieut and Mrs James B.; Presidio
Evans, Mrs George S.; 141 Hancock st.   *Wednesday*
——Miss Hallie
Evans, L. J.; NW cor. Haight and Gough sts.
Evans, Judge and Mrs O. P.; 2416 Washington st.   *Friday*
Everett, Mr and Mrs E.; The Bella Vista
——E.
Everts, Mr and Mrs P.; The Bella Vista   *Thursday*
Eyre, Colonel and Mrs E. E.; 2119 California st.   *Monday* **Menlo Park**
——Miss
——Perry P.
Eyre, Mr and Mrs Edwin L.; 1804 Octavia st.
Fagan, Mr and Mrs E.; The Berkshire   *Monday*
Fair, Charles L.   Abroad
Fair, James G.; Occidental Hotel   Virginia City, Nev.
——James G. Jr.
Fair, Mrs Theresa; 1120 Pine st.   *Thursday*   Del Monte
——Miss Birdie
Fairchild, Harriet M.; The Berkshire
Faison, Lieut S. L., U. S. A.; Benicia Barracks   Benicia
Falkenstein, Mr and Mrs H.; Palace Hotel   *Monday*
——Miss
Fallon, J. H.; 438 Geary st.
Fargo, Calvin F.; Pacific-Union Club

Fargo, Mr and Mrs Earl A.; 1919 Sutter st.   *Wednesday*
Fargo, Jerome B.; 1310 O'Farrell st.   *3d and 4th Fridays*
————Miss Lulu
Farnfield, Charles P.; Cosmos Club
Farnsworth, Mr and Mrs; 125 Golden Gate ave.
————Miss Lotta
Farnsworth, E. D.; 105 Scott st.
Faroe, Dr K; 841 Market st.   *Friday*   Paris, France
————Miss A. M.
Farquharson, Charles; 620 Sutter st.
Farquharson, David; Baldwin Hotel
————D. F.
Farren, Mr and Mrs John W.; 500 Harrison st.
————The Misses
————John W., Jr.
Farwell, Mr and Mrs Willard B.; 2318 Steiner st.   *Friday*
————Miss Edith
Fasanotti, Rev. A.; 620 Vallejo st.
Fassett, Mr and Mrs J. S.   New York
Faull, Mr and Mrs John A.; 1209 Sutter st.   *Tuesday*
————Miss Mary
Fay, Mr and Mrs Edward; 2315 California st.   *Tuesday*
Featherston, Mrs Mary; 1805 Jones st.   *Thursday*   Santa Cruz
————Miss Lillian
————Miss Minnie
————John N.
Fechheimer, Benjamin C.; 1453 Franklin st.
Felton, Hon Chas. N.; Palace Hotel   Menlo Park
————Chas. N., Jr.
Felton, Walter W.; 1460 O'Farrell st.   Mazatlan, Mexico
Fenn, Mr and Mrs T. W.; 3027 California st.
Fennell, Gerald M.; Palace Hotel
Fennimore, Mr and Mrs Watson D.; 501 Geary st.
Ferguson, Mr and Mrs G. B.; The Renton   *Monday*
Ferguson, Mrs W. S.; 448 Guerrero st.
Fernald, Commander and Mrs; Hotel Pleasanton   *Monday*
————C. B.
Ferral, Judge and Mrs Robert; 2518 California st.
Ferrer, Mrs Henry; 320 Geary st.
Ferrer, Manuel Y.; 1810 Pine st.   *Friday*
————Miss Carmelita
————Miss Eugenie
————Miss Adele
————Richard

28

Field, Mr and Mrs Hampton S.; 1608 Post st. *Monday*
Field, Justice and Mrs Stephen J.; Pacific-Union Club **Washington, D. C.**
Fielding, W. B.; 621 Bush st.
Fillmore, Mr and Mrs Jerome A.; Occidental Hotel *Monday* **Del Monte**
Findley, Mrs Thomas; 2316 Clay st. **Sausalito**
——Miss Mamie
——Miss Edith
——Miss Lulu
——Thomas
Finlay, Mr and Mrs John; SW cor. Jones and Chestnut sts.
Finley, Lieut and Mrs J. P.; Hotel Pleasanton
Finley, Mrs M. J.; SE cor. Francisco and Leavenworth { *Friday* **Santa Cruz**
——Miss Jennie
——Miss Rose
——Miss Mary C.
——P.
Finn, Judge and Mrs John F.; 902 Van Ness ave.
Finigan, Col and Mrs P. A.; 1248 California st. **Del Monte**
Fish, Mrs Jennie F.; 1310 O'Farrell st. *3d and 4th Fridays*
Fish, Mr and Mrs Azel H.; 129 Haight st.
Fish, Mr and Mrs T. F.; The Bella Vista *Thursday*
Fisher, Mr and Mrs Charles A.; 309 Jones st.
Fisher, Mr and Mrs E. F.; The Berkshire *Monday*
Fisher, Mrs Jennie; 210 Powell st. **Carson City, Nevada**
Fisher, Dr Walter E.; Occidental Hotel
Fisher, Will E.; Hotel Pleasanton **Monterey**
Fisher, Wm. H.; 1512 California st. and 410 Sacramento st.
Fiske, Dr and Mrs Henry M.; 2100 Bush st. *Tuesday*
Fitch, Mr and Mrs George K.; 703 Bush st.
——Miss
——Miss Florence
Fitch, Mrs S. L.; 1008 Green st.
Fitch, Mrs H. A.; 1021 Polk st.
Fitch, J. R.; 2409 Jackson st.
Fitch, Mr and Mrs Thos, Jr.; Hotel Pleasanton
Flack, Mr and Mrs George D.; 2909 Folsom st. *Thursday*
——Miss Minnie
Flagg, C. C.; The Berkshire
Flavin, Mr and Mrs M. J.; 914 Sutter st. **Menlo Park**
Fletcher, Mr and Mrs George W.; 714 Waller st. *Thursday*
Fletcher, Lieut and Mrs Robert H.; The Bella Vista *Thursday*
Flint, Mr and Mrs B. P.; 1121 Hyde st.
Flint, Dr and Mrs Thomas; Grand Hotel *Monday* **San Juan**
——Miss
Flood, John W.; 422 Eddy st.

29

Flood, Mr and Mrs George W. F.; 1424 Mission st.   **Del Monte**
Flood, Mrs James C.; 1010 California st.   **Menlo Park**
——Miss
——James L.
Flournoy, Colonel and Mrs George; 1140 Twenty-first st.
——Miss Marguerite
Flournoy, Mr and Mrs George Jr.; 24th and Ellen sts.
Floyd, Mrs R. S.; 415 First st.   *Wednesday*   **Clear Lake, Kelseyville**
——Miss Harry
Folger, J. A.; 110 California st.   **Oakland**
Folger, Daniel W.; 1916 Franklin st.
Follis, Mr and Mrs R. H.; 2534 Mission st.
Folsom, Mr and Mrs A.; 2918 Sacramento st.   *Wednesday*
Folsom, Mr and Mrs George A.; 1509 Jackson st.   *Thursday*
Folsom, George S.; Cosmos Club
Folsom, J. R.; Cosmos Club
Fonda, William M.; 3011 Sacramento st.
——Charles P.
——Henry S.
——Mr and Mrs William F.
Foote, General and Mrs Lucius H.; 800 McAllister st.
Forbes, Mrs Alexander; 2115 Broadway   **San Rafael**
——Miss Kate
——Miss Edith
Forbes, William D.; 2214 Jackson st.
Forbes, A. B.; 29 Essex st.
——Cleveland
Forchheimer, Mr and Mrs A.; 1603 Scott st.   *Thursday*
Ford, Mr and Mrs Alfred B.; 1620 Broadway st.
Ford, Mr C. W. R.; 532 Market st. and Commercial Hotel
Ford, Joseph A.; Palace Hotel
Forman, Robert B.; 2120 Broadway   **Menlo Park**
Forman, Mr and Mrs Sands W.; Occidental Hotel
Forney, Stehman, U. S. Coast Survey; Cosmos Club
Forsaith, E. W.; Grand Hotel
Forsyth, Colonel and Mrs Wm.; Fresno
Foss, Oscar; 428 Geary st.
Foster, Mr and Mrs Samuel; Hotel Pleasanton   *Monday*
Foster, William   **Honolulu, H. I.**
Foulkes, Dr and Mrs John F.; NW cor.Wash. & Fillmore sts. *Wednesday*
Foute, Rev and Mrs R. C.; 2125 Jackson st   *Monday*
Fowler, Bishop & Mrs Charles H.; SW cor. Oak & Buchanan sts. *Thurs.*
——Carl H.
——William
Fox, Dr and Mrs C.W.; Baldwin Hotel *Monday* **Coronado or PasoRobles**

30

Foye, W. R. S.; 1619 Howard st.

Frank, Mr and Mrs F. A.; 2001 Van Ness ave.

Franks, Mr Chris; U. S. Building, City

Francis, Mr and Mrs D. B.; 2320 California st.

Fraser, Mr and Mrs T. E.; Lick House   *Monday*

Freeborn, Mr and Mrs James; NE cor. Jackson and Gough sts.

French, Mr and Mrs Frank J.; 1617 Jackson st.   *Friday*

Freud, Mr and Mrs L ; 1816 Sacramento st.

Friedlander, Mrs Isaac; 1913 Clay st.   Santa Cruz

——Miss Fannie

——Miss May

——T. Cary

Friedlander, Joseph; Anglo-Cal. Bank

Friedman, J.; Palace Hotel

Fries, Mr and Mrs William; 1814 Washington st.

Frill, Captain and Mrs D. E.; Palace Hotel · *Monday*

Frink, Mr and Mrs Geo. W.; Hotel Pleasanton

Frisbie, General and Mrs.; 1308 Geary st.

Froelich, Christian, Jr.; Pacific-Union Club

Frölich, Mrs T. H.; 1216 Clay st.

Frost, Mr A. S.; 1514 Sacramento st.

Fry, Colonel and Mrs J. D.; 1812 Jackson st.

——Mr and Mrs Robert D.

Fuendeling, Pastor J.; 705 Bush st.

Fulda, Mr and Mrs L. R.; 106 Ellis st.

Fuller, Mr and Mrs William P., Jr.; 922 Fillmore st.   San Jose

Fulweiler, Judge J. M.; Cosmos Club   Auburn

Fuller, Mrs William P.; Hotel Pleasanton

——Miss Nellie

——Miss Bertha

Fulton, Mrs Paymaster   Washington, D. C.

Fulton, Mrs William, Jr.; 2418 Washington st.

Fulton, Miss A. M.; 1215 Sutter st.   *Thursday*

Gage, Mr and Mrs William S.; 822 Bush st.

——William S., Jr.

Gallagher, Mr and Mrs Henry; 224 Castro st.   *Tuesday*

Gallatin, Mr and Mrs Albert; 1840 California st.   *Tuesday*   Sacramento

——Miss Jennie

——Albert, Jr.

Galloway, W. T.; 2203 Devisadero st.

Galpin, Philip G.; 1736 Broadway st.

Galvini, Signor G. B.; 325 O'Farrell st.   · Europe

Gamble, Mrs S. B.; 1222 Pine

——Mr and Mrs J. W.

——Miss Clara

Garber, Miss E. B.; Palace Hotel   **Napa Soda Springs**

Garber, Judge and Mrs Eugene R.; Palace Hotel *Monday* **Napa Soda Springs**

Garber, Miss Margaret M.; 1534 Sutter st.   *Friday*

Gardet, Mr and Mrs Victor; 2310 Webster st.   *Wednesday* } **Santa Clara and Willows**

Gardiner, Miss; The Berkshire   *Monday*

Gariepy, Mrs.; 533 Taylor st.

Garnett, Mr and Mrs Louis A.; 35 Essex st.

——Miss

——Edgar M.

——Malcolm

——William H.

Garniss, Mr and Mrs James R.; Palace Hotel   *Thursday*

Garratt, Mrs W. T.; 405 Sixth st.   *Monday*

——Mr and Mrs William T., Jr.

——Miss Julia

Garrett, L. M., U. S. N.; Cosmos Club

Garvin, Rev and Mrs Thos. D.; Oriel Hotel   *Monday*

Garwood, Dr and Mrs William T.; 1523 Bush st.

Gashwiler, Mr and Mrs S. F.; 1820 Vallejo st.

Gately, Miss Mamie; 718 O'Farrell st.

Gattig, L.; 526 Calitornia st.

Gauld, Mr and Mrs James G.; 2220 Webster st.   *Friday*

Geldermann, Mr and Mrs E.; 1923 Broderick st.   *Friday*

Gerald, E. F.; Pacific-Union Club

Gerberding, A.; Bohemian Club

Gere, Miss Lucia; The Bella Vista   *Thursday*

Gerstle, Mr and Mrs Lewis; 1517 Van Ness ave.

——Frederick

Ghietelin, Dr J. F.; Occidental Hotel

Gibbon, A. D.   **Mare Island**

Gibbons, Dr and Mrs H., Jr.; 920 Polk st.   *Monday*

Gibbons, Lieut John H.; U. S. N.   **Mare Island**

Gibbons, Mrs T. P.; Hotel Pleasanton   *Monday*

Gibbon, Maj-Gen and Mrs John, U. S. A.; Hotel Pleasanton   **Fort Mason**

——Miss

Gibbs, Mr and Mrs C. V. S.; 722 Post st.   **San Rafael**

——Miss Mattie

——Harry T.

Gibbs, Mr and Mrs Charles E.; 833 Post st.   *Tuesday*

——Miss Lena J.

——Miss Mary P.

Gibbs, Mr and Mrs Frederick A.; 431 Bartlett st.   *Wednesday*

Gibbs, Mr and Mrs George W.; 2857 Sixteenth st.

Gibson, Mrs E.; 520 Bush st.

Gibson, Mrs F. A.; 15 Hill st.   Florence, Santa Clara Co.
Gibson, Mr and Mrs M. P.; 626½ Seventeenth st.   *Tuesday*   Mountain View
Giffard, Mme E. C.; 1222 Pine st.
Giffin, Mrs H. E; 2621 Sacramento st.
Giffin, Mr and Mrs O. F.; 2621 Sacramento st.
——Oscar F., Jr
Gillette, D. B.
——Miss

Gillig, Mr and Mrs John; The Bella Vista   *Thursday*   Virginia, Nev.
Gillig, Mr and Mrs Harry   Abroad

Gilliland, Mr and Mrs Adam; 923 Fillmore st.   *Tuesday*
Gillon, James; Baldwin Hotel
Gilman, Capt H.; Hotel Pleasanton
Gilmore, F. P.; 1104 Market st.
Gilmore, Mr and Mrs John H.; Hotel Pleasanton   *Monday*

Gilson, Mr and Mrs L.; Palace Hotel   *Monday*
Girvin, Mr and Mrs R. D.; 2224 California st.   *Friday*
Givens, C. S.; Occidental Hotel
Glass, Mr Louis ; Pacific-Union Club
Gleason, Miss Annie (Mlle. Anita Alameda), 2415 Fillmore st.
Glover, Mrs George F.
——Miss

Gnudelmyn,, Joseph ; Lick House
Goad, Mr and Mrs W. Frank ; cor. Washington and Gough   Hotel del Monte
——Miss Ella
——Aileen
——Genevieve
——Hattie Belle

Godley, Mr and Mrs Montgomery ; 1818 Sacramento st.
——Jesse E.

Godsey, G. P. ; Lick House
Goewey, James M. ; 300 Page st.   *Tuesday*   Monterey
——Miss Gertrude
——Charles H.
——Frank B.
——J. Monroe

Goetze, Mrs Henry ; 1006 Fillmore st.
Goggin, Mr and Mrs E. W. ; 1913 Van Ness ave.   *Friday*
Golcher, Mr and Mrs Henry C.; 105 Broderick st.   *Thursday*
Golcher, Mr and Mrs J. W.; 1506 Taylor st.   *Wednesday*
Goldberg, Mr and Mrs J.; 2620 California st.
Gonzales, A.; 300 Van Ness ave.
Gonzales, Mrs J. S.; 1114 Powell st.
Goodall, Mr and Mrs C. M.; 1062 Fulton st.

Goodall, Capt and Mrs Charles ; SE cor. McAllister and Pierce sts.
——Edward S.   San Mateo
——Harry W.
Goodman, Mr and Mrs T. H.; Palace Hotel   *Monday*   Del Monte
Goodman, Mrs J. H.; Palace Hotel
Goodrich, E. D.; Palace Hotel
Goodrich, Taylor ; 513 Taylor st.
Goodspeed, Mrs R. C.; 300 Fair Oaks st.
——Miss Annie
——O. C.
Gordon, Mrs ; The Renton   *Monday*
——Miss
——C. P.
Gordon, Major and Mrs D. S.; U. S. A.; 720 Pine st. *Monday* **Hotel Vendome**
Gordon, Geo. W.; Grand Hotel
Gorom, Nelson; U. S. Building, City
Gottig, Lawrence; 1806 Pine st.
Gottlob, Mr J. J.; 3¼ Monroe st.   *Tuesday*   Tiburon
——Miss Annie F.
Gove, Mr and Mrs Andrew J.; 925 Vallejo st.
——Miss Alice
Gove, Lieut and Mrs C. A.; U. S. N.; Hotel Pleasanton   *Monday*
Gould, Mr and Mrs E. H.; Lick House   *Monday*
Gould, Major and Mrs Wm. O.; 904 Van Ness ave.   *Tuesday*   Santa Cruz
——Miss Carrie L.
Graham, General and Mrs W. M.; U. S. A.; Presidio
——Miss Mary
——Miss Hattie
——Miss Meta
Graham, Mrs C. Tempest; Bush st.   Boulder Creek
——Miss Maud
——Miss Lily
Grannis, Col and Mrs George W.; 19 Hawthorne st.   *Wednesday*
Grant, Mr and Mrs Adam; 1112 Bush st.   *Thursday*   Hotel Rafael
——Joseph D.
Grant, Mr and Mrs Charles W.; 2011 Lyon st.   *Thursday*
——Miss Belle
Grant, Mr and Mrs George F.; 1420 California st.   *Thursday*
Grant, Mr and Mrs Jesse; Palace Hotel   *Monday*
Grant, Mr and Mrs Thomas C.; 213 Sansome st.   Napa
——Miss Mary
Grattan, Mr and Mrs W. H.   St. Helena, Napa Co.
Graves, Ernest; Cosmos Club   San Luis Obispo
Graves, Hiram T.; 204 Lombard st.
Graves, Mr and Mrs Robert N.   Hotel Rafael
——Miss Elma

Graves, Mr and Mrs Walker C.; 2131 Howard st. *Wednesday* **Fresno**
——Jefferson James
——Walker C., Jr.
Gray, George E.; 1115 Bush st.
——Miss Anna
——George Vernon
Gray, George F.; 432 Ellis st.
Gray, Henry W.; 208 Jones st.
Gray, Rev and Mrs John; 616 Folsom st. *Thursday*
——Miss Dottie
Green, Mr and Mrs Charles E.; 2607 Fillmore st.
Green, Mrs Duff; The Bella Vista *Thursday*
——Miss F.
Green, Mrs O.; The Pleasanton
Green, Mr and Mrs F. H.; Hotel Pleasanton *Monday*
Greenbaum, Mrs L.; 1026 Ellis st. *Tuesday* **Napa Soda Springs**
——William L.
Greenberg, Mr and Mrs S. H.: 2418 Webster st.
Greenblatt, Mr and Mrs M.; 1300 Laguna st.
Greene, Mr and Mrs Harry A.; 38 Eleventh st. *Friday* **Pacific Grove**
——Miss
Greene, Mr and Mrs N.; 1437 McAllister st. *Wednesday* **Agua Caliente**
Greenebaum, Mr and Mrs Alfred; 1296 Van Ness ave. *Friday*
Greenebaum, William, 2100 Van Ness ave.
Greenway, Edward M.; New California Hotel and Room 4, Nevada Block
Greer, Miss Anna P.; 1216 Hyde st. *Tuesday*
——Miss Mary M.
Gregoire, Mr and Mrs Louis; 816 Capp st. *Tuesday*
Gregory, Mrs H. P.; NW cor Jackson and Durant *Wednesday* **Soquel**
Grey, Miss Jane; St. Ann's Building, cor Eddy and Powell sts.
Griffin, William D.; 134 Haight st. *Tuesday*
——Miss Mollie E.
——Mrs M.
Griffing, Mrs A.; 1416 Jackson st.
——The Misses
Griffith, Capt and Mrs Millen; 569 Harrison st.
——Miss Jennie
——Miss Carrie
——Miss Alice
Grim, Mr and Mrs A. K.; 1810 Gough st.
——Alfred R.
Grim, Mr and Mrs Alonzo M.; 3026 Washington st.
Griswold, N. L.; 809 Haight st.
Griswold, Mr and Mrs N. W.; 2105 Pine st. } *Last Thursday* "Malrem Hall," Los Guilicos
——Miss

Gros, Mr and Mrs Alfred; 1113 Hyde st.
Grosvener, Mrs Frederica; The Berkshire   *Monday*
Grow, Mr and Mrs Charles A.; The Bella Vista   *Thursday*
Gruenhagen, Mr and Mrs W.; 412½ Post st.   *Friday*
Gummer, Mrs C. V.; The Bella Vista   *Thursday*
Gülich, E. L.; The Bella Vista
Gump, Solomon; 1224 Geary st.
Gunn, Mr and Mrs J. O'B.; 1833 Clay st.   *Friday*
Gunnison, A. J.; 1404 Van Ness ave.
Gunst, Mr and Mrs Si; 203 Kearny st.
——Mr and Mrs Lee
——Mr and Mrs A.
Gunst, Mr and Mrs M. A.; 1508 Pine st.
Gurney, Mr and Mrs J. Theodore ; Occidental Hotel   Boston, Mass.
Gutte, Isador; 217 Leavenworth st.
Gutte, Julius; 2202 Jackson st.
Gutzkow, Mr and Mrs Frederick; 18 Columbia square   *Wednesday*
——Miss Minnie
Gwin, Mrs Sarah C.; 1603 Gough st.
——Miss Maggie
Gwin, Mrs M. E. H.; 1450 Sacramento st.
——Miss Carrie
Gwin, Mr and Mrs William M.; 1512 California st.

Haas, Mr and Mrs George; 612 Ellis st.   *Wednesday*
Habenicht, F.; 1321 Pine st.
Haber, Mr and Mrs F. A.; 1603 Scott st.   *Thursday*
——Miss Ruth S.
——Louis F.
Hackett, 506 Battery st.
Hadley, Mr and Mrs Frederick W.; 518 Capp st.
Hagar, Col and Mrs George: Occidental Hotel   Colusa
——Miss Alice
Hageman, Mr and Mrs George; 723 Bush st.
——Miss Lillie
Hagar, Mrs John S.; NE cor. Jackson and Gough sts.   *Friday*   Menlo Park
——Miss
——Alice
Hager, Mrs L. T.; Palace Hotel
Haggin, Mr and Mrs J. B.; 1250 Taylor st.   *Tuesday*
——Miss Rita
Hahn, Mr and Mrs Eugene; 1013 Leavenworth st.
——Miss Theresa
Haight, Mr and Mrs George   Stege Station, Contra Costa Co.
Haight, Mrs W. A.; 710 Leavenworth st.
Haines, Dr and Mrs Byron W.; The Pleasanton   *Wednesday*

36

Hair, Mr and Mrs James; Florence House
Haker, G. F.; 2117 California st.
———William
Hale, Miss; 2518 Broadway st.
Hale, Mr and Mrs Joseph P.; Occidental Hotel   *Monday*   **Mountain View**
Haley, Mr and Mrs J. J.; 601 Buchanan st.
Hall, Mr and Mrs A. A.; The Bella Vista   *Thursday*
Hall, George; Bohemian Club   " Miramar" **Santa Barbara Co.**
Hall, Mr and Mrs Wm. H.; 1307 Hayes st.
———Miss Anna
Hall, Mr and Mrs Harry F.; Pacific-Union Club   **San Rafael**
Hall, Mr and Mrs Jennison C.; 2323 Pacific ave.   *Monday*
Hall, Mr and Mrs John C.; 2034 Bush st.   *Tuesday*
Hall, Mrs N. C.; Palace Hotel   *Monday*
Hall, Mr and Mrs Milton R.; Hotel Pleasanton   *Monday*
Hall, Mrs Robert C.; 2512 Washington st.   *Thursday*
Hall, Mr and Mrs William P.   *Thursday*   **Petaluma**
———Miss Hattie
Hall, Will S.; 1460 O'Farrell st.
Hallett, Mr and Mrs George H.; Palace Hotel   *Monday*
Hallett, William T.; Palace Hotel
Hallidie, Mr and Mrs A. S.; 1026 Washington st.
Halsey, Mr and Mrs A.; Palace Hotel   *Monday*
Halstead, Mr and Mrs J. L.; 612 Webster st.
———John B.
Halstead, Mr and Mrs W. A.; 814 Scott st.   *Wednesday*
Haley, Dr Charles S.; 110 McAllister st.
———Miss
Hamer, Susie C., Palace Hotel   *Thursday*   **Ventura**
Hamill, John E., 25 Dorland st.
Hamilton, Claude T.; Cosmos Club   **Sausalito**
Hamilton, Mr and Mrs F. F.; The Renton   *Monday*   **Erolia**
Hamilton, James T.; 1013 Scott st.
Hamilton, Mrs Lulu; 905 Sutter st.   *Monday*
Hamilton, Mr and Mrs Robert M.; 1015 California st.   *Tuesday*
———Miss May
———Miss Lelia
———Alexander
———Robert, Jr.
Hamilton, Dr and Mrs W.; The Oriel   *Monday*
———Miss
Hamilton, Mr and Mrs Alex. F. Fisher; 951 Chesnut st.
Hamilton, William; Grand Hotel
Hamlin, Miss Sarah D.; 1408 Van Ness ave.
Hamm, Mr and Mrs L. J.; Cosmos Club   **San Rafael**

Perrier-Jouët & Co., Champagnes To be had at All First-Class Hotels and Restaurants

Hammersley, George H.; 1028 Hyde st.
Hammersley, George H., Jr.; 1512 Sacramento st.
Hammersmith, Mr and Mrs John A.; 1920 Broadway st.
Hammond, John; 714 Geary st.
Hammond, Mrs John Hays; 2504 Scott st.   *Friday*
Hammond, Rev John D.; 627 Hayes st.
Hammond, Major Richard P.; Pacific-Union Club, 2504 Scott st.
Hammond, General Richard P., Jr.; 2504 Scott st.   **Monterey**   **San Rafael**
Hampton, John C.   **Sacramento**   **Virginia City, Nev.**
Hancock, Mrs. Ida; 1621 Larkin st.   **Los Angeles**
Hancock, Lieut and Mrs W. F.   **Alcatraz Island**
Hand, John S.; 314 Kearny st.
Hanlon, Mr and Mrs Daniel; 1627 Jackson st.   *Friday*
——Miss
——Miss Josie
——John F.
——Daniel M.

Hanlon, Mr and Mrs John D.; 1915 Baker st.   *Thursday*
Haquette, Mr and Mrs Ernest; 1613 Post st.   *Thursday*   **Belmont**
——Miss Daisy
Haraszthy, Arpad; 1301 Leavenworth st.   **Los Angeles**
Hardin, Mr & Mrs C. H. E.; 1404 McAllister st.   *Tuesday* **Tallac, L. Tahoe**
Harding, Mr and Mrs George J.   **Philadelphia**
Hare, Mr and Mrs E. C.; 510 San Jose ave.
——Miss Eva
——F. E.

Harkness, Dr.; Lick House
Harlan, Miss Addie   **San Ramon, Contra Costa County**
Harmon, Samuel H.; 3 Essex Place
——Edward N.
——Miss Lyle, A.

Harney, Mr and Mrs William; 1212 Washington st.
Harpham, Lee; The Berkshire
Harron, Mr. John O.; Cosmos Club
Harring, William; 1604 Stockton st.
Harrington, Miss Sarah; Oriel Hotel   *Monday*
Harris, Miss Bessie; 829 Oak st.   **Oakland**
Harris, Lieut H. L.; Presidio
Harrison, Capt and Mrs C. H.; Palace Hotel   *Monday*   **Sausalito**
Harrison, Dalton; 406 California st.   **Alameda**
Harrison, Lieut and Mrs G. F. E., U. S. A.; 2507 Sacramento st.   *Thursday*
Harrison, Mr Ralph C.; 919 Pine st.
——Richard
Harrison, Mr and Mrs Randolph; 1912 Vallejo st.   *Friday*

Harrison, Mr and Mrs William Greer; 2507 Pacific ave.   *Saturday*
——The Misses
Harrold, John F.; 232 Page st.   *Thursday*
——Miss E. E.
——Miss May E.
——Miss Nellie A.
Hart, Judge C. F.; 1309 Taylor st.
Hart, Mr and Mrs Harry; 903 Sutter st.   *Monday*
Hart, Jerome A.; Pacific-Union Club
Hart, Miss Susie; 24 Clinton Park   *Friday*
Hartwell, Mr and Mrs William H.; 243 Oak st.
Harvey, Mrs Josephine ; 1416 Clay st.
Harvey, Mrs M. Joseph; 804 Taylor st.   *Thursday*
Harvey, Mr and Mrs J. Downey; Palace Hotel   *Monday*   Los Medanos
Harwood, Miss Jennie; 1024 Washington st.   *Tuesday*
Hasbrouck, Mr and Mrs; 908 Sutter st.   *Tuesday*   Santa Cruz
Haselton, Mr G. B.; 801 Leavenworth st.
Haskell, Miss Ernestine
Haslehurst, Dr and Mrs O. A.; 1411 Octavia st.   *Wednesday*   Del Monte
——Miss G. M.   *Thursday*
Hassell, J. J.; 2751 Bush st.
Hastings, C. F. D.; 2400 Fillmore st.
Hastings, Mrs E. L.; 700 Post st.
——Miss Bettie
Hastings, Mr and Mrs D. N.; The Bella Vista   *Thursday*
Hastings, Mrs Dio; 2400 Fillmore st.   *Friday*
Hastings, Judge and Mrs E. O. F.; 1506 Pine st.
Hastings, Dr J.; The Bella Vista   *Thursday*
——Misses
Hastings, Mrs Robert P.; 2024 Jackson st.   *Friday* Azalea, Cordelia, Cal.
Hastings, Judge and Mrs S. Clinton; 120 Phelan Building   Portland, Or.
Hastings, Mr and Mrs J. Uhler; 1912 Pacific ave.   *Friday*
Haswell, Charles H., Jr.; Pacific-Union Club   San Rafael
Hatch, Dr and Mrs James H.; 213 Geary st.   Del Monte
Hatch, Miss Mary ; The Bella Vista   *Thursday*
Hathaway, Dr and Mrs E. V.; 38 South Park   *Tuesday*
——Miss
——Henry R.
Hatton, George F.; Palace Hotel   Santa Monica
Hausman, Frederick H.; 907 Pine st.
Havens, Mr and Mrs H. B.; Occidental Hotel
Havens, Charles I.; 2835 Howard st.
Hawes, Col and Mrs Alexander G.; The Bella Vista   *Thursday*
Hawkins, Mr and Mrs John E.; Lick House   *Monday*
Hawkins, Mr William; 340 Fremont st.

·39 ·

Hawkins, Mr and Mrs V. A. Cæsar ; Hotel Pleasanton
Hawkins, Gen'l and Mrs J. P., U. S. A.; Hotel Pleasanton   *Monday*
Hawks, Harry D.; 1514 Larkin st.
———J. Lawrence
Hayes, Mr and Mrs Thos. R.; Hotel Pleasanton
———The Misses
Hayes, George R. B.; 1814 Buchanan st.
Hayes, Mr and Mrs C. E.; The Beresford   *1st & 3d Mondays*   Del Monte
Hayman, Mr and Mrs Al; Occidental Hotel   *Thursday*   New York
Haymond, Creed; 501 Harrison st.   "Bella Vista," San Mateo Co.
Hayne, Duncan; 522 Montgomery st. and 206 Powell st.
———Brewton, A.   Berkeley
Hayne, Miss Mae; 908 Sutter st.   *Tuesday*
Haynes, Dr and Mrs B. W.; Hotel Pleasanton   *Monday*
Hays, Mr and Mrs Ira C.; 528 Geary st.   *Tuesday*
Hays, Mr and Mrs John C.   Visalia, Tulare Co.
Hays, T. Abe; 721 Hayes st.
Hays, Dr W. W.   San Luis Obispo
Hays, Mr and Mrs William C.; 1022 Golden Gate ave.   *Tuesday*
Haywood, Mr and Mrs Franklin; NE cor Hayes and Baker sts.   *Monday*
Head, Mr and Mrs E. L.; 314 Ellis st.   *Tuesday*   Dixon, Cal.
Head, Mr and Mrs A. E.; 1105 Taylor st.
———Miss Anna
Heald, E. P.; 1406 Polk st.   Napa
Healy, Capt and Mrs M. A.; Occidental Hotel   *Monday*
Hearst, Sen and Mrs George; Occidental Hotel   Washington, D. C.
———William R.; 508 Montgomery st.
Heath, Mrs R. W.; 1512 Taylor st.
———Miss Virginia D.
———Miss Roberta Lee
———William R.
Heath, Richard W.   San Anselmo
Heathcote, Mr and Mrs Basil; Pacific ave and Steiner st.   San Rafael
Heazelton, Mr George, "Evening Post"; Grand Hotel
Hecht, Mr and Mrs Isaac ; Palace Hotel   Lake Tahoe
Hecht, Mr and Mrs M. H.; Washington and Octavia sts.
Heim, J. F. H.; 120 Sutter st.
Heimey, Mr William ; 2413 Fillmore st.   *Thursday*
———Fannie M.
———William Francis
Heise, Mr and Mrs Charles E.; 2517 Pacific ave.   *Friday*
Heitschu, Mr and Mrs Samuel ; Cosmos Club   Portland, Or.
Hellen, Mr and Mrs C. C.; Occidental Hotel   *Monday*
———Miss
Heller, Mr and Mrs Moses ; Lick House   *Monday*

Helmer, J. S.; 1118 Taylor st.
Hellman, Horace G.; 226 Stockton st.
Hellman, Mr Richard; 525 Front st.
——George N.
Henarie, D. V. B.; Palace Hotel
Hencke, Mr and Mrs William; 1008 Vallejo st.
Henderson, J. H.; Cosmos Club   Oakland
Henderson, Mr and Mrs John C.; 2511 California st.   *Friday*
Hendrickson, W.; 1137 Bush st.
Hendry, Mr and Mrs C. J.; 430 Ellis st.
Hendy, Mr and Mrs Samuel J.; 102 Bartlett st.   *Thursday*
——Joshua
——John
Henley, Senator and Mrs Barclay; 2131 Green st.   Santa Rosa
Hennessey, Mr and Mrs H.; 909 Broderick st.   *Tuesday*
——Miss Minnie
Henricksen, B. E.; 1320 Fell st.
Henzel, E. F.; 1908 Steiner st.
Heppner, J. O.; Cosmos Club
Herman, Mrs Lucien; 1427 Washington st.   *Friday*
Herold, Mrs A.; 1716 Bush street
——Oscar
——Roderick
——Hugo
Herold, Rudolph; 1612 Van Ness ave.
Herrin, Mr and Mrs; W. F.; 1919 Baker st.
Herrman, Mr and Mrs George; 1500 Larkin st.   *Tuesday*   **Pasadena**
——Mr and Mrs S.
Herrman, Mr and Mrs Oscar; 2414 Webster st.   *Friday*
Herrman, Mr and Mrs William; 623 Turk st.   *Wednesday*
Herron, J. O.; Cosmos Club
Herzstein, Dr Morris; 323 Sutter st.
Hess, Mr and Mrs Frederick; 821 California st.   *Tuesday*
Heuer, Major William H.; 1814 Sacramento st.
Hewes, Mr and Mrs David   Europe
Hewett, Mr and Mrs J. M.; 415 Powell st.   *Wednesday*
Hewlett, Mrs Elizabeth; 410 Buchanan st.   *Wednesday*   Auburn
Hewlett, Mr and Mrs H. H.; Palace Hotel   *Monday*   { Residence, Stockton
                                                         { Hotel Del Monte
Heydenfeldt, Solomon, Jr.; 1607 California st.
Heyer, Albert; 500 Third st.
Heydenfeldt, Mrs Solomon; 1016 Post st.
——Miss Ziela
——Thomas O.
Heyman, Henry; 623 Eddy st., Bohemian Club

Heyneman, Mr and Mrs Charles H.; 2306 Post st.
Heyneman, Mr and Mrs Manfred H.; 1409 Hyde st.
Heywood, Mr and Mrs Franklin ; NE cor. Hayes and Baker sts.
Hiester, Mr and Mrs Amos C.; 2641 Howard st.
———The Misses
— ——William A.
Higgins, Mrs A. E.; Hotel Pleasanton   *Monday*
———Maurice
———Miss Libbie

Highton, Mr and Mrs H. E.; Baldwin Hotel   { *Monday*
                                            { McCloud River, P. O. Baird
———Mrs A. N.
———Miss Edith
Hihn, Mr and Mrs F. A.   Santa Cruz

Hill, Dr and Mrs Thomas L.; 1609 Gough st. { *Thursday and Tuesday Eve.*
                                            { Sausalito

Hill, Mr and Mrs A. B.   *Thursday*   Petaluma
Hill, Mr and Mrs Horace L.   East
———Miss
Hill, Mr and Mrs Morgan ; Occidental Hotel   *Monday*   Santa Cruz
Hiller, Dr and Mrs Albert ; 1011 Sutter st.
Hillman, Mrs Richard ; SW cor. Pacific and Gough sts.   *Friday*
Hillyer, Miss Nellie ; 2629 Bush st.
Hinkle, Miss Kate ; Sutter and Pierce sts.   *Thursday*   Petaluma
Hinsdale, G. S.; Lick House
Hirsch, Mr and Mrs Charles J.; 614 Sutter st.   *Tuesdays*   Del Monte
Hitchcock, H. R.   Honolulu, H. I.
Hitchcock, Mrs Helen M.; 1010 Powell st.   *Tuesday*
———Miss Nellie
Hittell, John S.; 1216 Hyde st.
Hittell, Mr and Mrs T. H.; 808 Turk st.   *Friday*   San Pablo
———Miss Catherine
———Franklin
Hoag, Jared C.; 1460 O'Farrell st.   *Thursday*   Sonoma Co.
———Charles C.
———Jed J.
Hobart, Mr and Mrs W. S.; Van Ness ave. and Washington st.
———Miss Alice
Hobbs, Mr and Mrs Frederick ; 1016 Bush st.
———Miss Annie
———Frederick, Jr.
Hobbs, Mr and Mrs Hiram H.; 1708 Geary st.   *Friday*   Santa Cruz
———Miss Jennie
———Miss Anna
Hobbs, Mr and Mrs John K.; 37 Hill st.
Hoburg, Mr and Mrs Frank T.; 431 Bartlett st.   *Wednesday*

42

Hochkofler, Rudolph ; 1825 Sacramento st.
Hoeflech, Morris ; 310 Stockton st.
Hochstadter, Wm. S.; 1528 Sutter st.
———Robert B.
———Edgar S.
Hodge, Mr and Mrs F. H.; 1114 Seventeenth st.   *Thursday*
Hoffman, Judge Ogden ; Pacific-Union Club   **San Rafael**
———Mr and Mrs Southard ; 1113 Bush st.
———Ogden, Jr.
———Southard, Jr.
———Miss May
Hoge, Judge Joseph P.; 1323 Geary st.
———Miss Blanche
———Miss Octavia
———Charles J.
Hogg, Mr and Mrs James ; 815 Eddy st.   *Friday*
Hohweisner, Mr and Mrs Frederick; 2706 Sacramento st.
Holbrook, Mr and Mrs Charles ; 1901 Van Ness ave.   *Friday*   **Menlo Park**
———Miss Mary
———H. M.
Holbrook, Mrs Cornelia F.; 1724 Broadway   *Friday*   **Tucson, Ariz.**
———Mr Edward
———Mr George
———Mr Herbert
Holcombe, Mr Walter G.; 1915 Sacramento st.
———Miss E. A.
Holden, Professor E. S.   **Mount Hamilton**
Holladay, Mr and Mrs Jesse ; Washington and Gough sts.
Holladay, Mr and Mrs S. W.; NE cor. Clay and Octavia sts.   *Wednesday*
———Miss Louise Ord
———Edmond Burke
Holland, Mr and Mrs Nathaniel ; 1414 Taylor st.
Hollis, Mr and Mrs William ; The Renton   *Monday*
Holmes, Mr and Mrs ; 1214 Lafayette st.   *Tuesday*
Holmes, Mr and Mrs A. J.; 1219 McAllister st.
Holmes, Mr and Mrs Henry T.; 1922 Pine st.
Holmes, Captain J. W.   **Ship "Chalmers"**
Holt, Mrs Thos. ; 1411 Hyde st.   *Friday*
Holway, Mrs S. P. ; 822 Sutter st.
Homer, Mrs Charles ; NW cor. Broadway and Taylor sts.
Hooker, Mr and Mrs Charles G. ; 917 Bush st.
———Miss Jennie
———Miss Bessie
———Robert G.
———C. Osgood ; Bohemian Club

43

Hooker. Mrs H. C. ; Occidental Hotel
Hooker, Richard C. ; 336 Pine st.
Hooper, Mr and Mrs Geo. F. ; Occidental Hotel   **Wanoma**
Hooper, Mr and Mrs George W. ; 824 Sutter st.
Hooper, Mr and Mrs John A. ; NW cor. Clay and Laguna sts.
Hooper, Mr and Mrs R. B. ; The Bella Vista   *Thursday*
Hopkins, Mr and Mrs C. H. ; The Pleasanton
Hopkins, Mr and Mrs E.W.; cor. Cal. & Laguna sts. *Thursday* **Menlo Park**
——Miss Maud
Hopkins, F. C. ; The Berkshire
Hopkins, Mr and Mrs Moses ; NE cor. Clay and Buchanan   **Redwood City**
Hopkins, Mr and Mrs Peter ; 2000 Broadway st.   *Friday*
——Miss Jennie
——Peter, Jr.
Hopkins, Dr and Mrs W. E. ; U. S. A. ; Presidio
Hopps, Mr and Mrs George H. ; 1719 Webster st.
Hord, Jos. ; New California Hotel
Horning, C. C. ; 917 Mission st.
Horsburg, Mr and Mrs David W. ; 1517 Washington st.   *Wednesday*
——James, Jr.
Hort, Mr and Mrs Samuel ; 1920 Jackson st.   *1st and 3d Fridays*
Horton, Frank H. ; 411 Eddy st.
Horton, Mrs P. B. ; 1615 Clay st. *Wednesday* **San Rafael & Santa Cruz Mts**
——Miss Minnie
Horton, Mr and Mrs Robert L. ; 1033 Ellis st.   *Thursday*
——Miss Mabel
——Mortimer
Hosmer, Mr and Mrs J. A. ; 2517½ Sutter st.
Hotaling, Mr & Mrs Anson P.; NE cor. Franklin & California st. **Menlo Park**
——Richard
Houseworth, Mr and Mrs Harrison ; 1235 Hyde st.
——Harrison, Jr.
Houghton, General and Mrs J. F.; 801 Sutter st.   *Monday*   **Del Monte**
——Miss Minnie
——Harry B.
Houseworth, Thomas; 1218 Ellis st.
——Frederick A.
Housman, John I.; 2704 Laguna st.
Hovey, Mr and Mrs S. D.; Palace Hotel   *Monday*
Howard, Mr and Mrs Charles Webb; 2123 Buchanan st.   **San Mateo**
——Miss Maud
——O. Shafter   **Salt Lake City**
Howard, Mr and Mrs George H.; 1812 Gough st.   **San Mateo**
——Miss Babette

Howard, Mr and Mrs William H.   San Mateo
Howe, Mr and Mrs Chas. M.; Phelan Building, rooms 314 and 316
Howell, Mrs; 512 Folsom st.
Howitt, R.; Hotel Pleasanton
Howland, George; 1312 Taylor st.
Howland, Mr and Mrs Robert M.; 1215 Sutter st.   Santa Cruz Mts.
———Miss Edith
———Miss Loula
Hoyt, F. T.; 324 Montgomery st.
Hubbard, Mrs Van Dyke; Van Ness, bet. Turk and Golden Gate ave.
Hubbard, Mr and Mrs H. C.; 427 Franklin st.   *Friday*
Huddart, Mrs E. J.; 923 Hyde st.
———George F.
Hudson, Mr and Mrs Horace R.; 1611 Washington st.
———Madame
Hueter, Ernest L.; 2312 Howard st.
Hug, Mr and Mrs Joseph; 1525 Sutter st.   *Thursday*
———Miss Annie
———Miss Hattie
———Charles
Hughes, Mr and Mrs; Oriel Hotel   *Monday*
Hughes, Mr and Mrs E. C.; 1321 Clay st.
Hughes, C. V.; 735 O'Farrell st.
Hughes, Mrs F. M.; 806 Bush st.   *Tuesday*
———Miss Emily
———Miss Fanny
———Edward O.
Hughes, Dr Jerome; 54 Oak st.
Hughes, Colonel Robert P.; 2318 Clay st.
Huie, Mrs S. E.; 1932 Pine st.   *Wednesday*
———Miss
———Robert B.
———William H. T.
———George B. and Edward M.
Hunt, Mrs M. E.; Palace Hotel   *Thursday*   Ventura
Hull, Capt G. A.; 36 New Montgomery st.
Humbert, Mrs P. A.; 531 Bush st.
Hume, Hugh ; 1227 Pine st.
Humes, Miss ; 1419 Post st.
Humphreys, Mr and Mrs William P.; 816 Chestnut st.   *Thursday*
Hunt, Mr and Mrs W. B.; 1437 Pacific ave.   *Tuesday*
———Wm. F.
———George Elliott
Hunt, Charles W.; 2409 Webster st.
Hunt, Judge and Mrs John, Jr.; 1703 Octavia st.

Hunt, John D.; 1026 Hyde st.
——Miss Sarah
——Miss Carrie
Hunt, Mr and Mrs Randol ; The Bella Vista   *Thursday*
Hunt, William B.; 410 Leavenworth st.
Hunter, Lieut and Mrs Charles H.; Presidio
Huntington, Mr and Mrs W. V.; Hotel Pleasanton
Huntsman, Mrs George H.; Hotel Bella Vista   *Thursday*
——The Misses
——Mrs Louise
——Miss

Hurlbut, Dr ; The Berkshire
Huston, John ; Lick House
Hutchins, Dr and Mrs C. B.; 617 Bush st.
Hutchins, Mr and Mrs ; 712 Sutter st., The Renton
Hutchinson, Mr and Mrs Joseph ; 110 Liberty st.   *Thursday*
Hutchinson, Miss; 1620 California st.
Hutchinson, Mrs C. I.; 1620 California st.
Hutchinson, Mr and Mrs Eli J.; 1329 Pine st.   *Monday*
Hutchinson, Mr and Mrs Frederick W.; 2409 Webster st.   *Friday*
Hutchinson, H. T.; 2504 California st.
Hutchinson, Mr and Mrs N. L.; Hotel Pleasanton   *Monday*   **Europe**
Hutchinson, Miss K.; 1910 Howard st.
Hyde, Mrs George ; 719 Geary st.   *Thursday*
——Miss Mamie
——Miss Gertrude
Hyde, Miss Helen ; SW cor. Pierce and Union sts.   *Friday*
Hyde, Mr and Mrs Henry C.; Occidental Hotel   *Monday*   **San Rafael**
——Miss Bertie
Hyde, Miss Marie C. ; 507½ Hyde st.
Hyde, Rothwell ; 1631 Sacramento st.
Hyman, Mr and Mrs J. ; 1946 California st.

Ils, Mrs M. ; 1310 Jones st.   *2d, 3d and 4th Wednesdays*
——Miss Lena
——Miss Mollie
——John G., Jr.
Ingram, Charles M. ; 2312 Steiner st.
Irelan, Mr and Mrs William J. ; 827 Post st.
Irvine, Mrs J. ; Occidental Hotel.   *Monday*
Irwin, Joseph N. H. ; 14 Grant ave.   **San Jose**
Irwin, Capt John ; U. S. N. ; 1001 Pine st.
Irwin, Mrs William ; 1221 California st.   *Friday*   **Yreka**
——Miss Emma

46

Irwin, Mr and Mrs William G.   Honolulu
Isaacs, Wm. B. ; 1428 Post st.
Itsell, Col and Mrs A. Jackson ; 1832 O'Farrell st.   *Thursday*   **San Rafael**
——Miss May
——Miss Maud
——Miss Alice Irene
——W. F.
Ives, Stephen D. ; Cosmos Club or 401 California st.
Ives, Miss Florence.   **San Jose**
Izer, Rev Dr and Mrs Geo W. ; Hotel Oriel, 1904 Market st.   *Monday*

Jackson, Miss Hattie ; 1805 Stockton st.   **Sacramento**
Jackson, Mr and Mrs John ; 326 Seventeenth st.   *Wednesday*   **San Mateo**
——Miss Edith Lyle
Jackson, S. M.   **London and San Francisco**
Jackson, Mr and Mrs Byron ; 941 Golden Gate ave.   *Thursday*
Jackson, Miss Caroline C. ; 1606 Van Ness ave.   **Oakland**
Jackson, J. ; Hotel Pleasanton
Jackson, Mr and Mrs Charles H. ; 517 Mason st.   **Napa Soda Springs**
Jackson, Colonel and Mrs John P.; 720 Sutter st. *Thursday* **Napa Soda Spgs**
——Jackson, Stanley H.
——Andrew
——Mr and Mrs John P., Jr.
——Mr and Mrs George T.
Jackson, Mr and Mrs G. H. T.; 308 Haight st.   **Napa Soda Springs**
Jacobi, Mr and Mrs Frederick ; 1320 Sutter st.
Jacobs, Mr and Mrs B. M. ; Lick House   *Monday*
Jacobs, Edward L. ; 1912 Broadway st.
Jacobs, Julius ; 423 California st.
Jacobs, Mr and Mrs Henry ; 612 Van Ness ave.
Jacobs, Mr and Mrs Isador ; 505 Golden Gate ave.
Jacoby, Franz ; 2601 Sacramento st.
James, Arthur R. ; 615 Sutter st.
James, Mr and Mrs D. H. ; 14 Oak st.
James, George ; 905 Fillmore st.
James, Mr and Mrs Jefferson; 2131 Howard st.
James, Mr and Mrs N. T.; 721 Ashbury st.   *Tuesday*
Janeway, John H.; Cosmos Club
Jarboe, Mr and Mrs John R.; 917 Pine st.   *Thursday*   **Santa Cruz**
——Miss Kate
——Paul
Jaynes, Mr and Mrs Frank; 2934 Sacramento st.
Jeffries, Mr and Mrs; Oriel Hotel   *Monday*
Jenisch, M.; Palace Hotel

Jenks, Dr and Mrs George H.; 321 Geary st.   *Wednesday*   **Petaluma**
——J. Shepherd
Jenner, Miss May; 510 Geary st.
Jennings, Mr and Mrs D. A.; 2105 Devisadero st.   *Thursday*
Jennings, Mrs Thomas, Jr.; 941 Fifteenth st.   *Friday*
——Miss A.
Jerome, Ed B.; Custom House
Jessen, G. M.; 1524 Jackson st.
Jessup, Mr and Mrs J. D.; 116 Liberty st.   *1st and 3d Fridays*   **Santa Cruz**
Jewell, Rev F. F.; 610 Buchanan st.
Jewell, Dr and Mrs J. G.   **Europe**
Jewell, T. E.; Grand Hotel
Jewett, Miss Fidelia; The Berkshire   *Monday*
Jobson, Mr and Mrs William G.; 19 Hill st.
Johnson, C. R.; Cosmos Club   **Fort Bragg**
Johnson, Mr and Mrs Frederick S.; 1503 Jackson st.
Johnson, George A.; 1513 Pierce st.
Johnson, Mr and Mrs J. C.; 1620 California st.
Johnson, Mr and Mrs James A.; 1707 Octavia st.
Johnson, Mr and Mrs J. M.; 1721 Jackson st.   *Friday*
Johnson, Mrs Robert C.; 605 O'Farrell st.
Johnson, Mrs Loring M.   **Mexico**
Johnston, Mrs Samuel; Hotel Oriel   *Monday*   **Del Monte**
Jolliffe, Mrs W. H.; 1225 Pine st.   *Thursday*
——Miss Nellie
Jones, Mr and Mrs Charles A.; 525 Fell st.
Jones, Mr and Mrs C. W.; 246 Chattanooga st.
Jones, Senator and Mrs John P.; Palace Hotel
Jones, Mr and Mrs Charles; The Berkshire   *Monday*
Jones, Mr and Mrs D. H.; Palace Hotel   *Monday*
Jones, Mr and Mrs H. B.; 2305 Sacramento st.
Jones, Mr and Mrs M. B.. 1121 Pine st.   *Thursday*
Jones, Mr and Mrs Webster; NE cor. Gough and Clay sts.
Jones, Winfield S.; 1313 Hyde st.
——W. Brooks
Jones, Mr and Mrs Witcher   **Salt Lake**
——Miss Maggie
Joost, Herman ; 307 Battery st.
Jordan, H. C.; 227 Capp st.
Jordan, R.; 897 Fulton st.
Joseph, Mrs E.; Palace Hotel   *Monday*
Josselyn, Mr and Mrs Charles; 1815 Gough st.   *Friday*
Jost, Charles, Jr.; 1108 Post st.
——William R.
——Joseph
Joullin, Mr and Mrs Amadio ; 611 Clay st.

Jourden, Mr J. P.; Windsor Hotel
Joyce, Martin; The Berkshire
Judge, Mr and Mrs H.; The Bella Vista   *Monday*
Judkins, Mr and Mrs P. C.; The Renton   *Monday*
Judson, Russell H.; 2305 Devisadero st.
Jungen, Lieutenant and Mrs Carl W.; U. S. N.   Mare Is'and
Junkins, Mr and Mrs; 1032 Twenty-fourth st.

Kahler, Mrs C.; 11 Guerrero st.   *Thursday*
———Henry S.
Kahn, Miss Henriette; 2213 Sutter st.   *Thursday*
Kahn, Dr and Mrs Adolph; 2821 Pine st.
Kane, Mrs Thomas; 340 Page st.
Kane, Mrs E.; 2857 Sixteenth st.
Kauzee, Miss Letitia; 726 Turk st.   *Wednesday*
Kast, Mr and Mrs L. S.; 1150 Guerrero st.
Katten, Mrs Simon; 2213 Sutter st.   *Thursday*
Kaufman, J.; 1201 Van Ness ave.
Kaufman, Mrs Rosalie; 1521 Jackson st.
———Charles H.
———Miss Emma
———Miss Laura
———Miss Jessica
Katz, Mr and Mrs R.; 203 Kearny st.
Kavanagh, Miss M.; 1534 Bush st.   *Friday*
Kavanagh, J. T.; 911 McAllister st.
Kavanagh, G. H.; 2017 Pacific ave.
Keane, Mr and Mrs Thomas; 340 Page st.   *Wednesday*   Santa Cruz
Kearney, M. Theo.; Palace Hotel   Fresno
Kearns, E. J.; 613 Clay st.
Keeler, Mrs J. M.; NW cor. Clay and Laguna sts.   *Tuesday*
Keeney, Mr and Mrs Charles M.; 2423 Fillmore st.
Keeney, Dr and Mrs James W.; 2220 Clay st.   *Tuesday*   Monterey
Keith, Prof and Mrs N. S.; The Berkshire   *Monday*
Keith, Mrs William H.; 1509 Washington st.   *Tuesday*
———Miss Eliza D.
———William H., Jr.
Kelleher, Mr and Mrs Alfred J.; 2324 Clay st.   *1st and 3d Fridays*
———Alfred Galton
Kelley, Mr and Mrs L. A.; 1034 Pine st.   *Wednesday*   Santa Cruz
———L. A., Jr.
Kellogg, Miss; 7 Glen Park ave.
Kellogg, Mr and Mrs Fred S.; 2205 Fillmore st.
Kellogg, Lansing O.; care Wells, Fargo and Co.'s Bank
Kellogg, L. M.; The Bella Vista   *Thursday*
———Miss
Kellogg, Mr and Mrs M. B.; 2424 Pacific ave.   *Friday*

Kelly, James R.; 309 Leavenworth st.
Kelly, Miss Elise; 1315 Van Ness ave.
Kelton, Miss Ella; 804 Taylor st.   *Thursday*
Kenfield, Mrs Daniel M.; 2125 California st.
Kenitzer, Mr and Mrs Henry; Lick House   *Monday*
Kennedy, Mr and Mrs John F.; 1727 Pine st.
Kenny, Mr and Mrs George L.; 22 Lapidge st.   Oakville
Kenny, Kearn; 2503 California st.
Kentfield, Mrs. 331 Fremont st.   *Wednesday*   San Rafael
———Mr and Mrs E. E.
Kenyon, Dr and Mrs C. G.; The Pleasanton   *Monday*
Kern, F. W.; 118 Fair Oak st.
Kerr, Mark B.; 307 Powell st.
Kerr, Earl; The Berkshire
Kew, Mr and Mrs M.; The Pleasanton   *Monday*
Keyes, Mr Winfield S.; 915 Van Ness ave. *Thursday* Howell Mt , Napa Co.
———Alex. D.
———Miss A. C.
Kidd, James ; 505 Hyde st.
Kidder, Miss ; Oriel Hotel   *Monday*
Kilgarif, Mr and Mrs John M. ; 614 Sutter st.   Napa Soda Springs
Kimball, Mrs G. G. ; The Pleasanton   *Monday*   Red Bluff
Kimball, Mr and Mrs F. H. ; 264 Golden Gate ave.   *Thursday*
Kincaid, Miss C. B. ; 730 Seventeenth st.
Kincaid, Rev and Mrs William ; 930 Fillmore st.
Kindrick, Mrs ; 1711 Broderick st.
King, Mr and Mrs Fritz R.; 1732 Broadway st.
King, Mr and Mrs Homer S. ; 1001 Leavenworth st.   *Thursday*   East
Kingsbury, Frank ; Cosmos Club
Kingsley, C. H. ; Palace Hotel
Kingston, Mrs Paul F. ; 941 Fifteenth st.   *Friday*
Kinsey, Griffith J. ; 903 Sutter st.   El Paso de Robles
———Mrs H. G.

Kinsman, Charles F. ; Oriel Hotel
Kinzler, Mr and Mrs A. V. ; New California Hotel
Kip, Right Rev and Mrs William I. ; 901 Eddy st.
———Rev W. I., Jr.   Berkeley
Kirchoffer, Dr Frederick ; German Hospital
Kirk, Miss Florence ; The Berkshire   *Monday*
Kirketerp, Christian ; 1017 Bush st.
———Miss Emilie
Kirketerp, W. C. ; 1815 Broadway st.
Kirkham, Ralph W. ; Pacific Club
Kirkland, Miss Cordelia S. ; 1306 California st.   *Thursday*

Kirkpatrick, Mr E. ; Palace Hotel   *Monday*
Kirkpatrick, Mrs E. L. ; 808 Leavenworth st.
Kittle, Mrs N. G. ; Pacific ave. and Steiner st.
——John G. Jr.
——Nicholas G. Jr.
——William S.
——Miss Maggie

Kleinhans, Mr and Mrs John ; 640 Fell st.
——Miss Lucy
Knight, Mr and Mrs George A. ; 2209 Buchanan st.
Knighton, R. ; Hotel Pleasanton
Knoderer, Theodore ; 1217 Clay st.
Knoph, Mr and Mrs M. E. ; 21 Eleventh st.   *Tuesday*   San Mateo
Knorp, Albert ; 706 Larkin st.
Knowles, Mr and Mrs Charles S.   Boston, Mass.
Knox, Mrs Mary F. ; 2222 Washington st.   *Friday*
Knox, Mr and Mrs C. C. ; 21 Eleventh st.
Kohl, Captain and Mrs William ; New California Hotel *Monday* San Mateo
——Miss Mamie E.
——Charles
——C. F.

Kohler, Mrs Elise ; 1358 Post st.
——Charles
——H. H.
——Miss Emma
——Caroline

Kohler, Mr and Mrs Henry C. ; 807 Sutter st.
——Miss Hennie
——Henry, Jr.
Kohn, Mr and Mrs I. ; 1316 Sutter st.   *4th Wednesday*
Kruse, Edward ; 620 Turk st.   Del Monte
——Edward, Jr.
——Emil
——William H.
Krusi, Herman ; 1232 Golden Gate ave.

Lachman, Samuel; 603 Sutter st.
Lacy, Mr and Mrs Benjamin T.; 615 Chestnut st.
Lake, Mrs M. C.; 1905 Pacific ave.   *Tuesday*
——Frederick Billings
Lake, Miss Mary; 1534 Sutter st.   *Friday*
Lambert, Wm. P.; 117 Stockton st.
Lampson, Mrs Sarah F.; 608 Nineteenth st.
——Miss Lillie

51

Landers, Mr and Mrs John; 1121 Bush st.   San Jose
——-Miss
Landsberger, Mr and Mrs I.; 717 Fillmore st.   *Friday*   A'ameda
——Miss Lillie
Landsberger, Mr and Mrs Henry   A'ameda
——Miss Florence
——Julius A.
Lane, Dr and Mrs Levi C.; 2302 Clay st.
Langhorne, Mr and Mrs James P.; 2419 Pacific ave.
Langley, Mrs Melanie; 234 Haight Street
Lansing, Miss Ada M.; 1418 Sutter st.   *Friday*   Santa Barbara
Lansing, Mr and Mrs G. L.; 2613 Pacific ave.
Larcher, Prof Edward; 811 Geary st.
Latham, Mrs J. K.; 2111 Pine st.
——Miss Edith
——Miss Florence
Latham, Mrs M. M.; 1104 Post st.   Del Monte
——Milton S.
Lathrop, Mr and Mrs Ariel; Palace Hotel
Lathrop, Charles G.; 2101 Van Ness ave.   *1st Friday*
Latimer, L. D.; Pacific Club   Winsor, Sonoma Co.
Laton, Mr and Mrs Chas. A.; Palace Hotel   *Monday*
Laton, Mr and Mrs M. E.; 821 Pine st.
Latson, Mr and Mrs Frank P.; 520 Oak st.
Latz, Mrs B.; 1006 Van Ness ave.   Portland, Or.
Lauden, Mr and Mrs M. E; 821 Pine st.
Lawler, Judge Frank W.; 1400 Golden Gate ave.
—— Miss Lillie
Lawless, Mrs E. J.; 1513 Larkin st.
Lawlor, Mr and Mrs J. M.; 3019 California st.   San Jose
——Miss Lillie
——William
Lawson, W.; 312 Pine st.
Lawyer, Mr and Mrs A. M.; 1422 Clay st.   *Tuesday*
Layman, Mr and Mrs Frederick O.; 330 Pine st.
Leach, G. W.; Lick House
Lean, Mr and Mrs W.; Oriel Hotel   *Monday*   Auburn
Leavenworth, Miss Grace; 116 Eddy st.   *Tuesday-Thursday*   Pac. Grove
Leavitt, S. B.; 2037 Howard st.
Le Breton, Mr and Mrs A. J.; 712 Sutter st.
——Miss Julia
Le Breton, Edward J.; 1414 Sutter st.
Le Breton, Mrs Julia; 1414 Sutter st.
Le Count, Mr and Mrs J. P.; 917 Van Ness ave.
——Miss Ella
——Miss Susie

HABITS A SPECIALTY
420 FIFTH AVENUE
N. Y.

BRANCHES

SACKVILLE ST., LONDON   9 PLACE DE LA BOURSE   2 WEST 38TH ST., N. Y.

Lee, Mrs B. F.; 2021 Webster st.
Lee, W. G.; Hotel Pleasanton
Lee, Dr W. M.; Grand Hotel
Lees, Captain and Mrs I. W.; 1022 Pine st.
———Mr and Mrs Fred W.
Lefavor, Lieut and Mrs F. H.
Leggett, Joseph; 918 Dolores st.
Leghorn, John G.; 1810 Leavenworth st.
Leichter, C.; 1722 Clay st.
Leigh, J. W.; 611 Commercial st.
Leighton, Mrs and Mrs J. B.; 932 Union st.   *Wednesday*
Lemmon, Geo.; 623½ Golden Gate ave.
Lent, Mr and Mrs William M.   **New York**
———George H.; Bohemian Club
Leonard, Charles L.; Bohemian Club
Le Roy, Gorges; 226 Stockton st.
———Eugene
Lessock, Mr and Mrs A. H.; 1258 California st.
———The Misses
Levison, Mr J. B.; 215 Montgomery st.
Levy, Eugene W.; 1516 O'Farrell st.
Levy, Mr and Mrs H. M.; 1302 Post st.
———Miss Dahlia
——— Martin H.
Levy, Mrs John; The Berkshire   *Monday*
———Miss Goldie
Levy, Judge and Mrs Walter H.; 661 Harrison st.
Levy, Mr and Mrs S. W.; 1296 Van Ness ave.
———Melville S.
Lewis, Dr and Mrs D. O., U. S. N.; The Bella Vista   *Monday*
Lewis, W. S.; Hotel Pleasanton
Lewis, William; 1212 Geary st.
Lewitt, Dr W. B.; 605 Laguna st.
Libby, Mr and Mrs Dorville; 822 Twenty-first st.
Libby, Mr and Mrs D. B.; 439½ Bryant st.
Lichtenberg, William; Cosmos Club   **San Rafael**
———The Misses   **San Rafael**
Liebes, Mr and Mrs Herman; 1714 Van Ness ave.
Lightner, I.; 1312 Golden Gate ave.
Lightner, Mrs Joel F.; 1759 Howard st.
Lilienthal, Mr and Mrs Ernest R.; 1818 California st.
Lilienthal, Mr and Mrs J. Leo; 1918 Jackson st.
Lilienthal, Mr and Mrs Philip N.; SW cor. Franklin and Clay sts.
Lilienthal, Dr and Mrs Samuel; 1316 Van Ness ave.

Limekin, Mr and Mrs; 927 Golden Gate ave.   *Thursday*
Lincoln, Mr and Mrs Jerome; 555 Harrison st.   **Hotel Del Monte**
———Miss Ethel
———Jerome B.
Linderman, Mr and Mrs Dell; 1501 Van Ness ave.
Linsay, Mr and Mrs J. A.; 1819 O'Farrell st.
Lion, Rev and Mrs Edgar J.; 812 Fulton st.
Lippman, George W.; 1151 Octavia st.
Lipscher, Mrs M.; 526 Ellis st.
Lissak, Louis S.; 409 California st.
Lissak, Mr and Mrs Adolphus H.; 1258 Cal. st. *Tuesdays* **The Vendome**
———Miss
———Miss Madeline
———Miss Edna
Little, Mr and Mrs John T.; 2515 Gough st.
———Miss Grace
———Miss Laura
———Miss Ada
Little, Mrs Amos R.; Baldwin Hotel
Little, Mr and Mrs W. H.; 311 Scott st.   *Thursday*
Littlefield, Miss Emma   **Salinas City**
———Miss Rose
Littlefield, Mr and Mrs J. H.; The Bella Vista   *Thursday*
Livermore, Mr and Mrs H. P.; 2021 Cal. st. { *Friday* **Rockridge Park, Oak.**
Livingston, Mr James M.; 2111 Pacific ave.   *Friday*
———Mr Howard
———Miss Gertrude
———Miss Alice
———Miss Florence
Livingston, C. H.; 621½ Post st.
Lloyd, Rueben H.; 1008 Folsom st.
Lockwood, Mr and Mrs Arthur D.; SE cor. Clay and Buchanan sts.
Lockwood, Miss Florence   **Redwood City**
Loewy, W.; 946 Geary st.
Logan, Mrs James C.; 1812 Webster st.
Logan, Mrs M. A.; Grand Hotel
Lohse, Mrs John F.; 2512 Washington st.   *Friday*
———Miss
Lohse, Miss Kittie; 1333 Pine st.
———Miss Lulu
Long, Mr and Mrs I. H.; 1812 Washington st.
Long, Mr and Mrs John T.; The Berkskire   *Monday*
Long, L. L.; The Bella Vista
Loomis, Mr and Mrs George; N. California Hotel *Monday* **Menlo Park**

Lord, Theodore A.; NE cor Vallejo and Octavia sts.
Loring, Mr and Mrs David W.; 2604 Jackson st.
——Miss Ruth
——F. H.
Loring, Mr and Mrs Prescott; 2521 Sutter st.
Loryea, Dr and Mrs A. M.; 1322 California st.   *First Tuesday of Month*
——Miss Amy L.
——James
Lotz, Miss Matilda   **Paris**
Loughborough, Mr and Mrs Alexander H.; 829 O'Farrell st.   { *Thursday* { **San Rafael**
——Miss Fannie
——Miss Josie
——A. Z.
——George A.
Loughhead, Henry W.; Cosmos Club
Loughery, Robert J.; 304 Bartlett st.
Love, John L.; 30 Glenn Park ave.
Love, Mrs Josie S.; 1714 Clay st.
——Miss
Loveland, Mrs Mary T.; 2243 Larkin st.
——Miss May
Lovell, Mansfield; 1312 Taylor st.
Low, Mr and Mrs Charles A.; 904 Taylor st.
Low, Mr and Mrs E. Louis, Jr.; 901 Fillmore st.   *Wednesday*
Low, Governor and Mrs F. F.; Gough and Sutter sts.   **Hotel Rafael**
——Miss Flora
Lowenberg, Mr and Mrs I. H.; 609 Van Ness ave.   *Thursday*
——Miss Ruby
——Albert J.
Lowenthal, Mr and Mrs M. S.; 1528 Sutter st.
Lowndes, Mrs A. O.; 613 Larkin st.
Lowndes, Mr and Mrs A. P.; 1212 Washington st.
——Miss Gertrude
——Miss Fiora
——Floyd, J.
Loyall, Miss Camilla; 2315 Scott st.
Luchsinger, Miss Rose Agnes; 1016 Franklin st.   *Tuesday*
Luckhardt, Cæsar; 1812 Howard st.
Ludovici, F. Woldemar; 1426 Clay st.
——Miss Alice E.
——Miss Frieda
——Miss Josephine
——Julius
——L. M.
——W. Oscar

Ludlow, Captain Nichol; Pacific-Union Club   Napa Soda Springs
——Miss
Ludwig, Ernest H.; 1206 Sutter st.
Lugsden, Mr and Mrs Jay; Palace Hotel   *Monday*   Del Monte
——Miss Flora
Luhrs, Mrs; Occidental Hotel
——Miss Annie
Lundborg, Dr and Mrs J.-A. W.; 1308 Jones st.   *Tuesday*
——Miss Florence
Lusk, F. C.; Pacific-Union Club   Chico
Luther, Mr and Mrs John B.; 336 O'Farrell st.
Lux, Mrs Charles; 1900 Jackson st.   *Friday*
Lyle, Mr and Mrs W. S.; 1922 Franklin st.   *Thursday*
Lyman, Mrs D. B.; The Bella Vista
Lyman, Colonel W. W.; Cosmos Club   —St. Helena
Lynde, William C.; 1416 Larkin st.
Lynds, A.; Lick House
Lyon, E. H.; 1419 Van Ness ave.
Lyons, Clarence; 208 Hyde St.
Lyons, Madame E. G.; 2022 Bush st.   *Tuesday*
Lyons, Mr and Mrs H.; 1431 Geary st.
——Miss Ida

MacCrellish, Mrs Frederick; SW cor. Pine and Mason sts. *Thursday*
Macdonald, Mr and Mrs Wm; 2219 Scott st.   *1st, and 3d Tuesdays*
——Miss Hildergarde
——Mr I. Burns
Macdougall, Miss Florence; 431 O'Farrell st.
MacGrotty, Mr and Mrs Alfred; 422 Franklin st.
Mackey, Mr and Mrs Duncan C.; 1419 Washington st.
Mackey, H.; The Berkshire
Mackey, Mr and Mrs Alexander; 619 Nineteenth st.
——Miss
——Walter S.
Mackenzie, Rev and Mrs Robert; 1452 Franklin st.   *Tuesday*
Macloon, Capt and Mrs C. H.; 2411 Washington st.   Europe
MacMurray, Major and Mrs J. W., Fort Mason   *Thursday*   Alaska
Macondray, Miss M. L.; The Bella Vista   *Thursday*
Macondray, William; 1821 Sacramento st.   Menlo Park
——Frederick W.
——Horatio N.
——Miss Nina; New California Hotel
——George N.
Macondray, Faxon A.; 1950 California st.   Menlo Park

Madden, Miss; 1100 California st.
Madison, Mrs S. E.; 1515 Sacramento st.   *Thursday*
———Frank D.; 1515 Sacramento st. and 324 Pine st.
Maddux, Mrs J. H.; 3009 Sacramento st.   *Wednesday*
———Miss Lulu
Maguire, Hon J. G.

Maguire, Mr and Mrs James Appleton, 516 Van Ness ave.
———George E.
Mahan, Lieut and Mrs Dennis H.; U. S. Str. "McArthur."
Mahan, Mr and Mrs H. H.; 2001 Eddy st.   *Thursday*
———Miss Addie
———Miss Bell
Mahon, Mrs Frank; 1429 Mason st.
Mailliard, Mr and Mrs John W.; 2716 California st.   San Rafael
Main, Mr and Mrs Charles; Palace Hotel   *Monday*
Maison, Mr and Mrs N. E.; 561 Seventeenth st.   *Wednesday*
Mallon, Mr and Mrs John; 2508 Sacramento st.
Mallory, Mrs M. B.; 1449 McAllister st.   *Thursday*
Malter, George H.; 912 Scott st.
Manchester, E. W. M.; Hotel Pleasanton
Manchester, Miss M. L.; The Bella Vista   *Thursday*
Mancusi, Guiseppe; 522 Sutter st.
Mangels, Claus; 2518 Howard st.
Manheim, Henry S.; 217 Sansome st.
Mann, Mr and Mrs Clarence M.; 2825 Jackson st.   *Tuesday*
Mann, Dr and Mrs F. P.; 2223 Sutter st.   *Tuesday*
———Hubert T.
———Miss Lelia A.
Mann, Mrs S. S.; 404 Turk st.   *Monday*
———C. S.
———F. A.
Mann, Seth; 2444 Howard st.
———Charles H.
Mann, Mr and Mrs Harry; Occidental Hotel   *Tuesday*
———Miss Tottie
Mann, Mr and Mrs Henry R.; 2011 California st.
Manning, Miss A. M.; The Renton   *Monday*
Manning, Mr and Mrs Seymour H.   Portland, Oregon
Marble, L.; Oriel Hotel
Margo, Mrs J. A.; 707 Bush st.   *Thursday*
Marks, Mr and Mrs Joseph; Palace Hotel
Marlin, Mr and Mrs A.; 230 Eleventh st.
Marriott, Mr and Mrs Frederick; Flood Building
Marsh, Mr and Mrs H. F.; 2507 Howard st.
Marshall, Dr and Mrs Benjamin; 924 Sutter st.

Marshall, General and Mrs E. C.; The Bélla Vista
——Miss Nellie
Marshall, Captain and Mrs J. H.   San Diego
Marshall, Mr and Mrs Louis; 2195 Devisadero st.   San Rafael
Marshutz, L. C.; 412 Eddy st.
Marston, Mr and Mrs C. A.   *Friday*   Hazel Glen Hotel, Sunol
Martel, Mr and Mrs James L.; 2226 California st.   {*Thursday* {Mountain View
——Miss Adele
——Miss Ethel
Martenstein, Mr and Mrs Jacob A.; 616 O'Farrell st.
Martenstein, Jacob; 1129 Turk st.
Martin, Mrs Ada N.; 3116 Washington st.   *Friday*
Martin, Mr and Mrs Camilo; 2412 Webster st.
Martin, Mrs Eleanor; Bryant and Second   Del Monte
Martin, Mrs H. B.; The Bella Vista   *Thursday*
Martin, Mr and Mrs Henry McL.; California and Taylor sts.   {Santa Cruz {*Tuesday*
Martin, Mrs J. M.   San Jose
Martin, Marie; 2220 Van Ness Ave.   *Tuesday*
Martin, Mr and Mrs J. P.; Palace Hotel   *Monday*
Martin, W. H.; Jackson and Franklin sts.
Martin, Dr William, U. S. N.; Cosmos Club
Martin, William; 2914 California st.
Martin, William C.; 314 Oak st.
Marvin, Mr and Mrs Harvey; 1911 Broderick st.
Marwedel, C. F.; 2011 Bush st.
——Charles W.
Marye, George T., Jr.; 234 Montgomery st.
Maskey, Mr and Mrs F.; 32 Kearny st.
Maslin, S. P.; 1500 Second st., Sacramento   Occidental Hotel, S. F.
Mason, Mrs N. H. A.; 1404 McAllister st.   *Tuesday* Mason Valley, Nev.
Mathews, Mr and Mrs Harvey; 1632 Clay st.   *Thursday* .
Mathews, Miss Lulu; 920 Jackson st.
Mathews, H. Allen; 614 Powell st.
Mathews, Mr and Mrs Henry E.; 803 Pine st.
Matthews, Miss Cora; 415 First st.   Clear Lake, Kelseyville
Matthews, Mrs M.; The Berkshire   *Monday*
Matthews, William; 2115 Sacramento st.
Mathieu, Mr and Mrs Julien; 1510 Larkin st.   *Thursday*
——Frank L.
——Mr and Mrs Julien, Jr.
Mau, Mrs H. Albert; 2215 Broadway   *Friday*   Larkspur
——Miss
——Miss Julia

Mau, Mr and Mrs William F.; 1327 Sutter st.   *Thursday*   Larkspur
Mauldin, Mr and Mrs Hugh; Hotel Bella Vista   *Thursday*
Maupay, Miss Emma; The Berkshire   *Monday*
Maxwell, Mr and Mrs J. D.; 801 Leavenworth st.
Maxwell, Mr and Mrs J. W. C.; 318 Van Ness ave.
——Miss Emily
Maxwell, Walter; Bohemian Club   Los Angeles
May, E. F.; 538 Guerrero st.
May, Mrs Edward; The Berkshire
——Miss Alice
May, Mr and Mrs Frederick   Washington, D. C.
May, Mr and Mrs Henry   Washington, D. C.
May, Dr and Mrs W. B.; 1114 Clay st.
Mayer, Albert M. S.; 412 Jones st.
Mayer, Charles, Jr.; 924 Fillmore st.
Mayer, J.; 1513 Pierce st.
Mayer, Miss Josephine; The Berkshire   *Monday*
Mayer, Colonel and Mrs Samuel D.; 825 California st.
Maynard, Mrs Geo. F.; 1512 California st.   *Wednesday*   San Mateo
——Miss Eva
——Miss Lena
——Miss Sallie
Maynard, Mr and Mrs John H.; Palace Hotel   *Monday*   San Mateo
Maynard, Mr and Mrs W. J.; Palace Hotel   *Monday*
Mayne, Charles; Pacific-Union Club   Del Monte
McAfee, Mrs J. C.; The Bella Vista   *Thursday*
——Edwin
McAfee, L. C.; 50 Nevada Block, S. F.   Bakersfield
McAfee, Mr and Mrs Carrol; Palace Hotel
McAffee, C. Wm.; 2919 California st.
McAlester, Miss A. E.; 8 Yerba Buena st.
McAllister, Elliott; 1419 Clay st.   Ross Valley
McAllister, Mrs Hall   Ross Valley
——Miss Eva
——Hall
McAllister, Mr and Mrs M. Hall; 1214 Hyde st.
McAllister, Mr and Mrs W. F. M.; Palace Hotel   *Monday*   Colorado
McAllister, Ward; Pacific-Union Club
McAron, Thos. P.; Palace Hotel   *Thursday*   San Jose
McBean, Mrs P. McG.; 2611 Pacific ave.   *Friday*
McCall, J. C.; 22 Montgomery st.
McCall, Robert A.; Westminster Hotel
McCabe, Mrs M. A.; Point Lobos ave., bet 18th and 19th aves.
McCarthy, Mr and Mrs F. F.; Palace Hotel   *Monday*

McCenery, Julius C.; Lick House
McClatchy, Mrs James; Grand Hotel   *Monday*   **Sacramento**
——Miss Emily
——Miss Fannie
McClung, Mr and Mrs J. W.; 1913 Devisadero st.
McClure. Mrs David; Occidental Hotel   *Monday*
McClure, Mr and Mrs Penuel; 408 Ellis st.   *Thursday*
McCombe, Mr and Mrs; 712 Golden Gate ave.
——Miss Eliot
McCoppin, Mr and Mrs Frank; Occidental Hotel   *Monday*
McCormick, Miss Eva; 924 Valencia st.
McCormick, Mr and Mrs William H.; 1715 Larkin st.
——Miss Lizzie R.; cor Pierce and Fulton sts. *Tuesday* **Skaggs' Spgs·**
—— Emanuel B.
M Coy, Henry J.; 724 Hayes st.
McCutchen, Mr and Mrs E. J.; 2602 California st. *Friday* **Ross Valley**
——Miss Alice
McDermott, Wm.; Hotel Pleasanton
McDonald, Mrs D. L.; 1800 Laguna st.
——Miss Laura
——Miss Blythe
McDonald, Captain James M.; 912 Union st.
McDonald, Mr and Mrs Mark L.; Occidental Hotel   **Santa Rosa**
McDonald, Mr and Mrs M. J.; 1701 Gough st.
McDonald, Dr R. H.; 813 Sutter st.   *Thursday*
——R. H., Jr.; Pine and Sansome sts.
McDonough, Mr and Mrs Joseph; New California Hotel   **Menlo Park**
McDonnell, Miss M.; 941 Fifteenth st.   *Friday*
McDonough, Mr and Mrs R.; Lick House   *Monday*
McElroy, Mrs; 704 Pine st.   *Thursday*
McElroy, Mr and Mrs Robert; SW cor. Buchanan and Haight sts.
——Robert D.
——Mr and Mrs James R.
——Mr and Mrs Robert D.; 1908 Valencia st.
McEwen, Mrs J A.; 1615 Clay st.
——Miss Susie
McFarlane, E. C.   **Honolulu, H. I.**
——George
McFarlane, A. G.; 1323 Oak st.
McGary, Mr and Mrs Edward; 1036 Mission st.   *Thursday*
McGauley, Mrs Julia F.; 1345 Union st.   *Monday*   **Mill Valley**
——Miss Julie C.
——James F.
McGavin, Mr and Mrs Walter J. T.; 910 Taylor st.   **San Rafael**
McGee, W. A.; 20 Montgomery st.   **Fruitvale**

McGill, Henry M.; 1808 Fillmore st.
McGilvray, Mr and Mrs James B.; 1322 Bush st.
McGlachlin, Lieut Edward F.; Presidio
McGlynn, Peter J.; 1500 Golden Gate ave.
McGuinness, J. P., U. S. N.; Cosmos Club
McKay, Thomas D.; Occidental Hotel
McKee, Mrs.; Bush and Mason sts.
——Miss
McKee, Mr and Mrs John; 26 Twelfth st.
McKenty, Mrs Lita; 1222 Pine st.   *Wednesday*
McKinley, Mr and Mrs D. A.; Palace Hotel   *Monday*
McKinstry, Judge and Mrs E. W.; 1237 O'Farrell st.
——Miss Laura
——James C.
McKisick, Judge and Mrs L. D.; 1311 Hyde st.   *Tuesday*   Alameda
——Miss Williette Ross
——Mr Lewis
——Mr R. T.
McKittrick, Mr and Mrs Wm. Holmes; Angel Island
McLaine, Mrs Laughlin; 2226 Clay st.   *Friday*
——Miss
McLaren, Norman; 614 Sutter st.
McLaughlin, Leo; 309 California st.
McLean, Mrs Robert A.; Pacific ave. near Broderick st.   *Friday*
McLean, Sterling; Cosmos Club
McLennan, Mr and Mrs Frank P.; 1515 Clay st.   Santa Barbara
McLeod, Mr and Mrs Daniel; Occidental Hotel   *Monday*
McMahon, Mr and Mrs B.; The Berkshire   *Monday*
——Miss Marion
——Miss Paralee
——Miss Alice
McMahon, Miss; 716 Jones st.
McMillan, Robert; 202 Ridley st.   *1st and 3d Fridays*   Yosemite
——Miss Jennie
——Miss Emma
MacMonagle, Dr Beverly; 3118 Sacramento st. and 430 Kearny st.
McMullen, Mr and Mrs Frank; 820 Grove st.   *Tuesday*
McMullin, Mrs George O.; 1104 Post st.
——Miss Mamie
——George O.
McMullin, Mrs John.   Casa Blanca, San Joaquin Co.
McMullin, Morgan D.; 1935 Clay st.   *Friday*   Lathrop
——Beauregard
——D. M.

Printing Department, THE BANCROFT COMPANY, 49 First street, do not claim to be the cheapest printers in town, but give full value to their patrons.

McMullin, Thurlow; 1104 Post st.
McMullin, Mrs Thurlow; 1252 California st.   *Tuesday*   Santa Cruz
——Latham
McMurtry, W. S., Jr.; Pacific-Union Club   San Jose
McNear, Geo. W. J.   Port Costa
McNeil, Miss; 1019 California st.   *Tuesday*
McNulty, Mrs Charles A.; 1252 California st.   *Tuesday*
——Bert
McNutt, Dr and Mrs W. F.; 1805 California st.
McPherson, Dr and Mrs Maynard; 609 Polk st.   *Wednesday*
——Miss Belle F.
——William
McRuer, Mr and Mrs Donald C.; 18 Laurel Place
McVay, Miss Nellie, 1919 Sutter st.   *Wednesday*
Mead, Mr and Mrs Charles H.; 1505 Larkin st.   *Wednesday*
Mead, Mr and Mrs Lewis R.; 2606 California st.   Byron Springs
Mead, Mr and Mrs Walter; 1611 Sacramento st.   *Wednesday*
Meagher, Mr and Mrs Thomas F.; 926 Clay st.   Del Monte
Medan, Mr and Mrs J. P.; 2324 Pine st.   *Tuesday*
——Miss Dora
——Miss Emma
——Mr Emil
Mehlert, Mrs E.; 1717 Laguna st.
Meinecke, Mr and Mrs Charles; 1917 Franklin st.   *1st and 3d Tuesdays*
——Miss Inez
——Miss Minnie
Meinecke, George H.; 405 Geary st.
Mellis, Mr and Mrs D. E. (*née* Bolton); 1531 Sacramento st.   *Thursday*
Melone, Mr and Mrs Drury; Palace Hotel   Oak Knoll, Napa Co.
Melrose, Mr and Mrs Kenneth; 2517 Octavia st.
Melsome, G. E.; 3220 Clay st.   Wiltshire, England
——Miss Mamie
Melville, William R.   Blithedale
Mendell, Colonel and Mrs George H.; 2310 Clay st.
——George H., Jr.
Merle, Charles F.; 302 O'Farrell st.
Merrill, Mr and Mrs John C.; 14 Stanley Place
——Miss Daisy
——John C., Jr.
Merrill, Mr and Mrs John F.; 1732 Washington st.   *Friday*
Merrill, Louis; 207 Thirteenth st.
Merry, Mr and Mrs W. L.; 2030 Pacific ave.   *Friday*
Merten, Mr and Mrs August F.; 923 Fillmore st.
Mesick, Richard S.; 24 Montgomery st.

Messer, Mr and Mrs N. T.; Hotel Pleasanton
Messersmith, E. T.; Hotel Bella Vista
Messing, Rev Dr A. J.; 708 O'Farrell st.
Meux, J. P.; Hotel Pleasanton
Myer, Capt and Mrs; 1610 Van Ness Ave.
Meyer, Miss Emma; The Berkshire *Monday*
Meyer, Em.; 1319 Gough st.
Meyer, Mr and Mrs Eugene; 1730 Pine st.
——Miss
Meyerfeld, Mr and Mrs J.; 1513 Pierce st.
Meylert, Dr and Mrs A. P.; Palace Hotel *Monday*
Mezes, Sidney; 530 California st.   **Berkeley**
Michael, Frank; Bohemian Club
Michalitschke, Mr and Mrs A.; 2102 California st.
Middleton, Mr and Mrs Samuel P.; 600 Bush st.
Middleton, Mr and Mrs John; 2311 Jackson st. *Friday*
Miel, Rev C. L.; 206 Lombard st.
Mighell, William E.; 514 Eddy st.
Miles, General and Mrs Nelson A.; U. S. A., Presidio
——Miss Cecelia
Miller, Mr and Mrs Chas. E.; 312 Haight st. *Wednesday*
Miller, H. Clay; 1137 Bush st.
Miller, Mr and Mrs H. M. A.; 1111 Pine st. *Monday*
Miller, Ed.; 105 Montgomery st.
Miller, E. E. W.; Hotel Bella Vista
Miller, Mr and Mrs Henry; 1240 Howard st.
Miller, Herbert; Oriel Hotel
Miller, Mr and Mrs W. S.; 712 Sutter st. (The Renton)
Miller, Miss Ida; Hotel Pleasanton *Monday*
Miller, Louis, Jr.; 807 Van Ness ave.
Miller, Mr and Mrs Samuel; 1011 Pine st.   **Yosemite Valley**
Mills, Mrs C. T.   **Mills Seminary, Cal.**
Mills, Mrs D. O.   **Millbrae and New York**
Mills, Mr Edgar.   **Pacific Union Club**
Mills, Mr and Mrs Edward T.; 322 Haight st. *1st and 3d Thursdays*
Mills, Mrs James E.; 2106 Van Ness ave.
Mills, Mrs W. L. B.; 1918 Sutter st.
Mills, Mr and Mrs William H.; 1707 Octavia st.
Miner, Mr and Mrs W. H.; 2025 California st.
——Frank G.
Minott, Joseph Otis; 577 Market st.
Mitchell, Edward H.; 6 Ford st.
Mitchell, Mr and Mrs G. H.; The Renton *Monday*
Mitchell, Mr and Mrs George M.; 813 Grove st.
Mitchell, Senator John H.   **Portland, Or.**

Mitchell, Mr and Mrs Robert B. ; 727 Ashbury st.
Mitchell, Mr and Mrs R. W.   Portland, Or.
Mizner, Mr and Mrs L. B.   Guatemala, Central America
——Edgar A.
——Lansing, Jr.; Bohemian Club.   Benicia
——Dr William G. Cooper Medical Institute, S. F.   Benicia
Mizner, Henry W.; 2415 California st.   Benicia
Moale, Colonel and Mrs Edward; U. S. A.
Moffatt, Mr and Mrs; 1419 Post st.
——Miss
Molera, Mr and Mrs E. J. ; 850 Van Ness ave.   *Thursday*   Monterey
Molineux, Mr and Mrs Henry; 216 Bush st
Molloy, Miss Bessie; The Renton   *Monday*
Montague, Mr and Mrs W. W.; 1103 Bush st.   Santa Clara
——Miss
Monteagle, Mr and Mrs Louis F. ; 2002 Pacific ave.   *Friday*
——Miss Jennie
Monteagle, Mr and Mrs Robert C. ; 209 Turk st.
Montealegre, Mrs Carlos F.; 512 Sutter st.
——Miss
Montealegre, Mrs S. J.; 1114 Bush st.   *Thursday*
Montgomery, George S.; Grand Hotel
Montpellier A.; California and Battery sts.
Moody, Mrs; NW cor. Pacific and Gough sts.   New York
Moody, Mr and Mrs Joseph L.; SE cor. Lombard and Jones sts. *Friday*
——Miss Eda
——Frederick L.
Moore, H. H. ; 411 Montgomery st.
Moore, Mr and Mrs Alfred S. ; 1711 Jones st.   *Wednesday*
Moore, Mr and Mrs Alfred ; 1511 Gough st.
Moore, Mr and Mrs Arthur W.; 2520 Pacific ave.   *Friday*
Moore, Mr and Mrs Austin D. ; 2728 Pacific ave. *Friday*
Moore, Mr and Mrs Charles A.   Port Townsend
Moore, Mr and Mrs Percy P.   King Landing, Visalia
Moore, Edward ; 2122 Bush st.
Moore, Mr and Mrs George A. ; 1511 Gough st.
Moore, Harry P. ; 518 Golden Gate ave.
Moore, Howell C. ; Cosmos Club
Moore, Mr and Mrs James; Nevada Bank   San Rafael
Moore, Mrs E. J. ; 711½ Hayes st.   *Thursday*
——William S.
Moore, Mrs Robert S. ; 619 Valencia st.   Paso Robles
Moore, Mrs Samuel   *Monday*   San Jose
——Miss Maude
Moore, Mr and Mrs Walter ; Palace Hotel (when in S. F.) Los Angeles

Mooreland, Mr and Mrs ; Hotel Oriel   *Monday*

Mooser, Mr and Mrs Wm.; 2709 Pierce st.   *Friday*   **Bradley, Monterey**

——Mr and Mrs Joseph H.

——Miss Alice

——William, Jr.

——Chas. E.

Mooser, Mr and Mrs Louis H.; 646 Folsom st.   *Wednesday*

Morgan, Major M. R.; Phelan Building

Morgan, Mr and Mrs; 413 Van Ness ave.

Morgan, Edward D.; 2312 Clay st.   *Friday*   **Del Monte**

——Miss Alice M.

——Miss Laura R.

——Miss Susie D.

Morgan, Percy T.; Cosmos Club

Morgan, Mr and Mrs William P.; 1451 Franklin st.   *Friday*

Morrill, Grant A.; 706 Taylor st.

Morrill, Mrs Paul ; Taylor and Bush sts.

——Miss

Morris, Sam F.; 707 Mason st.   *Tuesday*

Morris, Mrs R.; 2118 Bush st.

Morrison, Miss; SW cor. Union and Fillmore sts.   *2d and 4th Fridays*

Morrison, Col and Mrs George H.; 908 Guerrero st.   *Wednesday* **Carson City, Nev.**

Morrow, Robert F.; 916 Leavenworth st.

Morrow, Hon and Mrs W. W.; 600 Bush st.   **Hotel del Monte**

——Miss Maud

——William H.

Morse, Mr and Mrs George D.; 826 Market st.

Morse, Capt and Mrs H. G.; Palace Hotel   *Monday* **Str. "Alameda"**

Morse, I. H.; 1216 Jones st.

Mortimer, C. White, (British Vice-Consul)   **Los Angeles**

Morton, Mr and Mrs H. D.; Taylor and Ellis sts.   *1st and 3d Wednesdays*

——Mr and Mrs John

Morton, Sargent S.; 321 Oak st.

Morton, Mr and Mrs; 712 Sutter st. (The Renton)

Morton, W. R.; 309 Taylor st.

Mosby, Colonel John S.; 501 Geary st.

Mosely, Mr and Mrs Andrew S.; Hotel Pleasanton   *Monday*

Moses, Mr and Mrs Charles S.; Lick House   *Tuesday*

Mott, Lieut T. B.; U. S. A.   **Fortress Monroe**

Mott, Baldwin E.; 2820 Clay st.

Moulder, Hon and Mrs A. J.; 812 Bush st   *Thursday*

——Miss Maude

——Mr Augustus B.

Moulton, Mrs Adeline; 1120 Gough st *Wednesday* Blithedale
——Miss Florence
Moulton, Mr and Mrs Frank; 607 Harrison st.
Moulton, Mrs Josials; 925 Pine st.
Moultrie, Mrs L. M.; The Berkshire *Monday*
——Miss
Mozart, Mr and Mrs E. H.; Hotel Oriel *Monday*
Mozley, Mrs Brandon; Hotel Pleasanton *Monday*
Mulberforce, Mr Alex.; 1506 California st. San Rafael
Mulcreave, Miss Alice; 621 Octavia st. *Tuesday* Sacramento
Mulcreevy, Miss Josie; 321 Octavia st. *Tuesday* Menlo Park
Mullan, Capt and Mrs D. W.; U. S. N.; 818 Powell st. *Tuesday*
Mullin, Mr and Mrs Jas.; 422 Ellis st. *Thursday*
——Geo. A.
Millins, Mr and Mrs Charles F.; 1809 Gough st. *2d and 4th Friday*
Mundy, J. H.; Occidental Hotel
Munro, Mr and Mrs George R.; 1114 Seventeenth st. *Thursday*
——Miss Minnie
Murphy, Mrs D. T.; Occidental Hotel Abroad
——Miss Nellie
——Miss Fannie
Murphy, Daniel T; Pacific-Union Club
Murphy, Judge Daniel J.; 119 Liberty st.
Murphy, Mr and Mrs Eugene P.; 1304 Guerrero st.
Murphy, James T.; Cosmos Club San Jose
Murphy, P. W.; Pacific-Union Club San Luis Obispo
Murphy, Mr and Mrs Samuel G.
Murray, Mrs Jean ; 1708 Clay st.
Murray, Alexander S.; 1025 O'Farrell st.
Myrick, Judge and Mrs Milton H.; Palace Hotel *Monday*
——Miss

Nager, H. I.; Hotel Pleasanton *Monday*
——Miss A.
——Miss E.
Nager, Mrs S.; 908 Van Ness ave. Woodland
——Miss Annie
——Miss Emily
——Mr H. I.
Nagle, George W.; Bohemian Club, 520 Golden Gate ave.
Napthaly, Benjamin F.; 2315 Webster st.
Narjot, Mr and Mrs Ernest; 1601 Hyde st.
——Miss
Nash, H. C.; SW cor. Powell and California sts.
Nash, Jay T.; 916 Hyde st.

Nash, Joseph ; 3100 Pacific ave.
Naughton, Mr and Mrs J. F.; 2209 California st.
Natorp, Bernard ; 517 Mason st.
Nauton, R. H. ; 1418 Clay st.
——-R. H., Jr.
——George
Neal, Robert W.; Florence House
Neill, Mr and Mrs James; 1123 California st.   *Tuesday*
Nesfield, Mrs D. W. C.; 1503 Pacific ave.
Neuberger, Mr and Mrs Gustave; 1628 Octavia st.
Neville, Mrs A. E.; 1631 O'Farrell st.   *Thursday*
Nevin, Mr and Mrs C. W.; American Exchange Hotel   **Santa Cruz**
Newell, Mr and Mrs David ; 5 Pearl st.
Newell, Mr and Mrs W. H.   **Seattle**
Newell, Mr and Mrs; 703 Bush st.
Newhall, Mr and Mrs E. W.; 2200 Broadway
Newhall, Mrs H. M.; 1299 Van Ness ave.   *4th Fridays* **Hotel Rafael**
——Walter S.
——George A.
Newhall, Mr and Mrs W. Mayo; 1206 Post st.   **San Rafael**
Newlands, Mr and Mrs Francis G.; Palace Hotel   **Carson City, Nev.**
Newlands, James; 2902 Clay st.
——Miss Jessie
——James, Jr.;
Newmark, Mrs M. J.; 1101 Laguna st.   *2d and 4th Tuesdays*
Newton Mr and Mrs Morris; 207 Larkin st.   { *1st and 3d Wednesdays* **Mosean Cottage**
Niblack, Lieut A. P.   **Navy Dept., Washington, D. C.**
Nichols, Mr and Mrs D. C.; Palace Hotel   *Monday*
Nicholson, Mr and Mrs Peter; Hotel Pleasanton   *Monday*
——Alexander
Nicholson, Mr and Mrs W. A. S.; 510 Baker st.
Nickel, Mr and Mrs J. Le Roy; 1415 Jones st.   **Menlo Park**
Nickerson, Mr and Mrs A. A.; 2016 Pine st.   *Wednesday*
——Miss Maude
——Miss Myra
——A. A., Jr.
Nightingale, Mr and Mrs John; 300 Haight st.   { *Wednesday* **Napa Soda Springs**
——Miss Minnie
——Miss Georgie
——Dr John
——Joseph B.
Noble, F. L. H.; 216 Bush st.
Noble, Burr; 36 New Montgomery st.

Noble, Mr and Mrs Patrick; 1914 Webster st.   *Tuesday*

Noble, Mrs C. G.; 3006 Sacramento st.

Noble, Lieutenant Robert H.; U. S. A. **St. John's Col., Annapolis, Md.**

Noble, Rev and Mrs Thomas K.; 711 Jones st.

Nojot, Ernest; 711 Howard st.

Nolan, Lieut James E.; U. S. A., Presidio

Nolan, J. C.; 1329 Golden Gate ave.

Nolan, Mr and Mrs Patrick F.; 1428 Golden Gate ave.   { *Thursday*
—————Miss Kittie   { **Del Monte**

—————Mr and Mrs William M.

Norcross, Daniel; 413 O'Farrell st.

Norfleet, Dr Ernest; U. S. N.   **Mare Island**

Norris, Mr and Mrs B. F.; 1322 Sacramento st.   *Friday*

Norris, Miss F. L; 835 California st.   *Tuesday*

Norris, Dr Basil; Occidental Hotel

Norris, Mr and Mrs William; 927 Bush st.   *Thursday*

North, Mr and Mrs G. L.; Hotel Pleasanton   *Monda*

Norton, Mr and Mrs G. N.; 2414 Washington st.

Norton, Mr and Mrs Harry D.; The Clifton

Norton, Miss M. E.; The Renton   *Monday*

Norton, Miss May; 1708 Geary st.

Norton, J. F.; 237 Kearny st.

Norton, Mrs S. J.; 1511 Jones st.

Nougues, Mr and Mrs Joseph M.; 2226 California st.   **Napa Co.**

Nugent, John F.; 426 Geary st.

Nugent, Miss Sybil; 320 Harrison st.

Nunan, Mr and Mrs Matthew; 422 Oak st.

Nuttall, Mr and Mrs J. Robert K.; 1819 Jackson   *Monday*

Nye, Mrs U. S.   **Albeto, near Willows**

Nutting, Mr and Mrs Calvin S.; 1521 Golden Gate ave.

—————Miss Grace

O'Brien, Mr and Mrs J. J.; 300 Van Ness ave.

O'Brien, Mr and Mrs James; 910 McAllister st.   *Thursday*

O'Callahan, Daniel; 16 Twelfth st.   *Tuesday*

—————Miss Maggie

O'Connell, Daniel; 1624 Broadway st.

O'Connell, Miss Maggie; 806 McAllister st.   *Thursday*

O'Connor, Mr and Mrs Cornelius; 825 O'Farrell st.   *Wed.* **Del Coronado**

—————Miss Lillie

—————Miss Maud

O'Connor, Mrs J.; Occidental Hotel   **San Rafael**

—————The Misses

O'Farrell, Mrs John J.; 2035 Howard st.

O'Kane, Mr and Mrs William ; Lick House
O'Leary, Fergus ; Grand Hotel
O'Sullivan, Mrs Cornelius D. ; 1025 Bush st.   *Thursday*
——Cornelius D., Jr.
Oesting, Mr and Mrs Paul ; 1410 Taylor st.   *Thursdays*   **New York City**
Ogden, Mrs Richard L. ; Pacific ave. and Pierce st.   *Friday*
Okell, Charles J. ; Cosmos Club
Oliver, J. H., U. S. N. ; Cosmos Club
Oliver, Miss Mattie ; San Jose ave and Twenty-fourth st.   *Thursday*
Oliver, Mr and Mrs Wm. G. ; 233 Fair Oak st.   *Wednesday*
Onesti, George ; 1213 Taylor st.
Orcutt, F. L. ; Cosmos Club
Orena, Mr and Mrs Gaspard ; 729 Geary st.   *Wednesday*
——Orestes
Orena, Mr and Mrs Dario ; 527 Geary st.
Ortez, Miss Julia ; 2531 Pine st.
Otis, Mr and Mrs James, Jr. ; 1900 Washington st.   **San Rafael**
——Mrs James
——Miss Helen
——Fred

Oullahan, D. J. ; Occidental Hotel
Oulton, Mrs Geo. ; Hotel Pleasanton
Overton, Mrs Alice C. ; 1414 Geary st.
——Victor G.
——Robert H.
——Charles P.
——Elias P.
Owens, Frank ; Hotel Pleasanton
Owens, Mr and Mrs W. J. ; Hotel Pleasanton   *Monday*
——Miss Alice
Oxnard, Robert ; 623 Mason st.

Pace, Mr Charles ; 1018 Jackson st
Pacheco, Mr and Mrs Romualdo ; The Bella Vista   *Thursday*   **Mexico**
Page, Mr and Mrs Arthur ; 1805 Pierce st.   **San Rafael**
Page, Mr and Mrs Charles ; 2518 Pacific ave.
Page, Mr and Mrs Hamilton ; 201 Buchanan st.   **Napa Soda Springs**
Page, Mr and Mrs James D.; 2002 Jackson st.   **Martinez**
Page, Olaf   **Valparaiso, Chili**
Page, Miss Meta ; 2200 California st.   **San Rafael**
——William D.
——Mr and Mrs George F.
Paige, Calvin ; 116 Leidesdorf st.

Paige, Mr and Mrs Timothy; 2002 Pacific ave.   *Friday*
——Cutler.
Paine, Colonel and Mrs J. C.; Palace Hotel
——Miss Florence
——Miss Helen
Painter, Mr and Mrs Edgar; 1514½ Vallejo st.   *Friday*   **Alameda**
Painter, Mrs Caroline A.; 2709 Buchanan st. **Coyote Valley, Lake Co.**
——Walter M.
——Edgar
——Arthur
——Oscar
Palache, Mr and Mrs G.; 900 Eddy *1st & 3d Wednesday* **Hotel Vendome**
——Miss Ida
——Miss
——Thomas H.
Palache, Robert K.; 1910 Devisadero st.
Palmer, Jr., Mr and Mrs George; 824 Powell st.   *Friday*
Palmer, Mr and Mrs C. M.; The Bella Vista   *Thursday*
Pariser, James A.; 49 First st
Parke, Lyman C.; 1118 Gough st.
Parker, Mr and Mrs L. M.; 901 Larkin st.   *Thursday*
Parker, Mrs M. W.; Grand Hotel   *Monday*
Parker, E. L.; 1512 California st.
——Stafford H.
Parkhurst, Mr and Mrs John W.; 1419 Taylor st.   *Thursday*   **Martinez**
Parks, Mr and Mrs R. F.; Westminster Hotel
Parrish, E. H.; 738 Capp st.   **Boulder Creek**
Parrott, Mrs A. M.; 517 Sutter st.   **San Mateo**
Parrott, Mr and Mrs Louis B.; 1913 Franklin st.   **San Rafael**
Parrott, Mr and Mrs Tiburcio; 414 Montgomery st.   **St. Helena**
Parson, Dr Edward; Pacific-Union Club
Partridge, A. C.; 1414 Leavenworth st.   *Tuesday*
——Miss Ella S.
——Miss Jessie E.
Partridge, Mr and Mrs George; 812 Twenty-first st.
——Miss Jennie
——Miss Alice
Partridge, Mr and Mrs John; 2120 Jackson st.   *Friday*
Partridge, Mr and Mrs Samuel C.; 1307 Leavenworth st.   **Oakland**
Paterson, Lieut and Mrs Robert H.; Presidio
Paterson, Judge and Mrs A. Van R.; 310 Haight st.
Paterson, William T.; New City Hall
Patterson, Miss Martha; 59 Hoff ave.
——Miss Isabel
Patton, Mrs Charles L.; 1910 Broadway st.

Patton, Jasper N.; 1825 Carlos ave.
Pawlici, Dr and Mrs L.; 700 Sutter st.
Paxton, Mrs John A.; Palace Hotel *Monday*
Payne, S. W.; 759 Market st.
Payne, Redmond W., M. D.; 8-9-16 New Chronicle Building
Payne, Dr Eugene; 8-9-16 New Chronicle Building
——Sylvanus W.
——Clyde S.
Payne, Mr and Mrs Theodore F.; 1409 Sutter st.
Payne, Warren R.; Bohemian Club
Payot, Mr Henry; 922 Ellis st. *Wednesday*
——Mr Leonce
——Miss Henriette
——Miss Louise
Payson, Capt and Mrs A. H. Residence San Mateo
Payton, Clifford; The Clifton *Monday* Suisun
——Mrs
Pearce, C. W.; Cosmos Club
Pearson, Mr and Mrs H. H. Santa Monica
Pease, Mr and Mrs R. H., Jr.; 2600 Pacific ave. *Friday*
Peck, Mr and Mrs J.E.; 424 Haight st. *Wednesday* { Portland, Me. Syracuse, N. Y. Santa Cruz, Cal.
Peele, Mrs.; The Renton *Monday*
Pendleton, Mrs M. E.; Hotel Pleasanton
Pennell, Prof Robert F.; 214 Castro st.
Pennell, Mr and Mrs Charles C.; 1414 Taylor st.
Pennell, Henry E.; 1702 Larkin st.
——Thomas M.
Perine, Mr and Mrs J. H.; Grand Hotel *Monday*
Perine, Mr and Mrs George M.; 113 Page st. *Thursday*
Perkins, Mr and Mrs Samuel; 1454 Franklin st.
Perrault, Dr and Mrs Julian; 1400 Jackson st. *Friday* Santa Cruz
——Mrs. H.
——Miss Grace
——Mr Julien
Perrin, Dr and Mrs E. B.; 1935 Clay st.
——Miss Addie
Perry, Mrs M. L.; 2034 Bush st. *Tuesday*
Perry, Henry; 504 Geary st.
Perry, John, Jr.; Occidental Hotel
Pescia, Dr and Mrs Joseph; 1520 Taylor st.
Peters, Mrs Mary; 1016 Sutter st.
——Charles R. San Rafael

Society as I have Found It By Ward McAllister. The New Society Book.

The Bancroft Company, 721 Market Street.

Peterson, S. B.; 314 Haight st.   *Wednesday*
Peterson, Mr and Mrs Frank B.
——Seabury B.
——Miss Carrie
Peterson, Mr and Mrs A. S.; 337 Eddy st.   *Wednesday*
Peterson, Mr and Mrs Frank; Hotel Pleasanton   *Monday*
Peterson, Mrs G. H.; 109 Oak st.   *Wednesday*
--——Miss Louise
——Miss Leona
Pettit, Mr and Mrs E.; 818 Powell st.   *Tuesday*
——Miss Eva
Peterson, Mr and Mrs F. C.; 1034 Mission st.
Peyton, Colonel and Mrs Bernard   Santa Cruz
——Miss Julia
Phelan, Mr and Mrs James; SW cor. Valencia and 17th sts. { *Monday* Santa Cruz
——Miss Mollie
--——James D.
Phelps, Mrs C. A.; 313 Devisadero st.   *Wednesday*
——Miss Mary
——Miss Inez
——Walter J.
——Louis J.
——George
Phillips, Mr and Mrs T. K.; 1817 O'Farrell st.
Phillips, Miss; 2728 Pacific ave.   *Friday*
Phippen, Miss; 2008 Jackson st.
Pichoir, H. F.; Pacific-Union Club
Pickens, Mr and Mrs J. R.; 1925 Webster st.
Pickering, Mr and Mrs Loring; 1018 Bush st.   *Thursday*   **Niles**
Pickering, Mr and Mrs F. M.; 2444 Jackson st.   **Santa Barbara**
Pickett, Mrs; 1332 Bush st.
——Charles E.
Pidwell, C. T.; Room 1, Odd Fellows' Building
Pierce, Henry   **Oakland**
Pierce, Mr and Mrs Orestes   **Oakland**
Pierce, Mr and Mrs Charles D.; 1416 Grove st.   **Oakland**
Pierce, Mr and Mrs Ira; 1730 Jackson st.   **Napa Soda Springs**
Pierce, J. M.; 2413 Fillmore st.
Pierce, Mr and Mrs R. T.; Hotel Pleasanton   **Santa Clara**
·——Miss Annie
——Miss Grace
——Miss Florence
Pierson, Mr and Mrs Arthur B.; 1609 Washington st.
Pierson, Mr and Mrs H. H.; Baldwin Hotel

Pierson, Mr and Mrs Fred H. ; 2214 Van Ness ave.
Pierson, Mr and Mrs Lawrence H. ; 1520 Vallejo st.   *Friday*
Pierson, Mr and Mrs William M.; 2214 Van Ness ave.   *Friday*
Pike, Mr and Mrs Charles W. ; 1716 Baker st.   **Alameda**
——Frank W.
Pillsbury, Mr and Mrs Frank W.; 700 Jones st.
Pillsbury, Mr and Mrs T. W.; 700 Jones st.   *1st and 3d Mondays*
Pillsbury, Miss; 1802 Pacific ave.   *Friday*
Pillsbury, E. S. ; Pacific-Union Club ; 1310 Taylor st.
——Miss
Pinckard, Mr and Mrs George M. ; 2119 California st.   **San Rafael**
Pinkham, Miss Ella M.; 1036 Valencia st.
Pinney, Mrs W. E.; Hotel Rafael
Pinto, Mrs Nellie S; 1801 Van Ness ave.   *Friday*   **Central America**
Piper, W. A.; Lick House
Pitman, Mrs Francis Henry; 1404 McAllister st. } *Tuesday* **Mason Valley, Nev.**
Pitts, Miss N. A. ; 115 Ridley st.
Pixley, Mr and Mrs Frank M.; Union & Fillmore sts. { *2d & 4th Fridays* **Owl's Wood** **Ross Valley**
Platt, Mr and Mrs C. B. ; Hotel Pleasanton   *Monday*
Platt, Miss Carrie; 1428 Golden Gate ave.   *Wednesday*
Platt, Horace G.; 701 Stockton st., Pacific-Union Club
Plum, Charles M. ; 308 Page st.   *Last Wednesday*   **Ætna Springs**
——Miss
——Miss F. Anita
——Charles M., Jr.
Plummer, Mr and Mrs C. Moody ; 408 California st.
Plummer, Dr Richard H.; 652 Mission st.
Poag, Mr and Mrs A. C.   **Hotel Rafael**
Poett, Mr and Mrs Alfred ; 507 Montgomery st.   **Santa Barbara**
Pond, Mayor and Mrs E. B.; 1019 California st.   *Tuesday*
Ponton De Arce, Mr. and Mrs Lucas; 950 Bryant st.
——Miss Marie
——Stanley
Poole, Miss Ermentine; 1506 Washington st.   *2d and 4th Tuesdays*
Pool, Mr and Mrs I. Lawrence ; 1726 Broadway   **San Rafael**
Pope, Mrs A. J. ; 1601 Van Ness ave.   **St. Helena**
——Miss Mary E.
——George A.
Popper, Max; 1065 Mission st.
Porteous, Miss ; Care J. P. Hale, Occidental Hotel
Porter, Mrs A. A. ; Hotel Pleasanton   *Monday*
Porter, Miss Florence ; 120 Turk st.

Perrier-Jouët & Co., Champagnes To be had at All First-Class
Hotels and Restaurants

Porter, Mrs. W. H. ; 116 Eddy st. $\begin{cases} Tuesday \\ Thursday\ Evening \end{cases}$ Pacific Grove
——H. C.
Porter, Mr and Mrs B. F. ; The Berkshire *Monday* Soquel
——Miss Sadie
——Miss May
Porter, Mr and Mrs G. K. ; 1717 California st. *Tuesday* San Fernando
Poulson, Mrs Edna S. ; Hotel Pleasanton $\begin{cases} Monday \\ Snell's\ Seminary,\ Oakland \end{cases}$
Poultney, Mrs Jennie; 2111 Bush st.
Pounds, H. H.; Hotel Pleasanton
Powell, W. ; California and Sansome sts.
Powell, Mr and Mrs Thomas; 2213 Webster st. *Thursday* New Hope
Powers, Dr and Mrs G. H.; 1602 Taylor st. *Tuesday* San Rafael
Powers, Mrs Lucius; 1502½ California st.
Prather, John M.; 11 Kearny st.
Pratt, Judge and Mrs O. C. ; 731 Sutter st. *Thursday* $\begin{cases} Durham, \\ Butte\ Co. \end{cases}$
——O. C., Jr.
Pratt, Mr and Mrs. R. H. ; 929 Post st. *Monday* St. Helena
Pratt, William H. ; 708 Howard st.
Pray, Mrs A. B. ; 1222 Pine st.
Pray, Mr and Mrs Frank Pierce; 611 Chestnut st. *Friday* Santa Cruz
Prendergast, Rev J. J.; 628 California st.
Prentiss, Mr and Mrs S. R.; Hotel Pleasanton
Presby, F. L.; Hotel Pleasanton
Prescott, Mr and Mrs George W. ; Palace Hotel *Monday*
Presson, General and Mrs; 712 Sutter st., "The Renton"
Preston, Mr and Mrs Edgar F.; 1922 Sacramento st.
Preston, Otis J.; 1431 Mission st.
Preston, Ralph J.; 614 Sutter st.
Priber, C. E. ; 26 Webster st.
Price, Lieutenant and Mrs David; U. S. A.
Price, Prof Thomas San Mateo
——Miss Anna
——Miss Minnie
——Miss Lollie
——Miss Ida
——Arthur F.
Price, Dr and Mrs W. E. ; 527 Haight st.
Pritchard, Mr and Mrs Miguel G. ; 2523 Octavia st. $\begin{cases} Wednesday \\ Monterey \end{cases}$
Pritchard, Mr and Mrs M. G.; 2553 Octavia st. *Wednesday*
——Mrs Ygnacia Gamboa
——Miss Linda
Proll, Dr and Mrs R. B. ; 2710 California st. *Tuesday*
Provine, Judge and Mrs; The Renton *Monday*

Latest Stationery Of Every Description, Fine Paper, Envelopes and Writing Paper. *The Bancroft Company, 721 Market Street.*

W. B. CHAPMAN, 123 California Street   Fine Burgundies· from the
                   IMPORTER OF   Old Established House of
                                 Bouchard, Père & Fils, Beaune

Purdy, Mrs I. B.   Menlo Park
Putnam, Miss Caroline R.; 1223 Pine st.
——Miss E. W.
——Miss Minnie
Putnam, Mr and Mrs S. O.; 1012 Washington st.

Qualtrough, Lieut and Mrs Edward F.; U. S. N. *Wednesday* Mare Island
Quarré, Emile; 206 Powell st.   Bradley, Monterey Co., Cal.
Quay, Joseph M.; Pacific-Union Club
Quinan, Capt and Mrs W. R.   Pinole, Cal.
Quint, Mr and Mrs Leander; 1309 Mason st.   Alameda

Radovich, Bozo
Rafferty, Lieut W. C.   New York Harbor
Rail, Mrs E. B.; The Bella Vista
Raisch, Mr and Mrs Albert J.; Castro st. near 16th st.
Ralston, Mr and Mrs William C.   Auburn
Randall, George C.; Cosmos Club
Randell, Mrs H. V.; 105 Montgomery st.
Randol, J. B.; Pacific-Union Club   New Almaden
Rank, W. M.; 622 Haight st.
Rankin, Mr and Mrs Ira P.; 725 Geary st.
Rattenbury, Mrs W. H.; 1017 Pierce st.
Rapp, Mr and Mrs John; 903 Filmore st.
——Miss
Raum, Mr and Mrs George E.; The Pleasanton *Monday* San Rafael
Rawlings, Mr and Mrs Loyd; The Bella Vista *Thursday*
Ray, Lieut and Mrs C. M., U. S. N.   Washington, D. C.
Raymond, Mrs Wm. H.; 1030 Post st.   *Wednesday*
——Miss H.
Raymond, George A.; 1411 Hyde st.
Raymond, Mr and Mrs R.; 563 17th st.   *Wednesday*
——Miss Emma
Raymond, Mrs Samuel A.; 920 Polk st.   *Monday*
Read, Mr and Mrs W. D.   San Mateo
Reamer, Mr and Mrs George C. W.; 410 Buchanan st. { *Wednesday*
                                         { Auburn
——I. Lynne
Rearden, Judge and Mrs T. H.; 1910 Golden Gate ave.
Redington, Alfred; 2444 Jackson st.
Redington, Henry W.; 302 Calif. st., New California Hotel San Rafael
Redington, Mrs John H.; Bay and Larkin sts.
Redington, Mr and Mrs William P.; 1510 Pine st.
Redding, Mrs B. B. ; 2100 California st.
Redding, Mr and Mrs A. P.; 2489 Jackson st.   Del Monte

Redding, Mr and Mrs Joseph D.; 2129 California st.
——George H. H.

Reddy, Mr and Mrs P.; Lick House   *Monday*
Reed, Mr and Mrs Charles F.; 1200 Van Ness ave.   *Wednesday*
——Miss Florence
Reed, Mrs Henry   Chico
Reed, Rev. J. Saunders; Occidental Hotel
Reed, Miss Minnie   Brighton, Sacramento, Co.
--——Miss Mabel
Regan, Mr and Mrs C. R.; 1106 Powell st.   *Wednesday*
——Miss Kate
Regensburger, Dr and Mrs Jacob; 1432 Geary st.   *Wednesday*
——Miss
——Miss Alice
Regensburger, Mr and Mrs Martin; 1919 Webster st.   *Wednesday*
Reid, Mrs A. C.   Milwaukee, Wis.
Reid, R. I., U. S. N.; Cosmos Club
Reis, Mr and Mrs Christian; 835 California st.   *Tuesday*
——Christian, Jr.
——Ferdinand

Reis, Mr and Mrs John; 699 Polk st.
Reiss, Bernard; 1245 Franklin st.
Reis, Mr and Mrs Julius C.; 2201 Sacramento st.
—— Miss May

Rolfe, Miss K.; Hotel Pleasanton   *Monday*
Reynolds, Mr and Mrs Frank B.; 1227 Eddy st.
——Miss Mamie
Rhodes, Mrs Susan; Hotel Oriel   *Monday*
——Raleigh E.
——W. H. L.

Rice, Mrs Lydia C.; 1122 Pine st.   *Thursday*
Rice, Mr and Mrs George H.; Palace Hotel   *Monday*
——Miss
Richards, Mrs A. S.; 1514 California st.   *Tuesday*
——Miss Ada
Richards, W. H.; 1021 Market st.
Richards, Mr and Mrs Charles O.; 1906 Webster st.   San Rafael
Richards, Mr and Mrs D.; 1310 Valencia st.
Richardson, Mr and Mrs M.; 1030 Pine st.
Richardson, Mr and Mrs W. G.; 2036 Scott st.
Richter, Dr and Mrs C. Max; 614 Geary st.   Santa Barbara
Rickey, Mr and Mrs T. B.; 37 Liberty st.
——Miss Carrie
——Miss Nellie

Ricord, Miss M. E.; 1421 Clay st.

Rideout, Mr and Mrs Norman D.; cor. Wash. and Gough sts.} *Monday* Marysville

————Miss Grace

Ridgeway, Lieut and Mrs Thomas; Presidio

Riordan, Most Rev Archbishop P. W.; 1122 Eddy st.

Rising, Judge Richard; Palace Hotel   **Virginia City, Nev.**

————B.

————Miss Nettie

Rix, Alfred, 743 Pine st.

Rix, Mr and Mrs Edward A.; 1910 Vallejo st.

Rix, Judge Hale; 30 Potter st.

Rixford, Emmet H.; 2815 Pine st.

Rixford, Mr and Mrs Gulian P.; 1713 Pierce st.   *Wednesday*

————Miss Geneve

Robbins, Henry R., Jr.; 114 Devisadero st.

Roberts, Dr H. S.; 202 Stockton st.

Roberts, Mr and Mrs G. F.; 2513 Clay st.   **Highland Park, Oakland**

Roberts, Mr and Mrs Steven; 2118 Pacific ave.

Robertson, Mrs E. R.; 614 Sutter st.

Robertson, Mr and Mrs George M.; 2217 Octavia st.

———— –Mr and Mrs Victor J.

Robertson, Dr and Mrs John W.; NE. cor. Stockton and Chestnut sts.

Robinson, Miss Margie C.; 1510 Jones st.

Robinson, Mr and Mrs C. H.; 1117 Twenty-first st,   } *Thursday* San Mateo

Robinson, Capt Frank W.; Presidio Reservation

Robinson, Mr and Mrs J. A; New Cal. Hotel   **Redwood Farm, R. C.**

————Miss Elina

Robinson, Miss Jessie; 1618 Folsom st.

Robinson, Miss Jessie Whipple; 1012 Pine st.   **Oakville, Napa Co.**

Robinson, Lester L.; 500 Van Ness ave.   **Los Medanos**

————Mrs S. E.

Robinson, Mr and Mrs Sanford; Grand Hotel   *Monday*   **Guatemala**

Robinson, Sanford; 593 Ellis st.   **Simmons, Tehama Co.**

Roe, Mr and Mrs Geo H.; 2618 Pacific ave. *Friday* **Napa Soda Springs**

Roe, Mrs P.; Hotel Pleasanton

————Miss

Roeding, F.; 1810 Washington st.

Rodgers, The Misses; 1010 Folsom st.   **Napa**

Rodgers, Mrs Isabella D.; 1036 Valencia st.   *Friday*   **Pacific Grove**

Rodgers, Arthur; Occidental-Hotel

Rodgers, Allen G.; Cosmos Club

Rogers, Mr and Mrs E. B.; Hotel Pleasanton

Rogers, B.; The Berkshire

Rogers, Mr and Mrs C. A.; 105 Stockton st.

Rogers, Mrs John J.; Presidio
Rogers, Miss Florence; (abroad)   **Marysville**
Rojas, Mr and Mrs José   *Monday*   San Jose, Costa Rica, C. A.
Roma, J. Mariano; 1212 Sutter st.
Romaine, Nicholas T.; 1701 Buchanan st.
Roman, Mr and Mrs Anton; 1020½ Pine st.
————Miss Nettie
Rooney, Thomas H.; 912 Guerrero st.
Roos, Mr and Mrs A.; Palace Hotel   *Monday*
Roos, Mr and Mrs Adolphe; 1362 Post st.   *2d and 3d Wednesdays*
Root, Henry; The Renton, 712 Sutter st.
Root, Miss Nellie; 907 Steiner st.
Rose, Mr and Mrs A. W. Jr.; 2000 Broadway st.   **San Mateo**
Rose, Herbert E.; The San Francisco *Chronicle*   **Del Monte**
Rosener, Mr and Mrs Samuel; 1131 Laguna st.
Rosenfeld, Mr and Mrs John; Lick House   *Monday*
Rosenstirn, Dr and Mrs Julius; 932 Sutter st.
Rosenstock, Mr and Mrs S. W.; Palace Hotel   *Monday*
Rosenthal, Adolph, Consul German Empire; 318 Sacramento st. **Alameda**
Rosenthal, I. L.; 304 Stockton st.
————M.
Rosewald, Mr J. H.; 922 Geary st.   {*1st and 3d Wednesday Afternoons* / *and 1st Wednesday Evening*}
————Mme Julie
Ross, Miss; 1200 Van Ness ave.   *Tuesday*
Ross, Mr and Mrs George; 929 O'Farrell st.
Ross, Mr and Mrs Thomas; 1035 Valencia st.
Rothchild, Mr and Mrs J. M.; 1700 Broadway st.   *1st and 3d Fridays*
Rothe, Mr and Mrs E.; 1324 Geary st.
————Miss
Rothschild, Joseph; 218 Stockton st.
Rothschild, Mrs Abe; 309 Powell st.   *Last Wednesday*   **Menlo Park**
Rothwell, R. Percy; 324 Geary st.
Rountree, James O.; 1814 Geary st.   *Friday*
————Miss Laura
————Miss Louise
————James, Jr.
Rountree, Mr and Mrs Newton; 729 Sutter st.
Rountree, Mr and Mrs Walter E.; 1729 Broadway st.
Rowan, Mr and Mrs Thomas; Palace Hotel   **Los Angeles**
————Thomas, Jr.
Rowand, Doctor and Mrs; Hotel Pleasanton   *Monday*
Rowell, Rev Joseph; 1416 Sacramento st.
Rowland, B. Ellis; 512 Jones st.
Rowley, Mr and Mrs B. N.; 14 Pierce st.   *Thursday*   **Napa Valley**

Roy, Mrs Robert; 1016 Vallejo st.
Ruddock, John C.; 2514 Pine st.
Ruger, Miss; Presidio   *Friday*
Ruggles, Mr and Mrs James D.; 2210 Jackson st.
——James D., Jr.
Rulofson, Mr Chas. H.; 1918 Sacramento st.   *Wednesday*   Santa Cruz
——Miss Carrie C.
Runyon, Mr and Mrs Frank W.; 1037 Post st.
Runyon, Mr and Mrs Edward W.; 1424 Ellis st.   *Friday*
Rush, Dr and Mrs G. W.; U. S. N.   Mare Island
Russ, Mr and Mrs Henry B.; 6 Columbia sq.   *Tuesday*
——Miss Florence
Russell, Mr and Mrs Alexander; 2010 Bush st.
Russell, Miss Susie; 1703 Broderick st., and   Sacramento
Rutherford, Mr and Mrs A. H.; 1105 Bush st.   *Thursday*   Del Monte
Rutherford, T. L.; Pacific Club; 419 Sutter st.   Rutherford, Napa Co.
Rutledge, Miss; 113 Scott st. .   *Wednesday*
Ryan, Mr and Mrs E. B.; 20 Stanley Place   *Wednesday*   Menlo Park
——Miss
——Miss Ruth S.
——Shirly B.
Ryan, John; New City Hall
Ryan, James H.; 916 Jackson st.
Ryer, Mr and Mrs John B.; 2513 Folsom st.   *Thursday*
Ryer, Mrs Mary; Hotel Pleasanton
——Mr and Mrs Fletcher F.
Ryland, Mrs J.; 512 Eddy st.

Sabin, Judge George M.   Carson City, Nev.
Sabin, Mr and Mrs John I.; 1800 Pierce st.
Sachs, Samuel L.; 601 Leavenworth st.
Sadler, Mr and Mrs Herrman J.; 906 Van Ness ave. *Thursday* Larkspur
Salazar, Mr and Mrs J. A.   Mission San Jose
Salisbury, Mr and Mrs Monroe; 2304 California st.
   3d Thursday
Samuel, Mr & Mrs M.; cor Geary & Van Ness ave. } Mt. Diablo Vineyard, Clayton
——Miss Helen
——Miss Lelia Joyce
——Mr B. C.
——William
——Lawrence
——Sanford
Sampson, Mr and Mrs John A.; 1412 California st.
Sanborn, Mr and Mrs F. G.; 1020 Dolores st.
Sanchez, Mr and Mrs R. B.; 31 Stanley Place

Sanders, Mr George H.; 923 Pine st.
——Miss
Sanderson, Mrs George R.; 2517 Broadway *Tuesday*
Sanderson, Lemuel A.; 1617 Larkin st.
——Miss

Sanderson, Mrs S. W. **Europe**
-——Miss Jennie
-——Miss Sibyl

Sanger, Capt Joseph P. **Port Townsend, Wash.**
Santeller, Mrs L. A.; Steiner and O'Farrell sts.
Santon, Mr and Mrs C. F. von; Grand Hotel *Wednesday*
Sargent, Mrs A. A.; 1630 Folsom st.
——The Misses
Sargent, Mr and Miss E. L.; 1819 Mason st. *Tuesday*
Saunders, E. **St. Helena**
Savage, Col and Mrs Richard H.; 927 Sutter st. *Thursday*
Sawtelle, H. W., M. D.; U. S. Marine Hospital
Sawyer, Dr and Mrs A. F.; Palace Hotel *Monday*
Sawyer, Mr and Mrs L. S. B.; 617 Hyde st. *Wednesday*
Sawyer, Judge Lorenzo; 734 Sutter st. **Cazadero**
Saxe, Col and Mrs P.; Lick House *Monday*
Schact, Mrs Henry; 745 Golden Gate ave.
Schafer, Mr and Mrs Frederick W.; 2023 Pine st.
Schenck, Mr and Mrs W. T. Y.; 1427 Post st.
Schilling, Mr and Mrs August; 2322 Clay st.
——Miss
——Arthur

Schmidt, Mr and Mrs Henry; 1023 Sutter st. *Thursday*
Schmidt, Mr and Mrs Val.; 2216 Van Ness ave. *1st Thursday in month*
——Miss Lizzie
Schmitt, Mr and Mrs Maurice; 1501 Gough st.
Schmiedell, Mr and Mrs Henry; 739 Post st. *Friday* **San Rafael**
-——Edward
Schoemann, O.; 1229 Ellis st.
Schram, Jacob / **Schramsburg, Napa Co.**
Schroeder, Mr and Mrs J. B. **Redwood City**
Schroeder, H., Jr.; NW cor. Fell and Gough sts.
Schulte, J. G. W.; 710 Haight st.
Schussler, Mr and Mrs Herman F. A.; 522 Ellis st.
Schussler, Mr and Mrs Henry; 541 McAllister st.
Schuyler, Thomas J.; 905 Sutter st.
Scott, Mr and Mrs A. W.; 305 Buchanan st. *2d and 4th Wednesdays*
——Albert W., Jr.
Scott, Mrs C. C. G.; 1840 California st. *Tuesday*

Scott, Mrs and Mrs Henry T.; SW cor. Clay and Laguna sts.
——Miss Josephine
Scott, Mr and Mrs Irving M.; 507 Harrison st.
——Miss Alice
Scott, Mr and Mrs E. B.   *Friday*   **Fair Hills Terrace, San Rafael**
Scott, J. A.; Cosmos Club; 2506 Washington st.
Scott, Mr and Mrs J. Harry; 526 Hayes st.   *Friday*
Scott, Dr and Mrs Winfield   **Fort Huachuca, Ariz. Ter.**
Scrivener, Mr Arthur; Pacific-Union Club
Scruggs, Miss Sarah L.; 1036 Valencia st.
Searby, Prof and Mrs Wm. M.; 859 Market st.   } *Thursday* {Occidental, Son. Co.
——Miss Mary
Searle, Mr and Mrs George; 1902 Baker st.
Searles, Mr and Mrs Edw. F.; SE cor. California and Mason sts. **New York**
Searles, Mr and Mrs Robt.; 206 Haight st.   *Monday*
Searls, Judge Niles; The Beresford
Seaton, Mr and Mrs Daniel; 614 Capp st.
——Miss Dollie
Seaver, Mr and Mrs W. A.; Lick House   *Monday*
Sedgwick, Mr John; 1000 Van Ness ave.
—— Miss Brownie
Selby, Mrs Thomas; 2119 Buchanan st.
——Miss Annie
Selfridge, Mr and Mrs E. A.; 2615 California st.
Seligman, Mr and Mrs Albert L.; Clay and Franklin sts.
Severance, H. W.; U. S. Consul   **Honolulu, H. I.**
——Miss May
Severance, J. Seymour; Grand Hotel   **Menlo Park**
Sewall, Oscar T.; 2610 Jackson st.
Sewell, Mr and Mrs Daniel; 1105 Shotwell st.   *Monday*   **Yosemite Val.**
——Miss L. Eldora
——Dell
——Dottie
Schaeffer, Mrs J. W.; 1512 Leavenworth st.
Shafter, Judge James McM.; 951 Chestnut st.   **Olema, Marin Co.**
Shafter, Colonel and Mrs W. R.; U. S. A.   **Angel Island**
Shainwald, Mr and Mrs N.; 2222 Clay st.   *Tuesday*
——Miss Martha
——Mr Herman
——Mr Julius C.
Sham, Mr and Mrs W. E.; Palace Hotel   **Virginia City**
Shannon, Michael; 2310 Jackson st.
Sharon, Mr and Mrs A. D.; Palace Hotel   *Monday*

81

Sharon, Mr and Mrs W. E.; Palace Hotel   *Monday*   Virginia City
Sharpstein, Judge John R.; 1007 Sutter st.
——William
Shattuck, Mr and Mrs C. H.; 520 Commercial st.
Shattuck, Mr and Mrs D. D.; 814 Powell st.   *Thursday*
——Miss Alice
Shaw, Mr and Mrs Charles N.; cor. Taylor and Calif. sts.   Del Monte
Shaw, Miss Annette N.; 2219 Scott st. *2d and 4th Fridays* Santa Cruz
Shaw, Dr and Mrs H. B.; 1416 Clay st.
Shaw, Miss May; 741 Golden Gate ave.   *Wednesday*
Shaw, Mr and Mrs Stephen W.; 334 Ellis st.
Shaw, Hon and Mrs William J.; 2219 Pacific ave.
Shawhan, Mr and Mrs; 712 Sutter st., The Renton
Shay, Mr and Mrs Frank; 2522 California st.   Alameda
Shea, Mr and Mrs James; 1325 Golden Gate ave.
——The Misses
Sheehan, Mr and Mrs John F.; { 407 Montgomery st. / 303 Devisadero st. } Redwood City
Sheehy, Mrs Robt.; 803 Van Ness ave.   *Thursday*
———Miss
Sheffield, Charles; 1517 Sacramento st.
Sheldon, Mr and Mrs Mark; 1001 Golden Gate ave.
Sheldon, Edward H.; 2413 Pierce st.
Shepard, Mr and Morgan; 1615 Clay st.
Shepard, Mrs Alice; 608 Nineteenth st.
Shepard, Miss Evelyn; Care Chas. P. Eells,2524 Washington st. Oakland
Shepard, Miss Maude; 300 Haight st.
Sherman, Mr and Mrs O. D.; 108 Turk st.
——Miss Lizzie
Sherwood, Mr and Mrs Eugene; 1357 Post st.   *Thursday* Salinas City
——Miss Jessie
——Miss Rosemary
—— Miss Isabel
——Miss Winnie
——Lionel Claude
Sherwood, Mr and Mrs Henry H.; 2121 California st. { *Friday* / San Rafael }
Sherwood, Mr and Mrs Robert; 1123 Cal. st. *Tuesday* Hotel Vendome
——William R.
——Mr and Mrs Robert L.; 1014 Pine st.
Shields, William; Occidental Hotel   East
Shipley, John H.; U. S. N., Cosmos Club
Shipman, Miss Elizabeth H.; 1012 Washington st.
Shirley, Paul   Martinez
——Guy

Shorb, Mr and Mrs J. de Barth; Occ. Hotel	*Monday* San Gabriel, L. A. Co.	
——Miss Inez		
Short, Capt and Mrs John; 1404 Jackson st.		
——Dr Edward		
Shotwell, Mr and Mrs J. M.		Sausalito
——Miss Grace		
——Miss Minnie		
Shreve, Mr and Mrs George C.; 1117 Pine st.		
——Miss Bessie		
——George R.		Napa Soda Springs
Shuhy, Mrs R.; 803 Van Ness ave.	*Thursday*	Napa
——The Misses		
Siebe, Mr and Mrs Frederick C.; 838 Fulton st.		
——Frederick C., Jr.		
-——George H.		
Siebe, Mr and Mrs John D.; 2322 California st.		
——Miss		
Simons, Mrs P. B.; 312 Haight st.	*Monday*	
——Miss Blanche		
——Mr G. Stuart		Alameda
Simpson, Mrs T. B.; 1135 Ellis st.	*Thursday*	Oakland
——Miss Mariana		
-——Robert N.		

Simpson, Mrs J.; 2418 Webster st.
Simpson, Dr James; 234 Post st.
Simpson, Consul and Mrs John; 1504 Pacific ave. *Thursday* Del Monte
Sims, Samuel J.; 1226 Treat ave.
Sims, Mr and Mrs J. F.; 2404 Mission st.
Sims, Mr and Mrs John R.; The Berkshire   *Monday*
Sinclair, Mr and Mrs; 633 Golden Gate ave.
——Norman
Sinton, Colonel and Mrs R. H.; The Bella Vista   *Thursday*
——Miss Lizzie
Sjöholm, Mrs Maria; 934 Bush st.
Skelton, E. W.; 335 Eddy st.
Skenner, Mrs Grace; The Berkshire   *Monday*
——John
——Harry
Slack, Mrs Charles W.; 825 Ellis st.
Sleight, Cornelius   Los Angeles
Slevin, Mr and Mrs Thomas E.; 2413 Sacramento st.
Sloan, J. Ralph; 1144 Green st.
Sloss, Mr and Mrs Leon; 1717 Jackson st.

Sloss, Mr and Mrs Louis ; 1500 Van Ness ave.
——Louis, Jr.
——Joseph
Slosson, Mr and Mrs Edward P. ; 2330 Fillmore st.
Small, A. H. ; 1312 Taylor st., or 316 California st.
Smart, Mr and Mrs George C. ; Hotel Pleasanton   *Monday*
Smedberg, Colonel and Mrs W. R. ; 1611 Larkin st.   *Tuesday*
——Miss Helen
Smiley, Samuel ; 1701 Gough st.
——Miss Nellie
Smith, Mr and Mrs Bayard ; Occidental Hotel
Smith, Mrs Bessie G. ; 1810 Gough st.
Smith, Arthur H. ; 716 Ellis st.
Smith, Mrs M. H. ; 1827 Pacific ave.
——Miss Lizzie Blacker
Smith, Mrs A. H. ; 831 Ellis st.   *Thursday*
Smith, Miss C. A. ; Hotel Pleasanton   *Monday*
Smith, George H.
Smith, Mrs C. B. ; The Berkshire   *Monday*
——Miss Clara
——Miss Minnie
Smith, Mr and Mrs C. W. M.; 1719 Clay st.
Smith, Mr and Mrs G. T. ; 712 Sutter st. (The Renton)
Smith, Mr and Mrs G. Frank; Hotel Pleasanton
——The Misses
Smith, Rev James K.; 801 Leavenworth st.
Smith, Charles W.; 1418 Geary st.
Smith, Colin McRae; Bohemian Club
Smith, Mr and Mrs A. H. H. ; 716 Ellis st.   *Thursday*
Smith, Miss Ella; 500 Van Ness ave.   *Friday*   **Sacramento**
Smith, Miss Cora; 2610 Jackson st.
Smith, Mr and Mrs F. M. ; Palace Hotel   *Monday*
Smith, Mr and Mrs George F. ; 1717 Clay st.   *Tuesday*
Smith, Capt and Mrs G. F. ; The Berkshire   *Monday*
——Walter
Smith, Mrs George Law.; 2226 Jackson st.   *Friday*
——Miss Maude A.
Smith, Hiram C.; 2115 Broadway st.   **Stockton**
Smith, Rev J. C.; The Berkshire
Smith, Mr and Mrs J. Henley; Occidental Hotel   *Monday*
Smith, Rev and Mrs J. K.; The Berkshire   *Monday*
——Miss Edith
Smith, Mr and Mrs Julius P. ; 2505 Washington st.   *Friday* **Livermore**
Smith, Capt and Mrs Nicholas T. ; 2129 California st.   *Friday*

84

Smith, Percy W.; 2212 Van Ness ave.

Smith, Mr and Mrs S. Harrison; Occidental Hotel

Smith, Mr and Mrs Sidney M.; 1910 Gough st. *Wednesday* **San Rafael**

———Miss Ethel S.

———Miss Helen J.

Smith, Mr and Mrs Theo. E.; 1619 Washington st. *Friday*

———Miss

———Miss J. M.

Smith, Mr and Mrs Tremaine **Sausalito**

Smith, Mr and Mrs William H.; 2201 Buchanan st. *1st and 2d Fridays*

———Miss Belle

Smith, Mr and Mrs William F.; 2515 Broadway st.

———Snead, Miss Minnie **Dixon, Cal.**

Snook, Mr and Mrs James Athearn; 2001 Eddy st. *Thursday*

Snowgrass, Miss Lily M.; 1526 Eddy st. *Wednesday*

Snowgrass, Mrs S. Louise; 2001 Eddy st. *Thursday*

Snyder, Mrs Julia Melville; 138 McAllister st.

Sobey, A. L.; 810 Twentieth st.

Somers, Dr George B.; 1034 Mission st. *Thursday* **Del Monte**

———Mrs W. J.

———Mr and Mrs James C.; 1034 Mission st.

Somers, Mr and Mrs H. C.; 2906 Folsom st. *Thursday*

———Miss Ida O.

———Frank A.

Somerville, William S.; 919 Post st.

Sonnenberg, Mrs J.; 1305 Octavia st. *1st and 2d Tuesdays*

———Miss Sara

Sonntag, Mr and Mrs Henry P.; Hotel Pleasanton

Sonntag, Mr and Mrs Charles; Hotel Pleasanton *Monday* **Del Monte**

Sonntag, Julian; 2201 Sacramento st.

———Lincoln; 2332 Mission st.

Spalding, Rev and Mrs Edward B.; 1534 Mission st.

Spalding, Mrs Volney; The Bella Vista

Sparhawk, Miss S.; Hotel Pleasanton *Monday*

Spaulding, Mr and Mrs George; 1109 Clay st. *Thursday*

———Mr and Mrs James G.

Spaulding, Fred D.; 1717 Clay st. *Tuesday*

Spaulding, N. W.; 17 Fremont st.

Spaulding, Jerome; 713 O'Farrell st.

Spaulding, John; 1715 Clay st.

Spaulding, Mrs S. M. **San Anselmo**

Spear, Capt and Mrs A. F.; 2908 Folsom st. *Thursday*

———Lewis

Spencer, Mrs T. F.; 1211 Mission st. *Tuesday*

Spencer, Mr and Mrs George W.; 2436 Jackson st.   *Friday*
Spencer, Dr and Mrs John C.; 813 Sutter st.   *Thursday*
——Mrs Mattie S.
Spencer, J. D.; Supreme Court Building, Post st.
Spence, Mr and Mrs Clark; Hotel Oriel   *Monday*
Sperry, Mr and Mrs George B.; 22 California st.   **Stockton**
Sperry, Mrs A. W.; Occidental Hotel   *Monday*   **Stockton**
——Miss Beth
Sperry, Miss Evelyn; 1036 Valencia st.
Speyer, Mrs Morris; 2412 Washington st.
——Miss Olga
Spiers, Mr and Mrs Jas.; NW cor. Laguna and Wash. sts. { *Friday* **Haywards**
——James, Jr.
Sprague, Major C. J.; Phelan Building
Sprague, Richard H.; 623 Mason st.
Spreckels, Mr and Mrs C. August   **Philadelphia, Pa.**
Spreckels, Mr and Mrs Claus; 2027 Howard st.
——Mr Adolph B.
Spreckels, Mr and Mrs John D.; 2504 Howard st.   **Del Coronado**
Spring, Mr and Mrs Edward S.; 802 Van Ness ave.
Spring, Miss Emma; 30 Hawthorne st.
——Miss Hattie
Sproule, James; 2336 Pacific ave.
Spruance, Mr and Mrs John; 1329 Sutter st.   *Monday*
Staab, Mr and Mrs H. G.; 614 Sutter st. (The Westminster)   *Thursday*
Staacke, Mr and Mrs George; 818 Bush st.
Stadtmuller, F. D.; 819 Eddy st.
Stadtfeld, Mr and Mrs J., Jr.; 1210 Jackson st.
Stadtfeld, Mr and Mrs William C.; 934 Broadway st.
Stafford, Mr and Mrs William G.; 1206 O'Farrell st.
Stahl, Mr and Mrs A. W.; U. S. Navy
Stanford, Mr and Mrs J. B.; 1711 Broderick st.   *Tuesday*
Stanford, Mr and Mrs Leland; Cal. & Powell sts. { *Tuesday* **Menlo Park** **Washington, D C.**
Stanley, Mrs E.; Palace Hotel
Stanley, Samuel L.; 1218 Hyde st.
——Samuel B.
——Mrs Fannie S.
Stanyan, Mrs.; Hotel Pleasanton
——Miss
——Charles
Staples, James W.; 217 Sansome st.
Staples, Mr and Mrs D. J.; 711 Taylor st   *Thursday*   **San Joaquin Co.**
——John C.

Starbird, Mr and Mrs A. W.; 1055 Golden Gate ave.
——Miss Sadie
Starr, Mr and Mrs A. M.; The Renton   *Monday*
Starr, Mr and Mrs William C.; 1115 Van Ness ave.
Stealey, Mr and Mrs Thomas; 1412 Folsom st.
——Miss Ida
——Thomas
Stearns, Mr and Mrs William H.; 1110 Jackson st.
——Miss Nellie

Stebbins, Rev Horatio; 1609 Larkin st.
Steel, William; 424 California st.
Steele, Mr and Mrs James G.; 899 Pine st. (Olive House)   *Thursday*
Steen, Mr and Mrs E. T.; 1812 Market st. (Van Ness House)   *Thursday*
Steil, Mr. Henry; 1030 Bush st.
——Miss Lillian
——Miss S.
Stern, Sigismund; 621 Leavenworth st.
——Lewis
——Jacob
——Abraham

Steinhart, Mr and Mrs Ignatz; 916 Sutter st.
Stetson, Mr and Mrs James B.; 1801 Van Ness ave.   *Friday*
——Albert L.
——Harry N.

Steuart, Mr and Mrs James; Geary st.
Stevens, Lieut G. W. S.; Presidio
Stevens, Mrs N. J.; The Pleasanton
Stevenson, A ; The Berkshire
Stewart, Miss; 1222 Pine st.
Stewart, Lieut-Col Charles S.; 533 Kearny st.
Stewart, Mrs A. B.   San Jose
Stewart, Dr and Mrs George T.   Los Angeles
Stewart, Mr and Mrs James; 2617 Bush st.
Stewart, Senator & Mrs Wm. M.; Hotel Pleasanton   Washington, D. C.
——Miss Maybelle

Stillman, Mr and Mrs Alfred; 2525 Broadway st.
Stillwell, Mr and Mrs George W.; 534 Turk st.
Stillwell, Mr and Mrs Henry C.; Hotel Pleasanton   *Monday*
Stinson, Miss Arlie; 816 Chestnut st.   *Thursday*
Stinson, W. H.; 806 Filbert st.
——Henry
Stock, Ernest C.; 617 Jones st.
Stokes, James Brett; Bohemian Club   Del Monte

87

Stone, Rev and Mrs A. L.; 2534 Washington st.   *Friday*
——Miss
Stone, Dr E. E.; 712 Sutter st., The Renton
Stone, Mr and Mrs F. P.; 1030 Dolores st.
Stone, J. C.; The Bella Vista
Stone, Miss Kittie; 1882 Washington st.
Stone, Mr and Mrs L. D.; 2520 Howard st.   *Thursday*   **Hotel** Vendome
——Miss Hattie
Stone, N. B.; 109 Montgomery st.
Stone, Mr and Mrs Charles B.; 130 Haight st.
Stone, Mr and Mrs N. J.; 1010 Dolores st.
Stone, Mr and Mrs Walter S.; 2318 Steiner st.
Stoney, Lieut and Mrs George M., U. S. N.; 2500 Pacific ave.
——Miss Kate M.
——Gateland
Stoney, Judge and Mrs Thomas P.; 31 Fair Oaks st   *Friday*
Story, Mr and Mrs Charles R.; 30 McAllister st.
——Miss
Stow, Mr and Mrs Vanderlyn; 1820 Pine st.
Stow, Mr and Mrs W. W.; 1013 Pine st.
——Miss Nellie
Strauss, Mr Levi; 621 Leavenworth st.
Strauss, Mr and Mrs M.; 1603 Steiner st.
Streeten, James M.; 330 Pine st.
Strickland, Lieut and Mrs Geo. D., U. S. N.   { *Wednesday* { **Los Angeles**
Stringer, C. P.; Hotel Pleasanton
Strong, Dr and Mrs C. G.; Hotel Pleasanton   *Monday*
Strother, Lieutenant L. H., U. S. A.   **Angel Island**
Strozynski, Stanislas; 19 Powell st.
Struve, H. G.   **Seattle, Wash.**
Stuart, Mr and Mrs A. C.; 1902 Broadway st.
Stuart, Charles A.; 1601 Hyde st.
Stuart, William A.; 1704 Larkin st.
——James F.
Stump, Miss Alice; 1434 Golden Gate ave.
Sturdivant, Mr and Robert O.; 318 Page st.   *Friday*
——Miss Belle
——Joseph H.
Sturtevant, Mr and Mrs Henry; 502 Powell st.   *Monday*
——Cullen K.
——Miss Faith
Sullivan, Hon and Mrs Frank J.; 525 Oak st.   **Santa Cruz**
——Miss Ada
——Miss M.

88

Sullivan, Judge J. F. ; 2721 Folsom st.
Sullivan, Dr and Mrs Maurice J.; 820 Scott st. *Thursday*
Sullivan, Mr and Mrs J. F. ; 1617 Jackson st. *Tuesday*
Sullivan, Mrs Thomas; Occidental Hotel *Monday*
——Miss M.
Sullivan, Dr and Mrs J. F.; 1105 Van Ness ave. { *Thursday* {Sunnywood, Santa Clara
——Miss Angela
Sumner, Mr and Mrs F. W.; 1810 Van Ness ave.
Sumner, W. B. ; 415 Front st.
Sumner, Miss Mary P. ; 1036 Valencia st. *Wednesday*
Sunderland, Mrs Thomas ; Palace Hotel *Monday*
——Miss
Sutherland, Mrs E. F. ; Lick House *Monday*
——Miss C.
Sutro, Adolph; Sutro Heights
Sutton, Mr and Mrs J. B.; 712 Golden Gate ave.
Swain, Miss Clara; 1714 Turk st.
Spitz, Mr and Mrs; 820 O'Farrell st.
——Miss Hannah
Sutro, Mrs Adolph; NW cor. Hayes and Fillmore sts. *Tuesday*
——Miss Clara
——Charles W.
——Edgar
Swain, Mr and Mrs R. A.; 729 Sutter st. **Mountain View**
——Miss Amy
Swain, Frank R; 1034 Pine st.
——Harry L.
——Russell
Swain, Mr and Mrs Edward R.; Baldwin Hotel *Tuesday*
Swain, Mr R. R.; 1714 O'Farrell st.
——Mr and Mrs Frank A.
Swasey, F. B. ; 26 Montgomery st.
Sweeney, Miles D.; Market and Montgomery sts.
Swett, John ; 1419 Taylor st. **Martinez**
Swift, Mr and Mrs Charles J. ; 2211 Washington st.
Swift, Hon and Mrs John F., U. S. Minister **Tokio, Japan**
Swinerton, Mr and Mrs W. A.; 1910 Baker st.
Symmes, Mr and Mrs Frank J.; 630 Harrison st. *Thursday*
——Miss Anita D.
Syz, Mr and Mrs Harry W. ; 2014 Webster st.

Taber, Mr and Mrs F. A. ; 113 Scott st. *Wednesday*
Taber, Mr and Mrs I. W.; 1351 Madison st. *Tuesday* **Oakland**
——Miss Daisy
Taggart, Miss; Palace Hotel *Monday*

Taggart, Mr and Mrs Clayton; 2417 Filmore st.
Talbot, Mr and Mrs C. F. A.; 1819 California st.
Talbot, Fred C.; 2311 Scott st.
Talbot, Mr and Mrs William H.; 2840 Buchanan st.
Talbot, William; 930 Haight st.
Talbot, Mrs W. C.; 1730 Jackson st.
Tallant, Mrs D. J.; 1001 Bush st.   *Thursday*
Tallant, Mr and Mrs Frederick W.; 1120 Hyde st., nr. Cal.
Tallant, Mr and Mrs John D.; Occidental Hotel
Tamm, Charles L.; 329 Bartlett st.   "Belgian Consulate," **Soledad**
——Mrs A. J.
Tams, Mr and Mrs Sampson; 1915 Van Ness ave. *Wednesday* **Monterey**
Tanner, Capt and Mrs Z. L.; Hotel Pleasanton   *Monday*
Tarnes, Mr and Mrs Juan; Palace Hotel   *Monday*
Tarrant, Dr and Mrs Wm. H.; Haight and Pierce sts.   *Thursday*
——Miss Rowena M.
Tatum, Mr and Mrs Henry L.; 2525 Pacific ave.   *Friday*
Tay, Mrs George H.; 1005 Leavenworth st.   **Napa Soda Springs**
——Miss Irene
——Miss Hattie
Taylor, Col and Mrs C. L.; 709 Bush st.
Taylor, Mrs Irene; 436 Oak st. *Wednesday*   **Napa Redwoods**
Taylor, Edward S.; 1023 Hyde st.
Taylor, Mr and Mrs W. Hinckley; 1253 Castro st.   **Oakland**
Taylor, Mr and Mrs Thomas G.; 1911 Pine st.   *Wednesday*
——Miss Minnie
Taylor, C. E.; 312 Pine st.
Taylor, Dr W. E.; Baldwin Hotel   *Monday*
——Miss Grace
Taylor, Capt and Mrs William H.; 2128 California st.   *Tuesday*
——Miss Edith
——Miss Carrie
——Augustus
——W. H., Jr.
Techau, Mrs R. J.; 1515 Scott st.
Teller, Mr and Mrs Philip S.   **Alameda**
——Miss Adelaide
——Fred
——Mr and Mrs J. D. P.
Temple, Jackson; Supreme Court Building, Post st.
Ten Bosch, Mr and Mrs J. M.; 1452 Franklin st.   *Thursday*
Ten Broeck, Mrs; Hotel Pleasanton
Tennant, Miss Emelie   **San Jose**
——Miss Mary

Terrill, Dr George M.; 400 Stockton st., Cosmos Club
Terry, Mr and Mrs H. M.; 141 Locust st.   Santa Cruz
———— Miss Alice
Tevis, Mr and Mrs William S.; 2548 Jackson st.   *Friday*
Tevis, Mr and Mrs Lloyd; 1316 Taylor st.   *Tuesday*   Del Monte
Tevis, Dr Harry.L.; care of W. F. & Co., 1316 Taylor st.   New York
———— Mr and Mrs Hugh
Tevis, Carter; care of Wells, Fargo & Co's Bank, Palace Hotel
Tevis, Dr Samuel G.; Pacific Mail S. S. Co.
Tewksbury, Mrs Emily; 6 Montague st.
Tharpe, Mr and Mrs E. H.; Grand Hotel   *Monday*
Thayer, Mr and Mrs Edward N.; 1519 Webster st.
———— Miss Rose
Thayer, Dr and Mrs Orson V.; 2514 Washington st. } *Tuesday* Jamul, S. Diego
Thellar, Edward A.; 1917 Pacific ave.
Thellar, Samuel L.; 2026 Pacific ave.
———— Samuel
Theobald, Mrs; 801 Leavenworth st.
Theobald, Mrs George J.; 3028 California st.
———— J. J.
Theobald, George Jr.; 1239 Pine st.
Thibault, Mrs Emma; 1317 Hyde st
———— Miss Sallie
Thomas, Miss L.; Hotel Pleasanton   *Monday*
Thomas, Leon B.; 727 O'Farrell st.
———— Miss
Thomas, Mr and Mrs J. H.; 31 Hawthorne st.   *Friday*
Thomas, Mr and Mrs P. J.; 1307 Vallejo st.   *2d and 4th Fridays*
———— The Misses
Thomas, Mr and Mrs E. D.   Berkeley
Thomas, Mr and Mrs R. P.; Palace Hotel   *Monday*   Berkeley
Thomas, Mr and Mrs S.; 104 Devisadero st.
Thomason, Edwin R.; 2514 Folsom st.
———— Edwin R., Jr.
Tompkins, Mrs Edward; Palace Hotel   *Monday*   San Leandro
———— Miss
———— Miss S. H.
———— Miss Juliet
———— Gilbert
Thompkins, Mr and Mrs M. M.; 1920 Jackson st. San Anselmo, San Rafael
———— Miss Susie
———— Miss Julia
———— M. M., Jr.
Thompson, Mrs Charles I.; Palace Hotel

Thompson, G. R.; 806 Ellis st.
——Miss Meta
Thompson, Mrs; Fillmore near Clay st.
Thompson, Bradford F.; Second and Brannan sts.
Thompson, General and Mrs R. R.; 1501 Van Ness ave. *Thursday*
Thompson, Miss Fannie Marysville
Thompson, Robert A.; 605 Polk st.
—— Miss Mary Nixon
——Miss Virginia

Thompson, Miss Roberta A.; 2213 Fillmore st.
Thore, C. P.; Palace Hotel
Thorn, Charles C.; 220 Market st. and 1115 Bush st.
Thornberg, Mr and Mrs Frederick A.; 507 Gough st.
Thornburg, Mrs. H. F.; The Baldwin.
Thorne. Owen; Westminster Hotel
Thornton, Mrs Crittenden; 2517 Pacific ave. *1st, 3d Fridays* Santa Cruz
Thornton, Mrs Geo. F.; 1935 Clay st.
Thornton, Mrs Bessie San Pablo
——Miss Lucille

Thornton, Colonel H. I.; 1123 Leavenworth st.
Thornton, Judge and Mrs J. D.; Occidental Hotel
Thors, Mr and Mrs Louis; 928 Sutter st. Berkeley
Thorson, Mr and Mrs N.; 813 Bush st. *Monday*
Throckmorton, Miss S.; The Bella Vista *Thursday*
Thurston, Mr and Mrs George B.; Hotel Pleasanton
Tibbe, Mr and Mrs A. A. Washington, D. C.
Tibbitts, Mrs Jennie; 504 Geary st.
——Howard C.

Tierney, John Lawrence; 110 Post st.
Tilden, Charles L.; 324 Post st.
Tilden, Mr and Mrs H. N.; 119 Mason st.
——Mr Heber C.
Tilford, E. A.; Palace Hotel
Tilley, Mrs T. A.; 1320 California st.
Tillinghast, Mr and Mrs J. J.; U. S. N. Mare Island
Tillman, F.; 1916 Larkin st.
Tillman, F., Jr.; 923 Grove st.
Tingle, Mr and Mrs George R.; Occidental Hotel *Monday*
——Miss

Tinney, T. J.; Palace Hotel
Tinnin, Mr and Mrs Wiley J.; 202 Broderick st. *1st and 2d Tuesdays*
Tisdall, Capt W. N., U. S. N.; Presidio Philadelphia, Pa.
Titus, Mr and Mrs Jessee; 712 Sutter st. (The Renton)
Tobin, Michael E.; The Bella Vista

Tobin, Mrs Mary A.; SE cor. California and Taylor sts.
——Miss Agnes
——Miss Beatrice
——Alfred
——Joseph
Tobin, Mr and Mrs James; 1307 Lyon st.
——Miss Florence
——F. K.
Tobin, Mr and Mrs Richard C.; 718 O'Farrell st.
Tobin, Robert J.; 513 Van Ness ave.
Toland, Dr Charles G.; 820 Filbert st.
Toland, Mrs M. B. M.; Occidental Hotel *Monday* **Del Monte**
Toohy, Hon D. J.
Topping, Miss; SW cor. Union and Fillmore sts. *2d and 4th Fridays*
Torreyson, J. D. **Carson City, Nev.**
Torbert, Mrs Chas. J.; 1300 Leavenworth st.
——Miss Mollie
Touhill, Miss Nellie; 403 Hyde st.
——Miss Anita
——Miss Mary
Tourny, Mr and Mrs George; 1316 Jones st.
Town, Dr F. L., U. S. A.; Presidio
Towne, Mr and Mrs A. N.; 2522 Pacific ave **Del Monte**
Towne, Mr and Mrs Arthur G.; Taylor and California sts.
Townsend, Mr & Mrs E. W.; 1001 Pine st., Hotel Bella Vista *Thursday*
Townsend, Mr and Mrs William R.; 1028 Pine st.
Tracy, Mrs A. F.; The Bella Vista *Thursday*
——Theodore F.
——William E.
Tracy, Miss Etta; 213 Geary st. *Wednesday* **Napa Soda Springs**
Trask, Dr and Mrs; 1033 Ellis st.
Treanor, Mr and Mrs J. P.; 2336 Pacific ave. *Friday*
Treadwell, Mrs Mabel; Palace Hotel *Monday*
Treadwell, John; Lick House
Treat, Warren **Martinez**
Truesdell, Mrs A. W.; 712 Sutter st.
Trumbo, Mr and Mrs I.; Palace Hotel *Monday*
Trumbo, J. W.; Palace Hotel
Trumbull, David **Valparaiso, Chili**
Tubbs, Mr and Mrs A. L. **Calistoga**
Tubbs, Mr and Mrs W. B. **Ca'istoga**
——Miss Nettie
Tubbs, Mr & Mrs Austin C.; Pacific-Union Club, 1001 Bush st. *Thursday*
——Alfred S.

93

Tucker, S. E.; Cosmos Club
Tuggle, H.; The Berkshire
Turk, Mr and Mrs James   *Monday*   Astoria, Oregon
——Charles
——William
Turnbull, General and Mrs Walter ; 1001 Pine st.
Turner, Lieut and Mrs J. A., U. S. N.; Cosmos Club   Mare Island
Turner, Mr and Mrs R.   Los Angeles
Turrell, M. H.; Palace Hotel
Twiggs, John W. ; 226 Post st.
Twist, Dr J. F.; 906 Market st.
Tyson, Mr and Mrs George H.; 518 Lombard st.   *Friday*

Underhill, Mr and Mrs George L.; 2111 Pine st.
Underhill, Mr and Mrs Henry B.; 1926 Pine st.   *Thursday*
Underhill; Mr and Mrs Jacob; Grand Hotel   *Monday*
Unger, Frank L.; Bohemian Club
Unruh, Mr and Mrs H. A.; Baldwin Hotel   *Monday*
Urioste, George de; 1916 Jackson st.
Urmy, Rev and Mrs W. S.; 1423 Jackson st.
Urruella, Mr and Mrs Juan ; 1916 Jackson st.

Vail, Mr and Mrs A. H.; 2702 Sacramento st.
——Frank A.
Vail, David H.; 2912 Clay st.
Vale, Mr and Mrs William ; 912 Pine st.
Valentine, John J.   East Oakland
Valette, William M.; 322 Geary st.
Van Bergen, Mr and Mrs J. W.; 1422 Larkin st.
——Edgar
Van Bergen, Mr and Mrs Edward ; 509 Post st.
Van Bergen, Mr and Mrs N.; 834 Post st.
——William
——George
——Theo
Van Buren, Gen. Thomas B.; 539 Geary st.
Van Daalen, Mr and Mrs; 212 Twenty-third st.
——Miss Florence
——B.
——E.
Van Dusen, Lieut and Mrs Geo. W.; U. S. A.   Fort Mason
Van Fleet, Judge and Mrs W. C.; 1609 Sutter st.
Van Heusen, Mrs Henry; 322 Ellis st.   *Monday*
Van Ness, Mr and Mrs T. C.; 1020 Green st.

Van Ness Seminary, Rev C. H. Willey, Director; 1222 Pine st.
Van Norden, Mr and Mrs Robert T.; Fairmount Hotel *Monday*
——Miss Kate
Van Orden, Mr and Mrs L.; 207 Twenty-fourth st. *Wednesday*
——Miss Emily
——T. Starr
Van Reynegom, Mr and Mrs F. W.; 630 Church st. *Wednesday* **Monterey**
Van Wyck, Mr and Mrs H. L.; 2548 Jackson st.
Van Wyck, Mrs Sydney; 1600 Taylor st.
——Sydney M., Jr.
——Crittenden
Van Winkle, Mr and Mrs H. L.; 2009 California st.
Van Winkle, Mrs I. S.; 2120 Jackson st.   **San Rafael**
——Miss
——Miss Belle
Vance, Mrs Bessie; 400 Franklin st.
Vanderslice, Mr and Mrs W. K.; 2702 California st.
——The Misses
Vandewater, Mrs R. J.; The Bella Vista *Thursday*
Vassault, Ferdinand; 1812 Sacramento st.
——Ferdinand I.
——Lawrence S.
——Miss Virginia
Veuve, Henry H.; Pacific-Union Club
Vidaver, Rev Dr Falk; 916 O'Farrell st.
Vincent, Clarence; The Berkshire
Vocke, G. C.; 1706 Leavenworth st.
Vodges, Lieut Charles B.; U. S. A.   **Presidio**
Volkmann, G.; NE cor. Hayes and Fillmore sts.
Vollmer, Miss Kate E.; 1900 Vallejo st.
Von Schmidt, Mr and Mrs Alexis W.; 2420 Mission st.
Von Schröder, Baron, and Baroness J. H.; 553 Harrison st. { **Eagle Ranch San Luis Obispo** } *Wednesday*
Voorhies, Dr and Mrs Alfred H.; 2111 California st.   **Del Monte**
——Miss Marie
——Miss Katie
Voorman, Mr and Mrs; 800 Bush st.
——Miss Viola

Wadham, Mr and Mrs L.; 1909 Leavenworth st.
Wadsworth, Mrs E.; The Bella Vista *Thursday*
Wadsworth, Henry; Pacific-Union Club
Wadsworth, J. C. L.; Pacific-Union Club

Wagner, H. L.; 1221 Washington st.
Wagoner, Luther; Cosmos Club
Wainright, Mr and Mrs William; 1409 Jackson st.   *Wednesday*
——————Miss Lizzie
——————Miss Annie
Wainright, Mr and Mrs James; 808 Taylor st.   *Tuesday*
-——————Miss Ella
——————Miss Amie
——————James W.
Wait, Mrs Frona E.; 117 Jones st.
Waites, Mr and Mrs C. B.; Palace Hotel   *Monday*
Wakefield, Mrs Lucinda; 1942½ Mission st.
Walcott, Earle A.; 631 Eddy st.
Walker, Judge George B.; 2531 Pine st.
Walker, Miss Annie   **San Rafael**
Walker, Dr M. M.; U. S. A.   **Fort Camby, W. T.**
Walker, N. S., Jr.; Cosmos Club   **New York**
Walker, Mr and Mrs Cyrus; 1920 Franklin st.
Walker, Mr and Mrs S. P.; 825 Sutter st.   *Monday*
Walkins, Mr and Mrs N. A.; 1302 Laguna st.
Walkington, Mrs E. J.   *Monday*
Walkington, Mr and Mrs T. G.; Hotel Pleasanton   *Monday* **Cazadero**
Wallace, Miss Belle   **Napa City**
Wallace, Mr and Mrs Ryland B.; 2324 Polk st.   *Friday*
Wallace, Judge and Mrs W. T.; 799 Van Ness ave. *Thursday* **San Rafael**
——————Miss Marguerite
——————Miss R.
Wallace, Mrs Ellen; 1419 Mason st.
Wallace, Mrs L. E.; 1811 Post st.
Wallace, Mrs Wm. H.; 2220 Broadway st. *Friday* **Rosamond, Tulare Co.**
——————Miss
——————Mr Wm. H.
Wallace, Mrs Coland
——————Miss Miriam
Wallenrod, Mr and Mrs George; 1209 Florida st.   *Thursday*
Wallis, Talbot H. (State Librarian)   **Sacramento**
Walsh, Mrs James A.; 712 Golden Gate ave.
Walsh, Mr and Mrs J. C.; The Berkshire   *Monday*
Walter, Mr and Mrs D. N.; 1700 Van Ness ave.
·——————Miss Adele
Walter, S. H.; 824 Geary st.
Walter, W. T.; Palace Hotel
Walthall, Miss Stella B.; 1222 Pine st.

Walton, Charles S.	Los Angeles
Wandesforde, Juan B.; 211 Sutter st.	Haywards
——Miss Ivy	
Warburton, Lieut and Mrs E. T.; Hotel Pleasanton *Monday*	
Ward, Miss Russella; 1534 Sutter st. *Friday*	
Ward, Mr and Mrs Wm.; 2905 Bush st.	
Wardwell, Mrs Mary; 1405 Van Ness ave.	
——Miss Fannie	
Warner, Dr and Mrs Alexander; 1120 Gough st. *Wednesday* Blithedale	
Warner, Mr and Mrs Charles H.; 712 Sutter (The Renton) *Wednesday*	
Warrin, Mrs M. A.; 1016 Sutter st.	
Washburn, Mr and Mrs Albert H.; 2525 Fillmore st.	**Wawona**
Washburn, Mrs Georgia; 1407 Van Ness ave.	
——George E.	
Washington, Frank B.; 707 Chestnut st.	
——John T.	
Waterhouse, Mr and Mrs Columbus; 2213 Howard st.	
——Frederick A.	
Waterman, Mrs T. J.	
Waterman, Charles S.; 2000 Broadway st.	
——Miss	
Waterman, Mr and Mrs Waldo S.	Chico
Waterworth, Henry W.; Cosmos Club	
Waters, Mrs G. L.; The Beresford	
Waters, George L.; Hotel Bella Vista *Thursday*	
——Miss Lillian	
Watkins, Mr and Mrs A. A.; 1302 Laguna st. *Thursday* Ben Lomond	
Watkins, Miss Emma	San Jose
Watson, Capt and Mrs J. Crittenden, U. S. N.; 1928 Sutter st.	
Watson, Jerome W.; 2440 Pacific ave.	
——Miss Jennie	
Watson, Martin V. B.; 2400 Pacific ave.	
Watson, Mr and Mrs Lawrence; 1122 Pine st. *Thursday*	
Watson, Mr and Mrs William; 728 Shotwell st.	
Watt, Rev and Mrs; Hotel Oriel *Monday*	
Wattles, Mr and Mrs William S.; Occidental Hotel	
Wattles, Mr and Mrs John B.; 1608 Washington st.	
Watts, W. P.; Cosmos Club	Tulare
Wayne, Mr and Mrs William	Washington
Webb, Judge and Mrs	Salinas City
Weber, Adolph C.; 840 Folsom st.	
——Adolph H.	
Webster, Mrs B. F.; 2411 Washington st. *Thursday*	
——Miss Sadie A.	
——Frank W.	

97

Webster, Fred R.; Pacific-Union Club
Webster, F. L.; Grand Hotel
Webster, Reginald H.; 2005 Fillmore st.
Weck, Mr and Mrs F. A.; 2107 Howard st.
Weight, Mr and Mrs John A.; 1615 Jackson st.   *Thursday*
——Miss Aggie
——Miss Jessie
Weihe, Mr and Mrs August; 2410 Fillmore st.
——Miss Florence
Weiland, Mr and Mrs Robert P.; Palace Hotel
Weill, Mr and Mrs Charles; The Berkshire   *Monday*
Weill, Henry; Palace Hotel
Weill, Raphael; Bohemian Club
Weill, Sylvin; Palace Hotel
Weir, Mrs Mary S.; 27 Oak st.   *Thursday*
Welch, Charles W.; 1422 Turk st.
Welch, Mr and Mrs Samuel B.; 2440 Pacific ave.
Weller, Mrs; Hotel Pleasanton
Weller, Mr and Mrs Charles L.; 2725 Jackson st.
Wells, Mr and Mrs W. H.   *Thursday*   **San Mateo**
——A. H.
Wells, F. Marion; 757 Mission st.   **Berkeley**
Wells, Mr & Mrs Asa R.; 1711 Van Ness ave.   *2d & 4th Wednesdays*
——Miss Laura Marcy
——Susanne Hadley
Wensinger, Mr and Mrs F. S.; Occidental Hotel *Monday* {"Rosedale," {Sonoma Co.
Wenzell, Prof and Mrs Wm. T.; 436 Oak st. *Wednesday* **Napa Redwoods**
West, Mary B.; 1900 Washington st. or 1606 Van Ness ave.   *Friday*
West, Miss H. R.; Hotel Pleasanton   *Monday*
West, Lieutenant Horace B., U. S. N.; Occidental Hotel   **"Rush"**
Westerfeld, L.; 1003 Geary st.
Westphal, Dr O. F.; 915 Fell st.
——Miss E.
——Mr C., Jr.
Wetherbee, Mr and Mrs Henry   *Monday*   **Fruitvale**
Wethered, Mr and Mrs Jas. S.; 320 Van Ness ave. **Summit Soda Springs**
——Miss E.
——Woodworth
Whartenby, Mrs James; 408 Ellis st.
Wheeler, Alfred A.; 621 Clay st.   **Sausalito**
Wheeler, Mr and Mrs Charles S.; 828 Green st.
Wheeler, Harold; 611 Bush st.   **Sausalito**
——Miss Helen
Wheeler, William R.; Cosmos Club

Wheeler, D. J.; 1400 Post st.
——Miss Agnes
Whipple, Mr and Mrs H. L.; Hotel Pleasanton
——G. H.
Whipple, George; 308 Van Ness ave.   *Tuesday*
——Miss Lizzie
White, Mr and Mrs George Knight   .   Sausalito
White, Miss Hattie, 37 Welsh st.
White, Mr and Mrs Lovell; 1616 Clay st.
White, Patrick J.; 2315 Bush st.
• White, Mrs Robert; 1216 Haight st.   *Wednesday*
——Miss Hattie F.
White, Robert; 1253 Octavia st.
Whitely, Harry M.; 2310 California st.
——Miss Carrie
Whiting, Mrs S. E.; 1501 Scott st.   *Friday*   Sisson
Whitney, Mrs A. L.; 1825 Turk st.
Whitney, Mr and Mrs Calvin E.; 1213 Jones st.
Whitney, C. W.; 1712 Pacific ave.
Whitney, Sumner; 113 Page st.
Whitney, Capt and Mrs F. A.; Hotel Pleasanton   *Monday*   San Diego
Whitney, Dr and Mrs J. D.; Palace Hotel   *Monday*
Whitney, Miss M. M.; Hotel Pleasanton   *Monday*
Whitney, Miss May; 113 Page st.   *Friday*
Whittell, Dr and Mrs Alexander; 1131 California st.   *Tuesday* **Los Gatos**
——Miss Florence
Whittell, Mr and Mrs George; 1155 California st.   *Tuesday*   **Los Gatos**
Whittier, W. Frank; 2400 Howard st.   *1st and 3d Wednesdays*
——Miss
Whittimore, D. H.; 230 Page st.
Whitwell, Dr and Mrs William S.; 907 Sutter st.
——Miss
Wholer, Mrs A. M.; 1928 Sacramento st.
Wickersham, Mr and Mrs   *Thursday*   Petaluma
--——Miss May
——Mr and Mrs, Jr.
Wickes, George W.; NE cor. Geary st. and Grant ave.
Wickham, Charles E.; 627 O'Farrell st.
Wicks, S. G.; Hotel Pleasanton
• Wickson, Mr and Mrs G. G.; 746 Twentieth st.   *Wednesday*
Wieland, H. W.; 236 Second st.
Wiggin, Mr and Mrs Samuel B.; 733 Bush st.
Wiggins, Mr and Mrs W. W.; 1810 Broadway st.
——James F.
Wightman, Mrs M. A.; Hotel Pleasanton

Wightman, Mrs John M.; Grand Hotel   *Monday*
Widmore, Mr and Mrs Alphonso A.; 1318 Leavenworth st.   *Wednesday*
Wilber, Miss Elida; 2228 California st.
Wilcox, Miss Jeannette; 1036 Valencia st.
Wilcox, Mrs A. H.; 912 Bush st.   *Tuesday*   San Diego
——Miss Fannie
Wilder, Mr and Mrs Charles J.; 1703 Broderick st.
Will, Mr and Mrs F. A.; 806 Van Ness ave.
Willard, Mrs Eleanor; 525 Harrison st.
——Miss Daisy
——Edward
Willey, Harry I.; 1526 Jackson st.
Wiley, Rev Dr and Mrs; 1222 Pine st.
Willey, Mr and Mrs O. F.; 2115 California st.   *Friday* Hotel Vendome
——Frank D.
Williams, Hon and Mrs A. P.; Palace Hotel   *Monday*
Williams, Mrs C. H.; 1417 Geary st.   *Monday*
Williams, Charles E.   Marysville
Williams, Mrs F. W.; 805 Leavenworth st.
Williams, Capt and Mrs Frank; 1309 Broadway st.
Williams, Mrs Fred; 406 Van Ness ave.   *Friday*
——Miss Flora
Williams, Mr and Mrs H.; 1925 Octavia st.   *Thursday* Hotel Vendome
——Miss M. A.
Williams, Mr and Mrs H. Alston; 2218 Devisadero st.   *Wednesday*
Williams, Mrs Henry B.; 2016 Van Ness ave.   San Jose
Williams, Mr and Mrs Henry F.; 2422 Howard st.
——Miss Charlotte
Williams, Mrs Mary; 1109 Clay st.   *Thursday*
Williams, Dr and Mrs Robert E.; 1235 Geary st.   *Wednesday*
——Miss Marie
Williams, Capt W. W.; U. S. A.   San Rafael
Williamson, Alex. B.; 316 California st. and 2120 Broadway st.
Williamson, Dr and Mrs John M.; 638 Haight st.   *Tuesday*
Williamson, R. W.; 1202 Leavenworth st.
Willis, Mrs William   Coronado Beach
Willis, Mr and Mrs A. M.; 28 Liberty st.
Wilmerding, J. C.; Pacific-Union Club
Wilshire, H. Gay   Los Angeles
Wilshire, Mr and Mrs W. B.; 1804 Sutter st.
Wilson, Mr and Mrs Horace; 1307 Taylor st.   *Tuesday* Santa Barbara
Wilson, Harry L.   Berkeley
Wilson, Mr & Mrs J. L.; Filbert st., bet. Van Ness ave. & Polk st. *Tuesday*
Wilson, Mr and Mrs Alexander W.; Palace Hotel

100

Wilson, Col C. L.; Baldwin Hotel   Butte Co.
Wilson, Dr Frank ; 711 Pine st.   New York
Wilson, Mr and Mrs Chas. E.; 629 Hayes st.
Wilson, Mr and Mrs Edgar M.; 2214 Jackson st.
Wilson, E. J.; Grand Hotel
Wilson, Miss E. S.; 920 Valencia st.
Wilson, Mr and Mrs Sam; 521 Post st.
Wilson, Mr and Mrs James K.; 2110 Broadway st.
Wilson, Mr and Mrs J. L.; 2514 Pine st.
Wilson, Mr and Mrs J. N. E.; cor. Union st. and Van Ness ave.
Wilson, Mr and Mrs John Scott; 2330 Pacific ave.
Wilson, Joseph; 1214 Mason st.
Wilson, Mrs K.; 1107 Bush st.
Wilson, Mrs L. S.; Hotel Pleasanton   *Monday*
Wilson, Mrs N. I.; Hotel Pleasanton
Wilson, Mr and Mrs Russell J.; 711 Pine st.   Hotel Rafael
——Mr and Mrs Samuel M.   Del Monte
——Mr and Mrs Mountford S.

Wilson, Mr and Mrs Ramon E.; Pacific-Union Club   Webber Lake
——Miss Marion
Wilson, C. H.; Hotel Pleasanton
Wilson, Mr and Mrs William A.; 1114 Bush st.
Wilson, Mrs M.; 3026 California st.
——Miss Marie E.
——Miss Kate

Winn, Mr and Mrs A. H.; The Berkshire   *Monday*
Winn, Lieut and Mrs F. L., U. S. A.; Angel Island
Winans, Mrs Joseph; 926 Clay st.   Del Monte
——Miss Lillie
——Joseph W., Jr.

Wingerter, Mr and Mrs C. J.; 2714 Sacramento st.   *Monday*
——Miss Minerva

Wingerter, Mr and Mrs E. J.; Pierce st.
Winslow, Mr and Mrs Chauncey R.; Boh. Club, 1801 Van Ness *Friday*
Winslow, Capt Gordon   Berkeley
Winter, William ; 710 Capp st.
Winterberg, Dr W.; 602 Sutter st.
Winton, Dr H. N.; 1325 Leavenworth st.
Wise, Mr and Mrs Everett E.   Healdsburg
Wise, Mr and Mrs John H.; 1409 Leavenworth st.   *Wednesday* Gilroy
——Harry E.

Wise, Miss A. M.; 2130 Market st.   *Tuesday*
Wissel, Albert F.; 904 Steiner st.
Witcher, Major John S.; 36 New Montgomery st.

101

Witham, Mr and Mrs Walter D.; 2019 Webster st.   *Friday*
Withrow, Mrs K. H.; 925 Pine st.
——Miss Eva
Witt, E.; 826 Powell st.
Wittram, Mr and Mrs Frederick; 2319 California st.   *Wednesday*
Wolcott, Capt C. C.; U. S. N.; Mare Island
Wolff, Mr and Mrs Wm.; 1322 Leavenworth st.   *Thursday*   **Monterey**
Wollweber, Mr and Mrs B.; The Berkshire   *Monday*
——Miss C. J.
Wood, Capt and Mrs A. E.; Presidio
Wood, Lieut A. N., U. S. N.; Cosmos Club
Wood, Charles; 1024 Bush st.
——Miss Dora
Wood, E.; Lick House
Wood, Mr and Mrs George M.; 1507 California st.
Wood, Dr and Mrs Leonard; Presidio
Wood, J. W.; Palace Hotel   *Monday*
——Miss Nellie
Wood, Lieut S. S., U. S. N.; Cosmos Club
Wood, William H.; Hotel Pleasanton
Wood, Mr and Mrs William S.; 1920 Clay st.   **Yosemite**
——Miss Eleanor
Wood, Willard M.; 2105 Webster st.
Woodman, Mrs; 916 Van Ness ave.
Woods, Frederick N.; 1021 Nineteenth st.
Woods, Miss May; The Berkshire   *Monday*
Woods, Mr and Mrs Robert J.; 2714 California st.   **San Rafael**
Woodward, Robert B.; NE cor. Geary st. and Grant ave.
Woodward, Gideon P.; 1429 O'Farrell st.
Woodward, J. H.; 21 Montgomery st.
Woodworth, Mr and Mrs   **Tomales**
Woodworth, Selim E.; 320 Van Ness ave.
Woodworth, Samuel   **Stony Point**
Woolrich, George L.; 2629 California st.
——Miss
Woolworth, Mr and Mrs R. C., 1626 Sacramento st.   **Del Monte**
——Miss
Wooster, Mr and Mrs F. L.; Hotel Pleasanton *Friday* **Napa Soda Springs**
Wooster, Mrs John B.; California near Laguna sts.
——Ellis
Wooster, Mr and Mrs Philip L.   **Napa Soda Springs**
Worden, Miss Lizzie; 1105 Shotwell st.   *Monday*   **Yosemite Valley**
Worden, Lieut and Mrs Chas A.   **Mare Island**
Worden, Clinton E.; Pacific-Union Club

Wormser, Mr and Mrs Samuel L; 1834 California st.   *Tuesday*
Worn, Miss A. S.   **Ross Valley**
Wrey, Mr and Mrs G. E. B.; The Berkshire   *Monday*
Worth, Mr and Mrs Henry C.; 1310 Golden Gate ave.
Wright, Mr and Mrs C. S.; 1407 Hyde st.   *Thursday*
Wright, Mr and Mrs Edward C.; 103 Broderick st.
Wright, Mr and Mrs J. B.   **Sacramento**
Wright, Mr and Mrs J. M.; 2812 Sacramento st. *Wednesday* **Santa Barbara**
Wright, John A.; 2222 Washington st.
Wright, Mr and Mrs Selden S.; 910 Lombard st.   *Friday*   **Haywards**
———Miss Roberta E. Lee
———Miss Annie
———Ralph K.
———William H.
Wyllie, Mr and Mrs Alexander   **San Jose**

Yates, Mrs R. H.; Hotel Fairmount   *Monday*
Yemans, Dr and Mrs Herbert W.; 711 Taylor st.   *1st and 3d Thursdays*
Yerington, Miss; 1255 California st.
Yoell, Mr and Mrs Alexander   **San Jose**
———Miss
Yost, Mr and Mrs D. Z.; Pacific-Union Club
Yost, Mrs John D.; 1422 Sutter st.   **Alameda**
———John D., Jr.
———Miss
Young, Andrew S.; 1716 Jackson st.
Young, Carlos G.; 1616 Geary st.
Young, Mrs H. J.; 1514 California st.   *Wednesday*
———Miss
———H. H.
———F. J.
Young, Charles F.; Laguna and McAllister sts.
Young, Frederick J.; 1213 Octavia st.
———Henry H.
———Henry J.
Young, George A.; 1904 Broadway st.
Young, Captain J. D.   **Sacramento**
Young, Mr and Mrs John P.; 1919 Devisadero st.   *Thursday*
Young, Mr and Mrs Thomas; 314 Lombard st.
Young, Mr and Mrs Thomas; 502 Powell st.
Young, Walter; 514 Twenty-Third st.
Young, William; 1811 Sutter st.
Younger, Dr Alexander S.   **Steamer " Oceanic "**
Younger, Dr and Mrs Wm. J.; 1414 California st.   *Tuesday*   **Del Monte**
———Miss Maud
———Miss Bessie
———Herbert
Younger, Dr and Mrs Edward A.   **Alameda**

Zadig, Mr and Mrs Hermann; 2297 Franklin st.
Zahn, Miss Olga; 2206½ Devisadero st.   *Tuesday*
——Mr R. Geo.
Zane, Miss Marie; 829 O'Farrell st.
Zech, August F.; 211 Scott st.   *Tuesday*
——Miss Tillie
——Miss Hattie
——Miss Gussie
Zech, Frederick, Jr.; 1229 Bush st.
Zeile, Mr and Mrs Frederick W.; 2023 California st.   *Friday*
Zeilin, W. S.; Cosmos Club   New York
Zifferer, Prof and Madame; The Bella Vista.   *Thursday*
Zimmerman, Mr and Mrs Frank C.; 1321 Sutter st.   *Thursday*
Ziska, Madame B.; 1606 California st.   *2d and 4th Thursdays*
——Miss Alice
Zook, Mr and Mrs Frank K.; 2136 Sutter st.

Be Beautiful

Every Lady Owes it to Herself to be as Beautiful as Possible

A Perfect Complexion ══════
Can be Acquired ══════

Madame A. Ruppert's World-Renowned Face Bleach positively removes by natural methods all discolorations of the skin, is not a cosmetic—but a thorough skin tonic—cleaning the callous pores of the skin of their poisonous

fillings, leaving them clear for the free passage of the blood's impurities, which nature demands be exuded from the blood, through the pores to the surface.

My method of treating skin diseases appeals to the most intelligent—and has the endorsement of eminent medical authority. Do not understand that *Face Bleach* destroys healthful color or gives you a "washout" appearance, as the word "bleaching" would imply—but on the contrary, it restores natural color—is in no way harmful—but positively beneficial to the most delicate complexion, and almost a necessity.

Face Bleach is guaranteed in every instance to remove Freckles, Tan, Moth Patches, Blackheads, Blotches, Pimples, Roughness, Eczema (wrinkles not caused by facial expression included), and in fact, any and all discolorations or blemishes, leaving the skin clear, smooth and firm, proof against sun or weather, thus preventing tan or sunburn. Thousands of the best ladies of the land will testify to the truth of the above statement.

Mme. A. Ruppert's world-renowned **Face Bleach** is put up in an 8-ounce glass-stoppered bottle, with name and address blown in the bottle, labeled with facsimile of photograph and signature of MME. A. RUPPERT, New York City. None other genuine. Face Bleach is never sold in bulk or in any other style bottle or label, either by my own agents or druggists. Price, single bottle, $2; three bottles (usually required to clear the complexion), $5. Sent to any part of the world securely packed, plain wrapper, on receipt of price. Send 4 cents postage or call for catalogue and particulars.

MME. A. RUPPERT

121 Post Street
OVER
O'Connor, Moffatt & Co.

PARLORS 7 and 8
San Francisco

OAKLAND

Pacific Carriage Co.

COUPE, ONE OR TWO PASSENGERS, $1.00. HACK, ONE OR TWO PASSENGERS, $1.00. HACK, THREE OR FOUR PASSENGERS, $1.50. HACK, THREE OR FOUR PASSENGERS, $2.00

Within district bounded by Broadway, Gough and Twelfth Streets, and the City Front, or for One Mile

Hacks and Coupes sent promptly in response to calls from the S. F. Dist. Tel. Co's Boxes and the Pacific Bell Telephone Co. or Messenger Service, at our Expense

RATES OF FARE

	COUPE	CARRIAGE
One or two passengers	$1 00	$1 50
Three or four passengers		2 00
Each additional mile (each passenger)		25
Calling and Shopping, first hour	1 50	2 00
Calling and Shopping, each subsequent hour	1 00	1 50
Theatres, Balls and Parties, both ways	3 00	4 00
Funerals	3 50	4 00
Alms House, Holy Cross Cemetery	6 00	6 00
Black Point, etc., via Park	5 00	6 00
Cliff House, via Park and return	2 50	3 00
Cliff House, via Park and return via Ocean House	6 00	8 00
City and County Hospital	2 00	2 50

	COUPE	CARRIAGE
German Hospital	2 00	$2 50
2nd Point (ferriage extra)	3 00	4 00
Oakland (ferriage extra)	5 00	6 00
etc., via Park	6 00	8 00
Park Drive	4 00	5 00
Park Drive to end of Beach Road	5 00	7 00
Presidio	3 00	4 00
Presidio and Fort Point Drive	5 00	6 00
Presidio, Fort Point and Park Drive	7 00	10 00
Presidio, Fort Point, Cliff House and Park Drive	10 00	12 00
St. Luke's Hospital	2 50	3 00
Villa	4 00	5 00
14-Mile House	10 00	12 00
Industrial School	4 00	5 00

Detentions after the time on which Carriages are ordered will be charged by the hour

GENERAL BUSINESS OFFICE, 48 EIGHTH STREET

Baldwin Hotel Stand

CENTRAL STANDS, 200 AND 207 SUTTER STREET

N. W. & S. W. CORNERS KEARNY AND SUTTER STREETS

Coupes and Carriages at the Baldwin Hotel and Central Stands, 200 & 207 Sutter Street at any Hour of the Day or Night

Special Rates by applying to the Superintendent or Foreman at the Baldwin or Central Stands

FOUR-IN-HAND WAGONETTES FOR PARTIES. • HORSES, BUGGIES AND ROCKAWAYS. • WORK HORSES TO LET

Oliver Hinkley, Supt.

TELEPHONE 1950

OAKLAND, ALAMEDA, BERKELEY
AND SURROUNDINGS

NOTE.—Where street only is mentioned Oakland should be understood.

———

Abbott, Rev and Mrs Granville S.; 569 Eleventh st.
———Granville S., Jr.
Ackinson, Miss Blanche; 1426 Tenth st., East Oakland
Adams, Mrs Edson; Bay Place and Oak ave.
———Edson, F.
———John
Adams, Harry; 1406 Alice st.
Agard, Dr A. H.; 1259 Alice st.
Ainsworth, Capt and Mrs J. C.; Rose Lawn, Claremont ave.   *Wednesday*
———Miss Daisy
———Miss Maude
———Miss Bella
———Harry B.
———John C.
———Capt and Mrs George J.
Akerly, Rev Benjamin; Adeline and Sixteenth sts.
———James C.
———Morris K.
Albrecht, Mrs; Fruitvale.
———Miss Laura
Aldrich, William A.; Piedmont
———Miss Helen
———Burt
Alexander, Mr and Mrs O.; 1406 Alice st.
———Mr and Mrs Charles O.
Alexander, Mr and Mrs S. T.; 1006 16th st.
———Miss Lottie
———The Misses
Allender, Mr and Mrs; 1107 Alice st.
Allen, Arthur; Alameda
Allen, Mr and Mrs C. R.; 318 14th st.
Allen, Mrs Frank Howard; 1231 Poplar st.   *Wednesday*
Allen, Mr and Mrs I. P.; Santa Clara ave., Alameda
Allen, Mr and Mrs James G.; 1325 Jackson st.   *Wednesday*

———

Ames, Judge and Mrs J. P.; 1132 Adeline st.   *Thursday*
Ames, Mr and Mrs John; The Windsor   *Monday*
Anderson, Mrs W. W.; Hopkins Academy   *Tuesday*
———Miss
———Miss Ethel
Angus, Mr and Mrs William; Third ave. and 12th st.   {*Wednesday* {East Oakland
Anthony, Mr and Mrs Edwin R.; Alameda ave., near Peru, Alameda
Anthony, Mr and Mrs John A.; Central ave., Alameda
———Miss
Anthony, Mr and Mrs R. M.; 964 Eighteenth st.
Applegate, J. Henry, Jr.; Alameda
Archibald, Mr and Mrs F. A.; 118 Ninth st.   *Thursday*
———James J.
Armes, Mr and Mrs C. W.; 1201 West st.
Armes, Mr and Mrs G. W.; Berkeley
———W. D.
Arthur, Mr and Mrs J. D.; NW cor. 12th and Castro sts.
———E. M.

Babcock, Allen H.; 1216 Webster st.
Bacon, Mrs Alonzo; Alameda
Bacon, Mr and Mrs Frank; 923 Linden st.
Bacon, Mr and Mrs Henry D.; 960 Oak st.   *Wednesday*
———Miss Carrie
Badger, William G.; Fruitvale
Baker, Mr and Mrs J. A.; 1234 Regent st., Alameda
Baker, James W.; Galindo Hotel
Baldwin, Mrs C.; 930 Adeline st.   *Monday*
———Miss
———Alexander
Baldwin, Mrs Lloyd; Vernon Heights   *Thursday*
———Mrs. J. G.
Bangs, Mr and Mrs Franklin; East Oakland
Barker, Mr and Mrs Joshua L.; Berkeley
Barker, Mr and Mrs Timothy L.; 1119 Castro st.
Barnard, Mr and Mrs George B.; 554 Thirty-fifth st.
Barnes, Mr and Mrs E. T.; Central ave., Alameda
Barney, Mr and Mrs Alfred S.; Vernon Heights
Barstow, Mr and Mrs Anson; 1356 Franklin st.
Barstow, Mr and Mrs Alfred; 1018 Eighteenth st.
———Miss
Barstow, Mrs Ellen F.; 1064 Twenty-second st.
Bartlett, Mr and Mrs Columbus; Alameda
Bartlett, Mrs Earl; East Oakland

Bartlett, N. C.; 447 Prospect ave.
Bartlett, Mr and Mrs Pliny; 1311 Franklin st.
Barton, Mr and Mrs John; Broadway and Central ave., Alameda
——Miss
——W. F.
Barton, Mr and Mrs P. W.; Clinton ave., Alameda
Barton, Mr and Mrs W. T.
Bassett, Mr and Mrs J. F.; 964 Market st.   *Thursday*
Bastian, Carl; Galindo Hotel   *Thursday*   **Dansville, N. Y.**
Bayley, Mr and Mrs George B.; 1307 Castro st.
——Miss Gertrude
Beck, Mr and Mrs Eugene B.; 1339 Alice st.
Beck, Mr and Mrs W. F.; 512 Charter st.
Bell, Mrs G. W.; Centennial and Fourteenth sts.
Benson, Maj and Mrs Henry M.; 1846 Santa Clara ave., Ala.   *Friday*
——Miss
——Miss M. B.
Bentley, Mr and Mrs W. R.; 220 Eleventh st.   *Wednesday*
Benton, Mr and Mrs J. E.; 533 Sixteenth st.
——Miss May
Benton, Rev and Mrs J. A.; 437 Hawthorne st.   *Monday*
Berryman, Mr and Mrs H. B.; Berkeley
Bigelow, Mr and Mrs Elijah; 1155 Brush st.
Bird, Mr Frank L.; 2048 Encinal ave., Alameda
——George R.
——W. O.
——Mrs R. I.
Bishop, Mr and Mrs A. W.; Jackson st.   *Wednesday*
Bissell, Mr and Mrs George R.; Alameda ave., Alameda
——The Misses
——Eugene
——Louis H.
Bissell, William A.; Alameda   **Del Coronado**
Blake-Alverson, Mrs; 961 Fourth ave., East Oakland   *Wednesday*
——William E.
——Alverson, D. W.
Blake, Mrs Frances; Telegraph ave., bet. Knox and Caledonia ave.
——Miss Alice
Blasdel, Capt and Mrs; 1123 Market st.   *Thursday*
——Miss Flora
——Miss Libbie
Blood, Mrs; Berkeley
——Miss May
——George

Blow, A. H.; 759 Harrison st.
Blow, Mr and Mrs W. W.
Boardman, Charles T.; Galindo Hotel
Boardman, Mr and Mrs Edward; Magnolia, near Eighth sts.
Boland, Mrs Archibald; Webster st.
Bonham, Mrs M. T.; 626 Eighth st.
Borden, Mrs; 1117 Adeline st.
———Miss
———Rhodes
Bonner, Mr and Mrs Thomas; Brook and Orchard sts.
Bonte, Rev and Mrs J. H. C.; Berkeley
Booth, Dr and Mrs E. B.; Alameda
Booth, Mr and Mrs Lucius A.; Hope ave., Piedmont   *Wednesday*
———Miss Booth
Booth, Mr and Mrs W. H.; Alameda
Booth, William F.; Berkeley
Bowen, Mr and Mrs P. M.; 1303 Chestnut st.
Bowen, Mr and Mrs C. R.; 1439 Market st.
Bowles, Mr and Mrs P. E.; Tenth near Market st.
Bowman, Mr and Mrs A. W.; Piedmont
———George F.
Bowman, Mr and Mrs H.; 630 Ninth st.
Bradley, Mr and Mrs John T.; 364 Fourteenth near Webster st.
———Miss
———Miss Lucy
———Mr Hiram T.
Bradley, Prof and Mrs C. B.; Berkeley
Bray, Mr and Mrs Watson A.; Fruitvale
———Edward M.
———Robert A.
Brayton, Mr and Mrs Albert P.; 1167 Jackson st.   *Wednesday*
———Miss Louise
———Albert P., Jr.
———Edward
Breck, Mr and Mrs Samuel; 678 Fourteenth st.
———Miss Nellie
———Miss Emma
———Miss Augusta
———Miss Louise
———Samuel, Jr.
———James
Brett, Mrs and Mrs John R.; 562 Thirteenth st.
Brigham, Mr and Mrs C. O.; 1019 Oak st.   *Friday*
———Miss Lena

108

Brigham, Mr and Mrs Frank E.; 1017 Oak st.   *Friday*
Brigham, Frank; Oak and Tenth sts.
Brooks, Mr and Mrs Welby A.; Alameda
Bromwell, Col and Mrs L. L.; Ninth and Madison sts.   *Wednesday*
——Miss Louise
Bronson, Miss Cora; Kelsey House
——Miss Mabel
Brown, Mr and Mrs Albert; 1387 Alice st.   *Wednesday*
Brown, Mr and Mrs J. E.
Brown, Mr and Mrs Arthur; 1031 Filbert st.
Brown, Mr and Mrs David; Alameda
Brown, Mr and Mrs Roland G.; 1389 Jackson st.   *Wednesday*
——Miss Lillian
——Miss Florence
Browne, Mrs; 6th Avenue, East Oakland
——Miss Effie
Rrowne, Mr and Mrs P. D.; Highland Park
Buck, Dr and Mrs E. W.; 1011 Webster st.
——Miss
Buffington, Mr and Mrs J. M.; 10th and Oak sts.
——Miss Laura
Bugbee, Mr and Mrs Sumner W.; Hotel Merritt
Bulkley, Mr and Mrs Milton; 545 Albion st.   *Friday*
Bunker, Miss Minnie; 150 Lake st.   *Friday*   Santa Clara
Bunnell, Prof and Mrs George W.; Caledonia and Telegraph ave.
Burk, F.; Blake House
Burnham, Mr and Mrs O. H.; 1017 Madison st.
——Lee

Caduc, Com and Mrs Philip; "Mosswood," Tel. ave.   {*Saturday*
                                                      {Del Coronado
——Miss Cora
Cahill, Mr and Mrs Edward F.; 1368 Tenth st.
Cambden, Mr and Mrs Charles; Tenth and Market sts.
Cameron, Mr and Mrs W. W.; 28th st., bet. Grove st. and Telegraph ave.
Campbell, Mr and Mrs Fred M.; 1262 Webster st. *Thursday* Los Angeles
——Miss Mary M.
Campbell, Miss Jessie; Orchard ave.
——Colin
——Daniel Y.
Campbell, Mr and Mrs J. C.; Twelfth and Chestnut sts.   *Monday*
Campbell, William; Alameda
Canoran, Mrs Arabella; Claremont ave., North Temescal   *Thursday*
Capwell, Mr and Mrs H. C.; 531 Twentieth st.   *1st and 3d Fridays*

Carmany, Mr and Mrs Cryus W.; East Oakland
Carmony, John; Thirteenth ave., beyond Lynn, East Oakland
——Miss Mary A.
Carneal, Thomas D.; Twelfth st., near Castro
Carpenter, Horace W.; Alice and Third sts.
Carrick, Mr and Mrs D.; cor. 12th ave. and 15th st., East Oakland
Chabot, Mrs A.; 104 East Fifteenth st., East Oakland
——Miss Nellie W.
Chabot, Mrs R.; Eleventh and Madison sts.
Chalmers, William L.; Kelsey House
——Miss Jean
Chamberlain, Mr and Mrs Charles H; 1571 Seventh ave., East Oakland
Chamberlain, Colonel and Mrs W. E.; Oakland
Chapman, E. B.; East Oakland
Chapman, Mr and Mrs T. F.; 120 East Fourteenth st.
Chapman, Rev and Mrs E. S.; 1264 Twelfth ave., East Oakland
Chase, Mr and Mrs John L.   **Sioux Falls, Dak.**
Chase, Mr and Mrs H. W.; 1157 Alice st. *2d & last Thursday* **Ben Lomond**
Chase, Mr and Mrs Q. A.; Broadway, near Moss ave.
Cheever, Mr and Mrs M. R.; 1401 Seventh ave., East Oakland *Wednesday*
Cheney, Mr and Mrs Warren; Berkeley   *Tuesday*
Chetwood, Rev Hobart; Hotel Merritt
——John
Chickering, Mr and Mrs William H.; 970 Sixteenth st.
Chipman, Miss Alice M.; Encinal Park, Alameda   *Tuesday*
——Miss Fannie J.
——Mr W. F.
——Mr S. H.
Clay, Mr and Mrs C. C.; E. Fourteenth st., Fruitvale
Clement, Mr and Mrs E. B.; 1264 Harrison st.
——Miss Katie
——Alfred
——Joe
Clement, Mr and Mrs H. N.; Berkeley
Cluff, Mr and Mrs Edwin H.; Fruitvale
Cockroft, Mr and Mrs L. F.; Prospect Heights   *Tuesday*
Coffin, Mr and Mrs Albert F.; 918 Sixteenth st.
Coffin, Mr and Mrs C. B.; 1387 Harrison st.
——Miss
Coghill, Mr and Mrs T. B.; 1304 Jackson st.   *Wednesday*
Cohen, Mrs Emily G.; Versailles and Buena Vista aves., Alameda
——Miss Mabel
——Miss Edith
——Miss Ethel
——W. G.
——Daniel Y.
——Mr and Mrs Edgar A.

Cohen, Mr and Mrs Alfred H.; Fruitvale
Coit, Mr and Mrs Griffith ; Booth and New Broadway sts.
Colby, Mr and Mrs G. E.; Claremont ave.   *Wednesday*
Cole, Mr and Mrs Leander G. ; 1545 Webster st.
Cole, Mrs R. E ; 512 Twelfth st.
——Miss
Coleman, Mr and Mrs John W.; 754 Eighth st.   **Del Monte**
——Miss Jessie
——Harry L.
Condron, Mrs. D. B.; Field Seminary   *Thursday*
Conklin, Mrs F. G.; Fourth ave. and Sixteenth sts., East Oakland
Conners, John; 1115 Jackson st.   *Wednesday*   **Pleasanton**
——Miss Mollie
——Miss Maggie
Cook, Mrs H. E.; 1227 Linden st.
Cook, Prof and Mrs Albert S.; Dwight way and Auburn st., Berkeley
Cooke, Mrs F. W.; 1309 Haight st.
Cooks, Mr and Mrs Louis; 1524 Eighth st.
Cookson, Mr and Mrs Frank; 1919 San Pablo ave.   *Wednesday*
——Miss Annie
——William B.
Cool, Dr and Mrs Russell H. ; Galindo Hotel
Coon, Mrs H. P.; 1159 Alice st.   *2d and last Thursdays*   **Ben Lomond**
Coon, Mr and Mrs Henry Irving; Fruitvale
Cooper, E. R.; 829 Grove st.
Cooper, Mrs Eugene; cor. Oak and Tenth sts.
Coplin, Mr and Mrs A.; 536 Thirty-first st.
——Miss Ethel
——Albert D.
Cordiell, Mr and Mrs Thomas; Sixteenth and Webster sts.   *Wednesday*
Cornwall, Dr and Mrs Ambrose; Vernon Heights
Corran, Mr and Mrs W. H. C.; Tubbs' Hotel
Costigan, Mr and Mrs James M.; 1305 Franklin st.
——Miss
Craig, Mr and Mrs Homer A.; 2223 Green st.
Craig, Mr and Mrs Hugh; Piedmont Hotel   *Thursday*
Crane, Mrs A. M.; 584 Thirty-fifth st.
——Lauren E.
Crane, Mrs S. H ; 971 Market st.
Crellin, Mr and Mrs John ; 1061 Oak st.
——Miss
——Arthur
Crockett, Mrs J. B.; Fruitvale
——Miss Emma

Crockett, Mrs Robert; Fruitvale
Crouch, Mr and Mrs E.; 1061 Seventh ave., East Oakland
Cullen, Mr and Mrs; 10th ave. between 14th and 15th, East Oakland
——Miss Alice
——W. O.
Cumming, Capt and Mrs George; Fruitvale
——A. M.
Cunningham, Mr and Mrs Loring; 479 Orchard ave.
Curtis, Mr and Mrs; 124 Ninth st.
Cushing, Mr and Mrs Volney; Berkeley
Cuvellier, Mr and Mrs B. C.; 1212 Poplar st.   *Wednesday*   **Inverness**

Dam, L. E.; 493 Locust st.
——Cleveland
Dargie, Mr and Mrs W. E.; 1168 Jackson st.   { *Wednesday* / Santa Barbara Co.
——Miss Annie R.
——Thomas T.
Dargie, Mr and Mrs T. T.; NW cor. Twelfth and Alice sts.
Davis, Mr and Mrs John W.; Alameda
Davis, Edward C.; Alameda
Davis, Mrs M. V.; 759 Sixteenth st.
Day, Mr and Mrs Clinton; Piedmont way, Berkeley
Dayton, Mrs J. B.   *Wednesday*
——Miss Jessie
——George
Dean, Mr and Mrs Carl; Oakland
Dean, Mr and Mrs Elisha B.; 1219 Grove st.
Dean, Mrs J. B.; 1325 Jackson st.   *Wednesday*
——John
Dean, Mr and Mrs Peter; Madison st.   **Hotel Rafael**
——Miss Sarah
Deane, Mrs John; Claremont   *Wednesday*
——Miss Esma
Dearborn, Mr and Mrs G. W.; cor. 12th ave. and 15th st. East Oakland
De Estrella, T.; Berkeley
de Fremery, Mrs H. S.;   **Abroad**
de Fremery, Mr James; 1305 Adeline st.   **Abroad**
de Fremery, Mr and Mrs William C. B.; Prospect ave.   *Wednesday*
——Miss Virginie
De Golia, Mrs George E,; 1390 Harrison st.   *Thursday*
De Gomez, Mr and Mrs F.; 463 Twenty-sixth st.   *Tuesday*
De la Montanya, A.; 656 Sixth st.
Delger, Mr and Mrs Edward F.; 1453 Telegraph ave.   *Wednesday*
Delger, Frederick; Telegraph ave. and Nineteenth st.

Denny, Horace; East Oakland
De Pue, E. J.; 1115 Third ave., East Oakland
Derby, Mrs; Fruitvale
——Oscar
——A. G.
Dewing, Mr and Mrs A. A.; 353 East 14th st., East Oakland   *Tuesday*
Dietz, Mr and Mrs Alfred C.; San Pablo ave.
——Miss
——Miss Alice
Dille, Rev Dr and Mrs E. R.; 1401 Castro st.
Dillon, Miss; Seventh and Oak sts.
Dingee, Mr and Mrs W. J.; Fernwood, Piedmont
Diss, Mr and Mrs J. Wallace F.; Regent st., Alameda   { *Saturday* *Los Palmitos*
Donnell, Mr and Mrs Arthur C.; 1227 Myrtle st.   *Tuesday*
Donnelly, Mrs Henry;   *Wednesday*   *Fruitvale*
——Miss
——Miss Henrietta
Dorhman, Mr and Mrs F.; 2214 Alameda ave., Alameda   *Friday*
——Miss M.
——Mr B.
Dornin, Mr and Mrs George D.; Dwight way, Berkeley
——Miss
——Mr and Mrs Oscar G.
Dougherty, Mr and Mrs Chas. M.; 2203 East 14th st., Oakland   *Tuesday*
——Miss Ada May
Driscoll, Mrs J. M.; Sixteeenth and Webster sts.   *Wednesday*
Drum, John S.; 953 Market st.
——Frank
Dunham, Mr and Mrs Benjamin F.; 1397 Alice st.   *Friday*
——Miss Mary
Durbrow, Mr and Mrs Pierson; 1932 Alameda ave., Alameda
Dwinell, Charles H.; Berkeley
Dwinelle, Mrs J. W.; Encinal Park, Alameda   *Tuesday*
Dyer, Mr and Mrs J. B.; 312 Fourteenth st.   *Friday*
——Miss Ruth
——Miss Minnie
——Mr and Mrs J. B., Jr.; Thirteenth and Webster sts.

Eastland, Mr and Mrs Joseph G.; Rockridge
Eastland, Mr and Mrs Van L.; 817 Grove st.
Eastman, Mr and Mrs C. H.; Twelfth st. and Seventh ave. { *Tuesday* East Oakland
Eaton, Mr and Mrs Joseph C.; 19th ave. and East 24th st., East Oakland

Edwards, Mr and Mrs George C.; 1568 Webster st.   *Thursday*
Edwards, Mr and Mrs J. G.; 520 Tenth st.   *Thursday*
Eels, Mr and Mrs Charles P.; San Pablo ave.   *Thursday*
Eels, Miss Emma L.; Mills Seminary, Seminary Park
Eldridge, Mr and Mrs S. A.; Harrison and Fourteenth sts.   *Wednesday*
Elliot, Mr and Mrs N. L.; 1022 Peralta st.
Elsey, Mr and Mrs Charles; SW cor. 11th and Grove sts.
Emery, J. C.; San Pablo ave.
Emery, Mrs Joseph; 1308 Webster st.
English, Mr and Mrs W. B.; cor. 10th and Madison sts.
Ernest, Dr J. T.; Oakland
Evarts, Mr and Mrs P.; 1115 Jackson st.   *Wednesday*
Everett, Mrs S. L.; 1116 Adeline st.
Everett, Mr and Mrs Edward; 719 Eighth st.
Everest, Mr and Mrs H. B.; 1375 Madison st.
——Miss Nellie
Everson, Mr and Mrs Wallace; 16th and Filbert sts.   *Friday*
——Miss
Ewing, Mr and Mrs Thomas; Vernon Heights

Fabens, Mr and Mrs George; Alameda
Farnam, Mr and Mrs Charles W.; 1226 Fruitvale ave.   { *Monday* / Fruitvale
Farham, Mr and Mrs J. E.; Oakland
Farquharson, Mr and Mrs David; 1167 Jackson st.   *Wednesday*
——Miss Mary
Farrier, Mr and Mrs H. L.; 1253 Sixth ave., East Oakland
——Miss Emma L.
——Miss Annie F.
Felton, Mrs Katherine; 930 Adeline st.   *Monday*
Fields, Mrs D. I.; Olive House   *Wednesday*
Fine, Mrs A.; Sixth ave. and 12th st., East Oakland   *Monday*
Fischer, Mr and Mrs; Haywards
——J. K.
Fish, Mr and Mrs Charles H.; 804 10th st.
Fish, Mr and Mrs Harvey; 918 Grove st.
Fish, Dr and Mrs M. W.; 461 East 14th st., East Oakland
——Miss Julia
Fisher, Mr and Mrs Hugo; Alameda
Fitzgerald, Mrs Kate; 313 Fourteenth st.
——Miss Maggie
——Miss May
——R. M.
——Edward L.
Fletcher, Frank A.; Oakland

Flint, Mr and Mrs E. Du Bois; Myrtle st.   *Tuesday*
Flint, Mr and Mrs Edward P.; 521 Thirteenth st.   *Tuesday*
———Miss Helen P.
———Miss Alice M.
Flint, Harry L.; Glen Echo, off Piedmont ave.
Folkers, G. A. W.; 915 Myrtle st.
Folger, Mrs James A.; 1308 Jackson st.   *Wednesday*
———Mr Earnest
———James A., Jr.
Foote, Mr and Mrs W. W.; 504 Thirteenth st.
Forrest, Mr and Mrs C. T.; Webster st.
Fox, Judge and Mrs Charles N.; 1057 Market st.
———Miss
———George H.
Francis, Miss; " Rose," Claremont ave.
Freeman, Captain and Mrs E. M.; 1019 Linden st.
———Miss
Freeman, Mr and Mrs Littlejohn; 1724 Lincoln st.
Fry, Mr and Mrs Willis B.; 513 Frederick st.   *Thursday*

Gage, Mr and Mrs Steven T.; 1300 Harrison st.
Gamble, Mr James; Piedmont
———The Misses
———Lenan
Garber, Judge and Mrs John; Claremont ave., North Temescal   *Thursday*
———Miss Belle
———John, Jr.
Garcelon, Mrs Kate; 1213 Madison st.
Garthwaite, Mr and Mrs W. W.; Prospect Heights   *Thursday*
———Mrs H.
———Mrs C. T.
———Mrs Alice
Gaskill, Mr and Mrs George C.; Oakland
Gaskill, Mrs Rollin C.; Oakland
Gaskill, Mr and Mrs D. W. C.; 1395 Harrison st.
———Burt
———Mr and Mrs Barney W.
Gibbons, William H.; Alameda
Gibbs, William C.; 154 Third st.
Gibson, Judge and Mrs E. M.; Hays' Canyon
Gibson, Miss G.; Olive House   *Wednesday*
Gifford, Mr and Mrs W. B.; Oakland
Gilbert, Charles W.; Oakland
Gilman, Dr and Mrs S. M.; Prospect ave.

Girvin, Mr & Mrs J. W.; Claremont ave., Lorin, Alameda Co. *Wednesday*
Glasscock, Mr and Mrs John R.; Sixth and Jackson sts.
Glen, Mr and Mrs A. G.; cor. Julia and Monroe   *Tuesday*   Fruitvale
Goldsmith, Paul; Blake House
Goodall, Capt and Mrs Edwin; Jackson st.   Europe
——Miss
——Arthur
Goodfellow, Mrs M. J.; 1353 Webster st.
——Miss Bessie
Goodfellow, Mr and Mrs W. S.; 1363 Sixth ave., East Oakland
Goodwin, Mr and Mrs Millard F.; 1628 Seventh st., East Oakland
Gordan, Mr and Mrs Harry F.; 1353 Webster st.
Gordan, Mr and Mrs J. E.; 473 Merrimac st.
Gordon, Mr and Mrs N. H.; 1431 Webster st.
Gowell, Mr and Mrs Orrin; 2121 East 14th st.   *Wednesday* **Nevada City**
——Miss Edyth L.
Grant, Mr and Mrs G. E.; 1303 Third ave., East Oakland
——Miss Abbie
Grant, Mr and Mrs George; Highland Park   *Wednesday*
Graves, Mr and Mrs W. H. H.; 512 Seventeenth st.
Grayson, Mr and Mrs George W.; cor. Ninth and Madison sts., Iowa Hill
——Robert R.
Green, Mr and Mrs Adam T.; Berkeley
Greene, Judge and Mrs W. E. 1226 Fourteenth st.
——Miss Mabel E.
——Miss Ethel
Gregory, Mr and Mrs H. P.; cor. Durant and Jackson sts.
Grey, Mr and Mrs Geo. B. M.; 767 Alice st.   *Monday*
Griffin, Mrs S. E.; Jackson and Lake sts.   *Wednesday*
——Miss Mamie
——Frank
——Morris
Grimes, Mr Everett M.; cor. East Fourteenth st. and Fifth ave.
——Miss
Grimwold, Mr and Mrs A. D.; Fruitvale
Gross, Miss Mable; Berkeley
Grove, Mr and Mrs S. E.; 810 East Fifteenth st.   *Tuesday*
Gild, Mr and Mrs C. B.; Oakland

Hackett, Capt and Mrs Edward; 1303 Jackson st.   *Wednesday*
——Capt John
Hager, Mr and Mrs E. C.; Prospect Heights
Haight, Mrs; Alice st.
——Miss Janet
——Harry Huntley
——Louis Montrose

Hale, Miss Mamie; 364 Peralta st.   *Tuesday*
Hale, Mr and Mrs W. E.; 1212 Castro st.   *Wednesday*
——Miss Sadie F.
Haley, Dr C. S.; Lake Shore ave.
Hall, Mr and Mrs E. M.; 1369 Jackson st.   *Wednesday*
——Miss Jennie
——Miss Hattie
Hamilton, Judge and Mrs Noble; 1271 Jackson st.   *Wednesday*
——Miss Nettie
——William B.
——Mr and Mrs Edward H.
Hamilton, Mr and Mrs William; 466½ Thirteenth st.   *Tuesday*
Handy, Mr and Mrs George W.; 1350 Madison st. { *Tuesday* "Glen Una," Santa Clara Co.
——Miss
Hanford, Mr and Mrs James N.; 1205 Peralta st.
——Miss
Hansen, Chas. R.; Golden Gate, Berkeley
——Chas. R., Jr.
Harmon, Mr and Mrs A. K. P.; 1568 Webster st.   *Thursday*
——Mr and Mrs A. K. P., Jr.; Fruitvale
Harmon, D.; 961 Jackson st.
Harmon, Mr and Mrs J. B.; Fruitvale
Harries, Mr and Mrs W. H.; 1361 Jackson st.
Harrington, Mrs L.; 1167 Jackson st.
——Miss Agnes
Harrison, Mr and Mrs R. T.; 616 Third st.
Harrison, A. D.; San Antonia ave. bet. Morton and Paru; Alameda
Harrul, W. B.; 3558 Pacific ave., West End, Alameda
Hart, Mr and Mrs Jackson; Twelfth and Market sts.
——Miss Frankie
Harvey, Mr and Mrs Le Roy G.; 1123 Filbert st.   *Thursday*
Hathaway, Mr and Mrs Charles W.; Sycamore Park, San Lorenzo
——Miss Minnie
Haven, Mr and Mrs Charles D.; Eighth and Chestnut sts.   Sonoma
Haven, Mr and Mrs James; Brooklyn Heights
Haven, Mr and Mrs William P.; 1124 Adeline st.
Havens, Mr and Mrs A. W.; 1652 Webster st.
Havens, Mr and Mrs Howard; Alameda
Havens, Frank C.; Vernon Heights
Hawley, Mr and Mrs C. J.; 1118 Seventh ave., East Oakland
Hawley, Mr and Mrs George T.; Summit ave., Prospect Heights
Hawley, Mr and Mrs George W.; Clinton ave.
Hawley, Mr and Mrs J. C.; 522 Knox Place

Hawley, Mr and Mrs Levi H.; 2100 Telegraph ave.
Hawley, Mrs L. M.; 1226 Fruitvale ave., Fruitvale   *Monday*
Hayes, Mr and Mrs C. E.; 527 East Eleventh st., East Oakland
Hayes, Mr and Mrs J. R.; Centre and Seventh sts.   *Monday*
——Miss
——Miss Mamie
Hayes, Mr and Mrs Thomas R.   Santa Cruz
———The Misses
——Mr and Mrs Edward
Hays, Mr and Mrs John C., Jr.; Alameda   *Wednesday*
Heim, Mr and Mrs J. F.; 1361 Market st.   *Wednesday*
Henderson, Miss Minnie; Fruitvale
Hendy, Dr and Mrs G. W.; Fifteenth and Madison sts.
Henry, Mr and Mrs A. C.; 1221 Harrison st.
Henshaw, Judge and Mrs Frederick W.; Eighth and Filbert sts.
Henshaw, Mr and Mrs W. G.; East Fourteenth st. and Fifth ave.
Henshaw, Mrs Sarah E.; 941 Myrtle st.
——Tyler
——Mr and Mrs E. T.
Hernden, Miss Norma; Alameda
Herrick, Mr and Mrs E. M.; Webster st.   *Wednesday* **Saratoga, Cal.**
——Lester
Herrick, Mr and Mrs W. F.; 1302 12th st.   *Tuesday*
——The Misses
——Wm. A.
Hesse, Prof Frederick G.; 801 Jackson st.
Hewes, Mr and Mrs David   Europe
Hickman, Mr and Mrs L. M.; 1360 Madison st.   *Wednesday*
——Miss Macie
Hickman, Mrs R. D.; 1006 Franklin st.
Hickock, Mr and Mrs Arthur M.; Central ave., Alameda
Hickock, Mr and Mrs B. E.; 1155 Madison st.   *Tuesday*
High, Mr and Mrs W. H., Jr; 1432 Webster st.   { *Tuesday* {Grimes, Colusa Co.
Hilgard, Prof and Mrs Eugene W.; Berkeley   *Tuesday* **Mission San Jose**
——Miss
——Miss Alice R.
Hilligess, Mrs Maria; Berkeley
——The Misses
Hinckley, Mr and Mrs D. B.; Fruitvale
Hinkle, Dr and Mrs J. M.; 268 East Tenth st.; East Oakland
Hinchman, Mr and Mrs T. W.; Railroad ave. and Morton st., Alameda
——The Misses
——Charles H.
——Woodworth H.

Hofer, Mr and Mrs Grandjan ; 1674 Telegraph ave.
Holbrook, Mr and Mrs E. A.; 107 Thirteenth st.   *Friday*
Hook, Dr and Mrs W. E.; Jackson st.
Hook, Mr E. ; Tenth and Madison sts.
——Miss Nellie
——Henry
Hopkins, C. T.; Oakland
Horton, Mrs Sarah W.; 964 Eighteenth st.
Hostetter, Mr and Mrs Frank ; Thirteenth ave. and Fifteenth st., East
·——Miss Etta   [Oakland
Houghton, Harry B.; NE cor. Eighth and Broadway
Howard, Mr and Mrs John L.; Vernon Heights.   *Thursday*
Howell, Mr and Mrs John G.; 669 Seventeenth st.
Howell, Albert; Oakland
Howell, Mr and Mrs M. D.; 1317 Alice st.
Hubbard, Mr and Mrs Samuel ; NE cor. Webster and Twenty-second sts.
——Charles P.   [*Thursday*
Hunt, Mrs Jonathan ; Glen Echo
——Miss
——Miss Daisy
——H. O.
——Mr and Mrs S. O.
Howard, Mrs Charles Webb; Alice st., nr. Thirteenth
——Miss
——O. S.
——Carl
Hush, Mr and Mrs V. G.; E. Fourteenth st., Fruitvale
——Miss Estelle; Brooklyn (summer)
——Miss Hattie   "   "
Hutchinson, Mr and Mrs; Eighth and Brush sts.   *Wednesday*
——Miss
Hyde, Wallace E.; Oakland
Hyde, Mrs W. B.; 1825 Telegraph ave.   *Thursday*

Ingram, Mr and Mrs H. C.; Washington, Cal., Irvington, Cal. *Tuesday*
Irish, Mr and Mrs John P.; 1438 Adeline st.
——Miss
Issacs, Mr and Mrs J. D.; Thirteenth and Alice sts.

Jackson, Mr and Mrs D. H.; Eighth ave. & Fifteenth st., East Oakland
——Miss Gail
Jackson, Mr and Mrs D. A.; 1211 7th ave., East Oakland   *Wednesday*
Jacobs, Mr and Mrs N. A.; 125 Thirteenth st.   *Mondays*
Janin, Mr and Mrs L. B.; 1355 Webster st.

Johnson, Mr and Mrs M. M.; 122 Ninth st.
——Miss Alice
Johnson, Mr and Mrs W. P.; Merrimac st., near Webster st.
Johnson, Mr and Mrs John; 767 Alice st.
Jones, Mr and Mrs N. G.; 4th ave., bet. 13th & 14th sts., East Oakland
Jones, Mrs Vernon; Orchard st., near Telegraph ave.
Jordan, Mr and Mrs Frank C.; Santa Clara and Central aves., Alameda
Jordan, Mr and Mrs W. S.; Market st. near Fourteenth st.
Jorgensen, Carl; 1363 Seventeenth st.

Kahn, Miss Henrietta; 778 Ninth st.   *Wednesday*
Kahn, Mr and Mrs Solomon; 762 Ninth st.   *Wednesday*
Keith, W.; Berkeley
Kellogg, Charles W.; 1253 Grove st.
Kellogg, Prof and Mrs Martin; Berkeley
Kelly, Mr and Mrs H. W.; 1214 Brush st.
Kelsey, Mr and Mrs Noah; 130 Ninth st.
Kendall, Mr and Mrs Frank I.; 1258 Grove st.
Kenna, P. J. G.; Fruitvale
Kimball, C. H.; 1350 Jackson st.
——The Misses
——Mr Fred
King, Mr and Mrs George Lyman; 779 Eighth st.   *Wednesday*
Kipp, W. I., Jr.; Berkeley
Kirkham, General and Mrs R. W.; Oak and Eighth sts.
——Miss Kate
Kirkland, Joseph B.; Alameda
Knight, Mr and Mrs Allen; 1424 Webster st.
——Mr N. R.
Knight, Mr and Mrs W. H.; 1300 Jackson st.
Knowles, Capt and Mrs Josiah N.; 1300 Webster st.
——The Misses
Knox, Dr and Mrs .H E.; 480 Merrimac st.
——Miss Mary
——Harry I.
Knox, Mr and Mrs Israel; Knox place and Telegraph ave.
Knox, Mrs R. G.; 1825 Telegraph ave.   *Thursday*   **Pacific Grove**
Koerber, Mr and Mrs August; Alameda
Kunath, Mr and Mrs Oscar; Alameda
Kurtz, Mrs B. C.; 521 Thirteenth st.   *Tuesday*

Lamreaux, Miss Mamie; Petaluma ave.   **San Rafael** *
Landsberger, Mr and Mrs Isador; Alameda
——Miss
——Mr and Mrs Henry M.

Langley, Miss Melanie ; 156 E. Twelfth st., East Oakland
———Charles F.
Lathrop, John ; 1263 Twelfth ave.
Lathrope, Rev and Mrs H. D. ; East Oakland
———John M.

Le Conte, Prof and Mrs John ; Dwight way, Berkeley
Le Conte, Prof and Mrs Joseph ; Bancroft way, Berkeley
Lewis, Dr and Mrs W. F. ; 810 E. 15th st.   *Tuesday* **Rio Vista Rancho**
———Irving C.
———John M.

Leckie, Mr and Mrs Robert ; 977 Sixth ave., East Oakland   *Monday*
Leiske, Mr and Mrs Robert ; East Oakland
Liliencrantz, Dr and Mrs August ; Thirteenth and Madison sts.
Little, Col and Mrs William C. ; Broadway near Moss ave.
Livermore, Mr and Mrs H. P. ; Rocridge Park   }   *Wednesday* **Monterol, Napa Co.**

———Miss Grace
Liewellyn, Mrs E. ; San Lorenzo
Lohman, Mrs Fannie E. ; Lake and Madison sts.   *Wednesday*
———Miss Jennie
———Miss Fannie
Lucas, Mrs William ; Twelfth st. and Third ave.
Lunt, Mr and Mrs O. A. ; Alameda
Lyon, Mr and Mrs W. Parker ; SW cor. Eleventh and Grove sts.

MacDonald, A. S. ; 468 Ninth st.
MacDonarld, Miss L. S. ; 484 Merrimac st.
Magee, Thos. H. ; Fruitvale
———Mr Tom
———Mr Will

Magill, Mr and Mrs Arthur E. ; 310 East Seventeenth st., East Oakland
Mallory, Miss M. B. ; Twelfth st. and Third ave.
Mangels, Christopher ; Alameda
Mansfeldt, Mr and Mrs Hugo ; 1163 Alice st.   *Thursday*
Marcellus, Mr and Mrs E. P. ; 555 Nineteenth st.
Marriot, Mr and Mrs F. ; Willow and Alameda ave., Alameda *Thursday*
Marsh, Mr and Mrs E. B ; Field Seminary
Marston, E. W. ; 1391 Webster st.
Martin, Mr and Mrs J. West ; 720 Fourteenth st.
———Shelby
———Richard

Martin, Miss Ruth E. ; Centennial House
Marwedel, Mr and Mrs Edward H. ; 163 Tenth st.   *Friday*
Masten, Mr and Mrs Joseph N. ; 1428 Webster st.

Masten, Mr and Mrs J. M.; 1232 Madison st.   *Wednesday*
——Mr and Mrs N. K.
——Miss Irene
——Georgie
——Louis
Mastick, Mr and Mrs C. L.; Central ave. and Oak st., Alameda
Mastick, Mr and Mrs E. B.; Pacific ave. and Prospect st., Alameda
——The Misses
Mastick, Mr and Mrs George H.; Pacific ave. and Wood st., Alameda
Mastick, Mr and Mrs R. W.; Santa Clara ave. and Willow st., Alameda
Mathews, Mr and Mrs E. G.; 104 E. 12th st., E. Oakland   *Wednesday*
Marweda, Mr and Mrs E. N.; 215 Ninth st.   *Friday*
Mauzy, Dr and Mrs R. D.; 730 Eleventh st.   *Tuesday*
——Miss Alice
——Byron
Mauzy, Dr and Mrs W. P.; 814 Fourteenth st.   *Wednesday*
Maxwell, Mr and Mrs George H.; Berkeley
May, Mr and Mrs A. W.; 527 East 11th st., East Oakland   *Thursday*
——Miss Rosa
McChesney, Prof and Mrs J. B.; 1350 Franklin st.
McClure, Rev and Mrs David; Caledonia ave.
McCoy, Mr and Mrs Charles; 62 East 12th st., East Oakland
McCurrie, John P.; Alameda
McCutchen, Mr and Mrs E. J.; Alameda
McDonald, Frank V.; Berkeley
McElrath, Major and Mrs J. E.; 668 Sixteenth st
——Miss M.
McGilvray, Mr and Mrs Wm. D.; 1267 Twelfth ave., East Oakland
McGillivray, Joseph; 1365 Franklin st.
——John
——William
McKee, Mrs Samuel B.; 1033 Adeline st.   *Monday*
——Miss Nellie
——Miss Amy
——Samuel B.
——J. C.
McKenna, James; Alameda
McKisick, Judge and Mrs L. D.; 1167 Castro st.   Del Monte
——Miss Rose
McKnight, Mr and Mrs Andrew J.; Fruitvale
McLean, Edward; Encinal Park, Alameda
McLean, Rev and Mrs J. K.; 520 Thirteenth st.
McNear, Mr and Mrs George W.; Linden and 10th sts.
——John A.
——George
——Seward

Mead, Mr and Mrs L. R.; Oakland   Hotel Rafael
Mead, Le Grande; Alameda
Mead, William H.; Temescal
Mead, Mr and Mrs Calvert; 1315 Myrtle st.
Mecartney, Mr and Mrs Amos; Bay Farm Island, Alameda
Meehan, Mr and Mrs Jesse P.; Oakland   Lake Tahoe
Meek, H. W.; San Lorenzo
Melvin, Mr and Mrs S. H.; 358 East Fourteenth st., East Oakland
Merriam, Mr and Mrs Charles; Berkeley
Merrill, Mr and Mrs Thomas L.; 457 Merrimac Place
Metcalf, Mr and Mrs George D.; Berkeley
Metcalf, Mr and Mrs Victor H.; 1263 Harrison st.
Meyer, Mr and Mrs J. Henry; Berkeley
Mhoon, Major John B.; 1017 Adeline st.
Miller, Mr and Mrs Geo.; cor. Alice and Thirteenth sts.
——Miss
Miller, Miss Agnes; 1224 Webster st.
Miller, Mr and Mrs Albert; Fourteenth and Union sts.   *Monday*
——Miss Charlotte
——Miss Annie
——Harry East
——Horace H.
Miller, Mr and Mrs Charles E.; Alameda
Miller, Mr and Mrs C. O.G.; 1001 Adeline st.
Miller, Edward H., Jr.; Alameda
Miller, Robert W.; Galindo Hotel
Miller, Mr and Mrs W. E.; 1277 Webster st.   *Wednesday*
Mills, Mrs C. T.; Seminary Park
Millnack, Miss Jessie; 836 Eighteenth st., Oakland   *Friday*
Mininger, Mrs Adeline; Broadway and R. R. ave; Alameda   *Thursday*
——Miss Grace
Moe, Mrs George W.; 520 Thirteenth st.
Moffit, Mr and Mrs James; Broadway and Twenty-second sts. *Wednesday*
Montague, Mrs Samuel C.; 1019 Filbert st.
Moore, Mr and Mrs A. A.; 6th ave. and 20th st. East Oakland *Tuesday*
-——Miss
Moore, Mr and Mrs J. P.; 1010 Franklin st.
Moore, Mr and Mrs R. S.; 1101 Adeline st.
Moore, Mr and Mrs Joseph; 1099 Adeline st.
——The Misses
Morgan, Mr and Mrs Benjamin; Berkeley
Morgan, Mr and Mrs C. B.; 1363 Castro st.
Morgan, Mr and Mrs Cosmo; Berkeley
Morgan, Mr and Mrs James; 120 East Fourteenth st.; East Oakland

Morris, Mr and Mrs William; 1428 Webster st.   *Tuesday*
Moses, Prof and Mrs B.; Berkeley
Moss, Prof Bernard; Berkeley
Mowe, Mrs George W.; 1313 Madison st.   *Wednesday*
Murdock, Mr and Mrs George H.; Alameda

Nagle, Mr and Mrs H. H.; 973 Fifth ave., East Oakland
Nahl, Mr and Mrs; Alameda
Naylor, Mr and Mrs Chas. E.; Alameda   *Thursday*
Neal, Mr and Mrs Charles S.; Morton station, Alameda
Nelson, Capt and Mrs Charles; Seminary Park
——Miss
——Miss Maggie
Nicholson, Dr and Mrs J. E.; 626 Eighth st.
——Miss
Newton, Mr and Mrs; Peralta Heights.   *Thursday*
·——Miss Alice
——Miss Jessie
——Miss Mabel
Nichols, Charles M; 1062 Seventh ave., East Oakland
Nicholson, Mr and Mrs J. H.; 462 Twenty-second st.
Noble, Mr and Mrs Burr; 1327 Broadway, Alameda.   *Tuesday*
——Miss Pearl
——Miss Maud
North, Mr and Mrs George L.; Alameda

O'Brien, Col and Mrs W. H.; Claremont ave.   *Friday*   **Napa Co.**
Oliver, William Letts; 1110 Twelfth st.   *Wednesday* { Yacht *Emerald* Santa Cruz
Olney, Mr and Mrs Warren D.; 481 Prospect ave.
Olsen, John; 1765 Lincoln st.
——Henry
O'Meara, Miss Jennie; Park st. station, Alameda
Orr, Mr and Mrs John K.; 928 Linden st.   *Thursday*
——Miss
——Miss Edna
Otis, Mr and Mrs Frank; Santa Clara ave. & Paru st., Alameda. *Thursday*
O'Toole, Dr and Mrs M. C.; North Berkeley
Ott, F. W.; Oakland
Owens, John K.; Alameda
——Miss Mamie

Palache, Mr and Mrs James Claremont ave. "Fairview." *Wednesday*
——The Misses
Palmer, Mr and Mrs C. T. H.; Piedmont ave., Berkeley

Palmer, Mr and Mrs Frank; 592 Sycamore st.
Pardee, Dr and Mrs E. H.; 672 Eleventh st.
Pardee, Dr and Mrs George C.; 1367 Eighth ave., East Oakland
Partridge, Mr and Mrs Samuel; 1222 Webster st.   *Thursday*
Patten, Mrs F. A.; 1628 Seventh ave., East Oakland
Paulsell, A. C.; 1319 Grove st.
Payne, George H.; West End, Alameda
Pannoyer, Mr & Mrs Albert A.; 1353 Alice st.   *Wednesday* P.O. Box 107
Perine, Miss Eva; 1317 Jackson st.   *Wednesday*
Perine, Mr and Mrs N. P.; Fruitvale
——Miss Florence
Perine, Mr and Mrs W. D.; 809 Oak st.
——Miss Madge
Perkins, Hon and Mrs George C.; cor. Vernon & Oakland ave.   *Thursday*
——Miss Susie   [Del Monte
Perry, Senator and Mrs George H.: Alameda
Pierce, Mr and Mrs C. D.; 1416 Grove st.   *Wednesday*   Lake Tahoe
Peterson, Capt S. B.; 1218 Grand st., Alameda
——Miss Carrie
——Mr and Mrs Frederick C.
——Frank B.
Pheby, Mr and Mrs Thomas B.; 1275 Alice st.   *Tuesday*
——Miss Elise
——Fred
Phillips, Mr and Mrs J. W.; 977 Sixth ave., East Oakland   *Monday*
——Miss
——Miss Mamie
Phillips, Mr and Mrs William A.; 1922 San Pablo ave.   *Wednesday*
——Robert B.
Pierce, Marshall; 459 Merrimac st.
——Miss Josephine
Pierce, Mr and Mrs Orestes; Vernon Heights
Pierce, W. Frank; 568 Eighteenth st.
Pillsbury, Miss Edith; Alameda
Pinkham, Frank; Galindo Hotel, Oakland
Pinkerton, Mrs G. H.; 1014 Broadway
Pitman, Mrs Capt H. C.; Berkeley
Poindexter, Mr and Mrs Frank H.; Alameda
Pond, Mrs Ella C.; Berkeley
Porter, Mrs W. H.; 1156 Madison st.   *1st and 3d Tuesdays*
Posey, Dr and Mrs A. C.; 11th ave. and 22d st., East Oakland
Potter, Mr and Mrs E. E.; 1305 Twelfth ave., East Oakland
Powell, Mr and Mrs Wm.; Berkeley
Powning, Mr and Mrs Joseph; 1115 Third ave. East Oakland   Pine Glen
——Will A.

Prather, Mr and Mrs Thomas; 1253 Alice st.   *Thursday*
Prather, Mr and Mrs W. L.; 507 Eleventh st.
——The Misses
Prescott, Mr and Mrs F. S.; 1366 Tenth ave., East Oakland   *Wednesday*
Pringle, Mr and Mrs E. J.; 826 East Nineteenth st., East Oakland
——Miss
——Edward

Rabe, Mr and Mrs William; 1406 Alice st.   *Wednesday*
——Miss Francis Louise
——W. H.
Ralston, Mr and Mrs A. Jackson; Hotel Crellen   *Thursday*   **Santa Cruz**
——Miss Claire
——Lewis
Ralston, Mrs Lizzie F.; 172 Thirteenth st   *Wednesday*   **Michigan Bluff**
——Miss B.,
Ralston, Mr and Mrs William C.; Visit at cor. Ninth & Madison   *Auburn*
Ramsden, Mr and Mrs Chas H.
Randall, Mr and Mrs Chas. W.; Piedmont
Randolph, Daniel L.; Alameda
Ransome, Mr and Mrs Ernest L.; 1505 Tenth ave., East Oakland
——Leslie
Redington, Mr and Mrs Joseph; Alice st.
Reed, Mr and Mrs George W.; 974 Sixteenth st.
Requa, Mr and Mrs Isaac L.; Highlands, Piedmont   *Wednesday*
——Miss Amy
——Mark L.
Reynolds, Major and Mrs G. P.; 1855 Central ave., Alameda
Riley, Mr and Mrs P. T.; Berkeley
Risdon, Mr and Mrs Robert; Eighth and Myrtle sts.
Rising, Miss S. A.; 914 Castro st.   *Tuesday*
Rising, Prof and Mrs W. B.; Allston and Chapel, Berkeley
Robinson, Mr and Mrs Samuel; Park Hotel, Alameda   *Friday*
Robinson, Miss May; 917 Peralta st.   *Thursday*   **San Rafael**
Rodolph, Mr and Mrs C. T.; 1409 Brush st.
Rogers, Mr and Mrs Henry; 1209 Jackson st.   *Wednesday*
Romer, Eugene; 1926 Alameda ave., Alameda
Roos, Joseph; Alameda
Rosborough, Judge & Mrs A. M.; 1769 19th ave., Highland Park *Tuesday*
——Miss Fannie
——Mr A. J.
Russ, Mr and Mrs Frederick; Claremont
Russell, Mr and Mrs John A.; Pacific and First ave., Alameda
——Miss Jean
——Miss Ada
Ruther, Mr and Mrs Fred; 1316 Tenth st.   *Wednesday*

162

Sargent, Mrs A. B.; 437 Hawthorne st.   *Monday*
Sather, Mrs Pedar; Twelfth and Grove sts.
Saunders, Mrs J. M.; Olive House   *Wednesday*
Savage, Mr and Mrs W. C.; Broadway   *Wednesday*
Sawyer, Mrs Anna M.; Berkeley
Scott, Mr and Mrs Paul; Alameda
Seabury, Capt and Mrs; Berkeley   Steamer "Rio Janeiro"
Seaman, Mr and Mrs George B; 1204 Harrison st.
Sears, Judge and Mrs; San Leandro
——Miss Stella
Sears, Mr and Mrs H. B.; Fourteenth and Chestnut sts.
——H. B., Jr.
Seaton, Mr and Mrs Horace H., cor. Jackson and Lake sts. *Wednesday*
——Mr and Mrs William
Selby, Mr and Mrs Prentiss; Alice st.   *Thursday*   Santa Cruz
——Prentiss, Jr.
Selfridge, Dr Grant; 312 Fourteenth st.   *Friday*
——Dr J. M.
Sessions, Mr and Mrs E. C.; Highland Park, East Oakland
Shanklin, Mr and Mrs J. W.; 938 Filbert st.
Shattuck, Mr and Mrs Charles H.; Central ave., Alameda   *Thursday*
Shattuck, Mr and Mrs F. K.; Shattuck ave., Berkeley
Shay, Mr and Mrs Frank; Alameda
Sheldon, John P.; 932 Fourteenth st.
Shephard, Mrs A. A.; Berkeley   *Tuesday*
Shephard, Mr and Mrs J. L. N.; San Pablo ave.   *Thursday*
——Miss Madeline
——Miss Louise
Shephard, Mr and Mrs Morgan; San Pablo ave.
Shephard, Capt and Mrs L. G.; 1303 Seventh ave.   *Friday*
Shepherd, John E; 1123 Peralta st.
Shepherd, L. F.; 1217 Franklin st.
Sherman, Mr and Mrs Richard M.; 620 Fourteenth st.
——The Misses
Sherman, William; 620 Fourteenth st.
——Miss Lizzie
Simons, Mrs O.; 277 Second st.
——J. E.
Simons, Mr and Mrs Stuart; Alameda
Simpson, Mr and Mrs A. M.; 1265 Grove st.
Simpson, Mrs T. B.; 1653 Telegraph ave.   *Thursday*
——Miss Marianna
——Miss Lucy
Smith, Mr and Mrs F. M.; Eighth ave. and E. Twenty-fourth st.

Smith, Mr and Mrs A. D.; 910 Myrtle st.   *Wednesday*
——Miss
——Leon D.
——Harry
——Frank

Smith, Mr and Mrs H. B., Jr.; cor. Berton and Central aves.   Alameda
Smith, Mr and Mrs George E.; 1063 Eleventh st.
Smith, Henry L.; 768 Ninth st.
Snell, Miss Mary E.; 568 Twelfth st.   *Tuesday*
——Miss Sarah H.
——Mr and Mrs R. B.

Snow, S. A.; 719 Eighth st.
Soule, Prof and Mrs Frank; Oak and Tenth sts.   *Tuesday*
Spaulding, Mr and Mrs Nathan W.; Highland Park, East Oakland *Friday*
Sperry, Mrs M. S.; Sixteenth and Jefferson sts.
——Miss Minnie
——Miss Beda

Squire, Henry P.; Eleventh st., near Alice st.
St. John, Chauncey M.; Oakland
Stanley, Judge and Mrs A.; 1221 Jackson st.   *Wednesday* **Del Monte**
Stanford, Mrs J.; 1218 Oak st.
—— –Mrs

Starr, Mr and Mrs A. D.; 1353 Grove st. *Monday*
Starr, Mrs L. M.; Fifth ave., East Oakland
Steele, Mr and Mrs Edward L. G.; 824 Jackson. st.   *Thursday*
——William

Stephenson, Mr and Mrs C. V.; 118 Ninth st.   *Thursday*
Stevens, Mrs Levi; Fruitvale
——Miss O. E.
——Miss Dollie

Stewart, Mrs Wm. M.; Alameda
Stolp, Mr and Mrs G. M.; 118 Thirteenth st., Oakland
——Fred A.

Stone, Mr; 1825 Telegraph ave.   *Thursday*   **Boston**
——Miss Sophie

Stone, Mr and Mrs Byron F.; 1311 Harrison st.
Stone, Mrs R. Catherine; Field Seminary   *Thursday*
Stubbs, David D.; Alameda
Swenarton, Mr and Mrs J. A.; 1374 Franklin st.
Swift, Mr and Mrs Samuel; 1112 East Sixteenth st., East Oakland
Swyney, W. J.; Railroad ave. and Benton st., Alameda
——The Misses
——Robert

128

Taber, Mr and Mrs I. W.; 1351 Madison st.   *Tuesday*
——Miss Daisy
Taft, H. C.; 1363 Harrison st.
Taylor, Mr and Mrs Arthur C.; East Oakland
Taylor, Mr and Mrs Chauncey; NW cor. Castro and Eighth sts.
Taylor, Mr and Mrs William H.; Fifteenth and Castro sts.
Theobald, Mr and Mrs R. W.; Alameda
Templeton, M. F.; E. Fourteenth st., Fruitvale
Tevis, Mr and Mrs Joshua; 2051 E. Fourteenth st., E. Oakland *Saturday*
——Carter
——Dr Samuel
Thomas, Mr and Mrs J. P.; Alameda
Thomas, Mr and Mrs R. P.; Berkeley
Thomas, Mr and Mrs W. D.; 561 E. Eleventh st., East Oakland
——Miss Clara S.
——Miss Maggie A.
Thompson, R. B.; Summit ave.
Thompson, Mrs M. J.; 17th ave. and E. 25th st., East Oakland *Thursday*
——Miss Josephine
Thomson, Mr and Mrs A. D.; 1115 Jackson st., Oakland   *Wednesday*
——Miss Mollie R. Conners
—— Miss Maggie Conners
Thors, Mr and Mrs Louis; College ave., Berkeley

Tibus, Frank F.
Tibus, F. E.; 956 Myrtle st., Oakland, Cal.
Tibus, Mr and Mrs Daniel.   *Wednesday*
——Miss Edith
Tibbey, Miss Sadie; Alameda
Tompkins, Mrs Sarah; 1271 Jackson st.   *Wednesday*   **San Leandro**
——The Misses
——Burt
Touchard, Mr and Mrs G. L.; 1077 Eighth st.
——Albert
Trembly, Dr and Mrs J. B.; Eighth and Myrtle sts.
Tubbs, Mr and Mrs Hiram; Fifth ave. and Twelfth st., East Oakland
——The Misses
Tucker, Dr and Mrs J. C.; 1051 Market st.
——Miss Etta B.
——Miss Mae
——Miss Clare
Tuttle, Mr and Mrs C. A., Madison and Tenth sts.
Tyler, Mrs Maud; Alameda
——W. B.

Upham, Mr and Mrs Isaac; Hotel Merritt
Upham, Mr and Mrs Isaac; 1157 Oak st.   *1st and 2d Wednesdays*
——Isaac
——Benjamin

Van Loben Sels, Mr and Mrs P. J.; 1305 Adeline st.
Van Sicklen, Mr and Mrs F. W.; Central ave. and Union sts., Alameda
Van Tress, Mr and Mrs Frank; 811 Harrison st.
Vandenberg, Mr and Mrs S. L.; 1018 Adeline st.   *Monday*
Vinzent, Edward; 460 Eighth st.
Vrooman, Mrs Henry

Wade, Mr and Mrs E. E.; 1373 Eleventh ave., East Oakland
Wade, Mr and Mrs S. H.; 1375 Eleventh ave., East Oakland
Wadsworth, Mr and Mrs Henry; 1347 Alice st.   *Wednesday*
——Miss
——Henry E.
Wainright, Mr and Mrs Edward W.; Alemada
Walcott, Mr and Mrs J.; Bancroft Way, Berkeley
——Miss Mabel
——Miss Maud
——Earl A.
Wall, Mrs; Berkeley
——Dr B. P.
Wall, Mr and Mrs Jesse S.; 1439 Market st.
——Miss Louise
——Miss Bessie
——Miss Ella
Wallace, Mrs William H.; 2220 Broadway. *Friday* Rosemead, Tulare Co
——Miss
——Mr W. H.
Wandesforde, Mr and Mrs J. B.; Haywards
Ward, Mr and Mrs D. H.; 1216 Webster st.
Ward, Mr and Mrs Joseph W.; 517 Frederick st.
——Miss Hortense
Ward, Mr and Mrs J. Walter, Jr.; 1239 Linden.   *Monday*
Watkinson, Mr and Mrs J. H. T.; Merrimac Place and Webster st.
Waters, Miss Jennie; 568 Twelfth st.   *Tuesday*
Watkins, Mrs P. T.; Webster st.
Watson, Captain; Twenty-sixth st., near Broadway
——Horace
Watt, Mr and Mrs Robert; 1204 Madison st
—— Miss Janet
—— Miss Elizabeth L.
Wattles, Mr and Mrs William S.; Berkeley

W. B. CHAPMAN, 123 California Street   Fine Burgundies from the
Old Established House of
IMPORTER OF   Bouchard. Père & Fils. Beaune

Wellman, Mrs Bela; East Fourteenth st., East Oakland
——The Misses
——William
Wellman, Mrs R. A.   *Wednesday*   Fruitvale
——Alice K.
——Emma R.
——Jeanne A.
——William B.
Wentworth, Mr and Mrs Ira M.; West Berkeley
West, Mr and Mrs Albert A.; 1977 Webster st.   *Wednesday*
Weston, Mr and Mrs B. F.; 150 Lake st.   *Friday*   Santa Clara
Weston, Mrs Sarah S.; 1245 Webster st.
——F. F.
Westover, Mr and Mrs C.; 610 Twelfth st.
Wetherbee, Mr and Mrs Henry; Fruitvale
Wharton, Mr and Mrs George H.; Oakland
——Miss Bessie
Wheaton, Mr and Mrs George H.; 160 Lake st.   *Tuesday*
——Miss Bessie
——George
——Will.
Wheaton, Mrs William R.; 1060 Poplar st.
——The Misses
Wheelar, Capt R. J.; Claremont ave.   Lorin, Cal.
Whitcomb, Frank R.; Berkeley
White, Mrs.; Claremont ave., North Temescal   *Thursday*
White, Capt and Mrs; Highland Park
——Miss
Whitney, Mr and Mrs George; Eighth and Jefferson sts.
——Miss Violet
——The Misses
Whitney, Mr and Mrs S. A.; 1155 Madison st.   *Wednesday*
Whittaker, Mr and Mrs A. E.; 722 Eleventh st.
Wildes, Mr and Mrs Henry; Third ave. and Twelfth st.   { East Oakland
                                                    { *Wednesday*
Wildes, Mrs J. H.; Oakland
Wilcox, Mr and Mrs David; 1201 Alice st.   *Thursday*   San Jose
——Miss Minnie
——Miss Bertha
Wilkinson, Warring; cor. Warring and Dwight way, Berkeley
Wilkinson, Prof & Mrs C.; Dwight way and Col. ave., Bkly   { *Wednesday*
                                                        { Sonoma
Willard, Mr and Mrs G. H.; 122 Eleventh st.
——Miss
Willcutt, Mr and Mrs J. L.; Eighteenth st.

Williams, Mrs A. F.; 2131 Telegraph ave. *Wednesday*
——Mr and Mrs G. F.
Willcutt, Mr and Mrs George; Jones st. near Telegraph ave.
Williams, Mr and Mrs E. C.; 969 Brush st.
——Miss May
——Miss Mary
Winchester, Mr & Mrs J. P.; Pacific ave. bet. Wood&Chapin sts., Alameda
Winton, Mr and Mrs N. A.; 123 Ninth st.
Wood, Mrs Annie; 815 Thirteenth st.
Wood, Mr and Mrs C. L.; Bay st. and Pacific ave., Alameda
——Miss Annie V.
——Miss Mary K.
——Ed. C.
Wood, Mr and Mrs C. E. P.; 8th st. and 5th ave., E. Oakland *Thursday*
——Miss May
Wood, Mrs Eliza; 1008 Ninth ave., East Oakland
Woodard, Col and Mrs J. H.; 404 E. Sixteenth st., East Oakland.
Woolsey, Dr E. H.; Twelfth and Jackson sts.
Wright, Mrs C. S.; 758 Eighteenth st.
Wright, Mr and Mrs Geo. T. San Antonio ave., {*1st and 3d Thursdays* bet. Morton and Paru { Alameda
——Landsberger H. M.
——Harrison, A. D.
Wright, Paxton; 122 Ninth st.

Yates, Mr and Mrs Charles M.; Alameda
Yelland, Mr and Mrs.R. D.; 1464 Seventh ave., East Oakland
Younger, Dr and Mrs Edward A.; Alameda

132

Alameda Tennis Club

The Alameda Tennis Club was first organized in April, 1886, and was incorporated November 1, 1889. The object of the Club is of course the promotion of the game of Tennis. We have two asphaltum courts, and a very comfortable club house, situated on Encinal Avenue near Morton Street Station, Alameda.

BOARD OF DIRECTORS

A. D. HARRISON   DAVID MORRIS
AUGUST WATERMAN   H. M. LANDSBERGER
S. M. HASLETT

OFFICERS

A. D. HARRISON - - - - - President
DAVID MORRIS - - - - Vice-President
S. M. HASLETT - - Secretary and Treasurer

MEMBERS

Arthur M. Brown	Robert H. Swayne
O. C. Haslett	Jas. J. Fagan
Fred. P. Moore	S. M. Haslett
A. Dalton Harrison	Fred. Maurer, Jr.
Geo. T. Wright	H. M. Landsberger
Edw. A. Younger	Chas. S. Neal
J. C. Welsh	August Waterman
G. F. Newell	Percy E. Haslett
A. Carpentier	Geo. H. Murdock
A. Newbold	W. M. Rank
David Morris	Alfred H. Cohen
Henry Michaels	Chas. L. Tisdale
E. J. Dubbs	Geo. Coffee
F. W. Van Sicklen	F. H. McCormick
W. P. Fuller	W. A. Bissell
Edgar A. Cohen	Sidney Haslett
Arthur F. Allen	Sidney Allen

Allen S. Neal

LOS ANGELES

LOS ANGELES

Ackerman, Mr and Mrs; St. James Park *Wednesday*
Ainsworth, Dr and Mrs F. K.; Westminster Hotel *Monday*
Anderson, Judge and Mrs; 52 Lovelace ave. *Wednesday*
Ayres, Col and Mrs J. J.; Pearl st. *Tuesday*

Bailey, Capt and Mrs H. K.; 65 Estrella ave. *Wednesday*
Baker, Mr and Mrs Charles; Bellevue Terrace *Monday*
Baker, Mr and Mrs W. A.; 242 N. Main st., Baker Block *Monday*
Baldwin, Miss; Thorn Block
Banning, Mrs Mary; 431 N. Broadway *Thursday*
——Miss Mary
Bartlett, Mr and Mrs A. G.; 331 S. Olive st. *Wednesday*
Blake, Mr J. Fred; Bellevue Terrace
Boal, Mr and Mrs James R.; Figueroa and King sts. *Wednesday*
Bonebrake, Major George H.; 1610 Figueroa st. *Wednesday*
——Miss Blanche
Bonsall, Mr and Mrs J. P.; cor. Lucas and Arnold aves. *Friday*
Bowring, Mr and Mrs Henry; Pearl st. *Tuesday*
Boyce, Col and Mrs; Grand ave. *Wednesday*
Bradbeer, Mr and Mrs George; King st. *Wednesday*
Bradbury, Miss; cor. Hill and Court House *Monday*
Briggs, Mr W. R.; Baker Block *Monday*
Brooks, Mr and Mrs Benj.; San Luis Obispo   Kern
Browne, Miss Mary; 538 S. Pearl st. *Wednesday*
Buell, Dr and Mrs E. C.; S. Broadway near Third st. *Friday*
Burnett, Mr; 804 W. Twenty-third st. *Wednesday*
——Miss Lucia
Butler, Mrs; St. James Park *Wednesday*
Butler, Miss Jessie; The Melrose *Monday*

Carpenter, Mr and Mrs Charles C.; 1635 Ingrain st. *Friday*
Carron, Mr and Mrs Thomas J.; 721 W. Twenty-third st. *Wednesday*
——Miss Clara L.
——Mr T. J., Jr.
Caswell, Mr and Mrs William; 400 Grand ave. *Thursday*
Chandler, Mr and Mrs Burdette; 545 E. First st. *Tuesday*
Cheney, Judge and Mrs William; 936 S. Hill st. *Thursday*
Chichester, Rev William R.; W. Burlington ave.

Childs, Mrs O. W.; 1011 S. Main st.   *Tuesday*
——Miss
——Mr O. W., Jr.
Clacius, Dr and Mrs; cor. Pico and Figueroa sts.   *Wednesday*
Clark, Mr and Mrs A. K.; 1112 S. Hill st.   *Tuesday*
Clarke, Miss Daisy; Olive st.   *Monday*
Clay, Lieut T. J.; 1200 S. Olive st.
Clemons, Miss; 1635 Ingrain st.   *Friday*
Collins, Lieut and Mrs Charles; Westminster Hotel   *Monday*
Collins, Mr and Mrs Holdridge O.; St. James Park   *Wednesday*
Cole, Willoughby
Cosby, Mr and Mrs James F. Walter; Figueroa c. Brooklyn *Wednesday*
Creighton, Mr and Mrs Telfair; Los Angeles Theater Building *Monday*
Culver, Mr and Mrs J. P.; Grand ave. near Sixteenth st.   *Wednesday*
——Miss Flora
Culver, Miss; 1041 S. Hill st.   *Wednesday*

Damarin, Mrs Edith   *Friday*
Davis, Dr and Mrs John L.; Scarff st.   *Wednesday*
Davisson, Dr and Mrs; cor. Aliso and Michigan ave.   *Tuesday*
Dennis, Mr and Mrs L. W.
De Szigethy, Dr and Mrs Charles; 14 Main st.   *Monday*
Dewey, Miss Blanche; W. Jefferson st.   *Wednesday*
Dewey, Miss Z.; 1105 S. Hill st.   *Tuesday*
Dodsworth, Mr and Mrs Metcalf; 501 S. Main st.   *Thursday*
Ducomunn, Mr and Mrs Charles; S. Grand ave.   *Monday*
Dunkelberger, Mr and Mrs T. R.; 1000 N. Ninth st.   *Tuesday*
Dunn, Mr and Mrs Poindexter; Adams st. cor. Flower   *Wednesday*
——Miss
Dupuy, Mr and Mrs James R.; 204 W. Pico st.   *Friday*
——Miss
Dupuy, Mr Lowe
——Mr Robert

Elderkin, Mr and Mrs W. A.; Estrella ave.   *Wednesday*
——Miss Elise G.
Ellis, Rev and Mrs; Ellis College   *Friday*
——Miss
Ellis, Mr and Mrs Charles J.; cor. Ellis ave. and Scarff st.   *Wednesday*
Embody, The Misses; 1102 Downey ave., E. Los Angeles   *Thursday*
English, Mr and Mrs Taylor; Ellis ave.   *Wednesday*

Farrar, Mrs Wm. H.; 1003 South Hope st.   *Tuesday*
Finlayson, Mr and Mrs Jas. A.; 105 Daly st., E. Los Angeles   *Monday*
Fletcher, Mrs E. F. L.; 1112 S. Hill st.   *Tuesday*

Foreman, Mr and Mrs Charles ; 731 W. Pico st.   *Wednesday*
——Miss
——Mr Charles, Jr.
Forrester, Mr and Mrs E. A. ; 865 W. Seventh st.   *Thursday*
——Miss Mae
——Mr Art
Forrester, Mr and Mrs Charles ; 740 S. Pearl st.   *Thursday*
—— Miss Lena
——Mr Frank
Frankenfield, The Misses ; 1007 S. Hill st.   *Wednesday*
Francisco, Mr and Mrs A. W. ; 825 W. Ninth st.   *Thursday*
——Miss
——Mr J. Bond
——Mr A. W., Jr.
Friesner, Mr and Mrs W. M. ; Figueroa and Twenty-third st. *Wednesday*
Frye, Col and Mrs William ; cor. Central ave. and Ninth st.   *Tuesday*
Furrey, Major and Mrs W. C. ; 214 S. Broadway

Gates, Mr and Mrs C. W. ; 138 Hill st. ;
——Mr and Mrs Carroll ; 138 S. Hill st.   *Thursday*
Gephard, Mrs ; Hotel Pleasanton   *Monday*
——The Misses
Germain, Mr and Mrs Eugene ; 1030 Olive st.
Glassell, Mr and Mrs ; Waters near Temple st.
——Miss
Goodwin, Mr and Mrs L. C. ; 441 S. Broadway   *Thursday*
Graves, Dr and Mrs ; cor. Ottawa and Pearl sts.   *Wednesday*

Haralson, Mr and Mrs Orr ; cor. Flower and Tenth sts.   *Thursday*
Hart, Mr and Mrs Frank J. ; 156 S. Olive st.   *Thursday*
Hawkins, Mrs H. D. ; 211 S. Olive st.   *Thursday*
Hazard, Mr and Mrs Henry ; 209 S. Broadway   *Friday*
Hellman, Mr and Mrs I. W. ; S. Main and Fourth sts.   *Monday*
——Mr Marco
Henderson, Mr and Mrs J. A. ; Adams st.   *Wednesday*
——Miss
Hicks, Mr and Mrs Frank S. ; cor. Main and Eleventh sts   *Tuesday*
Hough, Mr and Mrs Deacon ; 815 Pearl st.   *Tuesday*
Houghton, Judge and Mrs S. O. ; 34 Orange ave.   *Thursday*
——The Misses
Howell, Mr and Mrs ; 1014 S. Hill st.   *Thursday*
——Miss
Hoyt, Miss
Hubbell, Mr and Mrs S. C. ; Aliso ave., Brooklyn Heights   *Thursday*
Hughs, Mrs Margaret ; St. James Park   *Wednesday*

Johnson, Mr and Mrs E. P.; 823 S. Hope st.   *Thursday*
——Miss
——Mr Sparx
——Mr E. P., Jr.
——Mr Ben
Jones, Mr and Mrs A. C.; Rich st.   *Monday*
Jones, Mrs Doria; St. Elmo Hotel   *Monday*
——Miss

King, Mr and Mrs George W ; W. Twenty-third st.   *Wednesday*
——Miss Frank
Klokke, Mr and Mrs E. F. C; Figueroa and York sts.   *Wednesday*
——Miss

Lacy, Mr and Mrs Wm.; Downey ave.   *Thursday*
——Miss
——Mr William
——Mr Richard
Lankershim, Mr and Mrs James B.; 850 S. Olive st.   *Monday*
Leck, Mr and Mrs Henry V.; Manhattan ave.   *Wednesday*
Lee, Mr and Mrs Henry T.; W. Adams st.   *Wednesday*
Lee, Mr and Mrs Bradner W.; 1105 S. Hope st.   *Tuesday*
Lewis, Mr and Mrs S. B.; Hotel Lincoln   *Thursday*
Lindley, Dr and and Mrs Walter S.; Fort near Sixth st.   *Thursday*
Littleboy, Mrs; 956 E. First st.   *Tuesday*
Lockhart, Miss Fannie; Ottawa st.
Lynch, Mr and Mrs Joe; Westminster Hotel   *Monday*
Lyon, Mr and Mrs William S.; 1400 Seventh st.

MacGowan, Dr and Mrs Granville D.; Edgar Block   *Monday*
Macneil, Mr and Mrs H. L.; Sixth st.   *Monday*
McKinley, Judge and Mrs; Adams st.   *Wednesday*
Mansfield, Mr and Mrs John; 301 Hill st.   *Thursday*
Masser, Dr and Mrs W. H.; cor Temple st. & Bunker Hill ave.   *Friday*
Maxwell, Mr and Mrs Walter; 509 S. Main st.   *Thursday*
——Miss Leita
Mayo, Mrs M. H.; 211 S. Olive st.   *Thursday*
——Miss Anna W.
McFarland, Mr and Mrs Dan; cor. Figueroa st. & Ellis ave.   *Wednesday*
Merrill, Mr and Mrs John; Figueroa st.   *Wednesday*
——Miss
Miles, Miss Sadie; Orange ave.   *Tuesday*
Mott, Col and Mrs T. D.; 543 S. Main st.   *Thursday*
Moore, Mr and Mrs W. S.; 153 Figueroa st.   *Wednesday*

Mortimer, C. White; (British Vice-Consul)
Munday, Mr and Mrs M. E. C.; Manhattan ave.   *Friday*

Neal, Mrs J. A.; Los Angeles Theater Building   *Monday*
——Miss
——Mr John A.
——Mr Thomas
Newell, Mr and Mrs H. T.; cor. Hill and Second sts.   *Tuesday*
——Miss
Newmark, Mrs H.; cor. Grand ave. and Eleventh st.
Newton, Mr and Mrs J. C.; 320 S. Olive st.   *Thursday*
——The Misses

Obear, Mr and Mrs James; Pasadena ave.   *Friday*
——Miss
O'Melveny, Mr and Mrs Henry; 26 Hansen st., E. Los Angeles *Thursday*
O'Melveny, Miss Adele; 528 S. Pearl st.   *Tuesday*
Osborne, Mr and Mrs H. Z.; S. Hope st.   *Tuesday*
Otis, Col and Mrs H. G.; 322 S. Hill st.   *Monday*
——The Misses
Owens, Dr and Mrs Jas. Stormont; 939 Pearl st.   *Wednesday*
Owens, Dr and Mrs J. B.; 421 S. Fort st.   *Tuesday*

Park, Mr and Mrs John S.; The Melrose   *Monday*
Parsons, Mr and Mrs Charles; 15 Loma Drive   *Friday*
Patrick, Mr and Mrs Joe; 124 Diamond st.   *Friday*
——Mrs Mary
Patton, Miss Susie
Perry, Mr and Mrs Charles F.; Bellevue Terrace   *Tuesday*
Perry, Mr and Mrs W. H.; 507 S. Pearl st.   *Tuesday*
——Miss Florence
Place, George E.
Plater, Mr and Mrs John, Baker Block   *Monday*
Polk, Mr and Mrs W. H.; Ninth st.   *Tuesday*
Ponet, Mr and Mrs Victor; Adams st.   *Wednesday*
Prager, Mr and Mrs William; Baker Block   *Monday*
Preuss, Mr and Mrs Edward A.; 148 Broadway *Wednesday* **Santa Monica**
Pridham, Mr and Mrs William; Baker Block   *Monday*
Prussia, Mr and Mrs F. B.; 141 S. Fort st.   *Monday*

Rader, Mr and Mrs Frank; W. Jefferson st.   *Wednesday*
Rawson, Mrs A. W.; Canal near Loomis   *Tuesday*
——The Misses
Reed, Mr and Mrs G. W. M.; 726 W. Twenty-third st.   *Thursday*

139

Robbins, Mr and Mrs A. S.; 811 Pearl st. *Wednesday*
Roginat, Baron and Baroness; E. Los Angeles *Thursday*
Rhodes, Miss Jessica
Rose, Mr and Mrs L. J.; Grand ave. and Fourth st. *Monday*
——The Misses
Ross, Dr and Mrs F. B.; The Rossmoore *Monday*
Ross, Mr and Mrs Percy; 775 S. Hope st.
Ross, Mrs; Pearl st. *Tuesday*
Rowan, Mr and Mrs T. E.; 429 S. Main st.
——Miss Joe

Salisbury, Dr and Mrs; 538 S. Pearl st. *Wednesday*
Schallert, Mr and Mrs John; Pacheco st.
Schumacher, Mrs Carrie; 14 N. Broadway *Monday*
——Mr John H.
——Mr Frank J.
——Mr Percy F.
Scott, Mr and Mrs Lester; Hotel Westminster *Monday*
Seamans, Capt and Mrs; Washington st. *Wednesday*
——Miss
Severance, Mr and Mrs Mark; Adams st. *Wednesday*
Shoemaker, Mrs; St. James Park *Wednesday*
Silent, Mr and Mrs Charles; W. Adams st. *Wednesday*
——Mr and Mrs Ed.
——Miss Libbie
Silver, Mr and Mrs Herman; 941 Pearl st. *Wednesday*
——Miss Cora
Slauson, Mr. and Mrs J. S.; Figueroa st. *Wednesday*
Slauson, Mr and Mrs. James; Figueroa st.
——James
Small, Dr and Mrs Henry E.; 726 W. Twenty-third st. *Thursday*
Smith, Mr and Mrs; 535 Pearl st.
——Miss Leonora
Snedaker, Mr and Mrs; Manhattan ave. *Wednesday*
Solano, Mr and Mrs Alfred; 535 S. Main st. *Monday*
Spence, Mr. and Mrs E. F.; 337 S. Olive st. *Thursday*
——Miss Kate
Steele, Mrs John B.; San Luis Obispo **San Luis Obispo**
Stewart, Mr and Mrs Lyman; 1000 W. Seventh st. *Friday*
——Miss May
Stewart, Dr and Mrs; Main st. *Monday*
Stickel, George; 221½ S. Spring st.
Stoneman, Ex-Gov and Mrs; Grand ave. and Jenkins st. *Wednesday*
——The Misses

Teed, Mr and Mrs Freeman G.; 2367 Scarff st.   *Wednesday*
Thom, Capt and Mrs C. E.; 19 Mayo st.   *Thursday*
Tubbs, Miss; Beaudry st.   *Tuesday*
Tufts, Mr and Mrs John L.; S. Grand ave.   *Wednesday*
——Miss Eva
——Mr Edward B.

Unruh, Mr and Mrs H. A.; Arcadia   *Wednesday*

Vail, Mr and Mrs Hugh; Washington   *Wednesday*
Van Nuys, Mr and Mrs Isaach; 613 S. Spring st.   *Friday*
Vignes, Mr and Mrs L. J.; 13 Manhattan ave.   *Thursday*
Vosburg, Mr and Mrs John; S. Figueroa st.   *Wednesday*

Walton, Mr and Mrs Charles Strong; 2337 Thompson st.   *1st and 3rd*
——Mrs Wm. F.   [*Wednesdays*   **Hotel del Coronado**
Ward, Mr and Mrs J. S.; 1200 S. Hill st.   *Tuesday*
——Miss Annie
——Mr Shirley
Waterman, Mr and Mrs Jesse F.; 105 Bonsallo ave.   *Wednesday*
Wells, Mr G. Wiley; 915 S. Hill st.
Wheeler, Mrs J. O.; Baker Block   *Monday*
White, Hon and Mrs S. M.; cor. S. Main and Eleventh sts.   *Tuesday*
Whitney, Mr and Mrs O. C.; 258 S. Olive st.   *Tuesday*
Wicks, Mr and Mrs M. L.; The Melrose   *Monday*
Widney, Mr and Mrs Robert M.; 416 S. Olive st.   *Thursday*
——Miss Helen
——Mr R. J.
Wilson, Mrs C.; 532 S. Spring st.   *Wednesday*   **Los Angeles**
——Mr Wm. A.
——Miss Agnes
Woods, Mr and Mrs Modiné; 507 S. Pearl st.   *Tuesday*
Workman, Mr and Mrs W. H.; 157 Boyle ave. Boyle Heights   *Tuesday*
——Misses
——Mr A. Boyle
Worth, Mr and Mrs Charles; The Winona   *Wednesday*
Wright, Mr and Mrs Arthur L.; 111 Bonsallo ave.   *Wednesday*
——Miss
——Mr Will E.

California Club

OF LOS ANGELES

The California Club was founded May 20, 1887, and incorporate
December 24, 1888.

OFFICERS, 1889

DAN. FREEMAN	President
W. G. HUGHES	Vice-President
NICHOLAS D. COLEMAN	Secretary
F. B. PRUSSIA	Ass't Secretary

DIRECTORS

Dan Freeman   C. Cabot

W. G. Hughes   H. J. Stewart

Nicholas D. Coleman

MEMBERS

Ainsworth, Dr F. K.

Austin, J. M.

Bard, Thomas R.

Baker, P. C.

Baker, Robert S.

Banning, Joseph B.

Banning, Wm.

Banning, Hancock

Baruch, B.

Baruch, Jacob

Beaudry, P.

Bissell, H. L.

Blackman, W. R.

Bleecker, H.

Bonebrake, George H.

Bonsall, W. H.

Bowring, Edward

Bonynge, W. A.

Boyce, H. H.

Breed, L. N.

Broaddus, Charles

Brodrick, W. J.

Brown, Thomas B.

Cabot, C.

Campbell, Alexander

Childress, A. D.

Clark, W. H.

Chadbourne, F. S., S. F.

Chadwick, R. A.

Cohn, Kaspare

Cohn, Max

Cole, Seward

Coleman, Nicholas D.

Conrey, N. P.

Cook, J. E.

Cowles, W. N.

Cox, Ernest A.

Craig, James

Craig, M. R.

Crank, J. F.

Creighton, Telfair

Crocker, Charles F., S. F.

Crow, H. J.

Crandall, E. E.

Curlett, Wm.

Cuzner, James

Davies, James N.

Del Valle, R. F.

De Szigethy, Dr C. H.

Dickson, George E.

Dobinson, G. A.

Dunkelberger, Isaac R.

Dunn, Williamson

Dunton, C. H.

Dupuy, J. R.

Duque, Thomas L.

Egan, Richard

Elliott, John M.

Ellis, Charles J.

Ellis, J. Ellwood

English, W. Taylour

Estudillo, J. G.

Estudillo, Francisco

Fairchild, J. A.

Fallon, C. John

Fisher, C. L.

Fleishman, H. J.

Forman, Charles

Forman, Charles, Jr.

Forster, J. F.

Forster, M. A.

Fowler, E. W.

Fox, C. J.

Freeman, A. C.

Freeman, Dan.

Frink, George W.

Fullerton, J. T.

Furrey, W. C.

Gaffey, John T.

Garbutt, F. C.

Gardner, W. P.	Lacy, Sidney
Garvey, Richard	Larkin, Alf. O.
Germain, Eugene	Latham, H. W.
Gibbon, T. E.	Lee, H. T.
Gillig, H. M.	Lewis, S. B.
Glenn, George E.	Lindley, Hervey
Goss, Thomas	Lindley, Walter
Goucher, W. H.	Lion, Gus.
Graves, J. A.	Loeb, L.
Grierson, Lieut C. H.	Loew, Jacob
Griffith, F. T.	Lovell, John
Hagen, W. R.	Lowe, T. S. C.
Hall, A. I.	Mackey, C. E.
Hall, Col Robert H.	MacGowan, Dr D. Granville
Hall, E. E.	Macneil, H. L.
Hall, Wm. Ham.	Mathews, John R.
Harkness, Fred.	Maxwell, Walter S.
Harper, W. H.	Mellus, J. J.
Harrell, A. J.	Meredith, J. M.
Harris, Rusk	Miles, D. E.
Harvey, J. Downey, S. F.	Montgomery, J. W.
Haverstick, J. W.	Moore, Walter S.
Hazard, H. T.	Mortimer, C. White
Hellman, I. W.	Mossin, John G.
Hellman, H. W.	Mott, S. H.
Hicks, F. S.	Mott, T. D.
Hotchkiss, A. B.	Murray, Dr C. P.
Houghton, S. O.	Mosgrove, H.
Howard, F. H.	McCool, D.
Hughes, W. G.	McFarland, Charles
Hughes, Dr West	McFarland, Dan.
Hunter, J. E.	McIlhenny, S. K.
Jevne, H.	McLaughlin, Jas.
Jewett, S. P.	Nabor, H. H.
Johnson, E. P.	Newhall, H. G.
Jones, A. C.	Newhall, W. S.
Jones, E. W.	Newmark, H.
Judson, A. H.	Newmark, M. A.
Kerckhoff, W. G.	Newmark, M. H.
King, George W.	Newton, I. B.
Kinney, Abbot	Niles, Wm.
Lacy, Wm.	Northam, R. J.
Lacy, Wm., Jr.	O'Melveny, H. W.
Lacy, R. H.	Osborne, H. Z.

144

Outhwaite, J. H.	Slauson, J. S.
Patrick, J. H.	Slauson, Jas.
Patrick, Walter M.	Smith, George H.
Patton, George A.	Smith, Colonel J. R.
Parsons, Charles T.	Spence, E. F.
Perry, Lieut J. A.	Stern, E. L.
Plater, John E.	Stern, B.
Polk, I. H.	Stewart, Dr G. T.
Pogson, R. N.	Stewart, H. J.
Pomeroy, A. E.	Story, F. Q.
Reynolds, Merick	Sumner, C. A.
Rhodes, Thomas	Teed, Freeman G.
Richards, Clarence J.	Treichel, Colonel Charles
Rognait, Baron	Truman, Ben C., S. F.
Rose, L. J., Jr.	Vail, W. L.
Ross, Erskine M.	Van Nuys, I. N.
Rowan, T. E.	Variel, R. H. F.
Rowland. Wm. R	Vickery, O. A.
Robinson, J. C.	Volkmar, Col Wm.
Russell, H. M.	Watchtel, J. V.
Rutan, C. F.	Walton, C. S.
Safford, George S.	Walton, Fred A.
Schumaker, F. G.	Ward, Ben E.
Schuyler, J. D.	Ward, F. Minott
Scott, L. F.	Ward, Shirley C.
Seligman, Carl	Weldon, T. J.
Severance, Mark S.	White, Stephen M.
Seyler, Charles	Whiting, Dwight
Shaw, Charles N., S. F.	Wills, Dr W. Lemoyne
Sheldon, Lionel A.	Wilshire, H. G.
Shankland, J. H.	Wilson, H. T. D.
Silent, Charles	Wood, F. W.
Silent, Edward D.	Woollacott, H. J,
Silver, H.	Workman, W. H.
Simpkins, C. H.	Wright, E. T.
Simpkins, H. R.	

145

Los Angeles Tennis Club

The Los Angeles Tennis Club was organized in 1889. The courts are on the corner of Ninth and Pearl streets. Visitors are always welcome, Tuesdays and Fridays being especially devoted to ladies.

MEMBERS

Chase, Charles W.	Chase, Mrs Charles W.
Bowering, Edward	Bowering, Mrs Edward
Vail, Hugh	Vail, Mrs Hugh
Severance, Mark	Severance, Mrs Mark
Cosby, Walter	Patrick, Mrs Joe
Francisco, A. W., Jr.	Baker, Mrs Charles
Lawrence, George	Tufts, Miss Eva
Curtis, Goorge H.	Carran, Miss Clara
Tufts, E. B.	Lantz, Miss Annie Laurie
Forrester, F. L.	Perry, Miss Florence
Lantz, Charles	Haveman, Miss Jeanette
Wigmore, F. M.	Forrester, Miss Lena
Sinsabaugh, George	Culver, Miss Flora
Suffel, F. H.	Henderson, Miss Nellie
Steckel, George	Smith, Miss Lenora
Allen, A. W.	Chanslor, Miss Mamie
Coulter, R. T.	Francisco, Miss Beatrice
Hellman, Marco	Stout, Miss Neita
Lester, W. E.	Jordan, Miss Luta H.
Nicholson, W. B.	Howes, Miss Marie
Moore, J. R.	Howes, Miss Flora
Edwards, William	Wells, Miss M. R.
Pemberton, Charles	Riley, Miss Florence
Gushee, R. H.	Bonebrake, Miss Blanche
Barker, W. A.	Tonner, Miss Bessie
Arnold, Paul	Routh, Miss F. G.
Manning, M. F.	Cochran, Miss
Flint, Fred	Crisp, Miss
Germain, Harry	Orr, Miss Virginia
Cochran, G.	Jones, Miss Louise
Routh, Stanley	Hendron, Miss

146

*

MENLO PARK
REDWOOD CITY
SAN MATEO

*

MENLO PARK

Atherton, Faxon and Mrs
Atherton, Mrs
Adams, Mr and Mrs W. J.
Bassett, Mr and Mrs A. C.
Butterfield, Miss Ada
Callahan, Rev Father
Coleman, Mr James L.
Coon, Mrs Chas. M.
Dimond, Gen and Mrs W. H.
——Miss Eleanor
——Mr and Mrs E. R.
Donohoe, Mr and Mrs Joseph A.
——Mr and Mrs J. A., Jr.
——Mr Edward
Doyle, Mr and Mrs John T.
——Mr and Mrs John T.
——Miss Fannie
Eyre, Col and Mrs E. E.
——Mr and Mrs E. L.
——Mr Perry P.
——Miss
Flood, Mrs James C.
——Miss
Felton, Hon Chas.
——Chas. Jr.

Hager, Judge and Mrs John S.
——Miss
Hicks, Mr W. P.
Holbrook, Mr and Mrs Chas.
——Miss
Hopkins, Mr and Mrs E. W.
Hopkins, Mr and Mrs Timothy
Hecht, Mr and Mrs
Loomis, Mr and Mrs George
Mills, Mr Edgar
——Miss Addie
Macondry, Miss Nina
——Miss Inez
——Mr Fred. W.
Prior, Mr and Mrs J. K.
Patrick, Mr and Mrs
Ryan, Mr and Mrs E. B.
——Miss Daisy
Stanford, Gov and Mrs Leland
Selby, Mrs Thomas
——Miss Annie
——Mr and Mrs Percival W.
Watkins, Mrs Eleanor

REDWOOD CITY

Brittan, Mr and Mrs Nat.
Hopkins, Mr and Mrs Moses
Josselyn, Mr and Mrs Charles

Phelps, Mr and Mrs T. G.
Robinson, Mr and Mrs Jas. A.
Schroeder, Mr and Mrs J. B.

SAN MATEO

Andrus, Mr and Mrs Geo. H.
Barroilhet, Mr and Mrs Henry
Beylard, Mr and Mrs E. D.
Borel, Mr
Bowie, Mr and Mrs H. P.
Booth, Mr and Mrs H. J
——Miss
——Genevieve
Brewer, Rev and Mrs Alfred Lee
——Miss Adalene
——Miss Susie
——Rev William A.
——Edward C.
Corbitt, William
——Miss
——Miss Nellie
Crocker, Col Chas. Fred.

De Guigne, Mr and Mrs Chris.
Folsom, Rev De F.
Howard, Mr and Mrs W. H.
——Miss Babette
Hayne, Judge and Mrs Duncan
Hayward, Mr and Mrs Alonzo
Judah, Mr and Mrs Henry R.
——Mrs E. E.
Kohl, Captain and Mrs Wm.
——Miss Mamie
Lawrence, W. H.
Maynard, Mr and Mrs John
Parrott, Mr and Mrs John
Parrott, Mrs A. M.
Payson, Capt and Mrs A. H.
Rose, Mr and Mrs A. W.
Rose, Mr and Mrs A. H., Jr.
Sessions, George W.

148

Importer and Designer of Millinery

332 FIFTH AVENUE

NEAR 33D STREET

PARIS
39 Rue de Trévise

NEW YORK CITY

*B*EING constantly in receipt of the Latest Novelties from the leading Paris and London houses, and going to Europe twice yearly, enables me to offer the very newest Creations. Particular attention paid to out-of-town orders as we design special shapes and styles for each individual person.

J. J. McKENNA ✳

Samples sent by mail with instructions for measurement

LADIES' TAILOR

36 East Twenty-third Street

Ladies' Suits, Coats, Ulsters
AND RIDING HABITS

NEW YORK

ALL ORDERS PROMPTLY ATTENDED TO

Rheumatism no More!

THE WONDERFUL AND MARVELOUS CURES THAT
ARE PERFORMED DAILY BY

MRS. DR. BAKER'S

Magnetic ✳ Liniment

ARE PERFECTLY ASTOUNDING TO THE GENERAL
PUBLIC. FOR

Rheumatism

AND ALL OTHER ACHES AND PAINS NONE CAN
COMPETE WITH HER DISCOVERY. ALL USE
IT WITH PERFECT SATISFACTION

50 CTS. AND $1.00 PER BOTTLE

*Sent to any address C.O.D. from 23 East 14th Street (up-stairs),
Rooms 6 to 12, New York City. Ask your druggist for it.
Can be secured through R. W. Robinson & Son, 182 Green-
wich street, New York.*

AGENCY

612 Sixth Ave., New York

SACRAMENTO

Adams, Mr and Mrs F. B.; 1525 L st.
Adams, Miss Lizzie; 910 Seventh st
Alsip, Mr and Mrs E. K.; 1711 N st.
Armstrong, Judge and Mrs J. W.; 917 O st.
Atkinson, Prof and Mrs E. C.; 1711 I st.   *Tuesday*   **Lake Tahoe**

Bainbridge, Mr and Mrs J. C.; cor. of Eighth and J sts.
Barrett, Miss Mamie; 701 Twelfth st.
Beckman, Mr and Mrs William; Golden Eagle Hotel
Bennett, Miss Eva; 1411 K st.
Bernard, Miss Lizzie; Metropolitan Building
Birdsall, Mr and Mrs Fred; 727 Ninth st.   *Thursday*
——Miss Etta
Bonte, Mr and Mrs Charles; 909 F st.
Booth, Hon Newton
Bowers, Mr and Mrs W. O.; Golden Eagle Hotel   *Tuesday*
Boyd, Mrs J. W.; 912 G st.
——Miss Mabel
Breckenfeld, Mr and Mrs H. B.; 1316 I st.   *Tuesday*
Briggs, Dr and Mrs W. A.; 1300 I st.
Brusie, Mr and Mrs Jud. C.; 917 K st.
Buchanan, Mr and Mrs A. N.; Tenth and H sts.
Bullard, Miss Etta   **Davisville**
Burnham, Mr and Mrs C. E.; 916½ J st.

Carey, Mr and Mrs R. S.; 1003 H st.   *Thursday*
Carroll, Miss Liela; SW cor. Tenth and H sts.
Carroll, Edgar B.; 806 Ninth st.
——Miss Leila
Carroll, Miss Mae; 729 Seventh st. .
Chipman, Mr and Mrs H. C.; 914 N st.
Clark, Miss Minnie; 1128 Tenth st.
Clark, Mr and Mrs George H.; 1017 Fourth st.
Clark, Mr and Mrs C. W.; Tenth and H sts.
——Miss Laura
Cluness, Dr and Mrs W. R.; 805 H st.
——Miss Minnie

149

Coleman, Mr and Mrs W. P.; 325 J st.
Coleman, Mr and Mrs J. O.; 501 M st.
Cosby, Gen and Mrs George B.; 1208 P st.
——Miss Edith
Cothrin, Mr and Mrs W. K.; 1228 N st.
Cox, Mr and Mrs Frederick; Twenty-first and W sts.
——Mrs Genevieve
——Mr and Mrs Crawford J.
——Miss Fredda
Crocker, Mrs Margaret; Third and O sts.
Crocker, Mr and Mrs B. R.; 618 L st.
Crocker, Mr Elwood
Crouch, Mr and Mrs E. A.; 308 O st.
Crouch, Miss Bessie; 229 O st.
——Miss Mamie

Demming, Miss Mamie; Twenty-first and T sts.
——Miss Ella
Dénson, Judge and Mrs S. C.; 1021 H st.   *Thursday*
Devlin, Robert T.
Dillman, Mr and Mrs C. F.; 1214 N st.
Dillman, Mr and Mrs M. J.; 1420 O st.
Dixon, Dr and Mrs G. M.; 728 Ninth st.
Dray, Senator and Mrs F. R.; 1323 I st.   *Thursday*
Duel, Mr and Mrs S. J.; 1118 H st.   *Thursday*
——Miss Alice
——Miss Ethel
Dunn, Hon John P.

Earle, Mr and Mrs Dan O.

Faris, Mr and Mrs James; 1123 H st.   *Thursday*
Felter, Mr and Mrs J. I.; 619 Tenth st.
——Miss Emma
Felter, Mr and Mrs W. R.; 1700 H st.   *Thursday*
Folger, Mr and Mrs A. G.; 1122 H st.
Foye Mrs A. L.; 1228 N st.
Fraser, Mr and Mrs Ed.; N bet. Seventh and Eighth sts.

Gardner, Dr and Mrs M.; Sutter Building
Garfield, Miss Susie; 218 M st.
Gerber, Mr and Mrs W. E.; 1424 N st.
Gill, Mr and Mrs John A.; 1108 G st.

Gillis, Mrs J. L.; 1220 Seventh st.
Glover, Mrs J. T.; 1021½ Front st.
Gregory, Mayor and Mrs E. J.; 208 J st.
Gregory, Miss Millie; 128 J st.
———Miss Daisy
———Miss Malvene
Green, Miss Genevieve; 923 M st.
Griffith, Mr and Mrs Fred D.; 1812 H st.   *Thursday*
Griffith, Mr and Mrs J. T.; 1231 H st.   *Thursday*
———Miss Eva
Griffin, Miss Lizzie; 2512 H st.   *Tuesday*
Grissim, Mr and Mrs W. W.; 1417 I st.

Hahn, Miss Florence; 1309 H st.
Hale, Mrs E. W.; Fifteenth and O sts.
Hall, Mr and Mrs Charles P.
Hall, Mr and Mrs T. B.; 1236 O st.
Hall, Mr William H.
Hamilton, Col and Mrs E. R.; cor. Fifth and J sts.   *Tuesday*
Hanchette, Miss Louise; 1402 H st.
Harmon, Mr and Mrs R. B.; 604 Seventh st.
Hart, Gen and Mrs A. L.; 1027 L st.
Heilbron, Mr and Mrs Henry; 2017 M st.
Hendricks, Sec and Mrs W. C.; 1823 H st.   *Thursday*
Herold, Adam
Hetzel, Mr and Mrs Selden; 624 O st.
Hickman, Mr and Mrs Frank; 1313 I st.
Hoitt, Mr and Mrs Ira G.; 916 L st.
Holl, Judge and Mrs Solon; 1325 G st.
Houghton, Mr and Mrs C. S.; 1315 H st.   *Thursday*
Hopkins, Mr and Mrs A. S.; 1413 I st.
Hubbard, Mr and Mrs C. H.; 1429 I st.
Hughson, Miss Edith; 704 N st.
Hughson, Dr and Mrs; Seventh and N sts.
Huntington, Dr and Mrs T. W.; 515 Thirteenth st.
Huntoon, Miss Eva; 721 M st.
Hurd, Mrs Horatio; 1317 H st.   *Thursday*

Ingram, Mr and Mrs William,; 724 N st.
———Mr and Mrs W., Jr.
Irvine, Mr and Mrs R. C.; 1900 H st.   *Thursday*

Jackson, Mr and Mrs Geo. W.; Metropolitan Building
Jelly, A. C.
Johnson, Mr and Mrs Grove L.; 720 Hyde st.

151

Johnson, Miss Mollie B.; 1100 F st.
Johnson, Mr and Mrs A. J.; 1319 I st.

Kaseberg, Mr and Mrs J. W.; Roseville
———Miss Mary
———Miss Fannie
Katzenstein, Mr and Mrs G. B.; 1213 O st.
Keegan, Mr and Mrs J. J.; Metropolitan Building
Kennedy, Mrs M. A.; 1603 H st.
Kewen, Miss May; 930 M st.
———Colonel Perry

Laine, Dr and Mrs J. R.; 913 K st.
La Rue, Mr and Mrs H. M.; 1602 H st.
Leake, Mr and Mrs W. S.; 923 M st.   *Tuesday*
Lenoir, Mr and Mrs C. J.; 803 M st.   *Friday*
Lewis, Mr and Mrs L. L.; 1623 H st.   *Thursday*
———Miss
Lindley, Mr and Mrs D.; Seventh bet. L and M sts.   *Thursday*
Lindley, Miss Liela J.; 1314 H st.   *Thursday*
———Miss Helen
Locke, Miss Ella; 330 M st.
Lorenz, Mr and Mrs George W.; 1007 I st.   *Wednesday*
Lyon, Mr and Mrs William M.; 1601 Second st.

McClatchy, Mr and Mrs V. S.; 2207 J st.
McClatchy, Mr and Mrs C. K.; 1416 Third st.
McCord, Mr and Mrs J. L.; 1220 N st.
McCreary, Mr and Mrs Charles; 1128 Tenth st.
McKee, Mrs E. H.; 420 P st.
McKillip, Miss Hattie; 1415 J st.
McKune, Judge and Mrs J. H.; 1511 H st.
McLaughlin, Major and Mrs William; 1621 Second st.
McNassar, Col and Mrs James; 1200 Tenth st.
Mebius, Mr and Mrs L.; 1101 N st.
Merkeley, Mrs R. J.; P. O. Box 366
Miller, Mr and Mrs Frank; 831 N st.
Milliken, Mr and Mrs J. M.; 1108 H st.   *Thursday*
———Miss Louise
Mills, Mr and Mrs J. E.; 1526 Third st.
Mott, Mr and Mrs Geo. M.; 1515 I st.

Nichols, Dr and Mrs C. B.; 1601 L st.   *Thursday*
Nichols, Dr and Mrs H. L.; 909 F st.
Norris, Mrs W. E.; 1012 P st.

Orcutt, Mr and Mrs F. L.; 1803 H st.   *Thursday*

Parkinson, Dr and Mrs J. H.; 1030 I st.
Petrie, Miss Lottie; 622 J st.
Porter, Mr and Mrs J. N.; 722 Ninth st.
Post, Mr and Mrs C. N.; 1922 H st.

Ray, Mrs F. E.; 710 H st.
Richardson, Miss Jocey; 1503 H st.   *Thursday*
——Miss Minnie
Robin, Mr and Mrs Charles; 1420 I st.
Ross, Mrs Charles H.; 1202 H st.   *Thursday*
Ryan, Mr and Mrs F. D.; 1200 P st.

Safford, Judge and Mrs W. S.; Lull House
Sheehan, Gen and Mrs T. W.; Twenty-first and U sts.
Siddons, Mr and Mrs W. M.; 1421 I st.
——Miss Daisy
Simmons, Dr and Mrs G. L.; cor. Tenth and N sts.
——Miss Celia
Slight, Mrs S. P.; 1309 I st.   *Wednesday*
Smith, Mr and Mrs H. G.; 500 Ninth st.   *Wednesday*
Smith, Miss Alice, 1224 H st.
Smith, Mr and Mrs F. B.; G bet. 12th and 13th sts.   *Wednesday*
Smith, Mr and Mrs S. Prentiss; 2100 J st.
Snead, Miss Minnie   **Dixon**
——Miss Kate
Snider, Dr and Mrs T. A.; 913 M st.
——Miss Mary
Southworth, Dr S. S.; 1905 J st.   **Granda Vista, Bolinas, Marin Co.**
—— Dr E. L.
——Fred B.
——Scott S.
Speiker, Mr and Mrs J. J.; 1322 I st.   *Friday*
Steffens, Mr and Mrs Joseph; 1524 H st.   *Thursday*
——Miss Lulu
Steinman, Mr and Mrs B. U.; 717 I st.
Stephens, Mr and Mrs R. D.; 12th and N sts.
Stephenson, Miss Carrie; 1228 N st.
Stevenson, Miss Lela   **Vacaville**
——Miss Mable
Sullivan, Mrs J. H.; 1430 H. st.   *Thursday*
——Miss Julia
——Miss Sophie

BOVININE the Blood Maker

Talbot, Miss May F.; 1626 H st.
Taylor, Miss Carrie; 1621 H st.
Taylor, Miss Mary; 1810 H st.   *Thursday*
———Miss Clara
Taylor, Mr and Mrs L. S.; 1207 O st.
Tebbetts, Dr and Mrs F. F.; 914 6th st.
Terry, Mr and Mrs J. E.; 930 M st.
Terry, Mr and Mrs W. E.; Thirteenth and N sts.
———Miss May
Towle, Mr and Mrs Allan; Twenty-first and M sts.
———Miss Ora
Tozer, Gen and Mrs L.; 1429 H st.   *Thursday*
Tufts, Mr and Mrs A. C.; 1605 H st.
Tyrrell, Miss Lulu; 617 N st.

Upson, Mr and Mrs L. S.; 1010 F st.
———Miss Lucy|

Van Fleet, Judge and Mrs W. C.; 815 Eighteenth st.
Van Voorhies, Mr and Mrs A. A.; 1403 H st.   T*hursday*
Van Voorhies, Mr and Mrs R. J.; 800 J st.
Von Herrlich, Rev John F.; Rector St. Paul's Church

Willis, Mr and Mrs E. B.; M bet. Sixth and Seventh sts.
Waterman, Gov and Mrs R. W.; 1100 H st.
———Miss
Watson, Mrs J. R.; 731 F st.
Weinstock, Mr and Mrs H.; 1207 L st.
Wilcox, Miss Florence; 1020 F st.
———Miss Mellie
Williams, Mr and Mrs Fred Y.; 719 H st.
Wilson, Mr and Mrs J. W.; 516 M st.
———Miss Lutie
Wiseman, Miss Julia; 308 M st.
Wittenbrock, Miss Eliza; 1303 I st.
Wood, Dr and Mrs William; 814 Seventeenth st.
Wood, Mr and Mrs A. A.; 725 Seventh st.
———Miss May
Wright, Colonel and Mrs J. B.; 1402 H st.   T*hursday*

Sacramento Lawn Tennis Club

OFFICERS

D. A. LINDLEY - - - - - -	President
DR. W. C. RUTH - - - -	Vice-President
FRANK G. SMITH - - - - - -	Secretary
FRED. E. RAY - - - - - -	Treasurer

DIRECTORS

Lindley, D. A.   Carroll, Lelia
Carroll, May   Burke, J. E.
Pond, Jas. H.   McCreary, R. C.

Smith, Frank G.

ACTIVE MEMBERS

Aull, Miss
Bennett, Eva
Briggs, Lena
Birdsall, Etta
Blair, Mrs H. R.
Carroll, Lelia
Clarke, Miss Laura F.
Carroll, Miss May
Clarke, Miss Minnie
Cox, Miss Frédda
Cravens, Miss Fannie
Cluness, Miss Mabel
De Laguna, Miss Fredricka
Govan, Miss Jeannie
Goggins, Mrs Ida
Hurd, Mrs H.
Hubbard, Mrs C. H.
Hughson, Miss Edith
Hinkson, Miss Lucy

Huntington, Mrs I. W.
Johnson, Mrs A. J.
Johnson, Miss Mollie B.
Jones, Miss Minnie
Kirk, Miss Agnes
Knox, Mrs W. T., Jr.
Kaseberg, Miss Mary
Kaseberg, Miss Fannie
Lindley, Mrs D. A.
Lindley, Miss Helen
Lindley, Miss Edith
Lindley, Miss Alice
Milliken, Miss Louise
McKune, Miss Florence
Neale, Mrs C. A.
Nixon, Miss Alice
Orcutt, Mrs T. L.
Ray, Mrs F. E.
Richardson, Miss Minnie

Simmons, Miss Celia M.	McCreary, R. C.
Smith, Miss Alice M.	McCreary, Harry
Stanley, Miss Nellie	Miller, Dwight
Southworth, Mrs Mary	Miller, Cyrus
Shaw, Miss Nellie	Potter, W. A.
———Miss Minnie	Pond, J. H.
Twitchell, Miss Blanche	Ray, F. E.
Williams, Mrs F. Y	Smith, F. G.
Wilcox, Miss Mellie	Terry, Wallace
Wilcox, Miss Florence	Ripley, L. W.
Wilson, Miss Lutie	Upson, L. S.
Wood, Mrs William	Purnell, W.
Adams, Mrs F. B.	Simmons, Sam
Wilkins, Miss Belle	Word, Dr W.
Briggs, Miss Nina	Word, H. C.
Jones, Mrs F. A.	Simpson, E. M.
Gee, Miss Emma	Reith, Dr W. C.
Fogle, Miss	Hughes, J. W.
Baldwin, Mrs Dr.	Scheld, Adolph
Lindley, Miss Lelia	Carroll, E. B.
Johnson, Miss Mary	Smith, Fred F.
Evans, Miss Lillian	Cosby, Geo. B., Jr.
Adams, F. B.	Jones, Frank A
Briggs, Dr W. E.	Clarke, G. F.
Burke, J. E.	McCloughry, H. H.
Blair, H. R.	Abbott, G. A.
Cluness, W. R., Jr.	Gray, Jos H.
Duden, E. F.	LaRue, H. M., Jr.
Dwyer, E. J.	Hummel, Herman
Gallatin, A. J.	Luce, Chas
Hale, J. C.	Hartley, Vic
Hale, M. Jr.	Shannon, Geo.
Johnston, A. J.	Turner, Gus
Kirk, H. C.	Brown, J. D.
Knox, W. F., Jr.	Hale, R. B.
Lindley, D. A.	Lipman, C. K.

HONORARY MEMBERS

Miller, Frank	Lubin D.
McCreary, R.	Lindley, T. M.
McCreary, C.	Hamilton, Col.
Cummings, C. H.	Hubbard, C. H.
Cothrin, W. K.	Simmons, Dr.
Beckman, Wm.	Cox, Senator Fred
Weinstock, H.	

Young Ladies' Drill Corps

COMMANDER

MISS MAYE KEWEN

MEMBERS

Bennett, Eva	Magann, Alice
Bennett, Sybil	Magann, Delia
Brown, Phoebe	Massey, Mabel
Bassett, Florence	Massey, Teeny
Balsdon, Emma	McKillip, Hattie
Boyd, Mabel	Oatman, May
Carroll, Minnie	Pyran, Belle
Clark, Effie	Richardson, Jocey
Coghlan, Anna	Richardson, Minnie
Cravens, Fannie	Russell, Mamie
Cox, Fredricka	Robertson, Florence
Demming, Mamie	Schwartz, Sadie
Demming, Ella	Shaw, Minnie
Dunlap, Mamie	Shaw, Nellie
Evans, Lillie	Smith, Alice
Gregory, Millie	Smith, Alcie
Govan, Jeanne	Smith, Lillie
Gregory, Malvene	Sullivan, Sofie
Griffith, Eva	Sullivan, Alice
Gregory, Daisy	Simmons, Celia
Hinckson, Lucy	Siddons, Daisy
Henderson, Margaret	Steffens, Lulu
Huntoon, Eva	Siddons, Nellie
Harrison, Ella	Upson, Addie
Hess, Effie	Upson, Lucy
Hatch, Grace	Waterman, Helen
Henry, Genevieve	Waterman, Abby Law
Henry, Miss	Waddilove, Ella
Hughson, Edith	Waddilove, Carrie
Kaseberg, Fannie	Wilcox, Mellie
Kaseberg, Mary	Wilcox, Florence
Lindley, Helen	Wilson, Lutie
Lindley, Pipey	Weil, Florence
Lewis, Alida	

The Sutter Club

Organized in 1890, with a view to the promotion of social intercourse among its members.

MEMBERS

Abbott, A.	Duden, W. L.
Alsip, E. K.	Dray, F. R.
Andrew, A.	Dwyer, E. J.
Armstrong, J. W.	Dillman, C. F.
Adams, Fred.	Deming, Theodore
Anderson, Claus	Enright, Thos. L.
Booth, Newton	Ellis, C. J.
Burnham, C. E.	Earl, Edwin T.
Beckman, Wm.	Fox, Thos.
Briggs, Wm. Ellery	Frazier, E. F.
Briggs, W. A.	Gerber, W. E.
Burke, J. E.	Gerber, Henry
Blanchard, Geo. A.	Gregory, Eugene J.
Barnett, Robert	Gregory, Frank
Boruck, M. D.	Givens, C. S.
Bruner, Elwood	Gardner, Chas. F.
Baker, C. W.	Geary, Wm.
Coleman, J. O.	George, Wilbur F.
Coleman, W. P.	Grau, H. H.
Crouch, E. A.	Hart, A. L.
Comstock, W. D.	Hawley, R. H.
Cox, Fred.	Huntington, Thos. W.
Crouch, H. R.	Hopper, A. J.
Cothrin, W. K.	Hale, P. C.
Carroll, Edgar B.	Hale, E. W.
Clark, George H.	Houghton, C. S.
Clark, J. Frank	Hall, Thos. B.
Curtis, W. A.	Hinkson, Add C.
Cummings, C. H.	Heilbron, Aug.
Devlin, Robert T.	Heilbron, Adolph
Denson, S. C.	Hubbard, C. H.
Dillman, M. J.	Hopkins, A. S.

158

Holl, S. Solon	Platt, P. E.
Hahn, Joseph	Petrie, Wm. M.
Hughes, J. W.	Pickett, G. G.
Hamilton, Ed. R.	Perkins, Dana
Irvine, R. C.	Rideout, N. D.
Ingram, Wm., Jr.	Richardson, L. B.
Johnson, Grove L.	Richards, S. L.
Johnson, A. M.	Ryan, Frank D.
Johnson, A. G.	Roberts, J. H.
Johnston, A. J.	Robie, I. A.
Johnson, F. T.	Remele, F. R.
Jones, S.	Scheld, Adolph
Jones, F. A.	Scheld, A. P.
Knights, Wm. D.	Sheehan, T. W.
Knox, W. F., Jr.	Stephens, R. D.
Kinross, W. H.	Stephenson, G. H.
Kimbrough, Howard	Steffens, Jos.
Lubin, D.	Schaw, Wm.
Luhrs, C. A.	Smith, Ed. F.
Lindley, D. A.	Smith, H. G.
Lindley, T. M.	Steinman, B. U.
Lewis, L. L.	Simmons, G. C.
Luckett, E. M.	Small, H. J.
Lovdal, O. A.	Singer, Wm., Jr.
McClatchy, C. K.	Smith, S. P.
McClatchy, V. S.	Southworth, S. S.
McCreary, Byron	Sellinger, C. F.
McIntire, J. A.	Simmons, G. L.
Miller, J. H.	Terry, J. E.
Marshall, C. S.	Tebbetts, F. F.
Mott, George M.	Van Voorhies, A. A.
Mohr, L. B.	Van Fleet, W. C.
McCreary, Chas.	Weinstock, H.
Montford, L. C.	Whitbeck, D. D.
Mills, Jas. E.	Waterhouse, C. P.
Miller, Frank	Wright, J. B.
McMullen, Geo. C.	Weinrich, E. C.
Maslin, S. P.	Weiger, Chas.
Mackey, John	Weil, John
McLaughlin, Wm.	Wiseman, Geo. F.
Neilsen, Alex.	Williams, L.
Ormsby, W. R.	Wilson, J. W.
Orcutt, F. L.	Winning, W. H.
Osler, E. B.	Young, J. D.
Porter, Jas. N.	Yoerk, C. A.

BOVININE is a Sheet Anchor in Cholera Infantum

NON-RESIDENT MEMBERS

Aull, Chas.
Beatty, W. H.
Bates, Geo. E.
Bates, F. E.
Boggs, John
Burnham, Jas. H.
Clarkson, J. Booth
Cuthbertson, W. J.
Chase, C. M.
De Pue, Edgar J.
Dixon, W. H.
Ecklon, C. L.

Humbert, P. A.
Hollister, Dwight
Hickmott, R. H.
Hale, Marshal, Jr.
Hubbard, Henry C.
Harvey, Obed.
Johnson, H. W.
Mills, Wm. H.
Rideout, Norman A.
Smith, Brainard F.
Waterhouse, Columbus
Tuttle, F. P.

Plaiseur Club

SACRAMENTO

MEMBERS

Adams, Mrs Fred B.	1527 L street
Adams, Miss Lizzie	910 Seventh street
Alsip, Mrs E. K.	1711 N street
Armstrong, Mrs J. W.	917 O street
Barrett, Miss Mamie	701 Twelfth street
Bainbridge, Mrs J. C.	Cor. Eighth and J streets
Bernard, Miss Lizzie	Metropolitan Building
Bennett, Miss Eva	1411 K street
Beckman, Mrs William	Golden Eagle Hotel
Birdsall, Mrs F.	727 Ninth street
Birdsall, Miss Etta	727 Ninth street
Boyd, Mrs J. W.	912 G street
Boyd, Miss Mabel	912 G street
Bowers, Mrs W. O.	Golden Eagle Hotel
Brusie, Mrs Jud. C.	917 K street
Breckenfeld, Mrs H. B.	1315 I street
Bullard, Miss Etta	727 Ninth street
Carroll, Miss Maye	729 Seventh street
Carroll, Miss Flora	SW cor. Ninth and H streets
Chipman, Mrs H. C.	914 N street
Clark, Mrs Geo. H.	1017 Fourth street
Cothrin, Mrs William	1228 N street
Cosby, Miss Edith	1208 P street
Cox, Mrs Crawford	Twenty-first and T streets
Cox, Miss Fredda	Twenty-first and T streets
Crouch, Mrs E. A.	Mrs Crocker's, Third and O streets
Dillman, Mrs M. J.	1420 O street
Duell, Miss Alice	1118 H street
Felter, Mrs W. R.	720 Eighteenth street
Folger, Mrs A. G.	1122 H street
Garfield, Miss Susie	218 M street
Gardner, Mrs Dr	Metropolitan Building or 430 J st.
Gerber, Mrs W. E.	SW cor Fifteenth and N streets
Gill, Mrs John A.	1108 G street
Gillis, Mrs J. L.	1220 Seventh street

Gregory, Mrs E. J.	721 I street
Gregory, Miss Millie	126 J street
Gregory, Miss Maloene	126 J street
Gregory, Miss Daisy	126 J street
Grissim, Mrs W. W.	1417 I street
Hahn, Miss Florence	1309 H street
Hale, Mrs E. W.	Fifteenth and O streets
Hamilton, Mrs Ed R.	Sacramento Bank
Hanchette, Miss Virginia	1402 H street
Harmon, Mrs R. B.	606 Seventh street
Hall, Mrs T. B.	1236 O street
Hart, Mrs A. L.	1027 L street
Heilbron, Mrs Henry	604 N street
Hendrichs, Mrs W. C.	1812 H street
Hetzel, Mrs Selden	624 O street
Hickman, Mrs Frank	1313 I street
Holl, Mrs Solon	1329 G street
Houghton, Mrs C. S.	1315 H street
Hubbard, Mrs C. H.	1429 I street
Hughson, Miss Edith	704 N street
Huntoon, Miss Eva	721 M street
Huntington, Mrs T. W.	515 Thirteenth street
Irvine, Mrs R. C.	1900 H street
Jackson, Mrs Geo W.	Metropolitan Building
Jobson, Mrs Jennie	Twenty-first and T streets
Johnston, Mrs A. J.	1319 I street
Johnson, Miss Mollie B.	1100 F street
Kaseberg, Miss Fannie	Roseville
Kaseberg, Miss Mary	Roseville
Katzenstein, Mrs George B.	1213 O street
Laine, Mrs J. R.	913½ K street
Leake, Mrs W. S.	923 M st.
Lindley, Miss Helen	1314 H street
Lindley, Miss Mamie	1314 H street
Locke, Miss Ella	330 M street
McCord, Mrs J. L.	1220 N street
McKee, Mrs E. H.	420 P street
McKillip, Miss Hattie	1415 J street
McLaughlin, Mrs William	1621 Second street
Merkeley, Mrs R. J.	P. O. Box 366
Milliken, Miss May	1108 H street
Nichols, Mrs Dr	1603 L street
Norris, Mrs W. E.	1012 P street
Petrie, Miss Lottie	622 J street

Porter, Mrs James N.	722 Ninth street
Post, Mrs C. N.	1922 H street
Ray, Mrs F. E.	710 Eighth street
'Ross, Mrs Chas	1200 H street
Russell, Miss Susie	1029 H street
Siddons, Miss Daisy	1421 I street
Smith, Miss Alice	1224 H street
Snead, Miss Minnie	Dixon, Cal.
Snead, Miss Katie	Dixon, Cal.
Steffens, Mrs Joseph	1524 H street
Steffens, Miss A.	1524 H street
Steinman, Mrs B. U.	717 I street
Stephens, Mrs R. D.	Twelfth and N streets
Stevenson, Miss Lela	Vacaville, Cal.
Stevenson, Miss Mabel	Vacaville, Cal.
Sullivan, Miss Julia	1430 H street
Sullivan, Miss Sophie	1430 H street
Talbot, Miss May	1626 H street
Taylor, Miss Carrie	1613 H street
Tebbetts, Mrs Dr F.	914 Sixth street
Tozer, Mrs L.	1431 H street
Thayer, Miss E.	Booth & Co.
Tryon, Mrs E. H.	1116 Ninth street
Van Fleet, Mrs W. C.	821 Eighteenth street
Van Voorhies, Mrs A. A.	1403 H street
Weinstock, Mrs H.	1207 L street
Wilson, Miss Lulu	516 M street
Wiseman, Miss Julia	308 M street
Wright, Mrs J. B.	1402 H street
Wood, Miss May	725 Seventh street

McNeill Club

Organized in 1887

W. H. KINROSS   -   -   -   -   Musical Director
MISS AMELIA BOHL   -   -   -   -   Accompanist

CHARTER MEMBERS

FIRST TENOR

1 Beaumont, C. J.   2 Cohn, R. T.   3 Cook, John
4 Elliott, R. E.   5 Graham, J. S.   6 Irvine, R. C.
7 Kidder, F. N.   8 McCaslin, Wm.   9 Reeber, L.

SECOND TENOR

1 Ashworth, E. F.   2 Barrett, M. K.   3 Beard, M. R.
4 Buchanan, A. N.   5 Crowe, W. D.   6 Elliott, Chas.
7 Flint, F. V.   8 Jobson, E.   9 Kidder, H. A.
10 Millikin, C. T.   11 McNally, P. J.   12 Wilson, B.
                       13 Wiseman, T. T.

FIRST BASS

1 Bruner, Elwood   2 Graham, E. M.   3 Hansbrow, G. R.
4 Heilbron, F. H.   5 Kraft, A. A.   6 Lampert, Wm.
7 Littlejohn, J. W.   8 Lovdal, W. A.   9 McClatchy, V. S.
10 Osborn, W. E.   11 Parker, E. S.   12 Potter, W. A.
                       13 Pyburn, George

SECOND BASS

1 Auerbach, R. H.   2 Carroll, E. B.   3 Clinch, C.
4 Crocker, H. A.   5 Frost, A. L.   6 Genshlea, J. G.
7 Hickmott, Robert   8 Hubbs, Chas.   9 McNeill, John
          10 Schaden, J. C.   11 Winter, Charles

SAN DIEGO

Aitken, Judge and Mrs J. R.; cor. Second and A sts.   *Thursday*
Arey, Capt and Mrs; Sixth near Ash st.
————Miss
Arndt, Dr and Mrs H. R.; 1732 Third st·   *Wednesday*
Anderson, Mr and Mrs J. H.; 1269 Twelfth st.   *Wednesday*

Bartlett, Mrs H.; 1922 First st.
————Miss
Bailey, Mr W. J.; Florence Hotel
Burnham, Dr and Mrs F. R.; 1708 C st.
Brown, Mr Gratz K.; Florence Hotel
Brayton, Col and Mrs G. M.; U. S. A., Coronado Hotel
Britt, Mr and Mrs E. W.; Fourth and Maple sts.
Barker, Mr and Mrs R. W.; 958 Second st.
Brooks, Mr and Mrs J. T.; cor. Third and Juniper sts.
·Bailey, Mr and Mrs J. H.; The Brunswick
Bates, Mr Frank E.; cor. Fourth and Ash sts.
Beauregard, Mr H. T.; Florence Hotel
Balon, Mr James; Florence Hotel
Bloodgood, Mr and Mrs W. D.; University Heights
Beabazon, Capt and Mrs; 1146 Fourteenth st.
Bowers, Hon and Mrs W. W.; Florence Hotel
————The Misses
Bancroft, Mr and Mrs Hubert H.; Fourth and Fir   *Wednesday*·
Babcock, Mr and Mrs E. S.; Coronado Hotel
Berry, Mr and Mrs John; 1045 Eighth st
Buck, Mr and Mrs J. S.; Twenty-first and Fir   *Wednesday*
————Miss
Buck, Mr and Mrs A.; 2143 Fifth st.
————Miss
Brust, Mr and Mrs S. B.; B and Front st.
Beane, Mr and Mrs E. J.; Albemarle Hotel
Bushyhead, Mr and Mrs E. W.; Third and Cedar sts.   *Friday*
Britt, Mr and Mrs E. C.; Fifth and Maple
Bailhache, Major and Mrs; Fifteenth st. between C and D
————Miss
Bruce, Mr and Mrs L. M.; 1053 Tenth st.
Burleigh, Dr and Mrs; First and Fir sts.
Braley, Mr and Mrs J. H.; Fourth and Hawthorn   *Wednesday*

Burnham, Dr and Mrs L.; cor. Eighth and C sts.
Birdsall, Mrs M. A.; Commercial Hotel
Beckwith, Mr and Mrs F. A.; Florence Hotel
Brooks, Mrs H. N.; Third st. and Brooks ave.   *Thursday*
Brodrick, Mrs. I. D.; Second and Hawthorn sts.
Blancharde, Mrs M. E.; 1307 Twelfth st.   *Thursday*

Cadwallader, Gen and Mrs S.; Boston ave., bet. 32d and 33d sts.
Carson, Dr Edwin; Union and Cedar sts.
Cave, Dr and Mrs D.; Fifth and E sts. (Morena)
Covert, Mrs C. B.; 2430 Second st.
Carter, Mr and Mrs John; Fourth and Cedar sts.
Carter, Mr and Mrs Cassius; 918 Fir st.   *Tuesday*
Chambers, Mr and Mrs Gordon; Albemarle Hotel
Cleveland, Mr and Mrs M. C.; 1332 First st.
Collins, Mr J. W.; Brewster Hotel
Cothran, Mr and Mrs E. E.; Coronado Hotel
Cox, Mr and Mrs E. A.; Johnson Heights   *Saturday*
Capron, Mr and Mrs J. C.; Twelfth and D sts.
Conkling, Mr and Mrs H. N; Fifth and Ivy
Collier, Judge and Mrs D. C.; Sixth, near Cedar
Collier, Mr and Mrs W. M; 1540 Sixth st.
Clarke, Mr and Mrs W. H.; Fifth and Date sts.
Choate, Mr and Mrs D.; Fifth and Fir sts.
Chase, Major and Mrs Levi; D and Twelfth sts.   *Thursday*
Chase, Mr and Mrs H.; 1042 Eleventh st.
Copeland, Mr and Mrs J. L.; Florence Hotel
Copeland, Mr and Mrs G. D.; 1546 A st.
Christian, Mr and Mrs H. T.; 1440 Third st.   *Tuesday*
Crepin, Dr and Mrs H. N.; 1930 First st.
——Miss
Clark, Mr and Mrs R. G.; 2144 A st.   *Wednesday*
Clough, Mrs J. H.; Third and Date sts.
Culton, Mr and Mrs J. W.; G, bet. Twenty-fourth and Twenty-fifth sts.

Dudley, Mr Irving B.; Bancroft Building
Doolittle, Mr and Mrs L. F.; Second and Ash sts.
Dare, Mr and Mrs D. D.; Fifth st., between Juniper and Kalinia
Doig, Dr and Mrs J. R.; cor. D and Fifth sts.
Dare, Mr and Mrs D. D.; Brewster Hotel   *Wednesday*
Douthett, Mr and Mrs M. A.; cor. Eleventh and C sts.   *Tuesday*
Derby, Mrs E. C.; cor. Hawthorne and Ivy sts.   *Friday*
——Miss
Daley, Mr and Mrs Thos.; 713 Tenth st.   *Thursday*
Dalton, Mr and Mrs R. A.; cor. Tenth and Fir sts.

Davison, Mr and Mrs D. F.; Cedar, bet. Fourth and Fifth sts.
Dalton, Mr and Mrs R. H.; 1957 Fourth st.

Ensign, Col and Mrs E. J.; Seventh, near D st.　　*Thursday*
Edwards, Dr and Mrs William; Fourth and Fir sts.　　.
Ekings, Mr L.; 1254 First st.
————The Misses
Emerson, Mr and Mrs R. B.; 1253 Union st.
Eaton, Miss L.; Florence Hotel
Edwards, Miss Annie; 1837 Third st.
Ewing, Mr and Mrs F. E.; cor. Second and Juniper sts.
Edwards, Mrs S. A.; cor. Fourth and Fir sts.
Eigenmann, Prof and Mrs; cor. Eighth and C sts.

Furman, Mr and Mrs Robt H.; 720 Cedar st.　　*Wednesday*
Fields, Mr and Mrs M. S.; Coronado Beach, Third and C ave.
Fisher, Mr and Mrs J. C.; Brewster Hotel
Foltz, Mrs Clara; Front, near B st.　　*Monday evening*
Fairweather, Mr and Mrs Henry; cor. First and Date sts.
Fox, Mr and Mrs C. J.; 845 Tenth st.　　*Wednesday*
Fisher, Mr and Mrs Jas.; Albemarle Hotel
Frisbie, Mr and Mrs J. C.; cor. F and Ninth
Fisher, Mr and Mrs Walter; cor. D and Seventh sts.
Fish, Mr and Mrs John; 554 Eighteenth st.　　*Saturday*
Fishburn, Mr and Mrs D. G.; First and Juniper
————The Misses
Falkinhan, Mr and Mrs Jos.; cor. Hawthorn and Albatross

Gassen, Mr and Mrs A. G.; cor. E and Eleventh　　*Thursday*
Gillmore, Mr and Mrs Jessie; 1766 Front st.
Ginty, Mr and Mrs John; Seventh and Ash　　*Monday*
Ginty, Mr and Mrs Wm.; 1632 Seventh st.
————Miss Morton
Gordrich, Mr and Mrs Ben; 849 Eighth st.
————Misses
Geddis, Mr and Mrs George; 1066 First st.
German, Mr and Mrs M.; 1053 Tenth st.　　*Thursday*
Gilmore, Mr and Mrs M. T.; cor. Fourth and Beech
Geuchten, Mr and Mrs; cor. Ninth and C
Gochenauer, Dr and Mrs D.; First and Olive sts.
Gray, Mr and Mrs William; First and Grape sts.

Hadley, Mr and Mrs W. E.; Horton House
Howard, Mr and Mrs Bryant; cor. Tenth and B　　*Thursday*
Hildreth, Mr and Hrs H. R.; cor. Third and Ash
————Miss

167

Hale, Mr and Mrs B. H.; cor. Cedar and Third
——The Misses
Hewitt, Mr and Mrs H. E.; Albatross st.
Hannahs, Mr and Mrs Geo;; cor. Second and Laurel
Haight, Mrs E. G.; cor. Front and B
Hill, Mr and Mrs K. M.; 2044 Fourth st.   *Thursday*
Higgins, Mr and Mrs A.; Second and Beech
Hubbell, O. S.; cor. Sixth and C
Hastle, Mr and Mrs E. D.; 5th ave. block
Hodge, Mr and Mrs N.; cor. Union and Cedar
Hazzard, Mr and Mrs Geo. W.; 2418 Fifth st.
Heath, Mrs C. E.; 832 Tenth st.
Harrison, Mrs Abbey A.; 2056 Fourth st.   *Tuesday*
Holloway, Mr and Mrs; cor. Fourth and Elm sts.
——Miss
Havermale, Mr and Mrs S. G.; cor. Seventh and Ash sts.
——Mr W. O.
Henderson, Judge and Mrs J. J.; 2163 Bradt st.
Harper, Rev and Mrs W. F.; cor. Fourteenth and A   *Tuesday*
Hanbury, Mr and Mrs J. D.; Twelfth near D
Hamilton, Mr and Mrs Chas.; cor Seventh and Beech
Hamilton, Mr and Mrs F. N.; First and Ash
Henderson, Judge and Mrs J. J.; cor. Union and Date
Hunsaker, Judge and Mrs W. I.; First and Juniper sts.
Harbison, Mr H. R.; Twelfth, bet. A and B
——Miss
Howard, Mr and Mrs L. B.; Brewster Hotel   *Monday*
Hawley, Mr and Mrs A. W.; 2040 Twelfth st.
Henderson, Miss Lizzie; Tenth and B   *Thursday*
Hyde, Mr and Mrs G. F.; Fifth street near Cedar   *Friday*

Ingle, Mr and Mrs Heber; cor. Seventh and Ash
Ingle, Mr and Mrs S. G.; cor. Sixth and Beech
Ivers, Mrs Mary; 1922 First st.
——Miss

Julian, Mr and Mrs A. H.; cor. Union and Date sts.
——Miss
Jewett, Mr and Mrs S.; cor. Fifth and Palm sts.
Jones, Mr T. G. and Daughters; 1734 Third st.
Jenks, Mr and Mrs C. L.; cor. State and D sts.   *Monday*
Jorris, Mr and Mrs J. G.; cor. Union and A sts.
Jones, Mrs Johnstone; 2157 Fourth st.
Johnson, Dr and Mrs C. M.; Florence Hotel

Kirby, Mrs; 2324 F st.
——Miss
Kutchin, Mr and Mrs H. M.; 1832 Fourth st.   *Wednesday*
Kew, Mr and Mrs M; Third and Cedar sts.
Keating, Mrs A. C.; 1723 First st.
Keating, Mrs Geo. J.; Second st., bet. Juniper and Kalinia
King, Mr and Mrs W. M.; First and Laurel sts.
Kellogg, Dr and Mrs E. T.; cor. Third and Ivy sts.   *Thursday*
——Miss
Keenam, Mrs Wm.; Fifth, bet. Redwood and Spruce sts.
——Miss
King, Mr and Mrs Wm. Neil; NE cor. First and Kalinia sts.   *Friday*
——Miss
Kinney, Miss Mary F.; cor. Third and Elm sts.
Knapp, Mrs

Leach, Mrs M. H.; cor. First and D sts.
Loomis, Mrs M. E.; Horton House
Levi, Mr and Mrs S.; 1726 Ninth st.
Ludlum, Mrs F. M.; cor. Fourth and Fir sts.   *Wednesday*
——The Misses
Lonsbery, Mr and Mrs. E. P.; Second and Laurel sts.
Livingston, Mrs H. M.; Albermarle Hotel
——The Misses
Lane, Mr and Mrs L. M.; First and Fir sts.
Leland, Mrs M. E.; Cedar st.
Loring, Dr and Mrs Leonard, U. S. A.; Fourth and Fir sts.
Luce, Judge and Mrs M. A.; Second near Cedar st.
——The Misses
Lacey, Mr and Mrs D. S.; Seventh and Beech sts.
Leifchild, Mr and Mrs E. L.; 925 Thirteenth st.
Leifchild, Mrs E. L.; Fourth and Fir sts.
Levi, Mr and Mrs M. E.; 1701 First st.   *Friday*
Levet, Mr and Mrs J. B.; cor. First and Date sts.
——The Misses
Laurie, Mr A. K.; Florence Hotel
Lesem, Mr and Mrs M. A.; 2467 First st.   *Wednesday*
——The Misses
Long, Mr and Mrs J. D.; 1763 First st.   *Thursday*
——Miss
Loop, Mr and Mrs S. M.; 946 Twelfth st.
Leovy, Mr and Mrs G. J.; cor. Brandt and Ivy sts.

McKoon, Mr and Mrs Hosmer P.; Richelieu Block
Matthews, Mrs S. M.; 1807 Fourth st.
——Mr H. N.

McMillan, Mrs; Second and Ivy sts.
——Miss
Murray, Gov and Mrs Eli H. 2455 Front st.
Matfield, Mr and Mrs Geo. H.; cor. Sixth and E sts.   *Thursday*
Mannix, Mr and Mrs John B.; 1804 Fourth st.
Monteith, Mr and Mrs George W.; Upper Fourth st.   *Wednesday*
——Miss Alice G.   .   **Monterey**
Maize, Capt and Mrs W. R., U. S. A. (retired); c. First & Laurel *Friday*
Metcalf, Mr and Mrs T. E.; Fourth and Cedar sts.   *Friday*
——Miss
Moore, Mr and Mrs M. B.; 2044 Fourth st.   *Thursday*
McDaniel, Rev and Mrs B. F.; 734 Grape st.   *Thursday*
Marshall, Capt and Mrs John; cor. Fourth and Beech sts.
Miner, Mr and Mrs M. E.; 2242 D st.
Monohan, Mr and Mrs T. J.; 1456 First st.
Maginn, Mr and Mrs B. W.; 1618 First st.
McLure, Mr and Mrs L. S.; Twenty-fourth and H sts.   *Thursday*
McDonald, Mr and Mrs J. Wade; cor. Seventh and Ash sts.
McRea, Mr and Mrs J. W.; cor. Fifth and Grape sts.
Morse, Mr and Mrs E. W.; Tenth and G sts.
Marston, Mr and Mrs Geo.; cor. Third and Ash sts.
Mannasse, Mrs H.; 1343 Front st.
——Miss
Mills, Mr and Mrs A. P.; cor. State and A sts.
Murtzman, Dr and Mrs B. F.: cor. Twenty-second and E sts.
McKie, Mr and Mrs N.; 744 Hawthorn st.
——The Misses
McBride, Miss; 1922 First st.
Maxwell, Mrs A. M.; Front and Ash sts.

Nutt, Mr and Mrs A. E.; Fifth near Olive st.
Noble, Dr and Mrs W. B.; 941 Eleventh st.
Niles, Mr and Mrs J. H.; First and Beech sts.
Neeley, Mr and Mrs J. H.; Front and A sts.
Nerney, Mr and Mrs T. A.; 2031 Union st.   *Thursday*
Nason, Mr and Mrs A. G.; cor. Grape and Union sts.   *Thursday*
——Mr and Mrs H.
Nason, Miss; Albatross near Grape st.   *Thursday*
Nugent, Dr Edmond; 1146 Fourteenth st.   **Alpine, San Diego Co.**
——The Misses
——John George
Niles, Capt and Mrs Randolph; 1459 First st.

Overbaugh, Mr and Mrs George; Sixth and Beech sts.   *Wednesday*
——The Misses
Ord, Mrs Gen E. O. C.; 1725 Union st
——Miss

Pauly, Mr and Mrs C. W.; 1340 Cedar st., cor. Fifth   *Tuesday*
——Miss
Puterbaugh, Judge and Mrs Geo.; Fifth near Palm st.
Patterson, Mr and Mrs W. R.; cor. Fifteenth and C sts.
Pierce, Judge and Mrs W. L.; First and Olive sts.   *Friday*
——Miss
Parker, Judge and Mrs Edwin; 927 Seventh st.
Parker, Mr and Mrs T. S.; Palm and Fifth sts.
Pierce, Mrs E. M.; 1835 Third st.   *Friday*
Preston, Mrs J. W.; First and Laurel sts.   *Wednesday*
——Miss
Perry, O. H.; Fourth and Laurel st.
——The Misses
Parish, Mr and Mrs W.; Eleventh and D sts.
Perry, Mrs C. O.; cor. Ninth and D sts.
Patton, Dr and Mrs E.; Florence Hotel
Peck, Mrs C. M.; 639 Twentieth st.   *Wednesday*
——Miss
Phillips, Mr and Mrs G. K.; 2112 D st.
Parker, Mr and Mrs T. S.; Palmer and Fifth sts.   *Friday*
Pollok, Mrs; First st., bet. Hawthorne and Ivy
——The Misses
——Andrew
——Allan
Phillips, Dr and Mrs R. F.; Third st., bet. Elm and Fir
Parker, Mrs Albert; 1132 Cedar st.
Parker, Miss Alice; cor. Fourth and Beech sts.

Regan, Mrs; 1566 Sixth st.
——Miss
Richards, Mr and Mrs C. B.; Florence Hotel
Richards, Mr and Mrs Bert; Florence Hotel
Restarick, Rev and Mrs H. B.; cor. Eighth and C sts.   *Wednesday*
Rafferty, Mrs; 966 Tenth st.
Remondino, Dr and Mrs P. C.; St. James
Robertson, Lieut and Mrs E. B.; 1756 First st., U. S. A.
Robinson, Mr and Mrs W. E.; 2056 Tenth st.   *Tuesday*

Sherman, Capt and Mrs M.; cor. Twenty-second and H sts.   *Wednesday*
——Miss
Stockton, Dr and Mrs S. C.; Twelfth st., ne r D
Slade, Mr and Mrs Samuel; 1312 Front st.
Story, Mr and Mrs W. H.; First and Hawthorne sts.
Shaw, Mrs Victor E.; 1132 Cedar st.
Stevens, Mr and Mrs O. L.; 1745 Second st.

Surr, Mr and Mrs Joseph; Front and B sts.
Smith, Mr and Mrs C. K.; 1045 Eighth st.
Scones, Mr and Mrs T. J. E.; cor. Sixth and A sts.
Sill, Mr and Mrs S. J.; cor. Seventh and Ash sts.   *Monday*
Sprigg, Mr and Mrs J. C; Twentieth and K sts.   *Wednesday*
Sherman, Mr and Mrs John; Second and Fir sts.
——Miss
Scott, Mr and Mrs Chalmer; First and Elm sts.   *Tuesday*
Smith, Mr and Mrs J. H; 1168 Eighteenth st.   ,
Simpson, Capt and Mrs J. H.; 1141 Seventh st.
Smith, Mr and Mrs C.; cor. G and Ninth sts.
Seaton, Mr and Mrs M. E.; 1167 Union st.
Seghers, J. B., Jr.
Sevort, Mr and Mrs H.; cor. Fourteenth and F sts.
Smiley, Mr and Mrs V. W.; First and Elm sts.
Stough, Mr and Mrs O. J.; Fourth and Ivy sts.   *Friday*
Smith, Mr and Mrs W. M.; Third and B sts.
Shirley, Mrs Kate B.; State and E sts.
Story, Mr and Mrs Hampton L.; First and A sts.
Sefton, Mr and Mrs J. W.; Sixth, near Maple st.
Sherman, Mr and Mrs M.; Twenty-fourth and H sts.
Schellenberger, Mr and Mrs; Twenty-fourth and H sts.
Stattler, Mr and Mrs S.; 922 Eighth st.
Smith, Mr and Mrs C. P.; 738 Ninth
Schiller, Mr and Mrs M.; 1305 Front
Smart, Dr and Mrs W. N.; 1329 State st.
Sloane, Judge and Mrs W. A.; 2222 C st.
Summer, Mr and Mrs F. M.; 1307 Twelfth st.   *Thursday*

Thompson, Miss Bertha; 1456 First st.
Turner, Miss; 927 Seventh st.
Thomas, Mr and Mrs J. R.; 1742 Fifth st.
Titus, Mr and Mrs H.; Sixth, near Cedar sts.
Timpkin, Mr and Mrs H.; First and Laurel sts   *Friday*
——The Misses
Thomas, Mr and Mrs R. A.; cor. Ninth and D sts.
Thompson, Mr and Mrs J. W.; cor. Fourth and Beech sts.
Toles, Mr and Mrs Jerry; cor. Second and Laurel sts.   *Friday*
——Miss Gertrude
——Miss Trilla
Tibbitts, Miss; Twenty-fourth and H sts.   *Thursday*
Taft, Judge and Mrs Alphonso; cor. First and Laurel sts.
——Mr
Turner, Mr and Mrs C. H.; 1044 Seventh st.

Vivian, Rev and Mrs A. H.; cor. Third and Ash sts.
Van Arman, Mrs J.; cor. Fourth and Grape sts.   *Friday*
Van Norman, Dr and Mrs E. V.; Fifth and Maple sts.
——Miss

Ware, Mr and Mrs K. J.; 624 Tenth st.
Warfield, Mr and Mrs M. M.; Coronado Beach
Woolwine, Mr and Mrs W. D.; Sixth st., near D   · *Friday*
Witherby, Mr and Mrs J. G.; 1106 D st.
Woodward, Miss; Second and Juniper sts.
Walker, Mr and Mrs M.; 541 Twentieth st.
Wellborn, Mr and Mrs O. W.; Eleventh and D sts.
Walz, Mr and Mrs E. A.; Brewster
Wamplemier, Mr and Mrs T.; Tenth and G sts.
Woodward, Dr and Mrs W. B.; cor. Fifth and Laurel sts.   *Friday*
——Miss Elizabeth
Whitney, Mr and Mrs W. W.; Highland Villa
White, Mr and Mrs T. F.; 1343 Front st.
Wagoner, Mr and Mrs J. R.; Fifth and Palm sts.
Winterburn, Mr and Mrs W.; 1140 Fourteenth st.
Way, Miss Emma F.; cor. Elm and Third sts.
Wood, Mr and Mrs L. C.; NW cor. Fourth and L sts., Langham
Wittenmeyer, Lieut Edmund; U. S. A.; Cuyamaca Club
Wertheimer, Mr and Mrs I.; 731 Tenth st.
Waterman, Gov and Mrs R. W.; Brewster Hotel
——The Misses

Yeamans, Dr and Mrs H. W.; cor. Seventh and D sts.   *Thursday*
Young, Mr and Mrs J.; Sixth and Cedar sts.
Young, Mr and Mrs W. W.; 742 Fourteenth st.

Pianos and Organs

THE BANCROFT COMPANY
AGENCY

Miller & Sons' Piano · · · · ·
  THE BOSTON FAVORITE

Behning & Son's Piano · · · · ·
  A SUPERIOR ::: THOROUGHLY RELIABLE INSTRUMENT

Starr & Company's Piano · · · ·
  HAS NOT ITS EQUAL IN THE WORLD AT THE PRICE

ORGANS : : :
FROM $35 UP
{ Chapelette · ·
  Reed-Pipe · ·
  Farrand & Votey

PLEASE TAKE NOTICE

The instruments for which we have the agency are guaranteed the best of the kind made.

Purchasers with ready money can save Twenty-five per cent. by making their selection from our stock.

THE BANCROFT COMPANY
HISTORY BUILDING   721 MARKET ST.
SAN FRANCISCO, CAL.

RESIDENTS OF CORONADO BEACH

CORONADO, SAN DIEGO CO., CAL.

Applegate, Mr and Mrs. B. W.

Babcock, Mr and Mrs E. S.; Hotel del Coronado
Babcock, Mrs E. S.; Ninth st. cor E ave.
——Mrs Gip
——The Misses
Bailey, Dr and Mrs W. F.; Second st. cor. D ave.
Balch, Mr and Mrs D. M.; Sixth st. cor. A ave.
Barbour, Mr and Mrs J. H.; Hotel del Coronado
Bean, Mr and Mrs J. W.; F ave. bet. Third and Fourth sts.
Bierce, Mr and Mrs J.
Birdsall, Mrs M. J.
Blaisdell, Mr and Mrs S. G.; Second st. cor. C ave.
Bragg, Mr and Mrs L. C.; Orange ave.
Brayton, Col and Mrs Geo. M.; U. S. A.; Hotel del Coronado
Brown, Mr and Mrs Daniel; F ave. bet. Eighth and Ninth sts.
Bronwer, Mr and Mrs J. H.; Fourth st. and F ave.

Cameron, Mrs S.; Orange ave. bet. Seventh and Eighth sts.
——Miss
Campbell, Mr and Mrs J. R.; Tenth st. cor B ave.
Carey, Mr D.
——The Misses
Case, Mr and Mrs T.
Connolly, Capt and Mrs James
Cook, Mrs M. W.
Covey, Mr and Mrs A. L.
Cowing, Mrs W. R.
Cox, Mr and Mrs Thos; J avenue.
Currier, Mr and Mrs C.

Densmore, Mr and Mrs E.
Dow, Mrs H. G.; Orange ave. cor. Isabella ave.
Dryden, Mr and Mrs J. L.; Eighth st. cor D ave.
Durgin, Miss Hattie E.; Hotel Josephine

Fitch, Mrs Rene
Fischer, Mr and Mrs Geo. L.; Orange ave. bet. Eighth and Ninth sts.
Fischer, Mr and Mrs C. J.
Fitzgerald, Mr John; G ave. bet. Third and Fourth sts.

BOVININE is the only Raw Food

175

Foster, Mr. and Mrs Geo.; cor. Sixth st. and B ave.
Freeland, Mr and Mrs J. L.; Adita ave.

Golden, Miss Ester
Green, Mr and Mrs Geo. R.; F ave. and Third st.
Grinell, Mr H. A.
Gwyn, Major, H. G.; cor. Sixth st. and B ave.

Harney, Mr and Mrs; near Star Park
Harper, Mr and Mrs J. H.
Hartupee, Mr and Mrs J. H.; H ave. bet. Ninth and Tenth sts.
Hickman, Prof. and Mrs R. O.
Hill, Mr and Mrs J. R.; I ave. bet. Fourth and Fifth sts.
Hind, Capt and Mrs; C ave. near Ninth st.
Holmes, Mr and Mrs J.; B ave. and Tenth st.
Hoppen, Mr and Mrs F.
Huntington, Dr and Mrs, U. S. A.; Hotel del Coronada
———Miss

Jackson, Mrs J. T.; cor. Third st. and C ave.
Jackson, Mr and Mrs W. M.; G st. bet. Seventh and Eighth

Keating, Mr and Mrs W. H.; Adella ave. near Ninth st.
Kellogg, Mr and Mrs Giles; C ave. near Orange ave.
Kessler, Mrs H. S.
Kimball, Mr and Mrs F. E. A.; cor. G ave. and Third st.

Lake, Mrs Lucy
Lamb, Mr and Mrs T. B.; G ave. cor. Sixth st.
Lanktree, Mrs T.; B ave. bet. Seventh and Eighth sts.
Laycock, Mr Nelson; A ave. bet. Seventh and Eighth sts.

Manahan, Mr and Mrs J. R.
Martin, Mr and Mrs P. D.
Matthewson, Mr and Mrs J. A.
McConaughey, Mr and Mrs A. M.; Tenth st. near F
McConaughey, Mr and Mrs O. H.; cor. First st. and Orange ave.
Miles, Mr and Mrs R. G.; G ave. bet. Third and Fourth sts.
Miller, Rev F. D.
Miller, Mr and Mrs O. C.; I ave. bet. Ninth and Tenth sts.
Montieth, Mr John
———The Misses
Moody, Mr and Mrs W. C.; cor. Tenth and J ave.
Mullett, Mr and Mrs J. C.; Orange ave.

Nagle, Mrs M. E.; Orange ave. bet. Third and Fourth sts.
Nevins, Mr and Mrs D. P.
Nichols, Mr and Mrs L. C.
Nordhoff, Mr and Mrs Chas.; Hotel del Coronado

Latest Stationery Of Every Description, Fine Paper, Envelopes and Writing Paper. *The Bancroft Company, 721 Market Street.*

176

Palmer, Miss S. E.
Pierce, Mr and Mrs Edgar F.; B ave. cor. Ninth st.
——Miss
Pittmann, Mr and Mrs W. R.; F ave. bet. Third and Fourth st.
Polhamns, Mr and Mrs A. A.
Powers, Mrs C.; B ave. and Tenth st.
——Dr F. G.

Qnown, Mr and Mrs J. F.

Reed, Rev and Mrs A. C.; cor. Tenth st. and F ave.
Reed, Mrs J. P.
Riddell, Mrs L. G.
Riggs, Mr and Mrs W. M.; G ave. bet. First and Second sts.
Robbins, Mr Harry
Robinson, Mr and Mrs C. W.; Hotel del Coronada

Saunders, Mr J. W.; I ave. bet. Sixth and Seventh sts.
——The Misses
——Mr
Sawyer, Mrs H. M.; D ave. bet. Ninth and Tenth st.
Seeley, Mr and Mrs Chas. W.; C ave. bet. Sixth and Seventh sts.
Sharp, Mr Edgar; Third and D sts.
Smith, Mr and Mrs; cor. C ave. and Sixth st.
Spencer, Mr H. B.; Hotel del Coronado
Sprague, Mr and Mrs J. C.; Hotel del Coronado
Stiles, Mrs Sarah B.; cor. Tenth st. and Adella ave.
Stocking, Mr and Mrs H. F.; cor. Ninth st. and I ave.
Stone, Mr and Mrs W. P.

Tyson, Mr and Mrs M. C.; Orange ave. bet. Seventh and Eighth sts.

Vanderkloot, Mr and Mrs M. R.; cor. Third st. and G ave.
Vanderkloot, Mr and Mrs P. S.; Orange ave. bet. Fifth and Sixth sts.
Varnum, Dr and Mrs G. W.; H ave. bet. Second and Third sts.

Waller, Mr and Mrs J. W.
Warfield, Major and Mrs Alex.; C ave. cor. Ninth st.
——Miss
Watts, Mrs; Hotel del Coronado
——Miss
——Mr Nathan
Webb, Gen W. E.; C ave. cor. Ninth st.
White, Mr and Mrs Earnest; Ninth st. near F
Wiatt, Mr Henry
Wines, Mr and Mr S. J.; H ave. bet. Fifth and Sixth sts.
Woof, Mr E. G.
——Mr J. H.; cor. Seventh and F sts.
——Mr

GO TO
BANCROFT'S
FOR
NEW
BOOKS

WHERE TO GO

FOR A

VACATION OR HOLIDAY

THE FOLLOWING NAMED PLACES ARE WORTHY OF A VISIT

HOTEL DEL MONTE, MONTEREY

MOUNT SHASTA

LAKE TAHOE   YOSEMITE VALLEY

Byron Hot Springs	The Mammoth Cave
White Sulphur Springs	Santa Barbara
Napa Soda Springs	Santa Monica
Ætna Springs	Long Beach
Harbins Springs	Donner Lake
Anderson Springs	Webber Lake
Howard Springs	Independence Lake
Seigler Springs	Big Trees
Highland Springs	Lick Observatory
Bartlett Springs	Forest Grove
Santa Ysabel Springs	Santa Cruz Big Trees
Klamath Hot Springs	Pacific Congress Springs

THE GEYSERS   PACIFIC GROVE

SANTA CRUZ

For Information and Tickets ask any Agent of the

SOUTHERN PACIFIC COMPANY

MONTEREY, CALIFORNIA

AMERICA'S FAMOUS WINTER AND SUMMER RESORT

BIRDS-EYE VIEW of HOTEL del MONTE MONTEREY, CAL.

"Where the leaf never dies in the still blooming bowers
And the bee bang'ets on thro' a whole year of flowers."

SAN JOSE AND SURROUNDINGS

Adams, Miss Mary P.; cor. Fifteenth and William sts.
Adams, C. L.; 509 S. Third st.
Adel, Capt and Mrs W. F.; 516 N. First st.
Alexander, Mr and Mrs J. H.; 313 S. Tenth st.   *Thursday*
Alexander, Mr and Mrs Henry J.; cor. 8th & San Carlos ave.   *Thursday*
Allen, Prof and Mrs C. H.; 419 S. Third st.
Andrews, Mr and Mrs W. C.; 176 N. Third st.
——Miss Mabel
Andrews, Mr and Mrs Frank G.; St. James Hotel   *Thursday*
Archer, Judge and Mrs Lawrence; cor. Keyes and Senter st.
——Lawrence
Arques, Mrs Nellie G.; 361 Market street
——Miss Maud
Arguello, Mr and Mrs Louis; cor. Third and Hensley ave.

Austin, Mr and Mrs Paul Page; 121 E. St. James st.   { *Monday* **Pacific Grove**

Auzerais, Mr and Mrs John   *Monday*

Barbour, Mr and Mrs J. H.
Baker, Miss Mattie S.
Barnhart, Mr and Mrs O. H.; 142 N. Third st.
Beach, Mr and Mrs Tyler; St. James Hotel   *Thursday*
——H. S.
——Wm.
Beal, Mrs G. P.; Sunol st.   *Tuesday*
——Miss Flora
——Miss Etta
Beans, Mr and Mrs T. Ellard; 489 N. First st.   *Tuesday*
——Miss Mary
——Miss Fannie
Beans, Mr and Mrs W. K.; N. Third st.   *Tuesday*
Belden, Mrs David; cor. Eleventh and San Antonio
Bentley, Mr and Mrs I. R.; Washington st.   *Friday*
Bethel, Miss Laura; 298 S. First st.
Bishop, Mr and Mrs S.; Alameda ave.
Blackford, Miss Lillian; 53 S. Sixth st.
Blanchard, Mr and Mrs W. W.; Alameda ave.   *Tuesday*
Blanchard, Miss Blanche; 445 North First st.
——Miss N.

Blaney, Mr and Mrs Charles D.; Stevens' Creek ave.   *Tuesdays*
——Miss Clarissa
Booksin, Mr and Mrs Henry, Jr.; 72 South Sixth st.   *Wednesday·*
Boring, Mrs S. W.; 450 North Fourth ·st. .
Bowden, Mr and Mrs N.; cor. Fourth and Hensley ave.
Bowman, Mr and Mrs G. M.; 480 North First st.
——Miss Edna
Bowman, Mr and Mrs G. B.; North First st.
Brainard, Mr and Mrs Henry A.
Breyfogle, Dr and Mrs C. W.; cor. Third and St. James sts.
——Miss Stella
Brown, Mr and Mrs A. M.
Bryant, D. T.; Sainte Claire Club
Burchard, Mr and Mrs D. W.; 478 North Third st.
Burke, Mrs; Naglee Place
—— Mr and Mrs J. Naglee
——Miss C.
——Miss Mamie .
Burkholder, Mr and Mrs Frank; cor. Ninth and San Carlos sts.
Boulware, Mr and Mrs M. A.; 281 East St. James st.   *Wednesday*
Benson, Miss Maud; South Third st.
——Miss Ruth
Baker, Wm. B.; 217 South Eleventh st.
——Miss Mattie
Black, Mr and Mrs T. K.; cor. Tenth and Santa Clara sts.
Brackett, Miss Dora; 469 South Second st.
——J. N. B.
Bruce, Mr and Mrs G. M.; Stockton ave.
Ballou, Mr and Mrs J. Q. A.
——-Miss Allie
Burns, Mr and Mrs Paul O.; Seventh and William sts.
Burns, Mr and Mrs X. E.
Burns, Mr and Mrs D.; La Molle House

Cadwallader, Mrs N.; Alameda ave.   *Tuesday*
Campbell, Mr and Mrs J. H.; 65 Fox ave.
Casey, Mr and Mrs W. J.   *Monday*
Castle, Neville H.; Sainte Claire Club
Childs, Prof and Mrs C. W.; Almaden Road
Chipman, Mr and Mrs L. J.; 410 East San Salvador st.
Clark, Mr and Mrs James; Locust and Park aves.
Clayton, Mr and Mrs J. A.; 471 North First st.
——Miss Ethel
Clayton, Mr and Mrs W. S.; Sunol st.   *Tuesday*
Cole, Mr and Mrs L. R.; Alameda ave.

180

Columbet, Mr and Mrs Peter; Fifth and William sts.
Cook, Mr and Mrs J. W.; 388 S. First st.
Crandall, Senator and Mrs; Paul Block
——Miss Albertine
Clayton, Mr and Mrs Ed; North Sixth st.
Caldwell, Dr and Mrs R.; South Second st.
——Miss Carrie
Callisch, Mr and Mrs Louis; South Second st.
Campbell, Mr and Mrs J. H.; 65 Fox ave.
Cochrane, Dr and Mrs A. H.; 216 South Second st.
Columbet, Miss Annie; 731 East Santa Clara st.
——Joe F.

Dawson, Mr and Mrs E. L.; Alameda ave.   *Tuesday*
Day, Mr and Mrs John A.
Denicke, Mr and Mrs F. A.; West San Carlos st.
Dougherty, Mr and Mrs W. P.; First st. and Hensley ave.
Duffy, Miss Nellie; cor. Eleventh and San Antonio sts.
Dunne, Mrs Catherine; 436 South Third st.   *Wednesday*
——Miss Kate
Davis, Mrs E. Livingstone; cor. Hedding and Elm sts.
——Miss Fanny
Denny, Mrs Elizabeth A.; 339 South Third st.
——Miss Cora
De Saisset, Mr and Mrs Pedro; 243 Guadalupe st.
——Miss Yetta
Dunn, Mr and Mrs Peter J., Jr.
Dusing, H. F.

Earle, Mrs M.; 694 South Second st.
——Miss Mae
Edwards, Mr and Mrs H. W.; P.O. box 854 *Thursday* { "Oak Grove," Hillsdale, Cal.
——Miss Cora
——Wilbur J.
Elwood, Prof and Mrs J. H.; 223 South Second st.
Enright, Mr and Mrs J. E.; Stockton ave.
——Mr and Mrs Joseph G.
Estabrook; Miss F. M.; South Tenth st.
Etchebarne, Mr and Mrs Peter; 287 North Third st.
——Miss Josephine
——Miss Lolita
——Miss Leontie
Evans, Mrs M. C.

Field, Mr and Mrs Walter M.; 476 North Third st.   *Monday*
Field, Arthur G.; Sainte Claire Club

Flagg, Mr and Mrs E. C.; Sunol st.   *Tuesday*
Foote, Mr and Mrs H. S.; Campbell's Station
Friant, Mr and Mrs; 149 S. Second st.   *Thursday*
————Miss Louise
————Miss Felicia
————Antonio
————Alfred
Faull, Joseph H.; Alameda ave.
Finck, Mr and Mrs W. H.; S. Ninth st.
Fischer, Miss Amelia; cor. Fifth and William sts.
Foley, Miss Minnie; Milpitas Road
Foster, Mr and Mrs Fred; 152 N. Fourth st.
Findley, Miss Minnie
Finigan, Dr and Mrs L.; William st.

Gaines, Mr and Mrs W. S.; 503 N. Fourth st.
————Miss Addie
Gillespie, Mr and Mrs E. J.; 90 Orchard st.
Guppy, Mr and Mrs E. H.; 691 S. Third st.
————Miss Ruth
————Edward S.
George, Mrs Fanny; 193 N. Third st.
————Miss Mattie
Gill, Wm. L.; N. First st., Sainte Claire Club
Gosbey, P. F.; 325 N. Third st., office, 28 Porter Building

Haile, Mrs Cornelius
Hale, Mr and Mrs O. A.; 269 S. Second st.   *1st Monday*
Hale, Mr and Mrs; 231 Guadalupe st.
————Miss Jennie
————Marshal   .
Hall, Mrs C. M.; Alameda ave.   *Tuesday*
Haydock, Mr and Mrs C.; 433 N. Fifth st.   *Thursday*
Henry, Mr and Mrs J. H.; Alameda ave.   *Tuesday*
Higgins, Mr and Mrs R. L.; Santa Clara st.
Hill, Mr and Mrs Morgan; The Alameda
Hirst, Rev and Mrs A. C.; Alameda ave.   *Tuesday*
Hobbs, Miss Allie; Alameda ave.   *Tuesday*
Hobson, Mr and Mrs W. B.; 154 S. Second st.
Hobson, Mrs T. W.; Sainte Claire Club
Howell, Mr and Mrs John; cor. Fifteenth and William sts.
Huggins, Mr and Mrs A. G.; Alameda ave.   *Tuesday*
Hall, Dr and Mrs J. U.; 186 N. Third st.
———— Miss Pearl
Harmon, Mr and Mrs Chas. H.; 128 S. Ninth st.
Hill, Dr and Mrs W. B.; 715 West Julian st.

Holly, Mr and Mrs John R.; North First st.
Hoydock, C.
Hunkins, Mr and Mrs S. B.; cor. St. James and Fourth sts.
———Miss Eva
Hughes, Mr and Mrs W. F.; 351 South Fourth st.   *Monday*
———Miss Mamie P.

Ingalsbe, A. W.; Sainte Claire Club
———Miss Margaret

Johnson, Mr and Mrs T. E.; Schiele ave.
Johnson, Mr and Mrs S. N.; North Eighth st.
Johnson, Mr and Mrs S. R.;. cor. Fourth and Empire sts.
———Miss May
———Walter

Kalfus, Mr and Mrs J. L.; Rose Lawn
King, Mr and Mrs A.; Julian and Fourteenth sts.
Kirkpatrick, Mr and Mrs W. J.; 343 Marlaire st.
King, Prof and Mrs F. L.; 369 South Second st.
Knickerbocker, Mr and Mrs E.; 404 North First st.

Laine, Mrs T. H.; Santa Clara
Lauck, Mr and Mrs George
Ledyard, Dr and Mrs F. K.; 441 South Second st.   *Thursday*
———Miss May
Ledyard, Dr and Mrs F. K.; 439 S. Second st.   *Thursday*
Leonard, Mr and Mrs H. M.; Santa Clara
Lewis, Mr and Mrs E. B.; 130 East St. James st.
Lewis, Mrs E. M.; 223 Santa Clara st.
———Miss Helen
———Miss Carrie
Lusson, Dr and Mrs P. M.; 31 North Second st.   *Thursday*
———Miss Cornelia
Lux, Mr and Mrs H.; Alum Rock ave.
———Miss Lizzie
———Lena
Lacoste, J. Frank; 140 North Third st.
Leib, Mr and Mrs S. F.; Alameda ave.
Lowe, Ralph; Sainte Claire Club
Lowe, Mr and Mrs James R.; 195 W. St. James st.

Malarin, Mr and Mrs M.; Santa Clara st.
———Miss Paula
———Miss Mariana
Mask, Mr and Mrs I. N.
McClellan, Mrs G. W.; Alameda ave.   *Tuesday*
———Carrie Foster

Mauvais, Mr and Mrs Romeo; Stockton ave.   *Tuesday*   Victoria
——Romeo, Jr.
——Juliet C.
——Ernest
——Edith
May, Judge and Mrs; Stockton ave.
——Miss Cora
——Miss Emily
Maynard, Mr and Mrs E. W.
McGeehee, Mr and Mrs J. H.; San Pedro and St. James st.
McGeoghegan, Mr and Mrs J. T.; Alameda ave.
McGrow, Dr and Mrs; cor. Seventh and St. James sts.   *Thursday*
——Miss Jessie
——Miss Louise
——Mr Sidney
——Mr Cyril
——Mrs D. F.
McKiernan, Mr and Mrs Charles; 225 San Augustine
——Miss
McLaughlin, Mr and Mrs E.; cor. Seventh and Reed sts.
——Miss Tina
Miller, Rev and Mrs W. Y.; 177 S. Second st.   *Wednesday*
——Miss Letitia
——Miss Elizabeth
——Dr John
McMillan, Mr and Mrs J. Y.; N. Fourth st.
——Miss Ida
——Miss Meda
——John
Montgomery, Miss Fannie; S. Second st.
Montgomery, Mr and Mrs T. S.; N. First st.
Moody, Mr and Mrs A. E.; N. Sixth st.
Moody, Mr and Mrs D. B.; 57 Devine st.
Moore, Judge and Mrs John; Alameda ave.   *Tuesday*
——Miss Bessie
——Howell C.; Sainte Claire Club
——Murray
Morrison, Miss Julia; cor. Fourth and Julian sts.
——Miss Angela
——Miss Winnifred
——Miss Fannie
Muirson, Mr and Mrs George; S. Tenth street.   *Tuesday*
Murphy, Mrs Martin; 361 S. Market st.
——Isaac T.

184

Murphy, Mr and Mrs J. M.; San Augustine st.
Murphy, Dan M.; Sainte Claire Club
Murphy, Mr and Mrs B. D.; 357 S. Third st.
Maybury, H.; Alameda ave.
——Miss Blanche
——Miss Carlotta

Naglee, Miss Marie; Naglee Place
Nance, Mr and Mrs C. P.; 367 South First st   *Thursday*   **Pacific Grove**
——Hugh J.
Nance, Mr and Mrs John A.
Nesmith, L. G.; Sainte Claire Club
Newhall, Mr and Mrs Silvester; Willow Glen
——Miss Bessie

Owens, Mr and Mrs Fred; 215 South Second st.
Owen, Mr and Mrs C. J.; San Fernando and Delmes ave.
Owen, Mr and Mrs C. P.; 129 W. Julian st.
O'Connor, Judge and Mrs M. P.; Second st.

Park, Mrs C. T.; Empire and First sts.
Parkhurst, Mr and Mrs W. A.; 518 South Second st.
Phillips, Mr and Mrs Mitchell; 208 North Third st.
Pierce, Dr and Mrs R. E; Hotel Vendome   *Monday*
Pierce, Mr and Mrs R. T.; Santa Clara
Pierce, Mr and Mrs J. H.; Alameda ave.   *Tuesday*
Pierce, Mr J. P.; Santa Clara
——Miss Annie
——Miss Florence
——Miss Grace
Polhemus, Mr and Mrs George B.; Stockton ave.   *Tuesday*
——Miss M.
——Miss J.
——Miss Nellie
——Mr C. B.
Porter, Norman; 75 East St. James st.   *Wednesday*
——Miss Evangeline
——Miss Anna
——Miss Elizabeth
——Miss Mary
Potts, Dr and Mrs J. S.   *Monday*
Paulsell, Mr and Mrs A. C.; 763 South Second st.
Pfister, Mr and Mrs A.; 10 South Second st.
——Frank M.
——Herman
——Miss

185

Randol, J. B.; Almaden
Reed, Mr and Mrs E. P.; 269 North Market st.
——George
——E. C.; Sainte Claire Club

Reed, Mr and Mrs Elliot; 279 North San Pedro st.
Rhodes, Judge and Mrs A. L.; Alameda ave.   *Tuesday*
Rhiehl, Mr and Mrs A.; 253 N. Third st.
——Miss Emma
——Miss Tessie

Richards, Mr and Mrs W. S.; Third and San Salvador
——Miss Sadie

Rinaldo, Mr and Mrs Tobe; Julian and Third sts.   *Wednesday*
Rucker, Mr and Mrs J. H.; S. Third st.   *Tuesday*
Rucker, Mrs J. E.; 271 N. Fifth st.
——Miss Susie
——Miss Lucy

Rucker, Mr and Mrs James T.; N. Third st.
Rucker, Mayor S. N.; Sainte Claire Club.
Russell, Prof and Mrs F. P.; cor. Second and Keyes sts.
Ryder, Mr and Mrs G. W.; 356 S. Second st.   *Wednesday*
——Miss Georgie
——William

Ryland, Mr and Mrs C. T.; 431 N. First st.
——Miss Ada
——Miss Norma
——John W.
——Mr and Mrs C. T., Jr.
——Dwight
——Charles

Ryland, Mr and Mrs J. R.; Los Gatos
Reynolds, Judge and Mrs John; 177 Devine st.
Reen, Mr and Mrs Peter C.; Seventh and Washington sts.

Saunders, Mr and Mrs E. B.; Stockton ave.   *Tuesday*
Saxe, Mr and Mrs J. D.; East San Jose
Shaw, Miss Jeannette; Berryessa ave.   *Saturday*
Sheehan, Mr and Mrs J. M.; Alum Rock ave.
Shortridge, Mr and Mrs Charles M.; 479 N. Third st.
Smith, Mr and Mrs T. O.; George st.   *Wednesday*
Smith, Mr and Mrs R. J.; 470 N. Third st.
Smith, Mr and Mrs Frank; S. Second st.   *Friday*
Spence, Mr and Mrs A. A.; Alameda ave.
Spence, Mr and Mrs R. B.; Alameda ave.   *Tuesday*
Spence, Mr and Mrs D. J.

Spencer, Judge and Mrs Francis E. ; 216 Autumn st.   *Friday*
——Miss Grace
Simpson, Mrs H. ; 253 S. Second st.   **Monterey and Santa Cruz**
——Dr William
——Miss H. Jessie
Singletary, Mr and Mrs Chas. F. ; 257 S. Third st.
——Miss Loie
Spring, Mr and Mrs T. W. ; 171 Orchard st.
——H. M. N.
Singletery, Mr and Mrs J. E. ; 325 East San Antonio st.
——Mr and Mrs E. C. ; Stockton ave.

Taylor, Mr and Mrs F. A. ; Taylor Block   *1st Thursday*
Tennyson, Mr and Mrs D. D. ; 353 North Third st.
Thorn, Dr and Mrs W. S.   Vendome   *Monday*
——Miss Grace
Thorpe, Mr and Mrs J. M. ; 355 South Fifth st.
Thurston, Mr and Mrs G. P.
Tisdale, Mr and Mrs W. D. ; Alameda ave.   *Tuesday*
Tosetti, Mr and Mrs Ernest
Travis, Mr and Mrs J. C. ; 776 South Second st.   *Friday*   Lake Tahoe
Trimble, Mrs ; Milpitas Road
——Miss Maggie
——Miss Mattie
Tupper, Mr and Mrs O. M. ; South Third st.   *Wednesday*
Thayer, Mr and Mrs H. P. Guadalupe

Urmy, Prof C. ; Hotel Vendome

Wagener, Mr and Mrs S. H. ; cor. San Carlos and Third sts.
——Miss Effie
Walsh, Miss M. A.
Wallace, Mr & Mrs John T. ; SW. cor. South First & Floyd sts. { *Tuesday* Pescadero
——John T., Jr.
Wallace, Mr and Mrs J. W.   *Thursday*
Wapple, Mr and Mrs Geo. ; 27 East st.   *Tuesday*
Weber, Hon and Mrs C. M. ; Madrone
Welch, Mr and Mrs George ; 289 South Tenth st.
Whitton, Col and Mrs A. K. ; North First st.   *Wednesday*
Wilcox, Mr and Mrs E. J. ; South First st.
——Miss Annie
——Miss Edith
Williams, Mr and Mrs C. W. ; 530 North Second st.   *Thursday*
Williams, Mr and Mrs Ed ; 609 South Third st.
——Miss Edith
——Miss Emma

Williams, Mr and Mrs A. S.; 307 North First st.
Williams, Mrs E.; South Third st.
Wood, Mr and Mrs Uriah ; 425 South Second st.
Wooster, Mr and Mrs C. M.; Second and San Antonio sts.
Worcester, Mr and Mrs H. B. ; East Santa Clara st.   *Wednesday*
Wright, Mr and Mrs W. H.; Eighth st.
Wright, Mr and Mrs W. F.; 258 North Fourteenth st.
Wright, Mr and Mrs C. D. ; 217 North First st.   *Wednesday*
Wright, F.; Sainte Claire Club
Wright, Mr and Mrs H. W.; 357 South Third st.
Wright, Mr and Mrs Alexander; 72 South Sixth st.   *Wednesday*
Walthal, Mr and Mrs J. ; 304 South Second st.
Wharton, Wm. H.; West Santa Clara st.
Wakefield, Rev John B. ; 81 North Second st.
———Geo. F.
———Miss H.

Yoell, Mr and Mrs J. A.; Alameda ave.   *Tuesday*
———Miss Gertrude
———J. H.
Younger, Col and Mrs; Forest Home
———Miss Rosalie
———Miss Gussie
———Miss Florence
———Mr and Mrs Ed

Sainte Claire Club

SAN JOSE, CAL.

Incorporated 1888

Dr. R. E. Pierce	President
A. W. Ingalsbe	Secretary
W. K. Keans	Treasurer

BOARD OF DIRECTORS

Dr. R. E. Pierce   S. N. Rucker

J. H. Henry   Arthur G. Field

O. B. Barnhart   C. M. Wooster

I. Loeb

ROLL OF MEMBERSHIP

Andrews, F. G.

Ahlers, H. C.

Averett, A. E.

Alvord, H. B.

Albright, H. G.

Austin, P. P.

Barnhart, O. H.

Bryant, D. T.

Beans, W. K.

Beans, T. E.

Bragg, G. H.

Burchard, D. W.

Burk, J. N.

Bowden, N.

Bull, C.

Bowie, A. J.

Babcock, J.

Bassett, A. C.

Castle, N. H.

Chadbourne, F. S.

Clayton, E. W.

Clayton, W. S.

Cunningham, J. F.

Casey, W. J.

Derby, Thos.

Dawson, E. L.

Dunlap, R. B.

Dunne, J. F.

Dougherty, W. P.

Edwards, H. J.

Etchebarne, P.

Enright, J. G.

Field, Arthur G.

Field, W. M.

Findlay, J. W.

Flagg, E. C.

Friant, A.	Murphy, J. T.
Flickinger, J. H.	Nesmith, L. G.
Gill, W. L.	Owens, F.
Goodrich, E. E.	Pierce, Dr R. E.
Graves, G. E.	Polhemus, G. B.
Hagan, C. A.	Priest, R. T.
Hill, Morgan	Rea, J. W.
Hobson, T. W.	Reed, E. C.
Henry, J. H.	Roberts, J. R.
Hill, Dr W. B.	Rucker, J. H.
Jones, B. L.	Rucker, J. T.
Ingalsbe, A. W.	Rucker, S. N.
Kennedy, W. C.	Ryland, C. T.
Kellner, G. N.	Schemmel, H. L.
Lowe, R.	Shortridge, C. M.
Lacoste, J. F.	Spence, A. A.
Lefranc, H.	Smith, H. E.
Lenzen, J.	Spence., R. B
Loeb, I.	Sanford, F. C.
Lieb, S. F.	Simpson, Dr Wm.
Murphy, D. M.	Tully, J. A.
McCabe, A. M.	Todd, W. A.
McMurtry, G. S.	Thayer, H. P.
Miller, Dr J. J.	Whitton, Lt Col A. K.
Moore, H. C.	Wright, F. V.
Murphy, B. D.	Wright, W. H.
McMurtry, W. S., Jr.	Wright, H. W.
Martin, W. J.	Wooster, C. M.
McGraw, Dr D. F.	Weber, C. M.
Masson, P.	Yoell, J. H.

Germania Verein

OFFICERS

H. L. Schemmel	President
J. Lenzen	Vice-President
C. Piatti	Treasurer
G. Knoche	Secretary

LIST OF MEMBERS

Pfister, H. A.	Pfister, H. C.	Willard, T.
Piatti, C.	Feist, Jos.	Knoche, G.
Stock, R.	Otter, H.	Alexander, G. W.
Bohland, G.	Balbach, J.	Burke, Dr R. H.
Brassy, F.	Baumgärtner, F.	Bowden, N.
Claus, F.	Callisch, F.	Eberhardt, J.
Fischer, C. W.	Friant, Ant.	Haydock, C.
Harbeck, T.	Hirsch, P. S.	Hermann, A. T.
Hermann, Chas.	Heinberg, J.	Jenkins, Dr O. C.
Harmon, J. B.	Hobson, W. B.	Hagan, C. A.
Koch, V.	Koch, A. J.	Krumb, L.
Luther, F.	Lenzen, J.	Lenzen, T. W.
Lenzen, T.	Lenzen, M.	Lieber, L.
Levy, J. H.	Levy, J. M.	Loeb, J.
Lux, H.	Levy, S.	Lion, G.
Lion, E.	Loeb, G.	Marten, A. H.
Marten, G. A.	Marten, J. P.	Moody, A.
O'Keefe, R.	O'Brien, M.	Pfister, A.
Pabst, F.	Pott, F. S.	Promis, O.
Pfau, L.	Rank, T.	Rinaldo, T.
Rosenthal, E.	Riehl, A.	Rucker, S.
Rich, S.	Rinaldo, D.	Schroeder, J.
Schemmel, H. L.	Scherrer, G.	Stern, M.
Stern, F.	Sontheimer, J.	Schoen, L.
Scheller, V.	Seifert, Dr G. F.	Quilty, C.
Wislocky, K.	Waterman, J.	Walthall, J. W.
Simpson, Dr W.	Callisch, L.	Lenham, G. L.
Andrews, W. C.	Chapman, F. N.	Rhein, A. J.
Hart, A.	Masson, P.	Rucker, James T.
Andrews, W. H.	Kennedy, W. C.	Harrenstein, J. W.

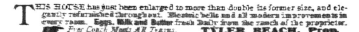

SAN RAFAEL

*

Hotel Rafael

Bowie, Mr and Mrs Aug J.
Bowie, Miss Bessie
Binsse, Mr C. W.
Briggs, Mr and Mrs Arthur R.
Christmas, Mrs R.
Crocker, Mr and Mrs H. J.
Cunningham, P. P.
Davidson, Mr and Mrs D. B.
Davidson, Miss Della
Donahoe, Mr and Mrs Dennis
Donahoe, Miss Rose
Friedlander, Mr Cary
Garber, Miss E.
Graves, Mr and Mrs R. N.
Graves, Miss Elma
Hall, Mr and Mrs H. E.
Hanna, Mrs S. C.

Holloway, Mr E. L.
Holloway, Mr and Mrs W. E.
Judd, E. T.
Lawton, Mrs T. D.
Lawton, Miss
McAllister, Mr Ward, Jr.
Moore, Mr and Mrs J. J.
Morse, Mrs A. C.
Morse, Miss Jessie
Morse, Miss Kate
Morse, Miss Sallie
Petersen, Mr Charles
Phillippe, Mr and Mrs
Poage, Mr and Mrs C. A.
Raum, Mr and Mrs Geo E.
Smith, Mr and Mrs Ward M.
Stanley, Mrs Edward

Ten Brock, Mrs M. C.

HOTEL RAFAEL

SAN RAFAEL, CAL.

or by the North Pacific Coast Railroad via Sausalito. Both routes crossing the Bay opposite the Golden Gate and running close to Alcatraz Island. The climate of San Rafael is not equaled by that of any other place on the Coast.

AS A SUMMER RESORT

it is an agreeable change from the fogs and smoke of San Francisco, and its warm equable climate makes it one of the most desirable resorts in California. It has not the oppressive heat of inland towns; yet it is protected from fogs and cold by the surrounding mountains.

AS A WINTER RESORT

for Eastern visitors, or for others desiring comfortable winter quarters, it has not an equal in the world. Its close proximity to San Francisco, the rapid and frequent communication with the large city, its warm winter days, and withal a magnificent hotel with every comfort and convenience that modern ideas can suggest, the RAFAEL has become the most popular Hotel in the State.

W. E. ZANDER, Manager

Alexander, Mr and Mrs Chas. O.
Alexander, Mr and Mrs R. S.
Alexander, Mr and Mrs J. E.
Ames, Mr and Mrs Pelham W.
——Miss Gertrude
——Miss Alice
Allen, Mr and Mrs Henry F.
Allen, Mr and Mrs Harry H.
——John De Witt
Boole, The Misses
Babcock, William
——Harry
Benedict, Mrs E. L.; Hotel Rafael
Bigelow, Mr and Mrs John F.
Bonneau, Mr Thomas
Berry, Mr and Mrs W. F.
Berry, Tom C.
Berry T. B.
Barker, Mr and Mrs William
——Miss Mary
——Miss Alice
Barstow, Mr and Mrs S. F.
Buckley, Dr and Mrs
Butler, Mr and Mrs Geo. E.
Bogart, Mr and Mrs William
Brander, Geo. L.
Boyd, Mr and Mrs John F.
Bourne, Mr and Mrs W. B.
Buck, Mr.
——Miss
Crane, Mr and Mrs
Crosby, Rev and Mrs Arthur
Cushing, Mr and Mrs Sidney B.
Coffin, Mr and Mrs James
Curlett, William
Curtis, Mr and Mrs Allen A.
Darwin, Chas. B.
Davidson, Mr and Mrs D. B.

Donohoe, Mr & Mrs D. (Brit. Cons.)
——Mr and Mrs Dennis, Jr.
——Miss Rose
Donahue, Mrs J. Mervyn
De Young, Mr and Mrs M. H.
Dibble, E. A.
Dodge, Mr and Mrs Geo.
Drake, Mrs Charles *Thursday*
Du Bois, Mr and Mrs Henry
Duffy, Mr and Mrs Thomas J.
Evans, Mr and Mrs Esau
Ferrer, Mrs
Francis, Harry
Favre, Mrs Otto
Forbes, William
——Mrs Alexander
——Miss Kate
——Miss Edith
Forbes, Mrs Johnson; Fair Hills *F'y*
Foster, Mr and Mrs A. W.
Fish, Mr and Mrs C. H.
Grant, Mr and Mrs Adam
Graves, Mr & Mrs R. N.; H. Rafael
——Miss Elma
Griffith, Mr and Mrs E. L.
Griffith, Mr and Mrs Millen
——The Misses
Glass, Capt and Mrs Henry
Green, Mr and Mrs Chas. E.
Gerstle, Mr and Mrs Lewis
Graham, Mr and Mrs Geo. S.
Heath, Mr and Mrs Frank
Hepburn, Miss
Henshelwood, Mr and Mrs Thomas
Hollaway, Mr and Mrs W. E.
——E. L.
Hyde, Mr and Mrs Henry C.
——Miss

Hoffman, Mr and Mrs Southard
Hoffman, Ogden
———Southard
———Miss
Heathcote, Mr and Mrs Basil
Jennings, Mr and Mrs C. B.
Jellett, Mr and Mrs
Johnson, Frank S.
Johnston, Mrs W. B.
Josselyn, Mr and Mrs G. M.
Kelsey, B.
Kittle, Mr and Mrs John G.
———Miss Lucia
Kent, Mr and Mrs A. E.
Kinne, Mr and Mrs C. Mason
———Miss Ella
———Miss Alice
Lawton, Mrs D. S.; Hotel Rafael
———Miss
Lancaster, Mr & Mrs E. A.; H. Rafael
Lucas, Robert H.
Lyman, Dr J. Chester
Lichtenberg, Mr and Mrs Wm.
———Mr and Mrs Rudolph
———The Misses
Locke, Mr and Mrs W. I.
Lilienthal, Mr and Mrs F. R.
———Mr and Mrs J. Leo
L'Amoureaux, Miss Mamie
———Miss Alice
Lord, Mrs J. M.
Latnam, Mr and Mrs F. B.
Moore, Mr and Mrs Jas P.
McDonald, Rev and Mrs Jas.
———Miss
McAllister, Mrs Hall
———Miss
———Elliott
———Hall
McCarthy, Mr and Mrs E. W.
Marshall, Mr and Mrs Louis
Mailliard, Mr and Mrs John
———Mr and Mrs A.
———The Misses

Morris, Mrs Thos.
Murison, Miss
Menzies, Mr and Mrs Thomas
Morse, Miss Jessie; Hotel Rafael
Nichols, Mrs A. C.
———Miss Belle
Neale, Mr and Mrs Vincent
Nichols, C. C.
Newhall, Mr and Mrs W. M.
O'Connor, Mrs M. J.
———The Misses
Oxenard, Mrs
———Miss
———Mr
Pinkard, Mr and Mrs Geo. M.
Pringle, Henry B.
Perry, Mr and Mrs Grattan
Page, Mr and Mrs Arthur
———Mr and Mrs Geo. T.
———Miss
———W. S.
Parrott, Mr and Mrs L. B.
Pomeroy, Mr and Mrs Carter P.
Poole, Mr and Mrs Lawrence
Park, Mrs T. W.
Regan, Mr and Mrs J. C.
Rose, O. G.
Redington, Henry W.
Redington, Mrs Lucy
Rolls, Mr and Mrs John S.
Ross, Mrs Ann S.
Scott, Mr and Mrs E.   *Friday*
Stoy, Sam.
Stoy, Rev Wm.
———The Misses
Sontag, Mr and Mrs Henry
———Mr and Mrs Chas.
Stewart, Irvine
Sweeney, Mr and Mrs L. H.
Scott, Mr and Mrs Eb.
Smith, Mrs Geo.
Smith, Mr and Mrs Sidney V.
Spencer, Mr and Mrs F. W.
Stetson, Mr and Mrs Edward G.

Sloss, Mr and Mrs Lewis
——Jr.
——Leon
Seibel, Mr and Mrs F.
——Miss Ella
——Miss Mollie
Smith, Mr and Mrs S. M.
——The Misses
Sherwood, Mr and Mrs H. H.
Tremper, Frank E.
Tomkins, Mr and Mrs Minthorne M.
——Miss Susie
——Miss Julia B.
——Miss Ethel
——Mr Minthorne, Jr.
——Philip W.

Van Winkle, Mrs I. S.
——Miss
——Miss Belle
Whiting, H. C.
Wilkins, Mr and Mrs Hepburn
Wright, Whitaker
Walker, Miss Annie
Wheeler, F. A.
Wood, Mr and Mrs H. P.
White, Dr and Mrs F. J.
Wilson, Mr and Mrs J. N. E.
Wintringham, Mr and Mrs Thos.
Worn, Mr and Mrs Geo. A.
——The Misses
Zander, Mr & Mrs. W. E.; H. Rafael

195

Mount Tamalpais Academy

A CORPORATION

Boarding and Day School

FOR BOYS

San Rafael, Cal.

REV. J. E. WHEELER, D. D.

PRINCIPAL

Assisted by a Corps of Competent Teachers

BOARD OF DIRECTORS

Wm. Babcock, Esq.
SAN RAFAEL

Robert Dickson, Esq.
SAN FRANCISCO

Geo. E. Goodman, Esq.
NAPA

J. R. Jarboe, Esq.
SAN FRANCISCO

Rev. Arthur Crosby
SAN RAFAEL

Rev. Thos. C. Eaton, D. D.
SAN FRANCISCO

Rev. H. C. Minton,
SAN JOSE

Hon. E. B. Conklin
SAN JOSE

Arthur W. Foster, Esq.
SAN RAFAEL

R. J. Trumbull, Esq.
SAN RAFAEL

For further information apply to

REV. J. E. WHEELER, D. D.

SAN RAFAEL

San Rafael Lawn Tennis Club

Club Grounds, Cullodon Avenue, San Rafael, Cal.

The San Rafael Lawn Tennis Club is composed of residents of San Rafael, and of San Franciscans who reside there during the Summer. It was organized October 14, 1880, and incorporated May 24, 1884. The object of the organization is the promotion of lawn tennis, and tournaments are annually held upon the Club grounds.

OFFICERS

WM. BABCOCK - - · - - - President
E. C. EVANS - - - Vice-President and Secretary
T. B. BERRY - - - - - -· Treasurer
T. C. BERRY - · - - - Ground Committee

DIRECTORS

Babcock, Wm.   Evans, E. C.
Berry, T. B.   Foster, A. W.
Berry, T. C.   Heathcote, Mrs Basil
            Page, Arthur

MEMBERS

REGULAR

Bennet, R. R.	Berry, T. B.	Berry, Wm.
Curlett, Wm.	Cushing, Mrs S. B.	Donahue, Mrs M.
Forbes, W. R.	Francis, H.	Gillette, D. B.
Hamm, Mrs	Heathcote, Mrs	O'Connor, Miss
O'Connor, Miss M.	Pomeroy, C. P.	Pringle, Harry
Severance, J. S.	Walker, Miss	Griffith, E. L.

MONTHLY

Bigelow, J. F.	Bunker, Paul	Campbell, D. Y.
Crockett, J. B.	Girvin, R. D.	Haymond, Mr.
Hoffman, O.	Hoffman, S.	Kittle, Miss M.
Kittle, Miss	McAllister, E.	McAllister, Hall
Oxnard, Robt.	Sherwood, Harry	Sherwood, Mrs
Sprague, E. H.	Stevens, Charles	Williamson, Alex. B.
Patton, Miss Ethel		

LIFE

Allen, John de Witt	Babcock, Wm.	Berry, Thos. C.
Bourn, W. B.	Boyd, John T.	Cushing, S. B.
Evans, E. C.	Foster, A. W.	Grant, J. D.
Heathcote, B	Newhall, H. M.	Newhall, G. A.
Page, Arthur	Page, Geo. T.	Sharon, F.

SANTA ROSA AND SURROUNDINGS

Anderson, Dr and Mrs T. H. B.   *Thursday*
——Miss Carrie
——Miss Lula
——Miss Lillian
——Edgar
——Thomas
Austian, Mr and Mrs J. S.; Beaver st.   *Thursday*
Brumpus, Mr and Mrs C. H.; 435 Mendocino st.
Carter, Mr and Mrs D. P.; 532 Mendocino st.
——Miss Mabel Mattoon
Coffey, Mr and Mrs H.; College ave. and Orchard st.
——Miss Minnie
——Miss Octavia
Chase, Miss M. E.; Santa Rosa Seminary   *Thursday*
Crawford, Mrs M. L.   Guatemala, C. A.
Doyle, Mrs M. E.; Fourth and Pierce sts.   *Thursday*
Dayton, Miss A.; Santa Rosa Seminary   *Thursday*
Frost, Mr and Mrs C. W.; 548 Mendocino st.
——Miss Jennie
Finlow, Dr and Mrs; Mendocino st.
Farmer, Mrs R. W.; B st.
——Miss Fannie
——Henry
Finley, Dr and Mrs W. A.; McDonald ave. and Seventeenth sts. *Friday*
Finley, Rev W. A.; McDonald ave.
Finley, Mrs S. E. L.; McDonald ave.   *Wednesday*
Goodyear, Mr and Mrs Andrew   Benicia
——Miss
——Mr and Mrs H. C.   Winters
Gordin, Mr and Mrs T. C.   Winters
——Miss Mary
——Miss Maggie
Hart, Mrs S. P.; 511 Mendocino st.
Hart, Mr and Mrs D. B.; 511 Mendocino st.   *Thursday*

Hardin, Col and Mrs J. A.; Fourth st.   *Wednesday*
——Miss Endora   .
—·——Miss Ethel
Hill, Mr and Mrs G. W.   Winters
Hunter, Mr F. A.; 720 Fourth st.
——Miss Mary
——Miss Lola
Hopkins, R. D.   Eureka Springs, Arkansas
——Mr R. D., Jr.   Napa
——Miss Minnie   Lakeport
Hopper, Mr and Mrs Thos; McDonald ave.   *Tuesday*
Hodgson, Mr and Mrs W. H.; McDonald ave.   Colusa
——Miss May Luman
——Mr Frank Luman

Jacobs, Mrs J. A.; 720 Fourth st.

Kinsey, Mrs Jennie   Winters
Krolck, Rev L.; Mendocino st.

Luding, Mrs E. J.; McDonald ave.   *Tuesday*

Middleton, Mr and Mrs W. V.; 443 Humbolt st.
Miller, Mr and Mrs J. M.; cor. Mendocino st.
——Miss Jennie
——Grace
McClain, Mrs Dr; College ave. and Orchard st.   *Thursday*
McFadyen, Mr and Mrs A.; B st.
——Miss Edith

Newton, Major and Mrs E. C. Newton   Kelseyville
——Horace B.

Oaten, Mrs F.; McDonald ave.   *Tuesday*
O'Meara, Mr and Mrs James; 650 Mendocino st
——Miss Frances L.
——Miss Polly A.
——Miss Julia A.

Parsons, Mr and Mrs; 309 King st.
——Miss Maggie
Petray, Mr and Mrs H. C.; 9 Cherry st.   *Wednesday*
Pope, Mrs C. S.; 117 Fifth st.
Pratt, Miss A. E.; Santa Rosa Seminary   *Thursday*
Pressley, Mrs; King st.'
——Miss Lulu
Prindle, Mr and Mrs Henry; Mendocino st.
Proctor, Mrs J.; College ave. and Humboldt st.
Purrington, Mr and Mrs Joseph; 648 Mendocino st.
——Miss Marguerite

Riley, Mr and Mrs A. W.; Mendocino st.
Robberson, Miss Ella; 404 Third st.
Runyon, Mrs Mary; 535 B st.

Sargent, Dr and Mrs J. S.
Sims, Mrs L. A.   Winters
——Miss Nora
Spotswood, Miss Belle; McDonald ave.   *Tuesday*

Thompson, Hon and Mrs T. L.; 804 McDonald ave.
——Miss Frances
——Miss Ethel
——Miss Grace
Thompson, Dr and Mrs C. H.; 312 Third st.
——Miss Cassie A.

Whipple, Mrs E. D.; 804 McDonald ave.
Wood, Mrs R. W.; Santa Rosa Seminary   *Thursday*

THE BANCROFT COMPANY

" Unrivalled for Sweetness and Sympathy of Touch."

It is my business to prepare striking and original advertisements for all commercial purposes. Additional samples of my work sent on receipt of request. H. C. BROWN, Advertising Sketches and Photo Engraving, 35 and 37 Frankfort Street, New York.

SAUSALITO

Avery, Francis; "The Nook"

Baker, Mr and Mrs Wakefield; "La Vuelta" *Wednesday*

Barrett, Mr and Mrs Moss; "Owl Cottage"

Barrett, Mr and Mrs W. G.; "Casa Madrona"

Bartlett, Mr and Mrs C. E.

Bass, Mr and Mrs T. J.; "Bellaggio"

——Miss Edith

Belknap, Mr and Mrs D. P.; "Admiral Bullfrog"

Bell, Mr and Mrs A. D.; "Elderberry Cottage"

Bell, James; "The Roost"

Boyle, Mr and Mrs H. A.; "Cypress Knoll"

——Miss

Brown, Miss Lizzie; "Mt. Thomas"

Burrey, Charles; "El Monte Hotel"

Burrows, Capt and Mrs; "Sunnyside"

——The Misses

Case, Dr and Mrs C.; "Sunnyside"

Campbell, Mr and Mrs H. C.; "The Heights"

Chandler, Mr and Mrs F. B.; "Cliff Haven"

Claussen, Mr and Mrs

——Thomas

Cobb, Major and Mrs Harry A.; "Bird's Nest Cottage" *Thursday*

——Miss Mamie

Cooper, Miss May

Cormack, T. E. K.

Crumpton, Dr and Mrs H. J.

Crall, Major and Mrs George A.; "Buckeye Cottage"

Dickenson, Col and Mrs John H.

Fiedler, Mr and Mrs F.; "Ivanhoe"

——The Misses

——Stephen

——Frederick

——James

Fleury, Paul; "Mira Mar"

——Miss

Foster, Mr and Mrs C. J.; "Hacienda"

Gardner, Mr and Mrs James H.; "The Bower" *Friday*

George, Mr and Mrs Robert; "Loma Vista"
——The Misses
Gray, Capt Emmet; "Cabana Bonita"
Gregory, Mr and Mrs J. N.; "Oak Cliff"
Groom, Mrs

Hall, H. H.; "Russell Cottage"
Harlan, Mr and Mrs Charles; "Monte Vista"   *Tuesday*
Harmes, Mr and Mrs J. T ; "Oak Knoll"
Harrison, Commodore and Mrs C. H.; "Hazel Mount"
Harrison, Mr and Mrs J. W.
Harrison, Mr and Mrs Robert
Hearst, W. R.; "Sea Point"
Heilbron, Theo.; "Lucretia Cottage"
Hellman, Mr and Mrs A. C.; "Chedder Villa"
Hill, Dr and Mrs Thomas L.; "Promontory"
Holmes, Mr and Mrs Walter
Hyman, Col P. C.; "Alcazar Cottage"

Jackson, Mr and Mrs T. W.; "Alta Mira Villa"
——Miss M
Jackson, W. A.; El Monte Hotel
Jerome, Mrs T. F.; "Gardner Cottage"

Lee, Mrs Rowland; El Monte Hotel
Little, Dr and Mrs Joseph R.; "Iroquois Villa"
Livermore, Col O.; "Gilead"
Low, Lieut and Mrs C. P.

Marvin, Mr and Mrs A. T.; "Cliff Cottage"
Meade, Mr and Mrs George W.; "Hollyoaks"
Miller, Major O. C.; "The Pines"
Mills, Mrs W. G.; "Barnstead Cottage"

Nation, Mr and Mrs G. M.; "Alta Mira Villa"
Nicholson, Miss Anna; "Vista de Mar"
Noble, Mr and Mrs H. H.
——Miss

Pariser, Mr and Mrs James A.; "Vista de Mar"
——Alfred D.
——Montagu H.
——The Misses
Penlington, Mr and Mrs T.
Pew, Mr and Mrs J. W.; "Toleda Cottage"

Ralph, Miss
Reade, F. William
Reed, Major and Mrs G. W.; "Mossbrae"
Richards, Mr and Mrs John; "Svea Cottage"

Roma, Mr and Mrs J. M.
———Miss

Sanderson, Miss Hilda; "Vista de Mar"
Schultz, Mr and Mrs Charles; "Vera Cottage"
———Miss Mary O.
Shoobert, Mr and Mrs J. E.
Stauf, Werner; "Wild Idles"
Slinkey, Col and Mrs J. E.; El Monte Hotel   *Monday*
———Miss Lillie
Sperry, Mr and Mrs J. W.

Tashiera, Mr and Mrs George; "Redonda Vista"
Theobald, Mr and Mrs George J.; "Magnolia Cottage"
Thomas, Capt and Mrs George W.   *Thursday*
Thomas, Mr and Mrs William J.; "Mt. Thomas"
Tillingast, D. F.; "The Bungalow"
———The Misses
———W. D.
Tiffany, William; "Alvaston Cottage"

Wheeler, Mrs S. G.; "Rose Bank".
———Miss Helen
Windsor, Mrs T.
Winterburn, Mr and Mrs George H.; El Monte Hotel
Woods, E. L.; "The Roost"
Wooley, Mr and Mrs D. M.

AT

The BANCROFT ✳ Company

Fall

and

Winter

1890

❋

DANIEL

BRADLEY © AGENT

Has the honor to inform you
that his New Stock for Fall and
Winter of 1890, is now complete
and ready for inspection.

The favor of your commands is solicited.

No. 235 Fifth Avenue

NEW YORK

STOCKTON

Adams, Mr and Mrs Henry; 171 El Dorado st.
Adams, Mr and Mrs H. E.; Magnolia, bet. Centre and Commerce sts.
Arnold, Mr and Mrs Fred; cor. El Dorado and Lindsay sts.
Ashe, Mrs W. L.   *Saturday*
Atherton, Mr and Mrs George A.; 162 Poplar st.
Atwood, Mr and Mrs Leroy S.; 387 Grant st.
Atwood, Mr and Mrs Oscar; 371 Stanislaus st.
Austin, Mr and Mrs W. B.; Flora, bet. Otter and Beaver sts.

Baggs, Mrs Wm. M.; 365 Beaver st.
Baldwin, Mr and Mrs Herbert; 129 Park st.
Baldwin, Judge and Mrs F. T.; Miner ave., bet. Aurora and Sacramento
Beecher, Mr and Mrs J. L.; cor. Lindsay and El Dorado sts.
Belding, Mr and Mrs Chas.; El Dorado, bet. Park and Flora sts.
Belding, Mrs W. J.; 543 Market st.
Bennet, Mr and Mrs C. O.; Channel, bet. American and Stanislaus sts.
Bennett, Mr and Mrs Paul W.; 158 El Dorado st.
Bidwell, W. E.; cor. Sutter and Lafayette sts.
——Miss Lena
Bogue, Mr and Mrs A. R.; Sutter, bet. Market and Lafayette sts.
Boissellier, Mrs H. G.; 273 Miner ave.
——Miss Emma
Botswick, Mr and Mrs I. S.; 245 Weber ave.
Bours, Mrs B. W.; North, bet. Hunter and San Joaquin sts.
——Wm. M.
Buck, Mr and Mrs T. B.; Yo Semite House
Buckley, Mr and Mrs W. D.; 365 Beaver st.
Budd, Mr and Mrs Jas. H.; Channel and Ophir sts.
Budd, Judge and Mrs Jos. H.; Sutter, bet. Channel st. and Miner ave.
Budd, Mr and Mrs J. E.; Acacia, bet. Beaver and Elk sts.
Buell, Mr and Mrs P. A.; SE cor. El Dorado and Flora sts.
Bunker, Mrs F. C.; 123 Park st.

Campbell, Mr and Mrs J. C.; Flora and Beaver sts.
Carter, Mr and Mrs S. L.; 135 Fremont st.
Chalmers, Mr and Mrs Alex.; cor. Lindsay and El Dorado sts.
-——Miss Anna

Chalmers, Mr and Mrs George; 215 Lindsay st.
——Miss Kittie
Chesnutwood, Mr and Mrs George; 327 Washington
Clark, Dr and Mrs Asa; Hunter and Park sts.
Clark, Mr and Mrs Geo. C.; Hunter and Park sts.
Clayes, Mr and Mrs J. R.; Acacia, bet. Centre and Commerce sts.
Clayes, Mrs J. C.; 207 Hunter st.
——Miss
——Miss Madge
Cobb, Mr and Mrs F. D.; Sutter, bet. Fremont and Lindsay sts.
Corcoran, Mr and Mrs H. J.; Flora, bet. Hunter and El Dorado sts.
Colnon, Mr and Mrs E. L.; El Dorado, bet. Wash. and Lafayette sts.
Condit, Mr and Mrs J. H.; 277 Miner ave.
Crawford, Mr and Mrs B. C.; 197 Flora st.
Crawford, Mr and Mrs B. B.; Centre and Flora sts.
Creanor, Mrs
——Miss Nan
——Miss Louise
Cross, Dr and Mrs L. E.; 348 Miner ave.
Cross, Dr and Mrs S. N.; 177 Park st.
Cutting, Mr and Mrs Francis; 97 Centre st.
Cutting, Mr and Mrs L. M.; 99 Centre st.

Daggett, Mr and Mrs W. C.; 235 Miner ave.
Davenport, Dr and Mrs; Centre and Acacia sts.
Davis, Miss Maggie; cor. Ophir and Sonora sts.
Davis, Mr and Mrs Frank; El Dorado and Acacia sts.
——Miss Maud
De Vinney, Dr and Mrs C. L.; Hunter st., bet. Acacia and Poplar sts.
Doak, Mr and Mrs J. K.; SW cor. Hunter and Fremont sts.
Dohrman, Mr and Mrs C. W.; 259 Oak st.
——Miss Gussie
——Miss Lou
Dorrance, H. T.; Yo Semite House
Dudley, Mr and Mrs W. L.; Flora and San Joaquin sts.
——Miss
——Miss Mamie
Dunham, Mr and Mrs Shubael; 180 El Dorado st.
Dunham, Mr and Mrs James S.; Hunter and Magnolia sts.

Earle, G. A.; 207 San Joaquin st.
Easton, Mr and Mrs A.; Beaver, bet. Lafayette and Sonora sts.
Elliott, Mr and Mrs L. W.; cor. Fremont and Commerce
——Miss Gertie

Diaries. Publishers of the Pacific Coast Diaries containing specially prepared information for the Pacific coast. *The Bancroft Company, 721 Market st.*

Farnum, Mrs R. G.; 206 El Dorado st.
Farrington, Mrs H. L.; 400 Sutter st.
——Miss Grace
Farrington , Mr and Mrs H. S.; 241 Flora st.
Folger, Mrs M. A.; cor. Centre and Acacia
——Miss Gussie
——Miss Mattie
Fraser, Mr and Mrs P. B.; 162 Lafayette st.

Garwood, Mr and Mrs John; 247 Fremont st.
Gerlach, Mr and Mrs Louis; Flora st., bet. Hunter and S. Joaquin
——Miss
——Miss Nellie
Grattan, Dr and Mrs C.; cor. Sutter and Lindsay sts.
Gray, Mr and Mrs George; 247 Fremont st.
——Miss Hannah
Greenwood, Mr and Mrs H.; 139 Lafayette st.
Gross, Mr and Mrs J. E.; 168 Park st.

Haas, Mr and Mrs C.; 186 Fremont st.
Haas, Mr and Mrs C. J.; Lindsay Point
Hamilton, Capt and Mrs J. C.; 157 Beaver st.
——Mrs Jeff
Hammond, Mr and Mrs John; 195 Hunter st.
Hansel, Mr and Mrs Joseph; 63 Aurora st.
Hansel, Mr and Mrs Louis; 77 San Joaquin st.
Hart, Mr and Mrs George; Acacia, bet. Beaver and Elk sts.
Hedges, Mr and Mrs E. R.; Commercial Hotel
Henderson, Mr and Mrs M. P.; Flora and San Joaquin sts.
Henderson, Dr and Mrs R. W.; Sutter, bet. Weber ave. and Channel st.
——Miss Ella
Hewlett, Mr and Mrs H. H.; 177 Oak st.
Hoisholt, Dr and Mrs A. W.; North, bet. Hunter and San Joaquin sts.
Hubbard, Mrs H. S.; El Dorado and Poplar sts.
—— —Miss May
Hudson, Dr and Mrs A. S.; 199 Hunter st.
——Dr and Mrs A. T.
Huggins, Mrs Emma; Weber Point
——-Miss Mamie
Hutchinson, C. F.; 156 Park st.
Hyatt, Mr and Mrs G. C.; 329 Miner ave.

Inglis, Wm.; 425 El Dorado st.

Johnson, Capt and Mrs R. S.; cor. Park and Centre sts.
——Miss Ida

Keagle, Mr and Mrs C. H.; Center st., bet. Rose and Magnolia
Keniston, Mr and Mrs C. M.; 349 Weber ave.
Kearns, Mr and Mrs J.
Kile, Mr and Mrs J. M.; Stanislaus st., bet. Weber ave. & Channel st.
Kelsey, Mrs A.; El Dorado and Oak sts.
——Miss Algae

Ladd, Mr and Mrs Geo. S.; El Dorado, bet. Poplar and Acacia sts.
Lane, Mr and Mrs F. E.; El Dorado and Oak sts.
Lane, Mr and Mrs R. P.; El Dorado, bet. Park and Flora sts.
Langdon, Dr and Mrs W. R.; Lindsay and American sts.
Levy, Mr and Mrs Chas.; cor. San Joaquin and Acacia sts.
Lehe, Col and Mrs Eugene; cor. Fremont and Stanislaus sts.
Levinsky, Miss Fay; 152 El Dorado st.
Littlehale, Mr and Mrs C. E.; El Dorado and Acacia sts.
Littlehale, Mr and Mrs S. S.; 125 El Dorado st.
Lothrop, Mr and Mrs I.; 203 Sutter st.
Lyons, Mrs G.; cor. El Dorado and Poplar sts.
——Mr and Mrs W. H.

Leitch, Mr and Mrs A.; cor. California and Flora sts.
——Miss Ada

Matteson, Mr and Mrs D. C.; 373 Main st.
McDougald, Mr and Mrs J. D.; Poplar, bet. Centre and Commerce sts.
McCarty, Mr and Mrs J. M.; California and Flora sts.
——Miss Nanie
McKenzie, Mr and Mrs Geo. A.; El Dorado, bet. Lindsay and Miner ave.
McKinnon, Mr and Mrs A.; 109 Commerce st.
——Miss Belle
Miller, Mr and Mrs W. P.; Lindsay, bet. California and American sts.
Miller, Mr and Mrs W. C.; Sutter and Fremont sts.
Moore, Mr and Mrs C. C.; Miner ave. and Aurora st.
McKee, Mrs L. M.; 213 Hunter st.
Moore, Mr and Mrs E.; 129 Flora st.
Moore, Mr and Mrs B. W.; El Dorado, bet. Park and Flora sts.
Moore, Mr and Mrs H. H.; 272 Lindsay st.
Moore, Mr and Mrs Thomas; 179 Park st.
Morrissey, Jas. A.; 525 Weber ave.
Mosely, Mr and Mrs J. F.; California and Magnolia sts.
Muenter, Mr and Mrs August; Channel and Sutter sts.

Newell, Mr and Mrs Sidney; 233 Miner ave.
Newell, Mr and Mrs T. W.; 231 Miner ave.
Newell, Mr and Mrs S. W.; San Joaquin and Magnolia sts.
Noble, Mr and Mrs A. M.; Hunter and Flora sts.
Noble, Mr and Mrs E. B.; 264 Flora st.

Nunan, Col and Mrs John J.; cor. Aurora and Oak sts.
Nutter, Mr and Mrs W. B.; Lafayette and Ophir sts.

Owen, Mr and Mrs C. E.; San Joaquin, bet. Magnolia and Rose sts.
Oullahan, Mr and Mrs Ed; 251 Fremont st.

Perrin, Mr and Mrs Otis; cor. El Dorado and Fremont sts.
Peters, Mr and Mrs J. D.; cor. El Dorado and Magnolia sts.   *Saturday*
———Miss Genevieve
———Miss Annie
Phelps, Mr and Mrs J. L.; Grant, bet. Miner ave. and Lindsay st.
Phillips, Dr and Mrs Thomas; 151 Beaver
Post, Mrs S. D.; Flora and El Dorado
———Miss Ida
Prugh, Mr and Mrs W. W.; Grand Central

Reid, Mr and Mrs J. C.; 165 El Dorado
———Miss Bessie
———Miss Lucy
Rhodes, Mr and Mrs Alonzo; cor. Sutter and Sonora
Rosenbaum, Mr and Mrs D. S.; 245 Fremont st.
Ruggles, Dr and Mrs Charles; 461 California
Ruggles, Mr and Mrs C. L.; 341 Miner ave.
Rucker, Dr and Mrs H. N.; State Insane Asylum

Sargent, Dr and Mrs C. S.; SW cor. Flora and San Joaquin
Sargent, Mr and Mrs H. S.; 123 Park st.
Simpson, Mr and Mrs A. W.; cor. Oak and El Dorado Occ. Hotel, S. F.
———Miss
———Miss Bertha
Smith, Mr and Mrs Ansel; cor. Hunter and Acacia
Smith, Mr and Mrs Frank H.; 487 Weber ave.
Smith, Mr and Mrs J. Jerome; NW cor. Hunter and Park
Smith, Capt and Mrs J. W.; 146 Sutter
Southworth, Mr and Mrs H. O.; 257 El Dorado
———Miss Mamie
Southworth, Miss Maud; cor. Grant and Miner ave.
———F. E.
Sperry, Mr and Mrs Austin B.; North st. near El Dorado
Sperry, Mr and Mrs George B.; cor. North st. and El Dorado
Starbird, Mr and Mrs W. B.; Sutter, bet. Miner ave. and Channel
Stewart, Frank A.; San Joaquin, bet. Main and Market
Swinnerton, Judge and Mrs J. G.; cor. Poplar and Commerce

Thomas, Mr and Mrs F. R.; 201 Commerce
Thompson, Mr and Mrs J. C.; 178 Flora
———Miss Allie
———Mr E. R.

211

Thompson, Mr and Mrs C. V.; 416 Sutter
Tresher, Mr and Mrs M. S.; cor. Fremont and Sutter
Thrift, Mr and Mrs E. E.; Channel, bet. California and Sutter
Trahern, Mr and Mrs G. W.; 206 El Dorado
——Miss
——Miss Lida
Tulley, Mr and Mrs R. W.; cor. Sutter and North
——Miss Annie

Wallace, Dr and Mrs U. G.; 319 Channel st.
Weaver, Mr and Mrs H. W.; Poplar and Commerce
Weber, Mrs Helen; Weber's Point
——Miss Julia A.
Weller, Mrs Mattie; 252 Fremont
——Miss
——Miss Grace
Welsh, Mr and Mrs J. M.; Poplar and El Dorado
West, Mrs and Mrs Fred M.; 153 Park st.
West, Mr and Mrs George; El Pinal Vineyard
——Miss
White, Mr and Mrs W. C.; Poplar, bet. El Dorado and Centre
White, Mr and Mrs John C.; Poplar and Commerce
Wilhoit, Mr and Mrs R. E.; Flora and Sutter sts.
——Miss Alice
Williams, Mr and Mrs C. E.; 144 Park st.
Wolf, Mr and Mrs Andrew; cor. Weber ave. and Grant st.
Woods, Mr and Mrs John N.; cor. Channel and Stanislaus sts.
——Miss Jessie
——Miss Mary

Yardley, Mr and Mrs John; 206 Sonora st.
Yolland, Mr and Mrs Charles W.; 152 Elk st.
Young, Dr and Mrs J. D.; Lindsay and American sts.

Yo Semite Club

STOCKTON, CAL.

BOARD OF DIRECTORS

Woods, S. D.	- - - - - - President
Starbird, W. B.	- - - - - Vice-President
West, F. A.	- - - - - - Secretary
Newell, Sidney	- - - - - Treasurer

Phillips, Dr. Thomas	Jackson, C. M.

Cobb, F. D.

Bell, F. P.	Earle, H. W.
Baldwin, F. T.	Ferris, John W.
Bennett, Paul W.	Funk, Lafayette
Budd, Gen James H.	Goodell, George
Bostwick, I. S.	Henderson, R. W.
Carter, Stanton L.	Henderson, W. R.
Claiborne, G. B.	Hewlett, H. H.
Close, O. H.	Haas, C. J.
Corcoran, Hugh J.	Haas, H. O.
Cross, Dr S. N.	Holden, I. D.
Chalmers, Alex.	Holt, Benjamin
Clark, Dr Asa	Inglis, Wm.
Cunningham, Thomas	Kitchener, S. A.
Campbell, J. C.	La Rue, J. M.
Dohrmann, C. W.	Littlehale, James M.
Dorrance, H. T.	Lane, F. E.
Dudley, W. L.	Lang, L. H.
Dudley, W. L., Jr.	Langridge, George W.
Dunham, James L.	Langford, B. F.

Levinsky, A. L.	Richards, L. A.
Louttit, J. A.	Sargent, Dr C. S.
Lauxen, Richard	Shelly, John C.
Minta, Wesley	Sperry, George B.
McKee, W. H.	Sperry, Austin B.
McCall, T. H.	Smith, H. C.
Mays, Dr W. H.	Smith, Capt J. W.
Moross, F. V.	Southworth, H. O.
Morrissey, James A.	Stackpole, Thos. W.
Mosely, J. F.	Shippee, L. U.
McKenzie, George A.	Sargent, R. C.
McDougald, John D.	Weber, T. J.
Noble, A. M.	West, George
Newell, T. W.	Wilhoit, George E.
Owen, C. E.	Wilhoit, E. L.
Parker, E. F.	Williams, Percy
Paulsell, A. C.	Williams, Thos. H., Jr.
Prugh, W. W.	Young, Dr J. D.
Post, W. H.	Young, David
Peters, J. D.	Wolf, A. I.
Reid, R. A.	

CALIFORNIA COLONY
IN NEW YORK

The California Colony in New York

Within some years past quite a number of San Franciscans have removed to the City of New York, and now form what is known there as the California Colony. It was not deemed by the publishers of the Blue Book that it would be complete without the names and addresses of these former residents, especially as many of them are at best only temporarily removed from their Pacific Coast homes. Accordingly these names and addresses have been secured and are here presented for the information of our readers, together with the names of Californians now resident in other Eastern cities.

Acheson, Mrs Thomas; 34 W. Nineteenth st.
Adams, Mrs Dr Samuel; Detroit, Michigan
Aldrich, Miss Letitia; Madison Square Theater
Alexander, Henry; 642 E. Ninth st.
Alexander, Mr and Mrs C. B. (*née* Hattie Crocker); 4 W. Fifty-eighth st.
———Miss
Alexander, Mrs Lieutenant (*née* Fanny Lent); 566 Fifth ave.
Aron, Joseph   Paris, France
Atherton, Mrs Gertrude; 340 W. Fifty-ninth st.
———Miss Muriel

Bacon, Mr and Mrs John P.; Coleman House
Baker, Thomas; Broadway Theater
Bean, Mr Fred W.; 13 W. Twenty-second st.
———Miss Alice P.
Belden, Mr and Mrs Josiah; 7 W. Fifty-first st.   Saratoga
———Miss
Belknap, Edwin S.; 5 Beekman st.
Berolzime, Mrs Kate; 44 W. Twenty-eighth st.
Best, Mrs John W.; Daly's Theater
———Miss
Barindo, Bernard; Hoffman House   Spokane Falls, W. T.
Belasco, David; 126 Waverly Place
Billings, Mr and Mrs Frederick; 279 Madison ave.   Woodstock, Vt.
Bierstadt, Mr and Mrs Albert; 1271 Broadway
Birch, Mr and Mrs William; 219 Seventh ave.
Boyer, Mrs
———Miss Lizzie

Bosqui, Frank; St. Nicholas ave. and 133d st.
Booker, Mr and Mrs Wm. Lane; New York Hotel
Bradford, J. Otey; 200 W. Sixty-ninth st.
——Miss Lucile
Brewster, Mr and Mrs Benjamin; 695 Fifth ave.
——R. E.; Pierrepont House, Brooklyn
Bullock, Mr and Mrs L. L.
Benfey, Miss Ida
Brown, Mr and Mrs H. C.; Hastings-on-Hudson
Brooks, Noah; Newark, N. J.
——Mrs B. S.; 241 W. Seventy-fifth st.
Bloss, Mr and Mrs A. C.; Bath Beach, L. I.
Butler, Mr and Mrs L. F. (née Linda Baby); 203 W. Fourteenth st.
Bacon, Frank P.; 119 E. Thirtieth st.
Baker, James A.; 917 Seventh ave.
Beyea, Dr J. L.; 216 E. Fourteenth st.
Barnes, Edwin D.; Gilsey House
Burling, Miss Jessie
Bullard, E. P.; 46 W. Twenty-fifth st.   City of Mexico
Butler, C. J.; 20 Lafayette Place, Brooklyn
Bugbee, Mr and Mrs Sumner W.; East New York, L. I.
Butterfield, Don Carlos, Mr and Mrs
Bacon, Mr and Mrs John P. (née Cunningham)
Burgoyne, Mr and Mrs Wm. M.; 155 W. Sixty-Third st.
——Wm. M., Jr.
——Miss
——Edgar
——Harry
Banner, Michael; 342 W. Seventieth st.

Connill, Miss Nora; 37 Gramercy Park
Clappe, Mrs Louise A. K.; Lexington ave.
Conness, Mr and Mrs John; Boston, Mass.
Chapman, Miss Sylvia; Madison Square Theater
Corcoran, Frank; St. James Hotel
Clemens, Mr and Mrs Sam B.; Hartford, Conn.
Casey, Capt Thos. L. U. S. A; The San Carlo, Broadway and 30th st.
Curtis, Miss Amy; National School of Design
Carpentier, Horace W.; 108 E. Thirty-seventh st.
Chenery, Leonard, U. S. N.; 45 E. Thirtieth st.
Clark, Smyth; Brooklyn
Cohn, Mr and Mrs Fred H.; 128 E. Seventy-ninth st.   Long Branch
Cox, Mr and Mrs Jennings S.; 76 W. Sixty-eighth st.   Huntington, L. I.
Convis, Charles E.; 6 Wall st.
Craddock, Miss Nannie; Madison Square Theater

BOVININE Gives Children Rosy Lips and Cheeks

Curtiss, Mr and Mrs Frank; 1902 Washington ave.
Crane, A. M.; Stewart Building
Clark, Joseph; Hotel Brunswick   The Hollywood, Long Branch

Dorland, Mrs A.
——Miss Blanche
Delafield, Robt. Hare; 20 N. Washington Square
Dorsey, Edward Bates; Union League Club
Dungan, Charles W.; La Normandie
Davis, Erwin; 121 Madison ave.   Rye, Winchester Co.
Dewey, Mr and Mrs Eugene E.; 14 E. Forty-seventh st.
Donahue, Peter J.; Hoffman House
Donaghue, Mr and Mrs O. B.; Yonkers, N. Y.
Dorris, Mrs; W. Forty-ninth st.
——Miss

Edmondson, Thos. J.; Delmonico's, Twenty-sixth st.
Ewen, Miss Mary
Edwards, Mr and Mrs Harry; 185 E. 116th st.
——Mr and Mrs Maze; Bath Beach, L. I.
Ellis, Mr and Mrs John S.; Bartow-on-Sound
——Samuel Cladius, 69 Madison ave.   Bartow-on-Sound
Eppstein, Fred J.; 203 West Forty-fifth st.
Eagan, Rev F. Dillon

Fuller, Dr and Mrs J. (*nee* Hastings); 47 West Fiftieth st.
Fair, Mrs Theresa; Hoffman House
——Birdie
Ferris, Mr and Mrs David C.; Harlem
Ferguson, George N.; 154 West Fifty-third st.
Foster, Mrs Lelia Love
Fonda, Mrs Alfred; The Effingham, West Fifty-eighth st.
Frank, Mr and Mrs Sam; 1071 Park ave.
Frank, L. P.
Freeman, Miss Lulu; Clarendon Hotel
Fritz, Henry
Fremont, Mrs John C.; Staten Island   Los Angeles
Funk, Charles C.; 46 West Twenty-fifth st.
Fearon, Mr and Mrs Robert (*nee* Torbert); New Brighton, Staten Island

Garvey, Mrs Wm. V.; 8 West Twenty-second st.
Gault, Mr and Mrs John; 200 West Fifty-seventh st.
George, Mr and Mrs Henry; 327 East Nineteenth st.
——Mr and Mrs Henry, Jr.
Gibson, Mr and Mrs George R. (*nee* Belden); 7 W. 51st st.   Saratoga
Gillette, Mr and Mrs Milton G.; 2101 Fifth ave.
——Miss

Gilmore, Harry
——Mrs
——Miss Grace
Glazier, Mr and Mrs Simon W.; 17 East Sixty-seventh st.   Long Branch
Gray, John; 346 Fourth st., Brooklyn
Gunter, Mr and Mrs Archie C.; 66 West Fifty-second st.
Goodman, Mr and Mrs A. J.; (*nee* Minnie Buchanan); 142 W. 16th st.
Greene, Mr and Mrs Clay M.; 27 West Eleventh st.   *Sunday*
Gutherie, Wm. D.; 281 Fifth ave.
Gall, Charles Funkenstein; 45 West Twenty-eighth st.
Greenebaum, Mr and Mrs Henry; 1607 Lexington ave.

Heppenheimer, Mr and Mrs W. C. (*nee* Blanche Miller); Jersey City
Hausman, F.; 8 West Twenty-eighth st.
Haggin, Mr and Mrs L. T. ; Albemarle Hotel
Harding, Mr and Mrs Geo. J.; 136 S. 23d st., Philadelphia { *Tuesday* {Catskill Mts.
Hubbard, T., 45 Broadway   Philadelphia, Pa.
Hubbard, Mr and Mrs Edmund Yates (*nee* Alice Grey); 21 East 64th st.
Haggin, Mr and Mrs Ben Ali; 10 E. Fifty-fourth st.
Hague, Mr and Mrs James D. ; The Dakota   Stockbridge, Mass.
Halpin, Mr and Mrs John J.; 47 W. Thirty-fifth st.
Hamlin, Mr and Mrs George; Mott Haven, N. Y.
-——Miss Florence Belle
Harpending, Mr and Mrs Asbury; Plainfield, N. J.
——Miss Genevieve
——Miss Clara
Harper, Miss Lulu; 24 W. Thirty-ninth st.
Harris, Mrs Lon; 4 Lafayette place
Harrison, Mr and Mrs J. M. (*nee* Florence Tyrrill)
Hartshorn, Ben M.; 24 W. Fifty-sixth st.   Pleasure Bay, N. J.
——The Misses
Hastings, Horace M.; Staten Island
Hastings, Charles S.; 13 W. Fifty-third st.
Haskins, Mr and Mrs D. C.; 313 W. Twenty-second st.
Hatch, Mr and Mrs S. D.; Murray Hill Hotel, New York { *Friday* {Swanton, Vt.
——Miss Gertrude
Haxton, Mrs H. R. (*nee* Agnes Thomas); 42 W. Thirty-fifth st.
Herman, M.; 34 E. Sixty-seventh st.
Henderson, Mr and Mrs John D.; Greenwood Lake, N. J.
Huntington, Mr and Mrs Collis P.; 65 Park ave.   Throg's Neck, Ct.
Homans, Harry S., Jr.; 60 Broadway
Hersey, Miss Blanche; 1418 Broadway
Hemphill, Rev and Mrs John (*nee* Mamie Coghill); Philadelphia, Pa.
Heitshu, Miss Gertrude; 32 W. Fifty-seventh st.

Hillyer, Dr and Mrs F. M. ; 132 W. Seventy-third st.
Hubbard, T. ; 45 Broadway

Irwin, Mrs Richard ; Hotel Victoria
Irwin, Benoni; Yonkers, N. Y.
——Miss Constance
Ivers, Mrs Richard ; Hotel Victoria
——Miss Arleen

Jackson, Mr and Mrs Schuyler (*nee* Angella Forbes); Newark, N. J.
Janin, Mr and Mrs Henry ; 20 E. Thirty-fifth st.   **West Point**
——H., Jr.
Jerome, Mr and Mrs H. (*nee* Lily Hastings); Stuyvesant Square
Jones, E. Perry ; 545 Lafayette place, Brooklyn

Keene, Mr and Mrs James R. ; Far Rockaway, L. I.
——The Misses
Keene, Foxhall; Far Rockaway, L. I.
Keene, Harry ; Delmonico's, Fifth ave.
Kelly, Mr and Mrs Eugene ; 33 W. Fifty-seventh st.   **Orange, N. J.**
Kelly, Eugene, Jr.; 19 Wash. Square
Kelly, Edward ; 33 W. Fifty-seventh st.
——Thomas
——Robert
Keefe, Mrs T. (*nee* Helm) ; The Vendome
Kelly, Edgar S.; 328 W. Thirty-second st.
——Miss Anna
Kent, Mr and Mrs W. A. ; Rochester, N. Y.
Kibbe, William C.; 45 Broadway
King, Miss Louise; Student's Art League
Kipp, William Ingraham, 3d ; Nineteenth st. and Ninth ave.

Ladd, Mrs George S.; Hotel Brunswick
Lamprecht, Mr and Mrs W. H. (*nee* Emma Pearson) ; Cleveland, O.
Lande, Mr and Mrs Bernard ; The Marlborough
——Master
Littauer, William; 578 Madison ave.
Lombard, I. D. ; Mr and Mrs; Fifth Avenue Hotel   **Augusta, Me.**
Lowell, Miss Augusta; Mt. Vernon, N. Y.
Locke, Mr and Mrs Chas. A.; 230 W. Fifty-ninth st.
——Miss
——Clarence
Lawton, Mr and Mrs Franklin; New Rochelle, N. Y.
——Frederick
Laffan, Mr and Mrs Wm. M. ; 335 Lexington ave.   **South Bay, L. I.**
La Grange, Gen and Mrs Oscar H.; 24 W. 46th st., Larchmont, N. Y.
Leverson, Montague M.

Lent, Mr and Mrs Wm. M.; 566 Fifth ave.
——Eugene
— ——Solomon
Leszynski, Julius; Park ave.
——Albert H.; 636 Lexington ave.
Lines, Rev and Mrs Sam'l Gregory; 65 East Eighty-ninth st.
Lounsberry, Mr & Mrs R. P. (*nee* Haggin); 102 E. 35th st. Bedford, N. Y.
Luning, Herman; 482 West Twenty-fourth st.
Lyster, Frederick; 18 West Twenty-third st.
Lynch, Mrs Dominick (*nee* Fonda); The Effingham, W. Fifty-eighth st.
Lane, Franklin R.; 132 East Twenty-fifth st.

Maguire, J. T.; 52 W. Ninth st.
McAllister, Miss Julia
Mahe, Dr and Mrs Gustave (*nee* Lande); 227 West Thirty-fourth st.
May, Mr and Mrs Fred.   Baltimore, Md.
——Henry
Morse, Mr and Mrs G. D.
Marvin, Azor S.; 18 Washington Place
Mayer, Marcus R.; 242 West Forty-second st.
Magagnos, James K.; 118 Sumner ave., Brooklyn, N. Y. ,
Mack, Julius J.; 80 Reade st.
Maguire, Mr and Mrs Thomas; 46 West Thirty-third st.
——Thomas, Jr.
Marks, Mrs Thomas (*nee* Fonda); .The Effingham, West Fifty-eighth st.
Martinez, Mr and Mrs Raoul; Hotel Vendome
Massett, Stephen C. ("Jeemes Pipes"); 102 East Twenty-second st.
Massen, Mr & Mrs Louis (*nee* Lillie Arrington); Madison Square Theater
McAneny, George B; The Cumberland   Coney Island
McCaulley, Mr and Mrs Wm.; Murray Hill Hotel
——Miss
McCormick, Mr and Mrs R. C.; Jamaica, L. I.
McDowell, Harry B.; 50 West Ninth st.
McKinney, Mrs (*nee* Dita Hopkins); Madison ave.
McAllister, Rev F. Marion; Elizabeth, N. J.
Minear, A. P.; Gilsey House
Mills, D. O.; 634 Fifth ave.
——Mr and Mrs D. O., Jr.; 2 East Sixty-ninth st.
Mills, Harry R.; 154 West Fifty-fifth st.
Mills, Frank J.; 74 East 109 st.
Miller, Mr and Mrs Charles; 14 E. Forty-fourth st.
——Elisha
——Miss Mary
Minturn, Mr and Mrs John; 338 E. Fifty-first st.
Monson, A. C ; 60 Madison ave.

Moore, Miss Robina; E. 24th and 7th ave., Windsor Hotel   *Thursday*
Murray, Mrs Henry B.; Roseville, N. J.

McAllister, Mr and Mrs Ward; 16 W. Thirty-sixth st.
——H. H.
McHarg, H. K.; 53 Broadway
McCullough, Mr and Mrs John G.; 507 Madison ave.   Rutland, Vt.
McDermot, Mrs Hugh F.; Jersey City, N. J.
McDowell, Mrs Gen Irwin; Brevoort House
McDonald, Mrs Alice R.; Fifth ave. near Fifty-seventh st.

Norton, Mrs Harry
Nutman, James E.; 70 Broadway
Neustadter, Mr and Mrs Henry; Windsor Hotel
Newton, Mr and Mrs Henry; 954 St. Nicholas ave.

Ogden, Com R. L.; The Aberdeen
Oelrichs, Mr and Mrs H. (*nee* Fair); 453 Fifth ave.   Seabright

Pearson, Mr and Mrs Henry H.; Coleman House
——Charles A.
Park, Mr and Mrs Trenor L.
Paige, Calvin; The Brunswick
Parmele, Charles R.; Staten Island
Parsons, Hubert; 45 Broadway
Peixotto, Ben. F.; 47 W. 130th st.
Pillsbury, C. J.; Boston, Mass.
——Samuel

Platt, Rev Horace; Rochester, N. Y.
Page, B. Frank
Phelps, Mr and Mrs Charles (*nee* Minnie Booth); 88 W. Washington Sq.
Parsons, George F; 17 E. Fifty-ninth st.

Regna, Mr and Mrs James L.; 18 Broadway
Rich, Gary; Orange, N. J.
Randall, Wm. W.; Rockville Center, N. J.
Randolph, Miss Maggie; 161 Madison ave.
Reynolds, Wm. T.; Brooklyn
Reid, Mr and Mrs Whitelaw (*nee* Mills) 451 Madison ave.   Rye, N. Y.
Riotte, Mr and Mrs E. N.; 102 W. 136th st.
Rix, Julian; 19 E. Sixteenth st.
Rich, David; Orange, N. J.
——A. L.

Rogers, George E.; 46 W. Twenty-fifth st.
Rogers, Mr and Mrs Ford, H.; Detroit, Michigan
Ruhl, Henry C.; 88 Clinton Place
Rosenfeld, Louis; Hoffman House

Rosener, Mr and Mrs Harry; Hoffman House
——Miss Fay
——Charles John
Reed, Mrs E. B.; 136 West Thirty-fourth st.
——Miss Lillian
Rosenbaum, Mr and Mrs A. S.; 44 East Sixty-ninth st.
Rosenfield, A.; 1270 Lexington ave.
Roberts, George D.; 45 Broadway
Roosevelt, Mr & Mrs Elbert C (*nee* Mabel Lawton); New Rochelle, N. Y.
Rosenbaum, Henry; West Sixty-first st.
Reynolds, Mrs E. H. (*nee* Fuller); 247 Fifth ave.
Ross, Harry; St. James Hotel
Rudkin, Mr and Mrs James T.; 315 Clinton st., Brooklyn
Sherwood, Mrs B. F.; 1002 Madison ave.
—— Miss Jennie
Seaman, Mr and Mrs Vernon; Brooklyn
Seaman, Dr & Mrs L. L. (*nee* Fannie Freeman); 18 West Thirty-first st.
Seligman, Mr and Mrs Jesse; 2 East Forty-sixth st.   Long Branch
——Henry
Seligman, Dewitt J.; 74 East Fifty-fifth st.   Long Branch
Seligman, Isaac W.; 58 West Fifty-fourth st.   Long Branch
Seligman, Jacob; 128 East Sixty-fifth st.   Long Branch
Severance, A. J.; The Aberdeen
Selover, Abla A.; Park Avenue Hotel
Sisson, Mr and Mrs Geo. H.; The Hanover, 15 Fifth ave.
Schroeder, Mr & Mrs Edward C. (*nee* Minnie Stebbins); Plainfield, N. J.
Schroeder, Charles; 1212 Broadway
Shainwald, Mr and Mrs R. L.; 1054 Lexington ave.
Shaffer, Col and Mrs W. F.; 35 West Fifty-first st.
Share, H. P.; 6 East Eighteenth st.
Sharon, Mr and Mrs F. W.; 323 Fifth ave.
Sherman, Miss Julia; Mt. Vernon, N. Y.
Somers, Frederick M.; 230 West Forty-second st.
Snow, Frank C.; Broadway and Thirtieth st.
Sperry, Miss Grace; E. 24th st. and 7th ave., Windsor Hotel *Thursday*
Steinhart, Ezekiel; Windsor Hotel
Staples, Mr and Mrs John
Stoat, Mr and Mrs Philip (*nee* Miss Van Wart)
Scoofey, Leonidas; New York Hotel
——Miss Ida
Snyder, Mr and Mrs Valentine (*nee* Sheda Trobert); 121 W. 97th st.
Siedenthop, Charles; Norwalk, Conn.
Smith, Mr and Mrs Edwin (*nee* Bullock); Hartford, Conn.
Stevens, Mr and Mrs Eugene; 182 West Seventy-fifth st.

Smith, Mr & Mrs F. M.; E. 24th st. & 7th ave., Windsor Hotel *Thursday*
Stanford, Mr and Mrs Philip
Stern, Benjamin, 1222 Broadway
Scholle, Mr and Mrs Wm; Lexington ave.
Searles, Mr and Mrs Hopkins; 60 Fifth ave.   **Block Isd.**

Tripp, Mr and Mrs Joseph (*nee* Chipman); 64 West Fifty-third st.
Ten Eyck, Samuel; Jersey City, N. J.
Thompson, Mrs G. (*nee* Stebbins); The Winchester
Taylor, Mrs Fred B.; 10 E. Sixty-fifth st.
——Miss
Taylor, Edward R.; New York Club
Taylor, Mr and Mrs Peter; 356 W. Fifty-eighth st.
——Miss Allie
Triest, Mr and Mrs Julian
Thurman, I. B.; 365 Fifth ave.
Taylor, Howard P.; 204 W. Twenty-third st.
· Teal, Ben; 327 W. Forty-second st.
Tefft, Mr and Mrs E. (*nee* Benchley); The Dakota, W. 72d st.
Thompson, Mr and Mrs J. Wm.; 101 W. Ninety-third st.
——Miss Ida
——Miss Rita
——Miss Alice
Thompson, Mr and Mrs Wm. Neely; Madison ave.
Thompson, Mrs K.; Plainfield, N. J.
Thompson, Mrs M. J.; E. 24th and 7th ave., Windsor Hotel   *Thursday*
Thompson, Mr and Mrs Henry; 40 W. Fifty-ninth st.
Tichenor, Mr and James F.; Newark, N. J
Toland, Mrs Annie; 41 W. Sixty-first st.   **West Point**
Uhler, J. Clem; Philadelphia, Pa.   **Yacht " Siesta "**
——Russell
——Miss Maud

Upshur, Mr and Mrs George L.; Staten Island

Van Vleck, Durbin; 55 Liberty st.
Verdenal, Mr and Mrs D. F.; The Dakota, W. Seventy-second st.
——Miss Blanche E.
——D. F., Jr.
Vernon, Col and Mrs George F. W.; Baltimore, Md.

Wright, George
Wallace, Thomas; Montreal, Canada
Williams, Mr and Mrs J. H. H.; The Grenoble
——Miss Lottie
——Miss Agnes
Withington, James H.; Binghamton, New York   **Long Branch, N. J.**

Willett, Ed. W.; 1005 Lexington ave.
Wilcox, Mr and Mrs Frederick P. (*nee* Bessie Garvey); 122 W. 79th st.
Wiggin, Mrs Kate
Wilson, Dr Francis P.; New York Hospital
Williams, Rev Albert
Whitlach, Mrs James; 220 First st., Brooklyn
Wolcott, A. F.; Delmonico's, Fifth ave.
Wormser, Louis; 2 E. Sixty-fifth st.   Long Branch
Wormser, Mr Simon; 836 Fifth ave.   Long Branch
———Mr and Mrs Isador
———Maurice
Weill, Alexander; Paris, France
Walter, Henry; Windsor Hotel
Watrous, Mr and Mrs Charles; 352 Lexington ave.
———Henry W.
———Walter W.
Wertheimer, L. E.
Wilmerding, Mr and Mrs J. C.; W. Thirty-third st.
Walker, Mr and Mrs J. S.; W. Eighty-sixth st.
Ward, Mrs Helen Danway; Hotel Vendome

ART ASSOCIATION

HANDEL AND HAYDN SOCIETY

LORING CLUB

THE
San Francisco Art Association

430 Pine Street

On March 28, 1871, the San Francisco Art Association was organized, with the worthy object of encouraging excellence in artists and a superior taste in the public. Incorporated, August 1, 1889. The School of design is also conducted by this Association. An exhibition by local artists is held annually, besides numerous other displays.

OFFICERS

D. P. BELKNAP	President
JAMES D. PHELAN	First Vice-President
JOHN I. SABIN	Second Vice-President
GEO. H. HOPPS	Treasurer
E. E. POTTER	Secretary
J. R. MARTIN	Assistant Secretary

DIRECTORS

Edward Bosqui	Wm. Keith	Wm. H. Crocker
Henry Heyman	Louis Sloss, Jr.	Fredk. W. Zeile

HONORARY MEMBERS

Alvord, Mrs. William; Palace Hotel	Crocker, Mrs E.B. {Washington st. & Van Ness av.
Bierstadt, Albert	Gilman, D. C.
Booth, Hon. Newton	Kip, Rt. Rev Wm. Ingraham; 901 Eddy st.
Breuil, Edmond	Mezzara, Joseph
Cerrutti, G. B.	Rogers, Ford H.

LIFE MEMBERS

Alvord, William	400 California street
Babcock, Harry	306 California street
Babcock, William, Jr.	306 California street
Bacon, Henry D.	3u7 Sansome street
Baird, Mrs J. H.	
Baker, Livingston L.	Pine and Davis streets
Bancroft, A. L.	132 Post street
Barnes, W. H. L.	426 California street
Barroilhet, Henry	524 Montgomery street
Beard, John L.	
Bell, Thomas	426 California street
Benson, John	803 Stockton street
Blakeney, T. J.	U. S. Appraiser's Building
Blanding, Gordon	324 Pine street
Bixler, David	330 Sansome street
Bixler, Mrs David	Union and Pierce streets
Booth, H. J.	
Bosqui, Edward	523 Clay street
Boyd, James T.	324 Pine street
Boyd, John F.	29 Nevada Block
Breede, Henry L.	
Brereton, Robert	
Brittan, N. J.	Stockton and Post streets
Burnett, W. C.	318 Pine street
Cahill, Edward	406 Montgomery street
Callandreau, J.	1307 Stockton street
Carlson, Chas. J.	
Coleman, Carlton C.	121 Market street
Coleman, J. W.	S. F. Stock and Exchange Bldg.
Coleman, William T.	121 Market street
Coleman, Mrs William T.	Occidental Hotel
Collins, W. J.	805 Howard street
Colton, Mrs D. D.	California and Taylor streets
Crocker, Geo.	
Crocker, John H.	327 Pine street
Cushing, Volney	
Deane, Coll	435 California street
Dean, W. E.	78 Nevada Block
Dennison, Mrs L.	
Dewey, E. E.	
Dewey, William P.	310 Pine street

Gruenhagen Leads in Bonbonniere Candies

226

DeYoung, M. H.	Market and Kearny streets
Dodge, Henry L.	114 Market street
Donohue, P. J.	
Donohoe, Joseph A.	
Downey, John G.	
Drexler, L. P.	
Duncan, William L.	304 Montgomery street
Eldridge, Oliver	303 California street
Eyre, E. E.	314 California street
Faull, John A.	1209 Sutter street
Felton, Charles N.	
Fitch, J. R.	322 Pine street
Forbes, A. B.	401 California street
Freeborn, James	420 Montgomery street
Fry, J. D.	326 Montgomery street
Garnett, Louis A.	524 Sacramento street
Gibbs, Frederick A	33 Fremont street
Gibbs, George W.	33 Fremont street
Giffin, O. F.	12 Annie street
Glazier, Isaac	
Grant, Adam	Bush and Sansome streets
Graves, Robert N.	406 Montgomery street
Gray, R. B.	328 Montgomery street
Haggin, James B.	50 Nevada Block
Haggin, Miss M. S.	
Hall, Harry P.	
Hanscom, John O.	3 Mission street
Harding, Chas. F. D·	
Harmon, A. K. P.	79 Nevada Block
Hastings, Charles F. D.	120 Phelan Building
Hayward, A.	224 California street
Head, A. E.	
Heald, E. P.	24 Post street
Hearst, Mrs George	1105 Taylor street
Hickox, George C.	43 Merchants' Exchange
Hill, Harry C.	
Hill, Horace L.	314 California street
Hochkofler, R.	38 California street
Holcomb, W. A.	
Hooper, George F.	
Hopkins, E. W.	
Hopkins, Mrs Moses	
Hopkins, W. S.	

227

Hotaling, A. P.	429 Jackson street
Howard, Mrs Chandler	
Irwin, R. B.	
Jackson, J. P.	538 California street
Janin, Henry	
Jarboe, Mrs Mary H.	
Keene, James R.	
Lent, William	
Livingston, Louis	25 Fremont street
Madden, Thomas P.	Occidental Hotel
May, John C.	
Mayne, Charles	524 Montgomery street
McLane, Louis	
Meinecke, Charles	314 Sacramento street
Merrill, John F.	225 Market street
Mills, D. O.	
Mills, Edgar, Jr.	
Moore, H. H.	423 Kearny street
Morrow, Robert F.	414 California street
Murphy, E. P.	1304 Guerrero street
Muybridge, E. J.	
Newhall, George A.	
Norris, William	516 California street
Norton, Edward	934 Pine street
Parrott, Mrs A. M.	414 Montgomery street
Parrott, Louis B.	306 California street
Parrott, Tiburcio	
Payot, Henry	204 Sansome street
Phelan, James G.	
Pierce, Henry	407 Market street
Platt, Rev W. H.	
Prescott, George W.	First and Mission streets
Redington, John H.	
Requa, Isaac L.	79 Nevada Block
Robinson, L. L.	320 Sansome street
Roman, Anton	331 Montgomery street
Rutherford, Mrs A. H.	
Sawyer, L. S. B.	U. S. Appraiser's Building
Seligman, Abraham	
Schmiedel, Henry	320 Pine street
Scott, Miss Alice W.	

Scott, Irving M.	First and Mission streets
Scott, Henry T.	First and Mission streets
Shaw, William J.	
Stanford, Leland	Fourth and Townsend streets
Stearns, J. H.	
Sutro, Adolph	Sutro Heights
Tevis, Lloyd	California and Sansome streets
Toland, Mrs M. B. M.	
Tubbs, A. L.	611 Front street
Underhill, Jacob	214 Sansome street
Upham, Isaac	204 Sansome street
Wallace, George	
Weil, Raphael	Kearny and Post streets
Whitcomb, A. C.	
Wiggins, W. W.	
Wilmerding, J. C.	214 Front street
Winter, William	710 Capp street
Woodbury, F. C.	
Woodworth, Selim	
Zeile, F. W.	

CONTRIBUTING MEMBERS

Abbott, Charles H.	Fifth and Bluxome streets
Allen, Henry	
Ames, Fisher	607 Kearny street
Ashe, R. P.	130 Sansome street
Bacon, Jacob	508 Clay street
Badlam, Alexander	322 Montgomery street
Baker, Mrs L. L.	
Bailey, James D.	710 California street
Barker, T. L.	126 Market street
Barner, Geo. E.	
Barron, Mrs E. S.	
Bass, T. J.	14 Ellis street
Belcher, W. C.	520 Montgomery street
Belknap, D. P.	405 Montgomery street
Beaver, George W.	418 California street
Bemis, Charles C.	435 California street -.
Bender, Miss E.	
Bidleman, E. G.	
Birmingham, J.	

Bendel, Herman	313 Battery street
Beyfuss, Ernest	126 Kearny street
Bigelow, S. C.	440 California street
Bishop, Thomas B.	327 Pine street
Blaisdell, N.	220 Sutter street
Boalt, John H.	438 California street
Bolton, Jefferson	
Bonnell, Edwin	619 Clay street
Borel, Antoine	311 Montgomery street
Boomer, Mrs A. H.	
Brady, Harry J.	29 Grant avenue
Brastow, S. D.	
Bray, Edward M.	
Brayfogle, Edwin S.	209 Geary street
Brisac, B. F.	
Britton, Joseph	525 Commercial street
Brookes, Samuel M.	Prospect ave. near 28th street
Brown, Arthur	
Brown, Mrs J. E.	120 Sutter street
Brown, W. E.	California and Sansome streets
Bruce, Robert	316 California street
Buckingham, Thomas H.	
Burr, E. C.	
Bush, Norton	420 Powell street
Bush, R. J.	Custom House
Capwell, Mrs C. A.	
Carlsen, Emil	
Carolan, F. J.	
Case, J. D.	Care of S. P. Co., Foot Market
Castner, Mrs C. A.	813 Haight street
Cebrian, J. C.	1801 Octavia street
Center, Wm.	
Chadbourne, F. S.	
Chalmers, W. L.	
Clarke, Martin	
Chismore, George	
Chittenden, Alice B.	
Coey, Gen James	
Coleman, E. J.	
Coney, Alex. K.	
Coon, H. J.	
Cope, W. W.	
Cornwall, P. B.	
Coulter, W. A.	

Glacé Fruits and Marrons at Gruenhagen's

Cowles, Wm. Northrop
Crocker, Mrs Clarke W.
Crocker, Henry J.   1609 Sutter street
Crocker, William H.   322 Pine street
Crockett, J. B., Jr.
Curlett, Wm.
Curtin, Miss K. T.

Dangerfield, W. B.
Davis, Horace
Davis, H. C.
Davis, J. B. F.
Davis, Mrs A. E.
Dapray, Lieut J. A., U. S. A.
D'Estrella, T.
De la Montanya, James   1508 Taylor street
Delong, Frank C.
Dibble, H. C.   45 Nevada Block
Dickenson, Mrs W. L.
Dimond, Gen W. H.
Dolheer, John   10 California street
Donahue, Mrs Annie   454 Bryant street
Douty, F. S.
Dornin, George D.   214 Sansome street
Dugan, Miss Susie
Dusbury, Horace
Duncan, H.
Dunham, Frank
Dutard, H.   126, 128 Davis street
Duval, W. S.

Eastland, Joseph G.   604 Commercial street
Easton, Wendell   618 Market street
Edwards, Miss Josephine
Elfelt, Joseph
English, John F.   313, 315 Davis street
English, F. M.
Epstein, Samuel
Erlanger, Miss Julia
Fair, Mrs Theresa   1120 Pine street
Farnfield, Charles P.   Cosmos Club
Farnham, John
Finegan, P. A.
Fisher, Hugo
Fonda, Harry S.
Ford, Joseph A.

231

Forman, R. B.   2120 Broadway street
Foote, L. H.
Freeman, Mrs Littlejohn
French, F. J.   528 California street
Friedrich, Gustave

Garrett, James H.
Gerberding, A   61 Merchants' Exchange
Gibbons, Mrs Dr. H., Jr.   920 Polk street
Gifford, W. B.
Goodall, Edwin   10 Market street
Goodall, Charles
Granniss, G. W.   24 Montgomery Block
Grant, Joseph D.   Cor. Bush and Sansome streets
Grant, Thomas C.
Grow, C. A.
Gample, M.
Gump, Solomon   581 Market street

Haber, F. A.
Hall, Geo. E.
Hamilton, Robert
Happersberger, F.
Harvey, Downey   1604 Stockton street
Harrison, R. C.   230 Montgomery street
Has Brouck, Joseph   607–13 Clay street
Hausman, F. H.   328 Montgomery street
Haviland, John F.
Hawes, A. G.   220 Sansome street
Herold, Rudolph
Hecht, M. H.   25-27 Sansome street
Hedger, H. A.   1608 Golden Gate avenue
Heyman, Henry   623 Eddy street
Higgins, Mrs Wm. L.   227 Geary street
Hill, Thomas
Hirschfeld, D.
Hittell, Mrs T. H.   23 Montgomery street
Hobart, W. S.   224 California street
Hobbs, Miss Jennie   100 Flood Building
Hofer, Mme Grandjean
Hoffman, Ogden
Holloway, W. E.   430 California street
Homere, S.
Hooker, Charles G.   917 Bush street
Hooker, C. Osgood

Hopps, George H.	429 Pine street
Houghton, Gen J. F.	
Hoyt, John G.	
Hughes, Dr Jerome	54 Oak street
Hume, Hugh	
Hyde, Rothwell	1631 Sacramento street
Irelan, William Jr.	Pioneer Building
Jacobi, Frederick	Cor. Bryant and Second streets
Johnson, J. C.	
Jones, W. S.	
Jones, J. A.	
Jorgensen, Christian	
Josselyn, Charles	611 Clay street
Joullin, A.	
Keith, William	
Kelley, Mrs H. W.	
Kelly, Jas. R.	
Kellogg, C. W.	611-13 Front street
Kenitzer, Henry	Lick House
Kinne, Col C. Mason	
Koerber, August	8 Montgomery avenue
Kunath, Oscar	
Lacy, B. F.	
Lash, Lee	
Latimer, L. P.	
Lauden, Mrs H. E.	
Lewis, Miss Rosa F.	
Lichtenburg, Wm.	
Lincoln, Jerome	228 Montgomery street
Linforth, Mrs E. J.	
Lissak, Louis	
Little, Mrs J. R.	
Livermore, Charles B.	
Lohse, John F.	230 California street
Loomis, Geo.	
Lotz, Miss Matilda	
Luther, J. B.	320 California street
Lutgen, Chas. F.	
Lynch, Jeremiah	538 California street
Magee, R. D.	
Magee, Thos.	
Mallon, John	

233

Malter, G. H.
Mandlebaum, F.
Manning, Miss A. M.   712 Sutter street
Marceau, T. C.
Marshall, Benjamin   924 Sutter street
McCeney, Julius C.
McCombe, John   402 Montgomery street
McCoppin, Frank
McCormick, William
McMullin, Frank
Martin, Mrs Eleanor   725 Sutter street
Martin, P. J.   2103 California street
Marye, George T.
Masten, N. K.   507-09 Montgomery street
Matthews, Arthur F.
Meade, Calvert   420 California street
Menzies, Stewart
Mesick, R. S.   60-61 Nevada Block
Michael, Francis
Michalitschke, Mme A.
Middleton, S. P.   22 Montgomery street
Miller, O. C.
Mizner, Lancing
Molera, E. J.   609 Sacramento street
Montague, W. W.   309-11 Market street
Monteagle, R. C.
Morgan, E. D.   315 Montgomery street
Morgan, C. A.
Morretti, A.
Morrison, Alex. F.
Moore, Eliot J.
Murphy, Daniel F.
Narjot, Ernest
Norton, Mrs S. J.

Otto, Ernest
Oxnard, Robert

Pariser, Jas. A.
Parrott, John, Jr.
Partridge, John   212-14 California street
Pease, R. H.
Pennie, J. C., Jr.
Perkins, Geo. C.   10 Market street
Perkins, Samuel   48 Market street

Pescia, Joseph J.	611 Washington street
Peters, Charles R.	1016 Sutter street
Phelps, Mrs T. G.	
Phelps, W. H.	
Pierce, Mrs Ira	1730 Jackson street
Pillsbury, E. S.	324 Pine street
Pissis, Albert	
Pixley, Mrs F. M.	SW cor. Union & Fillmore sts.
Pixley, Frank M.	
Potter, E. E.	428 California street
Powning, Joseph	230 California street
Rathbone, J. L.	
Rathbone, Mrs J. L.	
Rearden, T. H.	Dept. 7, New City Hall
Redding, Joseph D.	8 Montgomery street
Redington, W. P.	SE cor. Stevenson & Second sts.
Richardson, Mrs M. C.	
Richardson, W. G.	
Rithet, R. P.	
Rixford, G. P.	
Roberts, H. S.	7 Montgomery avenue
Roe, George H.	317 Mason street
Rollins, W. E.	
Roos, Joseph	857 Market street
Rosenstirn, Julius	NE cor. Sutter & Hyde streets
Royce, Clark E. K.	
Russ, Henry B.	203 Montgomery street
Russ, Frederick	
Sabin, John I.	323 Pine street
Samuels, B. C.	1257 Octavia street
Sanders, Geo. H.	923 Pine street
Sawyer, A. F.	302 Stockton street
Sawyer, Lorenzo	Appraiser's Building
Sayre, J. H.	
Schmid, R.	
Schnable, Herman	427 Second street
Schussler, Toby	27 Grant avenue
Scrivener, Arthur	London and S. F. Bank
Searls, Mrs M. T. S.	
Severance, J. S.	
Shafer, Frederick F.	
Shaw, S. W.	308 Phelan Building
Shehan, Gen John F.	

Sherman, L. S.
Sherwood, W. R.
Shinn, Chas. H.
Simpson, Major
Sloss, Louis, Jr.   310 Sansome street
Smedberg, W. R.   316 California street
Smith, Sidney M.   123, 125 Market street
Smith, C. W. M.   224 Sansome street
Smith, G. Frank   502 Montgomery street
Spiers, James
Sprague, R. H.
Spreckels, A. B.   California Sugar Refinery
Spreckels, Claus   327 Market street
Spreckels, C. A.   327 Market street
Spreckels, John D.   327 Market street
Stadtmiller, F. D.   819 Eddy street
Stafford Wm. G.
Starbird, A. W.   101; 107 Market street
Stanton, John A.   611 Clay street
Stearns, Miss Nellie
Stone, B. F.   Oakland
Strong, George H.   220 Market street
Sullivan, Frank J.   Phelan Building
Sumner, F. W.   810 Van Ness avenue
Swain, R. R.   603 Polk street
Swan, Benjamin R.   310 Stockton street
Syz, Harry W.   410 California street
Swayne, Robt. H.

Taber, I. W.   8 Montgomery street
Taylor, John
Taylor, John W.
Thors, Louis   1025 Larkin street
Tobin, Alfred   California and Taylor streets
Towne, A. N.   SE cor. Fourth and Townsend
Turnbull, Walter   228½ Montgomery street
Turner, William E.

Vail, A. H.   857 Market street
Van Wyck, H. L.   308 Pine street
Vinzent, Alice W.
Von Perbant, Carl
Von Schroder, Baron J. H.   108 California street

Wadhams, L.
Wallace, Mrs W. T.   Superior Court, Dept. 6, New
                                                    [City Hall

Walter, I. N.	529, 531 Market street
Wandesforde, J. B.	
Watkins, A. A.	309–17 Market street
Waymier, J. A.	402 Montgomery street
Weinert, Albert	
Welch, Samuel B.	
Wells, F. Marion	757 Mission street
Wheaton, Geo. H.	
Wheelan, Mrs A. Randal	
White, Lovell	532 California street
Whitney, George E.	
Whitney, J. O.	
Whittier, W. Frank	
Williams, Capt Frank	
Williams, H. A.	116 California street
Williams, Mrs Virgil	
Wilson, C. T.	
Wilson, Russell J.	
Wilson, M. S.	202 Sansome street
Wilson, S. M.	202 Sansome street
Winsinger, F. S.	
Withrow, Miss E	
Wood, Col Wm. S.	
Yates, Frederick	120 Sutter street
Yelland, R. D.	
Ziska, Madam	

Loring Club

Rooms, 413 Sutter Street

The Loring Club was founded in 1876 for the study of part songs and other music adapted to male voices, and consists of 60 active, or singing, and 250 associate members. The revenue of the Club is derived from the associate members, who pay $10 per annum as a subscription to defray necessary expenses. Rehearsals are held every Monday evening and the regular meeting on the first Monday of each month. The annual invitation concert is considered as one of the fashionable events of the year.

OFFICERS, 1889–90

WM. ALVORD - - - -	Anglo-California Bank
L. L. BAKER - - - - -	- Baker & Hamilton
W. C. STADTFELD, Secretary - -	- 69 Nevada Block
W. A. MURISON, Treasurer - -	- Occidental Hotel
C. W. PLATT, Librarian - - -	- Olympic Club
D. W. LORING, Musical Director -	- Bank of California

MUSIC COMMITTEE

Dr J. C. Spencer	514 Sutter street
W. F. Hooke	577 Market street
J. H. Mundy	16 Front street

VOICE COMMITTEE

R. Forster	616 Mason street
J. J. Morris	30 New Montgomery street
F. M. Goldstein	2106 Larkin street
H. M. Fortescue	Nevada Bank

ACTIVE MEMBERS

FIRST TENORS

Blum, S.	129 Kearny street
Bremner, Geo. St. J.	521 O'Farrell street
Davis, W. W.	1240 McAllister street
Fortescue, H. M.	Nevada Bank
Graham, J. H.	135 Fremont street
Husband, R.	101 Mission street
Morrissey, J. G.	304 Montgomery street
Nieman, H.	437 Sixth street
Purlenky, G.	D. N. and E. Walter & Co.
Park, R.	217 Front street
Stratton, C. A.	16 Front street
Sylvester, W. G.	935 Market street
Toler, J. H.	1008 Broadway, Oakland

SECOND TENORS

Emmons, E. S.	516 California street
Hutchinson, E. C.	30 California street
Howland, C. A.	724½ Market street
Husted, F. M.	610 Montgomery street
Keeley, Wm.	206 Post street
Morris, J. J.	30 New Montgomery street
Milner, C. H.	16 Post street
Snook, G. C.	630 Sacramento street
Spencer, Dr J. C.	514 Sutter street
Woods, W. G.	1360 Market street
Walsh, G. C.	6 Battery street

FIRST BASSES

Forster, R.	616 Mason Street
Hausman, F. H.	Safe Deposit Building, room 2
Hueter, E. L.	601 Market street
Helke, A.	617 Mission street
Humphrey, J. G.	1247 Market street
Loring, P.	317 California street
Mills, F. G. B.	620 East street
Mundy, J. H.	16 Front street
Mackay, W.	715 Market street
McGauley, J. F.	619 Clay street

Nachtrieb, J. J.   119 Clay street
Ruggles, J. D., Jr.   Bank of California
Stone, F. F.   410 Pine street
Stadtfeld, W. C.   69 Nevada Block
Tennent, T. H.   2310 Webster street

SECOND BASSES

Amos, J. P.   1581 Folsom street
Barney, A. S.   101 Sansome street
Bien, L.   315 Pine street
Egbert, H. H.   517 Clay street
Daly, S.   207 Eighth street
Dobbs, L. L.   210 Battery street
Goldstein, F. M.   2106 Larkin street
Greig, Jas.   Pier 12, Stewart street
Hooke, W. F.   318 First street
Maguire, Jos.
Murison, W. A.   Occidental Hotel
Nielsen, William   11 Yerba Buena street
Platt, C. W.   Olympic Club
Stone, C. B.   31 and 33 California street
Stark, J. G. W.   1659 Eighth street, Oakland

RETIRED ACTIVE MEMBERS

Atherstone, T. S.   22 Post street
Blair, Robt.   510 Montgomery street
Cutting, Jno. T.   23 California street
Clark, L. S.   224 Montgomery street
Duffy, Thos. J.   Safe Deposit Building
Elder, Alex.   129 California street
French, F. M.   35 Beale street
Gregory, S. O.   Alma, Santa Clara Co., Cal.
Hinz, Wm.   545 Market street
Low, C. P.   17 Main street
Mansfield, W. D.   202 Market street
Low, J. O.   17 Main street
Moore, Geo. A.   208 California street
Moore, Ed   2122 Bush street
Muller, H.   German Savings Bank
Nelle, Geo.   567 Market street
Sayre, J. H.   330 Pine street
Steuart, I.   218 California street

ASSOCIATE MEMBERS, 1889-90

Alvord, Wm.	Bank of California
Alvord, Mrs Wm.	Palace Hotel
Anthony, Jno. A.	S. P. R. R. Co.
Austin, B. C., Jr.	412 California street
Atherstone, T. S.	22 Post street
Breyfogle, Dr E. S.	209 Geary street.
Brown, Dr Chas. B.	Sutter st., bet. Polk and Van Ness
Bertheau, Caeser	209 Sansome street
Bandmann, C. J.	30 California street
Black, Mrs R. M.	1026 Geary street
Butler, Geo. E.	413 California street
Bond, Chas. A.	323 California street
Benjamin, Edward	215 Front street
Brandt, Herman	814 Sutter street
Bodwell, F. L.	577 Market street
Baker, A. S.	204 Sansome street
Bostwick, H. R.	219 Davis street
Babcock, Wm.	Parrott & Co.
Buckingham, A. E.	413 Montgomery street
Boysen, Ed C.	9 Montgomery street
Burton, Ben	2101 Hyde street
Barnard, H. W.	132 Market street
Behlow, C. J.	1807 Octavia street
Balfe, M. J.	2446 Jackson street
Bundschu, Chas.	With J. Gundlach & Co.
Bowers, G. W.	2610 Jackson street
Baker, L. L.	1882 Washington street
Belcher, W. C.	Palace Hotel
Belcher, E. A.	322 Geary street
Brüggemann, H.	526 Montgomery street
Cooper, Geo. D.	641 Market street
Carmany, J. W.	25 Kearny street
Carlson, Edward	2 Sutter street
Crocker, Chas. F.	915 Leavenworth street
Cook, Dr A. S.	224 Post street
Calame, Ed.	Lick House
Church, Rev Ed B.	1043 Valencia street
Cummings, H. A.	Treasurer's Office, S. P. R. R.
Center, Wm.	214 Shotwell street
Cummings, F.	420 Commercial street
Classen, F. H.	Del Monte Milling Co.

Gruenhagen Leads in Bonbonniere Candies

Carr, Col B.	805 Market street
Dewitt, Miss Cora A.	726 Eleventh street, Oakland
Dean, W. E.	79 Nevada Block
Davis, R. J.	Pacific Bank
Drown, A. N.	Cor Pierce and Jackson streets
Dutard, H.	Front and Sacramento streets
Donaldson, Jas	319 California street
Dobbs, L. L.	934 Leavenworth street
Dorn, D. S.	306 Pine street
DeGuigne, C.	414 Montgomery street
Duffy, T. J.	Safe Deposit Building
Denicke, E. A.	403 Market street
Ehrenberg, Dr. A. T.	225 Grant Avenue
Eldridge, Oliver	615 Sutter street
Emmons, G. W.	121 California street
Eastland, J. G.	604 Commercial street
Easton, Wendell	618 Market street
Eliot, J. B.	*Chronicle* office
Fox, Chas. W.	318 Pine street
Fredericks, Geo.	Union Iron works
Faymonville, Bernard	Box 2253, city
Fargo, E. A	316 Front street
Forderer, Jos. F.	226 Mission street
Fritch, J. Homer	143 East street
Fry, Willis B.	22 Post street
Galloway, W. T.	2203 Devisadero street
Gunn, J. O'B.	65 First street
Griffin, Frank, J.	101 Mission street
Gore, D. M.	Fillmore and California streets
Greenwood, F. M.	30 New Montgomery street
Greig, Wm.	1627 McAllister street
Glaser, E. F.	433 Kearny street
Hutchinson, E. C.	30 California street
Hammond, J. D.	1037 Market street
Hall, John C.	Nevada Block
Husband, Robt.	101 Mission street
Haight, Robt.	226 Front street
Harrison, R. C.	230 Montgomery street
Hunter, Mrs. David	903 Van Ness avenue
Husted, Mrs. F. M.	604 Merchant street
Hughes, Walter H.	1714 Market street
Hopkins, Moses	California and Buchanan streets
Hueter, E. L.	601 Market street

Haslett, Samuel	452 Spear street
Hooper, Maj. Wm. B.	Occidental Hotel
Howard, Chas. Webb	510 California street
Houghton, J. F.	101 Sansome street
Jordan, R.	897 Fulton street
Jones, W. S.	228 Montgomery street
Jones, J, D.	16 Front street
Jarboe, Jno. R.	917 Pine street
Jackson, G. H. T.	308 Haight street
Kalisher, Ed.	520 Market street
King, H. L., Jr.	Wells, Fargo & Co's Bank
Kern, F. W.	118 Fair Oaks street
Krogh, F. W.	51 Beale street
Klink, Miss Jean S.	1836 Eddy street
Kohler, Mrs E.	Second and Folsom streets
Kreutzmann, Dr H.	728 Sutter street
Larsen, C. G.	18 Eddy street
Low, F. F.	200 Sansome street
Lonergan, Geo. M	City of Paris
Lilienthal, P. N.	Anglo-Californian Bank
Lincoln, Jerome	228 Montgomery street
Lisser, Louis	1241 Franklin street
Loyd, Robt.	607 Sutter street
Ludovici, F. W.	206 Post street
Larzelare, W. R.	435 Paige street
Michaels, H.	40 First street
Murison, W. A.	Occidental Hotel
McKee, Jno.	234 California street
McLean, Dr. R. A	603 Merchant street
Melville, W. R.	Bank of California
McKowen, W. A.	Berkeley, Cala.
Marsh. H. F.	2507 Howard street
Martin, W. C.	314 Oak street
Murray, B. Jr.	Bank of California
Moore, R. S.	Riordan Iron Works
Murdock, C. A.	532 Clay street
Miller, H. M. A.	16 California street
Mitchler, A. G.	16 California street
Moore, Jas.	310 California street
Muller, W. M.	Pine and Front streets
Morgan, W. I.	512 California street
Milner, C. H.	Safe Deposit Company
Morgan, J. S.	509 Twenty-fifth street

McAllister, Hall M.	208 California street
McIntosh, C. K.	First National Bank
McMillan, Robt.	202 Ridley street
McCarthy, L. P.	814 California street
Meineke, Chas.	1917 Franklin street
Natorp, B.	109 California street
Nachtrieb, J. J.	119 Clay street
Nordwell, O. W.	218 Bush street
O'Toole, Dr. M. C.	St. Ann's Building
Payne, Geo. H.	West End, Alameda, Cal.
Pennell, Thos. M.	516 California street
Perry, J., Jr.	Occidental Hotel
Pidwell, C. T.	Odd Fellows' Hall
Paige, Timothy	2002 Pacific avenue
Pierson, Wm. M.	508 California street
Powers, Dr. Geo. H.	225 Geary street
Pierce, Jas. M.	2413 Fillmore street
Pinkham, Miss E. M.	1036 Valencia street
Probasco, Geo. H.	616 Taylor street
Pratt, R. H.	Fourth and Townsend streets
Pennie, J. C., Jr.	1506 Post street
Price, Thomas	524 Sacramento street
Powell, H. A.	207 Sansome street
Quinn, W. H.	Huntington, Hopkins & Co.
Robinson, L. L.	320 Sansome street
Ranlett, Horace D.	420 Montgomery street
Rideout, N. D.	2220 Broadway street
Reynolds, G. W.	406 Van Ness avenue
Reinstein, J. B.	217 Sansome street
Rosenstirn, Dr. Julius	cor. Hyde and Sutter
Rey, J. H. V.	829 Union street
Russell, Edwin	330 Pine street
Somers, B. S.	1034 Mission street
Stewart, I.	218 California street
Stadtmuller, F. D.	819 Eddy street
Schmidt, Max	21 Main street
Schilling, C.	1820 Post street
Shain, J. E.	Safe Deposit Bldg
Scobie, Jas.	324 Haight street
Sanders, G. H.	418 California street
Stone, Chas. B.	33 California street
Sharon, F. W.	Palace Hotel

Most Delicious Candies at Gruenhagen's

Smith, A. A.	122 California street
Siebe, Fr. C.	838 Fulton street
Smith, W. F.	206 Sansome street
Sobey, A. L.	810 20th street
Severance, J. S.	4th and Townsend streets
Smedberg, W. R.	316 California street
Spreckels, J. D.	327 Market street
Stadtfeld, Jacob, Jr.	56 Nevada Block
Selfridge, E. A.	2615 California street
Tubbs, A. L.	613 Front street
Tittle, Robt.	577 Market street
Thompson, G. H.	Bank of California
Trefethen, E. A.	Oakland, Cal
Wagener, Luther	Cosmos club
Walter, D. N.	529 Market street
White, Jas. A.	116 Leidesdorff street
Woodworth, Selim E.	1904 Webster street
Watkins, A. A.	care W. W. Montague & Co.
Whirlm, Miss H. E.	Berkeley, Cal.
Wright, Jno.	418 California street
Wilson, Mrs. N. I.	20 Drumm street
Wilson, Ramon E.	419 California street
Watson, Jas. E.	P. O. Box 1838
Whitcomb, G. F.	435½ Minna street
Wilson, Geo. E.	20 Drumm street
Wright, Jno. A.	208 Sansome street
Young, Wm. R.	132 Market street
Zeile, Fr. W.	220 California street
Ziliani, Signor F.	114 McAllister street

THE BANCROFT COMPANY

CLUBS

*

Pacific-Union Club

Club Building, Northwest Corner of Post and Stockton Streets

The Pacific-Union Club is a consolidation of the Pacific and the Union Clubs—two social organizations that existed in San Francisco: the former since the year 1852, and the latter since 1854. These two Clubs were consolidated in February, 1889, under the name of the Pacific-Union Club.

OFFICERS, 1889

THOS. C. VAN NESS, Pres.	- - - -	Nevada Block
WINFIELD S. KEYES, Vice-Pres.	- -	915 Van Ness Ave.
JOSEPH M. QUAY, Secretary	- -	124 Sansome street
JOHN McKEE, Treasurer	- - -	Care of Tallant & Co.

STANDING COMMITTEES

AUDITING COMMITTEE

Joseph M. Quay,	124 Sansome street
Horace G. Platt,	402 Montgomery street
John McKee	

RESTAURANT COMMITTEE

Frederick R. Webster,	Pacific-Union Club
William E. Holloway,	430 California street
John McKee	

WINE COMMITTEE

Austin C Tubbs	611 Front street
Winfield S. Keyes	915 Van Ness avenue
Joseph M. Quay	124 Sansome street

ROOM COMMITTEE

William E. Holloway	430 California street
Frederick R. Webster	Pacific-Union Club
Joseph M. Quay	124 Sansome street

BILLIARD COMMITTEE

Horace G. Platt	402 Montgomery street
Austin C. Tubbs	611 Front street
William E. Holloway	430 California street

READING-ROOM COMMITTEE

Winfield S. Keyes	915 Van Ness avenue
John McKee	Tallant & Co.
Horace G. Platt	402 Montgomery street

The President is ex-officio a member of all Standing Committees

ELECTION COMMITTEE

Russell J. Wilson	202 Sansome street
I. Lawrence Pool	
Horace F. Cutter	Pacific-Union Club
Louis B. Parrott	306 California street
Charles Page	316 California street
Tom C. Grant	213 Sansome street
John B. Wattles	Pacific-Union Club
John de Witt Allen	Pacific-Union Club
Jerome A. Hart	213 Grant avenue
Joseph D. Grant	N. E. cor. Bush and Sansome sts.
Henry Schmiedell	320 Pine street
William F. Goad	606 Montgomery street
John M. Adams	2510 Washington street
Daniel T. Murphy	Pacific-Union Club
Clinton Day	320 Sutter street

LIST OF MEMBERS

Abbot, George	
Abbott, Charles H.	Fifth and Bluxome streets
Adams, John M.	2510 Washington street
Aldrich, William A.	124 Sansome street
Allen, John De Witt	Pacific-Union Club
Alvord, William	400 California street

Composed of the Leading Musicians of San Francisco. Acknowledged by Artists, Press and Public to be the Greatest Musical Organization on the Pacific Coast

Late Successes of Ritzau's Orchestra

The best Band I have heard in my travels —*P. S. Gilmore at the serenade tendered him at the Palace Hotel.*

Historical Carnival at the Mechanics' Pavilion.—*Press and Public unanimous in their praise.*

Patti's Grand Italian Opera Company.—*Highly complimented by the greatest Operatic Conductor, Luigi Arditi.*

Concerts of the Loring Club.—*D. Loring, Conductor thanked one and all and expressed that it was the best Orchestra he had ever conducted.*

Concerts of Handel and Haydn Society.— *H. J. Stewart, Conductor, praised the Orchestra very highly.*

Concerts of Philharmonic Society—*H. Brandt, Conductor.*

Camille Urso Concert with Handel and Haydn Society at the Grand Opera House. Ovide Musin Concert at Grand Opera House. Finest Orchestra that accompanied me in San Francisco. Hotel Rafael, fashionable society highly pleased during the summer season. Reception at the Bella Vista Hotel in honor of Mr. H. Oelrichs and Miss T. Fair. Hotel Pleasanton musical fêtes and hops. You are cordially invited to hear the Orchestral Concerts at Blair's Park, Piedmont, Oakland, every Saturday afternoon.

Remember that on any occasion you require music to engage Ritzau's Organization and if excellence is what you want we are confident of a bright future.

MUSIC FURNISHED

For Concerts, Germans, Weddings, Receptions, Banquets, Kettledrums, etc. Special attention given to Private Parties. The orchestra will appear in full Evening Dress or Elegant Uniforms.

All communications addressed to SHERMAN & CLAY'S, corner of Sutter and Kearny Streets, will receive prompt attention.

Ames, George E.	First and Mission streets
Andrews, Horace D.	
Ashe, R. Porter	130 Sansome street
Babcock, Harry	306 California street
Babcock, William	306 California street
Baird, Andrew	438 California street
Baker, Livingston L.	Cor. Pine and Davis streets
Baker, Robert S.	
Baldwin, Archibald S.	830 Haight street
Baldwin, Charles A.	Pacific-Union Club
Balfour, Robert	316 California street
Bandman, Julius	30 California street
Barnes, William H. L.	Chronicle Building
Barrett, William G.	First and Natoma streets
Barroilhet, Henry	524 Montgomery street
Beale, Truxtun	307 California street
Beatty, William H.	121 Post street
Belden, Josiah	
Belknap, C. H.	
Bell, Thomas	426 California street
Belloc, Hippolyte	524 Montgomery street
Bender, David A.	
Benson, John	803 Stockton street
Berg, William	60 Merchant's Exchange
Bergin, Thomas I.	38 Nevada Block
Bermingham, John	318 California street
Beylard, F. Duplessis	
Bigelow, Samuel C.	440 California street
Bishop, Thomas B.	327 Pine street
Bissel, William A.	Phelan Building
Blanding, Gordon	324 Pine street
Bliss, Duane L.	
Boalt, John H.	327 Pine street
Boardman, George C.	514 California street
Bonnar, Chas. G.	
Bonny, George	106 Montgomery street
Bonynge, C. W.	
Boomer, Alexander H.	320 Sansome street
Booth, Newton	
Borel, Antoine	311 Montgomery street
Bostwick, I. S.	
Bosqui, E. L.	410 Pine street
Bourn, William D.	401 California street
Bowie, Augustus J.	217 Sansome street

249

Bowie, Henry P.	302 Montgomery street
Bowles, Philip E.	Oakland
Bowman, George F.	440 California street
Boyd, James T.	324 Pine street
Boyd, John F.	29 Nevada Block
Brander, George L.	218 Sansome street
Brigham, Chas. B., M. D.	703 Market street
Brittan, Nathaniel J.	Pacific-Union Club
Brewer, W. P. A.	1515 Fillmore street
Bromwell, Lewis L.	218 California street
Brown, A. Page	318 Pine street
Brown, Thomas	400 California street
Brown, William E.	Fourth and Townsend streets
Browne, Ross E.	307 Sansome street
Bruce, Robert	316 California street
Bruguiere, Emile A.	1800 Franklin street
Buckbee, S. C.	409 Montgomery street
Burke, Martin J.	401 Montgomery street
Bush, Frederick D.	
Butler, George E.	
Byrne, James W.	Pacific-Union Club
Cadwalader, Charles	
Cahill, Edward	406 Montgomery street
Cahn, David	3 Sansome street
Carey, John T.	
Carpentier, Alphonse	508 California street
Castle, Frederick L.	202 Davis street
Center, William	331 Montgomery street
Chapman, Wilfrid B.	123 California street
Chesebrough, A.	202 Market street
Clark, Joseph	
Clay, Clement C.	179 Kearny street
Cofran, John W. G.	313 California street
Coit, Griffith	308 Market street
Coleman, Carleton C.	121 Market street
Coleman, Evan J.	110 Sutter street
Coleman, James V.	Nevada Block
Coleman, John W.	S. F. Stock Exchange Bldg.
Coleman, William T.	121 Market street
Cooper, E. Mason	Wells, Fargo & Co.
Cooper, George D.	641 Market street
Cormac, Thomas E. K.	224 Sansome street
Cornwall, Pierre B.	450 Main street
Costigan, James M.	207 Battery street
Crocker, Charles F.	4th and Townsend streets

Glacé Fruits and Marrons at Gruenhagen's

Wedding and Party Invitations Engraved and Printed in Correct Form.

The Bancroft Company, 721 Market Street.

Crocker, George	Pacific-Union Club
Crocker, Henry J.	215 Bush street
Crocker, Henry S.	219 Bush street
Crocker, Wm. H.	322 Pine street
Crockett, Joseph B.	1st and Natoma streets
Culbertson, Arthur	
Cutter, Horace F.	Pacific-Union Club
Danforth, E. P.	723 Battery street
Day, Clinton	220 Sutter street
Dean, Walter E.	79 Nevada Block
De Crano, Edmund G.	
De Guigne, Christian	414 Montgomery street
Delafield, Robert H.	
Delmas, D. M.	310 Pine street
Denman, James	1201 Webster street
Denson, Samuel C.	
De Pue, Edgar J.	419 California street
Derby, Chancellor.	
Dewey, Eugene E.	
Dewey, William P.	310 Pine street
Dexter, Henry S.	401 Sacramento street
Dimond, William H.	400 California street
Dodge, Henry L.	116 Market street
Donahue, Peter J.	55 Nevada Block
Donohoe, Joseph A.	Montgy. and Sacramento sts.
·Donohoe, Joseph A., Jr.	Montgy. and Sacramento sts.
Dorn, Diademus S.	306 Pine street
Dorr, Dr. L. L.	405 Montgomery street
Douty, Frank S.	4th and Townsend streets
Doyle, John T.	101 Sansome street
Drown, Albert N.	621 Clay street
Dunham, Benjamin F.	17 Beale street
Dunphy, William	Flood Building
Dunsmuir, Alexander	620 East street
Dutton, William J.	401 California street
Earl, Daniel W.,	202 Sansome street
Eastland, Joseph G.	604 Commercial street
Eastman, Hosea B.	
Eells, Charles P.	316 California street
Eldridge, Oliver	303 California street
Evans, Oliver P.	230 Montgomery street
Everett, S. B.	
Ewing, Thomas	327 Pine street
Eyre, Edward E.	124 Sansome street

Gold Pens An endless variety of Gold Pens and Penholders from the celebrated Factory of Mabie, Todd & Co., New York.

The Bancroft Company, 721 Market Street

Fair, James G.	230 Montgomery street
Fargo, Calvin F.	Pacific-Union Club
Felton, Charles N.	Pacific-Union Club
Fillmore, Jerome A.	Fourth and Townsend streets
Fletcher, Montgomery	Pacific-Union Club
Flood, James L.	7 Nevada Block
Floyd, Richard S.	120 Sutter street
Follansbee, John G.	
Forbes, Andrew B.	401 California street
Forman, Charles	
Forman, Robert B.	316 California street
Foster, Arthur W.	322 Pine street
Fox, George H.	Fifth and Townsend streets
Fraser, Thomas E.	
Freeborn, James	420 Montgomery street
Froelich, Christian, Jr.	202 Market street
Fry, John D.	326 Montgomery street
Gallatin, Albert	21 First street
Galpin, Philip G.	101 Sansome street
Gamble, James	432 Montgomery street
Gansl, Albert	36 Nevada Block
Garber, Eugene R.	Palace Hotel
Garber, John	327 Pine street
Garthwaite, E. H.	Oakland
Gerald, E. F.	Pacific-Union Club
Gibbs, George W.	33 Fremont street
Gillette, Daniel B., Jr.	68 Nevada Block
Gilman, Byron	
Gilson, Livingston	211 Sansome street
Girvin, Richard D.	307 California street
Givens, Charles S.	221 Market street
Glass, Louis	323 Pine street
Glenat, Louis	
Goad, William F.	606 Montgomery street
Godeffroy, Alfred	10 Market street
Goewey, James M.	30 Page street
Goodall, Charles	10 Market street
Goodall, Edwin	10 Market street
Goucher, W. H.	
Grant, Adam	Bush and Sansome streets
Grant, George F.	217 Sansome street
Grant, Joseph D.	Bush and Sansome streets
Grant, Tom C.	217 Sansome street
Gray, George E.	1115 Bush street

Most Delicious Candies at Gruenhagen's

Grayson, George W.	327 Pine street
Grayson, Robert R.	327 Pine street
Green, Charles E.	Fourth and Townsend streets
Grow, Charles A.	Phelan Building
Gunn, James O'B	Mission and First streets
Guthrie, Alexander	316 California street
Hagar, George	
Haggin, James B.	50 Nevada Block
Haggin, Louis T.	45 Nevada Block
Hague, James D.	
Haldan, Edward B.	413 California street
Hale, Joseph P.	210 Battery street
Hall, Henry E.	528 Market street
Hall, John C.	Nevada Block
Hall, Marcus P.	318 Pine street
Hall, Wm. Hammond	Flood Building
Hallidie, A. S.	329 Market street
Hamilton, Alexander	Cor. Pine and Davis streets
Hamilton, Alonzo C.	
Hamilton, Robert M.	Cor. Pine and Davis streets
Hammond, John Hays	401 California street
Hammond, Richard P.	City Hall (old)
Hammond, Richard P., Jr.	10 Montgomery street
Hammond, William H.	
Hardin, C. H. E.	
Harkness, H. W., M. D.	Cor. California and Dupont sts.
Harmon, Albion K. P.	Nevada Block
Harries, William H.	426 California street
Harrington, W. P.	Palace Hotel
Harrison, Henry D.	
Harrison, Ralph C.	230 Montgomery street
Harrison, Robert	325 Montgomery street
Hart, James W.	302 California street
Hart, Jerome A.	213 Grant avenue
Harvey, J. Downey	Palace Hotel
Hastings, Robert P.	Phelan Building
Haswell, Charles H., Jr.	34 Montgomery street
Hawes, Alexander G.	220 Sansome street
Hayden, B.	
Hayne, Robert Y.	121 Post street
Hayward, Alvinza	224 Post street
Hearst, George	53 Nevada Block
Head, Addison E.	
Hearst, William R.	*Examiner*
Heatley, Edward D.	412 Battery street

Herrin, William F.	305 Sansome street
Hesketh, Sir Thomas	
Hewlett, Henry H.	Palace Hotel
Hewston, John Jr.	
Hill, Harry C.	
Hill, Horace L.	124 Sansome street
Hobart, W. S.	224 California street
Hochkofler, Rudolph	38 California street
Hodges, A. D., Jr.	
Hoffman, Ogden	U. S. Appraiser's Building
Hoffman, Southard	U. S. Appraiser's Building
Hoge, Joseph P.	Superior Court, Dept. 4
Holbrook, Charles	225 Market street
Holloway, William E.	430 California street
Hooker, C. G.	917 Bush street
Hooper, William B.	Occidental Hotel
Hopkins, Edward W.	Phelan Building
Hopkins, Moses	Phelan Building
Hopkins, Timothy	Fourth and Townsend streets
Hopkins, William S.	
Hotaling, Anson P.	429 Jackson street
Houghton, James F.	216 Sansome street
Howard, Charles Webb	516 California street
Howard, John L.	132 Market street
Howard, William H.	523 Montgomery street
Howland, George	
Hubbard, Samuel	
Hull, Edward	Occidental Hotel
Hunt, L. S. J.	
Huse, Frederic J. M. D.	2606 Pacific avenue
Hutchinson, Eli I.	419 California street
Hyde, Frederick A.	630 Commercial street
Ives, George I.	324 Pine street
Jackson, D. H.	
Janin, Henry	
Janin, Louis	211 Sansome street
Jackson, Andrew	
Jackson, A. W.	
Jarboe, John R.	230 Montgomery street
Jaynes, Frank	302 Montgomery street
Jennings, Hennen	
Jerome, Henry A.	
Jewett, John H.	931 Bush street
Johnson, Covington	Pacific-Union Club

Joice, Erastus V.	6 Merchants' Exchange
Jones, John P.	
Jones, Samuel L.	
Josselyn, Charles	38 Market street
Kellogg, Calvin W.	214 Front street
Kellogg, Marmaduke B.	530 California street
Kenney, Charles A.	
Keyes, Erasmus, D.	
Keyes, Winfield Scott	915 Van Ness avenue
Kimball, Gorham G.	
King, Homer S.	314 Pine street
Kinney, Abbot	
Kirkham, Ralph W.	
Kittle, Jonathan G.	202 California street
Knowles, Josiah N.	28 California street
Larkin, Alfred Otis	
Lawler, Frank W.	Superior Court, Dept. 8
Lawson, Wm.	120 Sansome street
Lent, Eugene	
Lent, Geo. H.	Bohemian Club
Lent, William M.	
Lincoln, I. B.	
Lincoln, Jerome	228 Montgomery street
Llewellyn, William H.	
Lloyd, H. C.	
Lloyd, Reuben H.	17 Nevada Block
Locan, Frank	1114 Post street
Lombard, Orville D.	
Loomis, George	13 Pine street
Low, George A.	208 California street
Low, Frederick F.	Sansome and Pine streets
Lukens, Edward G.	40 California street
Lusk, F. C.	
Lyle, William S.	25 Nevada Block
Lyons, Thomas L.	832 Bush street
Macdonald, William	410 Pine street
Macdonough, Joseph	41 Market street
Macdonough, J. M.	
Mackay, John W.	7 Nevada Block
Macneil, H. L.	
MacMonagle, Beverly, M. D.	California and Kearny sts.
Madden, Thomas P.	Occidental Hotel
Mann, Henry R.	324 California street
Marazzi, Count Jerome	506 Battery street

Marshall, Benjamin, M. D.	924 Sutter street
Martin, Henry MacLean	
Martin, William H.	1 Flood Building
Martinez, F. N. R.	
Marye, Geo. T., Jr.	232 Montgomery street
Mastick, Edwin B.	520 Montgomery street
Matthews, William	120 Sutter street
Maxwell, George H.	61 Nevada Block
Maxwell, John W. C.	318 Van Ness avenue
Maxwell, Walter S.	
Mayer, Josef	
Mayne, Charles	Palace Hotel
Menzies, Thomas	310 Pine street
Merrill, John F.	225 Market street
Mesick, Richard S.	61 Nevada Block
Meyer, Herman L. E.	210 Battery street
Meyer, William	
Middleton, Samuel P.	22 Montgomery street
Mills, Wm. O.	
Mills, Darius O.	
Mills, Edgar	Pacific-Union Club
Molera, Eusebius J.	609 Sacramento street
Montague, Wilfred W.	309 Market street
Moore, Austin D.	109 California street
Moore, Robert S.	Cor. Howard and Beale streets
Moore, John J.	302 California street
Morgan, Charles B.	Pacific-Union Club
Morgan, P. T.	323 Pine street
Morrow, Robert F.	414 California street
Moses, Charles S.	609 Brannan street
Mullins, Charles F.	301 California street
Murdock, W. C.	324 California street
Murphy, Daniel T.	Pacific-Union Club
Murphy, P. W.	
Murphy, Samuel G.	1st National Bank of S. F.
Murphy, Samuel J.	
McAfee, C. William	10 Montgomery street
McAfee, L. C.	
McAllister, Ward, Jr.	430 Montgomery street
McBean, P. McG.	2611 Pacific avenue
McCoppin, Frank	Pacific-Union Club
McFarland, Dan.	
McKee, John	Tallant & Co.
McKinley, Archibald	
McLaughlin, Frank	

New Books Received Daily Webster International Dictionary, a new book from cover to cover. In sheep, half morocco, half Russia and full morocco binding. Indexed.

The Bancroft Company, 721 Market Street.

McMullen, Frank	California and Battery streets
McMurray, Robert	
McMurtry, W. S., Jr.	Pacific-Union Club
McNear, George W.	306 California street
McNutt, Wm. F., M. D.	127 Montgomery street
McRuer, D. C.	
Murdock, W. C.	324 California street
Newhall, Edward W.	205 Bush street
Newhall, George A.	309 Sansome street
Newhall, G. D.	
Newhall, W. Mayo	809 Sansome street
Newhall, Walter S.	225 Bush street
Newlands, Francis G.	305 Sansome street
Nickel, J. Leroy	1415 Jones street
Nicholson, Alfred A.	Palace Hotel
Norris, William	516 California street
North, George L.	405 Montgomery street
Oxnard, James G.	
Oxnard, Robert	124 California street
Page, Charles	316 California street
Page, Henry	
Page, Wllfred	
Paige, Calvin	Lick House
Palache, G.	309 Sansome street
Parrott, John	414 Montgomery street
Parrott, Louis B.	306 California street
Parsons, Edward, M. D.	Phelan Building
Payne, Theodore F.	
Payson, A. H.	
Pease, Richard H., Jr.	557 Market street
Perkins, George C.	10 Market street
Perkins, H. C.	320 Sansome street
Perrin, Edw. B.	402 Kearny street
Petersen, Charles	124 Sansome street
Petre, Reginald W.	
Phelan, James D.	Phelan Building
Pichoir, Henry	320 Sansome street
Pierson, Wm. M.	75 Nevada Block
Pillsbury, Evans S.	324 Pine street
Pixley, Frank M.	213 Grant avenue
Plater, John E.	
Platt, Horace G.	402 Montgomery street
Polhemus, Charles B.	

Pool, I. Lawrence
Poudensan, P.
Powell, Walter   SE. cor California & Sansome sts.
Prentise, Samuel R.   401 California street
Prescott, Geo. W.   NW cor. First and Mission sts.
Preston, Edward F.   310 Pine street
Pringle, Edward J.   522 Montgomery street

Quay, Joseph M.   124 Sansome street

Ralston, William C.
Randol, James B.   320 Sansome street
Rathbone, Jared L.
Reade, Francis R.
Redding, Joseph D.   Chronicle Building
Reddington, William P.   Stevenson and Second streets
Reed, Simon G.
Reis, John O'N.   408 California street
Requa, Isaac L.   79 Nevada Block
Richards, Charles O.   46 Fremont street
Richards, Hugo
Rideout, N. D.
Rithet, R. P.   220 California street
Rix, Edward A.   225 First street
Robinson, James A.
Robinson, Lester L.   320 Sansome street
Robinson, Luke, M. D.   217 Geary street
Robinson, Sanford   320 Sansome street
Roe, George H.   227 Stevenson street
Rose, Andrew W., Jr.   224 California street
Russell, William F.   1 S. F. Stock Exchange Building
Rutherford, Thomas L.

Sabin, John I.   325 Pine street
Santa Marina, Eug. J. de
Sawyer, Alfred F., M. D.   302 Stockton street
Schmiedell, Henry   320 Pine street
Schroder, Baron J. H. von   109 California street
Schussler, Herman   27 Grant avenue
Scott, Henry T.   NW cor. First and Mission sts.
Scott, Irving M.   NW cor. First and Mission sts.
Scrivener, Authur   NW cor. Leidesdorff & Cala. sts.
Searls, Niles
Selby, Prentiss   416 Montgomery street
Sewall, Oscar T.   202 Market street
Shard, C.   412 Montgomery street
Sharon, Frederick W.   305 Sansome street

Gruenhagen Leads in Bonbonniere Candies

258

Sheldon, Mark	11 First street
Sherwood, Henry H.	212 Market street
Shiels, George F., M. D.	219 Powell st.
Shoobert, John E.	307 California street
Shorb, J. de Barth	
Shreve, George C.	106 Montgomery street
Simpkins, Charles H.	Palace Hotel
Simpson, Asa M.	48 Market street
Slauson, J. S.	
Smith, S. H.	New City Hall
Smith, Hamilton, Jr.	
Smith, Hiram C.	109 California street
Smith, J. Henly	110 Sutter street
Smith, S. Prentiss	
Smith, Sidney V.	212 Sansome street
Smith, William F.	206 Sansome street
Southgate, James J.	
Spencer, George W.	316 California street
Sprague, Richard H.	124 California street
Spreckels, Adolph B.	327 Market street
Spreckels, Claus	327 Market street
Spreckels, C. August	327 Market street
Spreckels, John D.	327 Market street
Stanford, Leland	Fourth and Townsend streets
Steele, Edward L. G.	208 California street
Steinhart, Ignatz	NE cor. Pine and Sansome streets
Steinhart, Sigismund	NE cor. Pine and Sansome streets
Steinbach, Rudolph	217 Sansome street
Stephens, John D.	
Stetson, Edward Gray	508 California street
Stewart, William M.	
Stillman, Alfred	307 California street
Stone, Charles B.	304 California street
Stoutenborough, Chas. H.	324 Pine street
Stringham, Irving	
Struve, H. G.	
Stubbs, John C.	Fourth and Townsend streets
Swan, Benjamin R., M. D.	310 Stockton street
Swift, John F.	814 Valencia street
Symmes, Frank J.	222 Sutter street
Talbot, William H.	2840 Buchanan street
Tallant, F. W.	Battery and California streets
Tallant, John D.	NE cor. Cal. and Battery streets
Tams, Sampson	Cosmos Club

Taylor, Chauncey	
Taylor, John W.	
Taylor, William H.	6 Merchants' Exchange
Ten Bosch, John M.	302 Montgomery street
Teschemacher, Henry F.	
Tevis, Wm. S.	14 Post street
Tevis, Lloyd	NW cor. Cal. and Sansome streets
Theller, Samuel L.	330 Pine street
Thomas, William	101 Sansome street
Thompson, Joseph P.	Pacific-Union Club
Thompson, Robert R.	NW cor. Van Ness ave. & Pine st.
Thornton, Harry I.	504 Kearny street
Tilford, E. A.	123 California street
Tobey, W. D.	
Tobin, Alfred	8 Montgomery street
Tobin, Robert J.	
Towne, A. N.	Fourth and Townsend streets
Townsend, Frederick	
Tritle, Frederick A.	
Tubbs, Austin C.	611 Front street
Tubbs, Alfred L.	611 Front street
Tubbs, Alfred S.	611 Front street
Tubbs, William B.	611 Front street
Tucker, James E.	U. S. Appraiser's Building
Upham, Isaac	214 Pine street
Valentine, John J.	Wells, Fargo & Co.
Van Ness, Thomas C.	Nevada Block
Veuve, H. Henry	Pacific-Union Club
Vouillemont, Eugene G.	
Wadsworth, Henry	Wells, Fargo & Co.
Wadsworth, James C. L.	Pacific-Union Club
Wallace, George	
Wallace, William T.	Superior Court, Dept. 6
Ward, D. Henshaw	204 California street
Watt, Robert	40 First street
Watson, Charles L.	641 Market street
Wattles, John B.	Pacific-Union Club
Webster, Frederick R.	Pacific-Union Club
Weighel, W. McM.	
Wenban, Simeon	
Wendt, A. F.	
Wensinger, Francis S.	624 Sacramento street
Wetherbee, Henry	111 Market street

Wheaton, George H.	221 Front street
Wheeler, Harold	621 Clay street
White, Josiah H.	79 Nevada Block
Whiting, Dwight	
Whiting, H. C	410 Mission street
Whitney, Francis L.	460 Townsend street
Whitney, Joel P.	
Whittell, George	130 Sansome street
Whittier, William F.	231 Front street
Wickes, George W.	419 California street
Wigmore, Alphonse A.	129 Spear street
Wilder, Charles J.	Fourth and Townsend streets
Willey, Harry I.	Pacific-Union Club
Williams, Evan	
Wilmerding, J. Clute	214 Front street
Wilshire, William B.	204 California street
Wilson, John Scott	2530 Pine street
Wilson, Ramon E.	419 California street
Wilson, Russell J.	202 Sansome street
Wilson, Samuel M.	202 Sansome street
Winslow, Chauncey R.	409 Market street
Wise, E. Everett	
Wood, William S.	Nevada Block
Woodward, Henry W.	309 California street
Woodward, Robert B.	419 California street
Woodworth, Selim E.	320 Van Ness avenue
Wooster, Fred L.	218 Front street
Worden, Clinton E.	NE cor. Ritch & Townsend sts.
Wright, Edward C.	Fourth and Townsend streets
Wright, John A.	212 Sansome street
Yerington, Henry M.	
Yost, Daniel Z.	
Zeile, Frederick W.	124 California street

Most Delicious Candies at Gruenhagen's

Cosmos Club

Club Building, 317 Powell Street

The Cosmos Club was organized in 1881 and incorporated in 1883. The membership is extensive, and the number of Army and Navy members is greater than in any of the other Clubs. The aim of the organizers to keep this Club the most select in the city has been pre-eminently successful, and its position as such is generally conceded. Every three months the members have a banquet in their elegantly furnished clubhouse.

OFFICERS, 1889-1890

SAMPSON TAMS	President
S. G. MURPHY	Vice-President
F. H. GREEN	Hon. Secretary
H. L. TATUM	Treasurer

DIRECTORS

Sampson Tams	F. H. Green
S. G. Murphy	J. P. Langhorne
J. R. Folsom	J. O. Heppner
H. L. Tatum	Wm. Anter
C. L. Weller	

MEMBERS

Abbott, Augustus	Sacramento, Cal.
Adams, Charles H.	Cosmos Club
Alexander, S. Cameron	London, England
Alvord, Henry B.	San Jose
Ball, H. M.	908 Stockton street
Bangs, Franklin	Oakland, Cal.
Barger, D. E.	1429 Sacramento street
Barry, Thomas F.	806 Lombard street
Bartlett, Columbus	Alameda

Beck, Eugene B.	Oakland
Beck, Walter F.	Oakland
Bishop, Thomas B.	1503 Larkin street
Boyd, Colin M.	American Exchange
Boyd, John F.	San Rafael
Bolling, Randolph	Portland
Bowen, J. J.	306 Jones street
Breeze, Charles K.	Contra Costa County
Brison, Wm. M.	539 Geary street
Browne, Christopher R.	Cosmos Club
Burns, Paul O.	San Jose
Cahill, Ed. J.	Grand Hotel
Campbell, W. S.	Washington
Carson, Samuel	2204 Pacific avenue
Center, William	214 Shotwell street
Chappell, J. J.	Cosmos Club
Clarke, E. K.	2119 California street
Clark, Warren D.	Cor. Cal. st. and Van Ness ave.
Clough, Charles L.	Cosmos Club
Cohen, Edgar A.	Alameda
Cole, E. P.	1521 Scott street
Cole, R. Beverly	218 Post street
Cole, Thomas	2006 Bush street
Coleman, Nicholas D.	Los Angeles
Commins, Frank	504 Geary street
Cunningham, J. M.	2518 Broadway street
Coon, F. A.	1239 Pine street
Danforth, E. P.	1200 Mason street
Davis, H. C.	Oakland
Davis, Wm.	Oakland
Dargie, Wm. E.	Oakland
Deering, Frank P.	929 Fillmore street
Degener, L. P.	Nicaragua
Dimond, Henry P.	Cosmos Club
Doe, Loring B.	Alameda
Donohue, Denis	2299 Sacramento street
Easton, A. M.	Millbrae
Easton, Wendell	Palace Hotel
Emerick, Harry F.	Occidental Hotel
Eliot, J. B.	325 Seventeenth street
Farnfield, C. P.	Cosmos Club
Ferris, John W.	320 Sansome street
Folger, J. A., Jr.	Oakland
Folsom, George S.	Cosmos Club

Folsom, J. R.	Cosmos Club
Friedlander, T. C.	1913 Clay street
Fulweiler, J. M.	Auburn, Cal.
Goodrich, Taylor	30 Post street
Gould, E. H.	
Graves, Ernest	San Luis Obispo
Green, F. H.	Pleasanton Hotel
Haggin, L. T.	1250 Taylor street
Hamilton, Claude Terry	Cosmos Club
Hamm, L. J.	San Rafael
Hanson, W.	
Harrison, A. Dalton	San Rafael
Harrison, W. Greer	2200 Broadway
Harron, John O.	Cosmos Club
Hayes, G. R. B.	1814 Buchanan street
Hayne, Robert Y.	San Mateo
Heitschu, Samuel	Portland, Oregon
Heppner, J. Otto	Cosmos Club
Hunt, John	1703 Octavia street
Ijams, P. M.	
Ives, Stephen D.	Cosmos Club
Jardine, W. H.	
Johnson, C. R.	Fort Bragg, Cal.
Kingsbury, Frank	Cosmos Club
Knight, N. R.	Alameda
Langhorne, J. P.	2419 Pacific street
Loughead, H. W.	Cosmos Club
Ludovici, F. W.	New York
Luckhardt, C. A.	1812 Howard street
Lyman, W. W.	St. Helena, Napa Co., Cal.
Macondray, Wm.	1821 Sacramento street
Marceau, F. C.	
Marwedel, E. H.	East Oakland
Martin, Henry	Palace Hotel
McCarthy, T. F.	San Mateo
McDonald, R. H., Jr.	813 Sutter street
McKinstry, E. W.	1515 Washington street
McGovern, Jno. F.	2513 California street
Melville, Wm. R.	Blythedale
Miller, J. H.	
Molera, E. J.	850 Van Ness avenue
Moore, Howell C.	San Jose

Morgan, Percy T.	Berkeley
Murphy, James T.	San Jose
Murphy, S. G.	931 Bush street
Murray, A. S.	1025 O'Farrell street
Naunton, R. H.	1418 Clay street
Northam, R. H.	Los Angeles
Nugent, J. F.	426 Geary street
Okell, Charles J.	Cosmos Club
Orcutt, F. L.	Sacramento, Cal.
Paterson, A. Van R.	310 Haight street
Perry, Henry	504 Geary street
Plummer, W. P.	
Pomeroy, C. P.	San Rafael
Powning, Joseph	646 Fell street
Price, Thomas	715 Post street
Randall, George C.	Cosmos Club
Randolph, D. L.	Alameda
Riordan, Thomas D.	1708 Octavia street
Roe, Edward A.	Cosmos Club
Rothwell, J. P.	Union League Club
Rountree, James O.	1814 Geary street
Schenck, W. T. Y.	1426 Post street
Scott, J. A.	Cosmos Club
Seifried, F. J.	
Sessions, G. W.	2621 California street
Simpson, James	234 Post street
Simpson, Wm. P.	234 Post street
Smith, B. T.	
Starr, Wm. C.	1910 Leavenworth street
Stone, W. L.	Washington, D. C.
Stone, Robt.	
Stoney, Geo. M.	2500 Pacific Avenue
Sullivan, Matthew I.	1218 Twenty-first street
Sullivan, Maurice J.	724 Gough street
Swift, Charles J.	1714 Pacific avenue
Tams, Sampson	Cor. Van Ness ave. & Jackson st.
Tatum, H. L.	2525 Pacific avenue
Ten Bosch, J. M.	1452 Franklin street
Terrill, Geo. N.	400 Stockton street
Thompson, R. A.;	605 Polk street
Thornton, Crittenden	1915 Webster street
Tillinghast, D. F.	Sausalito

Tilden, Chas. L.	Auburn, Cal.
Tucker, S. E.	Cor. Jackson st. & Van Ness ave.
Wagner, H. L.	506 Sutter street
Wagoner, Luther	Cosmos Club
Walker, N. S., Jr.	New York
Waterworth, H. W.	1312 Taylor street
Watts, W. P.	Cosmos Club
Weber, Arthur	Paris
Weller, Chas. L.	Bella Vista
Wheeler, Wm. R.	Cosmos Club
Whitney, F. L.	2030 Laguna street
Whitney, J. D.	Palace Hotel
Wickes, G. W.	Cor. Geary st. and Grant ave.
Wise, Jno. H.	1409 Leavenworth street
Wood, C. H.	1014 Bush street
Wood, David	
Wood, H. P.	San Rafael
Woodward, R. B.	Cor. Geary st. and Grant ave.
Young, Thos.	2316 Clay street
Younger, W. J.	300 Stockton street
Zeilin, W. S.	Cosmos Club

ARMY AND NAVY MEMBERS

Auzal, E. W.	McGuinness, J. P.
Bell, J. A.	Moale, Edward
Belknap, George E.	Niblack, A. P.
Bennett, F. T.	Noble, Robert H.
Brant, L. P.	Oliver, J. H.
Brumby, Thomas M.	Perry, T. B.
Dapray, J. A.	Poundstone, H. C.
Dougherty, W. E.	Reid, R. I.
Forney, Stehman	Rogers, Allen G.
Garrett, L. M.	Runcie, Jas. E.
Greble, E. St. John	Randolph, B. H.
Gibbons, John H.	Ruggles, Geo. D.
Gilmore, E. P.	Shipley, J. H.
Helm, J. M.	Tisdall, W. H.
Hill, F. K.	Tripp, Frederic A.
Harrison, G. F. E.	Watson, J. Crittenden
Hughes, R. P.	Wood, A. N.
Hunter, Edwd.	Wood, S. S.
Janeway, John H.	Winn, F. L.
Kerr, Mark B.	White, W. P.
Le Favor, F. H.	Whiting, Robert
Lovering, L. A.	Welles, Roger, Jr.
	Wilson, J. C.

It is an invariable rule with "Society that knows" when enter-
taining their friends to use the best of everything that can be procured.
When you depart from that time-honored custom, you lay yourself
open to very unpleasant criticism, and often from sources you would
and should least expect. To command success, every detail must be
looked into, the sending of invitations, the decorating of the rooms,
the programme of entertainment, which must be varied and not too
long, and last and not the least, the supper and refreshments, and when
you reach that point procure the finest brands of Champagnes, Clarets
and Sauternes, and you could not do better in that case than to make
your selections at Em. Meyer & Co's, at Nos. 413 and 415 Pine street,
where the best of everything in that particular line can be had—a fact
well known to our Connoisseurs and Society leaders.

The Bohemian Club

Club Rooms, 130 Post Street

The Bohemian Club was organized April 1, 1872. It was instituted for the association of gentlemen connected professionally with literature, art, music, the drama, and to those having appreciation of the same. The membership is limited to 600. The "High Jinks" held on or about the last Saturday evening of each month is the distinctive feature of this Club.

OFFICERS

James M. McDonald	President
James D. Phelan	Vice-President
E. B. Pomroy	Secretary
T. D. Brastow	Treasurer

DIRECTORS

George W. Granniss	H. J. Stewart
E. W. Townsend	Raphael Weill
Mountford T. Wilson	

MEMBERS

Abbott, S. L., Jr.	2411 Pierce street.
Abbott, Chas. H.	cor. Fifth and Bluxome streets
Abrams, John	Bohemian Club
Alexander, Chas. O.	121 California street
Alvord, William	Bank of California
Arditi, Luigi	London, England
Arnold, Dr J. D.	New Chronicle Building
Ashe, R. Porter	418 California street
Ashe, Gaston W.	407 California street
Austin, Joseph	Palace Hotel

Glacé Fruits and Marrons at Gruenhagen's

Babcock, Harry	306 California street
Babcock, William	306 California street
Baker, L. L.	6 Pine street
Baker, Wakefield	132 Post street
Barnes, W. H. L.	New Chronicle Building
Barrett, Lawrence	London, England
Bartlett, G. N.	96 Wall street, N. Y.
Barton, Willard T.	308 Market street
Bates, Morris T.	Seattle, Washington
Bayley, George D.	1307 Castro street, Oakland
Bayley, Robert	3 California street
Beach, Thomas T.	604 Merchant street
Beard, John L.	Warm Springs
Beaver, Geo. W.	414 California street
BeDell, Wm.	11 Montgomery street
Behr, Dr Herman H.	509 Kearny street
Belcher, W. C.	520 Montgomery street
Belknap, David P.	401 Montgomery street
Bender, A. S.	418 California street
Bennett, Thomas	420 Montgomery street
Benson, John	803 Stockton street
Berry, Fulton	Fresno
Belshaw, Mortimer	1626 Jackson street
Bigelow, Geo. T.	1816 Vallejo street
Bishop, Thos. B.	S. F. Stock Exchange Building
Boalt, John H.	S. F. Stock Exchange Building
Boardman, George C.	514 California street
Boericke, William	234 Sutter street
Bonestell, John T.	134 Sutter street
Bonynge, Chas. W.	Pacific-Union Club
Booth, Edwin	
Booth, Newton	
Boruck, Marcus D.	Sacramento
Bosworth, H. M.	2233 Taylor street
Bosqui, Edward	523 Clay street
Bourn, W. B.	401 California street
Bourne, John B.	12 Leidesdorff street
Bouvier, Alfred	Baldwin Theatre
Bowers, Mrs D. P.	
Bowers, Wm. F.	409 Market street
Bowie, Allan St. J.	314 Montgomery street
Boyd, James T.	Pacific-Union Club
Bowie, Augustus J., Jr.	202 Broderick street
Boomer, John H.	320 Sansome street
Brady, Henry J.	Bohemian Club

Most Delicious Candies at Gruenhagen's

.Latest Stationery Of Every Description, Fine Paper, Envelopes and Writing Paper. *The Bancroft Company, 721 Market Street.*

1

Brandt, Herman	738 Post street
Brastow, S. D.	Wells, Fargo & Co. Ex.
Breon, Paul	225 Front street
Brittan, Nathaniel J.	Pacific-Union Club
Bromley, Geo. T.	1418 Washington street
Bromley, Isaac H.	
Bromwell, Louis L.	318 California street
Brookes, Samuel M.	611 Clay street
Brooks, Wm.	516 California street
Brown, A. Page	318 Pine street
Brown, John William	920 Pine street
Brown, Roland G.	420 California street
Brown, Wm. E.	C. P. R. R. Office
Brown, Chas. A.	Honolulu, H. I.
Browne, J. Lewis	616 Folsom street
Buckbee, S. C.	407 Montgomery street
Budd, Wayman C.	Board of Trade, Chicago
Bullard, L. J.	35 Pine street, N. Y.
Bundschee, Chas.	Market and Second streets
Bunker, Wm. M.	*Daily Report*
Burgin, J. F.	New Chronicle Building
Burke, Hugh M.	Bohemian Club
Bush, David	316 Sutter street
Butler, George E.	413 California street
Burke, Jeremiah T.	211 Sansome street
Butler, Arthur P.	8 Bush street
Cahn, David	205 Sansome street
Camp, G. A.	Winona, Minn.
Campbell, Donald Y.	530 California street
Carlsen, Emil	Bohemian Club
Carlson, Chas. J.	523 Pine street
Cawlan, Francis J.	115 California street
Carroll, Edgar B.	Sacramento
Cartan, Francis M.	312 Sacramento street
Casserly, Augustine	507 Montgomery street
Castle, Fred. L.	312 Davis street
Castle, Michael	425 Market street
Carr, Byron O.	805 Market street
Ceuter, William	327 Market street
Chadbourne, Forrest S.	745 Market street
Chapman, Edmund B.	22 California street
Chapman, Wilfrid B.	123 California street
Chester, Frederick	Bohemian Club
Chismore, George	705 Sutter street
Churchill, Clark	Phoenix, A. T.

Chase, Horace B.	Napa Soda Springs
Clark, Benjamin	Bohemian Club
Clark, Wm. C.	328 Montgomery street
Clemens, Samuel L.	Hartford, Conn.
Clement, Henry N.	528 California street
Clough, Charles L.	Cosmos Club
Clunie, Thomas J.	334 Kearny street
Coleman, Evan J.	110 Sutter street
Coleman, Harry L.	Stock Exchange Building
Coleman, Wm. T.	123 Market street
Coney, Alex. K.	531 California street
Cook, Wm. Hoff.	319 California street
Coolbrith, Miss Ina D.	
Cope, Warner W.	324 Pine street
Cox, Jennings S.	17 Wall street, New York
Cowles, W. Northrope	308 Market street
Coleman Jas. V.	42 Nevada Block
Cramer, Francis A.	230 California street
Crocker, Chas F.	S. P. Office
Crocker, George	1100 California street
Crocker, William H.	322 Pine street
Crocker, Henry J.	217 Bush street
Crockett, Jos. B.	First and Natoma streets
Crowley, Dennis David	Twelfth and Broadway, Oakland
Culbertson, Arthur	
Cunningham, John S.	
Curlett, Wm.	Phelan Building
Currey, Montgomery S.	Dixon
Cuthbertson, Walter J.	St. Ann's Building
Cutter, Chester G.	80 Commercial street, Boston
Dam, Henry J. W.	Union Square Hotel, New York
Davis, Andrew McF.	3 Berkeley st., Cambridge, Mass.
Davis, Henry L.	317 Kearny street
Day, Clinton	220 Sutter street
Dean, Walter E.	79 Nevada Block
Deering, F. P.	206 Sansome street
Demis, S. W.	809 Market street
De Ojeda, Louis	San Salvador
De Pue, Edgar J.	409 California street
De Pue, Elmer H.	14 Montgomery street
De Vecchi, Paolo	700 Broadway
Dewey, Eugene C.	Paris, France
Dewey, William P.	Paris, France
Dibble, Henry C.	45 Nevada Block
Dickinson, John H.	402 Montgomery street

Dimond, W. H.	Union Block
Dodge, Wm. W.	406 Front street
Donahue, Peter J.	Bohemian Club
Dornin, George D.	214 Sansome street
Douty, F. S.	S. P. R. R. Building
Doxey, Wm.	631 Market street
Duffield, V. Cains	410 Pine street
Dungan, Chas. W.	
Dunsmuir, Alex	620 East street
Durbrow, Harry	324 California street
Duval, George L.	430 California street
Earnest, Joseph F.	314 California street
Edwards, Henry	Wallace Theatre, New York.
Edwards, John G.	320 Sansome street
Edwards, William	330 Pine street
Eddy, Richard A.	224 Front street
Eldridge, Z. S.	428 California street
Elliot, Charles	516 California street
English, Wm. D.	10 California street
Estee, Morris M.	419 California street
Ewen, Warren B.	220 Market street
Fargo, Calvin F.	Pacific-Union Club
Fargo, Jerome B.	316 Front street
Felton, Charles N.	Menlo Park
Field, Henry K.	324 Montgomery street
Fisher, Edward	Sehome, Wash.
Fisher, George A.	109 California street
Finn, Jno. F.	Palace Hotel
Fletcher, Geo. Wm.	613 Market street
Flint, Brilford P.	436 Townsend street
Flood, James L.	6 Nevada Block
Florence, Wm. J.	
Flemich, Oscar G.	Palace Hotel
Foley, M. D.	Reno, Nevada
Forte, Lucius H.	Bohemian Club
Forsyth, Wm.	Fresno, Cal.
Foster, A. W.	322 Pine street
Foster, Charles J.	110 Montgomery street
Foster, George H.	317 California street
Fox, Henry L.	339 Pine street
Fox, Joseph M.	Portland
Folsom, Joseph R.	Cosmos Club
Freeborn, James	Pacific-Union Club
French, Frank J.	319 Pine street

Froelich, Christian J.	202 Market street
Frcude, James A.	
Gallegos, Juan	Mission San Jose
Garter, Charles A.	Red Bluff
Gerberding, Albert	528 California street
Gibbes, Wm. C.	303 California street
Gillespy, John H.	123 California street
Gillette, Daniel B., Jr.	Pacific-Union Club
Gillig, Henry M.	Bohemian Club
Gilman, Chas. A.	Battery and Broadway
Gilman, D. C.	
Gilman, Granville B.	224 Front street
Godley, Montgomery	414 Montgomery street
Gordon, C. B.	Bohemian Club
Gover, Samuel J.	
Graham, James H.	143 Fremont street
Granniss, Geo. W.	24 Montgomery Block
Grant, Geo. F.	213 Sansome street
Grant, Joseph D.	Bush and Sansome streets
Grant, Tom C.	213 Sansome street
Grayson, Robert R.	Stock Exchange Building
Greathouse, Clarence R.	Yokohama, Japan
Green, Chas. E.	S. P. Building
Greene, Clay M.	27 W. Eleventh street, N. Y.
Grismer, Joseph R.	Bohemian Club
Gunter, Archibald C.	Delmonica, N. Y.
Gutter, Isador	303 California street
Haggin, James B.	50 Nevada Block
Haggin, Louis T.	Pacific-Union Club
Haldan, Edward B.	413 California st.
Hall, Frederick W.	401 California street
Hall, George E.	308 Market street
Hall, John C.	Nevada Block
Hamilton, Alex.	6 Pine street
Hamilton, Edward H.	Oakland
Hamilton, Robert M.	6 Pine street
Hamilton, James M.	6 Pine street
Hammond, R. P.	Pacific-Union Club
Hammond, R. P., Jr.	10 Montgomery street
Hampe, Theodore	1014 Geary street
Harasztby, Arpad	528 Washington street
Hardin, C. H. E.	Bohemian Club
Harney, Wm.	535 Market street
Harrisson, Ralph C.	230 Montgomery street
Harrisson, Wm. Greer	305 California street

Hart, Jerome A.	213 Grant avenue
Hartshorne, Benj. M.	
Harvey, J. Dovney	Pacific-Union Club
Hasbrouck, Joseph	613 Clay street
Hathaway, Wm. R.	516 California street
Haven, Chas. D.	422 California street
Hawes, Alex. G.	220 Sansome street
Hammond, Andrew B.	224 Front street
Head, Addison E.	1105 Taylor street
Hearst, George	50 Nevada Block
Hearst, Wm. R.	1105 Taylor street
Heazelton, George	*Evening Post*
Hellman, A. C.	308 California street
Hellman, Horace G.	525 Front street
Herold, Rudolph, Jr.	415 California street
Herzog, Theo. D.	612 Eddy street
Heskith, Thomas	
Hewston, John, Jr.	Mill's Seminary
Heyneau, Henry	623 Eddy street
Hickox, George C.	Merchants' Exchange Building
Hilborn, Samuel G.	401 California street
Hill, Barton	St. Paul, Minn.
Hill, Horace L.	Pacific-Union Club
Hill, Thomas	Wanona, Cal.
Hobart, Walter S.	224 California street
Hockkofler, Rudolph	32 California street
Holloway, Wm. E.	430 California street
Holmes, Oliver Wendell	Boston, Mass.
Hooker, C. Osgood	423 Market street
Hooker, Robert G.	917 Bush street
Hooper, Wm. B.	Occidental Hotel
Hopkins, Edw. W.	Phelan Building
Hotaling, Anson P.	431 Jackson street
Houghton, H. B.	908 Broadway, Oakland
Howard, Charles Webb	516 California street
Howell, Josia R.	303 Jones street
Hogg, James	134 California street
Hug, Chas. A.	327 Market street
Huse, Fred. J.	Bohemian Club
Hussey, Horace P.	Cleveland, Ohio
Hutchinson, E. C.	30 California street
Hutchinson, James	Sather Banking Co.
Hyde, Frederick A.	630 Commercial street
Irwin, Benoni	146 W. Fifty-fifth st., New York
Irwin, Joseph N. H.	San Jose

Irwin, J. H.	410 Kearny street
Ives, George I.	324 Pine street
Jarboe, John R.	230 Montgomery street
Jarboe, Paul R.	917 Pine street
Jefferson, Joseph	27 Madison Avenue, New York
Johnson, Chas. B.	1925 Taylor street
Johnson, Covington	Pacific-Union Club
Josselyn, Charles	40 Market street
Joullin, Anédeé	609 Sacramento street
Johnson, H. A.	1 Montgomery street
Keeny, James W.	14 Grant avenue
Kelley, Edgar S.	Chickering Hall, New York
King, Frederic R.	530 California street
Knight, Geo. A.	234 Montgomery street
Kohler, Charles	626 Montgomery street
Landers, John	240 Montgomery street
Landers, Wm. J.	P. O. B. 2180
Lansing, Gerritt L.	S. P. Building
Larkin, Alfred O.	Pacific-Union Club
Lash, Lee	1359 Post street
Lathrop, Barbour	Chicago, Ill.
Lathrop, John	Oakland
Leach, Stephen W.	Clinton House, Oakland
Leonard, Chas. L.	Anglo-California Bank
Leverson, Montague R.	
Lent, George H.	Bohemian Club
Lichtenberg, Wm.	321 Market street
Lloyd, Reuben H.	Nevada Block
Lorin, Francis H.	324 Montgomery street
Loryea, A. M.	218 Post street
Lynch, Jeremiah	402 Eddy street
Macdonough, Joseph	165 Taylor street
Macfarlane, Edward C.	
Maddox, Cabel H.	325 Montgomery street
Magill, Arthur E.	221 Sansome street
Malone, John T.	16 Grammercy Park, New York
Malpas, A.	Los Gatos
Malter, Geo. H.	Fresno
Marcus, George	232 California street
Marshall, Benj.	924 Sutter street
Marshall, Henry	Bohemian Club
Marshutz, L. C.	Main and Howard
Martin, J. P.	305 Sansome street
Martinez, Henry	413 Kearny street

Gruenhagen Leads in Bonbonniere Candies

Martinez, F. W. R.	99 Wall street, New York
Marye, Geo. T.	234 Montgomery street
Maslin, S. P.	Sacramento
Mathews, Arthur F.	728 Montgomery street
Man, Wm. F.	15 Beale street
Maxwell, Walter S.	Los Angeles
Mayer, Samuel D.	301 California street
Maynard, John B.	30 McAllister street
Maynard, John H.	Ann Harbor, Michigan
Mastick, Geo. H.	520 Montgomery street
McAllister, Elliott	328 Montgomery street
McAllister, M. Hall	208 California street
McComb, John	San Quentin
McDonald, James M.	Pacific Bank
McDonald, M. Jaspar	310 Pine street
McDonald, Mark L.	Santa Rosa
McIver, Charles C.	Mission San Jose
McCreary, Byron	Sacramento
McNutt, Wm. F.	137 Montgomery street
McEwen, Warren L.	737 Fourth street
McAllister, Hall	320 Montgomery street
McAfee, Clark Wm.	2919 California street
Mead, Lewis R.	SE cor. Howard and Beale sts.
Meade, Calvert	420 California street
Mellis, D. Ernest	1531 Sacramento street
Melone, Drury	Oak Knoll, Napa Co.
Menzies, Stewart	512 Battery street
Michael, Francis	402 Montgomery street
Mickle, Etting	
Miller, Albert	532 California street
Miller, C. O. G.	Pacific Gas Improvement Co.
Miller, Frank	Sacramento
Miller, Harry East	Annie and Stevenson streets
Miller, H. M. A.	18 California street
Miller, Joaquin	Oakland
Mills, Edgar	Pacific-Union Club
Mills, E. F. B.	31 California street
Mills, F. G. B.	620 East street
Mix, L. W.	Nogales, A. T.
Mizner, Edgar A.	Benicia
Mizner, Lansing, Jr.	Benicia
Mills, Wm. H.	Fourth and Townsend streets
Montealegra, C. F.	230 California street
Moore, Arthur W.	438 California street
Moore, Elliott J.	77 Montgomery Block

Moore, Horace H.	423 Kearny street
Morris, William	21 Post street
Morrow, Robt. F.	414 California street
Morrow, Wm. W.	600 Bush street
Morton, John M.	
Moulder, Andrew J.	812 Bush street
Mucke, G. A. E.	319 California street
Mundy, J. H.	16 Front street
Murphy, Daniel T.	Palace Hotel
Murphy, Eugene P.	Bohemian Club
Murphy, Samuel G.	First National Bank
Myrick, Milton H.	206 Sansome street
Nagle, George W.	Bohemian Club
Neal, Charles S.	230 Montgomery street
Neumann, Paul	Honolulu, H. I.
Newcomb, Thomas	Albany, N. Y.
Newhall, Geo. A.	309 Sansome street
Newhall, Geo. D.	Bohemian Club
Nesmith, Loring G.	San Jose
Noble, F. L. H.	1325 Leavenworth street
Noble, Patrick	P. O. Box 2032
Norris, William	516 California street
O'Connell, Daniel	Bohemian Club
Ogden, Richard L.	52 Broadway, N. Y.
Oliver, Wm. Letts	328 Montgomery street
Osten, E. van der	Baldwin Theater
Palmer, Clinton	17 Steuart street
Palmer, Edwin C.	Postoffice
Parrott, Louis B.	306 California street
Parsons, Thomas J.	Second and Brannan streets
Partridge, John	210 California street
Paton, R. W.	202 Market street
Payne, Theodore F.	Bohemian Club
Payne, Warren B.	Bohemian Club
Payne, William H.	Reno, Nev.
Payot, Henry	204 Sansome street
Palmer, Chas. M.	Bella Vista
Page, N. Clifford	Alameda
Pease, Richard A., Jr.	577 Market street
Perkins, Geo. C.	10 Market street
Peters, Chas. R.	609 Sacramento street
Pew, John W.	310 Pine street
Phelan, James D.	Phelan Building
Pillsbury, Evans S.	324 Pine street

Pissis, Albert	307 Sansome street
Pixley, Frank M.	*Argonaut* Office
Platt, Horace G.	402 Montgomery street
Pomroy B.	Bohemian Club
Pond, Edward B.	
Powers, George H.	215 Geary street
Powell, Abraham	Pier 3, Steuart street
Pratt, George C.	Seattle, Wash.
Prescott, Geo. W.	Palace Hotel
Preston, Edward T.	310 Pine street
Price, Arthur T.	524 Sacramento street
Raschen, Henry	408 California street
Rankin, James	Martinez, Cal.
Redding, Albert P.	328 Montgomery street
Redding, Joseph B.	Chronicle Building
Reynolds, Frank B.	203 Sansome street
Redding, Geo. H.	2100 California street
Richmond, Chas. A.	
Richter, C. Max	614 Geary street
Rix, Julian W.	Paterson, N. J.
Rickard, Thomas	21 Fremont street.
Robertson, Peter	321 Turk street
Robertson, Thomas T.	Seattle, Washington
Robinson, Cornelius P.	310 Pine street
Robinson, James A.	425 Market street
Robinson, Sanford	320 Sansome street
Rodger, Arthur	Nevada Block
Roeckel, Joseph	320 Post street
Rogers, Randolph	
Rogers, Robert C.	Washington, D. C.
Rollins, Edward W.	Denver, Colorado
Rose, Andrew W., Jr.	224 California street
Rosenstern, Julius	Sutter and Hyde streets
Rosewald, J. H.	938 Geary street
Rowell, Leonard F.	Wells, Fargo & Co.'s Express
Ruggles, Jas. D.	Bank of California
Runyon, E. W.	234 Sutter street
Rutherford, Alex H.	1105 Bush street
Rutherford, Thos L.	Rutherford, Napa County.
Rumbold, Thos. T.	219 Geary street
Salvini, Thomas V.	
Sanderson, George R.	319 Pine street
Satterlee, George A.	8 Mason street
Sanborn, William D.	32 Montgomery street

Rare Books   We have the most perfect system for recording orders and picking up Rare and out of print books.

The Bancroft Company, 721 Market Street.

Schmidt, Louis	810 Leavenworth
Schussler, Herman	516 California street
Scott, Irving M.	Union Iron Works
Severance, James S.	Fourth and Townsend streets
Sexton, Wm.	214 Sansome street
Sharon, Fred W.	305 Sansome street
Shaw, Chas. N.	Stock Exchange Building
Shaw, Stephens W.	305 Jones street
Sheehan, John F.	409 Montgomery street
Sherman, Harry M.	705 Sutter street
Sherwood, Wm. R.	1123 California street
Shockley, W. H.	Canderlaria, Nevada
Shreve, George R.	106 Montgomery street
Sherwood, John Dickinson	Spokane Falls
Sherman, M. H.	Phœnix, A. T.
Simpson, John H.	119 Market street
Simson, Robert	Mills' Seminary
Sloss, Leon	310 Sansome street
Sloss, Louis, Jr.	310 Sansome street
Small, A. H.	316 California street
Smedberg, W. R.	316 California street
Smith, Brainardt F.	121 Phelan Building
Smith, Chester M.	324 Sansome street
Smith, Colin M.	216 California street
Smith, Hiram C.	109 California street
Smith, Sidney M.	1150 Harrison street
Snelling, James F.	204 Sansome street
Somers, Frederick M.	30 West 23d street, New York
Spencer, Geo. W.	316 California street
Sperry, Geo. B.	134 California street
Spreckels, Adolph B.	325 Market street
Spreckels, C. August	325 Market street
Spreckels, John D.	325 Market street
Spery, James W.	134 California street
Stafford, Wm. G.	6 Battery street
Stanton, John A.	
Staples, David A.	401 California street
Steele, Edward L. G.	208 California street
Steinthar, S.	Anglo-California Bank
Stetson, James B.	Market and Beale streets
Stevens, Edwin	Casino Opera House, New York
Stewart, H. J.	2417 California street
Stitt, John G.	Pacific-Union Club
Stoddard, Charles Warren	Covington, Ky.
Stokes, James Brett	1006 Pine street

Stone, Charles B.	33 California street
Stone, Frank F.	410 Pine street
Stone, Lucius D.	2520 Howard street
Stone, Walter S.	132 Sutter street
Story, George A.	33 Post street
Stonenborough, Chas.	324 Pine street
Straus, Meyer	Flood Building
Strong, George H.	220 Market street
Strong, Joseph D., Jr.	Sydney, Australia
Stuart, Henry C.	Denver, Colorado
Stuart, James, E.	
Stuart, John	San Jose de Guatemala
Sullivan, Sir Arthur	London, England
Sullivan, Frank J.	Phelan Building
Sumner, Frank W.	415 Front street
Swan, Benj. R.	P. O. Box 1869
Swift, John F.	Tokio, Japan
Swett, John	1419 Taylor street
Syz, Harry W.	P. O. Box 1941
Taylor, Edward Graham	Union Club, New
Taylor, John W.	Promontory, Utah
Taylor, Stuart	1531 Sacramento street
Taylor, Wm. H.	Merchants' Exchange
Taylor, Wm. S.	314 Montgomery street
Teschemasche, H. F.	
Thompson, A Slason	Chicago, Ill.
Thompson, James A.	33 Post street
Thornton, Crittenden	426 California street
Tichenor, J. Fred.	322 Pine street
Tippett, J. E.	Boston, Mass.
Towne, Arthur S.	516 Sacramento street
Townsend, Edward N.	2003 California street
Truman, Benj. C.	Chicago, Ill.
Turnbull, Walter	228½ Montgomery street
Twigg, John W.	Bohemian Club
Uhler, J. C.	Philadelphia, Pa.
Unger, Frank L.	Bohemian Club
Upham, Isaac	204 Sansome street
Upton, Matthew G.	*Evening Bulletin*
Valentine, John J.	Wells, Fargo & Co.'s Ex.
Van Ness, Thomas C.	206 Sansome street
Van Wyck, H. L.	308 Pine street
Vickery, Wm. Kingston	108 Grant avenue
Von Huhn, Alex.	411 Bush street
Von Perbandt, A.	

279

Gold Pens An endless variety of Gold Pens and Penholders from the celebrated Factory of Mabie, Todd & Co., New York.

The Bancroft Company, 721 Market Street.

Wadsworth, Henry	Wells, Fargo & Co.'s Bank
Wadsworth, James C. L.	303 California street
Walker, James G.	224 Front street
Wallace, Wm. T.	324 Pine street
Walter, Solly H.	27 Main street
Walter, Wm.	131 Sansome street
Wandesforde, Juan B.	Haywards
Ward, Wm.	London, England
Warde, Frederick	
Washington, Frank B.	Bohemian Club
Waterhouse, Columbus	22 Beale street
Waterhouse, Waldo S.	Cuyamaca, Cal.
Watkins, A. A.	313 Market street
Waymire, James A.	402 Montgomery street
Webster, Fred. Rand	Pacific-Union Club
Weill, Raphael	Bohemian Club
Weill, Sylvain	585 Market street
Wells, F. Marion	West Berkeley
Wells, George R.	Nevada Block
Wethered, Wordworth	2109 Pacific street
Wheaton, Geo. H.	221 Front street
White, Wm. H.	316 Sacramento street
Whiting, Dwight	
Whitney, Geo. E.	Oakland
Whittell, A. P.	
Whitwell, Wm. S.	425 Sutter street
Wiggin, Marcus P.	Chronicle Office
Williams, A. P.	25 Fremont street
Williams, Frank	2224 Jackson street
Williamson, Jas. C.	
Williamson, J. M.	906 Market street
Willkomm, Adolph	405 Montgomery street
Wilson, Frank P.	711 Pine street
Wilson, Horace	Mechanics' Institute
Wilson, J. Crawford	
Wilson, James K.	Sather Banking Co.
Wilson, John Scott	324 California street
Wilson, Mountford S.	202 Sansome street
Wilson, Robert A.	1605 Golden Gate Avenue
Wilson, Russell J.	202 Sansome street
Wilson, Samuel M.	202 Sansome street
Wilson, C. H.	Chronicle Building
Winter, Wm.	
Wilkie, Alfred	834 O'Farrell street
Wood, James M.	California Theatre

Wood, John S.	Occidental Hotel
Woods, Robert J.	Front and Vallejo streets
Wores, Theodore	51 West 10th street, New York
Wright, Chas. W.	230 Montgomery street
Wright, Geo. S.	
Wright, John A.	212 Sansome street
Yale, Chas. G.	220 Market street
Yates, Frederick	215 Geary street
Younger, Wm. J.	Post and Stockton streets
Zeile, Frederick W.	220 California street

ARMY AND NAVY

Beck, Lieut-Col W. B. (A)	Alcatraz Island
Blunt, Lieut Albert C. (A)	Presidio
Borth, Capt Chas A. (A)	Occidental Hotel
Brechemin, Dr L. (A)	Presidio
Brown, Lieut R. A. (A)	Presidio
Burton, Col Geo. H. (A)	Phelan Building
Carlin, Lieut Jas. W. (N)	Bohemian Club
Cheney, Com'dt L. B. (N)	University Club, N. Y.
Coffin, Lieut Wm. H. (A)	Presidio
Darling, Maj John A. (A)	
Dietz, Dr N. W. (A)	Alcatraz Island
Dougherty, Capt W. E. (A)	Angel Island
Edgar, Dr John M. (N)	Mare Island
Erwin, Lieut Jas. B. (A)	Presidio
Faison, Lieut S. L. (A)	Angel Island
Fletcher, Lieut Robert H. (N)	Bella Vista
Gallup, Lieut C. C. (A)	Alcatraz Island
Gore, Lieut C. A. (N)	Navy Pay Office
Graham, Gen W. M. (A)	Presidio
Hancock, Lieut H. F. (A)	Presidio
Johnstone, Marbury (N)	Navy Pay Office
Kirkman, Lieut Geo. W. (A)	Angel Island
Lord, Maj Jas H. (A)	
Marbin, Dr Wm. (A)	21½ Third street
McGlachlin, Lieut E. F. (A)	Presidio
McCormick, C. M. (N)	Navy Pay Office
Nolan, Lieut Jas. E. (A)	Presidio

O'Connell, Capt J. J. (A)	Alcatraz Island
Osborn, Capt A. P. (N)	Navy Pay Office
Perley, Dr H. (A)	Fort Mason
Runcie, Lieut James E. (A)	Phelan Building
Schenck, Capt Casp. (N)	Norfolk Navy Yard
Strother, H. L. H. (A)	Angel Island
Town, Dr F. L. (A)	Presidio
Turner, Capt James A. (U. S. M. C.)	Mare Island
West, Ens H. B. (N)	Occidental Hotel
Wilson, Dr George B. (N)	Mare Island
Wilson, Lieut John C. (N)	Navy Pay Office
Williams, C. S. (N)	1728 Sutter street
Wood, Dr Leonard S. (A)	Presidio
Woodruff, Capt Chas A. (A)	36 New Montgomery street
Wood, H. O. W. (A)	Presidio

HONORARY MEMBERS

Arditi, Luigi	Holmes, Oliver Wendell
Behr, Dr. H. H.	Irwin, Benoin
Booth, Edwin	Joseph, Jefferson
Booth, Newton	Miller, Joaquin
Bowers, Mrs. D. P.	Newcomb, Thomas
Bromley, Isaac H.	Rogers, Randolph
Bromley, Geo. T.	Salvini, Tommaso
Brookes, Samuel M.	Stoddard, Charles Warren
Clemens, Samuel L.	Wallace, William T.
Coolbrith, Miss Ina D.	Wilson, J. Crawford
Froude, James Anthony	Winter, William

Concordia Club

Rooms, Corner Post Street and Van Ness Avenue

The Concordia Club was organized in 1864. It is the principal Jewish Society in the city, and composed chiefly of wholesale merchants. The rooms are only open evenings and Sundays, and the entertainments consist of monthly and bi-monthly receptions. The regular meeting of the members is held on the first Wednesday of each month. The financial standing of the Club is excellent. They are now located in their new and elegant quarters as above.

OFFICERS

J. M. ROTHCHILD, President   -   -   -   307 California street
SAMUEL SACHS, Vice-President   -   SW cor. Bush & Sansome sts.
G. M. BETTMAN, Recording Secretary
F. H. LEVY, Financial Secretary
A. HERMAN, Treasurer

DIRECTORS

Joseph Silverberg	29 Battery street
J. H. Neustadter	
Louis Stein	
Louis S. Haas	100–2 Front street
George A. Klein	
Henry Sinsheimer	37–39 Battery street

MEMBERS

Ach, Henry	303 California street
Ackerman, Charles L.	426 California street
Ackerman, I. S.	108 Pine street
Ackerman, Sig. H.	123 Kearny street
Ackerman, Edward	807 Market
Ackerman, Samuel J.	529–531 Market street

Glacé Fruits and Marrons at Gruenhagen's

Adler, A. A.	222 Sansome street
Adler, M.	423 California & 215 Sansome st.
Adler, Jacob	416 California street
Ahpel, Henry	410 Pine street
Alexander, Jos.	516 Market street
Anspacher, Simon	302 California street
Bachman, L. S.	10–12 Battery street
Bachman, Leopold I.	112 Sansome street
Bachman, Samuel N.	10–12 Battery street
Blum, Jacques	217 Battery street
Bine, S.	32–34 Sansome street
Brown, L.	121 Sansome street
Brown, M.	121 Sansome street
Brown, A.	121 Sansome street
Bastheim, J.	129 Sansome street
Block, D.	107 Sansome street
Bauer, M.	547 Market street
Bauer, S.	547 Market street
Brandenstein, M.	529 Clay street
Blum, Leon	201–03 California street
Bloom, Jonas	303 California street
Bettman, Gus M.	121 California street
Brown, A. L.	7 Montgomery street
Blaskower, M.	225 Montgomery street
Bachman, D. S.	10–12 Battery street
Baumgarten, Jos.	7 Montgomery
Blum, Chas.	116 Battery street
Blum, Maurice	116 Battery street
Bauman, Sig.	14–16 Battery street
Brooks, Max.	215 Sansome street
Blum, Mose	308 California street
Cahn, Israel	1120 Post street
Cahn, M. I.	129 Sansome street
Cerf, A.	111 Battery street
Cerf, J.	111 Battery street
Cahen, I. W.	418 Sacramento street
Dinkelspiel, Samuel	37–39 Battery and Pine sts.
Dinkelspiel, J. S.	120 Sutter street
Einstein, M.	206 Front street
Einstein, Z.	129 Sansome street
Eppinger, J.	305 California street
Eppinger, Herman	305 California street
Eisner, Milton S.	217 Sansome street
Ettlinger, B.	305 California street

Most Delicious Candies at Gruenhagen's

Emanuel, E.	432 Fourth street
Esberg, M.	California and Battery sts.
Erlanger, Jonas	304 Davis street
Elsasser, A.	117–19 Market street
Frank, M. J.	133 Sansome street
Frank, E. M.	1721 Sutter street
Frank, Geo. W.	217 Sansome street
Frowenfel l, J.	1307 Van Ness avenue
Foorman, I. S.	330 Pine street
Foorman, S.	330 Pine street
Falkenstein, H.	NE cor. Battery and Sac. sts.
Fenchtwagner, S.	133 Sansome street
Fisher, Ph. I.	14–16 Battery street
Fisher, Godfrey	7 Montgomery street
Frank, A.	406–08 Battery street
Gump, G.	581 Market street
Gump, S.	581 Market street
Guggenheimer, L.	11 Front street
Gunst, M. A.	203 Kearny street
Goodman, T.	547 Market street
Goldstein, Sanford	201–3 California street
Greenberg, Jos.	205 Fremont street
Gerst, G.	302 California street
Greenberg, S. H.	206 Kearny street
Goldstein, W.	123 California street
Greenebaum, Sig.	115–117 Bush street
Heller, Martin	112 Sansome street
Heller, E. M.	112 Sansome street
Heller, M., Jr.	112 Sansome street
Heller, E. L.	315 Pine street
Heller, S. W.	315 Pine street
Hoffman, J.	309 Front street
Hyman, M.	110 Sansome street
Hart, Chas.	106 Battery street
Herman, A.	324 Pine street
Helbing, D. A.	21–3 Battery street
Hochstadter, William S.	224 Sutter street
Haas, William	100–2 California street
Haas, Louis S.	100–02 Front street
Hoffman, S.	1157 Octavia street
Hart, Mose	1117 Post street
Hirsch, Chas.	310 Sansome street
Hirschfelder, S.	109 Sansome street
Hyman, Henry W.	214 California street

Wedding and Party Invitations Engraved and Printed in Correct Form.

The Bancroft Company, 721 Market Street.

Hart, Samuel	1120 Sutter street
Hausman, B.	18-20 Sutter street
Herzstein, D. M.	323 Sutter street
Hellman, I. W.	NW cor. Montgomery & Pine sts.
Jacobi, L.	509 Montgomery street
Jacobs, Henry	10-12 Main street
Jacobs, Isador	308 Market street
Judis, Alphonse	112 Sutter street
Kahn, Dr S. S.	14 Grant avenue
Kline, L.	302 California street
Klan, Edward	100-2 California street
Koshland, S.	220 California street
Kronthal, H.	16 Sansome street
Kullman, H.	106 Battery street
Kalisher, E.	21-23 Sutter street
Kahn, Jos.	7-9 Battery street
Koshland, M.	220 California street
Kline, George	Battery and Pine streets
Katten, Simon	547 Market street
Kohn, George A.	406 Front street
Klan, Karl	100-02 California street
Koch, Henry	21-23 Sansome street
Levi, H.	117-19 Market street
Levy, M. L.	420 Sansome street
Levy, Isaac	519 Clay street
Levy, W. H.	New City Hall
Levy, Fred. H.	104 Kearny street
Levy, Jos.	420 Sansome street
Levy, Oscar S.	529 Market street
Lewis, William	30 California street
Lyons, E. G.	508 Jackson street
Lowengrund, E. L.	318 Turk st., 432 Fourth street
Lyons, E. H.	539 Market street
Lilienthal, Dr. James E	1316 Van Ness Avenue
Levi, Jacob, Jr.	117-19 Market street
Loewe, Jos.	217 Battery street
Livingston, Jos.	200 Davis street
Lewis, Sol	320 Sansome street
Levy, Jules	5-7 Sansome street
Levy, Felix	209 Sutter street
Morgenthau, M.	108 Bush street
Morgenthau, G.	108 Bush street
Marx, D.	14-16 Battery street

Marks, Eli	413 California street
Mandel, E.	107 Sansome street
Manheim, H. S.	217 Sansome street
Manheim, Isaac	217 Sansome street
Meertief, A	100–2 California street
Meyer, C.	425 Eddy street
Meyer, Eugene	1-3 Sansome street
Meyer, M. C.	28–30 Sansome street
Meyer, L. C.	28–30 Sansome street
Meyer, Emmanuel	413 Pine street
Michels, Leopold	17-19 Sansome street
May, Jos.	25-27 Fremont street
Morgenthau, Henry	108 Bush street
Naphtaly, J.	426 California street
Neustadter, J. H.	133 Sansome street
Neustadter, D.	133 Sansome street
Newman, S.	117 Battery street
Newman, J.	117 Battery street
Nicklesburg, M.	129 Sansome street
Nicklesburg, S.	129 Sansome street
Newbauer, Herman	412 Front street
Oppenheimer, H.	117 Battery street
Oppenheimer, C.	5-7 Sansome street
Poly, Isaac	339 Kearny street
Patek, Fred.	519 Clay street
Roos, A., Sr.	319-21 Market street
Roos, A., Jr.	31 Kearny street
Roos, Achille	31 Kearny street
Rothchild, J. M.	303 California street
Regensburger, Dr. J.	1432 Geary street
Reiss, I.	24 Sutter street
Reiss, S.	24 Sutter street
Reiss, B.	516 Market street
Rosenbaum, A. M.	206 Front street
Rosenbaum, E. D.	116 California street
Rosenthal, M.	16 Sansome street
Rosenberg, B.	217 Battery street
Rosenberg, Joseph	29 Merchants' Exchange
Rothchild, T. H.	322 Clay street
Rosenthal, Meyer	107-11 Kearny street
Rosenthal, I. L.	107-11 Kearny street
Strauss, Levy	14-16 Battery street
Sachs, Martin	Bush and Battery streets

Sachs, Lippman	29-31 Sansome street
Sachs, Sam, Jr.	29-31 Sansome street
Sachs, David	29-31 Sansome street
Sachs, Ben	29-31 Sansome street
Sachs, S. L.	Bush and Battery streets
Sachs, Sanford	Bush and Battery streets
Sachs, D. M.	Bush and Battery streets
Steinhart, William	3-5 Battery street
Schweitza, J.	519 Clay street
Schweitza, B.	29-31 Battery street
Schweitza, M.	29-31 Battery street
Stern, Abe	14–16 Battery street
Stern, Louis	14–16 Battery street
Sutro, Chas.	408 Montgomery street
Straussberger,	316 1-2 Montgomery street
Stiner, Oscar	21–3 Sutter street
Seller, Fred	110 Battery street
Seller, Henry	110 Battery street
Salberg, M.	29–31 Battery street
Salz, Edward	106 Battery street
Sussmann, Sam'l	104 Front street
Stein, A.	SE cor. Market and Second sts.
Strauss, Louis	24-26 Sansome street
Silverberg, J.	29–31 Battery street
Son, A. A.	13-15 Sansome street
Schwabacher, Sigmund	319 California street
Schwabacher, Louis	319 California street
Schwabacher, A.	319 California street
Schmitt, Chas. A.	6 Merchants' Exchange
Schmitt, 'M.	6 Merchants' Exchange
Sahlein, H.	14–16 Battery street
Stern, J.	14–16 Battery street
Stern, S.	14–16 Battery street
Scheeline, S.	319–21 Market street
Slessinger, L.	7-9 Battery street
Sinsheimer, H.	220 California street
Steinberger, A.	21–23 Sutter street
Scholle, A. W.	324 Pine street
Spitz, A.	13–15 Sansome street
Spitz, J.	13–15 Sansome street
Simpson, A. D.	121 Sansome street
Scheideman, B.	121 Sansome street
Samuels, D.	123 Post street
Strauss, S. J.	112 Sansome street

Sweet, S.	222 Sansome street
Sachs, Isaac	29–31 Battery street
Stone, M.	1515 California street
Salz, M. J.	106 Battery street
Strauss, M.	807 Market street
Sundheimer,	107–11 Kearny street
Tanzky, Edmund	508 California street
Tash, M.	547 Market street
Triest, Bernhard	116–18 Sansome street
Walter, David N.	529 Market street
Wangenheim, S.	117 Battery street
Wangenheim, E. S.	117 Battery street
Weil, M.	Market and Sansome streets
Weil, Louis P.	25–27 Sansome street
Weil, Leopold	17–19 Sansome street
Weil, Alex. L.	15 Front street
Weiglien, J. J.	2204 California street
Weyl, Cerf	129 Sansome street
Wolf, Max	304 Battery street

San Francisco Verein

Rooms, Corner Sutter St. and Grant Avenue

The San Francisco Verein was incorporated in October, 1853, and is largely composed of prominent German citizens. The clubrooms were located at 430 Pine Street, (now occupied by the Bohemian Club) from 1869 until 1874, when they moved to their present rooms, which were fitted up at a cost of sixty-five thousand dollars. The membership is limited to 250.

OFFICERS

FREDERICK HESS	President
M. S. LOWENTHAL	First Vice-President
MAX ORDENSTEIN	Second Vice-President
S. W. Saalburg	Financial Secretary
S. BISSINGER	Recording Secretary
J. J. JACOBI	Treasurer
S. W. EHRMAN	Librarian

LIST OF MEMBERS

Abrams, Dr. Albert	435 Geary Street
Ackerman, Sigmund L.	320 Montgomery street
Adelsdorfer, Joseph	19 First street
Adler, Charles	816 Sutter street
Altschul, Charles	3 Sansome street
Arnstein, Ludwig	SE cor. Market and Second sts.
Arnhold, Benjamin	310 Sansome street
Aronstein, Dr. A.	1616 Sutter street
Bachman, D.	10-12 Battery street
Bachman, S.	SE cor. Battery and California
Bachman, N. S.	10-12 Battery street
Barth, Philip	440 California street
Beckh, G. W.	2211 Pacific avenue

Gruenhagen Leads in Bonbonniere Candies

Bergmann, J.	
Bissinger, S.	NE Townsend and 6th streets
Blach, Dr. Charles	305 Kearny street
Bloom, D.	Absent
Bloom, J.	303 California street
Bowman, John S.	215-17 Battery street
Brandenstein, Joseph	19 First street
Brandenstein, A. J.	SW cor. California and Gough sts.
Brandenstein, M. J.	118-20 Market street
Braverman, Sigmund L.	119 Montgomery street
Cahn, Mayer I.	129-31 Sansome street
Castel, W. M.	200-12 Davis street
Cohen, H.	19 Grant avenue
Cohn, Edward	225 Montgomery street
Cohn, Dr. D.	1404 Sutter street
Coleman, Charles	130 Kearny street
Dibbern, J. Hy.	217 Sansome street
Dinkelspiel, Hy.	39 Battery street
Dresbach, William	316 California street
Duchesne, Paul	312-18 Sansome street
Eckel, Dr. J. N.	324 Geary street
Ehrman, M.	104-10 Front street
Ehrman, Solomon	104-10 Front street
Ehrman, Joseph	104-10 Front street
Esberg, M.	SE cor. Battery and California
Fechheimer, Benjamin C.	706-20 Kearny street
Frank, William	1716 Sacramento street
Frank, E. M.	217 California street
Frankenthal, J.	6-10 Sutter street
Fredericks, Joseph	649-51 Market street
Freidenrich, D.	426 California street
Fries, William	306 Pine street
Friedlander, S. J.	21-23 Sansome street
Friedman, J.	484 Palace Hotel
Furth, Simon	207 Front street
Gensberger, M.	110 Bush street
Gerstle, Lewis	310 Sansome street
Goodkind, A.	120 Sansome street
Greenebaum, Sigmund	115-17 Bush street
Greenebaum, J.	232 Montgomery street
Greenebaum, Alfred	51-53 First street
Greenebaum, Emil	314 California street
Greenebaum, Moses	17-19 Sansome street

Ice Cream, Water Ices AND ICE CREAM SODA AT Gruenhagen's

The Bancroft Company, ^{49 FIRST STREET.} One of the largest and best
appointed Printing Offices on the coast. No
better work can be done anywhere.

Greenebaum, William	17-19 Sansome street
Greenewald, Otto. H.	117-19 Market street
Grinbaum, M. S.	215 Front street
Gutte, Isidore	307 California street
Gutte, Julius	307 California street
Haas, William	
Hausmann, B.	18-20 Sutter street
Hausmann, S.	123 Post street
Hausmeister, Julian	212 Pine street
Hecht, Isaac	25-27 Sansome street
Hecht, A. E.	25-27 Sansome street
Hecht, M. H.	25-27 Sansome street
Hecht, Bert R.	738-40 Market street
Heller, E. S.	303 California st., rooms 25-26
Hess, Frederick	411 Bush street
Hess, Joseph L.	300-03 Front street
Heilbronner, August	111 Sutter street
Heilbronner, Max	310 Sansome street
Heinecken, A. C.	220½ McAllister street.
Heynemann, Alexander	310 Pine street
Heynemann, H.	Merchants' Exchange, Room 28
Hofman, H.	
Hirsch, Charles	310 Sansome street
Hirsch, Louis	200-12 Davis street
Hyman, H. W.	214 California street
Hyman, M.	108 Sansome stree
Hellman, I. W.	Nevada Bank
Jacobi, F.	SE cor. Bryant and Second sts.
Jacobi, J. J.	SE cor. Bryant and Second sts.
Jacobs, Isidor	12 Main street
Jaffe, M.	316 Pine street
Joachimsen, H. L.	426 California street
Klau, Leopold	100-02 California street
Klauber, A.	16-18 Drumm street
Koch, Hy.	23 Sansome street
Kohler, Chas.	626 Montgomery street
Kohler, Hans H.	626 Montgomery street
Kronthal, H.	16 Sansome street
Kruse, E.	209-11 Front street
Keimer, Ignaz	322 Bush street
Landsberger, I.	127 California street
Lebenbaum, Louis	215-17 Sutter street
Levi, Jacob	117-19 Market street

Liebermann, Theodore	326 Pine street
Liebes, H.	111-13 Montgomery street
Lilienthal, J. Leo	100-02 Front street
Lilienthal, E. R.	100-02 Front street
Lilienthal, P. N.	NE cor Sansome and Pine sts.
Lipman, L.	325 Pine street
Livingston, Jos.	200-12 Davis street
Lloyd, R. H.	9-13 Nevada Block
Lowenthal, M. S.	320 California street
Loupe, L.	218 California street
Mack, A. A.	11 Front street
Mandlebaum, F.	4 Sutter street
Mandlebaum, R.	4 Sutter street
Marks, Eli	413 California street
Marks, Joseph	306 Montgomery street
Marx, I.	108 Sansome
May, Joseph	25-27 Fremont street
Mayne, Charles	524 Montgomery street
Mendheim, H.	417 Mason street
Meyer, Albert	212 Pine street
Meyer, Daniel	212 Pine street
Meyer, Hy.	212 Pine street
Meyer, Moritz	212 Pine street
Meyer, Moritz	102 Battery street
Meussdorffer, J. C.	810 Market street
Michels, Leopold	17-19 Sansome street
Moore, I. C.	117 Front street
Müser, Otto	541 Market street
Neuman, Rud.	310 Sansome street
Neuman, Dr Leopold	24 Montgomery street
Neustadter, I.	SW cor. Sansome and Pine sts
Neustadter, J.	SW cor. Sansome and Pine sts
Nielsen, H.	30 California
Ordenstein, M.	306 Battery street
Perutz, Alfred	London, Paris & American Bank
Pollitz, Edward	304 California street
Rehfisch, M.	316 Pine street
Rose, L. S.	406 Montgomery street
Rosener, Samuel	1430 Geary street
Rosenfield, John	202 Sansome street
Rosenthal, A.	318 Sacramento street
Rothschild, Hugo	118 Front street

Saalburg, S. W.	111-13 Montgomery street
Samson, R.	228½ Montgomery
Scheeline M.	
Scheeline, S. C.	328 Montgomery street
Scheeline, Solomon E.	212 Pine street
Schmolz, William	420 Montgomery street
Scholle, Albert W.	324 Pine street
Schussler, H.	516 California street
Schwabacher, Louis	319 California street
Schwabacher, S.	319 California street
Schwartz, Isidor	215 Sansome street
Seller, F.	112 Battery street
Shainwald, H.	404-06 Montgomery street
Shainwald, I: C.	404-06 Montgomery street
Shoenfeld, Albert	
Simon, H. L	SE cor. Market and 2d streets
Simon, Louis	SE cor. Market and 2d streets
Sloss, Leon	310 Sansome street
Sloss, Louis, Jr.	310 Sansome street
Sloss, Louis	310 Sansome street
Son, A.	13-15 Sansome street
Speyer, D. E.	10-12 Battery street
Spreckels, A. B.	327 Market street
Spreckels, Claus	327 Market street
Spreckels, C. A.	327 Market street
Spreckels, J. D.	327 Market street
Steinberger, N.	116-18 Sansome street
Steinhart, Ignatz	NE cor. Sansome and Pine streets
Steinhart Sig.	
Straus, Jacob	102 Battery street
Strassburger, I.	326½ Montgomery street
Strybing, C. H.	1212 Mason street
Sussman, Samuel	104-10 Front street
Sutro, A.	408 Montgomery street
Sutro, Charles	408 Montgomery street
Sutro, E.	408 Montgomery street
Sutro Gustav.	408 Montgomery street
Sweet, S.	222 Sansome street
Thannhauser, August	311 California street
Thannhauser, S. M.	311 California street
Triest, B.	116-18 Sansome street
Triest, Jesse E.	116-18 Sansome street
Toklas, F.	219 Bush street
Voorman, H.	506 Battery street

Waldeck, Hugo	SW cor. Bush & Sansome streets
Walter, D. N.	529–31 Market street
Walter, Isaac	529–31 Market street
Walter, H. N.	529–31 Market street
Waterman, H.	314 California street
Weil, Leopold	17–19 Sansome street
Wiel, L. P.	27 Sansome street
Wolff, William	105 Front street
Wollberg, Joseph	306 Montgomery street
Wormser, I.	107 Front street
Wormser, Samuel I.	107 Front street
Wunsch, M.	111 Sutter street
Zadig, H.	306 Montgomery street

Merchants' Club

I wish I had ∴ ∴ Some of Gruenhagen's Ice Cream Soda

Alexander, C. O.	10 California street
Armsby, J. K.	204 California street
Briggs, A. R.	321 Pine street
Beck, E. B.	32 Fremont street
Beck, W. F.	205 Front street
Brigham, F. E.	129 California street
Bothin, H. E.	213 Market street
Barker, T. L.	126 Market street
Brandenstein, M. J.	118 Market street
Brison, W. M.	116 California street
Bunker, H. C.	400 Front street
Bowles, P. E.	306 California street
Baldwin, Barry	307 California street
Bannister, Alfred	16 California street
Bruce, Robert	316 California street
Beyfuss, Carl	123 California street
Bowers, W. F.	407 Market street
Brown, Ed.	508 California street
Bolton, J. D.	1314 Jones street
Brooks, Peyton H.	S W cor. Spear and Mission
Brayton, A. P., Jr.	
Coleman, W. T.	121 Market street
Cutler, A. D.	125 Market street
Carolan, Jas.	115 California street
Craig, Hugh	312 California street
Cutting, J. T.	25 California street
Cluff, Wm.	Cor. Pine and Front streets
Cutting, Francis	125 Market street
Coburn, C. W.	6 Battery street
Coit, Griffith	308 Market street
Coogan, T. C.	310 Pine street
Clement, E. B.	405 Montgomery street
Chapman, W. B.	123 California street
Chickering, W. H.	206 Sansome street
Carpentier, A.	508 California street
Coffin, James	307 Montgomery street
Costigan, J. H.	
Cheesebrough, H. C.	48 Market street
Dalton, Frank	308 Davis street
Dodge, H. L.	114 Market street
Detrick, E.	6 California street
Dutard, H.	126 Davis street
Donnell, A. C.	318 California street

Deming, Jay	405 Front street
De Young, M. H.	Cor. Kearny and Market streets
De Long, F. C.	Novato, Cal.
Duval, W. S.	
Ehrman, M.	104 Front street
Evans, E. C.	302 California street
Ehrman, S. W.	104 Front street
Eldridge, S. A.	Oakland
Esberg, Mandel	SE cor. California and Battery
English, John F.	313 Davis street
Folger, J. A., Jr.	104 California street
Field, A. B.	126 California street
Freeman, A. G.	202 California street
Fontana, M. J.	116 California street
Fagan, Jas. J.	
Ghirardelli, D., Jr.	411 Jackson street
Gorrill, R. W.	4 California street
Girvin, R. D.	307 California street
Gillan, James	318 Pine street
Greenebaum, E.	314 California street
Gilman, C. H.	716 Battery street
Haas, William	100 California street
Hughes, H.	123 California street
Hogg, Jas.	134 California street
Haslett, Sam'l	452 Spear street
Herrick, E. M.	17 Steuart street
Holmes, C. L.	Pier 3, Steuart street
Hanson, W. H.	48 Market street
Hinsdale, G. S.	22 California street
Hueter, E. L.	601 Market street
Haslett, S. M.	1203 Battery street
Hewlett, Fred'k	300 Davis street
Harrison, W. G.	305 California street
Hoffman, Ed.	116 California street
Hirshfeld, D.	323 California street
Hooper, J. A.	4 California street
Haslett, P. E.	Cor. Front and Broadway
Huddleston, H.	52 Market street
Harrington, W. B.	Hotel Pleasanton
Husband, Robt.	SW cor. Spear and Mission sts.
Heron, James	405 Geary street
Hammond, John	

Gruenhagen Leads in Bonbonniere Candies

Hooper, F. P.	4 California street
Howard, John L.	Oakland
Ingersoll, G. S.	Alameda
Johnson, F. S.	204 Front street
Jennings, C. B.	121 California street
Jacobs, Isidor	409 Washington street
Jones, E. D.	207 California street
Jackson, A. W.	204 California street
Johnson, W. P.	401 California street
Jones, Webster	26-28 Fremont street
Kittredge, E. H.	113 Market street
Kendall, F. P.	125 Market street
Kohler, H. H.	1802 Pacific avenue
Kline, Geo. W.	First National Bank
Knight, Benj. A.	308 Market street
Lowenthal, M. S.	320 California street
Levi, Jacob, Jr.	117 Market street
Levi, H.	117 Market street
Low, J. O.	125 Market street
Lilienthal, E. R.	100 Front street
Laidlaw, R. D.	217 Front street
Lund, Henry	214 California street
Locke, W. L.	204 Front street
Lemcke, Martin	16 Drumm street
Low, C. P.	Front street
Livingston, John	320 California street
Lawson, William	Sansome street
Lovell, M.	116 California street
Mau, William F.	9 Beale street
Merry, William L.	125 California street
Meade, G. W.	132 Market street
Moore, J. J.	302 California street
Moore, A. D.	Pier 10, Steuart street
Meigs, A. W.	Front street
Montague, W. W.	309 Market street
McGlauflin, L. W.	309 California street
McNear, G. W.	306 California street
Morrow, Geo. P.	39 Clay street
Morgan, E. H.	9 Beale street
Miller, C. E.	18 Fremont street
Miner, W. H.	29 Stevenson street

Glacé Fruits and Marrons at Gruenhagen's

Miles, D. E.	405 California street
McCormick, F. H.	219 Front street
McCann, Frank	9 Beale street
Newton, Morris	132 Market street
Nagle, H. H.	306 California street
Noble, H. H.	325 Montgomery street
Owen, J. B.	Market and California streets
Palache, J.	202 California street
Polhemus, E.	208 California street
Page, Arthur	302 California street
Page, G. T.	302 California street
Potter, E. E.	428 California street
Platt, C. B.	104 California street
Philips, L. A.	109 California street
Peterson, F. C.	301 California street
Rowley, B. N.	321 Market street
Ruggles, J. E.	114 Market street
Risdon, R. N.	Cor. Front and Clay streets
Raymond, G. A.	206 California street
Root, E. M.	122 Market street
Rithett, R. P.	220 California street
Rohlffs, C. C.	1 Mission street
Stone, B. F.	126 California street
Stone, C. B.	204 California street
Sweeney, L. H.	114 Market street
Sanderson, G. H.	122 Market street
Siegfried, J. C.	118 Market street
Sussman, Samuel	104 Front street
Sperry, James W.	134 California street
Schenck, W. T. Y.	256 Market street
Sadler, H. J.	9 Beale street
Sutton, A. M.	122 Front street
Savage, W. C.	126 Market street
Smith, S. M.	125 Market street
Schmidt, M.	25 Main street
Smith, H. C.	Pier 10, Steuart street
Spreckels, Claus	327 Market street
Stratton, F. S.	325 Montgomery street
Swayne, R. H.	504 Battery street
Schacht, H.	16 Drumm street
Spaulding, N. W.	17 Fremont street
Shattuck, C. H.	520 Commercial street
Street, C. H.	415 Montgomery street

Simons, G. S.	220 Sutter street
Somers, H. C.	Pier 22, Steuart street
Simpson, A: M.	48 Market street
Stillman, Alfred	314 California street
Tilley, W. J.	126 Market street
Talbot, W. H.	204 California street
Talbot, F. C.	204 California street
Tallant, N. W.	125 Market street
Thomas, J. P.	112 Davis street
Thore, C. P.	
Townsend, W. R.	Cor. California and Battery sts.
Taylor, S. J.	414 Clay street
Voigt, R. E.	207 California street
Van Slyke, E. W. S.	124 Sansome street
Van Sicklen, F. W.	114 Market street
Whitney, C. E.	101 California street
Woods, F. N.	Cor. Front and Pine streets
Walker, Cyrus	
Wightman, John, Jr.	309 California street
Watson, G. W.	48 Market street
Wormser, S. I.	104 Front street
Weilman, W. B.	126 Market street
Wolff, Wm.	329 Market street
Woods, R. J.	Front and Vallejo streets
Watson, H. H.	218 Sansome street
White, C. F.	221 Front street
Wilson, J. K.	Pine and Sansome streets
Weil, Mayer	Battery and Market streets
Whitney, A. L.	Petaluma
Williamson, A. B.	316 California street
Young, C. G.	25 Davis street
Yates, C. M.	101 Front street

Cercle Français

The Cercle Français was organized April 12, 1884, and was incorporated, June 9, 1888. The membership is mostly composed of French merchants, a good number residing outside of San Francisco. The regular meetings take place on the second Thursday of each month.

Brandt, L. J.

Brand, A.

Brandt, J. B. L.

Bernard, B.

Cailleau, A.

Cahen, A.

Cahn, N.

Carpy, C.

Charonnot, E.

Chesney, D.

Coblentz, J.

Coblentz, F.

Coblentz, G.

Chauché, A. G.

Dahlman, N.

Debret, M.

Dubedat, E.

Dubedat, Ed.

Eisenberg, A.

Eisner, M. S.

Elder, James

Etchebarne, C.

Fagothy, J. G.

Falk, J.

Flamant, E.

Fleury, P.

Frank, G. W.

Fusenot, J.

Gallois, E.

Godchaux, A.

Godchaux, E.

Godchaux, Laz.

Godchaux, Lue.

Gros, A.

Grogan, A. E.

Grothwell, Leonce

Gregoire, L.

Greenzweig, G.

Hainque, M.

Hallgarten, B.

Hirsch, L.

Hirschfeld, E.

Hirschfeld, A.

Husson, P.

Husted, F.

Kahn, H.

Kahn, J.

Kahn, M.

Kauffman, L.

Kelly, Louis

Klein, L.

Koenig, A.

Koenig, F.

Kullman, A.

Kullman, S.

Labadie, E. L.

Leonard, C. S.

Lacoste, F.

Ladagnous, J.

Le Roy, E.

Levy, B.

Levy, I. B.

Levy, Jules

Levy, J. W.

Levy, Laz.

Levy, Max.

Levy, M.

Levy, N.

Leibes, Geo.

Lippmann, J.

Loaiza, L.

Loaiza, W.

Lohse, J. F.

Lonjou, J.

Loviza, W.

Lowenberg, E.

Lyons, E. G.

Mathey, H.

Marks, J.

Marrais, L. P.

Masson, F.

Martin, H. S.

Mather, H.

Mayer, J.

Mayer, N.

Meyer, E.

Menézes, P. de

Messager, E.

Meyer, Eug.

Meyer, L.

Myers, L. R.

Neale, Geo. S.

Nerson, A.

Neuberger, G.

Payot, H.

Paul, A. B.

Pereira, S. L.

Pesoli, E. A.

Pike, B. D.

Pissis, A.

Pierron, Emil

Poudenson, P.

Priet, P.

Puttman, H.

Raas, E.

Reiss, B.

Reiss, J.

Reiss, S.

Rens, A.

Richards, C. W.

Roeckel, J.

Roos, A.

Rothchild, E.

Roth, D.

Roth, J.

Routier, Senator

Solomon, S.

Schmidt, A.

Schmidt, M.

Schul, M.

Seigel, M.

Siegel, L.

Simon, A.

Simon, E.

Simon, J.

Somps, P. G.

Sondag, J.

St. Germain, F. De

Swyney, W. G.

Thomas, L.

Tronchet, L.

Verneil, J. L.

Wartenweiler, A.

Waters, W. E.

Weil, Ach.

Weil, M.

Weill, A.

Weill, H.

Weill, R.

Weill, S.

Willard, J.

Willard, L.

Wolf, J.

Yemans, H. W.

HONORARY MEMBERS

Mackay, J. W.

Carrey, Ed.

Yale Club

The Yale Club of California was organized September 1, 1877, and is composed of residents of this State who have formerly attended at Yale College. The regular meetings are held on the Second Friday of January, April and October, at place designated by the Executive Committee. The annual meeting and banquet is held on the last Friday of October of each year.

OFFICERS

MARTIN KELLOGG, President - - - - Berkeley, Cal.
GORDON BLANDING, 1st Vice-Pres. • - 324 Pine street
ELY I. HUTCHINSON, 2d Vice-Pres. - - 419 California street
MOUNTFORD S. WILSON, Secretary - 202 Sansome street
DONALD Y. CAMPBELL, Treasurer - - 130 Sansome street

MEMBERS

Allen, James M.   305 Sansome street
Andrews, Wellington M.   San Francisco

Bacon, Joseph S.   218 California street
Barnes, W. H. L.   426 California street
Barrett, C. H.   Oakland, Cal.
Beaver, George W.   1300 Taylor street
Benton, Joseph A.   Oakland, Cal.
Blake, Charles E.   200 Stockton street
Blake, Charles T.   4 Vernon Place
Blanding, Gordon   324 Pine street
Booth, William F.   220 Market street
Brewer, John H.   430 California street

Campbell, Donald Y.   130 Sansome street
Carpenter, E. W.   410 California street
Clarke, Samuel J.   506 Battery street
Crocker, William H.   322 Pine street

Society as I have Found It By Ward McAllister. The New Society Book.

The Bancroft Company, 721 Market Street.

Cunningham, James	2518 Broadway street
Cunningham, John	329 Sansome street
Day, Sherman	San Francisco
Drew, George W.	512 Jones street
Du Bois, H. A., Jr.	San Rafael, Cal.
Dwinelle, Charles H.	Berkeley, Cal.
Folsom, D. F.	San Mateo, Cal.
Forbes, Cleveland	29 Essex street
Foster, William	Honolulu, H. I.
Galpin, Philip G.	432 Montgomery street
Goodale, Charles	Berkeley, Cal.
Gordon, George W.	320 Sansome street
Gordon, Moses S.	Oakland, Cal.
Green, Edmund F.	508 California street
Hillyer, Curtis J.	Virginia City, Nevada
Hutchinson, Ely I.	419 California street
Janin, Louis	211 Sansome street
Janvier, Allen E.	Oakland, Cal.
Jarboe, John R.	230 Montgomery street
Johnson, Francis	402 Montgomery street
Johnson, Sidney L.	523 Montgomery street
Jordan, William H.	Oakland, Cal.
Kellogg, Martin	530 California street
Kendall, Wesley	San Francisco, Cal.
Keys, Winfield S.	915 Van Ness avenue
King, Clarence	San Francisco, Cal.
Lockwood, Arthur A.	San Francisco, Cal.
Loomis, H. B.	Portland, Or.
Lord, Theodore A.	1828 Vallejo street
Love, John Lord	116 Leidesdorff street
Lyman, J. Chester	325 Twenty-seventh street
McLean, Edward	113 Fair Oaks street
Metcalf, George D.	Oakland, Cal.
Metcalf, Victor H.	Oakland, Cal.
Naphtaly, Joseph	426 California street
Newhall, Henry G.	309 Sansome street
Newhall, William Mayo	309 Sansome street
Newlands, Francis G.	305 Sansome street
Page, Charles	316 California street
Page, Olaff	316 California street

Palmer, Charles T. H.	Berkeley, Cal.
Pearson, William	439 California street
Poston, John M.	Oakland, Cal.
Pratt, W. A.	507 Montgomery street
Reade, William	216 Sansome street
Roberts, E. P.	516 California street
Robinson, Sanford	320 Sansome street
Rothchild, Joseph	303 California street
Rowell, Joseph	1416 Sacramento street
Schofield, William	224 Third street
Sill, Edward R.	Berkeley, Cal.
Sleight, Cornelius	Los Angeles, Cal.
Smith, Sidney V., Jr.	212 Sansome street
Trumbull, David	Valparaiso, Chili
Torreyson J. D.	Carson City, Nev.
Tuttle, Frederick P.	Auburn, Cal.
Wilson, Mountford S.	202 Sansome street

Harvard Club

The Harvard Club of San Francisco was organized January 15, 1874, for the purpose of promoting social intercourse among its members. It is composed of the Pacific Coast Alumni of Harvard University, and numbers 120 members. Business meetings are held on the third Thursdays of January, April and July, and the annual meeting on the third Thursday of October.

OFFICERS

PELHAM WARREN AMES - - -	President
FRDK. RANDOLPH KING - -	First Vice-President
WILLIAM C. LITTLE - -	Second Vice-President
HAROLD WHEELER - - - -	Secretary
H. H. SHERWOOD - - - -	Treasurer

LIST OF MEMBERS

Abbot, George	Pacific-Union Club
Ames, Pelham W.	516 California street
Anderson, Dr Walter D.	Vallejo, Cal.
Ashe, Gaston M.	2315 Sacramento street
Ayer, Dr Washington	1622 Clay street
Baker, Wakefield	1882 Washington street
Barnes, Charles L.	Care of *Daily Examiner*
Barnes, William S.	821 Sutter street
Baum, Alexander, R.	330 Pine street
Belshaw, Charles M.	Antioch, Cal.
Bigelow, Samuel C.	440 California street
Bonestel, Chesley K.	438 California street
Boyd, Dr Samuel G.	715 Clay street
Bridge, Samuel J.	Roxbury, Mass.
Briggs, Frederick H.	Care of *Daily Examiner*
Brigham, Dr Charles B.	703 Market Street
Buck, Geo. F.	Stockton, Cal.
Bush, Walter N.	S. F. Boys' High school

Comte, Auguste, Jr.	534½ California street
Cook, William Hoff	319 California street
Courtis, William M.	West Point, Cal.
Davidson, George F.	1117 Hyde street
Davidson, Thomas D,	1117 Hyde street
Davis, Horace	41 First street
Davis, Hon John F.	2323 Sacramento street
Delger, Edward F.	1151 Broadway, Oakland
Du Bois, Pierre C.	313 Capp street
Faulkner, Dr Henry W.	906 Market street
Follansbee, John Gilbert	Pacific-Union Club
Foster, Samuel L.	434 Bartlett street
Frank, George W.	313 California street •
Friedlander, T. Cary	1913 Clay street
Garnett, Edgar M.	35 Essex street
Gibbs, Frederick A.	35 Fremont street
Gillig, Henry M.	Bohemian Club
Grimm, Dr Charles H.	Nevada City, Cal.
Grayson, Robert R.	327 Pine street
Haggin, Louis T.	Nevada Block
Hammond, Charles M.	Upper Lake, Lake Co., Cal.
Hammond, Gardiner G., Jr.	Upper Lake, Lake Co., Cal.
Handy, Dr George W.	Cor. 15th & Madison sts., Oak.
Hastings, Robert P.	Pacific-Union Club
Hardin, Charles H. E.	Bohemian Club
Hearst, William R.	Care of *Daily Examiner*
Hinchman, Augustus F.	610 Commercial street
Hoffman, Charles F.	Iowa Hill, Placer Co., Cal.
Holloway, William E.	Pacific-Union Club
Howard, Oscar Schafter	516 California street
Howard. Albert A.	University of Cal, Berkeley,Cal.
Huntington, Dr Thomas W.	S. P. Co.'s Hospital, Sac., Cal.
Jackson, Charles Hooper	426 California street
Jelly, Arthur C.	123 Boylston st., Boston, Mass.
Kendall, Frank Irving	509 Montgomery street
King, Frederick R.	530 California street
Lake, Frederick B.	1905 Pacific avenue
Le Conte, Prof. Joseph	University of Cal,Berkeley,Cal.
Lent, Eugene	699 Polk street. (Nevada Block)
Little, William Coffin	Cor. Mission and Main streets
Lux, Dr Frederick W.	703 Market street

Maxfield, Joseph E.	302 Montgomery street
McAllister, Hall	San Rafael, Cal.
McElrath, John E.	NE 8th & Broadw'y, Oak., Cal.
McLellan, George F.	Los Angeles, Cal.
McMonagle, Dr Beverly	703 Market street
McNutt, Dr William F.	405 Montgomery street
Merrill, Geo. B.	Nevada Block
Michael, Francis	1317 Gough street
Miller, Adolph Caspar	Berkeley, Cal.
Mills, James E.	2106 Van Ness avenue
Minns, Prof George W.	1819 Broadway street
Noble, Francis L.	Care of *Daily Examiner*
Otis, George Edmunds	San Bernardino, Cal.
Paterson, Dr Edward M.	1117 Washington st., Oakland.
Pennell, Robt. Franklin	Marysville, Cal.
Pinkerton, Thomas H.	1155 Broadway, Oakland, Cal.
Powers, Dr Geo. H.	215 Geary street
Prentiss, Samuel R.	Pacific-Union Club
Pringle, Edward J.	522 Montgomery street
Putnam, Osgood	1012 Washington street
Redding, Joseph D.	Hibernia Bank Building
Reid, William T.	Belmont, San Mateo Co., Cal.
Reis, Ferdinand, Jr.	835 California street
Richardson, George Morey	Berkeley, Cal.
Ryer, Fletcher F.	102 Montgomery street
Sanderson, George R.	312 Pine street
Sawyer, Dr Albert F.	302 Stockton street
Sawyer, Dr Wesley C.	San Jose, Cal.
Sawyer, William T.	422 Battery street
Severance, James S.	Cor. Fourth and Townsend sts.
Sharon, Frederick W.	Palace Hotel
Sharkey, Dr James M.	634 Washington street
Sherwood, John D.	Spokane Falls, Washington
Sherwood, Henry H.	212 Market street
Southard, Dr William F.	Oakland, Cal.
Stebbins, Rev Horatio	1609 Larkin street
Stetson, Edward G.	508 California street
Stow, Vanderlynn	222 Sutter street
Stringham, Prof Irving	University of Cal., Berkeley
Symmes, Frank J.	222 Sutter street
Taylor, John W.	Blue Creek, Box Elder Co., U.T.
Tevis, Hugh	Benson, Arizona

Thomas, William	206 Sansome street
Troutt, James M.	2217 Fillmore street
Tubbs, Alfred S.	611 Front street
Tubbs, Austin C.	611 Front street
Ward, David Henshaw	Room 4, 220 California street
Ward, John T.	Room 4, 220 California street
Watkins, James T.	Nevada Bank
Winn, Prof Able T.	230 Hermann street
Wigmore, John H.	133 Spear street
Wilson, Ramon C.	419 California street
Wheelan, Fairfax H.	San Luis Obispo, Cal.
Wheeler, Alfred A.	Care of H. Wheeler, 621 Clay st.
Wheeler, Harold	621 Clay street
Whitney, Calvin E.	1213 Jones street
Whitwell, Dr William S.	907 Sutter street
Zinkeisen, Oscar T.	Cosmos Club, 317 Powell street

Princeton University Club

San Francisco, California

LIST OF MEMBERS

Adams, James C.	320 California street
Alexander, Charles B.	Cor. Cal. & Mason sts., S. F.
Armstrong, James	220 Sutter street, S. F.
Austin, John M.	Los Angeles, Cal.
Avery, Rev H. R.	San Jose, Cal.
Bandman, Charles J.	908 Van Ness Avenue
Barretto, Francis J.	Downey City, Cal.
Benton, Samuel Hart	San Jose, Cal.
Berry, T. C.	202 California street
Bigelow, G. H.	San Francisco, Cal.
Bingham, Rev J. Shepherd	Baker City, Oregon
Blaney, Charles B.	San Jose, Cal.
Boyd, Rev T. M.	Pendleton, Or.
Brown, Thomas B.	122 N. Spring st., Los Angeles
Brown, Harrington	122 N. Spring st., Los Angeles
Burt, A. H., M. D.	Santa Barbara, Cal.
Burrows, Rev George, D. D.	19 Haight street, S. F.

Charlton, James	Albany, Or.
Chetwood, John, Jr.	318 Pine street, S. F.
Cory, Lewis	Fresno, Cal.
Condit, Rev E. N.	Albany, Or.
Critchlow, E. B.	Salt Lake City, Utah
Croco, Rev A. H.	Sonora, Cal.
Culbreth, Robert E.	City Argus, S. F.
Cuvellier, B. C.	410 Battery street, S. F.
Darden, Rev W. H.	Petaluma, Cal.
Dobbins, Hugh T.	Berkeley, Cal.
Gillingham, Rev H. C.	Modesta, Cal.
Green, W. H.	Seattle, Washington
Gurnee, Clinton	612 Commercial street, S. F.
Halsey, Abraham	328 Montgomery street, S. F.
Hickman, Lewis McL.	355 Madison st., Oakland, Cal.
Hicks, Frank S.	122 N. Spring st., Los Angeles
Higgins, William M., M. D.	Anaheim, Cal.
Kelly, Hon James Kerr	Portland, Or.
Kerr, Rev Alex. J.	1224 Jackson street, S. F.
Kittle, William Scott	202 California street
Lewis, L. A.	Portland, Or.
Lewis, David C.	Portland, Or.
Lewis, V. Courtney	Portland, Or.
Liston, Rev R. T.	Benson, Arizona
Marcellus, Rev A.	Lebanon, Or.
Mhoon, Major John B.	401 California street, S. F.
Mitchell, Robert B.	508 California street, S. F.
Moore, Sidney H.	San Fernando, Cal.
Moore, Austin D.	Pacific ave & Devisadero st, S.F.
McAllister, Hon Ward, Jr.	430 Montgomery street
McClain, Rev J.	Ogden, Utah
McDonald, Mark L. Jr.	Santa Rosa, Cal.
McMullin, Hon. John	1414 California street
Peck, Rev Harlan Page	Sedalia, Wash.
Reed, T. M., Jr.	Olympia, Wash.
Roberts, Bolivar	Salt Lake City, Utah
Sayre, Rev Sylvanus	Skipanon, Or.
Scudder, Rev. W. W.	Alameda, Cal.
Sessions, D. R.	The History Company, S. F.
Shearer, Rev F. E., D. D.	19 Montgomery street, S. F.

Fine Pineapple, Butternut and Assorted Bonbons at Gruenhagen's

Shearer, George Louis	Santa Rosa, Cal.
Shields, Rev Calvin R.	Joseph, Or.
Smith, Rev J. A. L.	Payson, Utah
Smith, Hon J. Henley	Occidental Hotel, S. F.
Smith, Prof Leigh Richmond	San Jose, Cal.
Stevens, Rev R. L.	La Grande, Or.
Stinson, John H.	Eureka, Cal.
Stokes, James B.	108 California, street S. F.
Strong, Rev Robert	Pasadena, Cal.
Thomas, J. N.	Santa Rosa, Cal.
Thornton, Col Harry I.	504 Kearny street, F. S.
Trask, James L.	6 Montgomery avenue, S. F.
Tupper, Henry Clay	Fresno, Cal.
Van Doran, Hon Peter A.	Pasadena, Cal.
Van Dyke, T. S.	San Diego, Cal.
Voorhees, Rev L. B.	Santa Ana, Cal.
White, E. J.	Los Angeles, Cal.
Whiting, Rev S. P.	Santa Rosa, Cal.
Whittlesey, W. H.	Seattle, Wash.
Whittlesey, C. F.	Seattle, Wash.
Wikoff, Rev H. H.	1908½ Mason street, S. F.
Willis, A. H.	Reno, Nevada
Wylie, Rev Richard	Napa, Cal.
Zahner, Peter	Pendleton, Or.

The Olympic Club.

Rooms and Gymnasium at Alcazar Building, 120 O'Farrell St.

The Olympic is the oldest and one of the best athletic clubs in the United states. It was founded in 1860 and the history of the organization has been one of uninterrupted prosperity. The accommodations for members are unsurpassed. Although the building they now occupy is large and commodious, owing to the constant increase of the membership and the consequent addition to the funds, the club has contracted for the erection of a new building, to be owned by them, and which, when completed, will excel both in its size and appointments any similar construction in this country.

There are 17 Charter, 75 Life and nearly 1,300 Active Members.

OFFICERS

W. Greer Harrison, Pres. - -	305 California street
E. A. Rix, Vice-Pres. - - -	227 First street
W. E. Holloway, Secretary - -	430 California street
Henry B. Russ, Treasurer - -	6 Columbia Square
E. A. Kolb, Leader - - -	422 Montgomery street
Walter A. Scott, Captain - -	2 Pine street

DIRECTORS

A. C. Forsyth	217 Bush street
M. H. Weed	327 Market street
A. J. Treat	S. P. Co.
J. H. Gilhuly	17 Beale street
John Elliott	31 Sixth street

Glacé Fruits and Marrons at Gruenhagen's

STANDING COMMITTEES

ADVISORY BUILDING COMMITTEE

E. A. Rix   A. C. Forsyth
W. E. Holloway   M. H. Reed

INDOOR ATHLETIC COMMITTEE

E. A. Kolb   E. A. Rix
W. E. Holloway   A. J. Treat   J. H. Gilhuly

OUTDOOR ATHLETIC COMMITTEE

W. A. Scott   E. A. Rix   John Elliott

MEMBERSHIP COMMITTEE

W. E. Holloway
A. C. Forsyth   John Elliott

HOUSE COMMITTEE

A. C. Forsyth   J. H. Gilhuly   M. H. Reed

FINANCE COMMITTEE

H. B. Russ   M. H. Weed   A. J. Treat

SOCIAL COMMITTEE

M. H. Weed   H. B. Russ   J. H. Gilhuly

The President is a member *ex-officio* of all Committees.

California Lawn Tennis Club

Club Grounds, Southeast Corner of Bush and Scott Streets

The California Lawn Tennis Club of San Francisco organized September 13, 1884. Club grounds, southeast corner of Bush and Scott streets. Club colors: red and white.

The Club comprises about 160 members, including some of the most prominent people in the city. The grounds are conveniently located, under lease for 10 years, and have three asphalt courts, a clubhouse with dressing-rooms, shower bath facilities and reading-room; a driveway on the Bush street side enables carriages to enter the grounds. Tournaments are held in the Spring and Fall of each year, and on Saturday afternoons, Club day, games are always in progress.

The grounds are open every day in charge of a keeper; and visitors are welcome at any time.

OFFICERS

DELL LINDERMAN, Pres. -   -   506½ Commercial street
MISS SUSIE MORGAN, Vice-Pres   -   - 2312 Clay street
GEORGE V. GRAY, Secretary   -   -   252 Market street
R. J. WOODS, Treasurer -   -   Vallejo and Front streets

BOARD OF DIRECTORS

Dell Linderman   506½ Commercial street
Miss Susie Morgan   2312 Clay street
George V. Gray   252 Market street
R. J. Woods   Vallejo and Front streets
Ward McAllister, Jr.   430 Montgomery street
H. H. Sherwood   212 Market street
W. H. Taylor, Jr.   Risdon Iron Works

317

LIFE MEMBERS

Alvord, William	Bank of California
Balfour, Robert	
Brander, George L.	
Coleman, Mrs W. T	1229 Taylor street
Crocker, Charles F.	
Fair, James G.	
Fair, Mrs Theresa	
Flood, Miss J.	
Forman, Robert B.	
Hager, Mrs. John F.	
Mackay, John W.	
Parrott, Mrs. A. M.	
Perine, George M.	
Scott, Henry T.	
Taylor, William H.	
Tubbs, A. L.	

REGULAR MEMBERS

Ashe, Mrs. Wm.	405 California street
Beaver, Fred H.	418 California street
Balnave, Wm.	Balfour, Guthrie & Co.
Bee, Everett N.	208 California street
Bigelow, J. F.	Nevada Bank
Blair, Miss Jennie	1315 Van Ness avenue
Boardman, F. D.	316 California street
Bolado, Miss Dulce	528 Sutter street
Bourn, W. B.	1300 Hyde street
Breeze, T. H.	1300 Sutter street
Browne, C. E.	Fireman's Fund Insurance Co.
Brust, Miss Lillie	Bella Vista
Carrigan, Miss	2124 California street
Carrigan, A.	2124 California street
Casserly, J. B.	2123 Buchanan street
Chase, H. B.	Napa Soda Springs
Clarke, Miss Lottie	2119 California street
Code, J. A.	1217 Bryant street
Coggins, E. B.	614 Sutter street
Coleman, Robert L.	1299 Taylor street
Collier, W. B.	226 Post street

Dargie, T. T.	Oakland
Davis, R. J.	Pacific Bank
Deane, E. B.	402 Montgomery street
Dillon, Miss Kate	501 Van Ness avenue
Dimond, Miss Eleanor	2204 Pacific avenue
Eyre, Edward L.	405 California street
Eyre, Miss Mary	Menlo Park
Eyre, Perry P.	307 California street
Eyre, Robert	307 California street
Fisher, Mrs Edward	The Berkshire
Floya, Mrs R. S.	415 First street
Forbes, S.	Spring Valley Water Works
Fuller, W. P.	Pine and Front sts.
Gadesden, Valentine	1111 Sutter street
Gibbs, Miss Martha	722 Post street
Girvin, R. D.	307 California street
Godley, Jessie E.	16 California street
Godley, Philip	302 California street
Goodall, Arthur	Oakland
Grant, J. D.	Sansome & Bush streets
Gray, Geo. V.	252 Market street
Harcus, H. B.	
Harcus, Mrs H. B.	23 Nevada Block
Hawkins, V. A. C.	
Hawkins, Mrs V. A. C.	436 California street
Harrison, R.	919 Pine street
Heathcote, Mrs. Basil	410 Sutter street
Hellmann, George	1829 Pacific avenue
Herd, Miss	
Hoffman, Ogden	302 California street
Hoffman, Southard	1113 Bush street
Hooker, Miss Jennie	917 Bush street
Houghton, Miss Minnie	801 Sutter street
Howard, G. H.	1812 Gough street
Howard, O. Shafter	1812 Gough street
Hubbard, C. P.	Oakland
Husband, J. T.	316 California street
Ivers, Miss Ailene	Palace Hotel
Jackson, S. M.	L. & S. F. Bank
Jacobs, E. L.	Nevada Bank

Wedding and Party Invitations. Engraved and Printed in Correct Form.

The Bancroft Company, 721 Market Street.

Kilgarif, J. M.	418 California street
King, Thompson	1501 Van Ness avenue
Kittle, John G.	1610 Franklin street
Kittle, Miss	1610 Franklin street
Lent, G. H.	699 Polk street
Linderman, Dell	1501 Van Ness avenue
Lockwood, Miss	Clay and Buchanan
Loughborough, Geo.	829 O'Farrell street
Loughead, H. W.	L. & S. F. Bank
Macondray, William	1821 Sacramento street
Madison, F. D.	512 Market street
Magee, F. E.	
Magee, W. A.	800 Van Ness ave.
Magee, Thos., Jr.	800 Van Ness avenue
McCutchen, E. J.	419 California street
McAllister, Ward	430 Montgomery street
McGavin, Walter	Nevada Bank
McKerrow, A. J.	Easton & Eldridge
McKinstry, Miss Laura	1515 Washington street
McPherson, William	1001 Pine street
Melville, William R.	Bank of California
Moore, Percy P.	2121 Buchanan street
Morgan, Miss Susie	2312 Clay street
Newhall, George A.	309 Sansome street
Newhall, W. Mayo	309 Sansome street
O'Connor, Miss Lily	825 O'Farrell street
Ortiz, Miss Julia	1512 California street
Otis, James	1900 Washington street
Page, Wm.	San Rafael
Paige, Cutler	2002 Pacific avenue
Parrott, John	414 Montgomery street
Payson, A. H.	San Mateo
Pope, Miss Mary	1601 Van Ness avenue
Requa, Mark	Oakland
Rutherford, Mrs A. H.	1105 Bush street
Salazar, A. J.	508 Sutter street
Schmiedell, E.	Post and Leavenworth sts.
Severance, J. S.	Fourth and Townsend sts.
Sherwood, H. H.	212 Market street
Sherwood, Mrs H. H.	212 Market street

Sherwood, R. L.	212 Market street
Simpkins, Miss Alice	2100 California street
Simpkins, Henry	2100 California street
Skae, Miss Alice	Palace Hotel
Small, A. H.	1312 Taylor street
Somerville, Philip	914 Howard street
Spencer, Dr J. C.	614 Sutter street
Spiers, Miss	2200 Washington street
Stetson, H. N.	1801 Van Ness avenue
Stringer, Ö. P.	800 Sutter street
Taylor, Augustus	2128 California street
Taylor, W. H.	2128 California street
Tevis, W. S.	W. F. & Co's Bank
Tevis, Mrs W. S.	1311 Hyde street
Thompson, Frank	1501 Van Ness avenue
Tobin, Joseph	SE cor. California and Taylor
Tubbs, A. S.	611 Front street
Tubbs, Miss Nettie	611 Front street
Tubbs, W. B.	611 Front street
Tucker, S. C.	28 California street
Van Fleet, Mrs. W. C.	Sacramento
Wilberforce, Alex.	123 California street
Williamson, Alex.	316 California street
Wilson, Mountford S.	202 Sansome street
Winslow, Chauncey R.	709 Sutter street
Wise, H. E.	1409 Leavenworth street
Wood, Miss Eleanor	1920 Clay street
Woods, Robert J.	NW cor. Vallejo and Front sts.
Wooster, Ellis	
Wrey, George	The Berkshire
Wright, W. Q.	Sebastopol, Sonoma Co.
Wright, C. W.	220 Montgomery street
Yates, C. R.	The Berkshire
Younger, Miss Maud	1414 California street

ABSENT MEMBERS

Baldwin, Charles A.	Preston, R. J.
Cook, Joseph E.	Schofield, W. B.
Hicks, Frank S.	Stetson, Mrs. E. G.
Wilshire, H. G.	

San Francisco Yacht Club

Club House, Sausalito, Cal.

The San Francisco Yacht Club was organized in July, 1869, and reorganized in July, 1873. The directors meet monthly. The Secretary can be communicated with at Wells, Fargo & Co.'s Bank.

OFFICERS, 1890

I. GUTTE, Commodore

J. MACDONOUGH, Vice-Commodore

FRED. B. CHANDLER, Secretary

CHAS. W. KELLOGG, Treasurer -   -   611-13 Front street

GEO. W. REED, Financial Secretary   -   502 Battery street

MATTHEW TURNER, Measurer

DIRECTORS

C. H. Harrison   E. W. Newhall

A. C. Hellman   John D. Spreckels

W. N. McCarthy.

MEMBERS

Alexander, Chas. O.   Barrett, W. G.
Adams, J.   Bromwell, L. L.
Barrett, M. M.   Baehi, Wm.
Bohen, Geo.   Berg, Wm.
Blum, Leon   Bates, M. U.
Berry, Fulton G.   Baker, Wakefield
Belknap, D. P.   Bent, E. F.
Baker, L. L.   Burrowe, Capt M.
Banning, Hancock   Bowen, H. A.

Boyd, Clair	Kruse, Wm.
Brown, J. W.	Kellogg, Chas. W.
Bonnell, J. F.	Kohler, Hans
Bass, T. J.	Kelly, J. C.
Bryant, G. H.	Kerr, E. T.
Chandler, F. B.	Lukins, E. J.
Chapman, L. B.	Le Count, J. P.
Cartan, F. M.	Larson, Henry
Cole, E. P.	Livingston, J.
Currier, J. P.	Lee, John
Chittenden, Chas.	Latser, S. H.
Cullen, E. F.	Merritt, Dr Samuel
Costle, Col A. E.	McDonough, J.
Crompton, H. J.	Musser, Otto
Dowling, T.	May, Joseph
Dowling, Thos.	Moore, R. S.
Durbrow, H.	Marcus, George
Davis, Dr G. E.	McCarthy, William
Duval, W. S.	Malter, G. H.
Davidson, G. F.	Moore, Joseph
Davidson, T. D.	McNear, Geo. W.
English, John F.	Metcalf, Geo. D.
Eppinger, Jacob	Morrell, C. H.
Engleberg, Emil	Madison, J.
Floyd, R. S.	Murray, Wm.
Franks, J.	McAfee, E.
Flood, J. L.	McFarland, D.
Folsom, J. R.	Miller, J. R.
Gutte, I.	Miles, D. E.
Guerry, Alfred	Murphy, F.
Gibbs, H.	Murray, A. S.
Greenbaum, E.	Newhall, E. W.
Harrison, J. W.	Newman, Dr L.
Hirsch, Louis	Noble, H. H.
Hellmann, A. C.	Oliver, W. L.
Hobbs, Wm.	Pew, John W.
Hayes, D. E.	Presson, Geo. R.
Harrison, C. H.	Pereira, S. L.
Herold, R.	Russell, E.
Harmes, J. T.	Reed, Geo. W.
Hyde, F. A.	Regensberger, Dr A.
Hendry, G. W.	Riordan, J. H.
Hopkins, F. C.	Rosenfeld, J.
Hamilton, C. T.	Ruyter, J. E.
Hecht, B. R.	Sloss, Louis, Jr.

323

Sloss, Leon
Shoobert, J. E.
Streeten, J. M.
Shotwell, J. M.
Spreckels, J. S.
Smith, F. M.
Sperry, J. W.
Stone, L. D.
Stickney, B.
Sawyer, Prescott
Seligiman, A.
Shelly, W. N.
Sheppard, A. D.
Schloh, B. A.
Slauf, W.

Spinney, W. S.
Turner, Mathew
Taylor, W. H.
Tillinghast, D. F.
Tashura, Geo.
Tallant, F. W.
Turner, L. H.
Thomas, L. B.
Thompson, J. A.
Tormey, T. J.
White, George Knight
Watson, Thos.
Woodlock, J.
Wormser, S.
Yale, Chas. G.

Oakland Canoe Club

Oakland Creek, foot of Alice St., Oakland

The Oakland Canoe Club was organized January 23, 1886, and the boathouse of the Mystic Boat Club purchased and remodeled to suit the purpose of its new owners. The building is easy of access by several local railroad lines and has a good landing-place at all stages of the tide.

OFFICERS

W. W. Blow	Commodore
A. D. Harrison	Vice-Commodore
G. W. Rodolph	Secretary
S. A. Hackett	Treasurer

LIFE MEMBERS

W. W. Blow	A. D. Harrison
George T. Wright	Henry M. Landsberger
Henry Olsen	W. G. Morrow
Abe Gump	T. E. Kent

HONORARY MEMBERS

Beasley, Thomas D.	San Diego, Cal.
De la Montanya, A.	656 6th street, Oakland
Engelbrecht, Mrs H.	834 Turk street
Platt, A. G.	Lakeport, Cal.
Richards, B. W.	Ontario, Cal.
Yates, Charles	Oakland, Cal.

ACTIVE MEMBERS

Blow, A. H.	454 Ninth street, Oakland
Blow, W. W.	454 Ninth street, Oakland
Darneal, Hervey	65 Nevada Block, San Francisco
Folkers, G. A. W.	118 Montgomery street, S. F.
Guiler, Jas. H.	1309 Taylor street, S. F.
Gump, Abe	581 Market street, San Francisco
Hackett, S. A.	Davis Block, Oakland
Harms, R. G. C.	118 Montgomery street, S. F.
Harrison, A. D.	406 California street
Havens, A. W.	23 Nevada Block
Jackson, Robt.	Tenth st., n. Broadway, Oakland
Kenna, J. G.	Phelan Building, S. F.
Kent, T. E.	597 Mission street
Kuster, H. C.	Los Angeles
Landsberger, H. M.	123 California street, S. F.
Morrow, W. G.	916 Leavenworth street, S. F.
McCormick, —.	323 California, S. F.
Olsen, Harry	1765 Lincoln street, Oakland
Olsen, John	1765 Lincoln street, Oakland
Rodolph, G. W.	1169 Broadway st., Oakland
Stanley, S. B.	410 Front street, S. F.
Warder, G. A.	454 Ninth street, Oakland
Wright, Geo. T.	71 Nevada Block

ABSENTEES

Allen, Arthur	Alameda
Earle, Alfred	406 California street, S. F.
Engelbrecht, R. T.	834 Turk street, S. F.
Hasslocher, E. A. Von	567 Market street, S. F.
Mathieu, Frank L.	41 First street, San Francisco

Ready for Shipment 1, 2, 3, 4, 5 and 10LB Boxes at Gruenhagen'

Society of California Pioneers

Rooms, Pioneer Building, Fourth Street

The Society of California Pioneers was organized in August, 1850. The object of the Society is to collect and preserve information of the early settlement of the country, and to perpetuate the memory of the founders of this State, and also the male descendants of members. All who were in California prior to January 1, 1850, are eligible to membership. The regular meetings are held on the first Monday of each month, and the annual election of officers on the seventh day of July.

OFFICERS

ALEXANDER MONTGOMERY, President
LIVINGSTON L. BAKER, Vice-President - - San Francisco
FREDERICK LUX, " " - - San Francisco
HENRY MATHEWS, " " - - - - Oakland
CAIUS T. RYLAND, " " - - - San Jose
GEORGE F. HOOPER, " " - - - - Sonoma
HOWARD HAVENS, Treasurer
E. P. MARSELLUS, Secretary

DIRECTORS

A. W. Von Schmidt	John I. Spear
Samuel Deal	Christian Reis
Henry B. Buss	John Brickell
Aug. E. Phelps	Geo. T. Marye, Jr.

John Nightingale, Jr., M. D.

The Press Club of San Francisco

Club Rooms, 430 Pine Street

The Press Club of San Francisco was organized August 30, 1880, with 80 charter members. The object of the Club is to bring members of the newspapers and other literary professions together in close personal relations, and to advance the interests of professional journalism. The active membership consists of 211 members, which number is constantly being increased.

OFFICERS

MARCUS P. WIGGIN	President
ALLEN P. KELLY	First Vice-President
JOHN TIMMINS	Second Vice-President
JAS. H. LOVE	Secretary
A. L. POUNSTONE	Librarian

BOARD OF MANAGERS

Jeremiah Lynch	H. H. Eggbert
A. C. Cook	Geo. H. Meyer
F. S. Vassault	H. W. Horton

LIST OF MEMBERS

Adam, L. D.	Briggs, H. H.
Allen, I.	Bartlett, W. C.
Bancroft, H. H.	Bacon, E. H.
Barber, J. E.	Bogart, W. F.
Barendt, A. H.	Backus, S. W.
Bigelow, H.	Bruer, H. J.
Black, O.	Brown, W. L.
Bonner, John	Bush, H. P.
Bonnet, T. F.	Bishop, A. W.
Brooke, H. L.	Benton, W. G.

Carroll, J. B.	Francis, G. M.
Carson, Will	Gates, Harry
Chamberlain, W. H.	Gill, Ed S.
Clemens, W. M.	Gagan, W. H.
Cooney, J. T.	Gibson, Robert
Cowles, P.	Greenway, E. M.
Cook, A. C.	Groom, J. J.
Cooke, W. B.	Gunzendorffer, Gus.
Coe, C. M.	Goldsmith, Paul
Corey, J. J.	Gaskell, V. W.
Cosgrave, J. O'H.	Garrett, T.
Cosgrave, John P.	Hahn, Eugene
Chamberlain, S. S.	Hart, W. N.
Coleman, Jas. V.	Haycock, Judson
Carpenter, L. G.	Haxton, H. R.
Calhoun, J. A.	Horton, S. W.
Culver, E. S.	Hume, Hugh
Coffey, J. V.	Hamilton, E. H.
Chalmers, W.	Hoyt, F. T.
Camp, Geo. K.	Haezelton, G. B.
Clarke, A. L.	High, Gavin D.
Davis, Sam	Hearst, W. R.
Dement, Edward D.	Hirsch, C. J.
De Forrest, H. L.	Hoesch, Jno.
De Young, M. H.	Irvine, Leigh
Dressler, W. D.	Irwin, J. N. H.
Drury, Wells	Isaac, John
Dunning, J. P.	Jackson, A. C.
Dye, Wm. P.	Jordan, J. S.
Dargie, Wm. E.	Jackson, J. Ross
Donahue, James	Kelly, Allen P.
Dewey, A. T.	Kelly, G. P.
Denny, J. O.	Kerr, J. P.
Dunne, F. H.	Krauth, F. K.
Davis, J. M.	Knight, Geo. A.
Daley, J. S.	Lane, F. K.
Davis, Washington	Lawrence, A. M.
Eggbert, H. H.	Love, J. H.
Elwert, Max	Low, C. A.
Ewing, S. M.	Lyon, Geo. E.
Finley, John	Levy, M. S.
Forman, Sands W.	Lynch, Jeremiah
Flynn, Thos. E.	McArdle, J. D.
Francouer, F. I.	Meyer, Geo. H.
Farmer, Fred	Michelson, Chas.

Moffett, S. E.	Simpson, James
McMullen, Jas.	Smythe, J. B.
McCormick, J. S.	Stowell, F. W.
Moran, E. F.	Shinn, C. H.
Murphy, F. J.	Simpson, J. C.
Murphy, P. J.	Stone, F. J.
McComb, John	Siebold, Louis
Moffitt, F. J.	Sarcander, J. F.
Mills, Wm. H.	Scott, W.
McLellan, J. H.	Slaven, Jas.
Murphy, Al	Sheridan, Sol N.
McEwen, Arthur	Shoemaker, R.
Moulder, A. J.	Thompson, Walter
Maxwell, Geo. H.	Timmins, John
McGillwrey, J. D.	Townsend, E. W.
McNaught, Jno.	Truman, B. C.
Morrow, W. C.	Turnbull, Walter
McCraney, H. A.	Trevathan, Chas.
Moore, C. W.	Thrum, J. F.
Norcross, Daniel	Tozer, R.
Naughton, W. W.	Ulrich, Charles
Noble, F. L. H.	Uhlhorn, J. A.
Older, Fremont	Vassault, L. S.
Owen, J. J.	Vivian, T. J.
Painter, E.	Vassault, F. I.
Powell, E. L.	Ward, J. M.
Pixley, Frank M.	Washington, John
Pounstone, A. L.	Wetmore, C. A.
Pratt, J. W.	Weeks, G. F.
Prendergast, T. F.	Whitty, J. H.
Palmer, Chas. M.	Wiggins, Marcus P.
Palmer, J. J.	Williamson, D. E.
Parsons, W. B.	Wishaar, E. B.
Price, E. T.	Woodard, J. A.
Phillips, E. A.	Williams, T. T.
Phelps, G. W.	Wells, W. R.
Reckard, E. L.	Waugh, A. P.
Ricord, W. C.	White, Douglas
Roberts, Percy W.	Yale, C. G.
Rice, Irwin H.	York, R. B. S.
Squires, Geo. D.	Zeehandelaar, F, J.
Shortridge, C. M.	Zeigenfuss, C. O.
Sheehan, J. F.	

Gruenhagen Leads in Bonbonniere Candies

The Union League Club

Club House, 322 Geary Street

W. H. Chamberlain	- - - - President
W. H. Crocker	- - - - First Vice-President
Wendell Easton	- - - Second Vice-President
John S. Mumaugh	- - - - - Secretary
M. H. de Young	- - - - - - Treasurer

BOARD OF DIRECTORS

W. H. Chamberlain
Albert E. Castle
M. H. de Young
Wendell Easton
W. H. Crocker

Frank J. French
John H. Hegler
A. S. Hallidie
J. M. Litchfield
T. H. Minor

John S. Mumaugh

LIFE MEMBERS

Crocker, Charles F. Crocker, William H.
Stanford, Leland

MEMBERS

Ackerman, J. D.
Alexander, Charles O.
Babcock, Madison
Backus, Samuel W.
Badlam, Alexander
Bailey, James D.
Bandmann, Charles J.
Barnes, William S.
Barth, Phil.

Bass, Thomas J.
Beamish, Percy
Belcher, Edward A.
Belshaw, Mortimer W.
Blake, F. L.
Bonnell, Allison C.
Booth, Andrew G.
Breyfogle, Dr. Edwin S.
Brown, Henry W.

Glacé Fruits and Marrons at Gruenhagen's

Brown, J. Frank	Friedrich, R. A.
Brown, William E.	French, Frank J.
Bucknall, Dr George J.	Gawthorne, J. F.
Bull, Franklin P.	Gerstle, Lewis
Carmany, John W.	Gibbons, Dr Henry
Cashin, D. M.	Giesting, Joseph G.
Castle, Albert E.	Grant, Joseph D.
Chadbourne, Forrest S.	Grismer, Joseph R.
Chamberlain, William H.	Gunn, J. O'B.
Chesley, James G.	Hallidie, A. S.
Clark, Zerah P.	Haslett, Samuel
Clement, Lyman H.	Hawes, Alexander G.
Cluff, William	Heazleton, George ·
Conly, William H.	Hecht, Marcus H.
Cook, Carroll ·	Begler, John H.
Cooney, Michael ·	Heynemann, Alexander
Coulson, Dr Nathaniel T.	Hilborn, Samuel G.
Crocker, Charles H.	Hinkle, Walter S.
Crocker, Henry J.	Hooper, Ralph R.
Danforth, Edward P.	Hopkins, Edward W.
Danforth, Edwin	Horton, Frank H.
Dare, John T.	Howe, Leonard W.
Davis, Dr George E.	Huey, Walter E.
Davis, Horace	Hunt, John
Deane, John J.	Hurlburt, W. H. ·
Deane, William A.	Irelan, William, Jr.
Decker, Dr Charles W.	Jennings, Cassius M.
DeHaven, Rhodes	Johnson, Frank S.
DeVeuve, James H.	Keeney, Charles M.
DeYoung, M. H.	Keeney, Dr James W.
Dibble, Henry C.	Kelly, James V. ·
Dickinson, John H.	Kerr, Earl T.
Dimond, William H.	Kilburn, Paris
Dodge, Henry L.	Kimball, Curtis H.
Donnelly, Edward T.	Knight, George A.
Dorn, Marcellus A.	Knox, Thomas R.
Durst, John H.	Kohler, Hans H.
Duval, William S.	Koscialowski, Philip L.
Easton, George	Koster, John A.
Easton, Wendell	Kron, Oscar J.
Edwards, George D.	Kruse, William H.
Edwards, Lemuel B.	Lawlor, Dr William M.
Ellert, L. R.	Lengfeld, Dr A. L.
Estee, Morris M.	Le Tourneux, Dr Thomas J.

Most Delicious Candies at Gruenhagen's

Lilienthal, Philip N.	Richards, James S.
Lippman, George W.	Rothwell, J. Percy
Litchfield, Joseph M.	Sanborn, W. D.
Livingston, Joseph	Schenck, W. T. Y.
Lloyd, Reuben H.	Scott, Irving M.
Long, Dr Seely F.	Sheehan, John F.
Long, W. G.	Sherwood, H. H.
Macdonald, William	Shortridge, Samuel M.
Macdonough, Joseph	Sime, Hugh T.
Mann, Abner S.	Simonson, Joseph
Martin, Henry	Simpson, Dr James
Masten, N. K.	Simpson, John H.
Mau, William F.	Sloss, Leon
Maxwell, George H.	Sloss, Louis
May, Joseph	Sloss, Louis, Jr.
Mays, Dr William H.	Smith, George W.
Middleton, John	Snedaker, W. H.
Miles, D. E.	Spear, Joseph S., Jr.
Minor, Theodore H.	Spreckels, Claus
Montague, W. W.	Stanford, Jerome B.
Moore, Harry P.	Stolp, Gordon M.
Mocre, O. E.	Stump, Irwin C.
Morrow, William W.	Sumner, Frank W.
Morton, John M.	Swan, Dr Benjamin R.
Mumaugh, John S.	Talbot, William H.
Murphy, Daniel J.	Tarrant, Charles E.
McCarthy, William N.	Thornton, Samuel K.
McDougall, Charles C.	Tilden, Charles L.
McLaughlin, Dr William H.	Troutt, James M.
Nash, Herbert C.	Trumbo, Isaac
O'Connor, Cornelius	Vail, Frank A.
Olsen, Justinius B.	Wagoner, Luther
Otis, Fred M.	Warner, Dr Alexander
Pardee, Dr George C.	Watt, J. Alva
Patton, Charles L.	Waymire, James A.
Paxton, Charles E.	Wharff, William H.
Pease, Jr., Richard H.	White, H. T.
Pippy, George H.	Willey, Frank D.
Pollock, Alexander F.	Willey, O. F.
Pratt, William H.	Williams, Abram P.
Rank, W. M.	Wood, William S.
Redding, Joseph D.	Wooster, Fred L.
Reed, Charles F.	Worth, Dr Sidney
Regensburger, Dr Martin	Young, S. P.

COUNTRY MEMBERS

Bailey, W. H.   Morehouse, M. V.
Campbell, George J.   Murphy, Daniel M.
Clark, Walter A.   Myers, Fred R.
Coombs, Frank L.   McComb, John
Dargie, William E.   Rea, James W.
Denison, Eli S.   Seaman, George B.
Hale, W. E.   Spence, Rudolph B.
Harrier, L. G.   Wickersham, Fred A.

STATE MEMBERS

Belshaw, Charles M.   Johnson, Grove L.
Bonebrake, George H.   Johnston, A. J.
Branch, L. C.   Kidder, John H.
Carr, Byron O.   Knight, D. E.
Champlin, George   Lindley, Hervey
Chipman, M. P.   Lindsey, Charles T.
Cole, Daniel T.   Markham, Henry H.
Cone, Joseph S.   Maxwell, Walter S.
Davis, John F.   Merrill, Isaac M.
Dunn, R. L.   Minor, Charles A.
Flint, Thomas, Jr.   Mosher, L. E.
Ford, Tirey L.   McLaughlin, Frank
Furlong, A. W.   McMurray, Robert
Garoutte, Chas. H.   Northam, R. J.
Garter, Charles A.   Otis, Harrison G.
Grattan, W. H.   Porter, John T.
Greeley, F. H.   Runyon, George P.
Green, Milton J.   Ryan, Frank D.
Gregory, Eugene J.   Sexton, Warren
Hanmore, H. M.   Sperry, Austin B.
Hersey, George E.   Sperry, George B.
Hilby, Francis M.   Sullivan, John T.
Hoitt, Ira G.   Van Fleet, W. C.
Hollister, C. E.   Warren, L. F.
Jewett, John H.   Wilde, W. H.
Johnson, Edward P.

NON-RESIDENT MEMBERS

Foley, M. D.   McNear, John A.
Howard, B. Chandler   Taylor, John W.

The Byron Mauzy Musical Club

The above Club was organized in the early part of the year 1888, and now numbers over three hundred members. Its object is to foster a love for the best music, to encourage teachers to bring forward their best pupils, thus striving by competition and emulation to incite them to ambitious work and to bring forward aspirants for the Lyric stage. A large Orchestra is connected with the club. Concerts are given twice each month, and members are entitled to two invitations for each concert. The fees are $1.00 per quarter.

A. A. Batkin is the Secretary, and Prof. H. R. Austin is the Conductor of the Orchestra, which is composed of the following members:

FIRST VIOLINS

Allenberg, Leo.	507 Golden Gate avenue
Austin, F. Victor	1609½ Clay street
Cragin, V. R.	1921 Buchanan street
Weigel, E. E.	1524 Bush street

SECOND VIOLINS

Beckedorff, G. H.	42 Russ street
Denton, C.	1311 Larkin street
Dowdell, R.	324 Eighth street
Schoenberg, M.	1019 Sutter street

VIOLA

Belnig, R.	308 Post street
Werner, A.	918 Market street

CELLO

Classell, J.	314 Post street
Lada, Adolph	213 Powell street

CONTRA BASS

Isreal, E. A.	551 Stevenson street

CLARIONETS

Habbish, Geo.   310 Post street.
Johnson, C.   310 Post street

FLUTES

Fleissner, H. J.   405 Octavia street
Toplitz, Mel.   1002 Van Ness avenue

CORNETS

Euphrat, M. T.   312 Post street
Mauzy, E. R.   308 Post street

TROMBONES

Moore, G. J.   1511 Gough street
Mocker, Wm.   725 Golden Gate avenue

HORNS

Batkin, A. A.   338 Oak street
Mauzy, Byron   308 Post street

TYMPANI

Burnett, G.   214 Haight street

DRUMS

Purnell, Alvin   308 Post street

NAMES OF PATRONS AND MEMBERS

Alexander, Mrs J.   2200 Pine street
Alferitz, Mr and Mrs   620 Green street
Allen, Mrs E. S.   510 Geary street
Allen, Mr and Mrs Charles D.   2500 Washington street
Argue, Miss A. E.
Ashton, Mrs M. J.
Austin, Mr and Mrs H. R.   1609½ Clay street
Austin, Miss Sissy
Austin, F. Victor   1609½ Clay street

Banch, Peter, Jr.
Band, Mr C. W.
Baker, Mr H. R.   122 Front street

Bearing, Miss B.	925½ Natoma street
Barr, Mr and Mrs	1010 Union street
Bartlett, Mr and Mrs C. S. M.	1828 O'Farrell street
Bartlett, Prof W. B.	123 Phelan Building
Bauman, Miss M.	
Bateman, Messrs.	
Bassett, Mrs Wm.	
Becker, Mr Geo.	
Belgrave, Mrs	
Bell, Mr M. L.	
Bernard, Miss Blanche	
Bernard, Miss Flora A.	
Berolzhime, Mrs	
Blote, Mr and Mrs H.	2422 California street
Birchall, Mrs M.	1537 Eddy street
Bretz, Mr A.	
Briggs, Mrs E. M.	
Brown, Miss	
Brown, Mrs. B.	1122 Market street
Brown, Mr J. E.	
Brun, C. B.	
Bruns, Carl	
Bruns, Miss Clara E.	
Bruns, W. G.	
Buchau, Professor	
Bull, Charles G.	Rossmore
Butler, M.	
Buchanan, Mrs Wm.	
Burness, Mr Robt. D.	
Bury, Miss May E.	1103 McAllister street
Buyer, Mr and Mrs C.	1719 Bush street
Buzard, Dr and Mrs A. E.	11 Seventh street

Cabanass, Mrs
Canton, Miss Maud
Capp, Mr S. M.
Carels, Mr J. H.
Carter, Miss Etta
Carrington, Mrs J. B.
Callahan, Miss Mary
Cellarus, Mr C.
Chamberlain, Mrs J. P.
Chase, Miss Minnie
Christian, Miss Bertha
Clark, Mrs J. J.

Connelly, Miss
Connelly, Mr and Mrs J. F.
Connelley, Mrs M. J. L.
Cockerell, Miss Ellie
Collins, Mr J. C.
Collins, Mr D. P.
Cooke, Mr and Mrs Walter B.
Cook, Mr and Mrs Chas.
Corliss, Mrs M. J.
Coursen, Miss Cathie
Coursen, Miss Ellen
Crandall, Mr E. S.

337

Crosby, Mrs. G. W.
Cushman, Mrs E. M.
Dannmeyer, Mr and Mrs. R.
Deasy, Mr J.
Denning, Misses
Denton, Mr Carl
Dickman, Mr and Mrs
Dockstader, Miss L. S.
Donigan, Mr John
Donovan, Mrs J.
Douglass, Mr John
Drake, J. H.
Dunbar, Miss E. M.
Dunn, Dr and Mrs R. K.
Dunn, Mr and Mrs
Dunn, Miss
Earhardt, Mrs E. V.
Eagan, Mrs J. P.
Eaton, Mrs H. J.
Eaton, Mrs E. J.
Elkington, Mr James E.
Ellsworth, J. W.
English, Mr and Mrs Francis
Ernst, Mr Henry
Fallon, Mr and Mrs William
Fabian, Mr Ernest M.
Farnham, Mr John
Fassonan, Mrs E.
Fitzgerald, Mrs B.
Fitzgerald, Miss
Flescher, Miss Nellie
Forbes, Mrs
Ford, Miss N.
Fowler, Miss L. F.
Fuller, Mr and Mrs W. P., Jr.
Fusier, Mrs
Galvin, Mr
Gamble, Mr J. M.
Ganghran, Mrs M.
Gansmer, Miss Flora
Garthorne, Mr G. H.
Geishaker, Miss M.
Gilmore, Miss F. A.
Goldman, Mrs C.
Goldman, Miss Ernestine

Gorman, Miss
Graves, Miss
Gray, Miss Annie L.
Gregg, Miss
Griffin, Miss Charlotte
Griffin, Mr W. D.
Grunhagen, Miss Charlotte
Gschwandner, Professor
Gummer, Miss Lillian
Hallihan, Mrs Thomas
Hamley, Mr J. S.
Hammond, Mrs
Hamilton, Mrs N.
Hanks, Mr W. S.
Handford, Miss E. V.
Harding, Miss E.
Harper, Miss Lulu
Hart, Mr
Hart Mrs H. S.
Hauseman, Mrs
Haymanson, Professor A.
Heiman, Mrs C.
Heney, Miss
Hewlett, Mr and Mrs Frederick
Heyman, Miss Kittie R.
Hill, Mr E. P.
Hill, Mr and Mrs E. W.
Hopkins, Miss
Hopkins, Mr and Mrs Moses
Hopkins, Mrs Peter
Hopkins, Miss Mae
Howe, Miss Susie
Hoyt, Mr F. W.
Huf, Miss Louise
Irish, Colonel and Mrs J. P.
James, Mrs T. K.
Jenkins, Miss Clara
Jenkins, Mr B. P.
Johnstone, Miss Imogen
Jordan, Mrs L.
Joseph, Miss Nellie
Keenan, Mrs L.
Keefe, Mrs K.
Kelly, Mrs J. F.
Kernan, Miss

338

Kilham, Mr H. D.

King, Mrs E. J.

Kline, Miss R. M.

Knapp, E. G.

Kneib, Mr and Mrs G. W.

Kohler, Miss M.

Kopp, Mrs Chas.

Koster, Mrs W. A.

Krebs, Mrs

Kuntze, Mr R.

Kupfer, Miss Rosina

Kusel, Mr S. A.

Lada, Madame

Lake, Mr Geo. W.

Lartigue, Mr J. P.

Lanfar, Mrs A. L.

Lavinson, Miss A.

Lawless, Mrs

Lawlor, Miss

Lawson, Mrs E.

Leckie, Mrs R. B.

Lejeal, Professor

Levy, I. G.

Levy, Mr and Mrs M.

Little, Mrs S. J.

Littlefield, Mrs

Littell, Mrs H. W.

Lopez, Mrs M.

Loring, Miss Grace

Lubbert, Miss

Lyons, Mr Thos. F.

Maguire, Miss

Maguire, Mr James

Maitland, Mrs M.

Manders, Mrs H.

Massen, Mr Alexander

Maxwell, Mr Henry

Martin, Mr Leslie W. R.

Marsh, Mrs H. D.

Mayers, Mrs J.

McChesney, Miss Alice

McChesney, Mr and Mrs J. B.

McClelland, Mr and Mrs John

McClure, Mrs J. P.

Melvin, Miss S. J.

McCrellis, Mrs B. F.

McDonough, Mrs A.

McDonough, Mr J. M., Jr.

McDonald, Mrs J. M.

McGregor, Maj. Thomas

McIntosh, Mr Charles

McIntosh, Mr and Mrs H. P.

McKinn, Mrs

McLean, H. W.

Mergenthaler, Miss

Merriman, Miss Fannie

Merrriman, Dr A. F., Jr.

Meyer, Mr Geo. H.

Michaels, Mr A.

Miller, Mr and Mrs

Miller, C. O. G.

Motte, Mme E. de la

Monk, Mrs H. P.

Moore, Miss Clara

Morris, Mrs M. E.

Morrison, Mrs T. H.

Mosher, Mr.

Mott, Ernest A.

Muncy, William G.

Murdock, Mrs William

Murphy, Miss Annie

Nippert, Mrs L.

Noble, Miss Pearl

Norman, F. G.

Norwood, Mrs R. E.

Palmer, Mr and Mrs George

Palmer, Prof H. C.

Pancoast, Dr F.

Parker, F. L.

Parkhurst, Mrs N. N.

Patrick, Mrs Lulu B.

Patterson, Mrs W. M.

Pattiani, Mr and Mrs W. L.

Peters, Miss Lillian

Pfund, Miss Amelia

Pieper, Mr Henry C.

Pierce, Mr and Mrs Joseph

Poulsen, Mrs M. S.

Ptetson, Mr M. B.

Pugsley, Mrs

Purdy, Mr A. J.
Purdy, Miss Eloise
Quinia, Mrs T.
Racoullait, Miss
Randall, Miss Mary
Rapp, Mrs J.
Rappin, Miss E.
Rappin, Miss Victoria
Raymond, Miss
Redmon, Dr and Mrs
Redmon, Miss Maud
Redmon, Miss Stella
Roeckle, Prof Joseph
Reid, Mrs G.
Reindl, Prof J. J.
Remillard, Mrs D.
Rendall, Miss May
Reynolds, Miss Alice
Reynolds, Prof Clark
Reynolds, Miss Edith
Reynolds, Miss Eva
Reynolds, Miss D. M.
Reynolds, Mr S. H.
Richards, Mrs T. E.
Richardson, Miss Lizzie
Roberts, Miss Zeno
Robertson, Mr E. B.
Robinson, Mrs J. J.
Rogers, Miss Lottie
Ross, Mr
Ross, Mrs George
Rutherford, Mrs H. M.
Ryan, Miss Fannie
Ryan, Miss Lizzie
Sadler, Mr and Mrs Caleb
Samuels, Mrs F. S.
Saunders, Mr Cole
Schaap, Mrs Charles
Schernstein, Prof Carl
Schneider, Miss Lily
Schram, Mrs H. A.
Schulz, Miss
Sesnon, Mr Robert F.
Shaner, Mr Charles
Shearer, Mrs George

Sherwood, Miss Lily
Sherwood, Miss Theresa
Sholl, Miss
Sichel, Prof Abe
Simmons, Mr Geo. O.
Smith, B. J.
Smith, Mrs F. L.
Smith, Mr Geo. O.
Smith, Miss Phoebe
Smith, Mrs R. B.
Smith, Mrs S. P.
Smith, Miss Theresa
Snyder, Mrs Melville
Solomons, Miss
Soto, Jose
St. Amant, Mr W. A.
Staples, Mr and Mrs D. J.
Staniels, Mrs C. B.
Starr, Mr and Mrs Geo. A.
Summers, Mrs E.
Starrs, Mr and Mrs A. E.
Starr, Mr and Mrs Geo. A.
Sullivan, Mrs J.
Taylor, Mrs
Taylor, Mrs S. H.
Taylor, Mrs W. C.
Taylor, Miss Emma
Thomas, Mrs Clara
Thomas, Miss Alice
Thomas, C. F.
Thomas, Miss T.
Thompson, Mrs Charles E.
Thompson, Mrs F. R.
Tittle, Miss Carrie
Turner, Miss
Tuttle, Miss Jennie
Ulrich, Mrs Alvin
Ulrich, J. Alvin
Vinzent, Mr E. G.
Walker, Mrs J. M.
Walker, Mrs William
Walker, Mrs C. H.
Walton, Mr
Ward, Dr and Mrs J. W.
Warren, Alfred

Weaver, Mrs
Webb, A. B.
Webb, Mrs C. H.
Webb, E. Carter
Weber, Mr C. F.
Weigel, Miss Ada
Werner, Mr
Watkins, Mrs H. W.
Whaites, Miss E. B.
Walsh, Mr J. C.
Whalin, Miss
Whalin, William
Wharf, F. L.
Wiehe, Mrs
Wilder, Mr E. H.
Williams, Mrs J. L.

Wilson, Miss M. Rey
Wilson, Alice
Wilson, C. M.
Wissell, Mr A.
Winslow, Herbert H.
Wood, Miss Isabel
Woolner, F. J.
Wrinkle, Mrs L. J. F.
Wysham, Professor H. Clay
Wysham, Mrs H. Clay
Wynne, Mr Chas.
Young, Miss S. M.
Zacharias, Mr and Mrs Z.
Zifferer, Professor
Zifferer, Mme. Billioni

311

Sadik Club

Rooms 2319 Mission Street, Excelsior Hall

The Sadik Club was organized February, 1887, with eight charter members.
objects are the promotion of acquaintance and the cultivation of social interec
among its members; also advancement in such literary and other subjects as
Club may decide upon. The membership is limited to 70 members, 35 active
35 associate.

OFFICERS

WALLACE L. THOMPSON	President
MISS FLOY A. SARLE	Vice-President
PHILIP A. FISHER	Secretary
MISS LILLIE M. WHITE	Treasurer
J. ALLEN PARSONS	Sergeant-at-Arms

HONORARY MEMBERS

Prof Silas A White   Hon Horace Davis
Prof Ebenezar Knowlton   Rev J. A. Cruzan
Judge Robert Ferral   Mr Chas. Murdock
Prof D. C. Stone   Mr H. W. Barnard
Mr Jas. D. Meeker   Mr Earnest McCullough
             Mr A. W. Gunnison

MEMBERS

ACTIVE

Andrews, Harry A.	Lindsley, Wm.
Curtis, Marvin	McQuitty, W. A.
Cookson, Wm. B.	Melendy, Harry W
Chapin, Geo.	McCullough, Chas.
Deacon, M. G.	Newkirk, John
Deacon, Frank	Parsons, J. A.
Fisher, Philip A.	Poland, Harry F.
Fisher, Lumon S.	Rix, Hale
Harris, Norman C.	Somers, Frank A.
Harper, Fred G.	Spear, Lewis E.
Hendry, J. Easton	Stone, Chas. F.
Haseltine, Chas. W.	Scott, Harry
Heywood, Fred	Symington, Samuel
Lightner, Harry	Thompson, Wallace L.
Libbey, Dorville	White, Henry, Jr.
Lindsley, Howard	Wheeler, George

ASSOCIATE

Ashton, Miss Lily	Moore, Miss Laura
Bartlett, Miss Finnie E.	Roberts, Miss Carrie
Brownell, Miss Alice R.	Reid, Miss Annie M.
Bullock, Mrs John	Ruthrauff, Mrs Wm.
Greene, Miss Bertie	Sankey, Miss May
Harris, Mrs N. C.	Stone, Miss Josie L.
Hilton, Miss Martie	Sarle, Miss Floy A.
Johnson, Miss Bertha	Sarle, Miss Hautie
Lightner, Miss Halcyon	Scott, Miss Edna
Lyman, Miss Isabel	White, Miss Lily M.
Lyman, Miss Emma L.	Warden, Miss Christie E.
Melendy, Miss Lelia	Warden, Miss Florence A.
McIllriach, Miss Effie	Winter, Miss Annie

Nos Ostros Dancing Club

Keenan, Miss Ala	Phoebe, Miss Elsie
Keenan, Mr Jos. B.	Phoebe, Mr Fred S
Kenna, Miss Blix	Pixley, Mr Will
Leviston, Miss Stella	Platt, Dr F. L.
Leviston, Mr F.	Sclingheyde, Mr C. E.
Lyons, Mr A. E.	Shannon, Miss May
Mays, Mr	Shell, Miss Lena
Macdonald, Mr B.	Skinner, Mr J.
Melrose, Miss May	Stoddard, Mr
Miller, Miss Mary E.	Sullivan, Miss Angela
Mooser, Mr Louis H.	Sullivan, Mr T.
Mooser, Mrs Louis H.	Sullivan, Mr W.
Mooser, Miss Alice	Sweeney, Mr Jas. P.
Mooser, Mr Chas. E.	Topping, Miss Daisy
Mooser, Jr., Mr Wm.	Topping, Mr F. E.
Morrison, Miss Fannie	Whitlock, Mr E. P.
Murphy, Mr E. J.	Wittram, Mr F.
Nelson, Miss Amelia	Wood, Miss Mattie
O'Connell, Mr R. C.	Woolrich, Mr Geo
Parker, Mr J. P.	

HOTELS

NAPA SODA SPRINGS

The LEADING SPA OF CALIFORNIA.

Climate Uniform and Agreeable, Free from Malaria and Cold Sea Air, Health Giving Natural Mineral Water, Natural Scenery Unsurpassed, Grand Mountain Landscape, Fragrant with Flowers, Health, Beauty, Satisfaction

For beauty of natural scenery, pleasant climate the year round, solidity of improvements and healthfulness of natural mineral water the noted NAPA SODA SPRINGS has no equal in the entire United States. Its natural advantages are rare and unsurpassed. Its pure sparkling springs of water, dry atmosphere, clear and balmy sunshine, even temperature, gentle breezes in the hottest seasons, varied and extensive views of mountains, plain and watered landscape and sweet aroma of fruit and flowers, make it a gratifying haven of rest for the pleasure seeker and a paradise for the invalid. Here the sojourners may treat themselves to most exhilarating Napa Soda Water baths—hot or cold—and drink the delightful natural beverage from fountains that flow on forever. The costly structures that adorn the premises are built of the solid rock, and will prove as enduring as the mountains on which they stand. Winter and Summer alike the place holds its charms and welcomes both the well and ailing. It stands on the mountain side one thousand feet above the valley. Oranges, lemons, palms. figs and olives, as well as other fruits and ornamental trees line its paths and beautify its broad acres, while the air is fragrant the year round with the incense of blooming flowers. The sunlight penetrates every sleeping-room, there are gas and water in every building, a music-hall for concerts and dancing, and billiards and ten-pin alleys for ladies and gentlemen. There is a fascination about the varied attractions of NAPA SODA SPRINGS that holds strangers and visitors by its charm and makes them bide at this point long beyond their allotted time. The place contains over one thousand acres and is a princely abode for pleasure-seekers as well as those in feeble health. OPEN ALL THE YEAR ROUND. Address,

JACKSON & WOOSTER,

NAPA SODA SPRINGS P. O.

RESIDENTS

Napa Soda Springs

Mrs. Edward Stanley (*Palace Hotel*)
Mr. and Mrs. H. W. Hyman & family
Mr. and Mrs. J. P. Jackson and family
Mr. S. J. Tripler and family
E. Rochat and family
Mr. and Mrs. C. H. Jackson
Mrs. Ira Pierce and family
Mrs. Jno. Garber
Miss Amy. McKee
Mrs. J. B. Wooster and family
Geo. R. Shreve
Mr. R. B. Woodward (*Maison Riche*)
Timothy Hopkins and family
Mr. and Mrs. Geo. H. Roe
Mrs. Henry Dutton
Miss Etta Tracy
Dr. and Mrs. Kenyon
Mr. and Mrs. Hiram B. Chase
Mr. & Mrs. Geo. Whipple } 308 Van Ness
Miiss Lizzie Whipple
D. G. Waldron and wife
A. H. Small
Mr. and Mrs. E. B. Pond
Mr. Walter M. Painter
Mr. and Mrs. Basil Heathcote
Geo. A. Low and family
Chas. L. Holbrook and family
John J. O'Brien
Miss Minnie Nightingale
Mr. and Mrs. John Nightingale
Mr and Mrs. Hamilton Page
Edw. P. Danforth and wife

Miss E. B. Garber
Mrs. Carlton C. Coleman
Louis Sachs and family
Mrs. Crowell and family
Mrs. Grant Boyd and family
F. T. Luty and family
Capt. Ludlow and Miss Ludlow
Miss Belle W. Garber
Miss Nellie McKee
Mr. and Mrs. J. M. Kilgarif
Mr. and Mrs. F. W. Hutchinson
N. P. Cole and family
Mr. & Mrs. P. S. Wooster (*H. Pleasanton*)
Mr. and Mrs. Samuel Middleton
Mrs. Geo. H. Tay and family
Dr. and Mrs. Albertson
Dr. McNutt and family
Mr. & Mrs. Albert Gallatin and family
Mr. and Mrs. Adam Grant
John Boggs and family
Miss Nellie Jolliffe
Miss Nettie Moyle
P. A. Finigan and family
Chauncey Taylor
Lieut. E. F. Qualtrugh and wife
J. H. Boalt and wife
S. L. Terry and wife
Miss Georgie Nightingale
Joseph B. Nightingale
H. S. Foote and family
Juo. A. Stanley and wife
Capt. John Metcalf and wife

Resort."

AUSTIN WALRATH, President   GEO. M. PERINE, Manager

TELEPHONE 991

SANTA CRUZ

 Rock Paving C.

BITUMINOUS ROCK

LAWN TENNIS COURTS A SPECIALTY

Office, 302 Montgomery Street SAN FRAN

VIEWS OF THE CELEBRATED HOTEL DEL MONTE, MONTEREY, CAL.
The most magnificent seaside establishment in the world.

BEACH AND GROVE

LIFE AT PACIFIC GROVE · MONTEREY, CALIFORNIA.

THE GREAT FAMILY RESORT OF THE PACIFIC COAST.

THE CALIFORNIA

(EUROPEAN)

SAN FRANCISCO

HORD & KINZLER, MANAGERS

This New and Elegant Hotel was opened for the
Reception of guests December 1, 1890

It is unquestionably *the* hotel of the Coast. The building is owned and built by the Macdonough estate, and neither time, money nor labor has been spared to make the hotel meet every demand of its patrons. The architect was originally J. M. Wood, of Chicago, but during the last year the building has had the personal supervision of Mr. E. F. Preston, the attorney for the estate. The style of architecture is Romanesque—round towers at the two ends fronting Bush street. The material used in construction is pressed brick and terra cotta. The general appearance of the building is severely chaste, and its correct outlines are a pleasing contrast to the broken lines and projecting windows seen in the majority of houses in this city. The hotel has eight entire stories; the ninth is a half story in the towers, from which a magnificent view is obtained, and considered already the choice location in the house. The finishing throughout is in hard woods, selected especially for this purpose and cut quartering, which gives the most beautiful markings of the grain. The lumber was bought in Chicago, cut, polished and carved there and sent here ready for use. The ninth, eighth and seventh floors are finished in natural oak, the sixth and fifth in red birch, the fourth and third in sycamore, the second in bird's-eye maple, and the ground floor in antique oak. The furniture of the rooms is in woods to match the wood finish. The hotel contains one hundred and thirty-five guest rooms, fitted up in the most complete manner, all *en suite*. The walls are finished in stippled oils in the most delicate tints, selected to harmonize with the colors of the carpets, and blending from wall tint to a lighter shade in the ceiling. The effect is soft and subdued, and is an immense improvement on the usual white wall. The wooden mantels are of the latest style, and the rooms are lighted with handsome bronze electroliers, arranged for the burning of gas as well.

The bath-rooms connected with the apartments have tiled floors and porcelain tubs. The plumbing is of the most approved pattern, all piping uncased and the system of ventilation perfect. There is not a single dark or inside room in the house. On the upper floor is a spacious ball-room, with supper-room attached, and in the tower at the west end is a delightful sitting-room for ladies.

The *loggia*, or seventh floor, is so called from the small balconies on which the front windows open. This is one of the many inviting features of the new hotel. The balconies are reached through long French windows, with stationary glass either side, thus giving admittance to a generous supply of sun and light. Filled with

FIC COAST.

THE CALIFORNIA

(EUROPEAN)

SAN FRANCISCO

HORD & KINZLER, MANAGERS

This New and Elegant Hotel was opened for the
Reception of guests December 1, 1890

It is unquestionably *the* hotel of the Coast. The building is owned and built by the
Macdonough estate, and neither time, money nor labor has been spared to make the
hotel meet every demand of its patrons. The architect was originally J. M. Wood, of
Chicago, but during the last year the building has had the personal supervision of Mr.
E. F. Preston, the attorney for the estate. The style of architecture is Romanesque—
round towers at the two ends fronting Bush street. The material used in construction
is pressed brick and terra cotta. The general appearance of the building is severely
chaste, and its correct outlines are a pleasing contrast to the broken lines and projecting windows seen in the majority of houses in this city. The hotel has eight entire
stories; the ninth is a half story in the towers, from which a magnificent view is
obtained, and considered already the choice location in the house. The finishing
throughout is in hard woods, selected especially for this purpose and cut quartering,
which gives the most beautiful markings of the grain. The lumber was bought in
Chicago, cut, polished and carved there and sent here ready for use. The ninth,
eighth and seventh floors are finished in natural oak, the sixth and fifth in red birch,
the fourth and third in sycamore, the second in bird's-eye maple, and the ground floor
in antique oak. The furniture of the rooms is in woods to match the wood finish.
The hotel contains one hundred and thirty-five guest rooms, fitted up in the most
complete manner, all *en suite*. The walls are finished in stippled oils in the most
delicate tints, selected to harmonize with the colors of the carpets, and blending from
wall tint to a lighter shade in the ceiling. The effect is soft and subdued, and is an
immense improvement on the usual white wall. The wooden mantels are of the latest
style, and the rooms are lighted with handsome bronze electroliers, arranged for the
burning of gas as well.

The bath-rooms connected with the apartments have tiled floors and porcelain
tubs. The plumbing is of the most approved pattern, all piping uucased and the
system of ventilation perfect. There is not a single dark or inside room in the house.
On the upper floor is a spacious ball-room, with supper-room attached, and in the
tower at the west end is a delightful sitting-room for ladies.

The *loggia*, or seventh floor, is so called from the small balconies on which the
front windows open. This is one of the many inviting features of the new hotel.
The balconies are reached through long French windows, with stationary glass either
side, thus giving admittance to a generous supply of sun and light. Filled with

plants and trailing vines the little balconies will be miniature hanging gardens, and be a delightful lounging place on a summer afternoon or moonlight night. When ready for occupation the hotel will be furnished throughout. The carpets will be of the finest material—Wilton in the choice rooms, others and halls in Moquette. The reception and ladies' reading-rooms, on the second floor, which are finished in bird's-eye maple of a satin-like texture are model apartments. The furniture of the reception rooms and private parlors are covered with magnificent brocades and Aubison tapestries, and the reading and writing room is fitted up with all the concomitants that can be desired. At the east end of the second floor are the billiard-room and the private dining-rooms, finished in antique oak. In the center of the hall is the promenade or balcony, which overlooks the spacious lobby below, and where the hotel guests can enjoy a postprandial stroll without the trouble of going on the street.

On the ground floor, in the center of the building, is the main office, handsomely finished in antique oak. Across one end is an immense fireplace, with carved oak panels and pillars. At the different openings into the office are panels of oak two and a half feet wide and nine feet high with beautiful markings. To the right of the office is the gentlemen's reading-room finished in Moorish arches and oriental frescoing and on the left is the smoking room. The broad oaken staircase winds up from the side, and next is the elevator opposite which is a cozy reception room for ladies with a street entrance. This avoids the publicity of walking through the office. At the extreme left of these rooms, opening from hall and street, also from a rear hall in the hotel is the Cafe, 125 feet long, finished in oak with mirror panels and tiled floor. At the end of the Cafe there are two round windows or grills, back of which a band of music will be stationed during dining hours. The table service of the Cafe is the same as that of the Cafe Savarin, the best appointed in New York—Baccarat cut-glass, rolled china and silver service. The Cafe will be governed by the most stringent rules, no ladies unaccompanied by escorts being admitted after five o'clock. The management proposes giving San Francisco a Delmonico, so that anyone wishing the best can find it, something hitherto impossible, hence it will compete with nothing on the Coast.

The electric system is simply perfect: · The lighting is from a plant in the basement of the hotel, where there are three 80-horse-power engines with 2,500 lights and also an arc-light machine. The dynamos are interchangeable, consequently the giving out of one cannot affect the lighting of the hotel, as the power will be at once supplied from another machine. In every room are return call-bells, one to the bell-boy's room on the same floor and one to the general office. Each room is also supplied with an automatic fire alarm. The danger from fire is rendered *nil* by the extreme precautions taken. In every hall are standing reels of fire hose, and the building is fire-proofed from floor to floor with concrete and iron lathing, so that no open space was left before putting up the partitions. There are also fire-escapes from the outside of the building.

The hotel will be under the management of Joseph Hord and A. F. Kinzler, who are thoroughly *au fait* in all matters pertaining to establishments of this kind, having many years' experience with the first houses of New York City. San Francisco will have for the first time a perfect hotel, built and furnished in the most complete manner—one that will challenge comparison with those of the Eastern cities, and of which the residents here may well be proud. The cuisine is of a peculiar excellence and service perfect.

Palace Hotel

S. F. THORN, MANAGER

Reception Day—*Monday*

Alvord, Mrs William
Ames, Mr and Mrs Fisher
Barton, Mr and Mrs John
Beebe, S. J.
Belcher, W. C.
Blanding, Mr and Mrs G.
Breyfogle, Dr and Mrs E. S.
Brown, W. E.
Carroll, Miss
——Miss F.
——John
——George L.
Chapman, Mr and Mrs W. S.
Clark, Mr and Mrs C. H.
Coit, Mrs L. H.
Collier, Mrs
Crocker, C. H.
Curry, Judge and Mrs J.
Deane, Mrs E. J.
Decker, Mrs Peter
Delmas, Mr and Mrs D. M.
Dennis, Dr and Mrs F. H.
Eastland, Mr and Mrs T. G.
Easton, Mr and Mrs Wendall
Estee, Mr and Mrs M. M.
English, Mr and Mrs J. M.
Ford, J. A.
Friel, Capt and Mrs D. F.
Friedman, Capt
Fries, Mr and Mrs Wm.
Gilson, Mr and Mrs L.
Goodman, Mr and Mrs T. H.

Goodman, Mrs J. H.
Goodrich, E. D.
Gregory, Mr and Mrs J. N.
Hallett, Mr and Mrs G. H.
Harvey, Mr and Mrs Downey
Herlztein, Dr M.
Hewlett, Mr and Mrs H. H.
Hovey, Mr and Mrs S. D.
Joseph, Mrs E.
Kearney, M. Theo.
Laton, Mr and Mrs C. A.
Liebenthal, Mr and Mrs A.
Lusk, Mr and Mrs A.
Lugsden, Mr and Mrs Jay
Main, Mr and Mrs Charles
Martin, Mr and Mrs J. P.
Mayne, Charles
Melone, Mr and Mrs Drury
——Miss
More, Mrs Sam
Morse, Capt and Mrs H. G.
Mudgett, J. G.
Myrick, Judge and Mrs M. H.
Prescott, Mr and Mrs Geo. W.
Rosenstock, Mr and Mrs S. W.
Ramsdell, Mr and Mrs Ira L.
Sachs, Mr and Mrs Sam
Sachs, Ben
Spruance, Mr and Mrs J.
Jacobs, Mr and Mrs C.
Sawyer, Dr and Mrs A. F.
Shaw, Mr and Mrs C. N.

Simpkins, Mr and Mrs C. H.
—— Miss
Simons, Mr and Mrs P. B.
—— Miss
Smith, Mr and Mrs H. C.
Taggart, Miss
Tilford, E. A.
Towne, Mr and Mrs A. N.
Tubbs, Mr and Mrs A. L.
—— Miss

Turrell, C. B.
—— M. H.
—— Miss
Walkington, Mr and Mrs T. G.
Wilson, Mr and Mrs A. W.
Wenban, Mr and Mrs S.
Whitney, Dr and Mrs J. D.
Wieland, Mr and Mr R. P.
Wood, Miss Nellie
—— J. W.

Lick House

Allen, Commodore T. H.
Andrews, Colonel and Mrs A.
Barnes, Mr and Mrs W. P.
Breon, Mr and Mrs Paul
Beyfuss, W. and family
Briggs, Mrs G. G.
Briggs, Mrs M. H.
Burns, Mrs I. R.
Clark, Dr and Mrs J. J.
Clements, John
Cohen, Mr and Mrs R.
Dana, Mrs D.
Ebbetts, Miss L.
Ebbetts, Mrs M. L.
Godsey, G. P.
Huston, John
Johnson, Mr and Mrs A. P.
Kenitzer, Mr and Mrs Henry
Klein, Mr and Mrs L.
Leach, Captain G. W.
McCreary, Judge J. J.
McKibbin, Mrs M. P.
Monteverdi, T. and family

Moses, Mr and Mrs W. L.
O'Kane, Mr and Mrs W. D.
Paige, C.
Piper, W. A.
Pratt, Mr and Mrs R. H.
Priest, Mr and Mrs P.
Reddy, Mr and Mrs P.
Reile, Mr and Mrs W. J.
Rosenfeldt, Mr and Mrs John
Saxe, Colonel and Mrs P.
Schmidt, Mrs
Soule, K. B. and family
Terry, Mrs D. S.
Thayre, Mrs B. B.
Thayer, Mrs L. H.
Treadwell, John
Trempor, F. E.
Walters, Mrs.
Walters, Miss
Weiland, Mr and Mrs J. H.
Weil, Mr and Mrs C. L.
White, W. H.
Whitney, Mr and Mrs J. R.

Grand Hotel

S. F. THORN, MANAGER

Reception Day — Monday

Allen, Hon J. M.
Becker, Dr G. F.
Becker, Mrs A. C.
Bennett, T. A.
Brice, Mr and Mrs Judge A. G.
Briggs, D. T.
Brown, Mr and Mrs A. M.
Burns, Mr and Mrs I.
Cahill, E. J.
Calm, C. E.
Cammack, J. M.
Curtis, Ed.
Curtis, S. S.
Carey, J. T.
Della Casa, A.
Forsaith, E. W.
Flint, Mr and Mrs Thos.

Flint, Thos., Jr.
Flint, Miss S.
Gordon, Jos.
Hauser, R. W.
Hoyt, Mr and Mrs F. T.
Jewell, T. E.
Leeds, E. F.
McClatchy, Mrs. C.
McClatchy, Misses
Mootrey, Thos., Jr.
O'Leary, F.
Severance, J. S.
Thorn, Mr. and Mrs S. F.
Underhill, Mr and Mrs J.
Wilson, E. J.
Yell, Hon and Mrs Arch

The Renton.

712 Sutter Street

MRS L. W. BROWN

Blethen, C. and family
Gordon, Mrs and Miss
Hennessy, Mrs and Miss
Hollis, Wm. H. and family
Judkins, Mr and Mrs T. C.
McKinne, Mr and Mrs A. W.

Peele, Mrs H. N.
Pressen, Gen and Mrs R.
Sterrett, Mrs and Miss
Smith, Mr and Mrs William T.
Tuttle, Mr A. D.
Tuttle, Mr and Mrs Chas.

Occidental Hotel

WILLIAM B. HOOPER, Manager

Reception Day—*Monday*

Alexander, W. W.
Allen, H. H. and wife
Ashe, W. L. and wife
Ashe, Master
Battams, W.
Bizette, Madam
Blakeman, I. Z. and wife
Blakeman, Miss
Booth, Capt and wife
Breeze, Mrs Thos..
Breeze, Misses
Breeze, W. F.
Brown, Gen W. H. and wife
Chapman, H. S.
Cole, M. B. and wife
Cutting, Gen I. T. and wife
Dewey, W. H.
Donnelly, L. E.
Dorsey, Mrs C. C.
Dorsey, Miss
Guard, Morris
Ellis, R. A. and wife
Fair, Senator Jas. G.
Feist, A and wife
Fillmore, J. A.
Fillmore, Mrs J. A.
Forman, Sands W. and wife
Ghisselin, Dr
Giffen, Miss
Givens, C. G.
Gordon, P. K.
Goodyear, H. G. and wife
Hager, Mrs J. S.
Hager, Miss
Hager, Miss Alice
Hager, Miss Ethel

Hale, I. P.
Hellen, C. C. and wife
Hellen, Master
Hooper, I. G.
Irvine, Jas.
Irwin, Col B. J. D.
Irwin, Mrs
Irwin, Miss
Irwin, Miss A. D.
Jones, Samuel
Kendall, C. B.
Kendig, Dr, U. S. A.
Lathrop, Ariel and wife
Luhrs, Mrs A. E.
Luhrs, Miss Christine
Madden, T. P.
Mann, Harry and wife
Marye, Mr G. T.
Marye, G. T., Jr.
Miller, Mrs Van Buren
Mills, Mrs Grace
Mills Miss
Moorhead, J.
Mundy, J. H.
McCone, James
McKay, T. D.
McMurray, Mr R. and wife.
Newland, Mrs Dr R. E.
Norris, Dr Basil
O'Connor, Mrs M. J.
O'Connor, Miss
O'Connor, Miss A.
O'Kane, W. D. and wife
O'Kane, Master
Payne, Dr Eugene
Perine, G. M. and wife

Perry, John, Jr.
Potter, Dr and Mrs
Powell, A. and wife
Powell, Miss Eva P.
Powell, Miss L. B.
Powell, Miss P. F.
Powers, S. S.
Reed, Rev J. Sanders and wife
Rogers, Arthur
Simpson, Col and Mrs J. H.
Smith, S. Harrison and wife
Stout, Geo. H. and wife

Stubbs, W. E.
Tevis, Miss L.
Toland, Mrs M. B. M.
Watson, C. L. and wife
Watson, Arthur
Watson, Douglas
Weighel, W. McM.
Wickware, G. C. and wife
Woods, Mrs
Woods, Miss
Woods, John S.
Wright, John T.

The Berkshire

711 Jones Street

MRS TRUESDELL

Abbey, Mr and Mrs
Addison, Mr and Mrs T.
Adler, C.
Adler, Misses
Barnett, Mrs Robert
Beck, A. J.
Bent, Mr and Mrs E. F.
Boobst, Mrs
Bottum, Mr
Bunker, Mr and Mrs R.
Bunker, Miss
Buttrick, Mrs
Buttrick, Miss Emma
Caswell, Mrs E.
Coggin, Mr
Davis, Mr
Deering, Mr and Mrs Charles J.
Dickey, Mr and Mrs J. R.
Dwyer, L.
Flagg, C. C.
Ferguson, Mr and Mrs
Forbes, R.
Frederica, Mrs Grosvenor

Hamlin, Mr
Hardy, Mr and Mrs William
Harkey, H. H.
Harding, John
Harpham, Lee
Harrison, Miss Virginia
Herndon, Miss
Hucks, Miss
Hollis, Mr and Mrs Wm.
Hopkins, Mr and Mrs W. B.
Jewett, Fidelia
Kerr, Earl
Keith, Prof and Mrs S. N.
Kinne, Mr and Mrs C. Mason
Kinne, Misses
Laurence, Mr and Mrs
Linderman, Mr and Mrs Dell
Martin, Miss Lillie
Mason, Mrs
Mayer, Josephine
McBride, Mrs
McBride, Misses
McLenegan, Lieut and Mrs

Meyer, Emily
Murray, W. H.
Parks, Dr
Porter, Mrs B. F.
Porter, Miss May
Porter, Miss Sadie
Rhodes, Mrs
Shawhan, Wm.

Storey, C.
Swan, Mr
Warburton, Mrs. H. R.
Wetzlar, Mr and Mrs A. J.
Williamson, S.
Wollweber, Mr and Mrs Theodore
Wollweber, Miss Clara

Hotel Bella Vista

1001 Pine Street

MRS VOLNEY SPALDING

Reception Day—*Thursday*

Brown, Mrs W. B. L.
Bunker, Mr and Mrs W. M.
Burling, J. W.
Bond, C. A.
Brush, Miss Lillie T.
Canfield, Mr and Mrs C. L.
Cecil, Mrs A. P.
Clement, Mr and Mrs L. H.
Dorn, Lieut and Mrs E. J., U. S. N.
Earl, Miss S.
Farquharson, Mr and Mrs C. D.
Fletcher, Lieut and Mrs R. H.
Foster, Mr and Mrs J. F.
Folsom, Mr and Mrs G. T.
Gillig, Mr and Mrs J.
Gummer, Mrs C. V.
Hatch, Miss M.
Hawes, Col and Mrs A. G.
Hooper, Mr and Mrs R. B.
Huntsman, Mrs L. M.
——The Misses
Kellogg, Mr and Miss
Lyon, Pay In'ptr and Mrs G. A.,U. S. N.
McAfee, Mr E.
McAfee, Mrs T. C.
Miller, Mr E. E. W.
Mauldin, Mr and Mrs H.

Mather, Mrs H.
Messersmith, Mr E. T.
Miles, Mr and Mrs D. E.
Marshall, Gen and Mrs E. C.
——Miss
Palmer, Mr and Mrs C. M.
Ryer, Mrs Mary
Ryer, Mr and Mrs F. F.
Ritchie, Mr and Mrs W. J.
Sherman, Dr and Mrs H. M.
Saunders, Col Cole and Mrs
Spalding, Mrs Volney
Sinton, Col and Mrs R. H.
——Miss Lizzie
Stone, Mr J. C.
Townsend, Mr and Mrs E. W.
Tracy, Mrs A. F.
Tracy, Mr T. F.
Tracy, Mr Wm. E.
Turnbull, Gen and Mrs W.
Throckmorton, Miss S.
Vandewater, Mrs R. J.
Wilson, Mr and Mrs F. M.
Waters, Miss Lillian
Wallace, Dr and Mrs W. S.
Weller, Mrs C. L.

Hotel Pleasanton

SUTTER STREET

MRS M. E. PENDLETON

Reception Day—*Monday*

Albertson, Dr and Mrs	Hall, Mr and Mrs M. R.
Allen, Mr R. J., Jr.	Hawkins, Mr and Mrs V. A. Caesar
Belden, Mrs D.	Jackson, Mr J.
Burns, Mr C. J.	Kenyon, Dr and Mrs C.
Baker, Mr and Mrs A.	Lewis, Mr and Mrs A. J.
Bovee, Mr and Mrs W. H.	McKay, Mrs E. J.
Bishop, Mr and Mrs Ira	Mozeley, Mrs B.
Clayton, Mrs Chas	Manchester, Mr E. W.
Cragin, Mr Geo. A.	Metcalfe, Capt J.
Cook, Mrs J. E.	North, Mr and Mrs Geo. L.
Cox-Edwards, Mr J. F.	Oulton, Mrs Geo.
Cristy, Mrs P. H.	Poulson, Mrs E. S.
Davis, Mr and Mrs E. G.	Platt, Mr and Mrs C. B.
Douglas, Mrs N. S.	Peterson, Mr E.
De Krafft, Mr J. C. P.	Porter, Mrs A.
Dayon, Mr and Mrs J. W.	Rumboldt, Dr Thos.
Duncan, Dr H. W.	——Miss
Easton, Mrs O. W.	Roe, Mrs P.
——Miss	——Miss
Earl, Mrs Edwin	Sonntag, Mr and Mrs A. P.
Fernald, Mr F. L.	Sonntag, Mr and Mrs Chas.
Fisher, Mr W. E.	Smith, Mr and Mrs G. Frank
Fuller, Mr and Mrs W. P.	Spencer, Mr N. McD.
Frink, Mrs Geo. W.	Smart, Mr and Mrs Geo. C.
Fitch, Mr and Mrs Thos., Jr.	Sheath, Mr A. G.
Finley, Lieut and Mrs J. P.	Shiels, Mr Chas.
Garrick, Mr F. C.	Sparhawk, Miss
Green, Mr and Mrs F.	Strong, Dr and Mrs
Gilmore, Mr and Mrs J. H.	Ten Broeck, Mrs
Gilman, Henry	Tappenbeck, Mr W.
Huntington, Mr and Mrs W. V.	Williams, Mr and Mrs C. H.
Haines, Dr and Mrs	Wooster, Mr and Mrs F. L.
Hawkins, Gen and Mrs	Wightman, Mrs M. A.
Herd, Mr and Miss	Whipple, Mr and Mrs H. L.
Hayes, Mr and Mrs T.	——Mr G. H.
Higgins, Mrs	Wilson, Mr C. H.
——Miss	Wilson, Mrs S.
Hutchon, Mr and Mrs H.	

THE SEA BEACH HOTEL

IS THE

NEWEST, LARGEST, MOST COMPLETE AND MOST

DELIGHTFULLY LOCATED HOTEL in Santa Cruz

Situated in the midst of commodious grounds, the house directly overlooks the broad and curving beach and the bay of Monterey, where is found the finest winter and summer surf-bathing in the world. From the wide verandas the most magnificent and varied marine and mountain views in California are seen on all sides. Its many rooms are handsomely furnished and sunny, while plenty of bath-rooms, fire-places, steam-heaters, electric lights and bells, gas, hot and cold water, are necessary comforts which will be appreciated by all.

❀ ❀ ❀

A Large Dining-Room, Excellent Table and the Best

of Service Throughout the House are Specialties

❀ ❀ ❀

The Beach Station of the Broad Gauge Road is just below the house, and Carriages await Trains at all Depots.

❀ ❀ ❀

For full Particulars, apply to **JOHN T. SULLIVAN, Proprietor**

PROMINENT RESIDENTS

PROMINENT RESIDENTS

PACIFIC COAST

Abbott, A. F.; Fruit-raiser	Marysville, Cal.
Abbott, J. P. Merchant	Antioch, Cal.
Abell, S. P.; Liveryman	Escondido, Cal.
Adams, T. W.; Postmaster	Escondido, Cal.
Adams, Alva; State Governor	South Pueblo, Colo.
Adams, Jewett W.; Ex-Governor	Carson City, Nev.
Allen, C. H.; Prof. State Normal School	San Jose, Cal.
Allen, Wm. L. N.	Salt Lake City, Utah
Allison, J. M.; Stock-raiser	San Diego, Cal.
Anderson, Elias; Real Estate Owner	Anderson, Cal.
Antes, S. G.; Farmer	Valley Center, Cal.
Antony, E. L.; Attorney	Cameron, Tex.
Aram, John	Grangeville, Idaho
Arem, Joseph; Farmer	San Jose, Cal.
Armbrust, B.	Virginia City, Nev.
Armold, C. B.; County Treasurer	Napa City, Cal.
Arnold, B. L.; Teacher	Corvalis, Or.
Arnold, Jesse H.; Merchant	Orange, Cal.
Ashenfelter, H. C.; Real Estate	San Jacinto, Cal.
Ashley, Mrs Mary A.	Santa Barbara, Cal.
Ashwell, George R.	Chilliwack, B. C.
Atkinson, George E.; Supt. Sawmill	Tacoma, Wash.
Atwood, Millen; Bishop	Salt Lake City, Utah
Atwood, Maj. E. B., U. S. A.	San Antonio, Tex.
Augustine, Henry W.; Real Estate	Spokane Falls
Austin, W. H.; Physician	Winters, Cal.
Ayers, C. M.; Farmer	Milpitas, Cal.
Bach, E. W.; Merchant	Helena, Mont.
Bailey, D. H.; Physician	Denison, Texas
Baird, John C.	Cheyenne, Wyo.
Baker, A. C.; Attorney	Phoenix, Arizona

BOVININE Never Becomes Rancid

357

Baker, George W.; Attorney	Eureka, Nevada
Bancroft, F. J.; Physician	Denver, Colo.
Bancroft, W. B.; Publisher.	San Francisco, Cal.
Barbour, A. K.; Attorney	Helena, Mont.
Barbour, Chauncey; Journalist	Walla Walla, Wash.
Barker, W. H.	Astoria, Oregon
Barncastle, J. D.	Las Cruces, N. M.
Barnes, E. H.; Banker	Healdsburg, Cal.
Barnes, L. S., M. D.; Physician	Laramie, Wyo.
Barnhart, G. H.; Maug. San Pedro Mine	Tuscon, Ariz.
Barton, H. M.; Banker ·	San Bernardino, Cal.
Bates, C. M.; Physician	Highland Springs, Cal.
Bates, Geo.; Principal Gymnasium	Berkeley, Cal.
Bates, Benj.; Farmer	Courtland, Cal.·
Bean, C. O.; Civil Engineer	New Tacoma, Wash.
Beans, T. Ellard; Banker	San Jose, Cal. -
Beard, Thos. K.	Prosser, Wash.
Beckman, Wm. Banker	Sacramento, Cal.
Belcher, E. A.; Attorney -	San Francisco, Cal.
Benton, H. M.; Farmer	North Yakima, Wash.
Belt, H. N.; Gen. Manager of Electric Road	Spokane Falls
Bettis, Frank A.; Member City Council	Spokane Falls
Blake, Mrs E. A. C.	Vacaville, Cal.
Blossom, J. A.; Mining Operator	Battle Mountain, Nev.
Blythe, C. E.; Farmer	Farmington, Cal.
Bowen, Robt.; Mining Operator	Silver King, A. T.
Bowman, C. E.; Farmer	Corralitos, Cal.
Boyd, J. H.; Pres. National Iron Works	Spokane Falls
Brackenridge, Geo. W.; Banker	San Antonio, Tex.
Bracht, Frank; Professor of Music	Spokane Falls
Bradley, Cyrus; Director Street Railroad	Spokane Falls
Breck, Geo.	Helena, Mont.
Breene, P. W.; Lieut.-Gov.	Leadville, Colo.
Brickell, E. J.; Pres. Spokane Mill Co.	Spokane Falls
Broadwater, C. A.; Banker	Helena, Mont.
Brook, Henry; Contractor and Builder	Spokane Falls
Brown, Leroy D.; Pres. State University	Reno, Nev.
Brown, Judge M. C.	Laramie, Wyo.
Browne, J. J.; Capitalist	Spokane Falls, Wash.
Brownson, J. M.; Banker	Victoria, Tex.
Bryan, Thos. J.	Miles City, Mont.
Bryne, Dr P. S.; Physician	Spokane Falls, Wash.
Buck, F. H.; Farmer	Vacaville, Cal.
Buckman, Geo. R.; Correspondent	Colorado Springs, Colo.
Bullard, Wm. H.	Miles City, Mont.

Burbank, David, M. D.; Physician	Los Angeles, Cal.
Burgess, F. P.; Newspaper Proprietor	National City, Cal.
Burleson, Rufus C.; Clergyman	Waco, Tex.
Burleigh, H. J.	Dillon, Mont.
Burns, Cyrus R.; Dir. Ross Park Electr. Line	Spokane Falls, Wash.
Butler, R. D.; Supt. Instruction	San Diego, Cal.
Caldwell, E. H.; Merchant	Corpus Christi, Tex.
Calhoun, George V.; Physician	La Conner, Wash.
Campbell, F. M.	Oakland, Cal.
Campbell, John G.; Merchant	Prescott, Ariz.
Cannon, A. M., Banker	Spokane Falls, Wash.
Clark, F. Lewis, Dir. of Spokane Sav. Bank	Spokane Falls, Wash.
Clough, C. F.; Mayor of Spokane Falls	Spokane Falls, Wash.
Cole, George E.; County Treasurer	Spokane Falls, Wash.
Cowley, H. T.; Editor *Chronicle*	Spokane Falls, Wash.
Cowley, M. M.; Cashier Traders' Nat. Bank	Spokane Falls, Wash.
Cushing, Theodore; Manufacturing Agent	Spokane Falls, Wash.
Cutter, Kirtland K.; Architect	Spokane Falls, Wash.
Cutter, Horace L.; Banker	Spokane Falls, Wash.
Campbell, J. C.; Merchant	Grant's Pass, Or.
Camron, W. W.; Capitalist	Oakland, Cal.
Cannon, A. M.; Banker	Spokane Falls, Wash.
Cardon, Thomas B.; Merchant	Logan, Utah
Carey, Alex. H.	Raton, New Mexico
Carlile, J. K.; Farmer	Malheur City, Or.
Carlson, Wm. E.; Real Estate	San Diego, Cal.
Carpenter, M. B.; State Senator	Denver, Col.
Carr, B. O.; Vineyardist	St. Helena, Cal.
Carr, Jessie D.	Salinas, Cal.
Carroll, Edgar B.	Sacramento, Cal.
Carson, George; Merchant	Compton, Cal.
Carson, John; Sawmill	New Tacoma, Wash.
Carver, D. B.; Banker	St. Helena, Cal.
Case, J. W.; Banker	Astoria, Or.
Cass, O. D.; Physician	Denver, Colo.
Castleman, R. M.; Pres. B. of T.	Austin, Tex.
Catlin, A. P.	Sacramento, Cal.
Chadwick, S. F.: Attorney	Salem, Or.
Chalmers, L. H.; Attorney	Phœnix, Ariz.
Chalmers, P. J.; Farmer	Farmington, Cal.
Chamberlain, M. Z.	Berkeley, Cal.
Chamberlain, J. B.	Horse Shoe Bend, Id.
Channel, B. F.; Capitalist	Berkeley, Cal.
Chandler, William S.	Nanaimo, B. C.
Chapin, O. S.; Real Estate	Poway, Cal.

Chapman, E. M.; Capitalist	San José, Cal.
Charles, J. Q.; Attorney	Denver, Colo.
Charles, William	Victoria, B. C.
Chase, Miss Martha	Santa Rosa, Cal.
Chase, John	Cheyenne, Wyo.
Chase, George W.; Capitalist	National City, Cal.
Cheney, A. E.; Attorney	Eureka, Cal.
Chipman, N. P.	Red Bluff, Cal.
Christy, William; Banker	Phœnix, Ariz.
Church, M. J.	Fresno, Cal.
Church, F.; County Treasurer	Denver, Colo.
Churchill, Clark; Attorney	Phœnix, Ariz.
Clapp, Miss H. K.	Carson City, Nev.
Clark, G. J.; Attorney	Kauffman, Tex.
Clark, George J.; Notary Public	Los Angeles, Cal.
Clark, Robert M.; Attorney	Carson City, Nev.
Clark, J. S.; Real Estate	San Diego, Cal.
Clark, H. H.	Helena, Mont.
Clarke, Asa; Physician	Stockton, Cal.
Clarke, W. J.	Buffalo, Wyoming Ty.
Clayton, N. W.	Salt Lake City, Utah
Clayton, A. W.	Salt Lake City, Utah
Clayton, James A.; Real Estate	San Jose, Cal.
Clayton, George R.; Physician	Sherman, Tex.
Cleveland, A. C.; Stock-raiser	Cleveland, Nev.
Cleveland, E. M.; Real Estate	Santa Ana, Cal.
Clindinning, J.	Lewiston, Idaho
Cluff, H. H.	Provo City, Utah
Cockrell, F. M.; Capitalist	Dallas, Tex.
Cochran, John H.; Speaker State Assembly	Dallas, Tex.
Cockburn, Frank Q.; Mining	Prescott, Ariz.
Cogswell, E. B.; Farmer	Bellota, Cal.
Coke, Richard; U. S. Senator	Waco, Tex.
Colby, L. J.; Horticulturist	Santa Ana, Cal.
Cole, R. E.; Physician	Oakland, Cal.
Cole, A. M.; Druggist	Virginia City, Nev.
Cole, C. K., M. D.; Banker	Helena, Mont.
Collier, J. A.; Merchant	Coquille, Or.
Collins, J. W.	San Diego, Cal.
Colman, James M.; Manager Coal Co.	Seattle, Wash.
Colombet, Mrs Murphy	San Jose, Cal.
Connell, Robert; Merchant	Prescott, Ariz.
Conner, Mrs Louisa A.	La Conner, Wash.
Converse, Mrs C. W.	Cheyenne, Wyo.
Cook, T. N.; Real Estate	Pacific Grove, Cal.

Cooper, E. H.	Eagle Pass, Tex.
Cooper, J. W.;. Farmer	Santa Barbara, Cal.
Corbett, H. W.; Banker	Portland, Or.
Corey, B., M. D.; Physician	San Jose, Cal.
Corlett, W. W.	Cheyenne, Wyo.
Cornwall, Clement T.; Lieut.-Governor	Victoria, B. C.
Corus, William C.; Farmer	Pomeroy, Wash.
Cory, David A.; Merchant	Helena, Mont.
Couch, Thomas	Butte, Mont.
Courteney, A. A.; Real Estate	San Bernardino, Cal.
Cowden, James; Farmer	Taison, Cal.
Cox, Frank; Attorney	Phœnix, Ariz.
Cox, J. H. D.; Real Estate	Riverside, Cal.
Cozzens, W. W.; Orchardist	San Jose, Cal.
Craig, L. W.	Salida, Colo.
Crane, G. B.; Physician	Helena, Cal.
Cravath, A. K.; Real Estate	Escondido, Cal.
Crepin, H.; Physician	Tuscon, A. T.
Cresswell, H. T.;`Attorney	Austin, Nev.
Crittenden, H. B.; Real Estate	San Diego, Cal.
Croaks, Edwin W.; Physician	Santa Barbara, Cal.
Cross, W. H.; Clergyman	Saratoga, Cal.
Cunningham, Ed. H.; Capitalist	San Antonio, Tex.
Curry, James E.; Farmer	Lodi, Cal.
Curtis, N. Green; Attorney	Sacramento, Cal.
Cushman, E. B.; Real Estate	Los Angeles, Cal.
Dale, F. W.	Liberty, N. M.
Daly, Marcus	Butte City, Mont.
Darcy, P. M.; Ex-Chief of Police	Los Angeles, Cal.
Dare, D. D.; Banker	San Diego, Cal.
Davis, M. M.; Banker	Yaquina, Or.
Davis, C. W.; Banker	Santa Rosa, Cal.
Davis, E. W.; Banker	Santa Rosa, Cal.
Davis, H. C.; Lieut.-Governor	Carson City, Nev.
Davenport, W.	Helena, Mont.
Dawson, W. J. G.; Physician	St. Helena, Cal.
Deady, Matthew P.; U. S. Judge	Portland, Or.
Dean, Peter; Banker	San Rafael, Cal.
Deal, W. E. F.; Attorney	Virginia City, Nev.
De Courcy, M. L.; Real Estate	Colorado Springs, Col.
Deegan, Ross	Helena, Mont.
Deemer, John A.; Mining, etc.	Georgetown, N. M.
Dennis, G. B.; Pres. Electric Street Railroad	Spokane Falls, Wash.
Diehl, C.	Salt Lake City, Utah
Dillman, L. C.; Real Estate and Inst. Broker	Spokane Falls, Wash.

261

Wedding and Party Invitations Engraved and Printed in Correct Form.

The Bancroft Company, 721 Market Street.

Dimmick, F. M.; Clergyman	Los Angeles, Cal.
Dimoud, William H.; Attorney	Menlo Park, Cal.
Dodge, J. M.; County Clerk	San Diego, Cal.
Doherty, Robert; Farmer	Hanford, Cal.
Dolph, J. N.; U. S. Senator	Portland, Or.
Dormer John; Secretary of State	Carson City, Nev.
Dorrington, J. W.; Journalist	Yuma, Ariz.
Dorsey, Stephen W.; Stock-raiser	Chico Springs, N. M.
Douglas, Benj.	New Westminster, B. C.
Dovey, W. C.; State Supt. Instruction	Carson City, Nev.
Downing, S. N. A.; Physician	Coquille City, Or.
Downs, Francis; Attorney	Santa Fé, N. M.
Drake, M. W. T.	Victoria, B. C.
Drake, B. F.; Capitalist	Salem, Or.
Drew, H. L.; Banker	San Bernardino, Cal.
Driffill, J. A.; Real Estate	Pomona, Cal.
Drumheller, D. M.; V. P. National Bank	Spokane Falls, Wash.
Drummond, J. H.; Vineyardist	Glen Ellen, Cal.
Dunn, E. C.; Pisah	Tombstone, Ariz.
Durham, Nelson W.; Editor	Spokane Falls, Wash.
Durkee, J. E.; Freighter	Tombstone, Ariz.
Dwyer, Col Jos. W.	Raton, N. M.
Dwyer, Edward; Capitalist	San Antonio, Tex.
Dyer, John C.	Rawlins, Wyoming Ter.
Eagan, M. J.	Clifton, Ariz.
Eaman, T. J.; Stock-raiser	Camp Verdi, Ariz.
Earp, Virgil W.; City Marshal	Colton, Cal.
Easton, G. A.; Chaplain	Berkeley, Cal.
Eccles, Thomas; Physician	Helena, Mont.
Eddy, William M.; Banker	Santa Barbara, Cal.
Edgar, G. A.; Merchant	Santa Ana, Cal.
Edgar, William F.; Physician	Los Angeles, Cal.
Edmonds, Henry V.	New Westminster, B. C.
Edwards, Melvin; Secretary of State	Denver, Col.
Edwards, John; Banker	Santa Barbara, Cal.
Edwards, E. J.; Livestock	Phœnix, Ariz.
Eisenbeis, Charles; Merchant	Port Townsend, Wash.
Eldredge, H. L.	Salt Lake City, Utah
Eldridge, E.; Farmer and Sawmill Owner	Whatcom, Wash.
Elliott, W. S.; Farmer	Linden, Cal.
Elliott, W. T.	Deer Lodge, Mont.
Ellis, Col L. A.; Sugar Planter	Austin, Tex.
Ellis, A. C.; Attorney	Carson City, Nev.
Elsner, J. E.; Physician	Denver, Colo.

Photograph Albums; a full line, bound in Morocco, Seal, Silk and Plush.
The Bancroft Company, 721 Market street

Embody, D.; Banker	Los Angeles, Cal.
Engel, Peter; Jeweler	Marysville, Cal.
Enright, Joe; Orchardist	San Jose, Cal.
Eppenetter, C. G.; Hotel	Santa Barbara, Cal.
Essig, Dr N. Fred; Physician	Spokane Falls, Wash.
Estes, H. W.; Farmer	Baker City, Or.
Evan, John; Ex-Governor	Denver, Colo.
Evans, Mrs. Jane	Chilliwack, B. C.
Evans, J. W.; Real Estate	Phœnix, Ariz.
Ewer, Seneca; Capitalist	St. Helena, Cal.
Failing, Henry; Banker	Portland, Or.
Fair, Mrs Theresa	San Francisco, Cal.
Fair, J. G.; U. S. Senator	Virginia City, Nevada
Fairbanks, H. S.; Banker	Petaluma, Cal,
Fairchild, E. W.; Real Estate	San Jacinto, Cal.
Fairchild, Mrs A.	Stockton, Cal.
Fairweather, H. W.; Banker	Sprague, Wash.
Fallon, E. F.	Hollister, Cal.
Farquharson, A. S.; Merchant	Puyallup, Wash.
Farrell, M. J.	Austin, Nev.
Farrington, Wm.; Capitalist	San Jose, Cal.
Feighan, Col D. B.; Lawyer	Spokane Falls, Wash.
Ferry, James L.; Hotel-owner	Marshfield, Or.
Finfrock, J. H.; Physician	Laramie, Wyo.
Fisher, W. J.; Real Estate	Los Angeles, Cal.
Fisher, Wm. V.; Farmer	Bellota, Cal.
Fisher, D. E.	Butte City, Mont.
Fitch, W. A.; Capitalist	Eagle Pass, Texas
Flanagan, W. H.; Physician	Grant's Pass, Or.
Fleming, John W.; Mining	Silver City, N. M.
Fleming, James; Horticulturist	National City, Cal.
Flint, Thomas	San Jose, Cal.
Flower, F. S.; Real Estate	San Diego, Cal.
Flynn, J. P.; Pres. Saredo Imp. Co.	Seredo, Texas
Flynn, S. R.; Editor	Spokane Falls, Wash.
Folsom, S. M.	Albuquerque, N. M.
Foote, A. D.	Boise City, Idaho
Foote, Frank M.	Evanston, Wyo.
Forman, Charles	Virginia City, Nev.
Forrest, Robert W.; Trader's Nat. Bank	Spokane Falls, Wash.
Fox, Richard; Orchardist	San Jose, Cal.
Fox, Charles A.	Raton, N. M.
Frank, A.	Yuma, Ariz.
Frazier, J. A.; Man. Mineral Water Co.	Carlsbad, Cal.
Freeman, Daniel; Agriculture	Los Angeles, Cal.

French, E. D.; Physician	Poway, Cal.
French, Wm. A.; Farmer	Stockton, Cal.
Fullerton, J. C.; Attorney	Roseburg, Or.
Fulton, R. L.; Journalist	Reno, Nev.
Fyre, Joseph S.; Real Estate	Spokane Falls
Gage, E. B.	Tombstone, Ariz.
Gaines, Judge R. R.; Justice Sup. Court	Austin, Texas
Gallatin, Albert; Merchant	Sacramento, Cal.
Galloway, J. C.; Real Estate	Santa Ana, Cal.
Ganz, Emil; Merchant	Phœnix, Ariz.
Garbatt, F. C.; Real Estate	Los Angeles, Cal.
Gardner, Dan.; Farmer	Saratoga, Cal.
Garrard, William; Supt. U. S. Mint	Carson City, Nev.
Gates, J. E.	Laramie, Wyo.
Geer, G. W.	Raton, N. M.
Geist, A. W.	Pueblo, Colo.
Germain, Edward; Merchant	Los Angeles, Cal.
Germain, Eugene; Merchant	Los Angeles, Cal.
Gibson, Paris; Real Estate	Great Falls, Mont.
Gillis, James; Farmer	Stockton, Cal.
Gilman, A.; Railroad Superintendent	Eureka, Nev.
Gilmer, J. F.	Salt Lake City, Utah
Gilpin, William	Denver, Colo.
Gilson, F. A.; County Recorder	Los Angeles, Cal.
Ginty, W. M.; Real Estate	Ensenada, L. Cal.
Gird, Richard; Capitalist	Pomona, Cal.
Gilliam, Lane C.; Real Estate	Spokane Falls, Wash.
Glass, Chester; Attorney	Spokane Falls, Wash.
Glover, James N.; Pres. First Nat. Bank	Spokane Falls, Wash.
Goodall, F. E.; Manager Wash. Nat. Bank	Spokane Falls, Wash.
Goodin, F. C.; Gen. Manager *Review*	Spokane Falls, Wash.
Goss, John W.; Hardware Dealer	Spokane Falls, Wash.
Gundlach, J. G.; Physician	Spokane Falls, Wash.
Graves, Jay P.; Real Estate	Spokane Falls, Wash.
Given, S. R.	Minidoka, Idaho
Glide, J. H.; Stock-raiser	Sacramento, Cal.
Glenn, J. H.; Merchant	Santa Rosa, Cal.
Glenn, M.; Farmer	Salinas, Cal.
Godbe, W. S.	Salt Lake City, Utah
Goddard, L. M.; District Judge	Leadville, Colo.
Goldschmidt, Adolf; Merchant	Tucson, Arizona
Goodfellow, G. E.; Physician	Phœnix, Ariz.
Goodyear, Mrs. C. V.	Benicia, Cal.
Gordon, J. E.; Farmer	Saratoga, Cal.

Bibles, Prayer Books, Oxford S. S. Teachers' Edition, Episcopal and Catholic. *The Bancroft Company, 721 Market st.*

364

Rare Books   We have the most perfect system for recording orders
                      and picking up Rare and out of print books.
                    The Bancroft Company, 721 Market Street.

Gorham, H. M.; Mining Superintendent	Gold Hill, Nev.
Gasper, J. J.; Real Estate	Los Angeles, Cal.
Graham, P. A.; Merchant	Escondido, Cal.
Graham, W. H.; Real Estate	Cuero, Texas
Grant, John; M. P.	Victoria, B. C.
Grant, James B.; Ex-Governor	Denver, Colo.
Graves, Amos; Physician	San Antonio, Texas
Graves, W. F.; Farmer	Salinas, Cal.
Gray, J. H.	Victoria, B. C.
Gray, John S.	Lewiston, Idaho
Gray, Gordon, Y.; Man. S. San Diego Co.	San Diego, Cal.
Greeg, Joseph W.; Stock-raiser	Monterey, Cal.
Gregg, E. P.; County Judge	Sherman, Texas
Green, E. K.; Capitalist	Los Angeles, Cal.
Green, P. M.; Banker	Pasadena, Cal.
Greene, L. D.; Farmer	Walnut Grove, Cal.
Greene, George B.; Farmer	Courtland, Cal.
Greenwell, Mrs A. C.	Santa Barbara, Cal.
Grether, John; Capitalist	San Diego, Cal.
Griffin, H. L.	Ogden, Utah
Grubbs, V. W.; Attorney	Greenville, Texas
Gruwell, J. D.; Farmer	Farmington, Cal.
Gunnell, A. T.; County Judge	Leadville, Colo.
Gunter Jot; Capitalist	Sherman, Texas
Gusdorf, Alex	Taos, N. M.
Ham, Daniel T.; Wheatgrower	Spokane Falls, Wash.
Hartson, Millard, T.; Probate Judge	Spokane Falls, Wash.
Herrick, Henry A.; Civil Engineer	Spokane Falls, Wash.
Houghton, H. E.; State Senator	Spokane Falls, Wash.
Houghton, Mrs H. E.; Real Estate	Spokane Falls, Wash.
Hoyt, H. M.; Lawyer	Spokane Falls, Wash.
Huber, Oscar; Civil Engineer	Spokane Falls, Wash.
Hughson, W.; Pres Arl'nHt'sMotorR.R.Co	Spokane Falls, Wash.
Hodges, Arthur	Princeville, Or.
Hagan, Martin, M. D.; Physician	Los Angeles, Cal.
Hagar, Geo. C.; Land Owner	Orange, Cal.
Hagerman, James J.; Capitalist	Colorado Springs, Colo.
Haight, E. J.; County Auditor	San Diego, Cal.
Hailey, John	Boise City, Mont.
Hale, O. A.; Merchant	San Jose, Cal.
Hall, Charles V.; Real Estate	Los Angeles, Cal.
Hall, George W.; Manufacturer	Seattle, Wash.
Hall, S. C.	Lewistown, Idaho
Hall, R. M.; Comm. General Land Office	Austin, Texas

Haller, Granville, O.; Major U. S. A.	Seattle, Wash.
Hallet, Moses; U. S. Judge	Denver, Colo.
Hallett, Mrs W. L.	Colorado Springs, Colo.
Haley, Ora	Laramie, Wy.
Hallock, J. F.; State Comptroller	Carson City, Nev.
Haléy, John; Representative	Boise City, Idaho
Hamilton, T. S.	Butte City, Mont.
Hammond, R. P.; U. Surveyor-General	San Francisco, Cal.
Hansl, A.; S. A. and A. P. R. R.	San Antonia, Tex.
Hanthorn, J. O.; Canner	Astoria, Or.
Hardenbrook, E. H.	Deer Lodge, Mont.
Hardesty, E. P.; State Senator	Wells, Nev.
Hardin, C. H. E.	Wabuska, Nev.
Harding, E. J.; Land Owner	Gervais, Or.
Harford, F. G.; Banker	Pataha City, Wash.
Harlocker, L.; Farmer	Coquille, Or.
Harlow, J. C.; State Printer	Carson City, Nev.
Harold, A. M.; Farmer	Farmington, Cal.
Harris, T. L.; Vineyardist	Santa Rosa, Cal.
Harris, M. C.; Merchant	Pataha City, Wash.
Harris, Wm. A.; Attorney	San Bernardino, Cal.
Harris, L. B.; Engineer	San Diego, Cal.
Harrison, F. H.; Physician	Evanston, Wy.
Hart, Archibald; Real Estate	San Diego, Cal.
Harvey, James	Nanaimo, B. C.
Harvey, J. S.; Horticulturist	San Diego, Cal.
Hawley, T. H.; Supreme Judge	Carson City, Nev.
Hawthorn, Mrs R. L.	East Portland, Or.
Hayford, J. H.; Physician	Laramie, Wy.
Haynes, J. P.; Farmer	Genoa, Nev.
Hazard, Henry T.; Attorney	Los Angeles, Cal.
Headley, J. H.	Bisbee, Ariz.
Heath, Russel; Assemblyman	Carpinteria, Cal.
Hecht, Charles	Cheyenne, Wy.
Hedges, Cornelius; Journalist	Helena, Mont.
Heilbron, August; Capitalist	Sacramento, Cal.
Heitman, F. M.	Eureka, Nev.
Hellman, I. W.; Banker	Pasadena, Cal.
Helm, J. C.; Supreme Justice	Denver, Colo.
Helmcken, J. S.; M. P. C. S.	Victoria, B. C.
Hemtz, J. E. P; Physician	Monterey, Cal.
Henderson, J. J.; Attorney	San Diego, Cal.
Henley, Barclay; Attorney	Santa Rosa, Cal.
Henry, John L.; Attorney-at-Law	Dallas, Texas
Henry, Francis	Olympia, Wash.

Henry, A.	Moscow, Idaho
Hensley, G. B.; Real Estate	San Diego, Cal.
Hereford, B. H.	Tuscon, Ariz.
Herff, F.	Laredo, Texas
Hauser, S. G.; Ex-Governor	Helena, Mont.
Hewlett, H. H.; Banker	Stockton, Cal.
Hilgard, E. W.; Prof in University	Berkeley, Cal.
Higgins, H. I.; Mining Operator	Denver, Colo.
Higginbottom, J. W.; M. E.	Grass Valley, Cal.
Hill, Harry C	Salt Lake City, Utah
Hill, William; President Water Works	Petaluma, Cal.
Hill, J. L.; Physician	Albany, Or.
Hinckley, H. G.; Stockraiser	Beowawe, Nev.
Hinds, George; Collector of Customs	Wilmington, Cal.
Hitchcock, Hollis; Capitalist	Petaluma, Cal.
Hobson, F. W.; Merchant	San Jose, Cal.
Hoefler, Joseph; Merchant	Tombstone, Ariz.
Holiday, William H.	Laramie, Wyo.
Holland, F. T.; Capitalist	San Jose, Cal.
Holden, E. S.; Director Lick Observatory	San Francisco, Cal.
Holgate, E.; Judge	Corvallis, Or.
Holmes, Charles	Bozeman, Mont.
Hood, Mrs E. A.	Santa Roza, Cal.
Hooks, J. F.; Physician	Paris, Texas
Horton, Dexter, Banker	Seattle, Wash.
Howard, Oliver O.; Major-General U.S.A.	Gov. Isl., N. Y.
Howard, Bryant; Banker	San Diego, Cal.
Howard, Judge Sumner	Prescott, Ariz.
Howbert, Irving; State Senator	Colorado Springs, Colo.
Howland, C. C. Man. Electric R. R.	Los Angeles, Cal.
Howell, J. W.	Bisbee, Ariz.
Hubbard, A. W.; Fruitraiser	Anderson, Cal.
Humphrey, J. F.; Mayor	Colorado Springs, Colo.
Hunton, John	Cheyenne, Wy.
Hurd, Columbus	Stockton, Cal.
Hurd, E. R.	Cheyenne, Wy.
Hurt, Judge J. M.; Court of Appeals	Dallas, Texas.
Hussey, J. C.; Capitalist	National City, Cal.
Hustler, J. G.; Merchant	Astoria, Or.
Hutton, C. E.; Principal High School	Santa Rosa, Cal.
Hutton, A. W.; Superior Judge	Los Angeles, Cal.
Ink, T. H.; Farmer	St. Helena, Cal.
Inman, M. F.; Farmer	St. Helena, Cal.
Irvine, Thomas H.	Miles City, Mont.

Jacks, David; Capitalist	Monterey, Cal.
James, W. S.	Gold Hill, Nev.
Jenkins, Col D. B.; Lawyer	Spokane Falls, Wash.
Jefferson, Thos. E.; R. Estate & F. Insur.	Spokane Falls, Wash.
Jennings, Frank W.	Salt Lake City, Utah
Jennings, Hyde; Attorney	Fort Worth, Tex.
Jewett, S. P.; Capitalist	Lamanda Park, Cal.
Johnson, Alex.	Granville, B. C.
Johnson, Joel H.	Kanab, Utah
Johnson, Thomas; Merchant	Ellensburg, Wash.
Johnson, S. S.; Manager Lumber Co.	National City, Cal.
Johnson, F. M.; Attorney	Corvallis, Or.
Johnson, A. R.	Nanaimo, B. C.
Johnson, A.; Farmer	Saratoga, Cal.
Johnson, A. R.; Attorney	Burnett, Tex.
Johnson, George; Lawyer	Spokane Falls, Wash.
Jones, J. P.; U. S. Senator	Gold Hill, Nev.
Jones, O. S.	Seattle, Wash.
Jones, J. H.	Helena, Mont.
Jorres, G. W.; Postmaster	San Diego, Cal.
Kampmann, Mrs Caroline	San Antonio, Tex.
Kaufman, I. S.; Real Estate	Spokane Falls, Wash.
Kearby, J. C.; Attorney	Dallas, Tex.
Keating, R. P.; Mining Supt.	Virginia City, Nev.
Keller, M. B.; Physician	San Diego, Cal.
Kellogg, Martin; Prof. in University	Berkeley, Cal.
Kelly, Henry; Mayor	Grant's Pass, Or.
Kendall, B. F.; Stock-raiser	Stone, Or.
Kenedy, Capt. Mifflin; Capitalist	Corpus Christi, Tex.
Kennedy, William F.; Real Estate	Spokane Falls, Wash.
Kettle, G. E.	Denver, Colo.
Kiesel, Fred J.	Salt Lake City, Utah
Kimball, Frank A.; Capitalist	National City, Cal.
Kimball, Nelson F.	Boise City, Idaho
Kimberlin, Prof. J. M.	Santa Clara, Cal.
King, T. H.; Stockman	Greenville, Tex.
Kinnaud, J. M.; Judge Superior Court	Spokane Falls, Wash.
Knapp, R. B.; Merchant	Portland, Or.
Knight, E. W.; Banker	Eagle Pass, Tex.
Knippenberg, Hon. H.; Mining	Glendale, Mont.
Koch, P.	Bozeman, Mont.
Lacy, A. E.	Tucson, Ariz.
Ladd, W. S.; Banker	Portland, Or.
La Dow, Stephen W.; Rancher	Los Angeles, Cal.

Diaries. Publishers of the Pacific Coast Diaries containing specially prepared information for the Pacific coast. *The Bancroft Company, 721 Market st.*

368

Laidlaw, J. A.	New Westminster, B. C.
Lamb, Charles C.	Los Angeles, Cal.
Lamb, John M.	Boise City, Idaho
Lampert, G. B.; Banker	Monrovia, Cal.
Lampert, Lockhart Henry	Socorro, N. M.
Land, William	Sacramento, Cal.
Landrum, R. W.; Real Estate	San Diego, Cal.
Langdon, W. W.	Moscow, Idaho
Langley, M. D.	Skull Valley, Ariz.
Langsdorf, J. M.	Ogden, Utah
Latz, James A.; Capitalist	San Jose, Cal.
Leach, A. M.; Lumber	Brownsville, Cal.
Le Bach, J. W.; Clergyman	Paris, Tex.
Lee, John	Lander, Wyo.
Lee, Hamilton; Clergyman	Oakland, Cal.
Lee, O. F.; Physician	Marysville, Cal.
Leech, Chas. W.; Mining Operator	Tombstone, Ariz.
Lehnherr, C.; Farmer	Myrtle Point, Or.
Leiser, J. J.; Physician	Helena, Mont.
Lewy, Augustus, Mayor	Temple, Texas.
Lemme, R. W.; Viticulturist	St. Helena, Cal.
Leonard, W. A.; Publisher	Silver City, N. M.
Leonard, O. R.; Supreme Judge	Carson City, Nev.
Leonard, H. C.; Real Estate Owner	Portland, Or.
Lerch, Frank, Real Estate	San Angelo, Texas
Lewin, Louis; Merchant	Los Angeles, Cal.
Lewis, W. R.	New Westminster, B. C.
Lewis, Meyer; Merchant	Los Angeles, Cal.
Lewis, T. T.	Ketchum, Idaho
Lindley, Hervey; Real Estate	Los Angeles, Cal.
Lindsay, John M.	Lewiston, Idaho
Lippett, E. S.; Attorney	Petaluma, Cal.
Lipscombe, J. M.; Farmer	Saratoga, Cal.
Littlefield, Sheldon; Capitalist	Santa Ana, Cal.
Look, P. H.; Stockman	Santa Ana, Cal.
Locke, George S.; Farmer	Lockeford, Cal.
Lockhart, Wilson; Physician	Spokane Falls, Wash.
Lockwood, Frank; Vineyardist	St Helena, Cal.
Logsdon, J. N.; Capitalist	San Jacinto, Cal.
Loomis, Abner	Fort Collins, Colo.
Love, John	Chico Springs, N. M.
Lowthian, Thomas	Denver, Colo.
Luce, M. A.; Attorney	San Diego, Cal.

Lynch, W. H.; Newspaper Correspondent	Spokane Falls, Wash.
Lyons, W. J.; Real Estate	San Diego, Cal.
Mabary, Frank; Real Estate	San Jose, Cal.
Macbeath, Donald; Contractor	San Jacinto, Cal.
Mack; C. E.; Attorney	Virginia City, Nev.
Macleay, Donald; Banker	Portland, Or.
Macniel, H. L.: Real Estate	Los Angeles, Cal.
Macy, Everett; Mining Operator	Pinal, Ariz.
Magee, S. L.; Farmer	Clements, Cal.
Magee, H. M.; Capitalist	Pasadena, Cal.
Malpas, A.; Farmer	Saratoga, Cal.
Mansfield, G. H.; Capitalist	Lakeside, Cal.
Manson, Peter; Physician	Goldhill, Nev.
Manville, H. S.	Cheyenne, Wyo.
Marcy, Russell	Raton, N. M.
Markham, V. D.; Attorney	Denver, Colo.
Markham, H. H.	Pasadena, Cal.
Marsh, T. E.; Farmer	Saratoga, Cal.
Marsh, R.	Laramie, Wyo.
Marshall, James T.	Leadville, Colo.
Marshall, C. H.; Rector	Denver, Colo.
Marshall, W. H.; Repres. No'rn R'way	Spokane Falls, Wash.
Martin, J. C.; Farmer	Dayville, Or.
Martin, C. J.; Capitalist	Santa Rosa, Cal.
Martin, J. H.; Lumber Operator	Carson City, Nev.
Mason, C. P.	Salt Lake City, Utah
Mast, D. B.; Farmer	Pomeroy, Wash.
Mater, Charles	Leadville, Colo.
Matthews, Judge J. C.; Attorney	Lampasas, Texas
Matz, N.; Catholic Pastor	Denver, Colo.
Maxey, S. B.; U. S. Senator	Paris, Texas
McAllister, James P.	Tombstone, Ariz.
McCarty, John; Physician	McKinney, Texas
McCarty, Daniel; Farmer	Sacramento, Cal.
McClelland, W. T.; Physician	Denver, Colo.
McCutcheon, Col I. D.; Attorney	Helena, Mont.
McDonald, A. D.; Express Agent	Saratoga, Cal.
McFadden, James; Real Estate	Santa Ana, Cal.
McFadden, John; Merchant	Santa Ana, Cal.
McGarvey, W. V.; Postmaster	Salinas, Cal.
McGraw, J. H.; Sheriff	Seattle, Wash.
McHaley, George W.; Farmer	Prairie City, Or.
McKay, Angus	Walla Walla, Wash.

McKinley, S.	Los Angeles, Cal.
McKisick, L. D.; Attorney-at-Law	Oakland, Cal.
McLane, A. L.; Capitalist	San Antonio, Texas
McLaren, John; Real Estate	San Jacinto, Cal.
McLaughlin, Ed.; Banker	San Jose, Cal.
McMeans, A. C.; Teacher	Santa Rosa, Cal.
McNaught, James; Attorney	Seattle, Wash.
McNaught, J. F.; Attorney	Seattle, Wash.
McVicker, John	Salt Lake City, Utah
Meacham, H. M.; Assessor	St. Helena, Cal.
Meigs, J. J.; Physician	Elko, Nev.
Melrose, Richard	Anaheim, Cal.
Menomy, J. B.	Lewiston, Idaho
Metcalf, James B.; Attorney	Seattle, Wash.
Meyers, John; Farmer	Oregon City, Or.
Millay, Jerry; Banker	Phœnix, Ariz.
Miller, John; Civil Engineer	Walnut Grove, Cal.
Miller, James; Dairyman	San Rafael, Cal.
Miller, Jacob; Livestock	Mayer, Ariz.
Miles, Nelson A.; General U. S. Army	Chicago, Ill.
Mills, Mrs	Mills Seminary, Cal.
Miley, James	Reddington, Ariz.
Minear, John I.; Mining	Jackson, Cal.
Ming, Mrs Katharine L.	Helena, Mont.
Mitchell, John H.; U. S. Senator	Portland, Or.
Mitchell, H. M.; Real Estate Owner	Los Angeles, Cal.
Mohr, Paul F.; Civil Engineer	Spokane Falls, Wash.
Monroe, W. N.	Monrovia, Cal.
Monteith, C. C.	Wallace, Idaho
Morgan, T. G.; Mining	Battle Mountain, Nev.
Moore, Frank R.; Capitalist	Spokane Falls, Wash.
Moore, F. L.; Merchant	Tombstone, Ariz.
Moore, F. Rockwood; Merchant	Spokane Falls, Wash.
Morehead, A. H.; County Clerk	Silver City, N. M.
Morgan, Hon W. C.; Mayor	Brownwood, Texas
Morris, Fred	St. Helena, Cal.
Morris, B. F.; Land Office	Mount Idaho, Idaho
Morrison, F. P.	Lugonia, Cal.
Morse, E. W.; Real Estate	San Diego, Cal.
Morse, E. H.; Real Estate	San Bernardino, Cal.
Morse, Phil; Lumber	San Diego, Cal.
Mott, T. D.; Capitalist	Los Angeles, Cal.
Mott, S. H.; Manager Lumber Co.	Los Angeles, Cal.
Moulton, L. F.; Farmer	Colusa, Cal.
Moynahan, James; State Senator	Denver, Colo.

The Bancroft Company 49 FIRST STREET, One of the largest and best appointed Printing Offices on the Coast
No better work can be done anywhere
371

Muir, B. L.; Real Estate	San Diego, Cal.
Muller, Judge C. F.	Cheyenne, Wyo.
Murdock, John A.	Beaver City, Utah
Murphy, Barney; Banker	San Jose, Cal.
Murphy, John T.	Helena, Mont.
Murphy, Mrs Mary	San Jose, Cal.
Murphy John	Helena, Mont.
Murphy, W. J.; Farmer	Phœnix, Ariz.
Murphey, Alonzo M; Memb. Loan Ass. Co.	Spokane Falls, Wash.
Murray, David; Capitalist	Ellensburg, Wash.
Murray, Carlisle; Physician	San Diego, Cal.
Murray, William; Stock-raiser	Dayville, Or.
Mussell, Jake; Stock-raiser	Caldwell, Idaho
Nadeau, Geo. A.; Rancher	Florence, Cal.
Naglee, Miss Marie	San Jose, Cal.
Nelson, George; Real Estate	San Diego, Cal.
Nelson, O. B.; Merchant	Spokane Falls
Nettleton, William O.; Real Estate	Spokane Falls
Newbery, A. A.; V. P. Spokane Falls & Northern R. R.,	Spokane Falls
Newlands, T. J.; Physician	Ellensburg, Wash.
Newman, G. O.; Engineer	Riverside, Cal.
Newmark, M. H.; Merchant	Los Angeles, Cal.
Nicholson, Dan W.; Attorney	Eagle Pass, Texas
Nicols, J. G.; Capitalist	Los Angeles, Cal.
Nichols, H. B.; Capitalist	Spokane Falls
Nolan, Geo. N.; Real Estate	San Diego, Cal.
Noland, George; Attorney	Astoria, Or.
Norman, N. S.; Journalist	Spokane Falls
Noon, John J.; Mining	Nogales, Ariz.
Norton, J. G.; Viticulturist	St. Helena, Cal.
Norton, O. O.; Farmer	Lodi, Cal.
Norton, E. S.; Farmer	Saratoga, Cal.
Norton, D. C.; Man. Land and Water Co.	Temecula, Cal.
Oates, J. W.; Attorney	Santa Rosa, Cal.
O'Brian, Morris; Capitalist	San Jose, Cal.
O'Brien, J. D.	Denver, Colo.
Obiston, F. F.; Mining Supt.	Idaho Springs, Idaho
O'Connell, Eugene; Catholic Clergyman	Los Angeles, Cal.
O'Connor, Thomas M.; Banker	Victoria, Texas
O'Connor, J. W.; Physician	Salida, Cal.
O'Connor, Myles P.; Farmer	San Jose, Cal.
Odle, James	Mt. Idaho, Idaho
Olmsted, E. D.; Physician	Spokane Falls

O'Neill, William O.; Journalist	Prescott, Ariz.
Orchard, G. F.; Banker	New Tacoma, Wash.
Ormsby, O. C.; Physician	Logan, Utah
Ornelas, P., M. D.; Mexican Consul	San Antonio, Texas
Ostrander, John Y.; Attorney	Seattle, Wash.
Oudin, Chas. P.; Pres. Wash. Pottery Co.	Spokane Falls
Packard, C. A ; Real Estate	Riverside, Cal.
Paine, Sumner; Farmer	Meridian, Cal.
Parchen, H. M.; Merchant	Helena, Mont.
Parish, J. L.; Clergyman	Salem, Or.
Parks, J. F.; Mining Supt.	Amador City, Cal.
Parkhurst, W. A.; Real Estate and Ins.	San Jose, Cal.
Parkhurst, A. L.; Real Estate	San Luis Obispo, Cal.
Parsons, R. J.	Woodbridge, Cal.
Patten, L. D.	Caldwell, Idaho
Patterson, T. M ; Attorney	Denver, Colo.
Paul, R. H.	Tuscon, Ariz.
Paul, Samuel	Salt Lake City, Utah
Pauly, A. J.; Real Estate	San Diego, Cal.
Pearson, Henry H.; Arcadia Hotel	Santa Monico, Cal.
Pearson, William C.	Grangeville, Idaho
Pearcy, Edmond	Lewiston, Idaho
Pellit, H. A.; Viticulturist	St. Helena, Cal.
Penfield, C. S.; Physician	Spokane Falls
Percival, D. T.; Banker	Cheney, Wash.
Perkins, A. O.; Real Estate	Santa Barbara, Cal.
Perkins, J. N.; Physician	Pomeroy, Wash.
Perry, Benj. F.; Physician	Aspen, Colo.
Personné, S.; Catholic Clergyman	Las Vegas, N. M.
Peshine, I. H. H.; Post Treasurer	Fort Mojave, Ariz.
Peters, T. W.	Cheyenne, Wyo.
Petsch, A.; Farmer	Cucamonga, Cal.
Pettibone, Jay	Cheyenne, Wyo.
Phipps, S. C.	Modesto, Cal.
Pierce, John B.	Boise City, Idaho
Pinney, James A.	Boise City, Idaho
Pitman, James M.; Searcher Records	San Jose, Cal.
Piutti, William; Professor of Music	Ontario, Cal.
Pleasants, James M.	Winters, Cal.
Foetz, J. G.; Architect	Spokane Falls
Pomeroy, H. E.; Real Estate	Los Angeles, Cal.
Pomeroy, A. E.; Real Estate	Los Angeles, Cal.
Pond, H. M.; Physician	St. Helena, Cal.
Porter, B.; Merchant	Salinas, Cal.

Porter, R. S.	Cameron, Texas
Potts, J. W.; Real Estate	Los Angeles, Cal.
Powell, E. M.; Civil Engineer	Dallas, Texas
Powning, C. C.	Reno, Nev.
Prather, Wm. T.; Farmer	Linden, Cal.
Pratt, William; Fruit-Grower	St. Helena, Cal.
Preble, C. S.; Ex-Surveyor General	Reno, Nev.
Prefontaine, F. X.; Catholic Pastor	Seattle, Wash.
Pressly, J. G.; District Judge	Santa Rosa, Cal.
Price, W. C.; Mining Operator	Tuscarora, Nev.
Price, W. E.; Farmer	Franktown, Nev.
Prim, P.; Superior Judge	Jacksonville, Or.
Preston, W. B.; Bishop	Salt Lake City, Utah
Preuss, E. A.; Postmaster	Los Angeles, Cal.
Preusse, H.; Architect	Spokane Falls
Proctor, E. C.; Artesian Wells	San Jacinto, Cal.
Prouty, C. C.; Farmer	Ione, Cal.
Quinby, S. J.; Physician	Cheyenne, Wyo.
Raas, Joseph C.; Merchant	San Angelo, Texas
Ragsdale, Prof P. C.; Supt. Public Schools	Brownwood, Texas
Ramsden, Charles H.; Banker	Oakland, Cal.
Raverdy, John D.; Catholic Pastor	Denver, Colo.
Raynolds, J.; Journalist	Las Vegas, N. M.
Reaves, J. R.; Newspaper Correspondent	Spokane Falls
Reaves, Thomas; Real Estate and Jeweler	San Bernardino, Cal.
Reed, Charles B.; Druggist	Ellensburg, Wash.
Reed, D. C.; Real Estate	San Diego, Cal.
Reid, William; Banker	Portland, Or.
Reel, A. H.	Cheyenne, Wy.
Renton, William; Sawmill Owner	Port Blakely, Wash.
Reynolds, Merick; Lumber Merchant	San Pedro, Cal.
Reynolds, J.; Physician	Salem, Or.
Rhea, James; Dentist	Denison, Texas
Rhodes, P. J.; County Recorder	Mt Idaho, Idaho
Rice, John C.; Farmer	Salinas, Cal.
Richards, F. S.	Ogden, Utah
Richards, C. J.; Real Estate Owner	Los Angeles, Cal.
Rickey, T. B.; Stock-raiser	Carson City, Nev.
Riebold, J.	Warren, Idaho
Riggins, G. A.; Pharmacist	St. Helena, Cal.
Rimpau, Theo.; Merchant	Anaheim, Cal.
Ringer, L. M.; Merchant	Almota, Wash.
Rives, Henry; Attorney	Eureka, Nev.
Robards, W. C.; Clerk U. S. Dist. Court	San Antonio, Texas

The Bancroft Company want to do some business with you, and are confident they can make prices satisfactory.

274

Roberts, George W.; Real Estate	National City, Cal.
Robertson, James; Farmer	Linden, Cal.
Robinson, H.; Catholic Pastor	Leadville, Colo.
Robinson, Mrs M. S. M.	Colo. Springs, Colo.
Robison, W. O.; Farmer	Stockton, Cal.
Robinson, W. E.; Real Estate	San Diego, Cal.
Robinson, Lyman	Cañon City, Colo.
Robinson, Chas. W.; Exposition Manager	Spokane Falls
Roder, Henry; Capitalist	Whatcom, Wash.
Rogers, W. W.; Gd. Master Odd Fellows	Elko, Nev.
Rogers, W. E.; Real Estate	Los Angeles, Cal.
Roller, Wm. W.	Salida, Colo.
Rose, Aron; Capitalist	Roseburg, Or.
Rose, Innis E.; Attorney	Myrtle Point, Or.
Ross, John E.	Jacksonville, Or.
Ross, A. J.; Vice-Pres. Exchange Bank	Spokane Falls, Wash.
Rossen, Mrs H. J.	Stockton, Cal.
Routt, John L.	Denver, Colo.
Rowe, William H.	Salt Lake City, Utah
Rourke, J. A.; Capitalist	Redington, Ariz.
Routhe, Major E. A.; Real Estate	Spokane Falls, Wash.
Rowell, C.; Physician	Fresno, Cal.
Rowland, Albert; Farmer	Puente, Cal.
Rowland, William R.; Capitalist	Los Angeles, Cal.
Russ, George W.; Capitalist	San Antonio, Texas
Russell, C. W. C.; Attorney	San Bernardino, Cal.
Russell, William H.; Farmer	Linden, Cal.
Russell, W. H. H.; Attorney-at-Law	San Diego, Cal.
Ryder, George W.; Jeweler	San Jose, Cal.
Ryland, C. T.; Capitalist	San Jose, Cal.
Ryerson, George; Governor	Ensenada, Lower Cal.
Sadler, R.; Merchant	Eureka, Nev.
Sampson, A. B.	Tuscon, Ariz.
Sanders, W. F.	Helena, Mont.
Sargent, Cyrus R.; Vineyardist	Minturn, Cal.
Sargent, J. B.; Real Estate	Spokane Falls, Wash.
Savage, James; Farmer	Woodville, Or.
Scheld, Philip; Brewer	Sacramento, Cal.
Schmidt, J., Jr.	Carson City, Nev.
Schmidt, George H.; Physician	San Diego, Cal.
Schneider, L.; Farmer	Redding, Cal.
Schneider, C. P.; Merchant	Santa Ana, Cal.
Schorn, L.; Real Estate	Anaheim, Cal.
Schroeder, J. B.	Raton, N. M.

Printing Department, THE BANCROFT COMPANY, 49 First street, do not claim to be the cheapest printers in town, but give full value to their patrons

Schryoer, A. C.; Merchant	San Antonio, Texas
Scofield, F. N.; Farmer	Phœnix, Ariz.
Scott, Joseph; Stock-raiser	Miles City, Mont.
Scott, Robert	Show Low, Ariz.
Scott, W. M.; Tax Collector	Sherman, Texas
Scott, E. B.; Real Estate	Encinitas, Cal.
Scott, Henry; Farmer	Salinas, Cal.
Scott, Chalmers	San Diego, Cal.
Scribner, C. I.; Editor	Pomona, Cal.
Seaton, T. H.; Capitalist	Honey Grove, Texas.
Seaton, Chauncey B.; Architect	Spokane Falls, Wash.
Seawall, J. A.; Prof State University	Boulder, Colo.
Seymour, S. E.; Lumber	San Bernardino, Cal.
Sharp, J. P.; Farmer	Ellensburg, Wash.
Shaw, T. C.; Farmer	Stockton, Cal.
Shaw, T. C.; County Judge	Salem, Or.
Shaw, Arthur Jay; Architect	Spokane Falls
Shelby, W. S.	Santa Fe, N. M.
Sheldon, Lionel A.; Governor	Pasadena, Cal.
Sheldon, A. Z.; Attorney	Colorado Springs, Colo.
Shelton, L. D. W.; Mngr. Lumber Mill Co.	Seattle, Wash.
Shelton, J. M.; Co. Commissioner	Ellensburg, Wash.
Shepard, Eli T.; Vineyardist	Glen Ellen, Cal.
Shepherd, Jesse; Capitalist	San Diego, Cal.
Shippy, B. J.; Farmer	Santa Clara, Cal.
Short, A. S.; Physician	Los Angeles, Cal.
Shortridge, C. M.; Journalist	San Jose, Cal.
Shuler, J. J.; Physician	Raton, N. M.
Shuler, B. J.; Farmer	Santa Clara, Cal.
Singleterry, E. C.; Banker	San Jose, Cal.
Singleterry, C. F.; County Clerk	San Jose, Cal.
Simmons, G. L.; Physician	Sacramento, Cal.
Simpson, S. P.; Banker	Eagle Pass, Texas
Simpson, William; Physician	San Jose, Cal.
Sisson, George H.; Vice-Pres. Intnl. Co.	Ensenada, Lower Cal.
Skinner, J. D.; County Treasurer	Placerville, Cal.
Slater, M. H.; Mining Supt.	Leadville, Colo.
Slattery, M.	La Cinta, N. M.
Slaughter, W. B.; Livestock	Albuquerque, N. M.
Smith, William; Merchant	Monrovia, Cal.
Smith, Derwent H.	Santa Fé, N. M.
Smith, E. G.; Soda Manufacturer	St. Helena, Cal.
Smith, Samuel C.; Capitalist	Carlsbad, Cal.
Smith, Isador	Idaho City, Idaho

Smith, W. T.; Merchant	Elko, Nev.
Smith, Mrs J.	Oakland, Cal.
Smith, M. D.; County Auditor	Spokane Falls, Wash.
Smythe, Mrs J. H.	Stockton, Cal.
Snyder, A. C.; Cattleman	Cheyenne, Wyo.
Soule, Frank; Prof in University	Berkeley, Cal.
Spalding, Jno.; Episcopal Bishop	Denver, Colo.
Sparks, John; Stock-raiser	Georgetown, Tex.
Spence, C. E.; Ex-Mayor	Los Angeles, Cal.
Spencer, Frank E.; Superior Judge	San Jose, Cal.
Splawn, A. J.; Farmer	N. Yakima, Wash.
Sprague, Otis; Railroad Supt	New Tacoma, Wash.
Sprague, John W.	New Tacoma, Wash.
Squire, W. C.; U. S. Senator	Seattle, Wash.
Stanley, A. C.; Physician	Sam's Valley, Or.
Stanton, Irving M.; Postmaster	Pueblo, Colo.
Stapleton, G. W.	Butte City, Mont.
Starkweather, Alfred; Farmer	Farmington, Cal.
Stayton, Jno. W.; Chief Justice, Sup. Ct.	Victoria, Texas
Stayton, R. W.; Attorney	Corpus Christi, Texas
Stead, J. H.; State Senator	Salida, Colo.
Steele, B. W.; Journalist	Col. Springs, Colo.
Stephens, R. D.; Postmaster	Sacramento, Cal.
Stephens, J. L.; Physician	Boise City, Idaho
Stephens, E. L.; Physician	Silver City, N. M.
Stevens, J. H.; Merchant	St. Helena, Cal.
Stephens, J. A.; District Attorney	Virginia City, Nev.
Stevens, James H.; Farmer	Ellensburg, Wash.
Stevenson, E. J.	Gold Hill, Nev.
Stewart, E.; Farmer	Dayville, Or.
Stewart, W. M.; U. S. Senator	Gold Hill, Nev.
Stocker, George K.; Real Estate	Spokane Falls, Wash.
Stoddard, Dr C. B.; Dentist	Austin, Texas
Stone, T. N.; Educator	Elko, Nev.
Stone, C. P.; Merchant	Seattle, Wash.
Stone, W. F.	Denver, Colo.
Stone, M. N.; Attorney	Virginia City, Nev.
Stone, C. P.; Merchant	Seattle, Wash.
Stone, John H.; Lumberman	Spokane Falls, Wash.
Stout, J. C.; Physician	San Jose, Cal.
Strouss, C. M.; Supt. Instruction	Prescott, Ariz.
Street, Webster; Attorney	Phœnix, Ariz.
Streeter, Rienzi; State Senator	Longmont, Colo.
Striplin, S.; Horticulturist	Valley Center, Cal.
Strong, F. R.; Attorney	Portland, Or.

Complete Line of American and English Poets From Cloth Binding to the very finest Polished Calf. *The Bancroft Company, 721 Market street.*

377

Strong, Solomon, Sr.	Woodland, Wash.
Stuart, Hon Granville; Merchant	Fort Maginnis, Mont.
Sullivan, E. H.; Attorney	Colfax, Wash.
Sullivan, Hon James; Auditor	Helena, Mont.
Swan, Thomas	Cheyenne, Wyo.
Swanholm, Henry	Rocky Bar, Idaho
Swayne, Mrs Belle	National City, Cal.
Syer, Robert; Farmer	San Jose, Cal.
Sylvester, C. W.; Real Estate	Riverside, Cal.
Symington, John; Physician	Santa Fé, N. M.
Tabor, H. A. W.; Ex-Senator, U. S.	Denver, Colo.
Talmage, James E.	Provo City, Utah
Tarke, Luis; Farmer	West Butte, Cal.
Tatum, F. J.; Merchant	Fort Worth, Texas
Taylor, S. W.	Hudson, N. M.
Taylor, Henry T.; Civil Engineer	Pomona, Cal.
Teague, John	Victoria, B. C.
Teller, H. M.; Ex-Secretary of Interior	Denver, Colo.
Temple, J. E.	Chico Springs, N. M.
Tenney, H. B.; Publisher	Tuscon, Ariz.
Thatcher, W. F.; Physician	Dallas, Texas
Thatcher, Moses	Logan, Utah
Thatcher, John A.	Pueblo, Colo.
Thomas, W. W.; Real Estate	Escondido, L. Cal.
Thomas, P. R.; Supt. Insane Asylum	Pueblo, Texas
Thombs, P. R.; Physician	Pueblo, Colo.
Thompson, John; Farmer	Woodbridge, Cal.
Thompson, E. W.	Beaver City, Utah
Thompson, D. P.; Banker	Portland, Or.
Thompson, Jesse E.; Physician	Las Cruces, N. M.
Thompson, W. F.; Horticulturist	Bernardo, Cal.
Thorne, William; Bishop	Salt Lake City, Utah
Threadgill, John; Capitalist	Taylor, Texas
Thurlow, George M.	Yuma, Ariz.
Tibbits, George W.	Squak, Wash.
Tillman, E. M.; Physician	Dallas, Texas.
Tilton, Henry L.; Real Estate	Spokane Falls, Wash.
Tisdale, W. D.; Banker	San Jose, Cal.
Todd, Robert B.	Phœnix, Ariz.
Torreyson, J. D.; District Attorney	Carson City, Nev.
Trenchard, C. J.; County Clerk.	Astoria, Or.
Llewellyn, W. H. H.	Las Cruces, N. M.
Trezevant, J. T., Jr.; Banker	Dallas, Texas
Tritle, F. A.; Governor	Prescott, Ariz.
Trullinger, J. C.; Mayor	Astoria, Or.

Tubbs, Silas; Farmer	Ione, Cal.
Tubbs, A. S.	Calistoga, Cal.
Tucker, E. P.	Dillon, Mont.
Tullidge, Edw. W.	Salt Lake City, Utah
Turner, D. McNeill; District Attorney	Corpus Christi, Texas
Turner, George; Lawyer	Spokane Falls, Wash.
Tustin, Mrs Mary	Tustin City, Cal.
Utt, Lysander; Merchant	Santa Ana, Cal.
Van Houten, B. C.; State Senator	Spokane Falls, Wash.
Van Zandt, Mrs F. S.	Menlo Park, Cal.
Van Alstine, J. R.; Farmer	Ellensburg, Wash.
Vanderherst, William; Merchant	Salinas, Cal.
Van Scoy, Thomas; Pres Williamette Univ	Salem, Or.
Vickers, J. V.	Tombstone, Ariz.
Violett, J. W.; Farmer.	Ione, Cal.
Wallace, Joseph; Capitalist	Pasadena, Cal.
Wallis, Talbot H.; State Librarian	Sacramento, Cal.
Walker, J. H.; Farmer	Pataha City, Wash.
Warburton, Joseph; Bishop	Salt Lake City, Utah
Ward, Rev William G.; Pres Spokane Col.	Spokane Falls, Wash.
Warfield, Mrs Kate	Glen Ellen, Cal.
Waring, George L.; Fruit-grower	Riverside, Cal.
Warner, Wm.; Farmer	Saratoga, Cal.
Warner, H. C.; Raisin-grower	Fresno, Cal.
Warren, F. E.; Governor	Cheyenne, Wyo.
Waters, Frank A.; Livestock	Colorado Springs, Colo.
Watson, Rev Thos. G.; Presb. Minister	Spokane Falls, Wash.
Weaks, W. P.; Vineyardist	St. Helena, Cal.
Webb, G. W.; State Treasurer	Salem, Or.
Weber, G.	Moscow, Idaho
Webster, D. J.; Attorney	Elko, Nev.
Webster, Edgar J.; Lawyer	Spokane Falls, Wash.
Weedin, Thos. F.	Florence, A. T.
Welch, C. H.; Capitalist	Taylor, Texas
Wells, E. W.; Mining Operator	Prescott, Ariz.
Whally, J. W.; Attorney	Portland, Or.
Whipple, J. C.	Cheyenne, Wyo.
Whitcomb, E. W.	Cheyenne, Wyo.
White, B. F.; Governor	Dillon, Mont.
White, Stephen M.; Lieut.-Governor	Los Angeles, Cal.
Whitehill, H. H.; Sheriff	Silver City, N. M.
Whitney, A. L.; Real Estate	Riverside, Cal.
Whittier, Mrs A. M.	Riverside, Cal.

Wilcox, A. W.; Physician	Laredo, Texas
Williams, Mat; Farmer	Salinas, Cal.
Williams, Ben	Bisbee, Ariz.
Williams, W. L.; Attorney	Dallas, Texas
Williams, D. B.; Farmer	Pataha City, Wash.
Williams, E.	Carson, Nev.
Williams, Mr and Mrs George Briggs, Jr.	Baird, Cal.
Williams, George H.; Attorney	Portland, Or.
Willis, Henry W.; Judge	San Bernardino, Cal.
Wilson, E. H.	Benicia, Cal.
Wilson, Mrs. B. D.	San Gabriel, Cal.
Wilson, B. F.; Mining Operator	Galena, Nev.
Wilson, Henry L.; Lawyer	Spokane Falls, Wash.
Wilson, A. J.; Methodist Minister	Spokane Falls, Wash.
Wise, H. A.; Farmer	Pomeroy, Wash.
Withers, G. G.; Journalist	Pueblo, Colo.
Witmer, H. C.; Real Estate	Los Angeles, Cal.
Wood, Chas. B.	Grangeville, Idaho
Wood, Fremont; Attorney	Boise City, Idaho
Wood, F. L.; Farmer	Dayville, Or.
Woodmansee, Chas.; Capitalist	Ogden, Utah
Wooldridge, A. P.; Banker	Austin, Texas
Wrathall, James; Stock-raiser	Grantsville, Utah
Wren, Thos.; Attorney	Eureka, Nev.
Yerrington, H. M.; Gen'l Supt V. & T. R.R.	Carson City, Nev.
Yesler, H. L.; Banker	Seattle, Wash.
York, W. E.; Vineyardist	St. Helena, Cal.
Yorkum, B. F.; Gen'l Mgr S. A. & A.P.R.R.	San Antonio, Texas
Young, J. W.	Salt Lake City, Utah
Young, C. S.; Ex-State Supt. Pub. Inst.	Carson City, Nev.
Zeiger, Charles; Merchant	Albuquerque, N. M.
Zulick, C. M.; Governor	Prescott, Ariz.

Rare Books We have the most perfect system for recording orders and picking up Rare and out of print books. *The Bancroft Company, 721 Market Street.*

380

STATE AND SAN FRANCISCO CITY AND

COUNTY OFFICIALS

ELECTED NOV. 4, 1890

Governor, Henry H. Markham
Lieutenant Governor, John B. Reddick
Secretary of State, Edwin G. Waite
Controller, Edward P. Colgan
State Treasurer, James R. McDonald
Attorney General, William H. H. Hart
Surveyor General, Theodore Reichert
Clerk of Supreme Court, Lewis H. Brown
Superintendent of Public Instruction, James W. Anderson
Congressman, First District, J. A. Barham
Congressman, Second District, G. G. Blanchard
Congressman, Third District, Jos. McKenna
Congressman, Fourth District, J. T. Cutting
Congressman, Fifth District, E. F. Loud
Congressman, Sixth District, W. W. Bowers
Railroad Commissioner, First District, Wm. Beckman
Railroad Commissioner, Second District, J. M. Litchfield
Railroad Commissioner, Third District, J. W. Rea
Board of Equalization, First District, J. S. Swan
Board of Equalization, Second District, L. C. Morehouse
Board of Equalization, Third District, Daniel Cole
Board of Equalization, Fourth District, J. R. Heffron
Chief Justice of the Supreme Court, William H. Beatty
Associate Justice of the Supreme Court, Ralph C. Harrison
Associate Justice of the Supreme Court, Charles H. Garoutte
Associate Justice of the Supreme Court, unexpired term, J. J. De Haven

State Senator, S. F., Cal., Nineteenth District, J. **Welsh**

State Senator, S. F., Cal., Twentieth District, **Geo. H. Williams**

State Senator, S. F., Cal., Twenty-first District, **W. O. Banks**

State Senator, S. F., Cal., Twenty-second District, **Dan'l H. Everett**

State Senator, S. F., Cal., Twenty-third District, **W. J. Williams**

State Senator, S. F., Cal., Twenty-fourth District, **J. H. Mahoney**

State Senator, S. F., Cal., Twenty-fifth District, **Jas. E. Britt**

State Senator, S. F., Cal., Twenty-sixth District, **Jno. T. Broderick**

State Senator, S. F., Cal., Twenty-seventh District, **J. E. Hamill**

State Senator, S. F., Cal., Twenty-eighth District, **T. C. Maher**

Mayor, **George H. Sanderson**

Auditor, **David Stern**

Assessor, John D. Siebe

Sheriff, **Charles S. Laumeister**

Tax Collector, **Thomas O'Brien**

Treasurer, **J. H. Widber**

Recorder, **Edward B. Read**

County Clerk, **William J. Blattner**

District Attorney, **Wm. S. Barnes**

Attorney and Counselor, John H. Durst

Coroner, **Wm. T. Garwood**

Public Administrator, **A. C. Freese**

Surveyor, **Charles S. Tilton**

Superintendent of Public Streets, Highways and Squares, **Jas. Gilleran**

Superintendent of Common Schools, **John Swett**

Judge of the Superior Court, John Hunt

Judge of the Superior Court, **Daniel J. Murphy**

Judge of the Superior Court, **J. C. B. Hebbard**

Judge of the Superior Court, **A. A. Sanderson**

Judge of the Police Court, **Hale Rix**

Judge of the Police Court, **A. E. T. Worley**

Judge of the Police Court, **H. L. Joachimsen**

Justice of the Peace, **C. F. Wood**

Justice of the Peace, **Frank J. Gray**

Justice of the Peace, **W. G. Brittan**

Justice of the Peace, **George W. F. Cook**

Justice of the Peace, **Charles A. Low**

Gold Pens An endless variety of Gold Pens and Penholders from the celebrated Factory of Mabie, Todd & Co., New York.

The Bancroft Company, 721 Market Street.

382

Supervisor of First Ward, **Henry Evans**

Supervisor of Second Ward, **David B. Jackson**

Supervisor of Third Ward, **James W. Burling**

Supervisor of Fourth Ward, **John B. Curtis**

Supervisor of Fifth Ward, **Washington Ayer**

Supervisor of Sixth Ward, **L. R. Ellert**

Supervisor of Seventh Ward, **George A. Carnes**

Supervisor of Eighth Ward, **P. J. Coffee**

Supervisor of Ninth Ward, **Albert Heyer**

Supervisor of Tenth Ward, **Dennis D. Hunt**

Supervisor of Eleventh Ward, **Charles W. Taber**

Supervisor of Twelfth Ward, **William Wilkinson**

School Director, **F. A. Hyde**

School Director, **Max Brooks**

School Director, **J. H. Culver**

School Director, **William Harney**

School Director, **S. E. Dutton**

School Director, **John I. Sabin**

School Director, **George W. Pennington**

School Director, **John J. Dunn**

School Director, **E. E. Ames**

School Director, **Charles W. Decker**

School Director, **Daniel Sewell**

School Director, **T. P. Woodward**

Judge of the Sup. Court, unexpired term, ending Jan.,'91, **J. McM. Shafter**

Judge of the Sup. Court, unexpired term, ending Jan., '93, **J. M. Troutt**

The Portland Blue Book

and

Pacific Coast Elite Directory

1890

NOTE—The *Italics* designate the Reception Day, the **Bold Face Type,**
the Country Residence

Ackerman, Mr and Mrs Henry; 194 Lownsdale st.
Adams, Edw. R.; 181 Sixth st.
Ahlstedt. Mr John A.; Union Block
Ahpel, Mrs Sarah; 189 Alder st.
Ainslie, Mr and Mrs George; 234 Eighth st.
Akin, Mr Frank S.; 327 W. Park
Alden, Dr H. R.; 167½ First st.
Allen, Mr and Mrs W. F.; 274 Q st., East Portland
Allen, Mr and Mrs Harry C.; Mrs Hill's, 10th and Morrison sts.   *Tuesday*
Allen, Mrs Will. H.; 148 Yamhill st.
Allen, Mr and Mrs H. S.; 321 J st.
Allen, Mr and Mrs E. W.; 171 Second st.
Alvord, W. C.; 228 Taylor st.
Amos, Mr and Mrs I. H.; 474 J st.
———Miss Tillie C.
———W. F.
Anderson, Mrs Alta B.; 320 Second st.
Anderson, Mrs C. C.; 221 B st.
———C. J.
———Miss Carrie
Andrew, Mr John; Oak Club, Sixth and Yamhill sts.
Andrews, Mr and Mrs Geo. H.; Mount Tabor
Andrews, Mr F. Vigne; 368 G st.
———Fred. H. V.
———Miss .

Aram, Mrs Mary A.; 287 Fourth st.
——Miss Mattie L.
——Miss Jennie
Arnold, Mr and Mrs F. K.; 135 Jefferson st.
Arthur, E. M.; Oak Club, Sixth and Yamhill sts.
Arthur, J. M.; 290 Morrison st.
Ashby, Mr and Mrs C. S.; 166 S. First st.
Ashley, Mr and Mrs M. A. A.; 629 S st.
Atkinson, Mr J. L.; 385 Third st.
Atwood, Miss Abbie L.; 111 Main st.
Atwood, Mr and Mrs J. R.; 338 Taylor st.
Atwood, Wm. T.; 191 Seventh st.
Aumack, Mr and Mrs Lyle N.; Seventh and Yamhill sts.
Averill, Wm. C.; 190 Yamhill st.
Ayer, Mr and Mrs W. B.; S. E. cor. King and Salmon sts.

Bach, Mr and Mrs Herman; 209½ Fourth st.
Baker, Mr and Mrs Ezra D.; Stout st., head of Main   *Friday*
Baker, Ernest B.; 168 Eleventh st.
Baker, Mrs Isabel; 231 Tenth st.
Ball, Mr and Mrs Robert L.; 135 W. Park st.
Ball, Mr and Mrs F. D.; 157 Fifteenth st.   *Monday*
Baltes, Mr and Mrs F. W.; 150 E. Park st.
Bartlett, T. Harris; 205 Madison
Baltimore, Mr and Mrs J. M.; 208 Twelfth st.   **Long Beach, Wash.**
Bangs, J. E.; 135 W. Park st.   **Clatsop Beach, Or.**
Barber, Mr and Mrs S. J.; 307 Yamhill st.   **Tioga, Wash.**
——Miss Attie
——Master Roy
Barchus, Mr and Mrs J. H.; 145½ Third st.
Bannore, Mr and Mrs W. H.; 160 S st.
Barnard, Mr and Mrs; 174 Washington st.
Barrett, Mr and Mrs John; cor. Nineteenth and L sts.   *Wednesday*
Bates; Mr Philip S.; 168 Eleventh st.
Battin, Mr and Mrs H. E.; Mount Tabor
Beach, Mr and Mrs Frank E.; 109 Clay st.
Beck, Mr and Mrs Wm.; 214 Taylor st.
Beck, Mr and Mrs John A.; 229 Sixth st.   *Thursday*
Beck, Mr and Mrs F. Allayne; 421 H st.
——Miss Gretchen
——Miss Mohl
——Foster, G.
Beebe, Mr and Mrs Chas. F.; cor. Seventeenth and L sts.
Belcher, Mr and Mrs J. H.; Twenty-first st., near B
——Miss Mabel

Bell, Capt and Mrs Miles; 669 O st., East Portland
——Miss Mary
Bellinger, Mr and Mrs C. B.; East Portland
——Victor C.
——Miss Daisy
——Emmett
Bergman, Mr. J.; 205 Alder st.
——Miss Ida
——N. J.
——Miss Clara
——Miss L.
Bernheim, Edmond; 338 E. Park st.
Bevan, Dr. A. D.; 163 Tenth st.
Biles, Judge and Mrs J. D.; C st., bet. Fifteenth and Sixteenth

——J. Norman
——Miss Bessie
——Miss Daisy
——Miss Leila

Bingham, Mr and Mrs Hugh T.; 407 G st., East Portland
Birmingham, Mr and Mrs J. M.; 404 Fourth st., East Portland
Blakely, Mr and Mrs C. O.; 969 Ninth st., East Portland
——Miss Blanche E.
Bloch, Rev. and Mrs Jacob; 135 Twelfth st.
Boise, Whitney L.; 188 Jefferson st.
Bosworth, Mrs and Mrs F. S.; 155 Alder St.   *Thursday*
Bourne, Jonathan, Jr.; 95 Salmon st.
Bowles, Mr and Mrs C. D.; 5 S. Seventh st.
——Mr and Mrs J. T.
Bowman, Mr and Mrs B. H.; cor. Twelfth and O sts., East Portland
Bradbury, Mrs Emeline; 272 Salmon
Bradley, Mr and Mrs Herbert; 390 C st.   *Tuesday*
Brady, Frank C.; 172 Yamhill st.
Brandes, Mr and Mrs Carl A.; 403 Fourth st.
Brayman, Mr and Mrs Arthur H.; 225 Third st., East Portland
——Miss
Bridges, Mr and Mrs J. B.; 289 Columbia st.
——J. B., Jr.
Brigham, Mr and Mrs P. E.; 71 North Seventeenth st.
Brockenbrough, Mr and Mrs J. B.; 468 East Park st.
Bronaugh, Mr and Mrs E. C.; 294 Morrison st.
——Earl C., Jr.
Brooke, Mr Lloyd; 111 Seventh st.
——Hamilton E.
——T. Scott
——Dr. J. M.

Brown, Rev. Arthur J. and Mrs.; 254 Alder st.   *Wednesday*
——Arthur, Jr.
——De Witt
Brown, Mr and Mrs Frank L.; Twenty-fifth and Hawthorne aves., E. P.
Brown, Capt and Mrs J. A.; 455 East st.
Brown, Clinton H.; Oak Club, Sixth and Yamhill sts.
——Edwd. L.
Buchtel, Mr and Mrs Joseph; 958 Twelfth st., East Portland
Buffum, Mr and Mrs Fred; 272 Salmon st.
Burell, Mr and Mrs A. H.; 54 Ella st.
Burke, Major D. W.; Vancouver Barracks
Burns, Mr and Mrs Walter J.; 153 North Eighteenth st.
Burns, Mr and Mrs W. B.; 187 Sixth st.
Burnside, Mrs Mary J.; cor. Twenty-fourth and J sts. ("Maplehurst")
——Davis W.
——Miss Helen
Burr, Lieut. and Mrs Edwd.; Cascade Licks
Burrell, Mrs M. S.; 204 Madison st.   **Clatsop Beach, Oregon**
——W. F.
——H. A.
——Miss H. S.
Bush, Mr and Mrs D. B.; 455 Fifth st.

Caesar, Eberhard; 229 Ninth st.
Caesar, Clemens; NW cor. Ninth and Taylor sts.
Cake, H. M.; 107 North Fifteenth st.
——Wm.
Cameron, Mr and Mrs J. K.; 227 Salmon st.
Campbell, Mr and Mrs; 48 Montgomery st.
Campbell, Mr and Mrs B; 66 North Twentieth st.
Campbell, Miss Mamie, 969 Ninth st., E. Portland
Canby, Major and Mrs Jas. P.; NW cor 11th and Alder sts.
——James
Capen, Mr and Mrs Ellery; 21 South Fourth st.
——Miss
——Miss Mina
——Frank
——George
Caples, Mr. John F.; 150 Taylor st.
——Miss Jennie
Cardwell, Mr. and Mrs. B. P.; 395 Fourth st.
——Dr H. W.
Carey, Mr. and Mrs. C. H.; 46 North Twentieth st.
Carr, Mrs. Matilda; 340 Second st.
——B. L.

Carson, Mr and Mrs John C.; 183 North Nineteenth st.
——Miss Lizzie
——Miss Ella
Carson, Mr and Mrs J. P.; 86 South Third st.   *Friday*
Carle, Mr and Mrs F. A.; 241 Twenty-first st.
Catlin, Judge John and Mrs; 221 North Eighth st.
——Robert
Cauthorn, Dr and Mrs F.; 115 Hall st.   *Thursday*
Chapman, Annie F.; 338 Taylor st.
Chapman, Mr and Mrs Wm. W.; 273 Twelfth st.
——Winfield S.
Chappell, Mr J. J.; Kamm Block
Charlton, Mr and Mrs A. D.; 155 Alder st.
Chenery, Chas. E.; 205 Madison st.
Child, Mr and Mrs John A.; 235 Ninth st.
Christie, Mr. and Mrs. C. J.; 89 Seventh st.
Clapp, Rev. and Mrs. T. E.; 223 West Park st.
Clark, Mrs J. Fred.; Belmont Park, Mt. Tabor
——Arthur S.
——Geo. Knight
Clarke, Mr. Louis G.; 190 Salmon st:
Clarke, Mrs Orlando; 330 C st.
Clarkson, Mr D. M., Jr.: 259 Ninth st.
Cleveland, Mr and Mrs Geo.; Seventeenth and D sts.
Cleveland, Mr and Mrs Geo. R.; 65 North Seventeenth st.
Coburn, Mrs C. A.; 956 Tenth st., East Portland
Coffee, Mr and Mrs A. J.; 13 North Eighth st.
Coffin, Mr and Mrs Laban; 520 I st., East Portland
Cohen, Mr and Mrs D. Solis; 289 Ninth st.
Cohen, Mr and Mrs Benj. I ; 508 G st.
Cohn, Mr and Mrs Frank M.; 547 G st.
Cohn, Mr and Mrs Henry M.; 245 Sixth st.
Cohn. Mr. Sig. L.; 214 Stark st.
Cole, Mr and Mrs Oliver H.; 60 North Twentieth st.   *Friday*
——Miss Alice Robbin
Cole, Mr and Mrs David; 203 Eleventh st.
Coleman, Mrs Albert G.; 194 Hall st.
Comstock, Mr and Mrs Crœsus; 155 Alder st.
——Artemus J.
Cook, Mr and Mrs E.; Abridgen Building
——Miss May
Cookingham, Mr and Mrs Edward; 51 North Twentieth st.
——Albert
Corbett, Mr and Mrs Henry J.; SE cor. West Park and Madison sts.
Corbett, Mr and Mrs Elijah; 275 Sixth st.
——William

Corbett, Mr and Mrs H. W.; Fifth between Yamhill and Taylor sts.
Colter, Mrs Annette; 160 Yamhill st.
——Miss
Cotton, Mr and Mrs W. W.; 155 Alder st.   *Thursday*
——Mrs. L. W.
Coursen, Mr and Mrs Edgar E.; 66 North Twenty-first st.
Cox, Mr Harry G.; 163 Tenth st.
Cox, Mr and Mrs L. B.; 195 Eleventh st.
Cox, Dr and Mrs Norris R.; West Main and Stout sts.   *Thursday*
Crau, Mr and Mrs John; 32 North Nineteenth st.
Crawford, Mr T. H.; 240 East Park
Croasman, Mr and Mrs A. B.; 254 Columbia st.
Crowell, Mr and Mrs C. H.; 201 Thirteenth st.
Cunningham, Mr and Mrs M. T.; 468 E st.
——Miss Eugenia
——Miss Josephine
Currier, Mr and Mrs Frederick I.; 123 Eighth st.   *Tuesday*

Dalton, Mrs Martha A.; 251 Alder st.
Dalton, Mr and Mrs Wm.; between 7th and 8th and I and J., E. P.
—— Miss
——Miss Carrie
——Willie
Davis, Mr and Mrs R. E.; 145 C st.
Davis, Mr Thomas A.; 163 West Park
Dawson, Mr I. R.; NE cor. F and Twenty-third sts.
Day, Mr and Mrs. L. L.; 422 F st.   *Thursday*   **Dayton**
Dayton, Mr and Mrs Frank; 291 West Park
Deady, Mr and Mrs Ed. N.; 153 Eleventh st.
Deady, Hon. and Mrs. M. P.; 163 Tenth st. *Tuesday* **Clatsop Beach, Or.**
——Paul R.
——Henderson
DeFrance, Mr and Mrs H. M.; 388 Seventh st.   *Tuesday*
——Alexander
——Miss Lillian
——Miss Mamie
DeHart, Mr and E. J.; SW cor. 18th and G *Tuesday* **Clatsop Beach, Or**
——Miss Ella
DeKune, Mr and Mrs Frank; 171 Eleventh st.
——Edward
——George P.
——Aolph
——Otto
DeLashmutt, Mr and Mrs Van B.; 285 Twelfth st.   *Thursday*
DePraus, Mrs. E., 233 Ninth st.

Dodd, Mr and Mrs C. H.; 403 Second st.
——Walter
Dodge, Mr Frank T.; 395 J st.
Dolph, Mr and Mrs C. A.; SW cor. Fifth and Jefferson sts. *Wednesday*
——Hon. and Mrs J. N.
Dosch, Mr and Mrs Henry E.; 193 West Park
Dudley, Mr and Mrs W. L.; 154 South Front st.
Dudley, Mr and Mrs John; 20 Meade st.
Duff, Mr and Mrs J. R.; 228 Yamhill st.
Dunbar, Mrs Agnes; 271 Alder st.
——William
——Dave
——Miss Helen
Dunckley, Mr and Mrs Wm. H.; 163 Tenth st.
Duniway, Mr and Mrs R. H.; East Portland
Dunlap, Mrs Caroline; 246 Washington st. *Tuesday*
——James L.
——Miss Ione
Dunne, Mr and Mrs D. M.; cor. Fifteenth and C sts.
Durham, Mr and Mrs Geo H.; Head of King st.
——Miss Nellie
——Miss Mary
Durham, Mr and Mrs Richard L.; 71 South Third st. *Wednesday*

Earding, Mr and Mrs Richard; 241 Eighth st.
Earhart, Mr and Mrs R. P.; cor. Tenth and Mill
——Miss
——Miss Clara
——Agnes L.
Eastwick, Mr Phil., Jr.; 334 East Park st.
Eaton, Gen. and Mrs Jos. H.; 424 F st.
——Dr. Frank B.
——Miss Louise
——Miss Daisy
Eckenberger, Mr and Mrs H. C.; 230 Taylor st.
Effinger, Mr and Mrs John; Nineteenth and F sts. *Wednesday*
Eggert, Mr and Mrs F.; 248 Columbia st.
Ehrman, Mr and Mrs Edw.; 57 North Nineteenth st.
Eliot, Rev. Mr and Mrs T. L.; 227 West Park st.
Emmons, Mr and Mrs Arthur C.; Riverdale (suburb of Portland)
Emmons, Mr and Mrs Ralph W.; Riverdale
Emmons, Mr and Mrs H. H.; Tibbett's Addition, East-Portland
Espey, Mr and Mrs W. W.; 140 South Water st.
——Miss
——Ella

Eugs, John S.; N. W. cor. Twenty-first and B sts.
Everett, Mr Edward; Oak Club, cor. Sixth and Yamhill sts.
Ewald, Mr and Mrs Ferdinand G.; 226 Twelfth st.
——Miss
Eweigh, Mr and Mrs J. D.; 248 Yamhill st.

Failing, Mr and Mrs Jas. F.; 243 Ninth st.
Failing, Mr Henry; Fifth, bet. Taylor and Salmon sts.
——Miss
——Miss May
——Miss Emily
Failing, Mr and Mrs Edward; 94 Yamhill st.
——Miss Henrietta
-——Miss Milly
Fairfowl, Mr Howard M.; NW cor. Nineteenth and F sts.
——Miss
Fallenius, Mr and Mrs Carl C.; Fulton Park   *Thursday*
Farrar, Mr and Mrs Louis C.; 243 Alder st.   *Tuesday*
Fechheimer, Mrs Clara; 383 West Park st.
Feldenheimer, Mr and Mrs Albert; 192 Lownsdale st.
Ferrera, Mr and Mrs A.; 236 B st.
——J. W.
——Albert
Fiereus, Rev. John F.; 80 Third st.
Flanders, Mr and Mrs Geo. C.; 6th and W sts., East Portland   *Friday*
Flanders, Capt and Mrs Geo. H.; Eighteenth and G sts.
——J. Couch
Fleischner, Mr and Mrs Marcus; 231 Seventh st.
Fleischner, Col. Louis; 107 Third st.
Fleischner, Mr and Mrs Jacob; 231 Seventh st.
——Isaac N.
——Miss Hattie
——Miss Minnie
Fliedner, Mr and Mrs C; 74 Fourth st.
——Miss
——Miss Lillie
Flinn, Dr. and Mrs W. A.; 8th and L sts., East Portland   *Wednesday*
Flower, Mr and Mrs Jas.; 150 Madison st.
Folger, Mr and Mrs Herbert; 163 Tenth st.   *Tuesday*
Forbes, Mr and Mrs C. M.; 126 Salmon st.
Foreman, Mrs H. A ; 201 Seventh st.   *Tuesday and Friday*
——Miss Lucille
Foster, Mr and Mrs John R ; 174 Taylor st.
Frank, Mr and Mrs Geo. P.; 301 Yamhill st.
Friedlander, Mr S. H.; Hotel Portland
——Miss Alice

Gambell, Mr and Mrs A. N.; 413 Seventh st.
——Miss
——Miss Lizzie
——W. B.
Gammons, Mr. Geo. G.; Oak Club, Sixth and Yamhill sts.
Garretson, Mr. and Mrs. W. L.; 82 South Third st.
Gaston, Mr and Mrs Jas.; Salmon, cor. of King st.
Gates, Mrs. John; 324 Second st.
Gautenbein, Rev. and Mrs John; 94 Ninth st.
——Miss Marie F.
——Miss Sophie
George, Mr and Mrs M. C.; 154 Columbia st.
Giesy, Dr. and Mrs. A. J.; 303 Twelfth st.   *Thursday*
Gilbert, Mr and Mrs Wm. B.; 149 Eleventh st.
Gill, Mr and Mrs John; cor. H and Twenty-second st.
Gilmore, Mr Fred. M.; 146 North Seventeenth st.
Gill, Mr and Mrs J. K.; Sixteenth and D sts.
——Mark W.
Gleason, Mr and Mrs Jas.; 502½ E st.
Glisan, Mrs Rodney; Eighteenth and I sts.
-——Miss Carrie
——Miss Florence
——Clarence
-——Rodney
Going, Mr and Mrs J. W.; 393 L st. ("Roselawn").   *Tuesday*
Goldsmith, Mr Berthold; 147 Eighth st.
Goldsmith, Mr and Mrs Bernard; 195 Eighth st.
——Miss Alice
——Milton M.
——Jas. C.
——Louis J.
Goldsmith, Mr and Mrs Solomon; 273 Alder st.   *First Thursdays*
——Hugo B.
——Milton P.
Good, Mr and Mrs Geo.; 467 Ninth st.
Goodsell, Mr and Mrs David; Mount Tabor
Gordon, Mr and Mrs Stuart; F st. near Twenty-Third
Gove, Mr Chas. H.; 468 Seventh st.
——Mrs Alice C.
Gove, Miss Ida; 355 Yamhill st.
Granger, Mr C. C.; 313 Twelfth st.
——J. L.
Green, Mrs H. D.; Cedar Hill
——H. J.
——Hal.

Griffin, Mr and Mrs M. G.; 454 Seventh st.
Gullixson, Mr and Mrs H. F.; 334 Morrison st.
——Miss Annie
Gunst. Mr and Mrs Silas; 384 East Park st.
Gurly, Mr. N.; 153 First st.

Habersham, Mr and Mrs F. E.; Tenth and Harrison sts.
Habersham, Rev. and Mrs B. Elliott; 484 Corbett st.
Habersham, Mr and Mrs Robert A.; 484 Corbett st.
——Elliott
——John P.
——Miss Emma
——Miss E. A.
Hageny, Mrs J. H.; 578 N st.   *Thursday*   Clatsop
Hall, Mr and Mrs Edward; 34 Hooker st.
Handbury, Major and Mrs Thos. H.; Head of King st.
Harbaugh, Mr and Mrs C. K.; 248 Yamhill st.
Harrington, Col and Mrs S. R.; 455 F st.
——The Misses
Harrison, Mr Carey H.; East Portland
Hart, Mr Frank E.; Oak Club, 65 Yamhill st.
Haussman, Mr and Mrs Henry; 194 Alder st.
Hawkins, Mr L. L.; 72 Oak st.
Hawthorne, Mrs J. C.; The Portland Hotel
——Miss
Hayes, Mr and Mrs J. W.; 48 Grant st.
Hegele, Mr and Mrs Charles; 161 12th st.
Heitshu, Mr and Mrs Samuel; L, between 18 and 19 st.   *Wednesday*
——Miss
——Alice
Hersey, Mr and Mrs S. O.; 514 D st. cor Twenty-first st.
——Miss Blanche
Hewett, Mr and Mrs Henry; Mt. Zion, Portland Heights
——Miss Isabella
Hexter, Mr and Mrs L.; 33 North 6th st.
——Miss Esther
Higgins, Mr Frank D.; 214 Main st.
Higgins, Mr and Mrs Wm. L.; 214 Main st.
——Frank D.
——James A.
Hill, Mr and Mrs H. C.; 1122 Eighth st., East Portland
——Chas. E.
Hill, Dr and Mrs Jos. W.; Eighteenth and B sts.
Hillman, Miss Jennie; 32 North Nineteenth st.
Hodgman, Mr M; 231 Main st.

Hogue, Mr and Mrs Harvey A.; 115 Twelfth st.   *Thursday*
——Harry W.
Holcomb, Mr and Mrs Cecil R.; 155 North Fifteenth st.
Holman, Mr and Mrs Edward; 271 Morrison st.   *Thursday*
Holman, Mrs Mary; 221 Tenth st.
——William C.
Holman, Mrs H.; 201 Lownsdale st.
——Frederick V.
——George F.
———Miss Frances A.
——Miss Katherine
Holt, Rev and Mrs W. S.; 331 South First st.   *Wednesday*
Honeyman, Mr. Benj. F.; 291 Tenth st.
Honeyman, Mr and Mrs John; 286 Tenth st.
Honeyman, Mr and Mrs Walter J.; 63 North Nineteenth st.
Howard, R. S., Jr.; 150 Madison st.
Howe, Mr and Mrs J. P.; 346 Eleventh st.   *Thursday*
Hoyt, Mr and Mrs Geo. W.; 153 North Fifteenth st.
——Miss Mattie
——George W., Jr.
Hoyt, Mr and Mrs Henry L.; 133 Seventh st.
——Ralph W.
Hudson, Mr and Mrs H. T.; 383 Ninth st.
———Miss Maud
Hughes, Mr and Mrs Chas A.; 261 Eleventh st.
Hughes, Mr and Mrs Ellis G.; 191 Yamhill st.
Humason, Mr and Mrs Ivan; 29 North Nineteenth st.
Hume, Mr and Mrs Wm. T.; 135 North Twenty-second st.
Hurlbuch, Mr and Mrs T. M.; 1370 Sixth st., East Portland
Idleman, Mr Cicero M.; 241 Sixth st.
Illidge, Mr and Mrs Wm.; 427 I st., East Portland
——Clarence
———Edwin

Irwin, Mr and Mrs Samuel R.; 81 Seventh st.

Jacobs, Mr and Mrs Isaac; 363 West Park st.
Jacobs, Mr and Mrs Ralph; 373 West Park st.   *First Thursday*
Janion, Mr and Mrs Robt. M.; N. E. cor D and Twenty-first sts.
Johnson, Mr and Mrs A. H.; S. W. cor Twenty-first and B sts.
Johnston, Mr and Mrs Thos. J.; 45 Ella st.
——Miss Hattie
Jones, Mr J. H.; 175 Taylor st.
——Miss Lovina
Jones, Dr Wm.; 49 North Sixteenth st.

Jones, Mr and Mrs Wm. P.; 310 Sixth st.
———Miss Jennie
———Benj. F.
———Lincoln
———Wm. H.
Jones, Miss Frankie; 71 South Third st.
Jones, Dr and Mrs Henry E.; 49 North Sixteenth st.
Jocelyn, Mr Frederick; The Portland Hotel

Kapus, Mr and Mrs Wm; 275 Morrison st.
———Wm. M.
Kaufman, Mr and Mrs Ralph; 351 E st.
———Miss
Kellogg, Capt and Mrs O.; 114 Mill st.
———Miss Stella
Kelly, Mr and Mrs Penumbra; East Portland
Kelly,Mr and Mrs Penumbra; Seventh st.,Brooklyn Heights, E. Portland
King, Mr and Mrs Wm. B.; 428 F st.
King, Amos N.; B bet. Nineteenth and Ella sts.
Knott, Mr and Mrs Gordon H.; 1211 Eighth st., East Portland
Knott, Mr and Mrs A. J.; 1224 Eighth st., East Portland
———George
———Harry G.
———Walter S.
Klosterman, Mr and Mrs John; 15 North Ninth st.   *Wednesday*
Knapp, Mr and Mrs Richard B.; 67 North Sixteenth st.
———Lawrence
Knapp, Mr Frank A.; 168 Eleventh st.
Koshland, Mr and Mrs Mathias; N. W. cor Eighteenth and J. *Wednesday*
Koehler, Mr and Mrs Richard; 274 Washington st.
Kohn, Mr and Mrs Charles; 147 Eleventh st.
Krumbein, Mr and Mrs Justus; 87 North Fifteenth st.

Ladd, Mr and Mrs C. E.; N. W. cor Sixth and Columbia sts.   *Monday*
Ladd, Mr and Mrs Wm. M; S. W. cor Main and W. Park st.   *Monday*
Ladd, Mr and Mrs Wm. S.; N.W. cor. of Sixth and Columbia sts. *Monday*
———Wesley
Laidlaw, Mr James; Seventeenth near I st.
Lamson, Mr and Mrs Roswell H.; Portland Heights
———Roswell B.
Landon, Rev and Mrs Warren H.; 214 Columbia st.
Lane, Capt and Mrs Nat H.; 215 East st., East Portland
Lane, Mr and Mrs John M. A.; 88 Main st.
Lang, Mr and Mrs Isadore; 363 W. Park st.
Lang, Mr and Mrs Max; cor. of Nineteenth and J sts.   *First Fridays*

Latz, Mr and Mrs Benjamin; 345 Ninth st.
Leland, Mr and Mrs Chas. E.; The Portland Hotel
Leland, Mrs Helen B.; 53 Washington Building
Levinson, Mr and Mrs Mark; 250 Tenth st.
Lewis, Mr and Mrs C.H.; Eighteenth, bet. G and H **Clatsop Beach, Or.**
——John C.
——L. Allen
——David
——Miss
——Evelyn
——Sallie
Lewis, Mr and Mrs Harry R.; East Portland
Lewis, V. Courtney; Head of King st.
Liebman, Mr Maurice; 209½ Fourth st.
——Joseph
Lindhard, Mr and Mrs Wm. L.; 502 East st.
Linthieum, Mr. S. B.; 163 Tenth st.
Loewenberg, Mr and Mrs Julius; 123 West Park
Logan, Rév. and Mrs W. H.; 386 Sixth st.
Lotan, Mr and Mrs James; 67 Ella st.
——W. Sam.
Lowengart, Mr and Mrs Philip; cor Sixteenth and D st.   *Tuesday*
Lownsdale, Mr and Mrs. J. P. O.; 43 South Third st.
——Chas. D.
———Fred R.
——John M.
Livingston, Mr Robt.; 45 North Twentieth st.

McAllen, Mr and Mrs D.; 111 South Third st.
McCraken, Mr and Mrs Henry E.; St. Clair near West Main *Wednesday*
McCraken, Col and Mrs John; 67 North Seventh st.
——Miss Ada
McCraken, Mr and Mrs Jas. R.; 369 E st.
McDougall, Mr Chas. J.; 225 Fifth st.
McFall, Mr and Mrs Wm.; 515 F st.
——Oliver P.
——John W. P.
——Miss Sue
McKay, Mr and Mrs David M.; 61 North Fifteenth st.
McKee, Mr and Mrs Edward D.; 215 Ninth st.
McMaster, Mr and Mrs Robt. M.; 54 Montgomery st.
McMillen, Mr and Mrs J. H.; 422 First st., East Portland
Mackay, Mr and Mrs Angus H.; Twenty-first st. near E st.
MacKenzie, Dr and Mrs K. A. J.; cor. Nineteenth and H sts.
——Miss
MacKenzie, Mr and Mrs W. R.; 329 H st.   *Monday* .

Macleay, Mr Donald; 189 Lownsdale st.
———Kenneth
Malarkey, Mr and Mrs Chas. A.; 253 Morrison st.   *Thursday*
———D. J.
———James A.
Malcolm, Mr and Mrs Philip S.; 22 North Tenth st.
Mallory, Mr Rufus, 193 Sixth st.
Markle, Mr and Mrs G. B.; Portland Heights   *Friday*
Marshall, Mr and Mrs John; cor. E and Sixteenth sts.
———Miss Augusta
Mason, Mr and Mrs A. B.; Eighth and J st. East Portland   **Clatsop**
Masten, Mr and Mrs E. C.; 502 E st.
Masters, Mr Wm.; 455 Sixth st.   *Wednesday*
———Mr and Mrs Wm. Y.
Maxwell, Mr and Mrs A. L.; 214 Mill st.
Mayer, Mr and Mrs F. J. Alex.; 32 North Tenth st.
Mayer, Mr and Mrs Jacob; 234 Morrison st.
———Mark A.
Meier, Mrs Aaron; 195 Morrison st.
Mellis, Mr and Mrs F. R.; 214 Salmon st.
Mesick, Mrs Dorothy; 391 B st.
Meyer, Mr and Mrs Emanuel; 164 Taylor st.
Meyer, Mr and Mrs Julius D.; 207 East Park st.
Miller, Dr and Mrs B. E.; 191 Sixth st.   *Thursday*
Mitchell, Mr and Mrs R. W.; 254 Market st.
Mitchell, Hon and Mrs Jno. H.; U. S. Senator, Washington, D. C.
———Miss Mattie
Mooney, Mr and Mrs Gustavus A; 252 Market st.
Montgomery, Mr and Mrs J. B.; 251 Seventh st.
———Harry
———Miss May
———Miss Antoinette
Moreland, Mr and Mrs Julius C.; 255 Eleventh st.
———Miss Susie
Morey, Mr P. F.; 91 South Second st.
Morden, Mr and Mrs G. P.; 350 E st.
Morgan, Mr and Mrs A. H.; 132 Taylor st.
———Miss Lena
Morgan, Mrs S. E.; 155 Fifteenth st.
———Miss Nellie E.
———E. Sheely
———Harry A.
Morris, Rt Rev and Mrs Wistar B.; NE cor. Nineteenth and E sts.
———Miss
———B. Wistar, Jr.

Morrow, Mr Robt. G. ; 195 Taylor st.
Mulkey, Mrs Marion F. ; 353 Tenth st.
Myrick, Capt and Mrs J. ; NE cor. Eighteenth and J sts.   *Wednesday*
——Miss
——Miss Lizzie
——Miss Winifred

Newkirk, J. W. ; 205 Ninth st.
Newton, Mr and Mrs Lyman ; 172 Yamhill st.
——Miss Hattie
——Frank
Nichols, Dr Clarence L.; 3 South Third st.
Niebling, Mr and Mrs E. T.; 155 Alder st.   *Thursday*
Noon, Mr and Mrs Wm. C.; 341 Tenth st.
——Miss Lulu
Norton, Mrs Catherine; 229 Eleventh st.
——Edward
——Miss Minnie
——Miss May
Northrup, Mrs Francis C.; 214 Eleventh st.
——Edwin P.
——Mr and Mrs Frank O.
Northrop, Mr and Mrs Frank E.; 54 North Twentieth st.

O'Connor, Mr and Mrs J. T.; cor. First and Corry sts.
——Miss Mae
Olds, Mr and Mrs Jay C.; 31 South First st.
Olds, Mr and Mrs Wm. P.; 427 Second st.
Oliphant, Mr and Mrs D. D.; 477 G. st.
Oppenheimer, Mr and Mrs J. L.: 247 Main st.   *Last Fridays*
Ordway, Mr and Mrs Julius; 380 Second st., East Portland
Ott, Mr Will S.; 195 Eleventh st.

Paddock, J. W.; 468 J st.
Page, Mr and Mrs J. H.; 432 F st.
——Fred H.
——Miss Fanny
Palmer, Mr and Mrs Ernest H.; 163 Tenth st.   *Tuesday*
Panton, Dr A. C.; Odd Fellows' Temple
Patterson, Miss Sarah E.; 248 Yamhill st.
Paxton, Mrs M. J.; 256 Ninth st.
——O. F.
——Miss Rota
Pendleton, Mr Fred N.; Oak Club, Sixth and Yamhill sts.
Pennoyer, Gov and Mrs Sylvester; 155 West Park st.
Pillsbury, Capt and Mrs A. B.; 956 Tenth st., East Portland

Pittock, Mr and Mrs H. L.; 115 West Park st.
——Fred F.
——Miss Carrie
Pope, Mr and Mrs Geo. H.; H st. bet. Nineteenth and Twentieth
Porter, Miss Alice; 53 Washington Building
Powell, Mr and Mrs T Cader; Eleventh and F sts., East Portland
Powers, Mr Ira F.; 240 Third st.
Prehu. Dr and Mrs Chas. T.; 655 I st., East Portland   *Wednesday*
Prehu, Dr and Mrs Fred W.; 1 South Sixth st.
Prentice, Mrs D. W.; 100 North Sixteenth st.
——Miss May
Protzman, Mr and Mrs Eugene C.; 15 NW Park st.
——Miss Edna

Raferty, Mr and Mrs Dave; Brooklyn Heights, East Portland
Raffety, Dr and Mrs C. H.; 526 L st., East Portland
Rate, Mr Geo. B.; 435 Tenth st.
Reed, Mr and Mrs C. J.; 55 North Twentieth st.
Reed, Mr and Mrs James S.; Hawthorne Terrace, Portland Heights
Reed, Mr Sanderson; 213 Eleventh st.
Reed, Mr and Mrs Simeon G.; First, bet. Montgomery and Harrison sts
Richardson, Mr and Mrs T. M.; 141 Eleventh st.
Rhoades, Lieut-Com and Mrs William Warland; 155 Alder st.   *Thursday*
Rieman, Mr and Mrs D.; 81 South Third st.
Robb, Mr and Mrs J. D.; 492 G st.
——Horace L.
——J. Howard
Roberts, Mr Andrew; 22 North Tenth st.
Robertson, Mr David; 381 Sixth st.
Roby, Mr and Mrs Chas. W.; 9 South Sixth st.
Rockwell, Mr and Mrs Cleveland; 395 Sixth st.   *Wednesday*
——Miss
Rodney, Miss Clementina; St. Helen's Hall
——Lydia
——Mary B.
Rogers. Mr and Mrs E. P.; 422 F st.
——Miss Lilian
Rowe, Mr and Mrs H. S.; 622 O st., East Portland
Rosenberg, Mr and Mrs F. H.; 246 Clay st.   *Tuesday*   **Centralia, Ill.**
Rosenberg, Mrs John; 246 Clay st.
——Frank H.
——William L.
Ross, Mrs A. G.; 5 South Third st.
Ross, Mr and Mrs C. D. W.; 329 Sixth st.

Rosenblatt, Mrs Simon; 141 Eighth st.
——Miss Caroline
——Edith
——Gus
——Leon S.
——Henry
Royce, Miss Susie; 123 Eighth st.
Russell, Mr and Mrs J. M.; 441 West Park st.
Russell, Mr and Mrs Geo. F.; 261 Eleventh st.

Sabin, Miss Ella C.; 255 Ninth st.
Savier, Miss Florence; 49 North Sixteenth st.
——Miss Helen
Samuel, Mr and Mrs L.; 381 Tenth st.
Sargent, Mr and Mrs E. M.; 577 G st., East Portland
Schuyler, Mrs Philip C.; 45 King st.
——Miss Genevieve
——Lucy
Scott, Mr and Mrs C. N. ; cor. Sherman and Front sts.
Scott, Mr and Mrs Harvey W.; NW cor. Tenth and Morrison sts.
Sealy, Mr and Mrs F.; 374 Second st.   *Wednesday*   **Long Beach, Wash.**
Selling, Mr and Mrs Ben; 203 Tenth st.
Shattuck, Judge and Mrs E. D.; 134 Hall st.
Sherlock, Mr and Mrs R.; cor. Twenty-first and B sts.
——Miss Kate
——Emma
Sherman, Mr and Mrs D. F.; 468 J st.
Shindler, Mr and Mrs G.; 274 Sixth st.   *Wednesday*
——Daniel A.
——Dodd D.
Shurtleff, Mr and Mrs F. A.; 194 Clay st.
Sibson, Mr and Mrs Wm. S.; 313 Eleventh st.
Sichel, Mr and Mrs Sig; 291 E st.   1st and 3d *Fridays*   **Clatsop**
Simon, Mr and Mrs David; 181 Pacific st.
——Miss
——Joseph
——Samuel
Simon, Mr and Mrs Nathan D.; 497 E st.
Sitton, Mrs Chas. E.; 293 Yamhill st.
Skiles, Mr and Mrs Robert; 84 College st.
Smith, Mr and Mrs Albert T. ; 17th and Jackson sts., Portland Heights
Smith, Miss Amanda J.; 175 Alder st.
Smith, Mr and Mrs C. C.; cor. Tenth and Harrison sts.   *Thursday*
Smith, Mr and Mrs C. J.; 152 North Seventeenth st.

Smith, Mr and Mrs Ferdinand C. ; 234 Salmon st.
——Miss Mamie
——Miss Florence
Smith, Mrs H. L. ; 229 Ninth st.
——Gilbert F.
——Miss Ella C.
Smith, Mr and Mrs Preston C. ; 215 Tenth st.
Smith, Mr and Mrs Saml. D, ; 181 Twelfth st.
——Miss Gertrude
——Fred
Smith, Judge Seneca, Corbett st. and First Ave.
——Miss
Smith,Mr and Mrs Walter V.; Portland Hotel *Saturday* **Portland Heights**
Smith, Mr and Mrs Wm. K. ; 351 Third st.   *Thursday*
——Miss Eugenie
——W. K., Jr.
——Joseph H.
.——Sumner
——Victor

Smithson, Mr and Mrs H. C.; 209 Alder st.
Snell, Mr and Mrs Geo. W. ; Seventeenth and D sts.
Snow, Mr and Mrs Zera ; 36 West Nineteenth st.   *Monday*
——Charles McCormac
Sommerville, Mr and Mrs John; cor. Twelfth and Washington sts.
——Frank
——Miss Maud
Spencer, Capt and Mrs E. W.; cor. Second and Irving's Add.,E. Portland
Sperry, Mr and Mrs J. L.; cor. Twelfth and G sts., East Portland
——Miss
——Miss Minnie
——Miss Dally
——Miss Etta
Spuhn, Carl; 274 Washington st.
Staver, Mr and Mrs Geo. ; 234 Clay st.   *Thursday*
——Miss
Steel, Mr and Mrs David; 409 First st.   *Thursday*
Steel, Mr and Mrs Geo. A.; 328 Sixth st.
Steel, Mr and Mrs James; 265 Sixth st.
Steel, W. G. ; 141 Morrison st,
Steinbach, Mr and Mrs A. B.; 341 Ninth st.   *2d Thursday of Month*
Stevens, Mr and Mrs E. T. C.; 166 Fourteenth st.
Stewart, Mr and Mrs John T.; cor. A and Fourth sts., East Portland
Stott, Mr Samuel R.; 188 Jefferson st.

Stott, Judge and Mrs Raleigh; 149 Jefferson st.
——Miss
——Miss Mary
——George
——Lansing
Story, Mr and Mrs Geo. L.; 55 North Seventh st.
—— Miss
Stratton, Mr and Mrs Howard C.; 48 South Third st.
Streibig, Mr and Mrs Frank J.; 129 Alder st.
Strong, Dr and Mrs Curtis C.; 225 West Park st.
Strong, Mr Fred R.; 427 B st.
Strong, Mr and Mrs T. N.; 189 Pacific st.
Stroud, Mr and Mrs Geo. M.; 720 I st., East Portland
——Geo. M., Jr.
——Miss
Strowbridge, Mr and Mrs J. A.; 365 Fifth st.   Fernwood
——George H.
——Joseph A., Jr.
——Alfred B.
Strowbridge, Mrs Alice J.; 163 Tenth st.
——Thomas A.
Taylor, Duncan O.; 272 Salmon st.
Taylor, Mr and Mrs George Jr.; cor. Twenty-first and E sts.
Teal, Mr and Mrs Joseph; 269 Taylor st.
——Joseph N.
——Miss Helen
——George
——Miss Clara
Therkelsen, Mr and Mrs L.; 335 Ninth st.
Thielsen, Mr and Mrs Hans; 181 Eleventh st.
——Julius E.
Thomas, Mr and Mrs W. E.; 293 Eleventh st.
Thompson, Mr and Mrs D. P.; 175 Tenth st.
——Miss Bessie
Towne, Mrs Lucy A.; 321 South Front st.   *1st and 3d Thursdays*
——Bert C.
——Miss Carrie
Townsend, Mr and Mrs Fredk.; 205 Tenth st.
Trevett, Mr and Mrs Theodore B.; F, bet. 22nd and 23d sts.   *Tuesday*
——Miss
——Emily Bancroft
Troup, Capt and Mrs J. W.; Irving's Addition, East Portland
Turrell, Mr and Mrs W. O.; 155 Alder st.   *Thursday*
Tuthill, Mr and Mrs D. S.; Seventeenth and D sts.
——Miss Helen
Tuttle, Mr and Mrs B. B.; 163 Tenth st.   *Tuesday*

Valentine, Mr and Mrs J. H.; 475 J st.
Van Schuyler, Mr and Mrs W. J.; 115 Tenth st.
——Miss Carrie
——William
Von Bolton, Mrs H.; 268 Yamhill st.
——Miss

Wadhams, Mr and Mrs Wm.; 343 West Park st.
Walker, Dr and Mrs David; 90 Jefferson st.
——Miss
——Blanche
——Maud
Wallace, Mr and Mrs Lucien; NE cor. Twenty-third and F sts.
Wallace, Mr and Mrs Wm. T.; 353 G st.
Wallace, Mrs Susan; 205 Ninth st.
——Robert H.
——Miss Jessie
Warren, Mr and Mrs Royal K.; 134 Montgomery st.
Wasserman, Mr and Mrs Philip; 194 Alder st.
——Miss Getta
Watson, Mr and Mrs Jas. F.; Eighteenth and E st.
Watson, Mr and Mrs J. Frank; 415 West Park st.
Watson, Mr and Mrs Edward B.; 331 Tenth st.
Weatherred, Mr and Mrs W. L.; 131 Oak st.
Watt, Miss; 5 South Third st.
Weidler, Mr and Mrs Milton; 221 Sixth st.
Weidler, Mr and Mrs Geo. W.; ccr. Eighteenth and L sts.   *Thursday*
Welch, Mr and Mrs Wm. B; Twenty-seventh and Base Line Road, E. Portland
Wetzel, Mr and Mrs W. A.; cor. Tenth and L sts., East Portland
Wetzell, Rev and Mrs David; 292 East Park st.
Wetzel, Mr and Mrs Wm. A. 1269 Tenth st., East Portland
Whalley, Mr and Mrs John W.; 393 West Park st.
——Miss
Wheeler, Mrs Fanny, Third and A sts., East Portland
Whidden, Mr and Mrs W. M.; 261 Eleventh st.
Whitcomb, Mr and Mrs F. C.; 191 East Park st.   *Wednesday*
White, Mr and Mrs Eugene D.; 201 Thirteenth st.   *Thursday*
White, Mr and Mrs Levi; cor. Nineteenth and G sts.
——Miss Ella
Whitehouse, Mr and Mrs B. G.; 175 Twelfth st.
——Miss
——Clara
Wilcox, Mr and Mrs Theo. B.; 311 Yamhill st.
Willey, Mr and Mrs S. B.; F st. near Seventeenth
Williams, Mr and Mrs David L.; 335 Ninth st.

Williams, Mr and Mrs Geo. H.; 49 North Seventeenth st.
Willett, Mr Geo. T.; First st., National Bank Building
Wilson, Dr and Mrs Holt C.; cor. Nineteenth and H sts.
Wilson, Mrs R. B.; cor. Nineteenth and H st.
——Miss Virginia
——Miss Clementina
——Miss Louisa
Wilson, Dr and Mrs Geo. F.; 101 North Seventeenth st.
Wilson, Mr Arthur; 163 Tenth st.
Winch, Mr and Mrs Martin; SW cor. First and Montgomery sts.
Winstick, Mr and Mrs N. G.; East Portland
Wisdom, Mr and Mrs W. M.; 274 Alder st.
Wisdom, Mr and Mrs M. D.; 252 Market st.
Withington, Mr and Mrs G. E.; 108 Salmon st.
Wolfe, Mr and Mrs M. F.; 231 Salmon st.
——George N.
Wood, Mr and Mrs C. E. S.; cor. King and Salmon sts.
——J. McI.
Woodard, Mr and Mrs C. H.; The Portland Hotel
Woodward, Mr and Mrs Tyler; cor. Eighth and Montgomery sts.
Woodworth, J. G.; 225 Fifth st.
Woolsey, Mr and Mrs Frank; 159 North Twenty-first st.
Wortman, Mr and Mrs H. C.; 227 B st.
Wygant, Mr and Mrs Theodore; cor. H and Nineteenth sts.
——Miss

Young, Mr and Mrs H. A.; 175 Alder st.   *Monday*

Field, Staff and Line Officers

First Regiment Infantry, 1st Brigade, Oregon National Guard

Colonel Chas. F. Beebe, Commanding
Lieut.-Colonel, O. Summers
Major, B. B. Tuttle
1st Lieut. Geo. F. Telfer, Adjutant
Captain A. J. Brown, Chaplain
Captain C. C. Strong, Surgeon
1st Lieut. J. A. Fulton (Astoria) Asst. Surgeon
1st Lieut. Ed. Bernheim, Quartermaster
1st Lieut. B. E. Smith, Commissary
1st Lieut. D. J. Moore, Signal Officer
1st Lieut. L. C. Jones, Inspector Rifle Practice

Co. A

Captain H. R. Alden, Commanding
1st Lieut., F. D. Kelsey
2d Lieut., J. C. Rutenick

Co. B (Hillsboro, Ore.)

Captain F. J. Bailey, Commanding
1st Lieut., W. L. Weatherred
2d Lieut., S. T. Linklater

Co. C

Captain M. G. Butterfield, Commanding
1st Lieut., B. C. Towne
2d Lieut., F. E. Casto

Co. D (Albina, Ore.)

Captain L. E. Simmons, Commanding
1st Lieut., J. Horton
2d Lieut., W. L. Gould

Co. E

Captain E. W. Moore, Commanding
1st Lieut , R. A. Hirsh
2d Lieut., Chas. Esplin, Jr.

Co. F (Oregon City)

Captain J. P. Shaw, Commanding
1st Lieut., E. S. Warren
2d Lieut., T. P. Randall

Co. G

Captain L. C. Farrar, Commanding
1st Lieut., R. E. Davis
2d Lieut., Geo. T. Willett

Co. H (Astoria, Ore.)

Captain H. J. Wherrity, Commanding
1st Lieut., L. E. Gillet
2d Lieut., Edward Hollock

Co. I

Captain A. J. Coffee, Commanding
1st Lieut., J. F. Case
2d Lieut., F. E. Cooper

Co. K

Captain H. L. Wells, Commanding
1st Lieut., W. E. Thomas
2d Lieut., J. P. Carson

The Assembly Club

This Organization, which was established some four years ago, is made up of prominent society leaders, and its object is to give social parties and dances during the Season, at which only members of the Club with their invited friends are present. They generally give one during each month of the Season, which is attended by all the fashion and wealth of Portland Society.

OFFICERS

JAMES LAIDLAW - - - -	President
GEO. F. WILSON - - -	Vice-President
W. F. BURRELL - - - -	Treasurer
F. R. STRONG - - - - -	Secretary

EXECUTIVE COMMITTEE

Laidlaw, James
Wilson, Geo. F.
Burrell, W. F.
Strong, F. R.

Nunn, Richard
Heitshue, Samuel
Brooks, T. Scott
Lombard, Ben

Howard, Jr., Robert

MEMBERS OF THE ASSEMBLY CLUB, 1890

Adams, E. R.
Ayer, W. B.
Allen, H. A.
Andrews, F. V. H.
Avery, Bailey
Burrell, Walter F.
Burrell, Herman
Beck, F. A.
Brown, C. H.
Beck, Foster
Brooke, Hamilton
Brooke, Scott, T.
Burnside, Davis, W.
Bartlet, Harris, T.
Buckley, Ed.
Brown, E. L.

Beebe, C. F.
Burns, W. J.
Boise, W. L.
Canby, Jas.
Cox, L. B.
Cæsar, Eberhardt
Coursen, E. E.
Cookingham, A.
Chenery, Chas. E.
Clarkson, D. M.
Deady, Paul R.
Davidson, H. R.
Deady, Edw. N.
Eaton, F. B.
Everett, E.
Effinger, Patterson

Effinger, John
Flower, Jas.
Frank, G. P.
Gilmore, Fred. M.
Good, Geo.
Green, H. J.
Granger, Jas.
Gordon, Stuart
Howard, Jr., R. S.
Heitshue, S.
Hoyt, Jr., Geo. W.
Hoyt, Ralph
Holman, Geo. F.
Holman, Fred. V.
Hart, Frank E.
Jones, Wm.
Janion, Robt. M.
Koehler, R.
Knapp, F. A.
King, W. B.
King, John
Linthicum, S. B.
Lewis, L. A.
Lewis, J. C.
Laidlaw, Jas.
Lombard, B. M.
Lombard, C. H.
McFall, O. P.
Mirris, Jr., Wistar B.
McCraken, E. H.
McCraken, Jas. R.
Muir, W. T.
Morrow, R. G.
Miller, E. H.

Malcolm, P. S.
Markle, Geo. B.
Nunn, Richard
Ott, W. S.
Palmer, E. H.
Panton, A. C.
Page, F. H.
Perry, Thos. B.
Reed, C. J.
Strong, F. R.
Strong, N.
Snow, Zera
Stott, Sam. R.
Strong, Thos. N.
Stevens, E. T. C.
Sherman, D. F.
Shepard, E. H.
Story, H. D.
Stout, Lansing
Smith, Jr., W. K.
Smith, P. C.
Thomas, W. E.
Tronsen, H. B.
Teal, J. N.
Tuthill, D. S.
Taylor, D. O.
Tuttle, B. B.
Wood, C. E. S.
Wilson, Arthur
Watson, Frank J.
Wallace, W. T.
Wilson, Geo. F.
Wells, H. L.
Wilcox, Theo. B.

The Arlington Club

This club, organized July 1, 1882, is composed of a large number of the city's leading commercial and professional men. The membership is limited to 250. They have a commodious clubhouse in the old Ainsworth Mansion, corner of Third and Pine streets. Following is a list of officers and members for 1890:

OFFICERS

D. P. THOMPSON - - - - - President
W. S. SIBSON - - - First Vice-President
T. B. WILCOX - - - Second Vice-President
GEO. GOOD - - - - - - Treasurer
F. A. BECK - - - - - - Secretary

DIRECTORS

C. H. Prescott   F. Townsend
D. D. Oliphant   John Kelly
Henry Failing

MEMBERS

Ankeny, A. P.	Cameron, J. R.
Arnold, F. K.	Charlton, A. D.
Ainsworth, G. J.	Colbert, T. J.
Ayer, W. B.	Cook, Vincent
Baillie, Alex.	Callender, M. P.
Bartlett, T. Harris	Campbell, B.
Beebe, Chas. F.	Carle, F. A.
Benn, Chas. E.	Carroll, James
Bloomfield, H.	Chappell, J. J.
Brown, F. L.	Cofran, J. W. G.
Burns, W. J.	Cook, J. W.
Beck, F. Alleyn	Cookingham, Edwd.
Bellinger, C. B.	Corbett, H. J.
Bevan, Arthur D.	Cotton, W. W.
Bourne, Jr., Jonathan	Craw, Geo. A.
Buckley, J. M.	Corbett, H. W.
Burrell, W. F.	Cran, John
Caesar, Clemens	Davis, T. A.

DeHart, E. J.
Dolph, C. A.
Downing, F. O.
Dunne, D. M.
Durham, R. L.
Darley, E. C.
Dawson, I. R.
Dement, R. M.
Dolph, J. N.
Durham, Geo. H.
Duval, W. S.
Earhart, R. P.
Effinger, W. H.
Eaton, F. B.
Evans, Dudley
Failing, Henry
Folger, Herbert
Fox, J. M.
Gearin, John M.
Good, George
Gilmore, F. M.
Ghiselin, J. T.
Green, John
Hawkins, L. L.
Hewett, Henry
Hall, M. G.
Henderson, M. W.
Hewison, J. G.
Holcomb, W. H.
Holman, F. V.
Honeyman, Wm.
Holman, Alfred
Holmes, Byron Z.
Hunt, G. W.
Idleman, C. M.
Jones, Wm.
Jones, H. E.
Kelly, John
Knapp, R. B.
King, W. B.
King, John C.
Koehler, Richard
Ladd, Chas. E.
Laidlaw, James
Lynch, Geo. W.

Lewis, C. H.
Lewis, L. Allen
Lotan, James
Linthicum, Stewart B.
Ladd, Wm. M.
Leonard, H. C.
Lombard, B. M.
Lewis, J. C.
Lewis, I.
Loring, David
Lombard, Chas. H.
Macdonald, H. G.
Mackenzie, K. A. J.
Mackintosh, Wm.
Macleay, Donald
Mackay, Donald
Mallony, Rufus
Macleay, Kenneth
Maxwell, A. L.
Markle, Geo. B.
McCaw, W. F.
McKee, A. D.
Michener, E. C.
Mitchell, John H.
Montgomery, J. B.
Oliphant, D. D.
Page, F. H.
Panton, A. C.
Paxton, O. F.
Pope, George
Powell, Chas. F., U. S. A.
Prescott, C. H.
Reid, John
Reed, S. G.
Roberts, Andrew
Robertson, David
Rowe, H. S.
Russell, J. M.
Schulze, Paul
Shackelford, Wm.
Sherman, D. F.
Shurtleff, F. N.
Sibson, Wm. T.
Sibson, M. H.
Smith, C. J.

Smith, Milton W.
Smith, Preston C.
Smith, Seneca
Smith, Walter V.
Smith, W. K. Jr.
Snow, Zera
Stott, Raleigh
Steel, R. M.
Scott, H. W.
Spuhn, Carl
Stratton, H. C.
Therkelsey, L.
Taylor, George
Thompson, D. P.
Thompson, H. Y.
Townsend, Fredk.
Tuthill, D. S.
Van Schuyver, W. J.

Walter, D. V.
Watson, J. F.
Weidler, Geo. W.
Whalley, J. W.
Whidden, W. M.
Willey, S. B.
Williams, Geo. H.
Wilson, Arthur
Winslow, Chauncey R.
Withington, G. E.
Woodard, C. H.
Wood, C. E. S.
Wilcox, J. D.
Wilcox, Theo. B.
Wallace, H. C.
Wilson, J. Frank
Wood, J. McI.

ARMY AND NAVY

Anderson, Thomas M. - - - U. S. A.
Cabell, Harry C. - - - "
Gibbon, John - - - "
Handbury, Thomas H. - -
Ingolls, Rufus - - - ..
Lee, J. C. G. - - -
Lovering, L. A. - - - ..
Lydecker, J. J. - - - "
Rhodes, W. W. - - - - U. S. N.
Sharpe, Henry G. - - - U. S. A.
Sumner, S. S. - - - - "
Symons, T. W. - - - "

The Portland Rowing Association

This Association is an incorporated institution, and its duration, in the Articles of Incorporation, is placed at fifty years. It was incorporated Nov. 13, 1879, and re-organized April 3, 1880. Its object is the mental and physical improvement and training of young men. It owns a fine boat house and a number of shells, pleasure boats, outriggers, etc., and among its membership are included the representative young men of Portland Society. During the summer the boat house is a favorite resort of all who like aquatic sports, and the club holds an annual regatta, at which prizes are competed for by the several crews which the club can muster.

OFFICERS, 1890

FRED. R. STRONG - - - -	President
J. P. MARSHALL - - - -	Secretary
E. M. ARCHER - - - -	Treasurer

DIRECTORS

F. R. Strong	J. P. Marshall
D. Loring	A. B. McAlpine
J. H. Shadone	E. H. Palmer
A. S. Whiting	E. M. Arthur

C. D. McLAIN - - - - Captain

MEMBERS

Arthur, E. M.	Coffee, A. J.
Andrew, John	Corbett, H. J.
Adler, Emil	Canby, James
Adams, E. R.	Crocker, A. M.
Baltes, F. W.	Collins, G. W.
Beach, F. E.	Carr, B. L.
Buffum, F. G.	Caesar, E.
Bills, J. Norman	Clark, W. J.
Bevan, A. D.	Coffey, J B.
Bourne, Jonathan, Jr.	Collins, A. S.
Brown, E. L.	Cawthorn, Dr F.
Brown, C. H.	Chappell, J. J.
Bellinger, J. E.	Davis, R. E.
Breyman, Otto	Dekum, E.
Campbell, John	Dunlap, J. L.

Dekum, Adolph	Morris, B. W. Jr.
Deady, Paul R.	Nun, Richd.
Eaton, F. B.	Nun, W. H.
Giltner, R. R.	Oppenheimer, S.
Gautenbein, C. U.	Oliphant, D. D.
Gordon, Stewart	Paxton, O. F.
Geer, J. C.	Powell, T. C.
Heintz, O. E.	Palmer, E. H.
Higgins, F. D.	Pendleton, F. H.
Holmcomb, Cecil	Prall, R. F.
Hughes, Ellis G.	Pilkington, H.
Hart, F. E.	Panie, J. W.
Hart, R. C.	Rosenberg, F. H.
Hoyt, Ralph W.	Russell, Lewis
Hogue, H. W.	Reed, Sanderson
Hahn, G. W.	Shindler, D. D.
Hetich, F. W.	Shindler, D. A.
Hudson, H. T.	Smith, Milton W.
Idleman, C. M.	Stoddard, J. R.
Jones, B. F.	Strong, F. R.
Jones, Dr Wm.	Strong, T. N.
Judge, H. E.	Swigert, C. F.
Kemera, E.	Shepherd, E. H.
King, W. B.	Starr, F. A. E.
Ladd, W. M.	Spadone, J. H.
Lewis, L. A.	Street, W. H.
Lownsdale, C. D.	Sommerville, F. B.
Ladd, Chas. E.	Strowbridge, T. H.
Loring, D.	Teel, J. N.
Lombard, B. M.	Thomas, A.
Lombard, C. H.	Towne, Bert
Lewis, John C.	Tronson, H. B.
Linthicum, G. B.	Todd, J. C.
Leland, E. W.	Tuttle, B. B.
Malarkey, C. J. B.	Thompson, R. W.
Maxwell, L. H.	Willey, S. B.
MacKenzie, D. H. K. A. J.	White, I. L.
Marshall, J. P.	Whiting, A. G.
McLain, C. D.	White, T. Brooke
Muir, W. T.	Woodworth, J. G.
McAlpine, A. B.	Warren, M.
Moore, E. W.	Wood, C. E. G.
Moore, D. J.	Wishart, F. V.
Martin, F. H.	Wolfe, Geo. N.
McGuire, Wm.	Zan, D. J.

The Concordia Club

This Club, which is the most prominent Jewish social organization in the city, was organized in October, 1878, and includes the best Jewish citizens of Portland among its membership. It is constantly adding to its list of members and is in a most flourishing condition; a project is now on foot to erect their own building. The present club-rooms, however, are handsomely fitted up and conveniently located in the Mulkey Block, corner Second and Morrison streets.

OFFICERS

B. Goldsmith - - - -	President
L. Liebman - - - -	Vice-President
Jul. Silverstone - - - -	Secretary
A. Greenebaum - - - -	Treasurer

BOARD OF TRUSTEES

The Board of Trustees is composed of the above officers and

Selling, B.	Fleischner, I. N.
Neustadter, B.	Simon, N. D.
Hausman, H.	Hexter, A. L.

HONORARY MEMBERS

Greenhcod, Louis, H.	Wasserman, P.

ACTIVE MEMBERS

Blumauer, Sol.	Hexter, A. L.
Baum, N.	Heilbronner, J.
Binswanger, Dr O.	Hass, J. L.
Bernheim, Ed.	Jacobs, I.
Cohn, Frank M.	Jacobs, R.
Cohn, Martin, L.	Koshland, M.
Dittenhoefer, H. T.	Liebman, J.
Feldenheimer, A.	Liebman, M.
Fleischner, L.	Lowengart, P.
Fleischner, Ike N.	Lowengart, I.
Fleischner, M.	Long, I.
Frank, Emil	Loewenstein, S.
Frank, Sig.	Loewenberg, J.
Goldsmith, B.	Lewis, L. H.
Goldsmith, R.	Monheimer, I.
Goldsmith, A.	Meyer, E.
Goldsmith, J.	Meyer, J. D.
Hirsb, S.	Mayer, M. A.
Hausman, H.	Mellis, F. R.

Neustadter, Ben.
Oppenheimer, Sol.
Oberdorffer, A.
Rothschild, E. S.
Rosenfeld, S. W.
Simon, Jos.
Simon, S.
Simon, G.

Selling, J.
Selling, B.
Selling, S.
Silverstone, J.
Thanhauser, L.
Thanhauser, H.
Taubenheimer, H.
Wolfe, A.

PASSIVE MEMBERS

Abrams, H.
Ackerman, J. S.
Ackerman, H.
Arnold, U. K.
Beck, S.
Bernheim, Th.
Bissinger, J.
Blumauer, P.
Blumauer, M.
Blumauer, S. M.
Durkheimer, M.
Ehrman, Ed.
Ellis, W. R.
Friedlander, S. H.
Ganz, M.
Goldsmith, Berth.
Goodman, Th.
Greenebaum, A.
Gunst, S. A.
Harris, H.
Herman, S. W.
Jacobs, A. G.
Jacobson, C. S.
Kahn, Felix
Kahn, J.
Kohn, N.
Kohn, Chas.

Kohlberg, E. L.
Kuhn, Louis
Levy, A. L.
Lowengart, Jos.
Lyon, M. C.
Mansfield, Th.
Marx, D.
Mayer, S. J.
Meier, A.
Meyers, Sam.
Rosenblatt, G.
Rosenfeld, Sol.
Scharff, J. D.
Schlussel, N.
Seller, Fred
Sichel, M.
Sichel, Sig.
Simon, N. D.
Sommers, A.
Steinbach, A. B.
Steinheiser, W.
Steinheiser, I.
Sterne, E. C.
Sternfels, M.
Strauss, D.
White, I.
White, I. L.

White, L.

The Willamette Rowing Club

This is the oldest institution in the city, or for that matter in the whole north. west, whose object has been aquatic sports, especially rowing. The Club was organized in 1877. Among its prominent early members were Messrs. James Laidlaw, W. W. Francis, George Good, H. G. McDonald, James S. Reed, George Piper, K. Macleay and other gentlemen who have always been prominent in amateur sporting matters. Until 188) the Club had always rented quarters with the different boat houses along the river, but last year built for themselves a very commodious and substantial boat house which at present is moored at the foot of Stark Street, near the Ferry Landing. Its position and means of access are the most convenient that can be procured. The house is illuminated by electric lights, has convenient dressing-rooms and bathing facilities, and being the most centrally located, affords what is very desirable in a Club of this kind, accessibility to its benefits and pleasures.

The Club possesses several four oar shells, one of which was built by the famous Salter Bros. of Oxford, England ; and another is the lightest and fastest model which Waters Bros. have ever turned out. Also a number of singles and doubles.

Up to the present year the Club has fostered shell rowing, but has found it necessary with its largely increasing membership to add new pleasure boats, and this spring nearly a dozen have been added.

The entrance fees and dues of the Willamette Club are a very small sum in comparison to those usually demanded by Clubs of this character, the entrance fee being $10.00, and the annual dues $1.00 per month during the rowing season, and 50c per month during the winter.

Application for membership can be made to any of the Club's officers. The present membership of the Club is about 100, than its working force is greater than it has ever been. The Club aims to hold its regatta about mid-summer, when it offers prizes for its own members and also for outside competition. Several of the Willamette's members are also members of other boating associations in the city, but having cast their lot with the Willamette have maintained their allegiance to the old organization. The charter members of the Club are mostly Englishmen, and the membership has always been composed largely of Britishers and Colonials. The present Captain, Mr. Charles H. Gallien, is a New Zealander, and has had a large experience in amateur racing in that country.

It is rumored that during the coming winter the Club will build for itself a larger house with gymnasium and all possible accessories for a metropolitan boating Club.

The list of members below is the enrollment June 1, 1890.

OFFICERS FOR 1890

JOHN GILL - - - - - -	President
J. S. DUNBAR - - - -	Vice-President
ALBERT WERLEIN - - -	Secretary
F. C. BRADEN - - - - -	Treasurer
C. H. GALLIEN - - - -	Captain
P. J. BANNON - - - -	Dep. Captain

MEMBERS

Braden, F. C.	Maxwell, J. M.
Blumlein, J.	Marion, J. V.
Buckemeyer, C.	Milner, Jos. H.
Brandes, C.	Mendenhall, M.
Bannon, P. J.	McCaw, W. F.
Conant, W.	McEvoy, P. A.
Coleman, P. J.	McKibbon, W.
Carey, F. W.	McNicholas, J. A.
Carroll, T.	McAlpin, A. B.
Crowne, E. P.	Neilson, C.
Dunbar, J.	Nicoll, B. H.
Finley, A.	Osborn, W. F.
Fitzgerald, J.	Owens, J. E.
Fitzgerald, W. J.	Protzman, L. F.
Farrell, J.	Povey, J.
Fooley, Wm.	Prichard, A. J.
Fairfowl, H.	Porter, W. D.
Gambell, W. B.	Peterson, J. S.
Gallien, C. L.	Palmer, E. H.
Gill, J.	Russell, L.
Grey, H.	Robbins, E. C.
Green, L. L.	Rogers, J. R.
Gatens, W.	Russell, F. G.
Harper, R. G.	Seliger, J.
Henion, F. N.	Smith, A. M.
Headley, A.	Sommers, E. A.
Hirsch, A.	Sinnott, W. P.
Hastie, S. T.	Tighe, J. P.
Howe, T. M.	Van Houten, J. H.
Jubitz, R.	Van Fridagh, P.
King, C. W.	Velton, A. K.
Kilham, E. H.	Willott, G. T.
Kilham, Howard	Worlain, E.
La Grande, C. A.	Worlain, A.
London, T. W.	Webber, H. A.
Lockwood, S. P.	Wallace, T. E.
Murphy, D.	Wasserman, F. E.
Morrill, A.	Wallace, B.
Martin, R.	Woodard, C. H.
Milner, J. T.	Wallace, W.
Mathiot, D.	Wenworth, W.

ALBINA, OREGON

Boyd, Dr W. H. and wife	Wood street
Brown, C. J. and wife	Russell street
Church, O. P. and wife	NE cor. Knott and Morgan streets
Cline, Mrs J. P.	Chapman near Stark
Corey, Dr J. W.	Russell street
Curtis, Mr and Mrs Anson	Corbett street
Delay, Mr and Mrs Joseph	Corbett, cor. Loring street
Donlon, Mr and Mrs Wm.	Russell street, cor. Rodney avenue
Evans, Mrs Charles	Wood street
Fisher, Dr J. J.	Grover street
Forbes, Rev W. O. and wife	Russell street
Foster, Capt W. H. and wife	Cor. Goldsmith and Page streets
Grimes, Mr and Mrs C. C.	Cor. Morris and Kerney streets
Hallowell, Mrs C.	Elliot street
Hershner, Rev J. L.	Gibbs street
Hillier, Mr and Mrs Albert	Grover street
Hill, Rev George W.	Russell street
Kent, Mr and Mrs W. G.	Russell street
Loomis, H. S. and wife	Page street
McEarchern, Mr and Mrs M. A.	Grover street
McKenzie, Mrs M. A.	Cor. Russell and Wood streets
McLauchlin, Mr and Mrs D. M.	Cor. Goldsmith and Page
Magoon, Mr and Mrs E. O.	NE cor. Borthwick and Russell sts
Manley, Mr and Mrs A. B.	Grover, SE cor. Goldsmith
Menefee, Mr and Mrs J. P.	Cor. Santa Barbara and Williams ave
O'Rourke, Mr and Mrs F. E.	Page street
Parker, Mr and Mrs John	Cor. Rodney ave and San Antonio
Peirce, Rev G. M.	Cor. Page and Abernathy avenue
Pittinger, Mr and Mrs T. W.	Grover street
Randall, Mrs J. A.	Borthwick street
Robbins, Mr and Mrs B. F.	Wood street
Sandercock, Mr and Mrs Wm.	Grover street
Smith, Mr and Mrs B. M.	Russell street
Smithson, Mr and Mrs A. J.	Helm street
Spiney, Dr N. S. and wife	Cardwell street
Steffen, J. H. and wife	Cor. Loring and Mitchell streets
Thompson, M. E. and wife	Williams avenue
Thompson, S. E. and wife	Goldsmith and Page streets
Wise, Dr W. S. and wife	Russell street
Young, A. M. and wife	Abernathy avenue
Young, Prof C. W. and wife	Lane near Russell street

YOUNG FOLKS

Barnes, Miss Katie	Goldsmith street
Beattie, Miss Laura E.	Elliot street
Bentgen, N. D.	Villard Hotel
Boggs, Miss Bertie	Elliot street
Burtch, J. H.	Cor. Goldsmith and Russell streets
Carter, W. N.	113½ Russell street
Eastes, James A.	Delay block
Fitzpatrick, Miss Agnes	Russell and Woodward streets
Gould, Wm. L.	Markel's block
Green, Miss Etta	Cor. Goldsmith and Page streets
Harris, D. J.	Albina
Holcomb, Dr Curtis	Russell and Goldsmith streets
Ladd, Will	Goldsmith and Page streets
Laurie, A. T.	Cor. Corbett and Goldsmith street
Musman, Hugo	Russell street
Menefee, R. E.	Williams ave. cor. Santa Barbara
Munk, Miss Jennie	Margaretta ave. near San Rafael
Tucker, Captain Clyde	Goldsmith and Page street

The Orchestral Union

This Society was organized during the winter of 1881 and gave its first concert at New Market Theatre, on Monday, February 20, 1882. A series of subscription concerts were given each season up to 1885, when it ceased rehearsals. It was re-organized the early part of 1888 and has since then given a series of subscription concerts each season with much success, both musically and financially. Rehearsals are held on Monday night, at the New Arion Hall, corner Park and Second Sts. The following are its

OFFICERS

CHAS. HEGELE, - - - - - - -	President
D. J. ZAN, - - - - - - -	Vice-President.

MUSICAL COMMITTEE

H. Wagner   O. Mangold

           S. Harris

Alex Wagner, - - - - - - -	Secretary
Simon Harris, - - - - - - -	Conductor

ALBANY, OREGON

Mr & Mrs S. E. Young
Mr & Mrs L. E. Blain
Rev & Mrs S. G. Irvine
Mr & Mrs C. Stewart
Mr & Mrs E. Sox
Mr & Mrs D. P. Mason
Miss Mason
Miss Vesta Mason
Mr & Mrs E. L. Thompson
Mr & Mrs H. H. Hewitt
Mr & Mrs J. V. Pipe
Mrs Thomas Monteith
Miss Tina Monteith
Rev and Mrs E. N. Condit
Mr & Mrs J. Irving
Mr & Mrs W. H. Lee
Mr & Mrs Redfield
Mr & Mrs Van Horn
Miss Van Horn
Miss Minnie Van Horn
Rev & Mrs Trumbull
Miss Rose Trumbull
Mr & Mrs F. Read
Mr & Mrs L. Flim
Mr & Mrs Powell
Mr & Mrs Blumberg
Mr & Mrs R. A. Irvine
Miss Winona Irvine
Mrs Tate
Miss Laura Tate
Mr & Mrs E. W. Langdon
Mr & Mrs F. P. Nutting
Miss Hettie Miller
Mr & Mrs T. S. Train
Mr & Mrs N. Henton
Mr & Mrs J. Althouse
Mrs S. Althouse
Miss Althouse
Miss Annie Althouse
Miss Katherine Althouse
Mr & Mrs C. Burkhart
Mr & Mrs D. G. Clark
Miss Lulu Clark
Mr & Mrs Duncan
Mr & Mrs D. P. Monteith
Mr & Mrs J. K. Weatherford
Mr & Mrs R. M. Robertson
Miss Robertson
Miss Ina Robertson
Mr & Mrs Crawford

Miss Helen Crawford
Miss Elizabeth Irvine
Mrs Henrietta Brown
Miss Lee Prather
Miss Jane Morris
Mr & Mrs Brink
Miss Margery Brink
Mr & Mrs J. W. Blain
Mr & Mrs W. Fortmiller
Rev E. R. Pritchard
Rev & Mrs Wilson
Mr & Mrs Townsend
Mr T. J. Overman
Mr & Mrs C. E. Wolverton
Mr & Mrs H. F. Merrill
Mr O. H. Irvine
Mr Collins Elkiers
Dr & Mrs G. W. Gray
Dr & Mrs Maston
Dr & Mrs Wallace
Mr & Mrs H. Bryant
Mrs Kirkpatrick
Mr & Mrs T. Wallace
Mr & Mrs LaForest
Mrs Barnes
Mr & Mrs Geo. Simpson
Miss Eva Simpson
Mr & Mrs Cundiff
Miss Mamie Cundiff
Mr & Mrs Hearst
Mr & Mrs E. Montague
Mr & Mrs A. B. McIlwain
Rev and Mrs R. C. Hill
Mr & Mrs I. Conn
Mr & Mrs P. Conn
Mr & Mrs D. Conn
Mr & Mrs R. Conn
Miss Conn
Mr & Mrs Wallace
Mr & Mrs Emerick
Mr & Mrs J. Briggs
Mr & Mrs W. R. Graham
Mr & Mrs Vunk
Mr & Mrs S. Gourley
Dr & Mrs Chamberlaine
Mr & Mrs A. B. Matthews
Mr & Mrs B. Johnson
Judge & Mrs D. R. N. Blackburn
Judge & Mrs J. J. Whitney
Mr John Crawford

Mrs Lisle
Mr & Mrs Crawford
Mr & Mrs A. B. Paxton
Mr & Mrs Blackman
Dr & Mrs Negus
Mr & Mrs W. R. Bilyen
Mr & Mrs Tatler
Mr & Mrs J. Stewart
Mr J. Ellison
Mr Backeusto
Mr & Mrs Elderkin
Mr & Mrs N. H. Allen
Mr & Mrs W Simpson
Mr & Mrs Curran
Mr & Mrs C. Meyer
Mr James Powell
Mr & Mrs Houston
Miss Artie Houston
Mr & Mrs Parker
Miss Nina Parker
Mr & Mrs V. Parker
Mr Walter Parker
Mr & Mrs L. Gray
Mrs Fish
Mr & Mrs C. Marshall
Mr & Mrs J. Wheeler
Mr & Mrs J. Schmeer
Mr & Mrs N. Payne
Mrs Muller
Mr Fred Muller
Mr & Mrs O'Connor
Mr & Mrs Garret
Mr & Mrs P. Pfeiffer
Mr & Mrs F. Pfeiffer
Mr & Mrs Isom
Mr & Mrs Lanning
Mrs Russell
Mr & Mrs J. W. Cusick
Mr & Mrs D. V. S. Reid
Mr & Mrs S. Froman
Mrs Helmick
Dr & Mrs J. M. Jones
Mrs G. Layton
Mr & Mrs W. Rayborn
Mr & Mrs W. Vance
Miss Vance
Miss Pearl Vance
Mr & Mrs Geo. Chamberlain
Mr & Mrs Dodder
Mr & Mrs A. Barker

Mr & Mrs Crosby
Mr & Mrs R. Crosby
Mrs D. Burmester
Miss Mildred Burmester
Mr Van Wilson
Mr Ed. Blodgett
Mr & Mrs F. French
Mr & Mrs W. Tiverdale
Miss Rhoda Hail
Mr J. Hail
Mr & Mrs M. Sternberg
Mrs S. Sternberg
Mr & Mrs A. Senders
Mr & Mrs A. Hackleman
Mr & Mrs T. Monteith, Jr.
Mr Thornton
Mr & Mrs Hoffman
Mr & Mrs R. Brown
Mr & Mrs O. Hendrikson
Mr & Mrs Wheeler
Miss T. Wheeler
Mr & Mrs Dannals
Mr & Mrs Caviness
Mr & Mrs Schlosser
Miss Schlosser
Mr Merrill Fish
Mr & Mrs Montanye
Mr & Mrs T. Hopkins
Mr & Mrs J. Milliard
Miss Yantis
Miss May Yantis
Mr & Mrs Standard
Mr & Mrs E. Searle
Mr F. Kenton
Mr & Mrs C. E. Brownell
Miss Frankie Hopkins
Mrs George
Miss Elsie George
Mr & Mrs D. Froman
Dr & Mrs M. H. Ellis
Dr & Mrs C. C. Kelly
Dr & Mrs G. A. Whitney
Mr John Foshay
Mr & Mrs Robson
Mr Ed. Cusick
Mr & Mrs J. M. Ralston
Mr & Mrs Oris Archibald-
Mr & Mrs W. H. Goltra
Mr & Mrs W. Ralston
Mr & Mrs W. Humphrey

SALEM, OREGON

Arnold, Mr and Mrs W. S. ; 367 Winter st.

Babcock, Mr and Mrs F. J.; 505 Commercial st.
Bagley, Mrs Ellen ; 180 High st.
Baker, Mr and Mrs J. A.; 357 Liberty st.
———Clair A.
Boggs, Mr and Mrs Wm. S.; 341 Summer st.
Boise, Judge and Mrs. R. P.; North Liberty st.
———Miss
———Mac
Breyman, Mr and Mrs Eugene ; 205 Court st.
———Miss
———Miss Minnie
———Miss Jessie
Brooks, Mr and Mrs J. H.; 130 High st.
Brown, Mr and Mrs J. F.; 347 High st.
Brown, Mr and Mrs Wm.; 188 State st.
Burnett, Mr and Mrs G. H.; SW cor. Centre and High sts.
Buss, Miss ; 251 Court st.
Bush, Mr. A.; Church st.
———Miss Sally
———Miss Eugenia
Bush, Mr and Mrs A. N.; 236 Ferry st.

Cannon, Mr and Mrs R. B.; 251 Ferry st.
———Miss Stella
Carpenter, Mrs S.; 205 Church st.
———Miss
Chadwick, Mr and Mrs S. F.; 369 Capital st.
———Miss Mar.
Church, Mr and Mrs S. W.; 385 Winter st.
Church, Miss Lizzie ; Court st.
Clarke, Mr and Mrs S. A ; 45 Commercial st.
———W. J.
Collins, Mr and Mrs George ; 197 Court st.
Casper, Miss Maggie ; 3 Marion st.
Cox, Mrs A. F.; 341 Summer st.
———Chas. A.
Crawford, Mr and Mrs J. W.; 344 Commercial st.
———Miss Emma

Cusick, Dr and Mrs J. W.; 357 Commercial st.
——Miss Ethel

Dalrymple, Mr and Mrs J. J.; 405 Winter st.
——Miss Kate
——Jessie
D'Arcy, Mr and Mrs P.; 465 Church st.
——Miss
——Miss Teresa E.
——P. H.
——W. J.
Dearborn, Mrs Helen ; SW cor. Commercial and Dearborn
——Miss
——Miss Ella
——Miss Kate
——F. S.

Edes, Mr and Mrs Ed. N.; 182 State st.
——Miss Helen
England, Mr and Mrs Wm.; 340 Liberty st.

Farrar, Mr and Mrs S.; 442 Commercial st.
——Joseph
Fleming, Mr and Mrs R. B.; NW cor. Centre and High sts.
Fry, Mr and Mrs J. D.; 458 Commercial st.

Gibson, Mr and Mrs H. L.; 367 Winter st.
Giesy, Mr and Mrs August ; 176 Cottage st.
Giesy, Mrs John ; 331 Liberty st.
——Miss Gussie
Gilbert, Mr and Mrs A. N.; 319 Liberty st.
——Ray
Gilbert, Mr and Mrs F. N.; 392 Cottage st.
Gilbert, Mrs I. K.; 48 Marion st.
——Miss Nellie
Gillingham, Mrs. Eugenia ; 314 Summer st.
——Miss Grace
——Charles W.
Giltner, Mr and Mrs Frank ; Liberty st., South Salem
Golden, Dr and Mrs T. L.; 310 Liberty st.
——Miss Belle
Gray, Mr and Mrs C. A.: 443 Court st.
Gray, Mr and Mrs D. B.; 204 Twelfth st.
——Miss Mabel
Gray, Mr and Mrs. G. B.; 265 Thirteenth st.
Gray, Mr and Mrs W. T.; 247 Thirteenth st.
Gregg, J. T. 347 High st.

Hall, Dr and Mrs C. H.; 359 Summer st.
——Miss Esther
Hendricks, Mr and Mrs R. J.; 311 Liberty st.
Hirsch, Mr and Mrs Edward ; 437 High st.
——Miss
——Miss Lulu
Hirsch, Mr and Mrs L.; 397 Cottage st.
Hodgkin, Mr and Mrs F. E.; cor. Court and Summer sts.
Holman, Mr and Mrs John ; 376 High st.
——Miss Minnie
Hubbard, Mr and Mrs T. H.; 396 Commercial st.
Hughes, Mr and Mrs John ; 47 High st.
——George P.
——J. Frank
——Miss Genevieve
——Northup, Miss Jessie
Howard, Mrs D. C.; 315 Capital st.
——T. A.

Jessup, Dr and Mrs S. R.; 178 State st.
Johnson, Mr and Mrs G. W.; 324 High st.
——Miss
——Miss Lulu
Jones, Mr and Mrs G. H.; cor. Commercial and Oak sts.
——Miss Frankie
Jordan, Mr and Mrs J. D.; 369 Liberty st.
——Harvey S.

Keller, Mr and Mrs C. L.; 196 State st.
——E. P.
——Harry P.
——Clyde L.
Kuhn, Mr and Mrs L.; 189 Court st.

Ladue, Mr and Mrs W. A.; 320 Capital st.
La Fore, Mr and Mrs E. M.; 339 High st.
Litchfield, Mr and Mrs G. C.; 406 Cottage st.
——Miss
——Miss Lillie
——Miss Nellie
Lunn, John N.; 375 Commercial st.

Manning, Mr and Mrs I. A.; 321 Chemekete st.
Martin, Mr and Mrs J. M.; SE cor. Court and Twelfth sts.
McNary, Miss Lizzie
Martin, Mr and Mrs W. W.; 385 Liberty st.
Myres, Miss Carrie

Mathews, Mr and Mrs D. W.; 391 Chemekete st.
——Miss Ruth
——Miss Mary
Messick, Mr and Mrs R. M.; 387 Marion st.
——Miss
——Miss Margaret
——Miss Mary
——J. Bruce
Monroe, Mrs A. J.; 313 Liberty st.
——Staiger, Will.
Moody, Mr and Mrs Z. F.; NE cor. Court and Winter sts.

——Miss Edna
Moores, Mr and Mrs A. N.; 395 Liberty st.
Moores, Mr and Mrs C. B.; 204 State st.
——Mrs J. H.
——Miss Carrie
Moores, Mrs Isaac; 407 Front st.
Mullon, Mr and Mrs J. T.; 347 High st.
Murphy, Mr and Mrs J. J.; Court st.
McBride, Hon. John H.; Capitol Building
McCully, Mr and Mrs J. D.; 315 Court st.
McElroy, Mr and Mrs E. B.; 357 Court st.
——Willis
McFadden, Miss Alice; 357 Court st.
McMeekin, Miss Margaret; 485 Commercial st.
McNary, Mr and Mrs H. M.; 400 Capital st.
——Miss
——Miss Lillian
——Hugh

Newal, Rev and Mrs H. A.; NE cor. Centre and Liberty sts.
Patterson, Mr and Mrs I. L.; 17 Commercial st.   *Thursday*
Patton, Mr and Mrs I. McF.; 251 Court st.
Parrish, Rev and Mrs J. L.; 404 Capitol st.
——Miss Grace
——Miss Josie
——Parish, Miss Ella
Parvin, Mr and Mrs Z. M.; NE cor. Capital and Chemekete sts.
——Miss Mamie

Richardson, Dr and Mrs J. A.; NE cor. Chemekete and Church sts.
——Miss Frankie
Rollins, Rev and Mrs W. E.; 226 Church st.
Rork, Rev and Mrs M. B.; 318 Chemekete st.
Rosenberg, Mr and Mrs J. W.; 143 Centre st.
Rowland, Dr and Mrs L. L.; 125 Court st.

Scott, Miss Mattie, 49 Marion st.
Sicka Joose, Rev and Mrs K. A.; 354 High st.
Smith, Mr and Mrs J. C.; NE cor. Court and Liberty sts.
Smith, Dr and Mrs J. N.; 175 Court st.
Starr, J, Benson ; 180 Cottage st.
Stotz, Mr and Mrs G.; 213 Winter st.
——Walter
Strang, Mr and Mrs A. E.; 205 Church st.
Strickler, Mr and Mrs J. H.; 461 Front st.
Strong, Mr and Mrs Amos ; 85 Commercial st.

Thomson, Mr and Mrs A. M.; 320 Liberty st.
Thompson, Mr and Mrs J. T.; 365 Commercial st.
——Hugh

Vandayer, Mr and Mrs I.; 390 Court st.
——Frank

Waite, Mr and Mrs E. M., 276 State st.
Wallace, Mr and Mrs R. S.; NW cor. Court and Capital sts.   *Monday*
Wheeler, Mrs A. A.; 335 Liberty st.
——Miss Emma
Williams, Major and Mrs. George ; 475 Front st.
Wilson, Mr and Mrs J. Q.; 326 Liberty st.
Willis, Mr and Mrs Leo; cor. Capital and Centre sts.
——Miss Leona
——Miss Eugene
——Percy
Woodworth, Mr and Mrs C S.; 29 Commercial st.   *Thursday*
Wright, Mr and Mrs J. G.; Church st. bet. Centre and Chemekete sts.

THE

PORTLAND BLUE BOOK

SHOPPING GUIDE

AND

ELITE BUSINESS DIRECTORY

EMBRACING NAMES AND ADDRESSES OF RELIABLE AND
PROMINENT HOUSES, CLASSIFIED UNDER
APPROPRIATE BUSINESS HEADINGS

Art Goods
S. & G. Gump, 184 First

Banks
Portland Savings Bank, SW. cor Second
and Washington

Boarding
The Comstock, cor. East Park and Alder

Booksellers
Stuart & Thompson, 105 First
Edward De Kum, De Kum's Building

Clothing
A. B. Steinbach & Co., 161-163 First

Cigars
Sichel & Mayer, 75 First

Carpets
Walter Bros., NW. cor. First and Yamhill

Crockery and Glassware
Olds & Summers, 189-191 First

Druggists
Wm. Phunder,
Wisdom & Co., First and Stark
Frank Nau, Hotel Portland Pharmacy
S. G. Skidmore, 151 First

Dry Goods
John Crau & Co., 131-133 First

Dentists
Ney Churchman, SW. cor. 3rd & Morrison

Dancing Academy
Mrs H. A. Foreman, 201 Seventh

Furniture
G. Shindler, 166 First and 167-169 Front

Grocers
Seeley, Mason & Co., 29-31 Yamhill
Portland Cash Grocery, 45 First

Jewelers
L. C. Henrichsen, 149 First
Albert Feldenheimer, NW. cor. First and
Morrison

Pianos
Klein & Day, 166 First

Purchasing Agency
Mrs Nina Larowe, 253 Sixth

Photographer
B. C. Towne, cor. First and Morrison

Theatres
Marquam Grand Opera House

Tailors
A. Polioka, Washington, bet. First and
Second
K. Stephan, Ladies' Tailor, First near
Washington

Choice Books in Fine Bindings, at STUART & THOMPSON'S, 105 First St.,
Portland.

Personnel of the Press

PERSONNEL OF THE PRESS

Daily Morning Examiner

BUSINESS OFFICE, 756 MARKET STREET, EDITORIAL ROOMS, 508 MONT-
GOMERY STREET

W. R. Hearst	Proprietor
C. M. Palmer	Business Manager
A. B. Henderson	Managing Editor
S. S. Chamberlain	Managing News Editor
Ralph Meeker	Night Editor
Mrs Adele Chretien	Dramatic Editor
F. L. H. Noble	Sunday Editor
E. A. Walcott	Weekly Editor
Samuel E. Moffitt	Editorial Writer
E. A. Walcott	Editorial Writer
A. G. Bierce	Editorial Writer
R. R. Livingstone	Commercial Editor
Allan Kelly	Special Writer
H. D. Bigelow	Special Writer
Chas. Michelson	Special Writer
E. H. Hamilton	Special Writer
A. McEwen	Special Writer
Ambrose G. Bierce	Special Writer
Sam Davis	Special Writer
C. E. Hamilton	Telegraph Editor
Weston Coyney	Telegraph Editor
C. A. Brant	Telegraph Editor
T. T. Williams	City Editor
J. M. Ward	Assistant City Editor
J. N. II. Irwin	Social Editor

LOCAL STAFF

W. D. Dressler	D. Mors Bowers
James P. Slevin	John Isaac
Samuel Ewing	Charles Low
Horace H. Briggs	M. E. Jackson
Alphonso Murphy	Winifred Sweet
A. M. Lawrence	W. Dorrance
F. W. Lawrence	J. P. Reynolds
S. P. Brady	Will N. Hart
Joseph Cooney	George H. Meyer
Chas. Trevathan	Alexander Allen
O. Black	H. Falkeneau

DAILY, including Sunday, per year,
        by mail.........................$7.80
DAILY, by carrier.........per month, .65
SUNDAY EXAMINER...........per year, 2.00
WEEKLY EXAMINER..........per year, 1.50

Morning ☙ Call

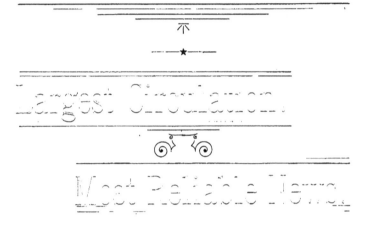

Largest Circulation

Most Reliable News

---★---

The Society News Department of the Morning Call is one of the features which attracts the attention of Society People. It presents the brightest, freshest and most reliable accounts of all the social events in the city

Daily Morning Call

BUSINESS OFFICE, 525 MONTGOMERY STREET. EDITORIAL ROOMS,
509 CLAY STREET.

Loring Pickering - - - ⎫
George K. Fitch - - - ⎬ Proprietors
Estate of J. W. Simonton - ⎭

Ernest C. Stock - - - Managing Editor

John Bonner - - - ⎫
G. B. Densmore - - - ⎬ Editorial Writers

W. S. Dewey - - - - Commercial Editor

Charles K. Graham - - - ⎫
John J. Corey - - - - ⎬ Telegraph Editor

Henry K. Goddard - - - News Editor
George E. Barnes - - - Dramatic Critic
L. D. Adam - . . - Social Editor
H. J. Lask - . - - Fraternal Editor
L. S. Whitcomb . - - - City Editor
Paul E. Vandor - - - - Assistant City Editor
M. J. Geary - - - - Sporting Editor

LOCAL STAFF

E. G. Wade   H. M. Tod
J. F. Klein   T. F. Pendergast
A. C. Jackson   C. Shaw
J. B. Smyth   W. C. Fenderson
F. H. Driscoll   J. McMullan

J. H. Witty

SPECIAL WRITERS

Mrs. S. M. Severance   Miss May E. Quigley
Mrs. L. E. Thane   Mrs. M. B. Watson
A. O. McGrew   J. Curtin

389

THE EVENING POST

The Leading Evening Newspaper

ON THE PACIFIC COAST

The Circulation of the POST is equal to that of all other evening news-papers combined.

THE EVENING POST.

SAN FRANCISCO.

COR. BUSH & KEARNEY STS.

The POST has endorsements from the leading advertisers of this city for being the best evening journal for advertising purposes.

The Evening POST Delivered by Carrier at 50 Cents Per Month.

The "Post" has agencies in Every City and Town in California and Nevada

BY MAIL, POSTAGE PAID

1 Year..................................$6.00	6 Months...................... $3.00
3 Months 1.50	1 Year, Weekly Post.......1.50

HEAZELTON & HIRSCH, Proprietors

SAN FRANCISCO, CAL.

The Evening Post

Geo. Heazelton and C. J. Hirsch, Proprietors

BUSINESS OFFICE AND EDITORIAL ROOMS

Corner of Bush and Kearny Streets

EDITORIAL DEPARTMENT

Geo. Heazelton	Editor
Thos. Garrett	Managing Editor
Jno. Finley	Mining Editor
Mr. Naughton	Sporting Editor
Mr. Horton	Horse Column Editor
Mr. Older	Reporter
Mr. Thompson	Reporter
Mr. McCarthy	Reporter
Mr. Carroll	Reporter
Mr. Slavin	Reporter
Mr. Jordan	Reporter
Mr. Phillips	Reporter
Mr. Cosgrave	Reporter
Mr. Gibson	Reporter
Mr. Denison	Reporter
Mr. French	Reporter
Mr. Carr	Reporter
Mr. Leavy	Reporter

BUSINESS DEPARTMENT

Chas. J. Hirsch	Business Manager
C. H. House	Cashier
W. C. Meagher	Accountant
J. E. Warren	Collector
Jno. F. Garvey	Mailing Clerk
F. Squire	Clerk
J. Moran	Clerk

Daily Evening Bulletin

BUSINESS OFFICE, 622 MONTGOMERY STREET

EDITORIAL ROOMS, 517 CLAY STREET

G. K. Fitch, - - - - - ⎫
L. Pickering, - - - - ⎬ Proprietors

George K. Fitch, - - - Managing Editor
R. L. C. Barnes, - - - Business Manager

W. C. Bartlett, - - ⎫
M. G. Upton, - - - ⎬ Editorial Writers

J. D. Lewis, - - - - - ⎫
W. M. Webster, - - - - ⎬ Editors

B. C. Wright, - - ⎫
W. B. Allen, - - ⎬ Commercial Editors

F. H. Sawyer, . - - - City Editor

LOCAL STAFF

H. S. Dalliba   Geo. D. Squires
C. S. Aiken   H. H. Egbert
Mrs. C. Nesfield   Jas. T. Coakley
J. A. Calhoun   D. H. Walker

The Daily Report

IS THE LEADING EVENING NEWSPAPER OF
THE PACIFIC COAST

Served by Carrier at 50 Cents per Month

Two Lightning Presses !   *Two Lightning Presses !*

Two Lightning Presses !   *Two Lightning Presses !*

Largest Circulation of Any Paper in San Francisco

The "Report" is the only Evening Newspaper in San Francisco with a
Circulation large enough to require Lightning Presses.
Daily Circulation 40,000.

Editorial Rooms: 320 Sansome St.   W. M. Bunker   **Business Office:** 238 Montgomery St.   A. C. Hiester

San Francisco Daily Report

BUSINESS OFFICE, 238 MONTGOMERY STREET.   EDITORIAL ROOMS, 320 SANSOME STREET.

William M. Bunker - - ⎫
Amos C. Hiester - - - ⎬ Proprietors
Daily Report Publishing Co. ⎭

Wm. M. Bunker - - - Editor

Amos C. Hiester - - - - Business Manager

S. F. Sutherland - - - ⎫
W. Booth - - - - ⎬ Editorial Writers
Edward Booth - - - - ⎭

S. F. Sutherland - - - City Editor

Gavin D. High - - - Assistant City Editor

Edward S. Spring - - - Commercial Editor

L. J. Kennedy - - - - Exchange Editor

Morris G. Jonas - - - Telegraph Editor

H. M. McKenney - - - Cashier

John M. Ward - - - ⎫
S. B. Morse - - - - ⎬ Assistants
Hub. A. Wood . - - ⎭

E. P. Fish - - - - Chief of Advertising Dept.

Wm. A. Hiester - - - -

C. H. Wall - - - -

M. Callinan - - - -

T. Coffey - - - -

LOCAL STAFF

Edgar T. Price	T. F. Bonnet	David E. Williamson
J. P. Booth	J. T. Hanna	L. D. Smith
C. A. Fraser	D. V. Clark	A. E. Shattuck
A. S. Jones	G. F. Brown.	A. Milling
Burnside Cromwell	C. F. Montague	H. L. Brooke
A. T. Brown	R. S. Merritt	S. N. Hencock
Thomas J. Reed	J. W. Harvey	L. H. Irvine
	George C. Williams	

Daily Alta California

BUSINESS OFFICE AND EDITORIAL ROOMS, 529 CALIFORNIA STREET

The Overland Monthly

1891 **1891**

The Overland Monthly is the Magazine of the Pacific Coast

Among the Features for 1891 will be

I. DESCRIPTIVE.
   1. Illustrated articles presenting the picturesque natural features, and the growth and possibilities of the different sections of the Coast.
   2. A series of articles on the social and industrial life of the Sandwich Islands.

II. HISTORICAL.
   1. Studies of disputed historical points in the history of the Coast, based upon the reminiscences of survivors.
   2. Personal reminiscences of life among the mines and on the frontier, preserving the tone and spirit of that life.
   3. Studies of the early Mexican and Indian life.

III. SOCIAL AND INDUSTRIAL.
   1. Discussions of the peculiar social conditions of the Coast.
   2. Descriptions of the various industrial interests, illustrated.
   3. Studies of the social and political problems of the day affecting the Pacific Coast.

IV. FICTION.
   1. Stories of early life on the frontier, and of contemporary Pacific Coast life.

V. TRAVELS AND ADVENTURES.
   1. Records, chiefly from the adventurers themselves, of explorations in the remote regions of the Continent.
   2. Sketches of hunting, prospecting and outing on the Pacific Coast.
   3. Accounts of miners' and gold hunters' life, and of pioneer experiences.

VI. INDIAN SKETCHES.
   Accounts of the Indian wars, customs, character, myths, and traditions.

VII. CURRENT THOUGHT.
   Comment on current thought of the day in editorials, and in articles commenting on recently published books in the field of education, history, science and political research.

Subscription, $4.00 a Year. Sample Copy, Twenty Cents.

Overland Monthly Publishing Company,

420 Montgomery Street, San Francisco, Cal.

The Overland Monthly

420 MONTGOMERY STREET, SAN FRANCISCO.

DIRECTORS

Judge John H. Boalt, President.

Irving M. Scott   Professor Martin Kellogg

L. L. Baker   Captain J. M. McDonald

George C. Perkins   W. E. Brown

F. M. Stocking - - - - - Manager

M. W. Shinn - - - - - Editor

Charles S. Greene - - Assistant Editor

The Argonaut

BUSINESS OFFICE AND EDITORIAL ADDRESS, 213 GRANT AVENUE

Argonaut Publishing Company - Proprietors

Frank M. Pixley - - - - Editor

Jerome A. Hart . - - - Managing Editor

Lawrence S. Vassault - - - Sub Editor

Walter B. Cooke - - - - Society Editor

A. P. Stanton - - . - Business Manager

San Francisco News Letter

AND

California Advertiser

OFFICES, FLOOD BUILDING, FOURTH AND MARKET STREETS

F. Marriott - - - Publisher and Proprietor

STAFF

A. S. Lowndes	Otto tum Suden
John Finley	W. D. Scurlock
Danl. O'Connell	W. W. Naughton
H. C. Beals	Mrs Kate Waters
Wm. M. Neilson	Miss E. D. Keith

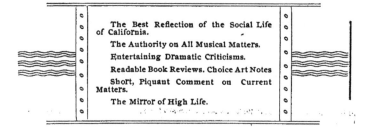

"THE WAVE"

A Journal for Those in the Swim

Business Office, Rooms 26-27, 331 Montgomery St.

J. O'H. COSGRAVE and *HUGH HUMF*, <u>Editors and Proprietors</u>

OAKLAND

TRIBUNE

The leading Daily Newspaper in Alameda County ; circulation Double that of all other Dailies combined.

Eight Pages, Fifty-six columns daily; a Peerless Twelve Page, Eighty-four column Daily, issued Saturday.

THE TRIBUNE is progressive, able, alert and metropolitan in all Departments.

A Brilliant Staff of Writers
Complete Associated Press Reports

Delivered by Carrier in Oakland, Alameda, Berkeley, Fruitvale, Piedmont, Temescal, San Leandro, Golden Gate, Lorin, Pleasanton and Livermore at 50 cents per month.   By mail, $6.00 per year.

THE Oakland Weekly Tribune

Is a Twelve Page, Eighty-four Column Paper, issued every Saturday.   By Mail, $1.50 per year.

TRIBUNE PUBLISHING COMPANY

W. E. DARGIE, President
T. T. DARGIE, Secretary
W. E. BOND, Business Manager

PUBLISHERS AND PROPRIETORS

Oakland Evening Tribune

BUSINESS OFFICE AND EDITORIAL ROOMS

413, 415, 417 AND 419 EIGHTH ST., NEAR BROADWAY, OAKLAND, CAL.

··o◇o··

TRIBUNE PUBLISHING CO., Publishers and Proprietors

W. E. Dargie   -   -   -   President

· T. T. Dargie   -   -   -   Secretary

W. E. Bond, Business Manager

LOCAL STAFF

E. F. Cahill	E. H. Clough
John Lathrop	Harry A. Melvin
J. F. Connors	J. E. Barber
E. H. Hamilton	Mrs M. G. C. Edholm
Geo. F. Hatton	E. H. Shaw
W. H. Monroe	Miss A. E. Knapp
Paul Goldsmith	Mrs L. E. Thane
W. F. Williamson	Miss A. M. Saul
H. S. Pugh	A. B. Taynton
C. W. Greene	Mrs M. A. Adams

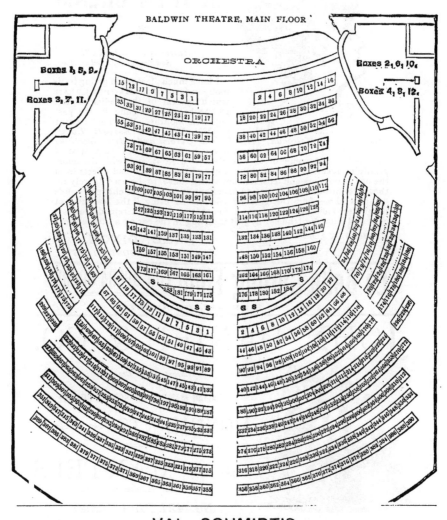

BALDWIN THEATRE, MAIN FLOOR

ORCHESTRA

Boxes 1, 5, 9.

Boxes 3, 7, 11.

Boxes 2, 6, 10.

Boxes 4, 8, 12.

KA-TI-LA CREAM

BALDWIN OPERA HOUSE,
San Francisco, April 25, 1890

I have much pleasure in giving testimony in favor of the KA-TI-LA CREAM which several of the ladies of our troupe have been using in the past eighteen months. When in Denver in 1889, *Miss Jesse Bartlett Davis, Miss Carlotta Malconda, Miss Juliette Corden and Miss Josephine Bartlett* tried the cream and were so much pleased with it that most of the ladies and some of the gentlemen tried it, and with the most gratifying results. It softens the skin and removes all bad effects from the use of powders and cosmetiques which have to be used largely in theatrical business. It is also an excellent preventive for chapped hands or lips, and we find the greatest comfort in using it the last thing at night after facing a cold wind. I found it an excellent remedy for earache and catarrh of the ear by just inserting in the ear on a little cotton.

FOR SALE BY ALL DRUGGISTS

FRED. DIXON,
Stage Director "BOSTONIANS"

La Belle Curling Fluid FOR OPERA GOERS

FOR SALE BY ALL DRUGGISTS

JOHN DANIEL & CO.

Importers and Dealers in

ITALIAN MARBLE AND SCOTCH GRANITE

MONUMENTS ✳ ✳

✳ ✳ MANTELS

No. 421 Pine Street

Between Montgomery and Kearny, and corner Central Avenue and Bush Street,
Opposite Entrance Laurel Hill Cemetery, San Francisco, Cal.

Manufacturers of *Monuments, Headstones, Mantel Pieces, Plumb-*
✳ *ers' Stones, Table and Counter Tops, Imposing Stones,*
✳ *etc.,* at Lowest Cash Prices : : : :

410

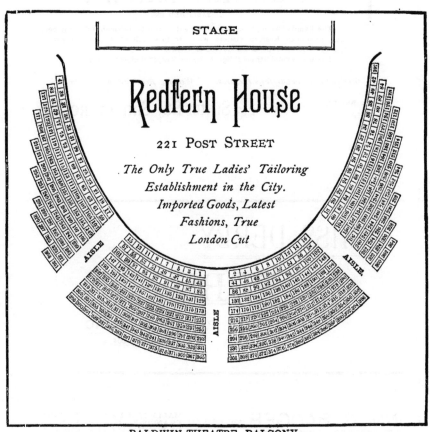

STAGE

Redfern House

221 POST STREET

*The Only True Ladies' Tailoring
Establishment in the City.
Imported Goods, Latest
Fashions, True
London Cut*

BALDWIN THEATRE, BALCONY.

412

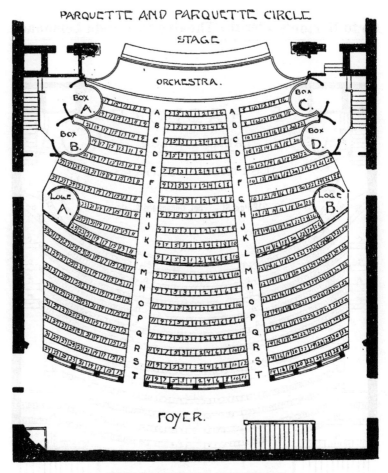

PARQUETTE AND PARQUETTE CIRCLE

NEW CALIFORNIA, MAIN FLOOR

CLARA MELVIN

EVERY LADY'S OPINION

Clara Melvin, of 126 Kearny Street,
Learn, as a Manicure can not be beat,
Attend and try her famed Complexion Bleach,
Rare Langtry Cream and Hair Shampoo for each,
And here in make-up doth a lesson teach.

Melvin Rouge! Forget-me-not! Citrine!
Eureka Face Powder, the best e'er seen.
Let Ivory Nail Cleaner and Nail Powder be
Valued by Ladies, their success we see:
Inspect, of manicures Miss Melvin's best,
Now is the Season, put this to the test.

French ★ ★
★ Method ★
★ ★ Manicure

SURGEON CHIROPODIST

126 KEARNY STREET, Room 25, Thurlow Block
San Francisco

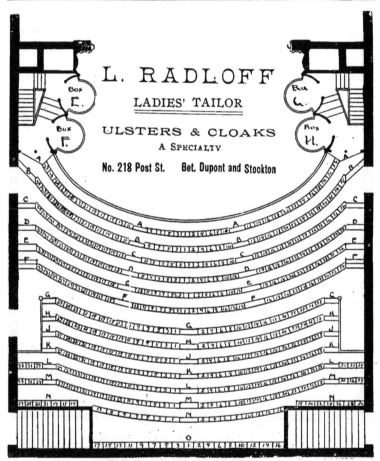

L. RADLOFF

LADIES' TAILOR

ULSTERS & CLOAKS
A Specialty

No. 218 Post St.   Bet. Dupont and Stockton

CALIFORNIA THEATRE, DRESS CIRCLE

ERNST H. LUDWIG

THE MODEL AMERICAN CATERER

1206 SUTTER ST.

TELEPHONE 2388

Supplies Wedding Breakfasts, Luncheons, Dinners,
Matinee Teas and Receptions on Shortest Notice.
Also Terrapin, Entrees for Luncheons and Dinners,
Ice Cream, Cakes, Etc.

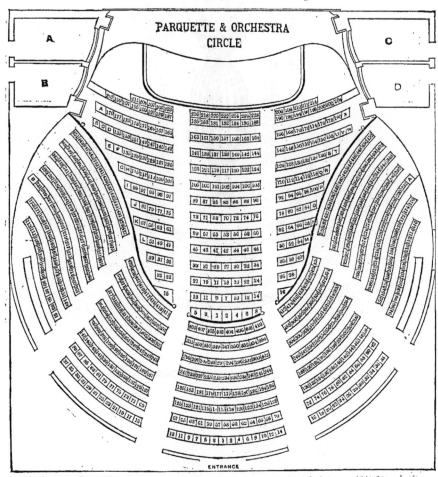

GRAND OPERA HOUSE. MAIN FLOOR.

MME. ANNA LEE

MANICURING

PHYSICAL CULTURE

405 SUTTER STREET

San Francisco

GRAND OPERA HOUSE

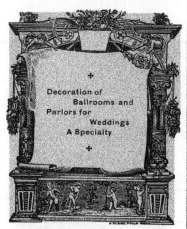

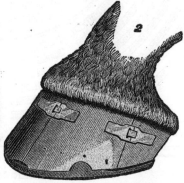

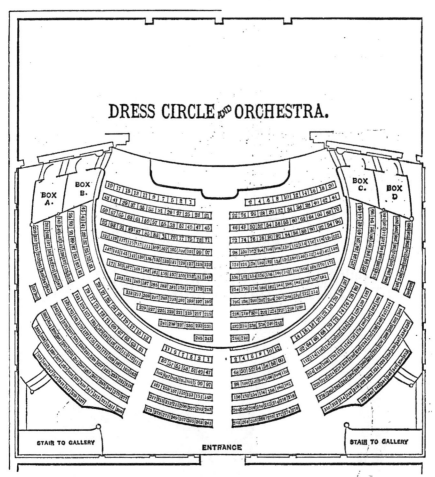

ALCAZAAR MAIN FLOOR.

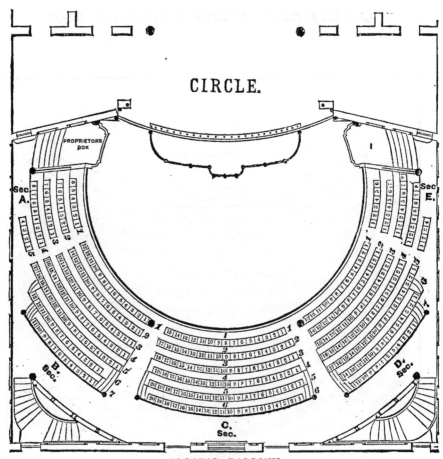

ALCAZAR BALCONY

Columbus Buggy Co.

Largest Carriage Manufacturers in the World

Buggies, Carriages, Phætons, Victorias

SURREYS, COUPES, KENSINGTONS, VILLAGE CARTS

Pacific Coast Headquarters
29 Market St., S. F. Latest Styles ! ❉ Newest Designs !

Finest and Lightest Repository West of the Rocky Mountains

A. G. GLENN, Manager

419

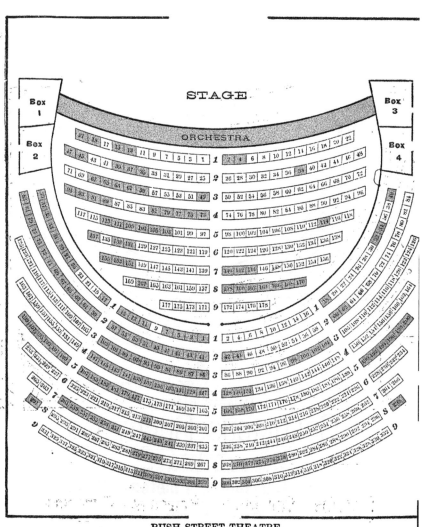

BUSH STREET THEATRE.

STAGE

ORCHESTRA

BOX A   BOX B

1
2
3
4
5
6
7
8
9
10
11
12
13
14
15
16
17
18
19
20
21
22
23
24
25
26
27
28
29

TIVOLI; MAIN FLOOR.

Portraits Enlarged

Artistic Portraits in India Ink
Water Colors, Crayons and Pastel

BY THE

Pacific Portrait Company

1221 MARKET STREET

T. J. O'BRIEN, Manager   Bet. Eighth and Ninth

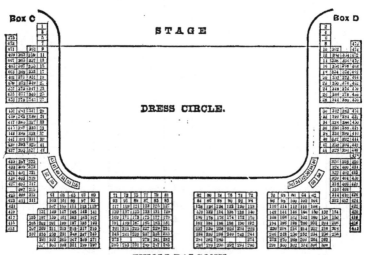

TIVOLI BALCONY.

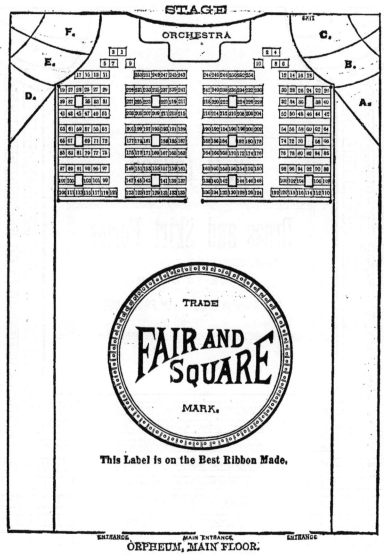

ORPHEUM, MAIN FLOOR.

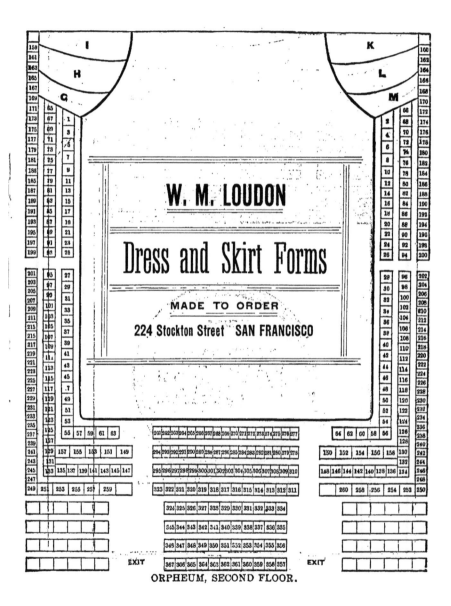

ORPHEUM, SECOND FLOOR.

Oakland Seminary For Young Ladies 528 ELEVENTH ST.,

Between Washington and Clay

and Eleventh and Twelfth Sts.

Oakland, Cal.

MRS. M. K. BLAKE, PRINCIPAL

MISS E. L. DICKINSON

ASSOCIATE PRINCIPAL

425

MISS LAKE'S SCHOOL FOR GIRLS
1534 SUTTER STREET, (Corner of Octavia)
SAN FRANCISCO

College of San Rafael

SAN RAFAEL, CAL.

The College is beautifully located, being only a short walk from either of the Railway Stations, and near that magnificent new hotel "THE R FAEL." The grounds costing $20,000, and the building $95,000. The building has a frontage of 219 feet with a uniform depth of 86 feet, and is a four-story structure. The approach to the College is by broad stairs twenty-eight feet wide. The corridors are twelve feet in width. As a precaution against fire there are five hose closets distributed throughout the building.

It is the intention of the Dominican Sisters to make this one of the Foremost Educational Institutions on the Pacific Coast. No expense has been spared to make this new Academy complete in all respects pertaining to the comfort and the convenience of its patrons.

FOR TERMS OF TUITION, ETC. APPLY to MOTHER SUPERIOR
San Rafael, Cal.

⇒St. Rose Academy⇐

WAS FOUNDED AND IS CONDUCTED BY

THE SISTERS OF ST. DOMINIC

An order of Ladies who have devoted their lives to the mission of teaching and
are as a consequence naturally adapted to that noble calling.

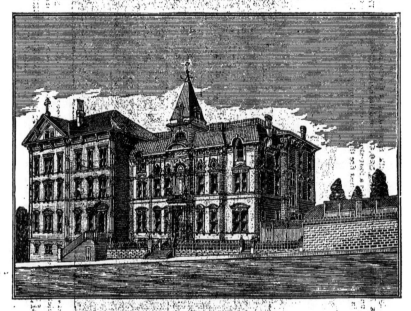

THE ACADEMY was established in San Francisco fourteen years
ago and has grown steadily into public favor as an educational
institution for young ladies. The course of study embraces all
that is required to obtain a thorough and refined education. The
Pupils have the careful supervision of home life, and the closest watch-
fulness is exercised in their mental, moral and physical training. A
careful examination is made so that no objectionable pupil is admitted.

❋ ❋ ❋

By addressing the SISTER SUPERIOR, St. Rose Academy,
Golden Gate Avenue and Steiner Street, San Francisco, full information, regarding terms, etc.. will be furnished.

THE

SAN FRANCISCO BLUE BOOK

SHOPPING GUIDE

AND

ELITE BUSINESS DIRECTORY

EMBRACING NAMES AND ADDRESSES OF RELIABLE AND
PROMINENT HOUSES, CLASSIFIED UNDER
APPROPRIATE BUSINESS HEADINGS

Advertisements

H. C. Brown, 35 and 37 Frankfort, N. Y.

Agricultural Implements

Thos. H. B. Varney, 42-44 Fremont

Ale and Porter

J. F. Burnell, 519 Sacramento
Sherwood & Sherwood, 212-214 Market
William Wolff & Co., 105 Front

Amusements—Places of

New California, Bush above Kearny
Alcazar Theatre, 116 O'Farrell
Baldwin Theatre, 932-936 Market
Bush Street Theatre, 325 Bush
Chinese Theatre, 626 Jackson
Chinese Theatre, Grand, 814 Washington
Chinese Theatre, New, 623 Jackson
Chinese Theatre, Royal, 836 Washington
Grand Opera House, N s Mission between
   Third and Fourth
Orpheum, S s O'Farrell bet. Stockton and
   Powell
Panorama, cor. Market and Tenth
Panorama, cor. Eddy and Mason
Standard Theatre, 320 Bush
Tivoli Opera House, 28-32 Eddy
Woodward's Gardens, Mission between
   Thirteenth and Fourteenth
Powell Street Theatre, Powell opposite
   Baldwin Hotel

Art Galleries

S. & G. Gump, 581 Market
San Francisco Art Association, 430 Pine

Artificial Stone

P. H. Jackson & Co., 223-230 First

Artist

Pacific Portrait Co., T. J. O'Brien, Manager, 1221 Market

Artists' Materials

The Bancroft Company, 721 Market
T. J. Bass & Co., 14 and 16 Ellis

Awning Makers

Neville & Co., 31 and 33 California

Banjos

T. W. Bree, 804 Larkin

Bands

Louis N. Ritzau, 803 O'Farrell

Baths

Dr. Loryea's Electric, Russian and Turk-
   ish, 218 Post
Byron Hot Springs, Mud, Hot Salt, and
   Sulphur, Byron, Cal.

Beds and Bedding

W. & J. Sloane & Co., 641-647 Market
F. S. Chadbourne & Co., 741 Market

Bell Founders

W. T. Garratt & Co., Fremont and Natoma

Bibles

Thomas Nelson & Sons, 33 E. 17th st.,
   New York

Billiard Table Manufacturers

The Brunswick-Balke Collender Co., 655
   Market
August Jungblut & Co., 10 and 12 Golden
   Gate Avenue

Bitters

Sherwood & Sherwood, 212-214 Market

Bill Posters

T. N. Dumphy & Co., 606 Commercial

Blackening
Sherwood & Sherwood, 212-214 Market,
(Day and Martin's)

Blacksmiths
T. Doyle, 57 New Montgomery

Bookbinders
The Bancroft Company, 721 Market

Booksellers—Law
The Bancroft Company, 721 Market

Booksellers and Publishers
The Bancroft Company, 721 Market

Books—Subscription Agents
The History Company, 723 Market

Brass Founders
Thos. Day & Co., 222 Sutter
W. T. Garratt & Co., Natoma & Fremont

Brass Goods
Thos. Day & Co., (Limited), 222 Sutter
W. T. Garratt & Co., Fremont & Natoma

Britannia Ware
Nathan, Dohrmann & Co., 126-130 Sutter
S. & G. Gump, 581 Market

Bronze Goods
Thomas Day & Co. (Limited), 222 Sutter
Nathan, Dohrmann & Co., 126 Sutter

Buggies
Columbus Buggy Co., 29 Market
Studebaker Bros. Mfg. Co., 201-3 Market

Callustro
For Cleaning, Scouring and Brightening

Candies and Confections
T. G. Gruenhagen & Co., San Jose
Norton, 27 Kearny

Cards, Fancy—Manufacturers
The Bancroft Company, 721 Market

Cards, Invitations, Etc.
The Bancroft Company, 721 Market

Carriages
Oliver Hinkley, 48 Eighth

Carpet Dealers
W. & J. Sloane & Co., 641 and 647 Market

Caterers
Ernest H. Ludwig, 1206 Sutter

Champagnes
W. B. Chapman (Perrier-Joüet), 123 California
J. F. Plumel, 18 Stockton (Roussillon)
Em. Meyer & Co., 413 and 415 Pine
Charles Meinecke & Co. (Deutz & Gildermann's "Gold Lac Sec")314 Sacramento
Sherwood & Sherwood (Moët & Chandon),
212 and 214 Market
William Wolff & Co., Pommery Sec, 105
Front

Chemists
A. H. Smith & Co., 1300 Polk, cor. Bush,
and 33 Grant ave., cor. Geary
Val Schmidt, 288 Kearny

Cider
Sherwood & Sherwood, 212 & 214 Market,
agents Ellenville Champagne Cider Co.

Cloaks
Miss Derby, Phelan Building
L. Radloff, 218 Post
Mrs F. R. Parr, 937 Sutter

Clocks, Chinas, Etc.
S. & G. Gump, 581 Market

Clothiers
Chicago Clothing Co., 34 to 40 Kearny

Complexion Powders
Dickey's Crème de Lis

Dr. Campbell, 220 Sixth ave., N. Y.
Mme. Elise Chalumeau, 12 W. Fourteenth,
N. Y.
Ferd. T. Hopkins, 37 Great Jones, N. Y.
Mme. A. Ruppert, 121 Post
M. K. Gentry, Ka-ti-la Cream, 1065 Washington, Oakland
Mrs Graham's Cucumber and Elder
Flower Cream, 103 Post

Dairy Produce, Etc.
Millbrae Dairy, Mission and Ninth

Decorators
G. W. Clark & Co., 653 Market
Auguste Duhem, 121 Sutter
W. & J. Sloane & Co., 641 and 643 Market

Dyes
Middleton's Household Dyes, the best
dyes in the world. The C. N. Middleton
Drug Co., 74 Courtlandt st., New York

Distilleries
Sherwood & Sherwood, 212 and 214 Market
(agents Kentucky Carlisle Whisky)

Dressmakers
Miss Ida E. Derby, 304 Phelan Building
Lumley, 43 Fifth ave., New York
Mme. Stoddard, 63 West Eleventh st., New
York
B. Schulich, 161 West Forty-fifth st., New
York
Redfern House, 221 Post

Dress Cutting
Taught by Studabecker Tailor Square
W. M. Loudon, 224 Stockton

Dress Forms
Patterns cut to measure, W. M. Loudon
224 Stockton

Dress and Skirt Forms
W. M. Loudon, 224 Stockton

Druggists and Perfumers
Val Schmidt, 238 Kearny
A. H. Smith, 1300 Polk
Garrett & Smith, 33 Grant ave.
Greenbaum & Co., 128 Post

Educational Agency
Mrs Fred M. Campbell, 721 Market

Educational Books
The Bancroft Company, 721 Market

Educational Institutions
Miss Bisbee's School for Young Ladies
and Little Girls, 7th ave. and 16th st.,
East Oakland
Miss J. Bolte, Boarding and Day School,
also, Kindergarten, 2127 Jackson
Field Seminary for Girls and Young
Ladies, Telegraph avenue and Knox
place, Oakland
Hopkins Academy, Oakland, W. W.
Anderson, Principal

Educational Institutions—*Cont'd*

Irving Institute for Young Ladies, 1036 Valencia; Rev Edward B. Church, A.M., Principal

Miss Lake's English, French and German Boarding and Day School for Girls, 1534 Sutter; Miss M. Lake, Principal

Mt. Tamalpais Academy, San Rafael

Oakland Seminary for Young Ladies, Mrs M. K. Blake, Principal; 528 Eleventh st., Oakland

Pacific Business College, 320 Post, T. A. Robinson, M. A., President

Miss West's School for Girls, 1616 Van Ness avenue

San Rafael College, San Rafael

St. Rose Academy, Golden Gate ave.

The Oaks, Madison and Eleventh sts., Oakland; Miss L. Tracy

Van Ness Seminary, 1222 Pine st., Dr. S. H. Willey

Electroplaters.

Thomas Day & Co., Limited, 222 Sutter.

Edward G. Dennistou, 653 Mission

Engravers and Designers

The Bancroft Company, 721 Market

Florists

A. Dubem, 121 Sutter

Fluid Food

Bovine, The J. P. Bush Manufacturing Co., 2 Barclay st., New York

Fretwork (Artistic)

Reynolds & Adams, 547 and 549 Brannan

Furniture

F. S. Chadbourne & Co., 741 Market

W. & J. Sloane & Co., 641 and 647 Market

Gas Fixtures

Thos. Day & Co., Limited, 222 Sutter

Ginger Ale Importers

Sherwood & Sherwood, 212 and 214 Market (Ross'. Royal Belfast)

Gold Pens

The Bancroft Company, 721 Market

Grocers

Sherwood & Sherwood, 212 & 214 Market

Hammocks

Neville & Co., 31 & 33 California

Heart Regulator

Dr. Campbell. 220 Sixth ave., New York

Hotels

The Baldwin, NE cor. Market and Powell

Hotel Bella Vista, 1001 Pine

The Berkshire, 711 Jones

New California, Bush bet. Kearny and Grant avenue

Hotel Del Monte, Monterey

El Monte Hotel, Sausalito, J. E. Slinkey, Proprietor

The Grand, Market and New Montgomery

Lick House, cor. Montgomery and Sutter

Occidental Hotel, Montgomery bet. Bush and Sutter

The Oriel, 1904 Market

Palace, Market and New Montgomery

Hotel Pleasanton, NW cor. Sutter and Jones

Hotels—*Cont'd*

Hotel Rafael, W. E. Zander, Manager, San Rafael. Cal.

The Renton, 712 Sutter

The Sea Beach Hotel, J. T. Sullivan, proprietor, Santa Cruz, Cal.

St. James Hotel, San Jose, Cal., Tyler Beach, Proprietor

The Westminster, 614 Sutter

Hotel Vendome, San Jose, Cal., E. E. Adams, Manager

Household Dyes

Middleton's—The best in the world—The C. N. Middleton Drug Co., 74 Courtlandt st., New York

Horseshoes

Thos. Doyle, 57 New Montgomery, the Sectional Expansion Horseshoe

Ice Cream Freezers

W. W. Montague & Co., 309-317 Market

Insurance Companies

Union Insurance Co., 416 California, Nathaniel T. James, President

Interior Decorators

Geo. W. Clark & Co., 653 Market

W. & J. Sloane & Co., 641-647 Market

Inlaid Flooring

Reynolds & Adams, 547 and 549 Brannan

Ladies' Tailors

L. Radloff, 218 Post

I. S. Weatherby, 420 Fifth Ave., New York

J. J. McKenna, 36 East Twenty-third st., New York

B. Schulich, 161 West Forty-fifth st., New York

Lager Beer, Imported

Sherwood & Sherwood, 212-214 Market

Lamps

Thomas Day & Co., Limited, 222 Sutter

Law Blanks

The Bancroft Company, 721 Market

Liniment

Mrs Dr Baker, 632 Sixth ave., New York

Liquors

See Wines and Liquors

Litographers

The Bancroft Company, 721 Market

Machine Threads

Neville & Co., 31 to 33 California

Manicure Parlors

Madame Lee, Beautifies the Hands, Nails, and Complexion, 405 Sutter

Clara Melvin. French Method Manicure Surgeon Chiropodist, 126 Kearny

La Verité Bazaar; 325½ Geary

Mrs F. R. Parr, 937 Sutter

Mantels

Thos. Day & Co., Limited, 222 Sutter

W. W. Montague & Co., 309-317 Market

W. & J. Sloane, 641-647 Market

Marble and Granite

John Daniel & Co., Importers and Dealers in Italian Marble and Scotch Granite Monuments, Mantels, etc., 421 Pine

Marbleized Iron Mantels

Thos. Day & Co., Limited, 222 Sutter
W. W. Montague & Co., 309 to 317 Market

Merchants—Commission

Wilfrid B. Chapman, 123 California
Sherwood & Sherwood, 212 Market and 15-17 Pine
Newell & Bro., 221 Davis
Macondray & Co., cor. Market and First

Milk

Millbrae Dairy (Pure Country Milk), Third and Brannan

Millinery Goods

Lillias Hurd, 332 Fifth ave., N. Y.

Mineral Waters

Sherwood & Sherwood (Henk's Waukesha), 212 214 Market
Jackson & Wooster, Napa Soda Water

Mucilage

The Bancroft Company, 721 Market

Monuments

John Daniels & Co., 421 Pine

Music Teacher

T. W. Bree, Mandolin, Guitar and Banjo, 804 Larkin

Newspapers

Alta California [daily and weekly], Alta California Publishing Co., 529 California
Argonaut [weekly], Argonaut Publishing Co., 213 Grant Ave.
Evening Bulletin [evening, weekly, overland, etc.], S. F. Bulletin Co., 622 Montgomery
Morning Call [daily and weekly], San Francisco Call Co., 525 Montgomery
Examiner [daily and weekly], W. R. Hearst, NE cor. Market and Grant Ave.
News Letter [weekly], Fred'k Marriott, Flood Bdg., SW cor. Market and Fourth
The Overland Monthly, Overland Publishing Co., 420 Montgomery
Evening Post [daily and weekly], Post Publishing Co., NE cor. Kearny and Bush
Oakland Tribune [daily and weekly], Tribune Publishing Co., Oakland
Report [daily], 238 Montgomery
The Wasp [weekly], John P. Jackson, 538 California
The Wave, 331 Montgomery.

Oil Cloths and Linoleum

W. and J. Sloane & Co., 641-643 Market

Olive Oil

Sherwood & Sherwood, 212-214 Market

Paper Hangers, Etc.

G. W. Clark & Co., 653 Market and 46 Third

Paper Hangings

G. W. Clark & Co., 653 Mkt. and 46 Third
W. and J. Sloane & Co., 641-643 Market

Papier Mache

Ladies' Jerseys in all sizes and made to order. W. M. Loudon, 224 Stockton

Patterns Cut to Measure

W. M. Loudon, Sirtk Forms, 224 Stockton

Parquetry (Hardwood Flooring)

Reynolds & Adams, 547 and 549 Brannan

Pavements

Santa Cruz Rock Paving Co., 302 Montgomery

Preparations for the Feet

The Pedine Co., World Building, N. Y.
Dr. J. Parker Pray, 56 W. Twenty-third, N. Y.

Pens

The Bancroft Co., 721 Market

Photograph Galleries

I. W. Taber, 8 Montgomery
Abell & Priest, 723 Market

Photographers' Supplies

Sam. C. Partridge, 226 Bush

Pianos and Organs

Wm. G. Badger, Sole Agent for Hallet & Davis Co's Pianos, Parlor and Vestry Organs, 725 Market
The Bancroft Company, 721 Market
Matthias Gray Co., 206 and 208 Post
Byron Mauzy, 308 and 314 Post
Schemmel & Pfister, San Jose

Pictures and Engravings

The Bancroft Company, 721 Market

Pickle Manufacturers

Sherwood & Sherwood, 212-214 Market, Agents Crosse & Blackwell's

Portraits

The Pacific Portrait Co., 1221 Market

Preserved Fruits

Sherwood & Sherwood, 212-214 Market, Agents Crosse & Blackwell's Jams and Marmalades

Printers

The Bancroft Company, 721 Market, 49 First. This book is a specimen of our work

Plumbers and Gas Fitters

Thos. Day & Co., Limited, 222 Sutter

Publishers

The Bancroft Company, 721 Market, make a specialty of Publishing Works for Authors

Pumps

W. T. Garratt & Co., cor. Fremont and Natoma
Joshua Hendy Machine Works, 39-51 Fremont
W. W. Montague & Co., 309-317 Market

Ranges

W. W. Montague & Co., 309-317 Market

Real Estate

Tevis & Fisher, 14 Post

Refrigerators

W. W. Montague & Co., 309-317 Market
Nathan, Dohrmann & Co., 126 Sutter

Resorts

Byron Hot Springs, Byron Cal.
Hotel del Monte, Monterey, Cal.
El Monte Hotel, Sausalito, Cal., J. E. Blinkey, Proprietor

Resorts—Cont'd

St. James Hotel, San Jose, Cal., Tyler Beach, Proprietor
Napa Soda Springs, Napa County
Pacific Grove, Monterey, Cal.
Hotel Vendome, San Jose, Cal., E. E. Adams, Manager

Restaurants

Swain Brothers, 213 Sutter

Ribbon

Joseph Loth & Co., 65 Green st., N. Y.

Robes

Costumes, Cloaks, Wraps, Coats, Ulsters, Tea Gowns, etc., I. Bloom, Manager, 287 Fifth Avenue, New York City
Mme. Stoddard, 63 W. 11th st., N. Y. City

Sail Duck and Twine

Neville & Co., 31-33 California

School Furniture

The Bancroft Company, 721 Market

Skirt Forms

Willow and all adjustible forms. W. M. Loudon, 24 Stockton

Stained Glass

T. C. Butterworth, 15 Polk

Stationers

The Bancroft Company, 721 Market

Stoves, Ranges, Etc.

W. W. Montague & Co., 309-317 Market

Table Delicacies

Sherwood & Sherwood, 212-214 Market

Tailors

N. Thorson, 633 Market
The J. Brennan Co., 835 Broadway, N. Y.
Daniel Bradley, Agent, 235 Fifth ave., N. Y.

Tents

Neville & Co., 31-33 California

Teas

Macondray & Co., cor. Market and First

Tiles

Thomas Day & Co., Limited, 222 Sutter Floor and Hearth
P. H. Jackson & Co., 228-2 0 First. Illuminating Tiles and Skylights
W. W. Montague & Co., 309-317 Market English, Encaustic and Plain

Toilet Preparations

Madam Elise Chalumeau, 12 W. Fourteenth st., New York
Ferd T. Hopkins, 37 Great Jones st., New York
Dr. J. Parker Pray, 56 West Twenty-third st., New York
La Verite Bazaar, 32½ Geary st.
Dr. Campbell, 220 Sixth Ave., New York

Undertakers

Porter & Scott, 116 Eddy st.

Upholsterers

F. S. Chadburne & Co , 743 Market
W. & J. Sloane & Co., 41 647 Market

Upholstery Goods

W. & J. Sloane & Co., 641 647 Market
F. S. Chadbourne & Co., 741-745 Market

Valentines

The Bancroft Co., 721 Market

Vault Lights

P. H. Jackson & Co., 230 First

Wainscoting

Reynolds & Adams, 1237 Market

Wall Paper

G. W. Clark & Co., 653 Market
W. & J. Sloane & Co., 611-647 Market

Washing

White Star Laundry, Vestibule, New Chronicle Building

Wedding Stationery

The Bancroft Co., 721 Market

Window Shades

G. W. Clark & Co., 653 Market
W. & J. Sloane & Co., 611-647 Market
F. S. Chadbourne & Co., 741 745 Market

Wines and Liquors

J. H. Burnell, 519 Sacramento
J. F. Plumel, 18 Stockton
Charles Meinecke & Co., 314 Sacramento
Sherwood & Sherwood, 212-214 Market and 15-17 Pine
William Wolf & Co., 105 Front
F. A. Haber & Co., 122 Sansome
Em. Meyers & Co., 413-415 Pine

Wooden Mantels

Thomas Day & Co. [Limited], 222 Sutter

Wood Carpet

Reynolds & Adams, 517 and 549 Brannan

THE CHARM

of music doubtless depends upon the "savage" who plays as certainly as upon the one to be "soothed". Of course some people "strum," and never will be musicians ; others delight in musical study and to these, anxious to secure in Church, School-room or Home a first-class Piano or Organ, we offer our assortment of Beautiful Instruments at satisfactory prices.

MILLBRAE COMPANY

Lightning Source UK Ltd.
Milton Keynes UK
UKHW011443160119
335572UK00010B/693/P